The Indianapolis
Automobile Industry

ALSO BY SIGUR E. WHITAKER
AND FROM MCFARLAND

---

*The Indy Car Wars: The 30-Year Fight
for Control of American Open-Wheel Racing* (2015)

*Tony Hulman: The Man Who Saved
the Indianapolis Motor Speedway* (2014)

*James Allison: A Biography of the Engine Manufacturer
and Indianapolis 500 Cofounder* (2011)

The Indianapolis Automobile Industry

A History, 1893–1939

SIGUR E. WHITAKER

McFarland & Company, Inc., Publishers
Jefferson, North Carolina

Library of Congress Cataloguing-in-Publication Data

Names: Whitaker, Sigur E., 1948– author.
Title: The Indianapolis automobile Industry : a history, 1893–1939 / Sigur E. Whitaker.
Description: Jefferson, North Carolina : McFarland & Company, Inc., 2018 | Includes bibliographical references and index.
Identifiers: LCCN 2017058862 | ISBN 9781476666914 (softcover : acid free paper) ♾
Subjects: LCSH: Automobile industry and trade—Indiana—Indianapolis—History. | Indianapolis Motor Speedway (Speedway, Ind.)—History. | Indianapolis (Ind.)—History.
Classification: LCC HD9710.U53 I65 2018 | DDC 338.4/7629222097725209041—dc23
LC record available at https://lccn.loc.gov/2017058862

British Library cataloguing data are available

ISBN (print) 978-1-4766-6691-4
ISBN (ebook) 978-1-4766-2938-4

© 2018 Sigur E. Whitaker. All rights reserved

No part of this book may be reproduced or transmitted in any form or by any means, electronic or mechanical, including photocopying or recording, or by any information storage and retrieval system, without permission in writing from the publisher.

On the cover: *clockwise from top* Ezra Meeker, who had traveled the Oregon Trail in an oxcart, took a trip across America in 1916 in a modified Pathfinder to memorialize the Oregon Trail (Bass Photo Company Collection, Indiana Historical Society); Duesenberg Straight Eight Coupe (Bass Photo Co. Collection, Indiana Historical Society); Peter DePaolo in the Duesenberg racer in which he won the 1925 Indianapolis 500 (Auburn Cord Duesenberg Automobile Museum)

Printed in the United States of America

McFarland & Company, Inc., Publishers
Box 611, Jefferson, North Carolina 28640
www.mcfarlandpub.com

Table of Contents

Preface   1

Introduction   2

1. In the Beginning   7
2. A Seed Is Planted   16
3. Indianapolis-Built Cars Dominate Racing   37
4. Indianapolis-Built Cars Continue to Dominate Racing   53
5. Stutz Cars Make an Entrance   78
6. National Leads the Way   94
7. Legislation Threatens the Indianapolis Auto Industry   106
8. Adopting the Six-Cylinder Car   121
9. Stutz Named Car of the Year   132
10. The Marvelous Marmon 34   148
11. The War Years   161
12. Peace Brings Significant Growth   174
13. Overcapacity and an Economic Recession   181
14. The Duesenberg Brothers Unveil Their Automobile   191
15. Industry Under Stress   197
16. Duesenberg Dominates Racing   218
17. E. L. Cord Buys Duesenberg   229
18. Then There Were Three   233
19. The End Comes   248

Chapter Notes   257
Bibliography   282
Index   307

Preface

Growing up in Indianapolis, I frequently heard that my hometown rivaled Detroit in the early 1900s and that the demise of the Indianapolis automobile industry was because it did not adapt to mass production techniques due to its dedication to high quality cars. I was aware of the major brands associated with Indianapolis ... Marmon, Stutz, Duesenberg, and National ... but did they really rival Detroit?

What I discovered was a vibrant industry with multiple brands which faded from the landscape years ago. It is true that the Indianapolis automobile industry was dedicated to building high quality, expensive cars. Did they rival Detroit? That depends on how rival is defined. If it is the number of cars produced, they were not close to Detroit's production. If the definition is narrowed to the production of high quality, expensive cars, I believe Indianapolis did, in fact, rival Detroit. The Indianapolis automobile industry made significant contributions to the innovation of the automobile. They were very supportive of Carl Fisher's idea to build the Lincoln Highway from the Atlantic Ocean to the Pacific Ocean. They joined forces to advertise Indianapolis-built cars and to provide training on salesmanship. Indianapolis was recognized as one of the industry's manufacturing centers, which attracted the Duesenberg brothers among others to locate in the town.

The other thing that became abundantly clear was the intertwined relationship between the Indianapolis automobile industry and the Indianapolis Motor Speedway. The Speedway was developed by four men involved in the industry. While they were fans of auto racing, their goal was to build a track where cars could be tested, leading to improvements in the automobile. I believe that without the track, the Indianapolis automobile industry would not have been as vibrant or long lived. Likewise, the track would not have been as successful without the Indianapolis-built cars which dominated auto racing in 1909 and 1910.

There are two primary sources of information for the book. The first is the *Indianapolis Star*, the local newspaper. Their archives are on line (www.indystar.com) on a subscription basis. I also used *Horseless Age* and its successor publication, *Automotive Industries*.

Pictures for the book were obtained from several sources. I reached out to the Stutz Club and the Marmon Club. It was fun learning from members of these clubs about their cars. I thank Carl Jensen, newsletter editor of the Stutz Club, for researching of the Club's archives, and Dave Marriner, Graeme Bristow, Warren Witherell, Norma Arsenalt, Butch Marcione, and Dennis Breeden for their contributions. I also thank Nadia Kousari of the Indiana Historical Society, Ethan Bowers of the Auburn Cord Duesenberg Automobile Museum, and Dick Bowman of the Gilmore Car Museum.

Introduction

Imagine living in the late 1880s and early 1890s when transportation centered around walking, biking, or horse power around town and trains for long distances. While today we think nothing of jumping into our automobile for a trip to visit family or to go to the store, the lives of the majority of people back then were centered very close to their homes.

All of a sudden, in 1891, a rudimentary automobile appeared on the streets of Indianapolis, causing great concern among the residents. Charles Pierson, a wholesale cigar dealer, received a large crate[1] containing a Benz automobile[2] from Germany.[3] The next day, Pierson, Charles Black, a local carriage builder, and Melvin Hunter, one of Black's employees, took the car on a spin through downtown Indianapolis. The citizens on the street had every reason to be very, very afraid of this contraption. Horses were frightened of the loud noises emanating from the smoke-belching machine. Drivers of carriages fought to control the horses from running away. People on the street stood watching in wonder and dismay. Although the total traveled that day was only six blocks, the route was filled with mayhem. After leaving Black's carriage business at 44 West Market, the car went through a plate glass window of the Occidental Hotel at the corner of Washington and Illinois Streets about a block and a half away and Pierson paid $25 to replace the window. Continuing, it ended up breaking a second plate glass window, this time at the corner of Pennsylvania and Washington streets, and another $25 was spent to replace it.[4]

In 1893, Black was the first to build an automobile in Indianapolis. Based upon the 1891 Benz, his car was a single cylinder with two seats.[5] Others, too, were interested in the automobile. Peter M. DeFreet built a car to participate in the Thanksgiving Day 1895 Chicago to Evanston race sponsored by the *Chicago Times-Herald*. Unfortunately, or perhaps fortunately for DeFreet given the cold snowy day, the car wasn't completed in time to participate in the race.[6] Robert H. Hassler built an experimental buggy in 1898.[7] The most enthusiastic of the early adopters was Carl Graham Fisher, who imported a French de Dion-Bouton in 1898 and would become a driving force of this new industry in Indianapolis by being among the first to open an automobile showroom.

Indianapolis was well equipped for the coming of the automobile age. It had a thriving bicycle industry, including manufacturers such as the Indiana Bicycle Company, which made the Waverley bicycle, and the Indianapolis Chain & Stamping Company, the world's leading manufacturer of bicycle chains. It also had a vibrant carriage and wagon industry, including the Parry Manufacturing Company which built a line of wagons, road carts and buckboards.

Introduction 3

Charles Black automobile (Auburn Cord Duesenberg Automobile Museum).

In 1896, Parry Manufacturing claimed to be the largest vehicle manufacturer in the world with 2,500 employees.[8]

When bicycles were at their zenith in the late 1890s, Indianapolis had a multitude of bicycle clubs established as social groups, including the Zig Zag Cycle Club. Although the club had disappeared by the early 1900s when the automobile supplanted the bicycle, the friendships that members developed riding their bicycles around town, on century runs, and at "smokers" where they would talk about the issues of the day allowed these men to form the backbone of the Indianapolis automobile industry.

Many members of the Zig Zag Cycle Club were among the early adopters of the automobile. Even though auto travel in those days was fraught with frequent breakdowns and tire failures, they enjoyed the increased freedom of being able to go further on their own timetable. They also took their love of speed from bicycle racing to automobile races. Not only were they regular race participants, but Carl Fisher, in particular, would organize automobile races on dirt fairground tracks throughout the Midwest. In those days, the races would sometimes involve some of the big names in racing—Barney Oldfield, "Wild" Bob Burman, and Earl Kiser—but most of the time it was local people who would race their own cars.

As automobile manufacturing began taking hold in Indianapolis, Fisher had the Premier Motor Manufacturing Company (Premier) build him a specialty racer with which he toured the Midwest along with Earl Kiser and Barney Oldfield. In the local circuit, Carl Fisher and Jim Allison were frequent participants, while Arthur Newby's National automobile would be raced by either Jap Clemens or Charlie Merz.

By 1908, auto racing was becoming more organized and there was a circuit of race tracks. Many manufacturers, including Stoddard-Dayton of Dayton, Ohio, Buick, National and

Indianapolis-based Marmon joined the professional racers in participating in the races. Perhaps it was a synergy of things coming together, but 1908 was also the year in which Jim Allison, Carl Fisher, Arthur Newby, and Frank Wheeler organized the Indianapolis Motor Speedway to promote the improvement of the automobile. Interest in racing exploded in 1909 when Indianapolis manufacturers Marmon and National dominated the racing circuit as the opening date for racing at the Indianapolis Motor Speedway approached in August.

The automobile industry was very good to these four men, who by that time were financially secure and among the industry leaders of Indianapolis. Fisher and Allison were the principals of Prest-O-Lite Company, which developed the first reliable system for automobile lighting, earning them millions of dollars. Arthur Newby was a principal in National Motor Vehicle Company (National), whose vehicle won the second Indianapolis 500. Frank Wheeler was the president of Wheeler-Schebler Carburetor Company, one of the multiple suppliers that developed in Indianapolis to support the burgeoning automobile trade. Allison, Fisher, and Newby had developed a strong friendship while members of the Zig Zag Cycle Club.

Another Zig Zag member was Walter Marmon, whose company, Nordyke & Marmon, would develop the Marmon Wasp, winner of the first Indianapolis 500. When Nordyke & Marmon began manufacturing cars in the early 1900s, they were already a well established manufacturer of flour milling equipment that was sold around the globe. There were also Howard O. Smith and George Weidley, the principals of Premier. Another member of the early Indianapolis automobile industry was Harry C. Stutz, who was employed for his engineering expertise by several Indianapolis automobile concerns before establishing the Ideal Motor Company, which built the first Stutz racer in 1911. Attracted to Indianapolis by the synergies of the town's automobile industry were Frederic and August Duesenberg, who developed the Duesenberg racing machine and later applied their engineering expertise to develop America's premier automobile.

Newby, Fisher and Allison had gained invaluable experience building and operating the Newby Oval, a wooden bicycle track built for the 1898 League of American Wheelmen national convention held in Indianapolis. They had been involved in local bicycle racing both as participants and as organizers for several years. So, in the days before automobile manufacturers had test tracks, the Indianapolis Motor Speedway was established by Fisher, Allison, Newby and Wheeler as a place for the testing and improvement of automobiles.

The development of the Indianapolis automobile industry was closely intertwined with that of the Indianapolis Motor Speedway. The Indianapolis-built cars used the Speedway for critical tests.

Without the interest in racing and the desire to build better cars, particularly those manufactured in Indianapolis, the track would not have been built. Conversely, without the Speedway, Indianapolis would not have been a center of innovation. Some companies, such as Duesenberg, used it to test every car that was manufactured before it was sold to a consumer. Others, such as Marmon, National, Cole, and Stutz, gleaned from it information about the quality of their racing machines which could be used in the manufacture of their stock cars. Participating in the first Indianapolis 500, an entry by Harry C. Stutz finished ninth in the race. Stutz would use the information gleaned through his racing activities to develop the Stutz brand, which became famous for the Stutz Bearcat.

How successful was the track in helping the automobile industry to improve the quality of its cars? In 1924, Charles Kettering, the founder of Delco and president of General Motors Research Corporation from 1920 until 1947, said,

> It has become a common laboratory for all of us—an ideal that Allison, Fisher, and Newby had in the beginning and one they have steadily clung to. Not only does the terrific strain of high speed develop all the faults and weaknesses of the automobile, but the very qualities which make for high speed when the car is geared up for racing make for economy when it is geared down to a working ratio.[9]

Indianapolis was a rival to Detroit and Cleveland in the early days of the automobile. The number of participants grew quickly as those interested in the new fangled machine ... or interested in making a quick buck ... started companies. Those companies, led by individuals who had a deep-seated interest in the automobile, such as Nordyke & Marmon, National Motor Vehicle Company, and Stutz, tended to thrive. Other Indianapolis-based manufacturers, such as Cole Motor Car Company, Premier Motor Manufacturing Company, Overland, American, and Marion Motor Company, also had a run of many years of successful business.

Indianapolis was proud of the craftsmen who built the fine automobiles, but craftsmanship was also the downfall of the Indianapolis automobile industry. With few exceptions, the Indianapolis manufacturers were at the medium to high end of automobile prices. Meanwhile, the Detroit manufacturers, following Henry Ford's lead, quickly adopted mass manufacturing techniques and appealed to the ordinary citizen. Did Indianapolis auto makers adopt the mass manufacturing techniques? Yes, but their machines tended to be among the leaders in engineering developments and they favored quality over quantity.

This is the story of the Indianapolis automobile industry from the 1890s through the 1930s. Today, when a person thinks about Indianapolis-built automobiles, the first to come to mind are usually Stutz and Duesenberg, and perhaps Marmon. Largely forgotten are the other manufacturers, including Premier, Marion, Frontenac, Monroe, Empire, National, Parry, Pathfinder, American, Hassler, Lyons-Atlas, Lafayette, Henderson, and Overland.

1

In the Beginning

It was possible to get a horseless carriage in the early 1890s but their appeal was limited. Not only were they expensive, but the two primary types available, an electric vehicle or a steam-powered vehicle, could travel only limited distances. By 1898, electrics had become the primary vehicle of choice as they were easy to drive and easy to make. However, the electric automobile had one huge drawback—its inability to travel far on a charge. Automobiles powered by gasoline were available, but were very expensive compared to the electric horseless carriages, which cost about $1,000.[1]

Long before his trip with Pierson around Indianapolis in the Benz, Charles Black was hooked on the horseless carriage. Without the money to order a Benz from Germany, Black began working in his shop. Black described his journey to building what might have been the first automobile in the United States.

> Well from 1865, I was a carriage builder in this city, and always interested in getting out the latest and most up-to-date vehicles for either business or pleasure, and so it was only natural that I should look for a self-propelled vehicle. In 1887, I came into possession of some literature showing a steam-driven motor wagon made in France, and, as I said, being interested, asked the United States consul at Paris to send me what additional matter he could get on the subject. He sent me some information, but I did not like the idea of a steam-propelled wagon, as it was too cumbersome and hard to manage, requiring a firebox like any locomotive, which I knew would never do for a wagon.
>
> A year or so later, I heard of the Otto gas engine in Germany, and from this sprang the idea from which I made my vehicle. The hint I needed was in the use of gasoline as fuel for power and I started to work immediately. In 1891, after making most of many parts in my blacksmith shop and having others made for me, I was ready with my first machine. I tried it out on the streets of Indianapolis in 1891, using the Circle and Delaware Street mostly, as they were paved.[2]

While Black built several automobiles, the first automobile manufacturer in Indianapolis with more than a nominal number of cars produced was the Waverley Electric Company (Waverley), which traced its roots back to the Indiana Bicycle Company and was subsequently acquired by Pope Manufacturing Company as part of the consolidation of the bicycle industry. In 1896, the company constructed its first electric car, a Stanhope model,[3] with the first delivery in 1897. By 1898, the company was manufacturing a full line of electric vehicles, including the Stanhope, a dos-a-dos, and a delivery truck, which were displayed at a bicycle show in New York City.[4] As an inducement to buy the car, Pope-Waverley Electric Company offered a five-year contract to keep the battery in order.[5]

The automobile was very much of a novelty for the rich. In 1897, there were 90 motor vehicle registrations in the United States. Unlike the bicycle industry, which had a brief moment of popularity during the late 1860s before fading from the landscape and later being revived, the automobile industry quickly expanded. A year later, in 1898, automobile registrations had grown to 800 nationwide.[6] During the early years of the industry, there were no parts manufacturers; those men who made an automobile had to rely upon metalworking companies or their own ingenuity to make the needed parts.[7] Just as the automobile industry grew quickly, entrepreneurs quickly started small companies to make the needed parts.

Financing for this industry was difficult, but the rewards were great for those who succeeded. Although six out of every seven companies failed in the early years[8] those who were successful could have a profit of 10 percent in 1900,[9] which would increase in some instances to around 20 percent.

The first New York Automobile Show, held in 1900, had four exhibitors, including Indianapolis manufacturer National Automobile & Electric Company,[10] which exhibited an electric model. National was begun by Arthur C. Newby, L. S. Dow and Phillip Goetz[11] with monies earned from the 1899 sale of the Indianapolis Chain and Stamping Company to the American Bicycle Company. By the end of June 1900, National had begun operations with 40 men and boys.[12] The first automobile produced by National was a New York Trap designed for city travel, which could go about 50 miles on a single charge. The car had 2½ horsepower with a maximum speed of 15 miles per hour.[13] One of the unique features of the first National model was that it had five forward and three reverse speeds. For the three backward speeds, each position of the controller had a different torque. Although the lowest position of the controller was usually adequate, there were times when greater torque was needed for backing up. Another feature of the National vehicle was that there were three positions for an extra controller operated by a handle. In the highest position, the car could run. In the second position, the motor could not be started. By locking the controller with a flat key, the owner could leave the car without fear of it being stolen. In the third (lowest) position, the controller acted as a brake.[14]

National planned to have seven to eight different models, including a Stanhope, a dos-a-dos, four passenger cars, and delivery wagons, priced from $1,000 for a runabout to $1,750.[15] As with the other vehicles of the time, the National automobile was very rudimentary. The motor was hung underneath the carriage and the car was driven by two gears, one on each of the rear wheels.[16]

National Electric Model 110 Park trap with fringed top (Bass Photo Co. Collection, Indiana Historical Society).

In July 1901, National was reorganized as the National Motor Vehicle Company with capitalization of $150,000. The principals, Arthur Newby and Charles Test, also incorporated the Western Storage Battery Company, which used the techniques of James K. Pumpelly, a Chicago battery storage inventor.[17] National also developed the first gasoline-powered car in Indianapolis,[18] which it brought to market in 1902.[19]

Waverley had six models on display at the second New York Auto Show, held in the fall of 1901, including a Stanhope (Model 21), a Stanhope with Victoria top (Model 22), a surrey (Model 20A), and a delivery truck. Waverley's storage battery supplier was the Sperry Storage Battery Company.[20]

Before 1900, Waverley automobiles had running gear of extremely rigid construction. This caused the premature failure of tires, often before 1,000 miles. By 1902, the company had adopted a more forgiving suspension design. With this change, tire life was extended to 5,000 miles.[21]

In March 1902, Waverley introduced a tonneau with 78-inch wheelbase. An 80-volt underslung battery powered two motors of two horsepower each, giving the car a maximum speed of 15 miles per hour. The delivery wagon had a capacity of 500 pounds plus two people in the front.[22]

George Weidley and Harold O. Smith also had a zest for the automobile. In 1902, in a small room on West Georgia Street, they began manufacturing a very rudimentary car and achieved initial success with a small air-cooled four-cylinder engine, designed by Weidley, mounted transversely in the front of a utility wagon.[23] Their company, the Premier Motor Manufacturing Company (Premier), soon outgrew the West Georgia Street facility and the company moved to the old Munger Bicycle Manufacturing Company facilities on Fort Wayne Avenue. They stayed in this facility for a year before moving to

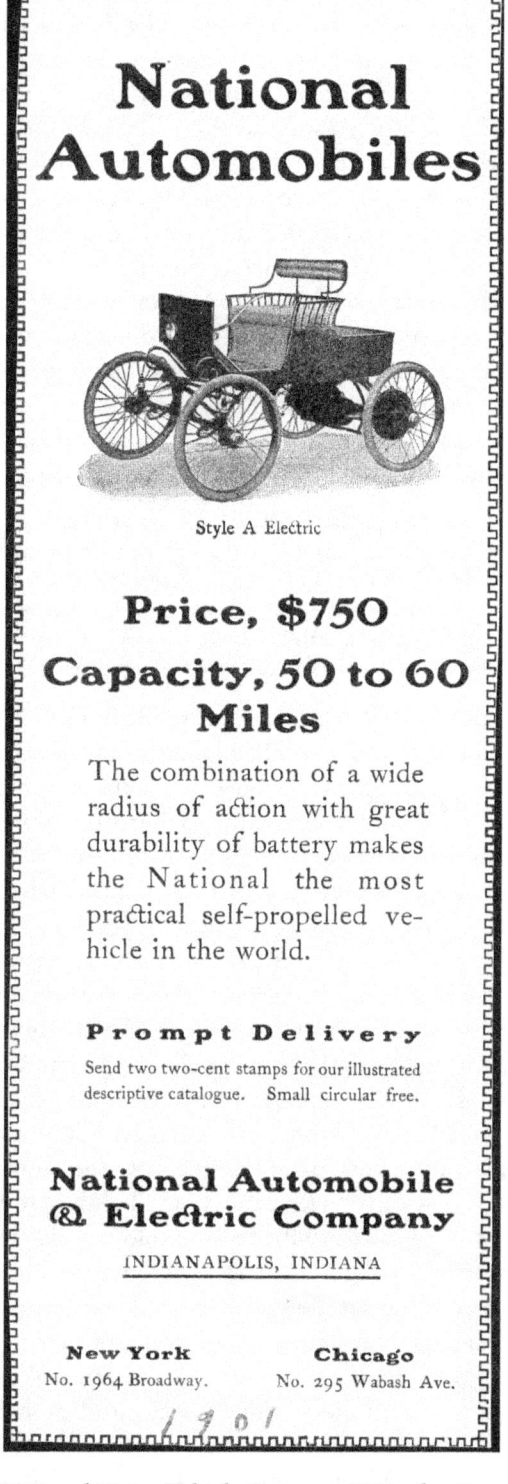

National Motor Vehicle Company 1901 advertisement (Indiana Historical Society, P0143).

another, larger facility.[24] The firm was incorporated in 1903 with authorized capitalization of $50,000. Premier claimed to be the first automobile manufacturer to use an emblem as a trademark on their cars—an oak leaf.[25]

The first Premier touring automobile model had three speeds forward and one reverse. The car's speed was controlled by a throttle governor which also eliminated "explosions" when the car was at rest. The frame of the car was of pressed steel with an 88-inch wheelbase. After studying the location of the seats to avoid the "teeter board" effect in the tonneau, the company placed the rear seat over the rear wheels.[26]

About 70 miles west of Indianapolis in Terre Haute, Indiana, Charles Minshall, owner of Standard Wheel Company, was also interested in the automobile. He learned that Clyde Cox, a student at nearby Rose Polytechnical Institute, had made a three-wheeled vehicle for his senior thesis. In 1902, Minshall hired Cox to design an automobile and to head a new automobile division at Standard Wheel in Terre Haute.[27] The Overland car had a two-cylinder water-cooled engine with five horsepower and a top speed of about 20 miles per hour. Standard Wheel promoted the Overland Runabout:

> The price of the "OVERLAND" was not fixed and the machine afterward built to suit, but it was designed and constructed to fill the growing demand for a light Runabout at a reasonable price—a price that the mass of the people can afford to pay for an automobile that will take them "there and back" seven days in the week, possess good speed, ride comfortably, be simple in construction, built of the best quality of materials by experienced workmen and offered to the public by an established and reliable concern, with a paid-up capital of One Million Dollars.[28]

Priced at $600, this car was first sold in 1903. In 1904 sales doubled to 24 vehicles, much quicker growth than the other fledgling Indianapolis automobile manufacturers had seen. When the demand for the Overland car quickly outstripped the manufacturing facilities in Terre Haute, Minshall moved operations to the former Standard Wheel plant in Indianapolis. Not long after this move, however, Minshall became convinced that the operation, which had yet to turn a profit, would continue to be a financial drain on Standard Wheel Company, so he decided to close the automotive division. Happily for Clyde Cox, a customer of Standard Wheel Company, David Parry of Indianapolis, was not only interested in getting into the business but had the financial wherewithal to do so and bought 51 percent of the company's stock.[29]

David Parry was the president of Parry Manufacturing Company. In 1882, at age 30, Parry purchased a carriage shop in Rushville. The company, enjoying success and needing more space, was relocated to an old wheel factory in Indianapolis in 1886, where Parry was joined by his brothers, St. Clair and Thomas, along with 40 employees. Parry had found a lucrative segment of the business and soon the company, which began by building two-wheeled carts for farmers and was building 100 carts per day in 1886, had expanded to building 1,000 carts a day with 2,500 employees. By 1890, the company's line had expanded to include a four-passenger surrey, a phaeton, road and spring wagons, and piano-boxed buggies at its large manufacturing plant located on Parry Avenue at the Vandalia railroad tracks. The company was the largest in the world, producing more wagons than the next five combined.[30] With the foresight to know that the automobile could become a threat to the carriage industry, David Parry was anxious to get into this growing industry. The purchase of the Overland automobile was his entrée.

The Marion Motor Car Company (Marion) was started in 1902 by Indianapolis Mayor Charles A. Bookwalter, Robert Hassler, Fred A. Joss, and J. Arthur Hittle.[31] The company was incorporated in December 1903 with a capitalization of $50,000 by Hassler, Hittle, and I. G. Besler.[32] Hoping to produce about $300,000 in automobiles per year, the company announced it would build a two-story brick factory at 323 West 15th Street at a cost of $7,050 in November 1904.[33]

In 1903, National introduced the Model 120, which was touted as a long distance electric car with all the earmarks of a gasoline car. Its appearance was similar to that of a gasoline car, with a brass hood, three front lights, a horn, and a steering wheel. Under the hood was a battery with sixteen cells, and an additional battery with twenty cells was in the rear of the vehicle.[34]

Arthur Newby enjoyed driving his personal car, a National Model 100. The 1,600-pound car sported Western Storage Battery Company batteries with 44 cells weighing 800 pounds. After the car had been driven about 200 miles, Newby drove 82 miles on smooth city streets on one charge. When the car had been driven 6,000 miles Newby reported an average fuel cost of 1.5 cents per mile. Other repairs were minimal at about $12 with the exception of new tires, which were put on after 4,000 miles of usage.[35]

Having begun in 1851, Nordyke & Marmon (Marmon) was another of Indianapolis' early automobile manufacturers. It was a well established and very successful company, constructing milling equipment distributed worldwide. Daniel Marmon, the head of the company, had been joined by his two sons, Walter and Howard. Walter's strengths were organization and finance and he had attended Earlham College in Richmond, Indiana. Mechanically oriented, Howard also attended Earlham, and subsequently graduated from the University of California at Berkeley with a degree in mechanical engineering. He started his career with Nordyke & Marmon in 1899 at age 20 and three years later was named a vice president and chief engineer of the firm.[36]

Howard Marmon was one of the early adopters of the automobile. By 1898, he had conceptually drafted a side entrance tonneau which he convinced his father to allow him to build in a corner of the Nordyke & Marmon factory. As Howard worked on the car in his spare hours, it began to take shape. Completed in 1902, the car had an air-cooled engine with the crankshaft in line with the frame. It had three forward speeds plus reverse and featured a unique lubrication system fed by a gear pump rather than the "dipper and splash" systems then in use by other manufacturers.[37] The side entrance tonneau, the first in the United States,[38] had some real advantages over other available tonneaus which were entered from the rear of the car. Instead of having a narrow aisle to gain access to the seats, the car permitted a single seat across the back, allowing passengers to easily alight from the car to the sidewalk.[39] The car was built of high quality wood. Quickly understanding that the wood couldn't stand up to the weather or the rough roads, Howard constructed the next model, built in 1903, of aluminum. The use of aluminum also allowed the car to be more stylish with curves.[40]

Wanting to make improvements to the car, Howard Marmon also designed a second car which had a piston displacement of 201 cubic inches. While smaller in size, the car had split front seats.[41]

In July 1903, the company built a 50-horsepower, four-cylinder touring car for Walter Marmon. Although the car had only been driven 100 miles,[42] some Indianapolis automobile enthusiasts wanted the Marmons to build a similar automobile for them. Walter Marmon talked about the thought process on whether to begin manufacturing automobiles.

It depends largely upon the success of the machine we have just built. My brother and I had it made right here in the plant and I think it will suit us better than any we have seen, either of American or European manufacture. There are unsatisfactory points about both makes, and I think we have avoided these faults in the car we built ourselves.

The plant has every facility for the manufacture of automobiles, and we could go into the business with practically no additional expense.[43]

Having made the decision in August 1904, Nordyke & Marmon began manufacturing automobiles.[44] Six Model A cars were sold during 1904. The company's 1907 catalog noted that of the cars produced, all were still running with three remaining with the original owners.[45] During a period when automobiles were very unreliable, this was a remarkable record.

In an era when auto racing was dominated by large, powerful gasoline cars, it seems almost counterintuitive that electric cars would engage in auto races. But they did. *Horseless Age* described a two-mile race for electric automobiles at the Narragansett racecourse as "almost a farce." Four Waverleys and one National entered the race, but only two of the Waverley automobiles showed up at the starting line. The winning car, a surrey, finished the two-mile course in 4 minutes 48.8 seconds. *Horseless Age* commented about the race that "the public hardly realiz[ed] the race was on."[46]

In January 1904, National began building two gasoline-powered tonneau models. Model A was a four-cylinder, 40-horsepower car with speeds up to 50 miles per hour. The car had three forward speeds and one reverse. It operated without chains, with the car being driven by shaft and bevel gear. There were three seats, with the front two seats being divided. Model B was a four-cylinder, 20-horsepower car which could achieve a speed of 40 miles per hour. The cars were built on an 86-inch wheelbase.[47]

At the New York Auto Show, National exhibited seven vehicles including a Model 50 Electromobile, a runabout with a piano box body. Model 75 was similar to the Model 50 with the exception of the body, which had a smoother line and a buggy top. The National Stanhope had a doctor's top. National also exhibited a custom-built model for a customer who wanted something different. While the car was an electric model, it had the appearance of a gasoline-powered car with the motor in the front under the hood. The car had two batteries—one in the front and the other in the rear.[48]

Pope-Waverley introduced the Surrey model in September 1904. Model 20 of this electric

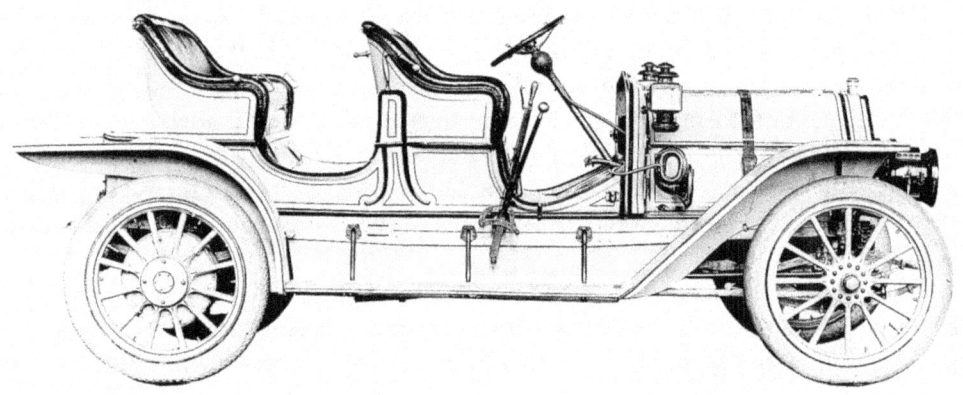

Marmon Motor Car (Bass Photo Co. Collection, Indiana Historical Society).

car was priced at $1,500. A canopy for the automobile cost an additional $75, while a full leather extension top was an additional $100. Pope-Waverley promoted this electric automobile as being "free from noise, odor, or mechanical complication."[49] The company also had an electric delivery car which "delivers the goods."[50]

With manufacturing on the rise in Indianapolis and strikes being a growing concern of management, David Parry called a meeting of various employers throughout the city. At the meeting in January 1904, the Employers' Association of Indianapolis was formed, with Walter Marmon elected as first vice president. The purpose of the organization was to have a city which was free from "industrial disturbance" including lockouts, strikes and boycotts.[51]

Premier and the Keyless Lock Company were hit by union activities in June 1904. Premier wanted its employees to work a 54-hour week; it had not signed the labor agreement with the Machinists' Union in 1903 in which the 50-hour week was part of the bargaining agreement. Sixteen men were impacted by the union action at Premier.[52] When the company had its machinists continuing to work more than 50 hours per week, the union posted pickets outside of the building. Premier responded by hiring non-union laborers. E. J. Collins, the machinists' business agent, explained that if Premier had its employees working overtime, then other companies would expect the same thing from their employees.[53]

Premier was also experiencing strong growth in its business. The company bought a quarter square and relocated to a two-story brick building at the corner of Georgia and Shelby Streets in February 1905.[54]

Several automobile manufacturers were determined that an American automobile would bring home the James Gordon Bennett Cup from Europe in 1905. As part of the desire to win the Cup, plans were made to construct a five-mile racing course in a swampy area of Michigan on which auto races as well as elimination trials for the James Gordon Bennett Cup could be held.

National Motor Vehicle Company automobile circa 1904 (Bass Photo Co. Collection, Indiana Historical Society).

George Weidley, one of the principals of Premier, designed the Premier Comet[55] for Carl Fisher, who had established a reputation for racing bicycles and later automobiles. In the Premier Comet, a specialty eight-cylinder racer,[56] Fisher established world records for the one- and two-mile marks with times of 59.4 seconds and 2 minutes 2 seconds respectively. Additionally, Fisher held the track records for Harlem and Chicago for all weight machines and the track records for Chicago, Cleveland, Columbus, and Dayton for the 1,400-pound class. Fisher's exploits in automobile racing were recognized by the Pope-Toledo Automobile Company, which sent him a contract to drive a specially built racer in the 1905 James Gordon Bennett Cup race.[57]

The Comet was the first vehicle to combine the overhead camshaft and the overhead valve, resulting in a very powerful car pioneering the straight-eight engine design. Weidley's engine had an over-square bore and stroke of 7 by 5.5 inches, resulting in total displacement of 846.6 cubic inches. In an era when the standard was a chain link drive, Weidley incorporated a shaft drive. Journalist Hugh Dolnar described his ride in the car on one of its first runs.

> A twelve-mile round trip on East Washington Street with trolleys in the middle and horse-drawn vehicles on the side, was not a tranquil joy to this writer. Mr. Weidley says that the seats on this racer are remarkably easy riding. This may be true in a comparative sense, or on a smooth track; to make it unreservedly true the car must be placed on a far better surface than the East Washington asphalt, which is not so bad, but is not good enough to drive a mile a minute on with comfort. This car can run fast, perhaps a mile in 40 seconds. It ran at about a mile a minute clip for a short distance on east Washington street with the throttle very slightly opened, and the exhaust muffled to a mild roar, not much louder than Niagara Falls and, say, a thousand threshing machines in active operation combined. What this racer will do with no muffler and the throttle wide open the writer does not know, and does not want to know, and never will know, of his own knowledge.[58]

At a race at the Indiana State Fairgrounds on November 4, Fisher driving the Comet won the five-mile handicapped race with an average speed of 59.21 miles per hour. He had wanted to enter the 100-mile race, but after the competitors saw the Comet, they refused to participate.[59]

By the end of 1904, Indianapolis had five automobile manufacturers: Waverley, National, Marion, Premier, and Marmon. Although the automobile was still a rich man's object, it wasn't the novelty it had been at the beginning of the century. Times were changing and so was the automobile, which was known for

Carl G. Fisher (Bretzman Collection, Indiana Historical Society).

Premier Motor Manufacturing Company automobile, circa 1904 (Bass Photo Co. Collection, Indiana Historical Society).

being unreliable. What was needed for broader acceptance was reliability. While racing had been for daredevils, run primarily on dirt tracks usually used for horse racing or on courses such as the Vanderbilt track, the need for improvement soon became a focus of racing. The automobile manufacturers saw this as a way to learn more about their automobiles, and when successful in their racing attempts, promote their product and hopefully see sales soar.

2

A Seed Is Planted

By February 1905, Premier had three models: a 16-horsepower runabout priced at $1,250, a four-passenger detachable tonneau car for $1,400, and a five-passenger side entrance tonneau for $1,500. One of the features touted by Premier was its engines, which were air cooled rather than water cooled like those of many other manufacturers. This meant that in cold weather, the cars could be used without worries about the engine freezing.[1]

Indianapolis manufacturer Premier also joined a new organization, the American Motor Car Manufacturers' Association (AMCMA), which represented the unlicensed manufacturers (those not paying a royalty for the use of the Selden patent). The new organization was headquartered in Detroit. One of the mainstay firms behind the AMCMA was the Ford Motor Car Company. The purpose of this new organization was believed to have been to make a concerted effort against the Association of Licensed Automobile Manufacturers (ALAM).[2]

In 1905 National introduced its Model C, a four-cylinder with a 24- to 30-horsepower gasoline motor which was more powerful than the previous gasoline-powered cars. It also featured a cylindrical bonnet with a circular radiator.[3]

The fourth annual Chicago Automobile Show, held in February 1905, had 220 manufacturers of automobiles and accessories showing their wares, including four from Indianapolis. To show the undersides of the automobiles, manufacturers used mirrors placed on the ground. Many manufacturers also removed the gear box covers to show the movement of gears, the change speed box, and the differential. National's exhibit included both electric and gas engine cars with Arthur Newby and Tom Hay manning the display, while Pope-Waverley displayed their electric model cars. Former Indianapolis Mayor Charles Bookwalter along with Hugh Landon displayed the Marion cars, with Bookwalter taking prospective customers for spins around the block. Also at the show was Frank L. Moore, sales manager, with the Premier exhibit. One account of the Chicago show said the autos outside had "eyes of acetylene gas," undoubtedly referring to Jim Allison and Carl Fisher's Prest-O-Lite apparatus which was exhibited.[4]

By March 1905 Nordyke & Marmon had created the Marmon Motor Company (Marmon) and its cars were in production. Described with the tag line of "A Mechanical Masterpiece," the auto's double three-point suspension system prevented dust from entering the suspension. It reportedly was the only car having a solid cast aluminum body, providing a durable but light strength to the car. Marmon also distinguished itself because, unlike most manufacturers of the time, the company built the majority of the component parts of its cars rather than being an assembler of the vehicle.[5] In 1905 Marmon introduced the Model B, which featured a longer 90-inch wheelbase and weighed 2,000 pounds. The company sold 25 of these cars priced at $2,500 each.[6]

Pope-Waverley built a combination police car and ambulance for the Los Angeles Police Department with seating capacity of 10 inside and two on the driver's seat. Before the car was shipped to Los Angeles, the Indianapolis police commissioners and Chief Krueger were taken out for a spin. They traveled north on Illinois Street to 34th Street before heading back to police headquarters on Meridian Street. Normal travel was 12 miles per hour, which could be increased to 20 miles per hour in an emergency. The vehicle sported a green body with red wheels and gearing. The inside was paneled in wood. At the time, electric patrol wagons were being introduced nationwide.[7]

Noticing that in many large cities the electric truck was replacing the horse-drawn dray for deliveries, Pope-Waverley promoted its various trucks, which had a capacity of one to five tons. The trucks were promoted as being quicker than the horse-drawn dray and also able to carry a heavier load. The company also boasted that the Pope-Waverley electrics were victorious in the service contests in New York City.[8] One of the specialty trucks built by Pope-Waverley was for the Indiana Brewing Company with a load capacity of 10,000 pounds. While the vehicle could handle a significant load, its speed was another matter. At an average speed of 5 miles per hour, it had a travel radius of 25 miles on a single charge. The truck was powered by a battery with 42 cells.[9]

Carl Fisher was very frustrated with the quality, or lack thereof, of American-produced automobiles. On a trip to Franklin, Indiana, after multiple breakdowns, he said, "There ought to be a track to test these cars out before the public gets 'em."[10] Fisher was convinced that the superiority of the European cars was because they raced against each other in factory teams.[11]

The need for a testing facility was underscored when Fisher was part of an American delegation to the James Gordon Bennett Cup races in France as a reserve driver for the Pope-Toledo team. The European drivers had a huge advantage in the races because of the hours they spent on the course testing their cars and becoming familiar with the route. During the testing, Fisher drove the 85.35 mile Circuit de l'Auvergne. Years later, Fisher recalled his experience at the James Gordon Bennett Cup. He wrote to Ray C. Thompson of the *Indianapolis News*:

> ...we had two very fast cars, but there was no place in America to test them over a continuous drive of more than two miles and in order to test them even the two miles in Toledo, we had to hire special guards and do the work at daylight; and even this testing was stopped because the cars made so much noise on the boulevard. So, we went to Europe with cars that were very fast but with no place to test them at high speed for a continuous run of 100 miles or so.... As a result, the French beat the tar out of us; in fact, we didn't have either car finish, and I could see that it was a lack of being able to test the cars over a continuous speed run; and I made up my mind then to build a speedway where cars could be run 1,000 miles in a test, if necessary.[12]

Like other manufacturers, Marion touted its racing successes as a form of advertising. A 16-horsepower car won a hill climbing contest sponsored by the Colorado Auto Club at Denver on July 1, 1905. That victory was followed with a successful eight-mile "Climb to the Clouds" at Mount Washington on July 18. The Marion was the only air-cooled car to succeed and later appeared at the Indiana State Fair. With a three model lineup for 1905 including a $1,000 and $1,250 two-person car and a four-cylinder $1,500 touring car, Marion reported a 50 percent increase in sales for fiscal year 1905.[13]

Upon his return to Indianapolis, Carl Fisher was convinced that the key to winning the James Gordon Bennett Cup was familiarity with the race course, and he announced he was giving up track racing. He commented to the *Indianapolis Star*, "It was not so much a case of familiar driving on the part of the contestants, but familiarity with the course over which the famous race was run." Fisher's plans for the future were unclear, but he planned to enter the Diamond Cup Race in Chicago and possibly the Vanderbilt Cup race.[14]

Fisher sounded the alarm about the quality of American-made automobiles, which he felt were in danger of being replaced by the superior European makes. He told the local automobile manufacturers that the European automobile makers "can take over the entire American market any time they decide to export cars in sufficient quantity to meet the demand."[15] His warning continued, "If you don't start building cars the public can buy with confidence, you won't even be able to give 'em away. The only way to gain the public's confidence quickly is to prove the dependability of your products on the race track. You'll learn ten times as much racing against each other as you will from listening to the complaints of your customers."[16] At the time, Indianapolis had a thriving automobile industry and the impact would be significant to the local economy.

Fisher set his sights on participating in the International Cup (Vanderbilt Cup) race. He applied to drive his Premier Comet and was accepted as one of three American entries. The other two American entries were Earl Kiser in a Winton and A. C. Webb in a Pope-Toledo. Other countries sending entries were France, England, Italy, and Germany, each of which entered three cars. The International Cup had five heats of five miles each with a final race of ten miles.[17]

Fisher's specially built Premier weighed 2,500 pounds. Unfortunately, the weight limit for the race was 2,200. In order to try to meet the weight requirements, Fisher had 256 half-dollar-sized holes cut in the frame, 28 ¾ inch holes cut in the rear axle, and 12 lug nuts removed from the wheels, without achieving his goal.[18] Despite these efforts, his car was still 150 pounds overweight.[19] He traveled to Long Island for the races, but only as a spectator.

Harry C. Stutz (Bretzman Collection, Indiana Historical Society).

With automobiles becoming a larger part of the Indianapolis business community, the YMCA began to offer some automobile courses in its night classes. Harry Stutz was put in charge of the class on the study of the automobile, which occurred in two of the city's repair shops. The students were expected to don overalls and get their hands greasy. Others involved in the teaching of the classes were National's W. Guy Wall and Premier factory superintendent Harry Hammond.[20]

2. A Seed Is Planted

Stutz had been born on a farm near Ansonia, Ohio, on September 12, 1876. Although his early years were spent working on the family farm and he had a love for growing things, his mechanical ability fixing farm equipment quickly became apparent. He became known as "that Stutz lad who can fix anything." He left the farm to seek employment as a mechanic in Dayton, Ohio, at age 18. After nine years in Dayton, Stutz came to Indianapolis in 1903[21] just as the automobile craze was taking off.

The Indianapolis Automobile Racing Association (IARA) was incorporated in April 1905 by James Allison, Charles Sommers and Frank B. Willis for "the development of speed possibilities and the science of manufacturing motor cars and other vehicles for speed."[22] In October, Arthur Newby was elected president, Howard Marmon vice president, and F. W. Hoblitt secretary/treasurer. The executive committee consisted of Newby (National), Howard O. Smith (Premier), Robert Hassler (Marion), Herbert Rice (Waverley), Walter Marmon (Marmon), and Fisher.[23]

The IARA planned an auto meet on October 21, 1905, at the Indiana State Fairgrounds. After discussing the possibility of holding some evening races, the executive committee decided not to due to the cool weather in mid–October. The meet organizers believed they would have several of the best race cars in the nation, including an Apperson which had been eliminated from the Vanderbilt Cup trials and the Premier built for Carl Fisher for the Vanderbilt Cup. The race card listed six races including the feature event, a 100-mile race.[24] Due to inclement weather the automobile races were postponed four times. On November 4, National driver Jap Clemens won the 100-mile feature event with a time of one hour 53 minutes 21.8 seconds, shaving 5 minutes off the world record. Ray McNamara, driving a Premier, took second place, finishing nearly a half-hour later. A feature of the racing card was an exhibition of Carl Fisher in the Premier Comet driving five miles.[25]

Two weeks later, Allison, Fisher, Newby and Indianapolis banker Stoughton Fletcher sponsored a 24-hour endurance test at the Indiana State Fairgrounds. Intimidated by the performance of the National automobiles in the recent automobile races, only two automobiles participated. Jap Clemens and Charlie Merz, both driving 40-horsepower Nationals, took to the track on November 16 at 2:45 p.m. Clemens quickly established the pace and set a new record for 150 miles with a time of 2 hours 52 minutes 32.8 seconds, which was 13 minutes 5.2 seconds faster than the previous record.[26]

Shortly after Clemens set the new record, the steering knuckle on his car broke. He lost control of the car, which knocked down "enough pickets to build a house" before being brought to a stop. Although the car was destroyed, Clemens was uninjured. After eating a brief meal, he took over the driving duties of the other National racer. Prest-O-Lite had furnished 500 lamps which were placed 25 feet apart and provided lighting for the nighttime driving.[27]

With Merz and Clemons alternating the driving duties every 50 miles, by 2:45 p.m. the next day, new records had been established not only for a 24-hour run but also for 1,000 miles being traveled in 21 hours 58 minutes 0.8 seconds, beating the record set by Guy Vaughn in a Decauville car at the Empire track in New York City by nearly two hours. The National's new 24-hour record of 1,094.2 miles shattered Vaughn's record of 1,015.8 miles.[28]

By 1905, Fisher clearly had the idea that a track to be used for testing cars was imperative for the long-term viability of the American automobile industry. He wrote *Motor Age* magazine:

The American manufacturers annually spend thousands of dollars in building high speed racing cars to compete with French cars and without possible chance of winning, and I think this is largely due to the fact that American drivers do not have a chance to thoroughly test their cars continuously at high speed for weak spots in construction, or to become entirely familiar with and have their car under perfect control at very high speeds.

There is no question in my mind that it takes weeks and months of practice handling a car at 75, 80 and 90 miles an hour to be able to properly gauge distances, numerous road conditions and the response of the car to such conditions. It has been my experience that quite a number of racing cars, when tested over the best roads we had in this country, seemed to have wonderful speed. There was no accurate way to time them for any distance, and the best anybody could do was to guess at what the cars were doing.

It seems to me a 5-mile track, properly laid out, without fences to endanger drivers, with proper grandstands, supply stores for gasoline and oil, and other accommodations would net for one meet such as the Vanderbilt Cup race a sufficient amount to pay half of the entire cost of the track.[29]

Whetted by Clemens' victory in the 100-mile race at the Indiana State Fairgrounds, National built its first race car with six cylinders and 60 horsepower to participate in the Ormond Beach races in mid–December 1905 with Fisher as the pilot.[30]

As 1905 drew to a conclusion, Indianapolis had five automobile manufacturers: Pope-Waverley, National, Premier, Marion, and Marmon. These five manufacturers anticipated building 2,000 automobiles during 1906 out of a projected 30,000 being built nationally. Premier and Pope-Waverley both anticipated building 600 units, National 350 units, Marion 300 units, and Marmon 200 units.[31]

Waverley general offices (Indiana Historical Society, P0235).

American touring car (*Horseless Age*, January 24, 1906).

A new entry to the Indianapolis automobile industry was the American Motor Car Company (American), founded by D. S. Menasco and V. A. Longaker, who had made their fortunes in the lumber industry.[32] They hired Harry Stutz as the chief engineer. At the New York car show, the company displayed a four-cylinder touring car with 35 to 40 horsepower. The wooden car had a 111-inch wheelbase with 32-inch wheels on both the front and rear.[33]

National displayed its Model D, which featured a four-cylinder generating 40 horsepower, at the New York Auto Show. The wheelbase on the car had been lengthened by six inches. The company also had a new six-cylinder car which generated between 50 and 60 horsepower. The wheelbase on this car was 121 inches. The tonneau could accommodate five passengers, all facing forward.[34]

Premier had two 1906 models featuring air-cooled engines. The Model F, little changed from the 1905 model, had a 16-horsepower engine and was available in a two-passenger doctor's special, a coupe, an open light delivery wagon, and a closed light delivery wagon. The new offering was the Model L with 20 to 24 horsepower. It was available in a touring car weighing 2,000 pounds, a deluxe touring car, and a limousine. The car featured a double braking system with a hand brake on the transmission shaft controlled by a foot pedal and a double internal hub brake on the rear wheels which was controlled by a side lever.[35] The crank shaft ran lengthwise of the chassis. The wheelbase was 104 inches. The car had three forward and one reverse speed.[36]

Meanwhile, Fisher's dream of having an auto track near Indianapolis appeared to be coming to fruition. He and Tom Taggart, Indianapolis' Mayor, were planning to build a track at French Lick, Indiana, at an estimated cost of $80,000. Provided the track was located at French Lick, Taggart promised $30,000 in funding. Fisher actively solicited investors for the project and by mid–December 1905 had commitments of $20,000 of the needed $50,000. Fisher hoped to raise additional funds from Eastern automobile manufacturers at the 1906 New York Auto Show, but his efforts failed as the manufacturers believed the track should be located in a more central location between Cleveland and Buffalo. Another impediment to the track was the hilly nature of French Lick, which would increase the construction cost.[37]

Marmon was focused on developing an eight-cylinder engine with 70 horsepower. The company anticipated using this engine in a seven-passenger touring car it planned to unveil in August 1906.[38]

Following a short parade through downtown Indianapolis, the first hill climb in the city was held on May 24, 1906, at the Glen Valley Hill, which was off of Three Notch Road (now South Meridian Street). In a course 440 yards long with a 10 percent grade, Edgar Apperson had the best time of all 42 contestants at 31.2 seconds. In the medium car contest, a Premier piloted by Cliff Waltman nosed out a Buick piloted by Whittle by two tenths of a second. Buick believed the cars had finished in a dead tie and suggested a runoff. When the runoff was denied, Buick threatened to file a protest. In a four-car field, Howard Marmon, driving a 30-horsepower Marmon with four passengers, had the strongest performance for a touring car at 40.6 seconds. In a second contest, Marmon finished second to a Stoddard-Dayton with a time of 36.6 seconds. Harry Stutz finished second to a Franklin in the light car contest (for cars weighing less than 1,432 pounds). In a contest for cars costing over $3,000, Harry Stutz driving a 25-horsepower Peerless was beaten by Edgar Apperson driving a 40-horsepower Apperson.[39]

The IARA sponsored Memorial Day races at the Indiana State Fairgrounds. Participants in the 100-mile race included Jap Clemens, who had broken the speed record in the previous November, driving a National, and Barney Oldfield, who had set his sights on setting a new record. Oldfield, driving a 24-horsepower Peerless, won in a close contest and established a new record for 50 miles.[40]

The feature event was the five-mile Hoosier Sweepstakes race with a $1,000 in gold coin prize to the winner. Also at stake was an additional $500 if the record or any intervening records were broken. After C. A. Coey withdrew from the race, Paul Kaiser driving the White Streak faced off against Jap Clemens piloting a National in the first heat. Clemens won the heat and then faced Oldfield at the wheel of the Green Dragon in the second heat, which Oldfield won.[41]

Disappointed by the lack of funds to build a race track in French Lick, Indiana, Fisher announced he was considering building an automobile racetrack at the Indiana State Fairgrounds. Envisioning a two-mile oval around the perimeter of the Fairgrounds, Fisher said he would either form a consortium to build the track or would finance it out of his own funds.[42] He said of the proposed track,

> This would give the association a track almost two miles in circumference. The plan at the present time is to hold a race meet of two or three days in conjunction with the auto show, which would give the visitors a chance to not only inspect the various makes of machines, and a chance to see the big machines in races. The manufacturers would also have an opportunity to try out their machines before the cup races.[43]

Pope-Waverley introduced the Chelsea electric coupe with a price tag of $1,700. Appealing to the convenience and ease of use of the electric car, H. T. Hearsey, Pope-Waverley sales agent, promoted it by saying, "No delay, no noise, no jar, no vibration, no cranking, no balking, no confusion or profanity!"[44]

Premier looked with anticipation to the auto races held in Detroit, Michigan, over the weekend of July 20–21, 1906, with A. C. Webb at the helm of the largest racer ever built, with a four-cylinder air-cooled engine generating 100 horsepower originally built for Carl Fisher's participation in the Vanderbilt Cup races. The car had recently traveled two miles in 2 minutes 1 second at Chicago. Organizers of the races anticipated large crowds, possibly the largest ever to see an automobile race. Despite threatening skies which limited the crowds to an esti-

Judge G. W. Stubbs in a Premier automobile (Bass Photo Co. Collection, Indiana Historical Society).

mated 3,000, Webb piloted the racer to victory with a time of 5 minutes 37 seconds.[45] After the Detroit victory, Premier entered races in St. Louis, Missouri. In a five-car field battling for a $600 prize, Webb was defeated by Bert Dingley driving a 90-horsepower Pope-Toledo in the feature ten-mile open race.[46]

Premier unveiled a two passenger, four-cylinder runabout fitted with a torpedo deck rather than the tonneau found on the Model L. The car, built upon a 106-inch wheelbase, was available in either carmine (deep red) or green.[47] To support the increased manufacturing effort, Premier stockholders authorized an increase of $100,000 in preferred stock.[48]

Auto enthusiasts planned a series of endurance runs throughout Indiana to assess the quality of the roads. Premier's president, Harold O. Smith, piloted a 24-horsepower Premier on a 138-mile endurance run to Louisville with a time of six hours.[49]

Robert Hassler, Marion's chief engineer, invented a new type of transmission which was available on the company's four-cylinder runabout. The transmission was a sliding type in an enclosed housing with the rear axles and the differential. The transmission was designed for cars with 10 to 24 horsepower with a maximum weight of 1,400 pounds.[50]

The murder of Indianapolis policeman Charles J. Russell was met with shock by the city. When it was discovered that Russell's family needed financial assistance, the Gentlemen's Driving Club and the IARA arranged a day of racing at the Indiana State Fairgrounds, including both horses and automobiles, for the benefit of his widow and children. Many Indianapolis auto enthusiasts, including Carl Fisher, Tom Kincaid, James Allison, Jap Clemens, A. C. Webb, and Harry Stutz, participated in the automobile races,[51] raising approximately $800 for the benefit of the Russell family. The 100-horsepower Premier driven by A. C. Webb set new track records for one mile and five miles in the five-mile open race. In the ten-mile event for stock cars costing over $2,000, the two Nationals finished first (Kincaid) and second (Allison), while Fisher in a Stoddard-Dayton finished third. The ten-mile stripped stock car race had the same results, with Kincaid finishing first, Allison finishing second, Fisher in the Stoddard-Dayton finishing third, and Joe Moore in the 16-horsepower Premier finishing fourth. In the five-mile handicapped race, the 60-horsepower National driven by Clemens finished first, Kincaid's 40-horsepower National finished second, and the 55-horsepower White Flyer finished third.[52] Buick took bragging rights, defeating a Mitchell, a Leader and an Indianapolis-built Premier in the three-mile class for runabouts with a 22-horsepower, two-cylinder car costing $1,150.[53]

To prove the worth of its cars, Premier had a policy of entering all contests where the "worthiness of the auto to the driving public could be established." One of the strategies employed was a reliability run where the car, along with other entrants, would take a pre-established route with success at the end being measured not only by whether or not the car had any mechanical breakdowns through the run but also a close physical inspection.[54] Premier entered an auto in an endurance run from Albany, New York to New York City by way of Springfield, Massachusetts in November. When the autos hit the Berkshire Hills in Massachusetts, they were greeted with a snowstorm described as a blizzard. Having started fifth, the Premier car, carrying five passengers, reached New York City first. It was one of two cars to finish the race.[55]

At the end of 1906, Premier introduced the Gentleman's Roadster, a runabout with a four-cylinder water-cooled engine. Built upon a shorter wheelbase, the car was very similar to the Model 24 touring car. It could accommodate three passengers through the use of a rumble seat. Unlike the tonneau, the rumble seat was not detachable.[56]

Premier 24 "Gentleman's Roadster" (*Horseless Age*, December 26, 1906).

National's 1907 Chicago Automobile Show advertisement (Indiana Historical Society, P0143).

Marmon offered two different models for 1907. The Model C-7 touring car was the same as the previous year except that the wheelbase was lengthened from 90 to 96 inches and some minor modifications were made to the planetary speed change gear. A new offering to the market was the Model F, which had a four-cylinder, air-cooled engine.[57]

National offered three different models for 1907. The Model F was a continuation of the four-cylinder, 40-horsepower, shaft-driven touring car offered in the previous year. The other two models were new and featured new engines: a four cylinder producing 50 horsepower and a six cylinder with 75 horsepower, designed by National's chief engineer, W. G. Wall. The four-cylinder car had a 112-inch wheelbase while the six-cylinder car was roomier with a 127-inch wheelbase. The cars had two separate ignition systems. One was a gear-driven magneto system with automobile governor while the other was a storage battery with a single coil and distributor. Both autos could carry up to seven passengers with five being seated in the tonneau. The standard color offered for both automobiles was carmine with a black stripe.[58] A month later, National unveiled a six-cylinder runabout built on a shorter frame than the six-cylinder tonneau. It had a small seat on the left running board for the mechanic, which was representative of the "extreme fashion" of the day.[59]

By 1907, Overland was building a four-cylinder car, the Model 22, with a sales price of $1,250. It was a shaft drive car with the transmission and the rear axle enclosed in one housing.[60] The company was reorganized with $100,000 in capital by C. E. Cox, David M. Parry, W. E. Oakes, F. N. Fitzgerald and W. E. Maxwell.[61] Running out of space, David Parry erected a building for Overland next to Standard Wheel's operation on Oliver Avenue. The building, measuring 308 feet by 80 feet, was for shops, with a second building planned for the future.[62]

Pope-Waverley offered three different models for 1907. The Model 65 Stanhope, a two-person vehicle priced at $1,500, could be fitted with a Victoria or buggy top. The Model 67 Victoria Phaeton, the "acme of style and luxuriousness," was priced at $1,600, while the two passenger Model 69 runabout was priced at $1,150 without a top or $1,225 with a top.[63]

National had one of the largest displays at the 1907 New York Auto Show. It included a 40-horsepower runabout, the 50-horsepower Model H touring car, and the Model L with both a seven-passenger limousine and a nine-passenger limousine. There were no major changes in the cars displayed other than that National had brought the design and construction of the engines in-house.[64]

American offered two 1907 models: a four-cylinder roadster and a five-passenger touring car. *Horseless Age* commented on the unique frame construction of the roadster, as the frame was hung beneath the axles by long lengths and raised forging, which, of course, was the underslung frame for which American is remembered. This resulted in the lower edge of the car being a low 10½ inches from the ground. The car featured a 24-gallon gas tank located in the rear. It reportedly could go 60 miles per hour at 1,200 rpm and its mileage was reported to be 11.5 miles per gallon when using the battery ignition and 14.25 miles per gallon when the magneto was in use. The touring car used a regular frame rather than being underslung like the roadster. The wheelbase for the touring car was 116 inches and it had an 18-gallon gas tank.[65] Needing capital to support its operations, in 1907 American increased its capital stock from $25,000 to $100,000.[66]

Marmon displayed its seven passenger, eight-cylinder touring car at the 1907 New York Auto Show. Built on a 128-inch wheelbase, the car had 60 horsepower and weighed 3,700 pounds. Marmon also displayed the Model F five passenger touring car and a Model F limousine which had a 35-horsepower engine. The wheelbase for the Model F was 104 inches. Marmon also had a Model C-7 four passenger touring car built on a 96-inch wheelbase.[67]

For 1907 Premier introduced a touring car with an interchangeable cooling system which could be either water or air based. Previously, all Premier cars had been air cooled. To support

American Underslung automobile (Bass Photo Co. Collection, Indiana Historical Society).

the interchangeable cooling system, the wheelbase of the car was extended by 2½ inches. The interchangeable system also weighed 70 pounds more than the air-cooled system alone due to the need for a radiator and the longer wheelbase. In spring 1907 the company also introduced a two-ton commercial truck equipped with a 24-horsepower Premier motor and a double sided chain drive. The truck averaged 11 miles per hour at 1,000 rpm and had a ten-gallon gasoline tank.[68]

The Vanderbilt Cup was the premier auto race in the United States. With a limited number of specialized racing automobiles entered and representing their countries of origin, Indianapolis automobile manufacturers believed there should be a race for stock cars. When Frederick H. Elliott, secretary of the American Automobile Association (AAA), visited Indianapolis, Edgar Apperson of the Apperson Brothers and George Weidley, Premier's chief engineer, advocated the idea of a separate race for stock touring autos to be run as soon as possible after the Vanderbilt Cup on the same track. They were appointed to the advisory technical committee for the AAA. The general parameters for this race were that, although the cars could have racing bodies, only stock cars were permitted. Participation in the race was limited to two autos per manufacturer. Premier, Franklin, and Apperson were among the early entrants in the race.[69]

By mid–June 1907, the details of the Stock Chassis Speed Endurance Contest were ironed out. Instead of having short races, the committee decided upon a three-day meet with each day having a race of 200 miles. On the second and third day, cars would start in the order of their finish on the previous day. It was hoped the races would show both the durability and the speed of the participating automobiles. Because the committee wanted the race to be a test of the cars and not the drivers, a change of drivers was permitted if they became injured or fatigued. The committee specified that the drivers and riding mechanics were to be American citizens because European professional drivers had more experience. The committee also rejected the idea of handicapping the cars in favor of establishing three classes based upon the cubic inches of displacement. The classes established were Class A for cars with a maximum engine displacement of 535 inches and a minimum wheel base of 105 inches; Class B for cars with a maximum engine displacement of 375 cubic inches and a wheel base of 100 inches; and Class C for cars with a maximum engine displacement of 250 cubic inches and a wheel base not to exceed 72 inches. The entry fee was $500 for the first car and $250 for a second car.[70]

In talking about the race, committee member and Premier president Howard Smith said,

> We believe a race in which will be entered the stock product of several manufacturers will enable the manufacturer and also the interested public to draw direct comparisons between the competing models, and the results of such a contest should, we believe, have the effect of raising the standard of stock cars very materially.[71]

The committee wanted to ensure that the cars were not specially made, which would defeat the purpose of the race. Smith explained,

> We have specified that the product must be that of a recognized established manufacturing firm. We desire, if possible, to make the rules such that a promoter could not produce a sample car, and on the strength of possible successes expect to enter the manufacturing field. This would be obviously an unfair advantage and also defeat the purposes of this race.[72]

Indiana manufacturers hoped to influence the AAA committee to route the 1907 Glidden Tour through Indiana. Edgar and Elmer Apperson of the Apperson Brothers Automobile Company met the AAA officials in Kokomo and traveled with them to Tipton, where they were joined by a delegation of 25 Indianapolis men including Fisher, Newby, Howard Smith, Howard Marmon, president of the Indiana Auto Club Louis Levey, and Indianapolis Mayor Bookwalter. The Appersons, the Indianapolis delegation, and the AAA officials then traveled to Indianapolis, where they were feted with a dinner and smoker at the Denison Hotel. Indiana anticipated being well represented in the Glidden tour by two Marmons, three Premiers, two Nationals, two Appersons, two Haynes, and a Fisher runabout.[73]

Sponsored by the AAA, the 1,590-mile 1907 Glidden Tour began in Cleveland, Ohio, on its way to New York City by way of Chicago, Illinois, with 73 cars. Forty-seven large touring cars competed for the Glidden Trophy, while 13 runabouts competed for the Hower Trophy. The other 13 cars were going to make the run but were not contestants.[74] Four Indianapolis cars participated, including a Premier runabout, two Premier touring cars, and a Marion runabout. A Premier 24 was selected to lead the Tour.[75] One of the Premiers was driven by Joe Moore for the Auto Club of the Americas, while Howard Smith drove another of the Premiers representing the Auto Club of Indianapolis. In the segment between Toledo and South Bend, the tour was marred when a 30-horsepower Packard skidded off the road and overturned with one of its occupants, J. T. Clarke of Chicago, suffering fatal injuries.[76] In the leg from South Bend, Indiana, to Chicago some hostility was shown to the automobiles near Hammond, Indiana, where a printer attempted to sabotage the trip by placing telephone poles across the road beyond a bend where they could not be seen by the drivers. Disaster was averted when another Hammond resident found the telephone poles and warned the oncoming cars of the danger. In another incident, some wooden planks were removed from a bridge, nearly causing the Premier pilot car to be wrecked.[77]

After a night's stay in South Bend, on the journey to Indianapolis the Marion runabout driven by Harry C. Stutz for the Auto Club of the Americas broke an axle after skidding into a ditch on roads slick from heavy rain. The occupants were thrown from the car but were not seriously injured. Although the Marion had to withdraw from the contest, the necessary repairs were made and the car journeyed through to New York City.[78]

When the Tour reached Indianapolis, cars and drivers were greeted by hundreds of automobiles of all makes lining the road into the city cheering the participants on. The participants enjoyed Hoosier hospitality with a social at the Indiana Auto Club's headquarters at the Denison Hotel.[79] The participating cars were all parked on the Circle overnight. According to the Tour's rules, after reaching a town, no inspection or changes could be made to an automobile until it left the control area the next day. The Indianapolis Police Department provided protection for the autos while they were parked on the Circle.[80]

Despite a perfect score when the tour reached Bedford Springs, Pennsylvania, the Premier runabout dropped out of the Glidden Trophy race when its driver, Harry Hammond, became ill. That left one car from Indianapolis to capture a trophy in the Tour.[81]

The Tour's end was at Park Circle in New York City. Of the 74 autos starting the trip, 55 were still running at the end. The Indianapolis Premier touring car had a perfect score along with 17 other competitors for the Glidden Trophy.[82] The strong performance of the Premier car in the Glidden Tour led the Gibson Automobile Company (Gibson), the sales agent for Premier, to take out a half page ad above the fold touting the car's performance.

The four-cylinder pilot car was the only car under $3,500 in price that did not have a demerit.[83]

Gibson also touted the performance of a $2,250 Premier Roadster in a 208-mile endurance run from New York City to Albany, some of it through drenching rains that resulted in muddy, rut-filled roads. Although the car finished in the top eight, it bragged that it defeated fourteen other cars costing $3,000, $4,000, $4,500 and even $6,500. The advertisement said,

> In other words, for all practical purposes, you get just as good service in the Premier as you do in any other car at two or three times the price. And as compared with most of the fancy priced rigs, you get even better service, better construction, more endurance and better durability in the $2,250 Premier.[84]

The roads of the early 1900s were primarily dirt. When it rained, the roads became muddy, frequently slippery and, in many instances, full of places where a car could bog down. One rainy evening, George Weidley, Premier's chief engineer, went into the Gibson shop. He found the proprietor, Cecil Gibson, bemoaning the fact of the weather and the muddy roads. Gibson had sold a new Ford runabout to a man from Shelbyville and took in trade a one-cylinder Cadillac. Gibson sent one of his employees to Shelbyville to pick up the Cadillac and bring it to Indianapolis. When he was about six miles outside of Shelbyville, the mud was so bad he was unable to continue his journey back to Indianapolis. Upon receiving word of this, Gibson sent a second car, nicknamed "Maud," to tow the Cadillac out of the mud. Unfortunately, Maud became mired in the mud about three miles before reaching the Cadillac. Gibson then sent a two-cylinder Rambler to pull both the Cadillac and Maud from the mud. About two miles from Maud, the Rambler met a farmer whose horse was frightened by the auto. So the driver and the farmer pushed the Rambler into a ditch. Upon hearing the tale of woe, Weidley told Gibson that he would tow all three cars with his six-cylinder Premier. Believing that Weidley was kidding, Gibson told him it was not a laughing matter. To show his seriousness, Weidley told Gibson, "I'll either tow them all in tonight or that Premier Six out there is yours." Bypassing the other two cars, Weidley reached the Cadillac and rescued it from the mire. With the Cadillac trailing behind, Weidley went back and the two cars pulled Maud from the mud. Then the Premier with two cars in tow went to fetch the Rambler. After about a half hour of work, the three cars freed the final auto. The procession then went back to Indianapolis. Mission accomplished.[85]

In 1907 the New York Auto Show, originally held at the beginning of the calendar year, was changed to October so that manufacturers could show off their newest models. Indiana, whose production of automobiles was second only to that of Michigan, was well represented at the auto show.[86]

National unveiled its 1908 model cars, displaying two six-cylinder and two four-cylinder cars. The larger of the six-cylinder cars had a 127-inch wheelbase while the smaller had a 116-inch wheelbase. Both four-cylinder cars were built upon a 112-inch wheelbase. For this model year, National adopted a curved cast aluminum body for the large six-cylinder car. The other three models were available in either a curved or a straight-lined body, and all cars featured a mahogany dash. The purchaser of the auto could also choose between the historic round radiator or a new rectangular radiator. All four models had three forward speeds and one reverse.[87]

Marmon introduced two four-cylinder models for 1908. The Model G was a five-passenger touring car with a 104-inch wheelbase and an air-cooled engine. The Model H was also a five-passenger car but its tonneau would allow for seating for seven passengers. The wheelbase for the Model H was 114 inches. The purchaser had the option of either an air-cooled or a water-cooled engine.[88]

For 1908, Marion displayed only water-cooled models. The company featured the Marion Flyer, a four-cylinder, 24-horsepower single rumble roadster weighing 1,850 pounds with a 102-inch wheelbase.[89] The company also exhibited a double rumble roadster and a six-cylinder gentleman's roadster with a 104-inch wheelbase and between 30 and 35 horsepower. The Hassler transmission permitted two forward speeds and one reverse.[90]

After two years of experimentation, Premier introduced the Premier 45, a six-cylinder car, for 1908.[91] The 1908 Premier Six was its first six-cylinder car.

In November 1907, Ray McNamara, driving a four-cylinder Premier 24, set a new record for a round-trip journey from Boston to New York with a time of 22 hours 59 minutes. Many found this new record remarkable, as much of the return trip was driven in the night without incident.[92] In the annual endurance run sponsored by the Chicago Auto Club, both the Premier and the National auto finished with a perfect score for the first day's effort. Johnny Aitken drove the National vehicle round trip from Chicago to South Bend. The second day's round trip journey was from Chicago to Ottawa, Illinois.[93]

John Willys formed the American Motor Car Sales Company for the national distribution of three Indianapolis manufacturers—Overland, Marion and American. Having a distributor was new to the industry, as previously all brands had undertaken their own distribution to sales agents around the country. Willys served as president of this organization with P. D. Stubbs as secretary.[94]

In December 1907, Arthur Newby and Howard Smith were among the seventeen men appointed to a new technical board of the AAA, which also included Edgar Apperson and Henry Ford. The function of the board was to run technical contests for automobiles.[95]

Prior to the opening of the Chicago Auto Show in early December 1907, there was a two-day reliability run with Premier, National and Marion participating. On the first day, the autos traveled round trip from Chicago to South Bend, Indiana and on the second day they traveled round trip from Chicago to Ottawa, Illinois. Because of the difficulties with the Glidden Tour, the organizers had an observer in each car from a different manufacturer who would have control of the tool kit which could be used should a car need repair.[96] A 30-horsepower Haynes runabout driven by Frank Nutt had a perfect score during the run. The run was disappointing for the Indianapolis manufacturers, as all were assessed penalty points for equipment failures.[97]

In January 1908, a group of Indianapolis auto enthusiasts, including Arthur Newby, Frank Wheeler, Carl Fisher, George Weidley (superintendent of Premier), and George M. Dickson (National's sales manager), traveled to Savannah, Georgia to support National's entry in the Grand Prize race. Their hopes for a National victory were soon dashed as the gasoline pipe of the car became clogged by some debris on the first lap. Despite that, all of the men were enthusiastic about the running of the race. Newby commented, "There has never been a race in America that has had such perfect management as this." He continued, "The course is a beautiful one, though it has a large number of turns and curves in it, and a magnificent roadbed had been built with the turns properly banked."[98]

In February 1908, a 40-horsepower Model G Marmon auto was entered in New England's motor car endurance test. The car, driven by F. E. Wing, Marmon's New England agent, traveled 135 miles from Boston to Providence to Worcester and back to Boston, turning in a perfect score with a time of five hours 20 minutes.[99]

In early December 1907, John N. Willys and E. B. Campbell, principals of the American Motor Car Sales Company, became aware that Overland was unable to deliver the cars they had ordered for the 1908 season. Having advanced monies in conjunction with the order, they found it necessary to advance additional monies to Overland in order to protect their investment. The principals of Overland agreed to give Willys and Campbell controlling interest in the company, with Willys ending up with 51 percent of the company stock. The American Motor Car Sales Company assumed the indebtedness of Overland, with other creditors agreeing to be paid 40 percent of what was owed.[100] Overland was reorganized as the Overland Automobile Company (Overland) in February 1908[101] with capital of $25,000.[102] Production of automobiles began in March.[103] In conjunction with the reorganization, Claude Cox resigned.[104] Officers of the new organization included J. N. Willys, president; Will H. Brown, formerly with Pope-Waverley, vice president; P. D. Stubbs, formerly with American, secretary and sales manager; and E. C. Hardegen, formerly with Pope-Waverley, plant superintendent. The directors included David M. Parry and Oliver H. Carson in addition to the officers. With the restructuring of the business accomplished, the plant began running at full capacity,[105] initially producing roadsters but quickly adding a touring car to its product lineup by May.[106] When the company reached the construction rate of three autos per day, it became clear that the factory was too small to handle the anticipated increase in production to five vehicles per day. This resulted in the company installing circus tents on the grounds for the final assembly.[107]

While Indianapolis leadership was excited with the possibility of this factory being reorganized, they were concerned that Overland was thinking about relocating away from Indianapolis. The company had received two or three offers. The Commercial Club and the Board of Trade were likely to try to prevent the move. In 1908, Overland anticipated 200 employees making 500 autos, while they had contracts for 1,500 automobiles in 1909 necessitating increasing the staff to 1,000 men.[108]

A special 360-mile race was planned for Savannah, Georgia. American planned to build a special 50-cylinder car to participate in the races[109] while Premier planned to send two entries for the 360-mile race. Adding further local interest was a $1,000 challenge from V. A. Longaker of American and Apperson Brothers of their runabouts.[110]

The kickoff for the 1908 Auto Week in Indianapolis began with a parade through downtown Indianapolis with Charles Newby, Harry Stutz' cousin, as the Parade Marshal.[111] An estimated crowd of between 50,000 and 100,000 people watched the parade, nearly six blocks long and consisting of 175 cars, which began at the Circle and processed down Meridian Street and on to North Street.[112] On Tuesday, March 21, a 0.4-mile hill climb of Michigan Hill was held. In one of the six races, which were broken into groups based upon automobile cost,[113] an Overland piloted by Carl Brockway won a very close contest, with the difference between the winning time and last place being 19.6 seconds. Howard Hodson in a Stoddard-Dayton won the heat for cars costing over $3,500 in which Fisher Auto entered three Nationals valued at $4,200 driven by Thomas Kincaid who finished second, Johnny Aitken who finished third, and Frank Clements who finished fourth.[114] A National touring car, valued at $5,000, also won its class in the hill climb.[115]

Willys was thrilled with the victory in the hill climb of the Overland vehicle, which had left the factory only five days before the contest.[116] "We had hardly hoped to win the hill climb in the face of so many competitors, and it is an added gratification to us that at least one Indianapolis built car should have come away with a trophy," he said. Willys also believed that the strong surge of orders for the Overland was attributable to its performance in the hill climb.[117]

Following the example of other automobile manufacturers, Overland entered a Model 24 roadster in a variety of hill climbing and endurance contests and, much to the delight of John Willys, was very successful. Driven by Carl Brockway, the car scored first in hill climbing contests in Indianapolis, Bridgeport, Connecticut, and Williamston, Pennsylvania, and second at Cincinnati, Ohio, Fort George, New York, and Bridgeport, Connecticut. Additionally, the car made four endurance runs with perfect scores.[118]

For its 1908 models, Premier introduced a water-cooled engine and its first six-cylinder car.[119]

The Indianapolis Automobile Trade Association (IATA) decided to sponsor an endurance run. Premier's George Weidley, National's W. G. Wall, and Marmon's Howard Marmon were appointed as technical observers for the run. These three men drew up the rules for the test and provided their observations of the race to three judges who determined the winner. The run utilized AAA rules and there were three classes of automobiles based upon cost.[120]

On May 20, 1908, there was a 150-mile endurance run for 37 big sealed-bonnet automobiles from University Square in Indianapolis to Noblesville, Anderson, Muncie, and Newcastle before returning to Indianapolis. Leading the pack were Frank L. Moore and A. E. Vinton in a Premier. The cars departed from Indianapolis at one minute intervals and it was anticipated that they would return to Indianapolis in one minute intervals. The participants were broken into three classes. The "A" class, comprised of 1907–1908 stock touring cars, runabouts or roadsters costing over $2,500, was expected to negotiate the course at 18 miles per hour. Class "B," comprised of 1907–1908 stock touring cars, runabouts or roadsters costing between $1,500 and $2,500, was expected to maintain a speed of 16 miles an hour, while the "C" class for 1907–1908 stock touring cars, runabouts or roadsters costing under $1,500 was to maintain the course at 14 miles per hour.[121]

Starting at the end of the pack was the technical car with Frank Staley, George Weidley, and W. G. Wall in a Marmon driven by Howard Marmon. During the endurance run, this car was expected to pass all the participants.[122] This car and two other Marmons had perfect scores in the contest.[123]

With the slogan "One hundred miles a day for 100 days or bust," Premier was determined to show the reliability of its cars. Starting at Monument Circle in downtown Indianapolis and under the watchful eyes of an observer, the same car would travel 100 miles each day. Driving a different route each day, the car would include parties of auto enthusiasts. The challenge would occur come rain or shine.[124]

The folks at Premier were delighted with the free publicity when one of their six-cylinder, 45-horsepower touring cars was chosen to determine the route for the 1908 Glidden Tour. The party of four for the route determination included Ray McNamara at the wheel, AAA touring board secretary Dal H. Lewis, Leon M. Bradley and N. Lanarnick of New York.[125] In a letter back to the company, McNamara described the difficulties of the trip.

> Arrived in Johnstown after a hard trip through the Alleghany Mountains in a rain and wind storm. Roads very slippery and bad, mostly soft clay. The only good road we had was a two mile climb on the first range of mountains encountered. Engine worked perfectly all the time.

> The car does not show any bad effects from the hard work it has been called upon to do, except the mud and slush is rapidly making the car look as though it has seen a season's service.[126]

The Glidden Tour promised to be the most difficult of all the tours, since it crossed five mountain ranges as it traveled from Buffalo, New York southward to Pittsburg, Pennsylvania before turning to the east. After reaching Pittsburg, it turned northward to Albany, New York, then on to Boston and Rangeley Lake, Maine. Turning southward once again, the tour went through Bethlehem, New Hampshire, before concluding in Saratoga, New York.[127]

The organizers changed the rules for the 1,700-mile 1908 Glidden Tour to have the cars divided into classes. Indianapolis manufacturers anticipated having 20 percent of all entries. Bested only by Pierce, which had six entries, Premier had five participants including the pilot car and the Century car, which took up the challenge of 100 miles a day for 100 days. Studebaker, Franklin and Reo had four entries each. Indiana was also represented by Marmon, Overland and Haynes.[128]

The Premier Century piloted by George Weidley, two Stoddard-Daytons and two Arrows had perfect scores, necessitating a runoff for the Hower Trophy. A two-day run was scheduled from Saratoga Springs, New York, to Buffalo with an overnight stop in Syracuse.[129] Weidley, driving a Premier Century in the runoff contest, suffered a broken axle when the car hit a rut.[130] A Stoddard-Dayton had a broken frame while a second Stoddard-Dayton experienced great difficulty. The contestants decided that the trophy should remain with Pierce, which had won it the previous year and still had two vehicles in the contest.[131] Weidley in a telephone conversation with officials at Premier headquarters said, "The roads are so bad that it is just a question of all the cars being broken except one."[132]

The Indianapolis automobile community was divided as to what type of race would do the most to put Indiana in the automobile spotlight. One faction, including Carl Fisher, P. D. Stubbs of Overland, Haynes and Apperson of Haynes-Apperson of Kokomo, and V. A. Longaker of American, believed the best way was a large race involving the best drivers and cars in the nation. The other faction, which included Premier's Howard Smith and Walter Marmon, felt that endurance runs were the most useful in attracting people to Indiana-built automobiles.[133]

The IATA arranged for a two-day endurance run to French Lick, Indiana. The technical committee arranging the run consisted of Premier's George Weidley, National's W. G. Wall, and Howard Marmon. The contest was believed to be the most difficult of the endurance runs in Indiana due to the hills around French Lick.[134]

The IATA also arranged for two days of racing at the Indiana State Fairgrounds on September 18–19, 1908. Walter Marmon, Arthur Newby and Howard Smith served as judges for the racing program while George Weidley and Frank Moore served as clerks of the lines.[135] The program began with motorcycle races with eight entries, including six Indians, one Thor and one Overland. Participating in the auto races were Barney Oldfield, Walter Christie and Charles Soules. Charles Soules put on a one-mile exhibition run in his "Red Devil." Christie also did a one-mile timed run. The organizers were also interested in getting Carl Fisher and Paul Smith to have a match race. The starter and announcer for the races was Ernest Moross.[136]

Walter Christie set a new one-mile track record with a speed of 52.2 seconds, winning the $500 prize for the fastest one-mile time in the two days of racing. Charles Merz piloted a Stoddard-Dayton sponsored by Fisher Automobile Company to the best performance by an amateur for one mile. Merz easily won a special five-mile match race consisting of two heats with Loring Wagner piloting a Haynes. Merz, the son of an Indianapolis policeman, won the free-for-all handicapped event with a 15-second handicap. Herb Lytle, who had participated in the 1904 Vanderbilt Cup and 1905 Grand Prix races, placed second driving an American racer built in Indianapolis. Third place was captured by Johnny Aitken driving a National racer.[137]

In late September 1908, a Marmon car was among 37 participants in a 375-mile reliability run from Boston to the White Mountains and didn't experience any difficulties.[138] Another reliability run was organized by the Kansas City Automobile Club through Kansas and Oklahoma in late September 1908. Although that part of the country is flat and the drivers didn't have to navigate through mountains, Ray McNamara driving a Premier explained that the course was still challenging because of all of the lakes and rivers they had to negotiate. Additionally, heavy rains had turned the red clay and black soil into a gummy mess, causing the drivers to use their low gear. The Kansas City Automobile Club had requested that the pilot car for the Glidden Tour participate in this tour.[139]

The Pope Motor Car Company, of which Waverley was a part, was put into receivership around 1907. The collapse of the Pope empire put the Waverley automobile in limbo. In an effort to save the large manufacturing facility, Herbert H. Rice, manager of the Waverley plant, and Wilbur C. Johnson, assistant manager, started talking to a variety of Indianapolis businessmen about forming a consortium to purchase the plant out of receivership. In Sep-

Madame C. J. Walker, Indianapolis entrepreneur of African-American hair care products, in her Waverley electric automobile (Madame C. J. Walker Collection, Indiana Historical Society).

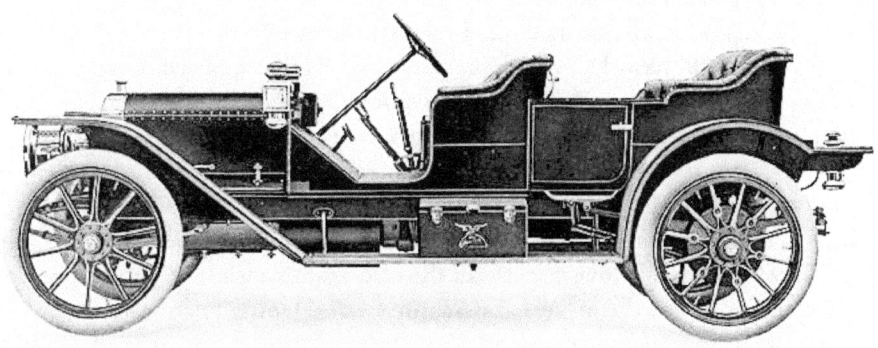

The American Gadabout was a five-passenger automobile built in 1909. It had 50 to 60 horsepower and retailed for $3,750 (courtesy New York Public Library).

tember 1908, the plant was purchased by a consortium of Indianapolis businessmen for $200,000.[140] One of the first people interested was William B. Cooley, the president of Blackford County Bank. Others joining Cooley, Rice, and Johnson in the purchase were Hugh Dougherty, William F. Kuhn, Carl Von Hake, William Kothe, Jr., John R. Love, Hugh M. Love, Joseph C. Schaf, and Burton E. Parrott. Cooley was named president of the new Waverley, Herbert Rice vice president, Von Hake secretary, and Johnson secretary.[141]

Waverley produced ten different models ranging from a runabout priced at $1,150 to a four-passenger coupe priced at $2,150. The cars used Exide, National, or Waverley batteries as their power source. Marketing focused on the ease of use which did not require a driver or chauffeur. It also featured the lower operating cost per mile compared to a gasoline or steam engine and lower maintenance costs.[142]

In October 1908, several manufacturers including Premier and Marmon participated in a reliability test to run 250 miles daily for four days. A Premier entered by Webb Jay and driven by Ray McNamara won the Standard Oil Company's trophy for the best fuel consumption. A 32-horsepower Premier tied with a 36-horsepower Haynes driven by Frank Nutt for a perfect score. In the touring car division, there were three cars with perfect scores— a Franklin, a Haynes, and a Pierce-Arrow. A 50-horsepower Marmon entered in this class had a one-point penalty for a fan belt coming off and a second one-point penalty for a leak in the air line causing too much pressure in the gasoline feed.[143]

Marmon unveiled its 1909 models in October 1908. These included the Marmon 32, the Marmon 50, and a roadster, the Marmon 45. Displayed at the New York Auto Show, the Marmon 32 was a low-slung five-passenger touring car and had somewhat of the appearance of a roadster. The Marmon 50 was a seven-passenger touring car.[144] American displayed the American Traveler which was priced at $4,000. All of the 250 cars American planned to produce in 1909 had been sold by the time of the auto show.[145]

Overland unveiled its lineup of automobiles for the 1909 season, which consisted of three different chassis equipped with roadster bodies with either a single or double rumble seat so that the automobiles could accommodate either three or four passengers. The four-cylinder, 30-horsepower Model 30 chassis was similar to the 1908 Model 20 chassis except that the length of the wheelbase had been increased to 105 inches. The Model 32 was identical to the Model 30 with the exception of a three-speed transmission that was controlled by levers on the side and a 110-inch wheelbase. The Model 34's four-cylinder engine could develop 35 horsepower. The car had a 116-inch wheelbase.[146]

In October 1908, John N. Willys, president of Overland, purchased 989 of the 1,000 shares of the stock of Marion. With this acquisition, production of the Marion automobile ceased and its factory was dedicated to the manufacture of Overland engines and other smaller parts.[147]

In early December 1908, the United States Post Office began collecting mail from outlying boxes in Indianapolis using two Overland vehicles. The two red, white and blue wagons were leased by the Federal Government for the one-year experiment. In addition to the two autos, Overland provided the drivers and maintenance. Deputy Postmaster John E. Shideler commented, "I feel sure that the experiment will be a big success. Indianapolis is well adapted to the automobile with good streets and absence of hills and from our experience the machines look like a most desirable innovation." Shideler had ridden in the mail wagon the previous day on a route which took the horse and cart three and one-half hours to complete but was done by the mail wagon in two hours.[148]

The Premier Century car, which had easily accomplished the task of 100 miles a day for 100 days, left in mid–December for a tour to the east, stopping by agencies which carried Premier automobiles on its way to the New York Auto Show where it would be part of Premier's display. Driven by Joe Moore, the car was greeted warmly in various towns, having garnered much attention with its century runs. Critics had predicted that a run like this would ruin the car, but after the challenge it was torn down and was in nearly perfect condition.[149]

Premier received an honor from a unique source in December 1908 when the Herreshoff Manufacturing Company of Bristol, Rhode Island ordered a Premier six-cylinder motor and the Premier ignition system including a magneto for use in a power boat they were building. Herreshoff was known for its design and building of sailing yachts entered in the America's Cup and had begun building power boats. Additionally, Herreshoff ordered a Premier Six auto.[150]

3

Indianapolis-Built Cars Dominate Racing

The New York Auto Show was a time for the manufacturers to talk about the various issues they faced, compare notes, and scope out what the competition was doing. At the ninth annual show, Indiana and Indianapolis were well represented with approximately 24 percent of the autos on display having been made in Indiana and 15 percent having been made in Indianapolis, including Overland with six autos on the floor, Marion with two, and Marmon with two 50s and three 32s—one each of the touring car, the roadster and the suburban. Also with displays were American with five models, National with four models, and Premier.[1]

Imagine riding in a car open to the elements on a run of hundreds of miles during the winter. That is exactly what the entrants in a two-day reliability run sponsored by the Philadelphia Quaker City Motor Car Club faced in early January 1909. A 1909 Model 30 Premier touring car left Philadelphia, traveled to Wilkes-Barre on the first day, and returned to Philadelphia by a different route the next day.[2] Although the Premier was the only contestant to finish with both a perfect score and a perfect technical score, it was disqualified because it did not carry the proper number of passengers for the whole trip, so Premier was denied the McDonald-Campbell Cup for its efforts. Caught in a blockade of cars, the Premier's passengers had exited the vehicle so that it could go around the blockade, a distance estimated at 50 yards. Disappointed by the ruling, Premier appealed the decision to disqualify the car without success to the AAA Contest Board's sanctioning committee.[3]

At the Chicago Auto Show, Marmon had an unusual twist to its display. Rather than lifting the hood to reveal the engine, the cars had glass hoods installed. The use of strategically placed lighting enabled spectators to clearly see the engine. Marmon autos on display at the Chicago Auto Show included a seven passenger 50 touring car, and four 32s: a roadster, a suburban, a touring car and a coupe.[4]

As a result of the Chicago Auto Show, Indianapolis automobile manufacturers were filled with hope that 1909 would be a banner year. P. D. Stubbs of Overland Automobile said,

> The quantity of business done was phenomenal, particularly as regards retail sales. It is recognized that the season of 1909 is going to be the biggest year that the automobile manufacturers have ever known and there was scarcely a sales manager at the Chicago show who had anything left to sell—that is on contract orders to agents.

The demand for moderately priced cars was the strongest. Stubbs continued,

> There is no doubt that the number of cars sold listing at prices between $1,000 and $2,000 will exceed that of the more expensive machines. This is only natural, for the $1,250 car is the car for the masses.[5]

One of Indianapolis' successful carriage companies, the Cole Carriage Company, was founded in 1902 as the Gates-Osborne Carriage Company.[6] In 1904, Joseph Cole and Lee Watson bought controlling interest in the firm[7] and by 1907 they were producing 3,000 carriages annually.[8] With the carriage trade being impacted by the Panic of 1907, Cole started thinking about the industry and its long-term outlook. Believing that the days of the industry were numbered, Cole decided that the key to the company's survival was to build a car.[9] With assistance from Charles Crawford, the first Cole automobile was built in a neighbor's garage. In a test run, Cole discovered that the builders had failed to put any brakes on the vehicle, so he circled Monument Circle until the car ran out of gas.[10]

The Cole Motor Car Company (Cole), an offshoot of the Cole Carriage Company, developed the Cole Solid Tire Automobile in 1909.[11] Not surprisingly, the car looked like a carriage.[12] One of the challenges the company had was to make sure that prospective buyers understood that this was an automobile, so the company placed an advertisement proclaiming that the car was "not a converted buggy." As a result, the company had some initial success, selling 170 vehicles. They had three models—a single rumble, a double rumble and a toy tonneau.[13] Not long after Cole delivered its first car in August 1909, Harvey S. Firestone, the president of Firestone Tire & Rubber Company, saw it. Impressed, he lent the company funds which allowed it to rapidly expand production to 42 cars in November 1909.[14]

Wanting to further differentiate from the buggy company, Joseph Cole, John F. Morrison, and Nellie Cole incorporated Cole with capitalization of $100,000 in June 1909.[15] A month later, the company leased the former Overland facility to build three versions of the Cole 30: a roadster selling for $1,400, a demi-tonneau selling for $1,450, and a touring car selling for $1,500. Within 60 days, the company also planned to add a four-cylinder car retailing from $900 to $1,000. Anticipating an output of automobiles of $1.5 million annually, Cole announced that it would hire between 500 and 700 men.[16] In August, the Henderson Motor

One of the original Cole automobiles, circa 1909 (Bass Photo Co. Collection, Indiana Historical Society).

Joseph and Nellie Cole riding in a Cole automobile (LeRoy Cole Collection, Gilmore Car Museum).

Sales Company (Henderson) was organized as the sales agent for Cole with Charles P. Henderson as the vice president and manager. There was a cross-relationship of the two companies, as Henderson was a director of Cole and Joseph Cole was a director of Henderson.[17]

After the success of the 1908 auto show, the Indianapolis automobile dealers held an auto show from March 23 through March 27 to display their wares to the local audience. Unlike the shows in Chicago and New York, in the Indianapolis one the auto dealers preferred to display their autos at their display rooms rather than in a large hall.[18] With the auto show being spread out over the several blocks of "auto row," people attending the car show enjoyed a variety of contests. An incline test of 134 feet in length and an incline of 33.3 percent was held at Carl Fisher's garage, with an Overland car making the test in twelve seconds.[19] Edgar Apperson won the tire change contest for detachable rims with a time of 43 seconds. For the women, there was the egg contest where a woman, riding as a passenger, would hold a parasol in her left hand while balancing an egg on a spoon with her right hand while the driver drove down the street with large pieces of timber placed every 12 feet or so apart. Concluding the auto show was a parade of 365 automobiles nearly five miles long led by Indianapolis' first police car, a 40-horsepower National touring car equipped with a gong, a heavy windshield, and upholstery to stand up to the anticipated excessive wear and tear.[20]

Strong demand for Indianapolis-built autos resulted in expansion by Marmon, Premier, and Gibson. Marmon announced that it was moving its showroom from its manufacturing facility to the ground floor of the new Central Union Telephone Building, located at the corner of Meridian and New York Streets. Before the move, prospective buyers could tour the plant to see where and how automobiles were made. Marmon planned to continue the tours of the manufacturing facilities if requested by a prospective auto buyer.[21] Premier expanded its manufacturing floor space by 50 percent and operated the factory 24 hours per day.[22] Gibson, the sales agent for Marmon, Premier, Ford, and Reo, announced the construction of a new $10,000 three-story brick showroom with a solid plate glass front on North Pennsylvania Street while retaining the existing showroom facilities located directly behind the new location on Massachusetts Avenue.[23] Another impact of the automobile boom was an increase in railroad traffic bringing raw materials into Indianapolis and shipping new automobiles out. A record 325 railroad cars left Indianapolis in March 1909 loaded with automobiles.[24]

A Premier 30 owned by R. M. Owen participated in a New York to Boston endurance run. Along with 19 other cars, the Premier, piloted by Ray McNamara, left under the cloak of darkness. Twelve hours later, 14 of the cars completed the 245 mile journey with a perfect score, including the Premier. Rather than having a runoff, the title was decided by a drawing.[25]

In late 1908, Carl Fisher gave Jim Allison a set of blueprints. Years later, Indianapolis journalist Russel Seeds recalled meeting with Allison at the Prest-O-Lite offices and, upon seeing the blueprints, asking him, "What the devil's that, Jim? Going to build a balloon or a boiled egg?" Allison responded, "It's another dream of Carl's." Allison continued,

> Does look a little bit like a balloon. He has dumped it on me to drive in a few brass tacks that will either explode it or hold it down to earth. I hope we can make it come true, for it would be a great thing for the automobile game, and I guess we owe it something. Anyway, I'm willing to take a chance, if it don't look too durn expensive.

Allison went on to explain that the blueprint was of an automobile race track which would serve the double purpose of increasing the public's interest in the automobile and improving its reliability.[26]

Allison obviously approved of the design of the track and believed that the cost of building it wasn't "too durn expensive," as the announcement was made on February 6, 1909, of the much talked about motor speedway in Indianapolis to rival the Vanderbilt and Savannah courses. The articles of incorporation were filed on February 8 for the Indianapolis Motor Speedway Corporation, with Carl Fisher as president, James Allison as secretary, Arthur Newby as first vice president and Frank Wheeler as second vice president. The company had an initial capitalization of $250,000,[27] with Fisher and Allison each contributing $75,000 while Newby and Wheeler each contributed $50,000. In addition to the officers, Frank E. Sweet served on the board of directors.[28]

The anticipated design of the track was described by the *Indianapolis Star*.

James A. Allison
(Indiana Historical Society, M1040).

The outer circular track is a course of two miles, fifty feet wide and banked at the curves to stand a racing speed of 100 or more miles per hour. Inside this track is a winding course, twenty-five feet wide banked to permit a racing speed of sixty miles per hour. The inner course connects with the outer one, and may be used, when desired, to give a five-mile lap, affording plenty of the curves without which no international race is deemed sufficiently strenuous for the cars or sufficiently exciting for the spectators.

The design of the track was promoted as the safest in the world because of the very broad curves, the smooth track surface, and the absence of buildings or fences within 50 feet of the racecourse. This prediction would soon be disproven. To give the spectators a view of the entire course, three large grandstands and 20 smaller individual ones at a height of ten feet were planned.[29]

National provided a racing machine to take visitors on a fast spin through town as part of the Indianapolis Auto Show. They reported that although most people talk about going sixty miles per hour, the average person had enough speed at fifty miles per hour. Visitors to the Auto Show could also tour the Indianapolis Motor Speedway site.[30] To the delight of the motorists who drove to the construction site, there was a model of the track on the Speedway grounds.[31]

During the Indianapolis Auto Show week, Carl Fisher announced that the contract for the grading of the Indianapolis Motor Speedway had been awarded to King Brothers and that construction of the track, estimated to take 60 days, would begin immediately.[32] By March 18, King Brothers had 100 men, 70 mules, and three 15-ton steam engines working on the track. Work had barely begun when Fisher gave an update on the progress in building the Speedway: "Work on the speedway is being pushed and the entire five-mile circuit has already been staked. The grading for the five miles of track is being done rapidly, with every expectation that the speedway will be completed in the early spring." In addition to the grandstands, the Speedway planned to build "training quarters" for the different teams entering the races.[33]

With shades of the Premier "100 miles per day for 100 days" test of its automobile, National planned a promotional test at the Indianapolis Motor Speedway when construction was completed. The company planned to rent the track for ten days and run one of its cars 1,000 miles a day.[34]

In addition to the work going on at the Indianapolis Motor Speedway and their ongoing businesses, Fisher, Allison, Newby, Charles E. Test, and Robert Hassler decided to start another automobile company in Indianapolis. Test had been a business partner with Newby in Indianapolis Chain and Stamping and National, while Hassler, who had built his first car in 1898, was one of the original organizers of Marion[35] and was later a mechanical engineer with National.[36] With capitalization of $100,000, the Empire Motor Car Company (Empire) was incorporated on April 22, 1909, to manufacture a "businessman's runabout" priced at $800. The manufacturing facility was located at the old Mohawk Cycle Company on West 29th Street at the Canal.[37]

As the opening day of auto racing at the Speedway approached, National was the first to register to participate in the upcoming races with four autos. Two cars were signed up for the Prest-O-Lite Trophy race of 250 miles, which was for cars weighing over 2,100 pounds with between 301 and 450 cubic inches of displacement. National entered two big six-cylinder racers weighing less than 2,400 pounds each with between 451 and 600 cubic inches of displacement in the 300-mile Wheeler-Schebler Trophy race. Although the drivers were not named, expectations were that one would be Johnny Aitken.[38]

Overland, whose motto was "Only Pedals To Push," introduced a four-cylinder model with 35 horsepower and a six-cylinder model with 45 horsepower in addition to the Overland 24 and Overland 26 in 1909.[39] The company also introduced a taxicab as part of its automobile lineup. The taxi had the ability to carry a trunk or luggage as well as five passengers, with three passengers accommodated in a back seat while the front of the taxi had a fold-down bench which could seat an additional two persons.[40]

By 1909, the Overland factory covered approximately four acres and employed over 1,500 workers. With demand soaring for its products, Overland was out of space to support the anticipated growth, causing the company to search for possible solutions including potential relocation outside of Indianapolis.

Incentives for businesses are not a new phenomenon, especially when localities believe that they can increase the number of available jobs. When it became known that Overland needed new facilities, three different localities made attractive offers. Shelbyville, Indiana, offered 40 acres of land and a bonus of $125,000 for the company's relocation; Peru, Indiana, was willing to provide 37 acres of land and $50,000; while Marion, Ohio, offered 87 acres of land and $65,000 in cash.[41] After the Marion, Ohio, delegation visit, Will H. Brown, vice president of Overland, said, "The Marion proposition looks mighty good to us." He continued, "We need more facilities for our growing business."

At the time Overland employed 1,027 people and was building 23 automobiles a day. Overland believed that within the next three weeks its daily volume would increase to 30 automobiles.[42] A special committee of the Commercial Club worked with officials of Overland on a proposal to erect a large factory in Indianapolis which would enable Overland to consolidate its four separate locations into one, thereby improving the efficiency of its operations. Will H. Brown implied that Indianapolis was in the driver's seat, although he clearly was keeping the door open for another town.

> We have an option on a fine factory site in this city. It will expire in thirty days and we hope to have the question of where we are going to locate this new plant settled before that time. We have had all kinds of offers from other cities the most flattering of which is from Marion, O. We have considered the offer made by people of that city, and we have not turned their proposition down.[43]

Imagine the surprise of the Commercial Club and other city officials when on April 6 Overland president John Willys reached an agreement to acquire the Toledo, Ohio, facilities previously owned by Colonel Albert Pope. The purchase included 24 buildings with 400,000 square feet of manufacturing space.[44] Although the news article about the agreement said that Willys planned to operate both the Toledo and Indianapolis facilities, A. A. Atwood, the Overland representative in Toledo, said Willys planned to move all three of the Overland facilities to Toledo.[45]

After touring Pope's Toledo manufacturing plant, Willys announced he was on his way to New York City to close the option to purchase the facility from Colonel Albert A. Pope. The Indianapolis Overland facility would remain open and it was estimated that the two plants would turn out between 10,000 and 15,000 automobiles annually.[46] Any fears of the Indianapolis community of Overland shuttering its facilities were allayed when the company announced the construction of three additional buildings in Indianapolis with an aggregate cost of $40,000 on the Oliver Street property. The new buildings would house a new enameling shop, a finishing and upholstery shop, and a power plant.[47]

As spring returned, the auto manufacturers turned their focus to the upcoming year of racing—hill climbs, endurance contests, and track racing. Howard Smith, president of Premier, felt that the endurance test not only provided good information to the manufacturer about the quality of the product but could also be of value to the consumer in deciding which car to purchase. He observed,

> When we reflect how little was known of the automobile even by the makers a few years ago, it is reasonable to suppose that the average buyer, and particularly one contemplating his first purchase, is not especially equipped with the knowledge to judge the value, actual and relative, of the various cars on the market. The public has the perfect right to know and demand proof of the worth of the automobile, and the great problem is to establish the basis of truth.
>
> Automobiles can no longer be classed as a luxury or a fad. The purchasers are interested in actual service and dependability. There is no doubt that some cars are better than others, and that some cars of a certain class or price are better than others of the same price or class. This value, however, is not altogether determined by the appearance of a car. It is what is in it, what constitutes the vital parts and how every part works with the other.

Smith concluded with how he thought the public could determine the value of the auto under consideration:

> Follow the contests which have been run under rigid rules and strict supervision, and the performances of the various cars entered. Information thus gained can be relied upon. Not only have these contests become more rigid as the cars have developed, but added to the ordinary rules governing the roads has been that of inspection at the finish, showing the actual effect that the undertaking itself had on the car.[48]

In late April 1909 Indianapolis was represented on a very muddy endurance run outside of Pittsburg, Pennsylvania, by Marmon and Premier. Both manufacturers showed well among the 47 entries on the first day of the three day event, with perfect scores on a 150-mile run.[49]

When National chose to participate in a hill climb at Fort George Hill in New York City, Arthur Newby traveled to the contest to support his two drivers, Charlie Merz and Johnny Aitken. The 60-horsepower six-cylinder National won the event for its class with a time of 34.2 seconds, nearly six seconds better than the second place finisher, a Stearns. Although it bettered its time to 33.6 seconds in the free-for-all race, the underpowered car finished third behind a 120-horsepower Benz and a Panhard. In the class for cars selling for less than $3,000, the 35-horsepower, four-cylinder National placed third with a time of 41.2 seconds. After the hill climb, the two Nationals took to the track at Jamaica, New York, where the six-cylinder vehicle circled the track at 91 miles per hour and the smaller 35-horsepower car recorded a speed of 68 miles per hour.[50]

Newby was pleased with the performance of his automobiles at the various trials sponsored by the new Motor Trade Association in New York. Upon returning to Indianapolis, he said,

> I was pleased with our victories, of course, not merely because they demonstrated the superiority of the National all-ballbearing construction, but because every event that brings Indianapolis to the front as a center of automobile manufacturing is helpful.

Newby continued to praise the quality of the automobiles built in Indianapolis:

> As a matter of fact, some of the best cars in the world are made right here in Indianapolis. The Indianapolis manufacturers have not gone in so much for quantity, but when it comes to quality, with the selection of the best materials and design, and to that extreme care in workmanship that insures the best construction, the Indianapolis factories take the highest rank.[51]

Braving a spring storm which brought rains and bad road conditions, a Premier 30 participated in a three-day endurance run from Pittsburg, Pennsylvania. Of the 37 cars that entered the contest, only ten finished, with a Premier, driven by Ray McNamara, finishing in third place. Although the first place finisher, an Oldsmobile, had 17 points in deductions, the Premier, with only 1.5 points in deductions, was penalized for not finishing the trip in the allocated time when the gasoline line became clogged.[52]

Indianapolis manufacturers were looking forward to showing the reliability of their autos in the sixth annual Glidden Tour, which departed from Detroit, Michigan and concluded in Denver, Colorado. Overland entered five vehicles in the tour.[53] Marmon entered two vehicles including one driven by Frank Wing of Boston with Joe Dawson as the riding mechanic. The other was driven by Howard Marmon with Harry Stillman as the riding mechanic.[54] Premier entered five autos including one piloted by Howard Smith.[55]

Smith was very supportive of the Glidden tours:

> The Glidden has worked wonders for the industry and pastime. I would like to see the 1909 tour be the best ever held. Makers learn a lot from it; besides, it affords the manufacturers the opportunity to try cars and to locate the strong and weak points. Running under schedule and strict regulations, the value of a test is more than a private test could provide.
>
> The buying public demands the Glidden and watches with keen interest the result and the progress of the cars during the event. Men feel safe in buying a car that goes through the test with a perfect score or even with a good showing. They look with suspicion on the makers who fail to enter the event, feeling that there must be something wrong with the car if the maker is publicly timid in demonstrating his product in such a strenuous test.[56]

At the conclusion of the 2,600 mile Glidden Tour, the Marmon driven by Howard Marmon and the two Premiers piloted by Webb Jay and Harry Hammond had perfect scores, giving the cars a good chance to win the Glidden Trophy. Other makes with perfect scores included Pierce-Arrow, Moline, Chalmers-Detroit, and Lexington.[57] Having achieved a perfect score in three consecutive Glidden Tours, Premier touted its performance in a 1909 *Motor Age* magazine advertisement: "Do not judge the Premier by its best performance. Judge it by its average performance."[58]

National did not participate in the Glidden Tour but rather entered automobile races sponsored by the Auto Club of Chicago and held in Lake County (Crown Point), Indiana, in June 1909.[59] Historically, Marmon did not enter any speed contests as the company preferred the Marmon car to be known for its reliability, durability and comfort as a family car. However, with an apparent change of mind about not participating in auto racing, Marmon also entered the races at Crown Point to compete for the Cobe Trophy with a two-car team.[60] Shortly after registering for the race, the company withdrew its entries after the death of Daniel Marmon, the patriarch of the Marmon family.[61]

Although not as active on the racing circuit, Marion also entered races and achieved some success with Harry Stutz as the chief engineer and superintendent.[62] Marion entered two cars to be driven by Charles Stutz and Adolph Monsen in the Indiana Trophy race at Crown Point.[63] Monsen won the Indiana Trophy with a time of 4 hours 42 minutes 3 seconds. During one of the Crown Point races, Gil Andersen, the riding mechanic for Monsen, had quite the introduction to auto racing. The car blew an air valve on the carburetor and for 25 miles, Andersen lay on top of the hood holding his hand over the top of the carburetor so that the car might have a chance to win.[64] Charles Stutz dropped out of the Indiana Trophy race on the eighth lap.[65] Two days later in races held at Wildwood, New Jersey, the Marion Flyer piloted by Charles Stutz won two races and also achieved a second and third place.[66]

National walked away with honors at the fourth annual hill climb of "Giant Despair" sponsored by the Wilkes-Barre (Pennsylvania) Auto Club. More than 70,000 spectators saw a National take first place in the event for cars priced at $3,000 with a time of 1 minute 48 seconds, bettering the speed from the previous year by four seconds. National also placed second in two additional events. In the race for autos with a weight of 2,400 pounds and between 401 and 600 cubic inches of displacement, National had a time of 1 minute 47.4 seconds, while in the class for autos weighing up to 2,100 pounds and between 301 and 450 cubic inches of displacement, the car had a time of 2 minutes 3.8 seconds.[67]

Driving a Marion automobile, Charles Stutz won the one-mile incline race at Plainfield, New Jersey, with a time of 1 minute 36 seconds. The car was designed by Harry Stutz, who believed that hill climbs and automobile races were the best tests of an automobile. "The public gets the best recommendation possible when a stock car goes at abnormal speed over a race course. This shows the average buyer what the same bore and stroke can do, and will do, for him under all circumstances."[68]

At an Atlantic City auto exhibition, Waverley unveiled a new driving system where the motor rested on cross bars which were attached to the frame. The effects of vibrations were reduced by rubber cushions.[69]

Demand for the various Marmon models was very strong and the company sold out of the entire stock of 1909 models by July 1909.[70] Anticipating the output of automobiles to increase to 300 for the 1910 year, American planned to increase its production facilities.[71]

Leading up to the automobile races at the Indianapolis Motor Speedway, Indianapolis fans were encouraged by the results when National racers swept every race at the Blue Grass track in Lexington, Kentucky.

At last, the long awaited day for the opening of the Indianapolis Motor Speedway arrived on Friday, August 13, with the Federation of American Motorcyclists races.[72]

When the Stoddard-Dayton team and others arrived at the Indianapolis Motor Speedway for testing, conditions weren't ideal as the course was being repaired from the motorcycle races. The drivers had to drive on one side of the track, leaving the remaining side for a crew of 300 men tamping down the course.[73] One of the drivers testing his racer on the new course was Len Zengel in a Chadwick six who, in a practice lap, recorded a speed of 73.74 miles per hour. Johnny Aitken thrilled the Indianapolis crowd when he went around the track in 2 minutes 2 seconds. This bettered Barney Oldfield's record in his National racer Old Glory with a recorded time of 2 minutes 15 seconds.[74]

The first day of auto racing at the Speedway was one of mayhem. In the featured Prest-O-Lite Race, Wilfred Bourque lost control of his Knox racer, which flipped upside down after hitting a ditch. Both Bourque and Harry Holcomb, his riding mechanic, were killed.[75] Officials from the AAA were very concerned with the condition of the track, which was breaking up due to the stress of the heavy cars and the ditches along the outside of the track. After assurances by Carl Fisher that the track would be repaired and the ditches would be covered, racing continued the next day.[76] Although the track held up on the second day, the third day was a different story. In the 300-mile Wheeler-Schebler Trophy Race, Herbert Lytle was the first to lose control of his car and ended up in a pile of dirt without injury to either himself or the riding mechanic.[77] At 175 miles, Charlie Merz lost control of his National racer when his right tire blew. The car flew through the air for 100 feet and ripped through five fence posts. Although Merz suffered minor injuries in the crash, his riding mechanic, Claude Kellum, and two spectators were killed.[78] Later, when Bruce Keene lost control of his Marmon racer and struck a pedestrian bridge support, AAA officials called off the remainder of the race. When the race was ended, Leigh Lynch in a Jackson was leading by a lap, having driven 235 miles. Since the race was declared "no contest" by the officials, the Wheeler-Schebler Trophy was not awarded.[79]

With business booming, Indianapolis manufacturers were expanding their facilities. National announced a $25,000 expansion to its manufacturing plant on 22nd Street at the L.E.W. Railway. The new two-story structure was 154 feet by 200 feet and was connected to the original structure by a bridge. Premier also expanded into a two-story brick structure at Georgia and Shelby Streets costing $15,000.[80]

Impacting the auto industry on a national level, Judge Charles M. Hough of the United States Circuit Court of Southern New Jersey sustained the validity of the Selden patent in October 1909. The Selden patent had a royalty fee attached for each vehicle sold, which went to the patent holder through the Association of Licensed Automobile Manufacturers (ALAM). Leading the charge against the Selden patent were the Ford Motor Company and the Winton Motor Company who were members of the AMCMA. When Judge Hough handed down his decision, seven members of the AMCMA joined the ALAM, including Reo, Stoddard-Dayton, Mitchell, Jackson, Maxwell, Regal, and Indianapolis-based Premier. Despite the unfavorable ruling, the Ford Motor Company vowed to continue the fight[81] and was ultimately successful in having Judge Hough's ruling overturned in 1911.

In October, National announced its three 1910 models. They added to their roster a four-cylinder, 40-horsepower, five-passenger car retailing for $2,500. This new car joined the six-cylinder National 60 and the smaller six-cylinder National 50. The new National 40 was available in either red or green with black seats[82] with a 125-inch wheelbase, which was slightly longer than previous National 40 models.[83]

Five Indianapolis manufacturers—Marmon, National, American, Marion, and Cole—entered the 1909 Vanderbilt Cup. Marmon entered two Model 32 stock cars, of which one would participate in the Vanderbilt Cup race and the other in the Wheatley Hills Trophy, a shorter race run concurrently. The Marmon drivers were Ray Harroun and Harry Stillman. Although there were faster cars entered in the Vanderbilt Cup and Wheatley Hills Trophy race, Marmon hoped the steady performance of its cars would lead to victory. National's entries included a 40 driven by Johnny Aitken, the world record holder for 100 miles, and a 60 driven by Charlie Merz. In testing after the races at the Indianapolis Motor Speedway, these two cars had achieved speeds of 75 miles per hour on the straightaway. The Cole entry in the shorter Wheatley Hills Trophy race was made by the New York sales agent for the car. Unlike the entries by Marmon and National, the Cole entry was not built to be a racer but was rather built to be a family car.[84] An Indianapolis-built American, driven by Willie Haupt, was entered in the Vanderbilt Cup. George Raiss, piloting a Marion, was entered in the Wheatley Hills Sweepstakes.[85]

Although Arthur Newby had said that National would no longer be involved in racing after the deadly races at the Indianapolis Motor Speedway, he traveled to New York to lead the National team in the races.[86] Ray Harroun, driving a Marmon 32, won the 189.6 mile Wheatley Hills Sweepstakes with a time of 3 hours 10 minutes 21.4 seconds.[87] The only other

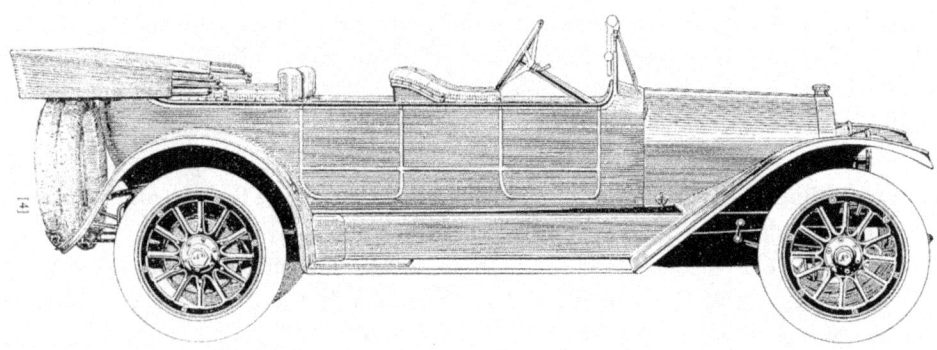

National 40 seven-passenger, four-cylinder touring car (Indiana Historical Society, P0130).

car to finish the Wheatley Hills Sweepstakes was a Columbia driven by Indianapolis resident Howdy Wilcox. The 1909 Vanderbilt Cup race was won by Harry Grant in a six-cylinder, 40-horsepower Alco with a time of 4 hours 25 minutes 42 seconds. Of the 16 cars entered in the Vanderbilt Cup, only five finished.[88]

Ernie Moross, promoter for the Speedway, announced his resignation on October 27, 1909, after meeting with investors planning to build a track similar to the Indianapolis Motor Speedway in Detroit. Moross explained, "My reason for leaving the Indianapolis course, which is now about to be duplicated at Detroit, and which has been copied at Atlanta, is to be able to devote my time to several interests instead of one alone."[89]

Waverley announced several new models including a four passenger Brougham, Model 75-C, which sported a 79-inch wheelbase; Model 70-C, a two-passenger coupe; and Model 76, a Victoria phaeton. The company also introduced its first gasoline-powered car—Model 78, a men's runabout with a folding rumble seat and an estimated speed of 25 miles per hour.[90]

In November 1909, Indianapolis racing teams traveled south to participate in races at the newly opened Atlanta Motor Speedway. The opening day 200-mile feature race was won by Louis Chevrolet in a Buick. Harry Stillman's Marmon was in second place when the car left the track. Stillman was slightly injured and his riding mechanic, Joe Dawson, escaped injury. With a handicap of 70 seconds, Johnny Aitken set a new world record in a ten-mile free-for-all handicap race at 8 minutes 2.41 seconds, upending Barney Oldfield's previous record. The race was won by Stillman followed closely by his Marmon teammate Ray Harroun. Aitken also won a second ten-mile stock chassis race followed closely by his teammate Tom Kincaid. Aitken finished third in both the ten-mile free-for-all and the two-mile free-for-all race.[91]

In a second day of racing at Atlanta, four cars participated in a 120-mile stock chassis race which was won by Harroun driving a Marmon 32 with a time of one hour 49 minutes 26.4 seconds, beating its nearest competitor by six laps.[92] He ran the race without a riding mechanic, driving the same car that had won the Wheatley Hills Trophy in the Vanderbilt races.[93]

On the third day of racing, Aitken established a new American record of 16 minutes 42.76 seconds in a 20-mile stock car race, breaking Barney Oldfield's record by 11.04 seconds. For the first four laps of the race, all five racers were only inches apart as the cars roared around the two-mile speedway. Aitken was closely followed by Stillman in a Marmon and Lee Lorimer in a Chalmers-Detroit. In a subsequent ten-mile handicap race, Aitken finished second and Stillman, driving a Marmon, finished third to George Robertson driving a Fiat.[94]

In the final day of racing at the Atlanta Motor Speedway, auto racing enthusiasts saw Robertson lower the world record for a 50-mile race by 4 minutes 7 seconds. The previous record had been established by Aitken at Indianapolis. In the Atlanta race, Aitken, at the wheel of a National, placed second and Stillman, piloting a Marmon, finished third. Both drivers also beat Aitken's old record, even though Aitken's time was slowed when he had to replace a tire on the 42nd mile.

The 12-mile stock chassis race had the crowd on its feet the whole time as Aitken, who had led for the first six miles, fell behind a Chalmers-Detroit racer piloted by Lee Lorimer, but came back to win by 20 yards. Harroun, piloting the Marmon 32, won a very close ten-mile race with a speed of 9 minutes 51.01 seconds. It was a good day of racing for the Indianapolis teams, with two wins and two seconds out of the seven races run.[95]

Both Marmon and National took pleasure in displaying the trophies won at the races. With its showroom at the very desirable location of Meridian and New York streets, Marmon showed off the trophies won at the Atlanta races, including the Atlanta Speedway Trophy for Harroun's victory in the 120-mile race.[96] National also returned to Indianapolis with five trophies from the Atlanta races. Aitken won four races, placed second in four, and placed third in three. His teammate, Tom Kincaid, won a cup for second place and scored fourth place in two additional races.[97]

Upon returning from the Atlanta races, Moross changed his mind and announced he would continue to promote all of the races at the Speedway for 1910. He began by promoting the upcoming races in December, announcing a full racing card. He predicted,

> Two miles a minute will surely be traveled over the new track and all the marks made in the South will surely be swept away. The Atlanta track was much faster than the old surface on our Speedway, but I do not think that it compares with our new track.[98]

Later in the month, Marmon took bragging rights, winning a 100-mile contest on a one-mile circular track at New Orleans in a time of 1 hour 47 minutes 14 seconds with a 32 piloted by Harroun.[99] Harroun's victory was assured when Aitken, driving a National and leading by a mile at the end of 80 miles, experienced ignition problems.[100] Harroun also won a 50-mile contest with a time of 54 minutes and a 20-mile race with a time of 21 minutes 28.4 seconds. Of the eight events it entered in the New Orleans contests, Marmon had these three first place finishes; second place finishes in the 5-mile race, the 5-mile amateur race and a 10-mile handicapped race; and third place finishes in two ten-mile handicapped races. Blowing its own horn, Marmon touted its success in an advertisement:

No other car has ever demonstrated such ability to endure the tremendous strain of a mile-a-minute speed for long distances without stopping as the Marmon did in the Vanderbilt, in the Indianapolis races, in the Atlanta races, and in the New Orleans races.[101]

For the 1910 season, Indianapolis Motor Speedway management announced six events, one each month from May until October, subject to approval by the AAA Contest Board. Five of the events would be automobile racing and the sixth an aviation meet.[102] Auto races were tentatively scheduled for Memorial Day weekend (May 27, 28, & 30); July 4 weekend (July 1, 2, & 4); a 24-hour race on August 12 & 13; a Labor Day race for September 3 & 5; and a final meet for October 7 & 8. An aviation event was scheduled in combination with the auto race on July 4. International aviators would participate in the aviation event scheduled for July 23.[103]

Anticipating that the paving of the Speedway with brick would be finished in late October 1909, management announced a series of record trials to be held on November 1.[104] Just as with the initial construction of the Indianapolis Motor Speedway, the timetable was aggressive and the track wasn't finished in time. The repaving was completed on November 27[105] at a cost of $170,000.[106] The project included doubling the number of seats and providing a wide berth on the outside of the track to lessen the possibility of injuries to spectators during crashes. The inner field of the Speedway was graded to allow for airplanes, and management anticpated that the Indianapolis Motor Speedway would be the finest facility for aviation in the nation.[107] Anxious to show off the completed track, Carl Fisher took James Jeffries, former World Heavyweight champion, for a spin around the track in Jim Allison's Stoddard-Dayton.[108]

Without much fanfare, Harry Stutz, Charles Stutz, and Henry F. Campbell incorporated the Stutz Auto Parts Company on November 29, 1909, with a capitalization of $10,000[109] to manufacture a transaxle designed by Harry Stutz.[110] Officers of the corporation were Harry Stutz, president; Campbell, vice president; and Charles Stutz, general manager.[111] In conjunction with the formation of Stutz Auto Parts, Harry Stutz resigned from Marion where he had been employed for four years.[112]

American anticipated producing 300 cars in 1910, an increase of 50 percent over the 200 1909 model cars. The company offered six different models: the Traveler, the Traveler Special, the Roadster, the Roadster Special, the Tourist, and the Limousine. For all cars with the exception of the Roadster Special and the Traveler Special, the engine was a four-cylinder generating 50 horsepower at 1,000 rpm. The Traveler Special and the Roadster Special were powered by a more powerful four-cylinder engine which developed 60 horsepower at 1,000 rpm. All models had four forward speeds and one reverse. The Roadster and Roadster Special, which could accommodate three passengers, had a wheelbase of 110 inches. The Traveler and Traveler Special could accommodate three passengers and had a wheelbase of 122 inches, while the Tourist and Limousine were built for seven passengers and had a wheelbase of 124 inches.[113]

At the New York Auto Show, Marion displayed two vehicles built upon a 112-inch wheelbase: a gentleman's speedster and a five-passenger touring car. Both cars had a four-cylinder engine and three forward speeds.[114]

To celebrate the paving of the track, management announced automobile races on December 17 and 18. The events, planned by Director of Contests Ernie Moross, included everything from a quarter mile to 100 miles and involved all five classes of the racing machines permitted by the AAA.[115]

While at the Atlanta races, Lewis Strang had told Arthur Newby he would come to Indianapolis for the reopening of the track. Strang was expected to bring his big 120-horsepower Fiat which had recorded a speed of 128 miles per hour on the Brooklands Speedway in England. Additionally, management anticipated that a big 200-horsepower Hemery Benz, which had gone 120 miles per hour, would be part of the festivities, driven by either George Robertson or Barney Oldfield. The Speedway owners hoped the Benz would recapture the speed title from the Fiat during the trials.[116]

As the date for the reopening of the Speedway approached, Walter Christie's racer and Strang's Fiat were being prepared in Fisher's garage.[117] After a tour of the track with Moross, Christie was looking forward to setting new records on the track and said, "I am more than happy over the fact that the track has turned out as successfully as it has, and I think that I shall break all records up to twenty-five miles when I get on it December 17 and 18."[118] Local manufacturers National, Marmon, Cole and Empire all indicated they would have race cars at the track to participate in the reopening festivities. Aitken predicted that he would set new records driving his National racer. Newell Motsinger also predicted that the small Empire would lower records for its class even though it was the first time an Empire would be raced.[119]

Cole racing vehicle, for Henderson Motor Sales Company, 1909 (Bass Photo Co. Collection, Indiana Historical Society).

David Maclean Parry and son Max Parry taking a drive in a Parry automobile (Indiana Historical Society, M1144).

Another entry at the reopening time trials was a Cole 30 built by Indianapolis manufacturer Cole. The demand for Cole's products was so strong that by December 1909, the company had found it necessary to expand from its original plant, located on West New York Street, to a second plant and factory showroom located at 742–778 East Washington Street.[120] The company had two models, a Cole 30 touring car and a Model H Flyer, both of which retailed for $1,500.[121]

The practices at the Speedway the day before the opening ceremonies raised anticipation of records being broken. Strang, in his Fiat, drove a half mile in 16.4 seconds. Aitken, piloting a National 40, recorded a time of 1 minute 59 seconds, while Stillman, driving a Marmon, recorded a time of 2 minutes 1 second for a trip around the 2½ mile oval.[122]

The December 17 reopening ceremonies for the Indianapolis Motor Speedway included the laying of a $500 gold brick by Indiana Governor Thomas R. Marshall.[123] The brick wasn't really gold; composed of brass, it had been manufactured by Wheeler-Schebler.[124] However, the best laid plans of the Indianapolis Motor Speedway for two days of speed trials were upended by very cold temperatures as the jet stream dipped down from Canada. Organizers, judges, and timers were surprised that approximately 150 men and women showed up at the track to watch the time trials. While the judges' box had a coal-fired oven to keep the judges and timers warm,[125] the drivers, support crews, and spectators didn't have that luxury. To battle the fierce cold, the drivers put on heavy chamois face cloths that had holes cut for eyes and were held on the head with rubber bands; goggles; and heavy caps made of either fur or felt to protect the ears. The exception to the winter gear was Lewis Strang, who drove in a red sweater and an automobile jacket,[126] while Walter Christie drove without gloves.[127]

Arthur Newby was unable to attend the event due to the bitter weather, but those who braved the cold witnessed world records being broken on the first day of racing. Johnny Aitken, a driver for the National team, set two new world records. He broke the 20-mile record for cars with 301 to 450 cubic inches of displacement with a time of 16 minutes 18.41 seconds. Then, driving a larger National, he also established a world record for cars with a piston displacement between 451 and 600 cubic inches, breaking the record previously set by George Robertson in a Fiat at Atlanta. Louis Strang bested Barney Oldfield's record for one mile with a time of 40.61 seconds. Letting loose in his Fiat racer, Walter Christie also set a new world record for the ¼ mile at 103 miles per hour, shattering the previous world record of 96 miles per hour set in the Atlanta races. Newell Motsinger in an Empire set a world record for a car with 160 cubic inches or less of displacement, running 20 miles in 25 minutes 50.23 seconds.[128]

On the second day of racing, only three drivers attempted runs on the track—Strang in a Fiat, Christie in a Christie racer, and Motsinger in an Empire. Strang lowered the world record for five miles established by Oldfield the previous August by nearly a minute with a time of 3 minutes 17.70 seconds. He also set a new Indianapolis Motor Speedway record for one mile, going the distance in 38.21 seconds. On the previous day, he had gone that distance in 40.61 seconds.[129]

Christie, who had a bet with Fisher that he could record a speed of 120 miles an hour around the track, was disappointed when a rear spring cracked as he was warming up the car. He did, however, set a new American record of 8.78 seconds for a quarter mile run on Friday and then lowered the record to 8.38 seconds on Saturday. Very shortly after Christie's run, Strang set a new record for the quarter mile at 8.05 seconds. Motsinger, driving an Empire, also lowered his record for the mile from 1 minute 20.46 seconds on Friday to 1 minute 17.08 seconds on Saturday.[130]

As 1909 came to a close, Indianapolis was home to ten automobile manufacturers: American, Cole, Empire, Marion, Marmon, National, Overland, Parry, Premier, and Waverley. The Parry Auto Company (Parry) was a new entrant to the Indianapolis automobile industry, started by David Parry after he recovered financially from personal bankruptcy. The manufacturers all expected a strong 1910, anticipating the sale of 20,000 automobiles with an aggregate value of $35 million. The automobile industry was a big employer in Indianapolis with an estimated 5,000 people dependent upon it. Leading the way in terms of sales was Overland with anticipated sales of 8,000 vehicles from its Indianapolis factory.[131] Parry, which had begun producing autos in the late summer, anticipated constructing 5,000 automobiles during 1910. Other manufacturers also anticipated an increase, but not of the size anticipated by Waverley, Overland and Marion.[132]

4

Indianapolis-Built Cars Continue to Dominate Racing

As 1910 dawned, Indianapolis produced the most racing car models (24) of any city in the United States. It seemed that virtually all of the Indianapolis manufacturers had been bitten by the racing bug. For the upcoming season, National was preparing six racers for drivers Johnny Aitken, Charlie Merz, and Tom Kincaid. Marmon was building a special racer under the supervision of Ray Harroun that was expected "to do great things in the realms of speed." Its driving stars were Harroun and Harry Stillman. Marion's team of drivers included Charles Stutz and Adolph Monsen. Empire, with Newell Motsinger at the wheel, planned to enter the races in the smallest engine category. Cole and American were also readying racing teams. Others planning to have teams, although they were not announced in January, included Atlas Engine Company and Parry, which was in discussions with George Robertson, winner of the 1908 Vanderbilt Cup and the 1908 Fairmount Park race, to be its pilot.[1]

Always a big event, the New York Auto Show in early January was an opportunity for the Indianapolis auto manufacturers to show off their wares. Getting a lot of attention were the displays by National and Marmon due to the race records these two companies had established during the prior year. While at the show, Marmon announced it was building two new racing chassis for the upcoming season. Arthur Newby, National's president, stated that the company was focused on the manufacture of automobiles for the general public, but when the racing season arrived, the company would be ready.[2] The Indianapolis Motor Speedway displayed the various trophies including the Wheeler-Schebler Trophy at the show.[3]

A topic dominating conversation at the New York Auto Show was the two competing organizations, each of which held its own auto show. The ALAM, which paid a royalty for the use of the Selden patent, had 52 member companies, including Overland and Premier, which had joined in late 1910. A well known branch manager from Indianapolis' "auto row" said, "It looks like the beginning of the end of the bitter opposition to the ALAM manufacturers who are willing to pay royalties under the Selden patent No. 549,160. The United States Court had decided that this basic patent is legal and that the contentions of the ALAM are sound."[4] During the show, an announcement was made that National and Marmon had joined the ranks of the ALAM.[5]

One of the Indianapolis companies opposed to paying the Selden royalty was newcomer Parry, which had been sued for infringement of the patent. David Parry was unfazed. He didn't believe the suit would impact his business and thought that it ultimately would be settled by the Supreme Court. He also pointed out that the application for the patent had been in the patent office from 1879 until 1895 and that it would expire within two years.[6]

While attending the Auto Show, Ernie Moross, publicity director for the Indianapolis Motor Speedway, took time to confer with AAA Contest Board officials about the upcoming race season. Moross was hopeful of adding a race involving foreign cars and drivers. Friction between the AAA and the Automobile Club of America prohibited foreign makes with foreign drivers from participating in any sanctioned events. Moross planned to propose an international amateur world championship race and hoped to attract some of the leading amateurs to the newly bricked Speedway.[7]

There was interest in an international racing event, as shown in a letter that Carl Fisher received from the clerk of the Brooklands track in England later in the month. He wrote,

> I have already approached the Automobile Club of America with the hope we may be able to organize some international contests at Brooklands this year, my suggestion being that we should have races in certain classes open to cars owned and driven by amateurs representing the two nations.
>
> I am sure that should we be able to institute such international contests our drivers would reciprocate by coming over to race on one of your American tracks, of which I understand yours is the most up-to-date, and such international contests would undoubtedly add enormously to public interest.[8]

The other item on Moross' list for discussion with the AAA officials was to try to secure the dates for racing at the Indianapolis Motor Speedway, including Memorial Day, July 4, July 23, August 12, August 23, September 2, and October 7, with each meet running for three or four days. Although the Speedway had made application for these dates, other race promoters opposed the granting of so many dates, especially for the highly sought after holiday weekends of Memorial Day, July 4, and Labor Day. Moross' argument to the AAA Contest Board was that the Speedway was the first in the field, cost the most money and set the pace for the entire country. In an attempt to limit the number of racing events, the AAA had announced that it would limit the number of events to 100 for 1910.[9]

After New York, Moross planned to go to Chicago, where he hoped to land the Cobe Trophy race for the Indianapolis Motor Speedway. A group was planning to build a speedway in Chicago and planned to hold the Cobe Trophy race on it in the spring. However, it was felt that there wasn't enough time for the construction of a speedway in Chicago to host the event even if they had men working on the new track 24 hours a day.[10]

With the expansion of the automobile industry in Indianapolis, there was a need for men trained in the maintenance of the gasoline engine. Various industry leaders including Howard Smith and George Weidley (Premier), Howard Marmon, Will H. Brown (Overland), Fred I. Tone (American), George Schebler (Wheeler-Schebler Carburetor Company), W. G. Wall (National), W. D. Oakes (Parry), F. L. Moore (Fisher Automobile Company) and Fred I. Willis (Hearsey Automobile Company) banded together to have a course in the gasoline engine to be taught at the YMCA.[11] The course attracted not only those interested in learning a trade but also motoring enthusiasts. Dealers began sending their customers to the course as they believed that participation would help the customers take better care of their cars and therefore save money.[12]

Howard Marmon, a strong proponent of auto racing, planned for his company to be involved in numerous events for the 1910 season. He said,

> I believe that the grueling pace of contests, the unusual strain on all parts, develops the necessity for more perfect equipment and better cars more than anything else.
>
> For years the foreigners have learned lessons from racing, while the American manufacturer was content to build and market his product and neglected, to a great extent, this part of the industry.

4. Indianapolis-Built Cars Continue to Dominate Racing

1910 Cole 30, Model E (Bass Photo Co. Collection, Indiana Historical Society, M1144).

I contend that the loser of a race learns more of the weaknesses of his car and benefits more thereby than the winner. In these days of keen competition all cars look good when filling the floor space of automobile shows, but what they will do under severe usage is the question that the public is asking.

Our cars sent out on the roads by demonstrators do not give us the information that we desire. A car cannot be properly observed while it is performing. Its wear and breakage may be caused by abuse and again it may not be put to a severe test by negligence of the operator, in which event what does the designer learn?

Practically nothing of the information that he seeks. Racing, however, creates sufficient interest to bring the owners and designers of the car to the scene of the strife. The preliminary work on the speedways or roads shows many weaknesses which are sometimes remedied before the day of the contest. Steering gears are made stronger or other parts strengthened as the case may be, while weight, that all important item, is reduced and still of sufficient strength to stand the severe strain.[13]

At its plant Marmon was busy building racers to participate in the 1910 season for a three-member team including Ray Harroun and Harry Stillman, both of whom had raced for Marmon in 1909. The third member of the team would be added later. The yellow and black six-cylinder racing car being constructed had special features which had never been seen before. The company was aiming to have air resistance reduced by having the driver seated in the center of the frame directly behind the engine with only his goggles visible above the hood of the car. The car would be pointed both front and rear to help reduce drag, and would be able to carry fuel and water for a 200-mile race without stopping. Ray Harroun was bullish about the new car, stating "that the only way to photograph him with a contestant will be when they are standing." Marmon expected the racer would be built by March 1, when it would be taken to the Indianapolis Motor Speedway for testing.[14]

In 1910, the Cole 30 was available in four models—the Cole Flyer (Model H), a light touring car (Model E), the Tourabout (Model F), and the Palace Touring Car (Model K). The Cole Flyer was the most popular car. Built on a 108-inch wheelbase, the Flyer was among the first cars to offer demountable rims as standard equipment.[15]

The racing season started early for the Indianapolis race teams. Marmon and Cole[16] headed toward Los Angeles to participate in the inaugural races on a board track. Marmon's effort centered around Harroun piloting the newly designed racer.[17] Cole entered one of its 30 racers to be driven by Bill Endicott. In addition, National and Cole had teams heading south to participate in the upcoming Mardi Gras Speed Carnival at New Orleans with two racers each.[18]

Early in the year, Charles Stutz sold his ownership interest in Stutz Auto Parts Company and quit the racing game, saying, "I don't want anyone saying about me, 'There he lies.' I want to live an ordinary life, so far as risks are concerned, and do not crave being mangled in a heap of motor car machinery as the chances are in racing."[19] Despite this announcement, by March he had changed his mind and he took a Marion racer to Amarillo, Texas.[20] His efforts were rewarded with wins in the five-mile, ten-mile, and 20-mile races.[21]

Indianapolis-based American struck a deal with Lafayette, Indiana, to move its manufacturing facilities. V. A. Longaker, president, attributed the decision to leave Indianapolis to the strong competition from the other automobile firms for skilled labor and the fact that American could not find a site on which to expand its business. The company planned to build a plant costing $250,000. In order to induce American to move, Lafayette officials agreed to purchase $125,000 in bonds and to raise an additional $25,000 from the sale of lots near the proposed site. American would be the first automobile manufacturer in Lafayette.[22] However, within three months the deal fell apart. Even though the bonds had been fully subscribed, the company wanted a $100,000 line of credit which the Lafayette bankers were unwilling to provide.[23]

By mid–February the racing calendar was becoming clearer. The Indianapolis Motor Speedway was granted four racing dates covering ten days including some of the best dates of the season's calendar. Racing would be held over the Memorial Day holiday on May 29, 30 and 31; the July 4 holiday on July 1, 2, and 4; and at an August meet on the 16th and 17th, The season would conclude with a September meet on the 16th, 17th, and 18th. Adjusting the calendar to reflect that the Speedway did not get the desired Labor Day weekend, officials planned to have a national balloon and aviation meet on September 2, 3, and 5. They continued to work on an international aviation meet for the period from October 18 through November 2.[24]

Marion was building two racers and planned to enter various racing events.[25] After Harry Stutz finished designing the two racers for Marion, he began making plans for his own racer.[26]

The Wheeler-Schebler Trophy, which was the center of a lawsuit by the Jackson Automobile Company, was on display at the Jackson sales agent's window in Chicago. Aided by a press release by the Jackson Automobile Company, its appearance led to the rumor that the trophy had been quietly awarded to Jackson and represented an acknowledgment that it was the rightful possessor of the trophy. The press release said,

> The exhibition of this trophy in the showrooms of a Jackson agent occasioned a great deal of comment among those who remembered that the $10,000 trophy was the first place prize in the big 300-mile race at Indianapolis, which was called off at 235 miles, when the Jackson car, driven by Leigh Lynch, was in the lead.
>
> As the Jackson car led its nearest competitor in the race at the time by 14 miles, the decision by Referee Stevens in calling the race off brought forth a vigorous protest from the Jackson Automobile Company, and because that concern advertised the fact of its leading position in the race the American Automobile Company disciplined the Jackson Company by barring it from AAA competition until December 31, 1909.

Therefore the fact of the trophy being shown in the window of the Jackson Company's Chicago agent is taken by those in the trade as indication that the big $10,000 trophy, the auto prize of the year, has been turned over to the Jackson Company as the real winners, and thus terminates a long-drawn-out legal battle for possession of same which seemed very imminent.

This statement was soundly rebuked by Ernie Moross:

The Speedway people could not award this trophy if they wanted to, because action must be taken by the Contest Board of the American Automobile Association. Action was taken by these men in stopping the race and in punishing the Jackson people because of their advertising that they had won the cup by suspending them from racing for several months. The Contest Board has not fixed matters up differently now, so that all there is to it is that Mr. Wheeler saw fit to loan the Jackson people the trophy for three weeks.

At New York, Mr. Wheeler loaned the trophy to the Buick people and it was photographed with their other trophies, and he also loaned it to the Marmon people at New York. The plan is to get the handsome trophy circulated over the country on exhibit as much as possible, and Mr. Wheeler simply gave the Jackson people a three weeks' favor.[27]

On March 16, a little later than the anticipated unveiling date, Harroun took his new six-cylinder Marmon racer to the Indianapolis Motor Speedway. Fresh from the factory, it was the first water-cooled race car produced in Indianapolis. Several friends and people from the Marmon organization were at the track when Howard Marmon took the wheel of the car for a spin around the track at almost 90 miles per hour. Also taking the car for a trip around the Speedway was Harry "Sunshine" Stillman. After its first appearance at the Speedway, the car was taken back to the factory, where it was evaluated by the experts. A second, more extensive run was anticipated a week later. The unveiling of the car for a race was expected to be at the Indianapolis Motor Speedway's Memorial Day races.[28] The car, nicknamed the "Yellow Jacket" due to its racing colors, was designed by Howard Marmon.[29]

Howard Marmon talked about the new racer:

We have built a special racing car for this class. It will race in Division 5, Class C for cars of from 450 to 600 inches of piston displacement. This six-cylinder will weigh close to 2,200 pounds, but with its pointed radiator and sharpened "fish" tail its speed is a matter of speculation at this time.

I have always contended that it is not as much a matter of weight to promote speed as it is a matter of reducing wind resistance. A motor properly turning up at its highest speed will carry a few hundred pounds, more or less, with or practically at the same speed. It requires more time to start a heavy car than a light one, but once started and well underway over a fine surface, such as is furnished at the Speedway, a couple of hundred pounds make but little difference.

But against a wind surface, that is the vital question. Under ordinary speed this is not as important, but as the speed is increased it takes additional horsepower to overcome the resistance, and as each additional mile is added the power required increases at a phenomenal rate.

Marmon continued,

I expect this special machine with wind resistance reduced to the minimum to travel 40 miles an hour faster than the same car which we are making into a stock model, but with the regular wind resisting radiator and construction such as is found in stock chassis.[30]

Racing fans expected new records to be set at the Los Angeles Motordrome, the nation's first one-mile board track ever raced on by motor cars, and they were not disappointed. Indianapolis manufacturers Cole and Marmon were among the cars setting new records. On the first day of racing, Harroun was in a tight duel with Frank Seifert driving a Dorris for 90 miles. Harroun took the lead and went on to win the 100-mile race, breaking his own record by 4 minutes 46.21 seconds. In a ten-mile race for cars with a piston displacement between 161 and 230 cubic inches, a Cole piloted by Bill Endicott took home the honors and set a new world record with a time of 9 minutes 3.25 seconds.[31] In a second day of racing, Harroun set another record, this time for five miles for cars with piston displacement between 231 and 300 cubic inches with a time of 3 minutes 55.97 seconds.[32] Harroun's competitors on the Los Angeles track nicknamed the car the "Yellow Peril."[33] The third day of racing on the Los Angeles Motordome was disappointing for Harroun and the Marmon team when a pit stop for a tire resulted in a third place finish in the feature 50-mile race. In the five-mile free-for-all handicapped race, Harroun placed second in a field of seven racers.[34] The fourth day of racing was a good one for Indianapolis-built cars. In a ten-mile race for cars with a piston displacement between 161 and 230 cubic inches, a Cole driven by Endicott came in second. In the featured 50-mile race for cars with a piston displacement between 301 and 450 cubic inches, Marmon racers finished first with Harroun at the wheel and second with Wade as the pilot. Harroun also finished third in a ten-mile free-for-all for cars with a piston displacement of 600 cubic inches.[35] In the fifth day of racing, Harroun again brought the winning honors home to Marmon. Eight racers took to the field for a two-hour free-for-all race. At the end of two hours, four racers were still on the track, with Harroun having traveled 148 miles. Helping Harroun to win the race was that he did not need any stops. Later in the day, the Marmon team finished second with Harroun at the wheel and third with Wade as the pilot in a five-mile race for cars with a piston displacement between 301 and 450 cubic inches.[36] In the final day of racing, Harroun, driving a Marmon in the 600-cubic-inch class, won the feature race, a 100-mile event, with a time of one hour 16 minutes 21.9 seconds. In the smaller 301 to 450 cubic inch class, Harroun finished second and Wade finished third in a ten-mile race.[37]

Wishing to capitalize on the victories at Los Angeles, Marmon ran an advertisement which noted,

> …the important point in these racing victories lies not the speed of the Marmon. We know that it has more speed than you'll ever care to use, and all the power you will ever need in any emergency. The thing that counts, the point that amazes the veterans of racing experience, is that the Marmon will stand up to better than mile-a-minute speed, with all the terrific strains involved, not merely for short dashes of ten or twenty miles, but for hundreds of miles without showing signs of distress. It takes a real car manufactured of the very best materials in every part and workmanship of high order to endure the strain.[38]

Having achieved success at the Los Angeles races, Cole also touted its success.

> The Cole 30 covered itself with glory at the Motordrome in Los Angeles Friday afternoon.
> After surprising achievements, speeding one mile and five miles against time, Endicott, driving the Cole, in a ten-mile race for stock cars of 161–230 displacement, won in 9:03, lowering the world's record for cars in this class by 46 seconds.
> In view of what the Cole 30 has already done, this victory is just what the public had come to expect of it.[39]

Believing long road trips were the best test of an automobile, Premier was an enthusiastic supporter of the Glidden Tour. For the 1910 tour, Premier entered two cars—a six-cylinder

4. Indianapolis-Built Cars Continue to Dominate Racing 59

Bill Endicott in his Cole 30 racer (LeRoy Cole Collection, Gilmore Car Museum).

60-horsepower car piloted by Ray McNamara, and a four-cylinder 40-horsepower car driven by Charles Ballinger, the company's head tester. After leaving Cincinnati, Ohio, the Tour traveled southwest to Dallas, Texas with stops in Kentucky, Tennessee, Alabama, and Arkansas. The return route went through Oklahoma, Kansas, Nebraska, and Iowa, and the Tour concluded in Chicago. One of the oddities of the trip was that at Terral, Oklahoma, the cars crossed the Red River on a mile and a half plank roadbed laid across the crossties of the Rock Island Railroad. The railroad posted train dispatchers at the bridge to ensure the safety of the autos crossing the river. Another unique feature of the trip was a sand road of about five-eighths of a mile between Oklahoma City, Oklahoma and Wichita, Kansas.[40] Crossing of the Mississippi River was accomplished by ferry. The 1910 Glidden Tour was the first time that a portion of the tour had been run at night.[41]

The trip was very difficult for the entrants. In the South, there were few roads and the route traveled through cypress swamps where cars became hopelessly mired and were difficult to extract. The cars were required to maintain an average speed of 21 miles per hour and the days were very long for the participants. One run took 17 hours and most nights the participants got only five hours of sleep. In Oklahoma, the tour experienced extreme heat with temperatures reaching 105 degrees.[42]

After traveling 2,850 miles, only six of the 14 cars that had been entered in the Tour finished. The Premier, driven by Ray McNamara, was declared to be the winner of the Glidden Trophy. Second place went to a Chalmers-Detroit driven by William Balger, third to the Maxwell entry, fourth to the Premier driven by Ballinger, fifth to a Glide manufactured by the Bartholomew Company, and sixth to Cino Automobile. Unhappy with the results, Chalmers-Detroit filed a protest stating that the oil tank and pump on the Premier were not stock. Referee A. H. Whiting quickly dismissed the protest.[43] That did not end the controversy, however, and three weeks later Whiting reversed his decision. Premier then filed suit in New York Supreme Court. Howard Smith explained the rationale for filing the legal action:[44]

> We have been of the opinion that contests of this character are conducted with the idea of giving the public the opportunity to judge various cars on their merits by a comparison of the results and rewards should be made in favor of the contestant whose car has made the best showing under the rules published at the start. Detailed descriptions of the two Premier cars entered in the Glidden Tour were filed with the AAA in advance of the commencement, and the hand oil pump and tank, as protested, were fully described, even as to their location. Members of the technical committee had access to the Premier factory before and during the event, and they inspected the two cars and accepted both without question.
>
> Both cars complied with the spirit and letter of the rules, and the winning Premier, in addition, was called upon to carry officials, including the pilot, Dal Lewis; the referee, and others on ten of the 16 running days because the official cars were incapacitated. No allowance was made for time or otherwise, and none asked on account of this additional work. The winning Premier not only finished with the best road score, but also with the best road and technical scores combined.[45]

Judge William P. Kelley issued a restraining order prohibiting the AAA from delivering the trophy to Chalmers Motor Company.[46] The AAA Contest Board responded by disqualifying Premier and Howard Smith from all future contests held under the AAA sanction. In taking this action, the AAA cited the contest rules, which specified that Premier as a contestant had agreed to recognize the authority of the Contest Board and that therefore its appeal to the courts was a breach of contest rules and prejudicial to the sport.[47] Smith responded, saying,

> The action of the board was not in accordance with the official rules of the AAA which governs the Glidden tour and other contests, and I might be charged with unsportsmanlike conduct by anyone who is not familiar with the occurrences during and since the tour. I entered this contest believing it was a sportsman's affair, but it is sufficient to say that three other companies, represented by officials of their concerns, concluded before the contest had progressed very far that they were warranted in employing a professional detective service to safeguard their interests.
>
> It was my determination upon entering the event that I would not protest any car, but the fact that I did not enter such a complaint does not indicate conditions did not arise which would warrant such action. We are perfectly willing that this matter should be presented to an impartial court, as our experience has convinced us that we have no other alternative. No one regrets more deeply than I this occurrence, as I have for years been a strong advocate of reliability contests.[48]

In September, Judge Putman ruled in favor of Chalmers-Detroit, much to the disappointment of Smith. Judge Putman opined that there was no evidence of fraud on the part of the AAA Contest Board and that since this was a sporting event, the decision of the Contest Board stood.[49]

In 1910, Marion entered the taxicab business with a four-cylinder, 30-horsepower chassis built on a 112-inch wheelbase. Equipped with a landaulet body, the car retailed for $2,250.[50]

National constructed a new 40,000 square foot facility adjacent to its existing facilities for transmission and engine assembly. This new two-story building brought total floor space to 90,000 square feet.[51]

With two models, Premier anticipated producing 1,000 cars in 1910. The 4–40, a four-cylinder car, was produced in three models: a five-passenger touring car, a four-passenger closed body car (the Clubman), and a two-passenger roadster. The 6–60, a six-cylinder 60-horsepower car, was the second longest standard automobile produced in the United States, with a wheelbase of 139.5 inches. The 6–60 came in three models: a seven-passenger touring car; a four-passenger closed car; and a two-passenger roadster model. With few exceptions, all of the parts for the Premier automobiles were built in Indianapolis by Premier's team of 400 craftsmen. Before the bodies were attached to the cars and finished, the cars were tested with a 100-mile run over rough roads.[52]

The National 40 model was available in a torpedo body style which sold for $2,800. This car, which accommodated four passengers, had doors which were unusually high while the seats backs were relatively low, giving the car a unique design.[53] American also offered two torpedo-styled cars. Build upon a 112-inch wheelbase, the cars had an underslung hang with 12½ inch clearance from the ground. The cars had rear doors on both sides but a door only on the left side in the front.[54]

The Waverley Company updated its Model 78 Gentleman's Roadster in 1910. Where all other Waverley automobiles were steered by a lever, this car featured a steering wheel which included a push button bell for warning others. The automobile had four forward speeds and four reverse speeds.[55]

When Indianapolis put out a contract for an "automobile fire wagon," Premier responded with a proposal to build a 40-horsepower vehicle on a 120-inch wheelbase. The design carried a chemical tank and provided for 12 firemen. One of the arguments Premier made for the local purchase of the "automobile fire wagon" was the speed and ease of repair in case of accident.[56] Until Premier presented its proposal to the Safety Board, only a Packard model was being considered. National was also interested in the possibility and showed the board a picture of one of its automobiles which it would modify.

National was the first to submit entry forms for the Memorial Day weekend races at the Indianapolis Motor Speedway with three entries in both the Prest-O-Lite and Wheeler-Schebler Trophy races. Drivers were identified as Johnny Aitken and Tom Kincaid. Marmon also submitted entries for three cars, with Harroun and Stillman as pilots. There was speculation that Howard Marmon might be the third driver.[57] Later in the month, Howard Marmon was seen circling the track at the Indianapolis Motor Speedway in his Marmon Wasp racer, adding fuel to the speculation. Marmon had two Class 3B racers in the class for cars with a piston displacement between 231 to 300 cubic inches taking practice laps at the Speedway.[58] An Empire car to be driven by Jack Reep was entered in the races for small cars.[59]

After the strong showing at the Los Angeles Motordrome, the Marmon team returned to Indianapolis for a few days before leaving for races at the Atlanta Speedway in early May. Getting ready to leave Indianapolis, Harroun expressed confidence that the Marmon team was going to bring home more honors. "The Speedway wasps have been disturbed and someone is sure to get a stinging when hornets known as the 'Yellow Peril' are turned loose over the surface of clay of the Atlanta track."[60]

Harroun also had his sights clearly set on doing well in the Memorial Day races at the Indianapolis Motor Speedway.

> The Indianapolis Motor Speedway is the spot I have set my highest hopes on. Why, do you know what the May 30 championship meet means to me? It means to win a race on that date carries with it the honor of being the champion of the United States for 1910. This will be my first championship race and I am doing my motordrome and Atlanta work simply as preparation for the greater meet to take place here.[61]

For the Memorial Day races at the Indianapolis Motor Speedway, Marmon had seven entries, followed closely by National with six. Cole, Marion, and Empire each had two racers registered while American had registered one team. Taking advantage of the hometown track, the cars regularly practiced at the Speedway. While Indianapolis manufacturers had signed up for the races at the Indianapolis Motor Speedway over the Memorial Day weekend, one of the keys to the success of the races was the participation of some of the big named racers. Ernie Moross went to the races at the Atlanta Speedway in early May to try to convince some of the national racers to come to Indianapolis.[62]

Marmon and Cole won honors at the first of three days of races at the Atlanta Speedway. Three cars finished first in their races while an additional two Indianapolis-built racers finished second. Harroun in the Marmon "Yellow Jacket" walked away as the winner of the feature 200-mile event with a time of 3 hours 2 minutes 31.25 seconds. The long grind saw Aitken crash his car on the 49th lap, ending his day of racing. At the time of the crash, Aitken had a two-mile lead and was going about 70 miles per hour. Aitken's crash handed the lead to Harroun, who maintained it throughout the remainder of the race. Harroun also won the ten-mile free-for-all race while Aitken in a National 40 finished third. Endicott in a Cole 30 won a ten-mile stock chassis race, the only one for which his car was eligible. Before crashing in the feature race, Aitken, driving a National 40, placed second in a 20-mile race for cars with a piston displacement between 451 and 600 cubic inches. W. J. Stoddard, driving a National 40, finished second in two special match races. In the first race, he lost to John A. Rutherford driving a Fiat Sixty while in the second race he lost to Asa Candler driving a Fiat Sixty.[63]

The second day of racing at Atlanta was a tremendous day for Indianapolis-built racers, who won four races and placed second in three and third in one. Harroun, piloting the Marmon Wasp, won a 12-mile free-for-all, while Herbert Lytle in an Indianapolis-built American racer finished second. In the ten-mile free-for-all for racers with piston displacement between 301 and 450 cubic inches, Kincaid in a National crossed the finish line first, followed by Harroun in a Marmon in second place. Bill Endicott, driving a Cole 30 racer, led the entire 60-mile race for cars with piston displacement between 161 and 230 cubic inches. The 50-mile free-for-all was a close race among three Indianapolis racers. The American jumped out in the lead for the first 19 miles, after which the National took the lead. In the final mile, the American racer again took the lead, winning the race with the National racer finishing second and a Marmon racer driven by Joe Dawson finishing third. Harroun, in a Marmon racer, had to withdraw from the race with tire trouble on the 28th lap. In the one-mile time trials, Herb Lytle piloting an American racer set the pace, followed by Harroun in the Marmon racer.[64]

The strong showing by Indianapolis-built cars continued on the third and final day of racing at the Atlanta Speedway when a National 40 swept the 200-mile feature race with an average speed of 65.79 miles per hour. Herb Lytle piloted the American racer to second place in the race. With the exception of two races during the three-day meet, Indiana-built cars won every race,[65] taking $3,700 of the $4,300 in prizes. Aitken and Kincaid of the National team walked away with $1,400, while Harroun of the Marmon team earned over $850.[66]

The drivers in auto racing were well compensated by their employers for risking their lives. Some companies, including National, also allowed the drivers to take home the earnings from the races as well as any additional monies offered by accessory companies, such as Remy. Aitken and Kincaid brought home their winnings from the Atlanta Speedway plus about $1,700 in bonuses paid by National, while the company paid all of the expenses of the driving team.[67]

Howard Marmon was very pleased with the results of his racers in the Los Angeles and Atlanta meets. He believed that wins on the racetrack translated to sales in the showroom.

Racing has put the Marmon car on the map. It is not altogether the winning of events, the remarkable speed shown and the world's records made that have attracted attention, but rather the consistent work of the car—its ability as demonstrated to win the long distance, hard grueling contests, one after another, in competition with Europe and America's best cars and to run these long races without stopping, without apparent mechanical distress and with wonderful freedom from tire troubles.

The results from an advertising standpoint are accordingly very satisfactory, the best drivers from every section having been attracted by the consistent performance of the cars and the public, too, has been quick to recognize quality as evidenced by the heavy demand the country over.[68]

Not surprisingly, Marmon used its victories in the Atlanta and Los Angeles races to promote its cars. An advertisement for a 40-horsepower Marmon stated,

Any manufacturer, any automobile engineer, any mechanic that understands motor cars will tell you that the supreme test of the quality of a car is its ability to go long distances at lightning speed and "hold together." The Marmon not only "holds together" and makes the long runs without a stop—but at the end of every one of these races it has been running as smoothly, as "sweetly" as at the start.[69]

Ernie Moross, the publicity director for the Indianapolis Motor Speedway, crowed with the very strong results of the Atlanta races and looked forward to a strong performance by local manufacturers at the upcoming three days of races at the Speedway. Moross said,

The eyes of the motor world are on Indianapolis racing cars. The way that Indianapolis cars and drivers cleaned up with things at Atlanta was certainly a shame. We expected and predicted that the Indiana racing machines would win half of the events, but no one would have dreamed they would have won nine of ten regularly programmed races.[70]

Cole continued the string of successes for Indianapolis-based manufacturers, winning the Chicago Auto Club's Economy Run of 191 miles. Carrying four passengers, a Cole 30 averaged 23.6 miles per gallon of gasoline. Joseph Cole said of the victory, "It is very gratifying to have our car be first in such a contest. For, in view of all its recent speed victories, it demonstrates beyond a doubt that in designing the car for speed the matter of fuel economy was not sacrificed."[71]

For the 1910 racing season, famed racer Louis Strang was added to Marion's stable of drivers, joining Gil Andersen and Charles Stutz for races at Brighton Beach. It was expected that Strang would head the team and would participate in the Indianapolis 500. Ed G. Sourbier, Cole's general manager, said, "We are negotiating with Strang and I believe the deal will be closed, as it looks as if the company and the driver could get together easily."[72]

The 24-hour race at Brighton Beach was marred by three crashes that killed one and injured two. In the first crash, Gil Andersen's Marion skidded into the fence and turned three somersaults. While Andersen wasn't injured, his riding mechanic, William F. Bradley, was killed. An hour later, Bill Endicott, piloting the Cole entry, skidded into the fence, doing serious damage to the car. In a third wreck, a Buick "turned turtle," severely injuring the riding mechanic.[73] Endicott, driving a Cole Thirty, ended his drive after 21 hours, having gone 760 miles and endured three crashes through fences. He emerged from the race with a sprained ankle and cuts to his face.[74] Despite having been damaged in the wrecks, the Marion car returned to the race. It finished seventh and the Cole car finished ninth out of the 12 cars entered in the race. The winner was Charles Basle driving a Simplex, with 1,145 miles recorded.[75]

The 24-hour event at Brighton Beach generated tales of woe and vows that the three Indianapolis racers would never again race on the one-mile cement and dirt track. Gil Andersen described the condition of the track: "The outer half of the track was paved with cement and the inner half with sand. Between the cement and the sand, there was the deep gutter."[76]

Arthur Newby, National's president, believed that the growth of the automobile industry was directly tied to the popularity of auto racing.

> It is the firm conviction of the National Motor Vehicle Company that motor racing has been a leading factor in the development of the self-propelled gasoline vehicle. The policy of this pioneer concern has always been to submit its product to the severest tests, and it found the superlative degree of severity in testing lay in speed events on track, hill and road. This, with the genuine love of the sport of racing, has kept the National car to the front in automobile speed events.
>
> From the beginning the company sent its machines through the most severe punishment. And it accounts much of its success to the improvements which were the direct result of information gained by engineers from the racing game. Nothing tears at every detail of a motor car more than long flights at high speed.[77]

Racing for the 1910 season at the Indianapolis Motor Speedway opened over Memorial Day weekend. Interestingly, the program for the first two days of racing wasn't announced until two days before the races were scheduled to be run. Although management had to cancel the event for cars with 600 to 750 cubic inches of displacement because of a lack of entries, Contest Director Ernie Moross was enthusiastic about the races. "It is the best program I ever have seen," Moross said. "The number of cars entered is not as great as in some other meetings, but the entries are distributed so that every event is designed to be a race—and a good one."[78]

Fifteen thousand race fans turned out for the opening day, which was highlighted by 14 different world records being shattered. The day started with one-mile time trials with Herb Lytle in an American finishing first with a time of 46.05 seconds, Tommy Kincaid in a National 60 finishing second, Aitken in a National 70 finishing third, and Harroun in a Marmon Six finishing fifth. In the feature Prest-O-Lite Trophy race, Kincaid, driving a National, shattered the world record for 100 miles by a half minute, winning the race. Amazingly, Kincaid had to stop three times during the race to replace worn out tires. His teammate, Charlie Merz, took second place in the Prest-O-Lite Trophy race, finishing about two minutes behind Kincaid. Joe Dawson, driving a Marmon, had held the lead in the race at 85 miles, setting new world records for 40, 50, 60, 70 and 85 miles. Dawson was ahead by a lap and appeared destined to win the race when a spark plug failed, causing him to take a pit stop and hand the lead over to Kincaid. Dawson's Marmon teammate, Harroun, set the early pace for the race, establishing new records for 10 and 20 miles. His chance for victory was destroyed by a valve failure.

Two Indianapolis-built cars battled for supremacy in a 5-mile race for cars with a piston displacement between 301 and 450 cubic inches. Kincaid, driving a National 40, was in a pitched battle with Dawson in a Marmon 32 and won the race at the tape. In the ten-mile race for cars with 231 to 300 cubic inches of displacement, the Marmon entries driven by Joe Dawson and Harroun left the other competitors far behind and battled each other for the victory. Harroun won the race, taking 47 seconds off the world record. The sixth race, for cars with a piston displacement between 451 and 600 cubic inches, was a sure victory for the National team. There were only four entries for this ten-mile event, three of which were Nationals. When Barney Oldfield's steering knuckle broke, it was only a question of which National driver would take home the honors. Aitken proved up to the task, beating Kincaid, who finished second, and Howdy Wilcox, who placed third. In a field of 14 cars, Art Greiner, driving a National, won the five-mile handicap race. Greiner also won the "millionaire's race," a five-mile event for private owners. The only other competitor in this race, William Tousey, also drove a National.[79]

Harroun, piloting the Marmon Wasp, won the Wheeler-Schebler Trophy race on the second day of racing before an estimated 25,000 spectators. In winning the race with an average speed of 72.12 miles per hour, Harroun shattered the national records for 150 and 200 miles. His strategy of keeping his racer at a steady speed throughout the contest would be utilized in the inaugural Indianapolis 500 in 1911. The steady but competitive speed saved his engine and tires from the excessive wear and tear some of the other cars experienced. Harroun took the lead in the fifteenth mile and led the field throughout the remainder of the race. Aitken driving a National finished third in the Wheeler-Schebler race. Dawson in a Marmon 32 saw his dream of winning the Wheeler-Schebler Trophy dashed when his car crashed through a fence. He was fortunate not to have been injured.[80]

Howard Marmon later talked about the strategy used by Harroun to win the race:

> In the greatest event of the meet, the Wheeler-Schebler Trophy, Harroun did not attempt to take the lead until many miles after the race had been won. At least two-thirds of the entrants were fighting it out for every inch, using every ounce of power to nose out the leaders. Harroun simply bided his time and after many of the drivers through necessity had been compelled to stop for repairs or tire changes, he slid into first place and held the lead to the finish opening a greater gap with every mile that he traveled. The fact that Harroun led for more than 150 miles is one of the greatest performances ever witnessed in a long race, and, as he won by several miles, it proved the quality of the car as well as his ability as a driver.[81]

On the second day of racing, Indianapolis-built machines had another strong showing. In the one-mile time trials where the cars could show what they could do, the Empire piloted by Newell Motsinger, the smallest car in the field, recorded a time of 1 minute 7.1 seconds. The American, driven by Herb Lytle, traversed the mile in 44.44 seconds while a National 70 with Aitken at the helm did the mile run in 46.3 seconds. Harroun in the Marmon 62 drove the mile in 42.33 seconds. Indianapolis-built cars swept the ten-mile race for cars with an engine displacement between 301 and 450 cubic inches with Aitken in a National finishing first, Harroun in a Marmon finishing second, and Merz in a National finishing in third place. This race was marred by the crash of Herb Lytle, who was thrown from his American racer on the last lap of the race after both rear tires blew within the space of 30 feet. While the winner of the five-mile race for cars with an engine displacement between 451 and 600 cubic inches was Barney Oldfield in his Knox Six, Don Herr and Aitken in National racers finished second and third respectively.[82] The ten-mile free-for-all handicap race, in which 19 cars started, was won by Howdy Wilcox piloting a National.[83]

Naturally, Marmon used the winning of the Wheeler-Schebler Trophy race as a springboard for another advertisement.

> The greatest contest of the Speedway meet—the 200-mile race for the $10,000 Wheeler-Schebler Trophy and $1,000 cash—was won by the Marmon Six, driven by Ray Harroun.
> This is the race all the big ones have been preparing for since last August. It was open to all cars up to 600 cubic inches piston displacement—minimum weight 2,300 pounds—and many of the fastest cars in the country struggled for the supremacy. Among them were several cars more powerful than the Marmon, whose piston displacement is 477 cubic inches, with a rating of 48 H.P.
> Harroun's time for the 200 miles was 2:46:31–200 miles in 166 ½ minutes averaging over 72 miles per hour. This captures the national record for 200 miles.

> The Marmon now holds all the national track records, regardless of class, from 55 miles to 200 miles, eclipsing Robertson's record for 150 miles in the Fiat and Chevrolet's record for 200 miles. The only big records Marmon did not break were the Marmon records made at Los Angeles by Harroun.
> The entire race was run by the Marmon without changing any of its Michelin tires—merely another demonstration of the remarkable tire economy of the Marmon. But one stop was made for gasoline only.[84]

The headliner for the third day of racing was Barney Oldfield, who was offered "more money than was ever paid before for a single mile."[85] Oldfield did not disappoint the crowd of about 50,000 gathered at the Indianapolis Motor Speedway. He set a new record not only for the mile but also for the kilometer. He drove the mile in 35.06 seconds, eclipsing his former record of 36 seconds set at Cheyenne, Wyoming. Likewise, he smashed the record for the kilometer at 21.45 seconds, beating his previous record of 23.7 seconds set at the Los Angeles Motordrome. Changing to a Knox Sixty, Oldfield also established a new record for five miles with a time of 4 minutes 1.3 seconds, breaking the time he had established earlier in the three-day meet.[86]

The crowd also witnessed the breaking of ten additional national track records. Harroun continued his winning ways, capturing the 50-mile Remy Grand Brassard, the feature event of the day, with a time of 41 minutes 42.33 seconds. For his efforts, Harroun received $50 per week as long as he defended the Remy Grand Brassard. Before winning this prize, Harroun had experienced a terrifying crash which could have ended his day of racing: the car straddled the retaining wall for 110 feet before crashing through a concrete barrier.[87] Meanwhile, Aitken again lowered the record for ten miles for cars in the 301–450 cubic inch of displacement class three times in three consecutive days.[88]

Over the three days of the meet, the Indianapolis-built cars won more places (45) than all of the other makes combined (25).[89] While the Marmon racers took the Wheeler-Schebler and Remy Grand Brassard races, and thus the majority of headlines, the National team had more places in the meet, with 32 compared to Marmon's 13.[90]

As the competitors were leaving town, Indianapolis Motor Speedway management began making preparations for the July 4 races. The featured event was the Cobe Trophy Race, to be run on July 4 for cars with a minimum weight of 2,300 pounds and an engine displacement under 600 cubic inches.[91] Anticipating increased crowds for the July 4 races, management constructed seating for 15,000 additional spectators. To encourage participation in the races, Speedway management offered $9,000 in prizes for the three-day meet.[92]

After the Memorial Day meet, several Indianapolis teams including Cole, Marmon, and Parry went to Louisville, Kentucky for a day of racing and came home with the victor's spoils. Of the nine races, they had seven first place finishes, eight seconds, and two thirds.[93]

Harroun of the Marmon team and Aitken and Kincaid of the National team left for a different type of test—a hill climb at Wilkes-Barre, Pennsylvania. The Marmon entry was a late one as the company was unsure if the Marmon Wasp could be repaired after its collision with a wall. However, other than having a bent front axle and being minus four wheels, the car was found to be in good shape. The National team hoped to repeat its prior performance by winning the majority of the titles. In the climb of "Giant's Despair"[94] Harroun, driving a Marmon 32, won the hill climb for cars with a piston displacement between 231 and 300 cubic inches with a first place prize of $75. However, it was a disappointing day for the National team, which placed third with Aitken at the wheel and fourth with Kincaid as the pilot in the hill climb for cars with a piston displacement between 301 and 450 cubic inches. Harroun finished second in that contest with a $25 prize. In the Hollenback Trophy race for cars with an engine displacement between 601 and 750 cubic inches and costing between $2,000 and $3,000, Kincaid finished third. In the Invitation Event for cars which failed to win the free-for-all race, Kincaid again finished in third place. Aitken took home third place honors in the final event of the day, which was for cars costing over $2,000; an Indianapolis-built Marion with Edward Habblett as the driver took home first place.[95]

Meanwhile, American entered a reliability run from Atlanta to New York City, a distance of 1,200 miles. The car, driven by J. P. Dick, finished the run with a perfect score and then took off for a 400-mile run on the "Montauk or Bust" Long Island run.[96]

Harroun went from his victory in the "Giant's Despair" hill climb to Memphis, Tennessee, for a day of racing where he won a five-mile handicap while Endicott, driving a Cole 30, finished second. A Cole 30 driven by Endicott won and another Cole driven by Louis Edmunds placed second in a five-mile race and in a 25-mile race. Harroun came in second to George Robertson driving a Simplex in two events—a five-mile free-for-all and a one-mile free-for-all. In a ten-mile free-for-all, Robertson continued his winning ways, with Marmons driven by Dawson and Harroun finishing second and third respectively. In the eighth race, Harroun, driving a Marmon 32, again placed second to Robertson's Simplex.[97] Putting a positive spin on the performances at Memphis, a Marmon advertisement said that the defeats were at the hands of a larger car.[98]

In a combination aviation and auto racing meet at the Twin City track at St. Paul, Minnesota, Harroun in a Marmon 32 won two events—a five-mile free-for-all handicap and a $1,000 ten-mile match race with J. M. McLane in a Buick.[99] After the race at St. Paul, Harroun and the Marmon Wasp returned to Indianapolis to prepare for the July 4 weekend meet at the Indianapolis Motor Speedway.

On the business side of things, due to a large number of orders for the Marion automobile, Harry Stutz made the decision in late June to temporarily quit the racing game.[100] Meanwhile, three shareholders in the American Motor Car Sales Company, Henry F. Campbell, Thomas P. C. Forbes, Jr., and Eben Forbes, brought various suits against Willys and the Willys-Overland Company. Forbes filed one suit in court demanding an accounting and a second suit in another court asking for the appointment of a receiver for American Motor Car Sales Company. Campbell filed suit in a Federal court seeking an accounting and alleged mismanagement of the firm by John N. Willys.[101] Campbell and Forbes alleged that Willys used corporate funds to pay himself $150,000 without consulting them. Prior to filing the suit, Forbes and Campbell offered to sell their stock to Willys for $2 million, an amount which Willys considered to be exorbitant. Willys offered to sell Campbell and Forbes his stock for the same amount, which they declined.[102] The parties reached a settlement for $1,000,000 from Willys with the payment of $150,000 in cash and a promissory note in the amount of $1 million secured by Willys-Overland stock by Willys. The repayment period for the promissory note was 36 months. With this transaction, Willys, who owned practically all of the stock in Willys-Overland and its various subsidiaries, planned to reorganize the Willys-Overland Company with a capitalization of $2 million and merge the Willys-Overland Company, the Overland Automobile Company, and the American Motor Car Sales Company.[103]

For 1911, Empire unveiled its Model C, which retailed for $850. This car featured a shaft drive rather than a chain drive. The car's standard colors were blue for the body and cream for the running gear. The company planned to devote its entire plant to this model.[104]

With the strong performance shown in the Memorial Day races at the Indianapolis Motor Speedway, there was great anticipation by the Indianapolis manufacturers of again dominating the July races. Having increased the seating capacity of the Speedway, management was also looking forward to the races bringing in more spectators. However, management would be disappointed, as were those spectators who came to the Speedway to see Indianapolis-built cars again dominate the action. In the ten events, only one, an amateur race, was won by an Indianapolis-manufactured car—and that race had only two entries, both Nationals.[105]

On the first day of racing at the July 4 meet, only 6,000 spectators came to the Speedway, as compared to 10,000 for the first day of racing during the Memorial Day meet.[106] Undoubtedly the low attendance at the race can be attributed in part to the weather. A heat wave was hanging over the Midwest and Indianapolis was hot and humid, with the thermometer reaching 94 degrees.[107] With the races beginning at 1 p.m., the spectators as well as the participants were subjected to the hottest part of the day.

The weekend of races was not disappointing to the spectators as they witnessed nine new speed records. The highlight of the first day was a quarter-mile run by "Wild" Bob Burman of the Buick team at 105.87 miles per hour, beating the record set by Barney Oldfield at the Memorial Day meet. Burman also established a new record of 8 minutes 14.46 seconds in a ten-miler and won the 50-mile G & J Trophy feature race some 11 seconds ahead of Dawson in a Marmon. Third place went to Harroun.[108] In a 15-mile race for cars with a piston displacement between 301 and 450 cubic inches, Aitken finished second to Burman in a Buick.[109] The ten-mile free-for-all Speedway Helmet race was won by Eddie Hearne driving the 200-horsepower Benz formerly owned by Oldfield. The win earned Hearne a $50 per week stipend as long as the Helmet was successfully defended. Aitken was forced out of the race on the third lap when his car's air valves failed, while Harroun finished second.[110]

In the second day of the meet, Burman continued his winning ways. During the feature Remy Grand Brassard race, nine new speed records were established during the 100-mile run. Driving a white Buick, Burman set the pace with an average speed of 74.44 miles per hour. At 20 and 30 miles, Kincaid was leading the pack and setting new records. When Kincaid

An Empire 20 introduced in 1910 (*Horseless Age*, June 29, 1910).

experienced tire trouble shortly after establishing the new speed record for 30 miles, Burman roared into the lead. Dawson, driving a Marmon, set the pace at 60, 70, and 75 miles. By mile 90, Burman was again in the lead and established a new speed record for 100 miles.[111]

The third day of racing featured the 200-mile Cobe Trophy race for cars in the 600 cubic inch class. Named for Ira M. Cobe, a Chicago banker and president of the Chicago Auto Club, the race was sponsored by the Chicago Auto Club.[112] The Indianapolis Motor Speedway offered $500 for the driver of the winning car, $300 for the second place car, $200 for the third place car, and $100 for the fourth place car. In addition, if the winning car was equipped with a Bosch magneto, it would be awarded an additional $300, the second place car would receive $200, and the third place car would receive $100. Eighteen cars were registered for the race, including three Nationals piloted by Aitken, Howdy Wilcox, and Kincaid and two Marmons driven by Harroun and Dawson.[113] The favorite to win the race was Burman, who had had a wonderful two days of racing. The crowd of 20,000 cheered wildly for Dawson, who was leading the race at the 190-mile mark. With his tires wearing down, he signaled the pits that he needed to come in for new tires, but the stop was denied for fear that he would lose the race. So he kept driving and was rewarded with winning the Cobe Trophy with a time of 2 hours 43 minutes 20.1 seconds. Burman, driving the Marquette-Buick, finished second after having a tire explode, resulting in a 45-second pit stop. Harroun, driving a Marmon, placed third. For his efforts, Dawson was awarded the $3,000 trophy and $1,200 in cash ($500 from the Indianapolis Motor Speedway, $300 from Bosch magneto, and $400 from Michelin Tire Company). Dawson was only 20 years old and had begun driving race cars in the spring. Sixteen new speed records were set during the Cobe Trophy race, including 20 miles by Arthur Chevrolet, 60 miles by Burman, 70, 80, 90, 100 and 110 miles by Arthur Chevrolet, 120, 130, 140, 150, 160, 170 and 180 miles by Burman, and 190 and 200 miles by Dawson.[114]

The Cobe Trophy race was the highlight of the day for the crowd. In the five-mile amateur race, Arthur Greiner, driving a National, finished second and William Tousey, driving another National, finished third behind Spencer Wishart in a Mercedes. In the 20-mile free-for-all, Aitken, driving a National, finished second to Eddie Hearne, driving a Benz, who set a new world record at 14 minutes 8.72 seconds. The previous record was 15 minutes 31.8 seconds.[115]

Next on the Marmon, Cole, and Parry calendar were the Grand Circuit automobile races, which opened at Churchill Downs on July 8. On the dirt track at Churchill Downs, Indianapolis-built cars returned to their winning format with seven firsts, eight seconds and two thirds in the nine races run. Marmon won four races, Cole won two, and Parry won one. The only races in which an Indianapolis-built racer didn't win were those for the class of less than 160 cubic inches, where an Indianapolis car did not participate.[116]

With the strong showing at Churchill Downs, the racers moved to the Latonia Race Track, where the results were similar with the Marmon team dominating the competition by winning five of the nine events while the Cole team won two. Five second place finishes were recorded by the Indianapolis-built cars, with four being recorded by Marmon and one by Cole. The two third place finishes were recorded by Cole.[117]

Having not done well in the races over the July 4th weekend, the National team went to the Indianapolis Motor Speedway to try to improve its cars' performance, with Aitken and Kincaid making 50-mile test drives. Aitken left the track after about 30 miles and was in the pits when Kincaid lost control of his car on the backstretch going an estimated 80 miles per hour. The crash killed him instantly. Based upon the physical evidence on the track, it was believed he lost control of the car and skidded sideways before jumping a ditch and crashing through a board fence. Just as with the first weekend of racing in 1909 at the Speedway, the loss of a National driver raised speculation that the company would exit the racing game.[118]

The Cole and Parry teams went on to Dayton, Ohio, for a day of racing on a dirt track. While the day was filled with both motorcycle and automobile races, Hughie Hughes driving a Parry and Bill Endicott in a Cole battled it out in a five-mile exhibition race, with Hughes emerging victorious. Hughes failed in his attempt to beat Barney Oldfield's world record for a mile.[119]

The Circuit races continued with a day of racing in Columbus, Ohio. Hughie Hughes in a Parry won the five-mile race for cars with displacement between 161 and 230 cubic inches. He also finished second in the five-mile handicap race for cars with under 600 cubic inches of displacement, as well as second in the five-mile race for cars with displacement between 301 and 450 cubic inches.[120]

Racing returned to Brighton Beach in late July, where Bill Endicott driving a Cole beat H. A. Neely's Patterson in a ten-mile race by about a third of a mile. Up until the final mile, the two racers had been neck and neck as they negotiated the race course, providing the most exciting race of the day. In a one-hour race for those cars which had participated in the 24-hour race in June, Louis Disbrow driving a Marion went 53 miles to finish second behind George Robertson's Simplex. Endicott went 51 miles to place fourth out of the seven cars participating.[121]

During the season, American announced a 10,000 square foot expansion of its plant, which would permit the company to build 400 automobiles a year. The company's racing activities were in limbo. Following Herb Lytle's wreck at the Indianapolis Motor Speedway, the company had been barred from participation in stock events by the AAA Contest Board. American was one of several companies barred from racing. Others had been reinstated and the company hoped to resume its racing team once Lytle had recovered from his injuries.[122]

In July Marmon showed off its 1911 line of automobiles at its Indianapolis showroom. The wheelbase had been lengthened to 120 inches, adding to the roominess and comfort of the car. The car featured a water-cooled four-cylinder engine generating between 32 and 40 horsepower. It had three forward speeds and one reverse speed.[123]

Ernest Moross, the Indianapolis Motor Speedway's publicity director, visited Detroit to encourage manufacturers there to enter the Speedway contests in September. Other than Buick, little interest was expressed. One unnamed manufacturer explained perhaps why many Michigan cars did not participate in the races:

> It is almost useless to us to enter our racing cars at the Speedway, as we are not prepared for special track events. The Marmon and other teams in Indianapolis have tuned their cars over the course and are better prepared to win the events than outsiders.

The unnamed source continued, telling Moross,

> Of the great classic events which have been held at the Speedway in 1910, the Wheeler-Schebler trophy, the Prest-O-Lite trophy and the Cobe cup, and the Remy Brassard, three have been captured by Indianapolis cars. The Marmon won the Wheeler-Schebler, the most valuable trophy in the world, and the Cobe cup, the most noted trophy in the middle west, while the National won the Prest-O-Lite trophy,

with the outsiders gleaning a sole prize when the Buick just nosed out the Marmon and won the Remy Brassard. Therefore, I cannot see how we can compete in Indianapolis until such time as we have a Speedway here to prepare properly for speed events.[124]

After his conversations with the Michigan manufacturers, Moross decided to relocate to Detroit to promote a speedway which would "surpass in design and construction any Speedway in the world." He believed a speedway in the Detroit area would allow the Michigan manufacturers to be competitive in racing, which would in turn result in more entries in various races around the nation.[125]

In late July the AAA Contest Board vacated the victories and the 26 records of the Marquette-Buicks set at the Indianapolis Motor Speedway meet over the July 4 weekend. The cars were disqualified because they were not stock cars, a prerequisite of running in the races. Two of the models were not offered for sale at the regular Buick or Marquette agencies. Also cited was the agreement to advertise their performance as Marquette-Buicks, which was violated when an advertisement of the "Buick" cars appeared in a New York newspaper on July 10. The car entered as the Buick Special was entered in a free-for-all contest and its performance was not part of the AAA Contest Board action. As a backdrop to this action, the AAA Contest Board had ruled out of competition several of the Buick team cars, declaring that they were not stock cars, at the Memorial Day weekend meet.[126]

This action by the AAA Contest Board resulted in the awarding of the Remy Grand Brassard to Ray Harroun of the Marmon team.[127] Although Burman had already received $200 from the Remy Company as part of the award, the company paid Harroun for the award back to the date of the race and continued to pay Bob Burman the $75 per week until the September races at the Indianapolis Motor Speedway, when the Remy Grand Brassard would again be up for grabs.[128] The decision also meant that the Marmon performance in the Cobe Cup race would be moved from third to second place in addition to its first place finish. The disqualification of the Marquette-Buicks also had a positive impact upon the National team results. At the time of the race, it was believed National had won two firsts, five seconds, and three thirds. After the decision, the National record was modified to six firsts, eight seconds and three thirds.[129]

In mid–August, Brighton Beach hosted another 24-hour event, with seven cars participating including a Cole driven by Bill Endicott.[130] A Stearns driven by Cyrus Patschke and Al Poole easily broke the track record of 1,106 miles, going 1,236 miles in the 24 hours. Endicott, with relief provided by Louis Edmunds, finished in fourth place, traveling 906 miles. Only four cars finished the 24-hour grind.[131]

With total prizes of $2,500, Indianapolis manufacturers were enthusiastic about entering the Elgin races sponsored by the Chicago Motor Club in late August. By the time the entries closed, 35 cars representing 22 different manufacturers were entered. Indianapolis was well represented, with National and Marmon entered in the featured 300-mile Elgin National Trophy race for cars with over 600 cubic inches of displacement. This race featured a $1,000 cash prize in addition to a trophy valued at $2,500 for first place, $300 for second, and $200 for third. National and Marmon also entered the 204-mile Illinois Trophy race for cars with piston displacement between 301 and 450 cubic inches, with a cash prize of $400 to the winner. Marmon, Overland, and Marion were registered to participate in the Kane County Trophy race for cars with between 231 and 300 cubic inches of displacement, with a cash prize of $400. Cole entered the Fox River Trophy race for cars under 231 cubic inches of displacement with a $300 cash prize.[132]

On behalf of the Marmon team, Harroun surveyed the Elgin course, which was under construction, and was impressed with the preparations for the race.

> The course is in excellent condition and will be much better before the race. It is not a boulevard, but a course that will really try out a car and a driver. Possibly an average of 60 miles an hour will be made in the races Friday and if the course stands the grind better may be done Saturday, but it is a matter of serious doubt. The four turns are very abrupt and will prove a severe test for drivers. The course is winding and picturesque and the race should be exciting in every respect.[133]

Indianapolis-built cars had terrific results on the first day of racing at the Elgin road races. In the 204-mile Illinois Trophy race, Al Livingston in a National 40 took home the honors with an average speed of 60.6 miles per hour, while Dawson placed third. Dave Buck, a new driver for Marmon, brought home the victory in the 169.5-mile Kane County Trophy race. In second place was Adolph Monsen in a Marion, while Louis Heinemann piloting a Marmon was third.[134] However, the Indianapolis-built cars failed to bring home the championship for the Elgin National Road Race held the next day, which was won by Ralph Mulford driving a Lozier with an average speed of 62.5 miles per hour. Finishing second, a lap behind on the 8.5-mile course, was Al Livingston in a National, while Art Greiner in another National finished third. Both Marmon cars were forced out of the race with mechanical issues. Harroun's car suffered a broken piston on the second lap while Dawson's car had a broken connecting rod on the twenty-seventh lap.[135]

American's 1911 automobiles had few significant changes with the exception of a coupe which was available in two-passenger and four-passenger models. The most significant innovation was the oiling system, which relied upon a gear-driven pump inside the engine case to force the oil. All of the automobiles had four-cylinder engines which had either 50 horsepower or 60 horsepower depending upon the size of the cylinders. Seven of the company's models used the underslung chassis. The tourist and limousine models had the traditional chassis.[136]

Marmon was the first manufacturer to enter the Labor Day weekend races at the Indianapolis Motor Speedway. Five cars with Dawson and Harroun as pilots were entered to run in 18 different events.[137] In preparation for the races, Marmon unveiled a new four-cylinder racer designed by Howard Marmon and Harroun for the Vanderbilt Cup races in October. Dawson and Harroun went to the Speedway to check out the new car, which had 413 cubic inches of displacement. The car's best time for a lap was 1 minute 43 seconds or 87 miles per hour.[138] Prior to being installed in the racer, the engine was tested out in Howard Marmon's touring car for 30 days.[139]

Eleven cars took to the starting line for the Remy Grand Brassard race, the feature event, on the first day of the September races at the Indianapolis Motor Speedway. After the dust settled, two Nationals took top honors in the 100-mile race, with Indianapolis resident Howdy Wilcox taking home $75 per week until the end of the racing season.[140] Overall, the Indianapolis racers performed well, winning five of the nine races, placing second four times, and placing third three times.[141]

A rainy day greeted the final day of racing, limiting the crowd to an estimated 20,000. It was another strong performance by the Indianapolis teams, which won four firsts, four seconds, and four thirds. The highlight of the day was the 200-mile Wheeler-Schebler Trophy race with 12 hopeful racers taking to the starting line. After the 200-mile grind, Aitken, driving a blue National with an average speed of 71.4 miles per hour, crossed the finish line first. In his winning run, Aitken smashed the record for 200 miles set by Dawson in the Cobe Trophy race in July. For his efforts, Aitken received $1,000 in cash from the Speedway management plus $300 from Bosch as his car was equipped with a Bosch magneto. Coming in second was Al Livingston, also driving a National, who received $500 from Speedway management and $200 from Bosch. Arthur Greiner's National placed fourth in the contest. It was a disappointing day for Ray Harroun, who led the majority of the way in the race until a coupling broke on his car on the 68th lap.[142] Meanwhile, in the 50-mile free-for-all event, Eddie Hearne in a Benz took home $800 for winning the race. Indianapolis-built cars finished second, with Harroun at the helm of the Marmon racer, and third, with Al Livingston piloting the National car.[143]

With the success of both Marmon and National on the track, Indianapolis was eagerly following the two teams as they traveled to the East. The first stop was Long Island for the Vanderbilt Cup and Grand Prize races. Of the 32 cars registered to participate, six were from Indianapolis, including three Nationals with drivers Aitken, Louis Disbrow, and Al Livingston, two Marmons with Harroun and Dawson, and one American with William Wallace. The Wheatley Falls Trophy race had nine cars registered, including two Marions with Marcel Basle and Fred Heinemann at the wheel. The Massapequa Trophy race had six cars entered, including two Cole entries piloted by Bill Endicott and Louis Edmonds.[144]

The Vanderbilt Cup race was marred by the deaths of four and injury to 19. Louis Chevrolet lost control of his Marquette-Buick when the steering gear failed. The car crashed through a fence into a parked touring car, sending that car's occupants high into the air. Chevrolet's riding mechanic, Charles Miller, died in the wreck, while Chevrolet, who suffered a broken arm, said he would never again race a car.[145] Dawson, of the Marmon team, also was contemplating quitting the racing game after his racer injured a man standing on the course arguing with a policeman. After striking the man, Dawson stopped and then stopped again at the pits to inquire as to the man's well-being.[146]

Harry Grant, piloting an Alco, repeated his 1909 victory in the 278.08 mile Vanderbilt Cup race with an average speed of 65.1 miles per hour. Dawson, at the helm of a Marmon, finished second at 20 seconds off the winning pace.[147] The two stops had cost him six minutes and the race. On a mile for mile comparison, Dawson's speed exceeded that of Harry Grant, the race winner.[148] While finishing second overall, Dawson finished first for his class for cars with a piston displacement between 301 and 450 cubic inches and took home the Donor's Trophy.[149] Aitken, driving a National, placed third, crossing the finish line about a minute after the Marmon car. Aitken's teammate Louis Disbrow finished fourth.[150]

The 189-mile Wheatley Hills Trophy race, which was run simultaneously with the Vanderbilt Cup, was won by Frank Gelnaw in a Falcar. The 126.4-mile Massapequa Trophy Race was won by Bill Endicott in an Indianapolis-built Cole with a time of 3 hours 8 minutes 4 seconds.[151]

After the Vanderbilt Cup race, the Grand Prize race to be held on the same Long Island route was called off due to the hazards of the course. Dr. Wadsworth Warren, manager of the Buick team, explained:

> I for one—and I know many of the other managers of the same kind—am pleased that the Grand Prize, with its 400 miles of contest, is taken from the Long Island Motor Parkway Course. Conditions there invite death. While the Long Island course might be made into a good race site, it is far from that now, and I believe the public and contestants are right in asking assurance of protection from death and accident.

Our drivers, Louis and Arthur Chevrolet, and Bob Burman, have told me that they never drove a more dangerous race than the Vanderbilt of 1910, and each asserted he would not drive it again under such conditions. I know them to be as fearless and efficient as any drivers in the world, so I believe they speak the sentiments of the majority of motor pilots.[152]

A week later, the National and Marmon teams were racing at Fairmount Park in Philadelphia. While practicing for the race, Harry Endicott's Cole racer lost a tire while going an estimated 70 miles per hour. Neither Endicott nor his riding mechanic, Dr. H. Simmeron, were seriously injured despite being thrown about 25 feet from the car.[153] In a highly choreographed effort, five races, divided by class, were run simultaneously. The races at Fairmount Park would be disappointing for the Indianapolis racers with the exception of Aitken, who won a 204.5-mile race for his auto's class, taking home a $1,000 cash prize and a silver trophy.[154]

The 1910 racing season concluded at the Atlanta Motor Speedway with a two-day meet. The first day of racing was a bonanza for the Marmon team, with six cars entered in three events. Dawson won three events including the featured 200-mile City of Atlanta Trophy race, crossing the finish line a mere 3.5 seconds before Ralph Mulford in a Lozier. In that race, Dawson took two minutes off the record for a 200-mile speedway event and took home $1,000 in cash and a trophy valued at $5,000.[155]

After being postponed for two days, the final day of racing at Atlanta including the 250-mile feature event. The charmed luck of the Marmon team did not hold up. Early in the race both Dawson and Harroun were among the leaders, but both dropped out after developing engine trouble. The race was won by Joe Horan driving a Lozier.[156]

After the cancellation of the Grand Prize race, Savannah, the Los Angeles Motordrome, and the Indianapolis Motor Speedway each pleaded its case to host it, with the Speedway offering a $10,000 purse. Given the strength of the Grand Prize race held in Savannah in 1908, Savannah was selected to hold the race, the longest road race in the United States, on November 12, subject to a review of the plans for crowd control.[157] Indianapolis manufacturers Marmon, National, and American quickly committed to participating in the race, with the Marmons being driven by Harroun and Dawson, the Nationals being driven by Aitken and Howdy Wilcox, and the American being driven by William Wallace. In all, 23 cars were entered in the race. On November 11, Savannah hosted two races, the Tiedeman Cup for cars with a piston displacement between 161 and 230 cubic inches and the Savannah Challenge Trophy for cars with a piston displacement between 231 and 300 cubic inches.[158]

A native of California, Al Livingston, known as a "dirt track king" for his racing skills, was driving a National racer at an estimated 90 miles per hour in a practice session at the Atlanta racetrack when his rear right tire suffered a puncture. The blowout caused Livingston to be ejected from the racer, rising an estimated 25 feet before falling to the ground. He suffered a crushed head and although taken to a hospital never regained consciousness.[159] His death caused Arthur Newby to cancel the National team's participation in the races at Atlanta and Savannah.[160]

Marmon ended its racing season in grand style, with Joe Dawson winning the 276.8-mile Savannah Challenge Cup race with a time of 4 hours 23 minutes 39.95 seconds. Cole had two entries in the Tiedeman Trophy race, one piloted by Bill Endicott and the other by Harry Knight, neither of which ended up winning any money for their efforts due to mechanical issues.[161]

Howard Marmon, captain of the Marmon racing team, unveiled the secrets of the team's success:

> The running of a race is usually mapped out before the cars start, and the driver knows the schedule decided for him to run on. He is signaled whether he is exceeding this schedule or falling behind it, and he is informed at all times of any important happenings in the running of the race.

Marmon continued his explanation:

> He wants to know whether he is in striking distance of the leader or how far behind he is from the leading car. If in the lead, he must know what advantage he holds on all competitors, so that he can use some judgment whether to increase his lead and drive harder or begin to take matters easy.[162]

Marmon sold all of its 1910 models by the end of June. With the success achieved on the race track, there was great interest in the 1911 models. The company was offering a five-passenger touring car and a four-person toy tonneau, both with a 120-inch wheelbase. The company would also build landaulets, coupes and limousines by special request. The four-cylinder engine in all of the Marmon cars was the same as the one used in its racing cars. The transmission offered three forward and one reverse speed. While the standard color for the Marmon automobile was blue-black with gray stripes, the company offered other color options upon request.[163]

Premier's 1911 automobiles included a six-cylinder car known as the 6–60 and a four-cylinder car known as the 4–40 in a variety of body styles including touring, closed-coupled clubman, roadster, and limousine. The 4–40 and 6–60 cars were relatively expensive. The selling price for the four-cylinder car was increased to $3,000 while the six-cylinder car sold for $3,500. The limousines were priced at $4,200 and $5,000. Premier boasted of a new type of front axle that resulted in a lower body profile for the car.[164] All of the cars had three forward speeds and one reverse. The cars were manufactured in a blue-black color with pin stripes and sported gray wheels.[165] One of the marketing ploys used by Premier was that the cars used the same steel as was used in U.S. Army gun carriages, which assured the strength of the automobile.[166]

Cole increased the power of its 1911 models to 36 horsepower. The company also increased the wheelbase by seven inches to 115 inches.[167] The company announced plans to produce 2,000 of the 1911 model cars, as compared with 800 cars produced in 1910. To accomplish this, the company increased its production space by constructing a 30,000 square foot building and leasing a second building.[168]

Waverley introduced the Model 81, a four-passenger brougham which was similar to the Model 75 unveiled in 1909. The Model 81's body was built in a single piece and was three inches wider than that of the Model 75.[169]

In late November, Harroun quit the racing game, returning to his hometown of Chicago to build airplane engines and airplanes. He had been driving for the Marmon team since the Indianapolis Motor Speedway opened in August 1909.[170]

Some tantalizing rumors were floating around Indianapolis that the French Grand Prix would be revived, having last been run in 1906. The Automobile Club of France had sanctioned the Automobile Club de la Sarthe to run an event of approximately 370 miles between May 15 and July 15, 1911. Although the details of the race's timing would be announced later, National, Marmon and Lozier were already champing at the bit to be part of the race.[171]

The 500-mile International Sweepstakes to be held at the Indianapolis Motor Speedway with a purse of $25,000 in gold coin was announced in early December 1910.¹⁷² Patrons of the Speedway had indicated to management a preference for long events with large purses.¹⁷³

Late 1910 brought difficult times for the Parry Automobile Company. The Webster & Parks Tool Company, which was owed $327.15, petitioned the court to place Parry into the hands of a receiver in December 1910. It was believed that the company owed all creditors in aggregate about $350,000 and didn't have the working capital to pay. Although Parry had $3.3 million in orders, the company's board agreed it would be in the firm's best interest to be placed in the hands of the receiver as it didn't have the funds to manufacture the cars.¹⁷⁴ In order to recover their monies, the company's creditors wanted the receiver to continue to manufacture automobiles with the parts that were available.¹⁷⁵ During the short period of operating under the receiver, three autos were assembled but were not sold. Against the wishes of the majority of the creditors, who believed that operations could be profitable, Judge Vinson Carter mandated that the factory be sold. It had a going concern value of

1910 Parry Automobile Company advertisement (Indiana Historical Society, M1144).

$139,000 and a non-going concern value of $25,000. The judge set a price of $50,000 for the factory. One of the parties interested in the property was W. C. Teasdale, Jr., son-in-law of David Parry, who indicated an offer of $45,000 to $55,000 depending upon the terms of the sale. The intention was to start a new auto company.[176]

In January, a syndicate purchased the Parry plant for $50,000. The syndicate, headed by W. K. Bromley of Indianapolis and G. O. Simon of Dayton, Ohio, included many of the creditors of Parry Automobile Company. The company, bolstered by $150,000 in additional capital, planned to manufacture 1,000 cars in the first year. Simon was named as the firm's general manager.[177] W. C. Teasdale was elected president of the company, called Motor Car Manufacturing Company, which produced the New Parry.[178]

5

Stutz Cars Make an Entrance

Concurrently with the 1911 New York Auto Show, the AAA held a meeting to discuss a wide range of topics including the Good Roads movement to improve highways throughout the United States. Indianapolis was well represented at the New York Auto Show, with Overland, National, Premier, Marmon, Cole, Marion, Empire, American, and the Wheeler-Schebler Carburetor Company in attendance.[1]

Howard Marmon, vice president of the ALAM, discussed proposed changes to the association's racing regulations. One of the primary points of agitation among manufacturers and drivers was Rule 238, which applied to long distance tracks but not 24-hour races. The rule stated:

> No driver shall be permitted to drive or have control of the car for more than three consecutive hours. After the expiration of such three-hour period he shall not again be permitted to drive until he has taken at least one hour's rest.

At the Chicago Auto Show, which was run by the ALAM, there was discussion about changing the rule to a five-hour period before the driver would need to step away from driving duties. Howard Marmon felt that the rule would probably stay as it was but give the referee more discretion in allowing a driver to remain at the wheel.[2]

Indianapolis was well represented on the AAA Contest Board rules committee, with Howard Marmon serving as the chairman and George A. Weidley of Premier as a member. One of the main topics the committee expected to take up was the future of the Glidden Reliability Tour. When rumors circulated that the AAA Contest Board would no longer be involved in the tour, the Chicago Auto Club expressed a desire to become the sanctioning body. Others thought that since the Glidden Tour had become a national event, a national organization should be the organizer.[3]

The other task of the committee was to establish a national grand circuit of automobile racing supplemented by a secondary circuit to include speedways, hill climbs, and road races. Automobile racing was expensive for the manufacturers and the committee hoped to put racing on a more business-like basis. Key among the goals was to eliminate the long distances between the races, which drove up the costs incurred for transportation of the cars, the drivers, and the support teams. The other goal was to eliminate the advertising of records which had not been officially recognized, such as the advertising by Jackson Motor Company after the 1909 Wheeler-Schebler race.[4]

Attempting to capitalize on the racing fever, Cole announced that it would build a Cole 30 roadster guaranteed to have a top speed of 70 miles per hour. Each racing roadster would

78

be tested at the Indianapolis Motor Speedway prior to shipment to the customer. The car could travel an estimated 700 miles on a single fill-up as it carried 40 gallons of gasoline and ten gallons of motor oil. Keeping with the racing theme, the cars had a gear ratio of 3 to 1.[5] The Cole racing roadster was one of five models built on the same chassis, with the others being a five-passenger touring car available in both an open and a closed configuration, a four-door, four-passenger toy tonneau, and a limousine. All of the Cole 30s had a water-based cooling system and a four-cylinder engine which produced 36 horsepower. One of the features of the Cole 30 was that it didn't need a dustpan because there were no exposed working parts.[6]

The National Motor Vehicle Company was very supportive of participating in auto races. W. G. Wall, chief engineer, explained,

> We have always felt that the car was better advertised by racing than touring with the same amount expended in each event. We are also able to learn more of the car's stability and it is much easier to correct any faults in construction that would show up in a race and never become noticed in a touring event.
>
> Such an extreme test we feel benefits the customer because of the strain placed on all parts. The strain exerted on a car in one 200-mile race is more than equal to a test of stability and perfection which 10,000 miles of touring would demand. While the racing expense and the attendant upkeep is very great, in fact it runs into the thousands, we have always considered that we were well repaid and that the customer in the end was the gainer.
>
> Building the cars for a racing team involves more work than the finishing of 25 regular cars, because the constant wear and tear on the cars in the long grinds will demand careful inspection on returning to the factory each time. The real reason for our racing campaigns and the teams we have in the field is that we think we are eventually doing the purchaser a great service, as we are able to detect the slightest fault and make the cars more perfect than would be otherwise possible.[7]

Ralph DePalma joined Howdy Wilcox and Charlie Merz on the National team of drivers for the 207.5-mile free-for-all in the Portola (Panama-Pacific) road race on February 22.[8] Merz won the 152.8-mile Panama-Pacific race with an average speed of 66.8 miles per hour[9] as Arthur Newby watched. While Wilcox, Merz, and DePalma were on the West Coast, National drivers Aitken and Louis Disbrow headed to New Orleans for the Mardi Gras race. While Disbrow joined the team for the Mardi Gras race, his participation in the 500-Mile International Sweepstakes would be as a pilot of a Pope-Hartford which was built in his garage in Jamaica, Long Island.[10] By early March, it was suspected that DePalma would not be driving a National in the Indianapolis race.[11]

Although not a significant player in the Indianapolis automobile industry, James I. Handley took over American and assumed the presidency in January, changing the name to American Motors Company (American). The deal was valued at $1,095,000. Joining Handley as directors of the company were A. D. Ogborn of Newcastle, Indiana, and James E. Kepperly of Indianapolis. V. A. Longaker of Indianapolis was named as chairman of the board and general manager of the company.[12]

American unveiled a new four-cylinder car priced under $2,000 at the Boston Auto Show in early March. The car, which had seating for five, was built upon a 115-inch wheelbase and was guaranteed to go 50 to 60 miles per hour.[13]

John Willys announced in March that the manufacture of the Overland car, including its engine, would be moved to Overland's Toledo facilities. The good news for Indianapolis and its automobile industry was that the space vacated and the men employed by Overland in Indianapolis would be reassigned to the building of Marion cars. Willys believed that when the Indianapolis facilities were dedicated to Marion automobiles, the volume of cars produced each year would increase from 2,000 to 5,000.[14]

The inaugural Indianapolis 500 was run by the AAA in 1911 as a Class E event for specialized auto racers. As such, speeds were expected to reach perhaps 100 miles per hour. To ensure the fast speeds, all participating cars were required to be able to run at least 75 miles per hour. Early ticket sales for seats to the event led management to believe that attendance at the race would exceed 100,000. In addition to the purse of $25,000 in gold offered by the Speedway, various automobile suppliers added special prizes to bring the total prizes offered to $40,000.[15]

In preparation for the first running of the Indianapolis 500, seats in the main grandstand and the adjacent one, which had previously been offered on a first-come basis, were changed to reserved seating.[16] By March 1, there were 29 entrants in the race. They included some of the biggest names in the sport, such as David Bruce-Brown, the winner of the 415-mile Grand Prize at Savannah; Harry Grant, twice winner of the Vanderbilt Cup; and Louis Strang, winner of three races in 1908 (the 342-mile Savannah race, the 259-mile Brier Cliff race, and the 250-mile Lowell race). Indianapolis-based companies entered six racers. The Marmon team entered Joe Dawson and an unnamed driver. To avoid the unlucky number 13, the unnamed Marmon entry was 12½ and the entry driven by Dawson was number 14. Representing the National team were Aitken in car number 4, and cars numbered 20 and 21 with unnamed drivers. Also on the list of entries was car number 10 from the Stutz Auto Parts Company, to be driven by Gil Andersen.[17] Harry Stutz had begun designing this car after he finished the two racers for Marion for the 1910 races. The car had a four-cylinder T-head Wisconsin engine producing 389.9 cubic inches of displacement and a transmission with three forward speeds and one reverse.[18] By early March 1911, Stutz had been enticed by Carl Fisher and the other owners of Empire to leave Marion and become the designer and factory manager for Empire.[19]

In conjunction with the running of the first Indianapolis 500, the AAA planned a 7,000-mile Grand Circuit to begin in Indianapolis following the race.[20] This circuit would benefit the manufacturers by lowering the transportation costs of racing, since the races would be held in geographic order. Additionally, there was talk of a special train, hotel, and garage bills that would further cut the costs.[21]

Famed racer Barney Oldfield was not in the field for the inaugural Indianapolis 500, having been suspended by the AAA until January 1, 1912, for driving in an unsanctioned race with Jack Johnson and subsequent unsanctioned races. In reaching agreement with the AAA, Oldfield and his manager, William Pickens, agreed to retire from auto racing for a year. As part of this agreement, Oldfield sold his three racing cars to E. A. Moross, the former publicity man of the Indianapolis Motor Speedway and the promoter of the Jacksonville and Galveston beach races. Moross planned to approach the AAA for reinstatement of the three cars: the Blitzen Benz, the Prince Henry Benz, and the giant Knox. Moross announced that an attempt would be made to lower the world speed record on the Jacksonville Beach with the Blitzen Benz with Bill Burman, Ray Harroun, or Louis Disbrow at the wheel.[22] Adding more interest in Indianapolis was the news that Moross had reached an agreement for a 300-horsepower Benz to participate in the Jacksonville Beach race. Moross contacted Howard Marmon to see if he could secure the services of Joe Dawson to drive the big Benz at Jacksonville. Both Ray Harroun and Johnny Aitken of the National team also initially agreed to be part of the races.[23]

However, the announcement that Ray Harroun would drive in the races at Jacksonville seemed to be more of a pipe dream than a reality. In late March, Harroun had reaffirmed his decision to quit the racing game and to concentrate on his new monoplane, which was entered in a race from San Francisco to New York and had its base of operations at the Indianapolis Motor Speedway. He had previously declined an offer to drive a car in the 500-mile International Sweepstakes at the Indianapolis Motor Speedway.[24]

Hoping that a new speed record would be set at the Pablo-Atlantic Beach races in Jacksonville, Ernie Moross hired an engineering firm to establish the kilometer, one-mile, two-mile, five-mile and ten-mile distances on the beach. The Warner horograph would be used to record the times and AAA officials would be there to verify the results. Bob Burman, driving the Blitzen Benz, was going to attempt to beat the world record of 145 miles per hour which had been established by a 350-horsepower Benz in France.[25]

Although Ray Harroun had decided he wasn't going to pilot one of the racers at Pablo-Atlantic Beaches, National sent five cars to be piloted by Howdy Wilcox and Charlie Merz, and Cole sent three cars to be piloted by Louis Edmunds and Tucker, a new participant in the racing game.[26]

Carl Fisher and Arthur Newby[27] were at the Pablo-Atlantic Beaches races to witness the National team win five races, take three seconds, and place third four times. Cole racers won one race, placed second three times, and placed third twice. The highlight of the races was Howdy Wilcox breaking Barney Oldfield's mile record by 0.03 seconds, with a time of 40.32 seconds.[28]

In what had appeared to be a settled issue, Howard Smith did not give up the fight to claim the 1910 Glidden Trophy awarded to Chalmers Motor Company. In April 1911, New York Supreme Court Judge Josiah T. Marean agreed to hear the case. At issue was whether or not the oil hand pump was a stock part. Judge Marean ruled that the burden of proof was on the AAA Contest Board and Chalmers to substantiate that 57 of the Premier 6–60s were not equipped with the oil pump. Howard Smith had testified that the company's records were incomplete as to this part. Judge Marean believed that since the AAA had agreed that the car was a stock car and let it participate in the race, it did not have the right to deny Premier the Trophy.[29] In late June Howard Smith gave up the fight for the 1910 Glidden Trophy,[30] and in January 1912 the suspension of Howard Smith and Premier in contests run by the AAA Contest Board ended.[31]

The Indianapolis Speedway hosted a very special visitor in mid–April. With the day off from baseball because of rain, Detroit slugger Ty Cobb took to the track in a National racer with Johnny Aitken at the wheel. After two trips around the track, Cobb was given the wheel of a new National roadster straight off of the showroom floor. With Aitken on his left hand side, after getting used to the track Cobb drove a mile in 45 seconds and made one lap in 1 minute 57 seconds.[32]

In April 1911, Nordyke & Marmon announced a $10,000 expansion to their manufacturing facilities. The one-story building, with dimensions of 100 feet by 200 feet, would be used for the storage of lumber and as a repair shop.[33]

With the settlement of the Selden Patent dispute, the ALAM was disbanded. Taking its place was the Automobile Board of Trade, with offices in New York City and the objective of taking care of the industry through investigation of adverse legislation, patent infringements, and bad business practices. One of the directors was Charles Hanch, treasurer of Nordyke & Marmon.

An issue vexing the industry at this time was used cars and price cutting. At a meeting of the IATA, Charles Hanch proposed that the various automobile dealers establish a company to be responsible for the handling of used cars taken in trade. He also urged the dealers to stop price cutting on new cars and naively suggested that customers would stop buying from a dealer if the price cutting didn't stop. Neither of these suggestions was adopted.[34]

After experiencing the theft of brass castings and aluminum automobile doors from its factory, Nordyke & Marmon hired a private detective. One night, the detective saw three men climb the fence surrounding the building and enter the building. They left a while later with 70 pounds of loot and were followed to a secluded spot on the banks of the White River. The private detective notified the bicycle policeman who had previously worked the case, who then witnessed the exchange of the loot. Five people were arrested for the theft, including the junk dealer who took possession of the stolen property.[35]

Cole was represented at a 24-hour race in Los Angeles and finished third out of the ten cars that started the race. The winning car, a Fiat with 60 horsepower, went 1,491 miles in the grind. The Cole entry, which completed 1,219 miles, experienced two broken cylinders, which took it out of the run for two hours.[36]

After months of maintaining that he had quit the racing game, Harroun agreed to pilot the Marmon Wasp in the upcoming inaugural Indianapolis 500 International Sweepstakes race. Harroun explained his change of mind:

> I returned to the game because I like it, and again I returned because of the large purse that is offered the winner of the 500-mile race. I have had countless offers to drive racing cars—indeed, the many requests for my services became wearisome—and I had just one pet phrase to give to one and all, "I am never going to race again." It has not been such a long time since I told the same phrase to the Marmons, but the more I thought about the big race and the prizes offered the more I longed to sit at the wheel of one of my old cars, smell the gasoline and see the brick track gliding swiftly under my car.
>
> When the race starts, I will roll my Wasp with which I have won many races up to the tape and I am going to go the 500 miles without a stop. I will go the long route and I am out to win.[37]

Marmon, National, Lozier, and Buick weren't interested in showcasing their cars only on the national stage; they had also expressed some interest in participating in the French Grand Prix. W. J. Morgan of New York traveled to Indianapolis to meet with Newby of National and Howard Marmon. Morgan said,

> A short time ago, I made the journey to France in order to inspect the course, so that I might be able to tell the prospective American entrants what kind of going their drivers could expect. I have already told all about the course. It is undoubtedly the fastest road course in the world, and I would not be surprised to see the winner average very close to 80 miles an hour for the 373 miles. It is my opinion that if four American cars were sent over we would be able to win the race for the United States, as our cars and men are now equal to any combination the world can produce.[38]

Ultimately, the four American manufacturers decided against entering the French Grand Prix, although American driver David Bruce-Brown participated driving a Fiat.[39]

Cole introduced the Cole Speedster, a 4-cylinder, 40-horsepower roadster, to the market in late April, 1911. Built upon a 118-inch wheelbase, the car was painted battleship gray with bright red seats and natural wood wheels.[40]

As entries closed for the 500-mile International Sweepstakes race, 44 cars were entered including two Marmon entries piloted by Dawson and Harroun, three National entries driven by Aitken, Merz, and Wilcox, two Cole entries, one of which was piloted by Bill Endicott, and the Stutz Auto Parts entry driven by Gil Andersen. Total prize money for the race had increased to $33,400, including $25,100 being offered by the Speedway management and $8,300 being offered by various accessory makers.[41] Two other entries postmarked by the entry deadline of May 1 were subsequently received by the Speedway management.

The Stutz entry, a specially built racer with 309 cubic inches of displacement, was the first on the track to get in some practice laps.[42] Harry Stutz talked about the creation of the 309 cubic inch racer:

> This is the first Stutz car I ever have built, but I believe I will be justified in making more, since this one has shown up so well. There seems to have been a misunderstood rumor that the Stutz car is a Marion. The car is not a Marion and is entirely different in every detail of construction. Probably this report gained credence through the fact I was an engineer for the Marion company for four years and took charge of the Marion racing team. Gilbert Anderson, who drives this new Stutz for me, was a driver of the Marion, but this car has no connection in any way with the Marion car or the Marion company.[43]

The second driver on the track was Joe Dawson, a young Marmon pilot, under the watchful eye of Howard Marmon.[44] Later in the week, the rebuilt Marmon Wasp, which had won the Wheeler-Schebler Trophy in the 1910 racing season, showed up for some practice laps with Harroun at the wheel.[45]

Joseph Cole, a proponent of racing, was eager to have his cars participate in the Indianapolis 500-mile International and other long races even though the cars had little possibility of winning when pitted against cars with greater power.

> It is in events like the 500-mile contests or the 24-hour races the manufacturer gets the best lessons. While an automobile may do well and show up to a great advantage in a five or ten-mile race, its actions in a long grind are entirely different.[46]

1911 Cole. Joseph Cole is on the far right hand side (LeRoy Cole Collection, Gilmore Car Museum).

Before the racers took to the Indianapolis Motor Speedway for the 500-mile race, there was a day of racing on the dirt track at Lavonia, Kentucky. It wasn't a very good racing day for the Indianapolis-built cars, which had four second place finishes. Emmett Meddock, piloting an Empire, finished second in a five-mile race and a ten-mile free-for-all, while H. F. Fulton of the Marmon team finished second in a 10-mile race and the 100-mile feature race. In the featured race Bill Endicott's Cole blew a rear tire. While hurtling toward the infield, Endicott tried to get out of the racers behind him by cutting across the field to the outside of the track. As his car swerved, it was hit in the middle by Mack Dermond's Schacht. The Schacht reared up and came down on the rear tire of the Cole, crushing it. A Buick driven by Zeke Hilliard couldn't avoid the two cars, and all three drivers were thrown from their racers. Endicott, who was not seriously injured, ran back down the track to warn the approaching cars of the wreck ahead to avert additional crashes. The race was immediately flagged off as 13,000 spectators surged from the stands to the site of the crash.[47]

Some were surprised that Harroun, the victor in many auto races, would choose to drive the Wasp rather than a newer car. He explained,

> A car that is built right is in better condition for a long race the second year than it is in the first. Any car that is built for one race and driven for the first time in a big event is uncertain, no matter how much work you do in practice. I know I can depend upon my car at every stage of the long grind.

He went on to predict victory in the 500-mile race:

> That is the real reason for getting back into the racing game. Judging from what it has done, I believe the "Wasp" can go the 500-mile route in better time than any other car entered.[48]

Ray Harroun in the Marmon Wasp (Bass Photo Co. Collection, Indiana Historical Society).

As race day dawned, the Marmon team was favored to win the race, with the three-car National team placing second in the bookies' favorites.[49] Starting at 10 a.m., Carl Fisher, accompanied by Jim Allison in Fisher's white Stoddard-Dayton, led the race cars around the track on the pace lap.[50] Employing his proven racing strategy, Harroun won the inaugural Indianapolis 500, averaging 74.62 miles per hour before 85,000 spectators in the Indianapolis-built Marmon Wasp. Ralph Mulford finished second five minutes later. Other Indianapolis cars finishing the race included Dawson in a second Marmon entry, who finished fifth; Charlie Merz driving a National, who finished seventh; and Gil Andersen in the Stutz racer, who finished eleventh.[51]

The Stutz entry, the first car Stutz produced, performed very well. Gilbert Andersen, who piloted the car, drove the entire 500 miles without a relief driver and the car didn't have any mechanical difficulties. The car, equipped with a four-cylinder motor, averaged 68.25 miles per hour even with 11 tire changes.[52] This led to the Stutz brand becoming known as "the car that made good in a day."[53]

Despite the apparent victory by Harroun, the race results were in disarray, causing rumors to be rampant at the Claypool Hotel where the announcement of the official results was expected. The rumor that gained the most support was that David Bruce-Brown had placed second rather than Ralph Mulford. After checking the results five times, the committee got Thomas Devine, the manager of the Columbia Phonograph Company, out of bed to help check the results. C. V. Weaver and C. P. Herdman were tasked with recording the results of the race utilizing the Columbia Phonograph Company's two dictaphones. The race was recorded on 51 wax rolls.[54]

Harroun earned $10,000 for his win, while second place finisher Mulford's paycheck was $5,000. Dawson earned $1,500 and Charlie Merz earned $700. The awarding of fifth place to Dawson was a change from the original recorded finishes. In reviewing the scoring, it was discovered that Dawson's car had completed 200 laps when given the green flag. On the 201st lap, his leaking radiator suffered a four-inch gap when a piece of metal went through it, resulting in the car breaking down on the backstretch.[55]

Not surprisingly, Harroun announced his retirement from the racing game although he would appear with the Marmon Wasp in some exhibition runs.[56] The Marmon Wasp and Dawson's fifth place car were displayed in Marmon's showroom.[57]

Marmon Motors placed an ad celebrating the Marmon victory:

> Ray Harroun, driving the Marmon Wasp, wins against a packed field of the fastest and highest priced cars in the world in the greatest race ever driven.
> This is a Fitting Climax to the Longest and Most Remarkable List of Important Racing Victories Ever Won by Any Make of Motor Car.
> There Can Be But One Logical Conclusion That Will Interest the Buyer—Marmon Design, Marmon Materials, Marmon Workmanship *Must Be Right.*[58]

Mulford, who had placed second in the race, calculated that his actual driving time was 14 minutes less than that of Harroun. The difference in the race, Mulford believed, was his 14 pit stops as compared to four for the Wasp.

Following the victory at the Indianapolis Motor Speedway, Harroun and the Marmon Wasp traveled to the Chicago area for a race at the Hawthorne track, where Harroun, Bob Burman, and Ralph DePalma made an exhibition drive for the crowd. Fellow Marmon driver Joe Dawson took the driving duties in the races in a different Marmon racer. Arthur Greiner drove a National racer, as did amateur racer Austin Harlan.[59] The first day of racing at the Hawthorne track was marred by a crash on the very first race, a five-miler, which took the life of Maurice Basle when he crashed through a fence going about 80 miles per hour. The second race was a close contest between Dawson, driving a Marmon, and Gus Monckmeier, piloting a Staver, with Dawson pulling ahead toward the end and winning the contest. When, during the second race, Joe Jagersberger went through the fence in the exact same location as the Basle accident, the race promoters and race officials halted the day of racing and spent three hours inspecting the track.[60]

Empire, American, National and Marmon entered a hill climbing contest in Cincinnati, Ohio, at the end of July with very satisfying results. Out of eight events, the Indianapolis-built cars won four, placed second in four, and placed third in two before an estimated crowd of 10,000.[61]

At a dinner before the Indianapolis 500 race for the sales agents for Cole Motor Company, Joseph Cole announced that Cole would consolidate its manufacturing efforts from three separate plants around town to a new facility.[62] In July, Cole bought the property it had been leasing at 744–750 East Washington Street for $150,000.[63] Several days later, the company announced the construction of a $60,000 four-story building behind the property recently purchased.[64]

Cole wasn't the only automobile manufacturer in Indianapolis to announce a new plant. American leased a plant at Meridian and the Belt Railroad formerly occupied by the Columbia Conserve Company, a cannery. The need for this new facility was driven by the company designing a lower priced four-passenger car, the American 30 underslung with a price tag of $2,250, in addition to a two-passenger car, the American underslung roadster with a retail price of $1,250. The company also produced a seven-passenger limousine.[65]

The Indiana automobile manufacturers planned a four-state tour to promote their automobiles beginning July 12. The route extended from Indianapolis to St. Louis, Missouri, and Dubuque, Iowa, before returning to Indianapolis. The organizing committee was dominated by Indianapolis manufacturers as this was easier for planning purposes. The advisory committee included Howard Smith (Premier), V. A. Longaker (American), Elmer Apperson (Apperson), Arthur Newby (National), Elwood Haynes (Haynes), Walter Marmon, William H. McIntyre (McIntyre), Will H. Brown (Mais), Carl Fisher (Empire), and Herbert Rice (Waverley).[66] George Dickson of National encouraged other Hoosier manufacturers to participate in the tour as well:

> Every one of the makers of motor trucks and automobiles in this state should enter at least one car in the proposed tour for Indiana-made cars. If conducted along the lines suggested, the tour will prove a big boost for the state makers.[67]

The most unusual car to participate in the four-state tour was a Waverley electric, given the challenges associated with the electric battery. The car's journey of 1,400 miles was done in 124 hours, setting a new record for electric automobiles. By way of comparison, the swiftest gasoline powered car made the trip in 73 hours.[68]

While hill climbs did not offer the lucrative prizes of other racing venues due to smaller crowds and the difficulty of collecting admission fees from the spectators, National continued to believe this was an important test of its vehicles. George Dickson, chief engineer, commented on its importance:

Hill climbing victories, and especially those made by stock cars, afford a very efficient index to a car's capability. This form of contest puts the machine under strains that would not be encountered in ordinary use, for the individual owner seldom attacks a grade with the high speed obtained in competition. For this reason, the National company prizes its victories of this kind and has been one of the most consistent entrants in this form of competition."[69]

During July and August National won more than 12 firsts, including eight by National 40s at a variety of hill climbing contests. National participated in a 2,000-foot hill climb with an average grade of 10 percent and a maximum grade of 15 percent in Port Jefferson, New York, in September. Don Herr won five events, including an event for cars costing between $2,001 and $3,000; a free-for-all for the Ardencraig Trophy; an event for cars with a piston displacement between 301 and 450 cubic inches; an event for cars with a piston displacement between 451 and 600 cubic inches; and a final event.[70]

In a race outside of Cincinnati as part of the celebration the opening of the Fernbank Dam, Johnny Jenkins' Cole racer finished second in a 200-mile contest. Leading the entire way, the winner, Eddie Hearne driving a Fiat, finished the race in 3 hours 29 minutes 3.2 seconds. Jenkins finished the 200 miles in 3 hours 40 minutes 4.4 seconds, or an average of 54 miles per hour on a course that was believed to be so dangerous that the starter, Fred Wagner, decreased the length of the drive from 250 miles. Jenkins finished first in a second event, a 150-mile race, with a time of 2 hours 46 minutes 29.84 seconds.[71]

Assistant Indianapolis Fire Department Chief Harry Johnson riding in a Stutz Bearcat (Indiana Historical Society, P0411).

Based upon the success of the Stutz racer in the Indianapolis 500, Harry Stutz decided to manufacture the car on a wide scale and incorporated the Ideal Motor Car Company. The company leased offices in a three-story building at Capitol Avenue and 10th Street built by Carl Fisher. The financial backing for the company was provided by local as well as Eastern capitalists. Harry Stutz was named the designer and factory manager of the new company.[72] Initially the factory, which was tooled to build 500 cars per year, produced three different models: a two-passenger roadster, a four-passenger toy tonneau, and a four-door five-passenger car.[73] Production began in August.[74] By September, the Ideal Motor Car Company announced the first shipments of the Stutz automobile and the establishment of a sales agency in New Zealand and Australia.[75]

Cole Motor announced that the Cole 34, a 40-horsepower car, would be available for the 1912 season in a five-passenger touring car, a four-passenger toy tonneau, a roadster speedster, a coupe, a limousine, and a five-seat London limousine. The Cole 34 cars all had Queen Anne style body panels and doors. A feature of the car was a gasoline sight gauge so that drivers would know when they were running low on fuel.[76] At the price of $3,250, the London limousine was built upon the Cole 30–40 chassis with an option to change the body out to any 1912 open body after the winter.[77]

Waverley also announced that it would be making a bigger electric car in 1912.[78] The five-passenger car featured "full view ahead," an unobstructed view for the driver, which was hailed as being a radical innovation. By the time the car was shown at the Chicago Automobile Show, the company had tested the innovative design for six months.[79]

SILENT WAVERLEY LIMOUSINE-FIVE
MODEL 98   (FULL VIEW AHEAD)   PRICE $3500

Silent Waverley Limousine Five (Bass Photo Co. Collection, Indiana Historical Society).

5. Stutz Cars Make an Entrance

With the departure of Harroun from the Marmon racing team, three new drivers were recruited, including Joe Nikrent, formerly of the Buick and Knox racing teams; Cyrus Patschke, the relief driver for Harroun in the winning effort in the first 500-mile International Sweepstakes race; and "Farmer Bill" Endicott, who had driven for Cole.[80] Harroun, who remained as the Marmon team captain, devised a new racing car body for Joe Dawson. The lines of the new car had the hood of the car making an upward curve in front of the steering wheel to throw the wind current over the driver's head. While the driver had good sightlines, this new design would protect him from the dust and wind of racing.[81]

Shortly after Harroun's retirement announcement, Aitken announced that he too was retiring, although he would remain employed by National. For the remainder of the 1911 racing season, National sponsored two teams. A team comprised of Len Zengel and Don Herr headed east for the Fairmount Park races while a team comprised of Charlie Merz and Howdy Wilcox headed to the West Coast for the Santa Monica races.[82] While Newby was hopeful he could convince Aitken to participate in the Santa Monica races, Aitken accepted a position as the first assistant to W. G. Wall, the company's engineer, in the National factory.[83]

The racing calendar was jam packed with opportunities to display the strength of the different cars. Eight different events were scheduled in October 1911, including the Glidden Tour, which left New York on October 14 on a 1,000-mile endurance run sponsored by the Chicago Motor Club (October 6–13), and a Harrisburg Motor Club reliability run (October 16–18). There were also a variety of track races including events at Danbury, Connecticut, Fairmount Park in Philadelphia, and the Springfield Auto Club on October 7, and events in Atlanta and Santa Monica the following weekend. Indianapolis-manufactured cars provided 13 entries for the Santa Monica and Fairmount races. National, Stutz, and Cole entered both races while Marmon entered only the Santa Monica races with entries for the two different classes. "Farmer Bill" Endicott and Joe Nikrent piloted the Marmon in the smaller class while Joe Dawson and Cyrus Patschke drove the larger class Marmon. Driving the National entries in Santa Monica were Charlie Merz and Howdy Wilcox. Stutz shipped a car to the West Coast for the Santa Monica race with the driver being supplied by the western Stutz distributor.[84]

It didn't take long for a Stutz car to be entered in an endurance run. Shortly after the first cars rolled off the assembly line, Harry Stutz announced that a Stutz would participate in the 500-mile Fairmount Park road race in Philadelphia in early October, which was divided into four groupings based upon the horsepower of the car. Each division had a $1,000 prize and there was a $2,500 prize for the overall winner. The Stutz car was piloted by Gil Andersen with Frank Agan as the riding mechanic.[85] Also entering the race were three Nationals with Don Herr, Len Zengel and Louis Disbrow at the helm. The overall winner of the Philadelphia race was Erwin Bergdoll, who averaged 61 miles per hour in a 90-horsepower Benz. Finishing fourth in the overall standings was Len Zengel, while Louis Disbrow in a National finished sixth. The Stutz car finished eighth, nearly 22 minutes slower than the winner. The final National entry finished ninth in the overall standings. In the division for cars with 301 to 450 cubic inches of displacement, Louis Disbrow's National finished first and took home a $1,000 prize. The Stutz car finished second with Gil Andersen at the helm and the National piloted by Don Herr finished third.[86]

As the 1911 racing season drew to a close, Marmon unveiled a new race car, the 36, piloted by Joe Dawson and Cyrus Patschke at the Santa Monica races. Spectators noticed the new body design which "protects the driver from the air currents without impeding his view of the track." The new car was very similar to the Marmon 30 except that it had a four-cylinder engine generating 36.1 horsepower and 496 cubic inches of displacement.[87]

After practicing on the Santa Monica course for a week, Dawson established a very fast pace of 75 miles per hour. If this pace could be maintained during the race, it would smash all of the then existing records. Team manager Harroun set a goal for the team to not only win the race but also establish a new world record.[88]

The Santa Monica races were a great showcase for Indianapolis-produced cars as National, Marmon, and Stutz walked away with honors and two world records were shattered in front of an estimated crowd of 100,000.[89] In addition to taking the top three spots in the feature race, National and Marmon both scored victories in two of the three remaining races. Marmon also scored a second place finish and Marmon and Stutz each scored a third.[90] For the featured 200-mile free-for-all contest, the National team developed a winning strategy to neutralize Teddy Tetzlaff and his big Fiat. The only car with any chance of beating Tetzlaff was a National 50 driven by Howdy Wilcox. As the race started, the Fiat and Wilcox's National set a dizzying pace with the other cars entered in the race running far behind. Mile after mile the two cars circled the track. Eventually, the fast pace began to take a toll on the two cars. Tires began to disintegrate. Then the two cars' pace began to slow. The National racing team strategy worked. The remainder of the field caught up and passed both Tetzlaff and Wilcox.[91] The National strategy benefitted both National and cross-town rival Marmon. In the last 20 miles of the race, Harvey Herrick, driving a blue National racer, established a new record for 200 miles with an average speed of 74.93 miles an hour. At times on the straightaways, he was doing close to 100 miles per hour. Driving a Marmon, Patschke finished a close second and Joe Dawson finished third.

Indianapolis expected to have three new automobile manufacturing facilities before 1912. In addition to the Ideal Motor Car Company's $2,000 three-story fireproof addition to its building,[92] Cole built a new plant and American leased a plant at Meridian Street and the

Pathfinder Martha Washington Coach introduced in 1912 (*Horseless Age*, November 27, 1912).

Belt Line railway. This last item was of particular interest to Indianapolis as the former American had been reorganized by J. I. Handley of New York. Under previous management, the company had focused on high priced underslung automobiles designed by Fred Tone and produced under the supervision of V. A. Longaker. Under the new management, the company expanded its product line to include a smaller, four passenger model known as the American 30 with a sales price of $2,250. The new plant was used for the production of the American 30, with the old plant on Henry Street continuing to produce the American 50 which had a sales price of $4,250 to $5,250.[93]

The Motor Car Manufacturing Company (formerly Parry) introduced its Pathfinder vehicle in October. The company planned to continue to build the New Parry in the old factory and to construct a new 150 by 500 foot factory at a cost of $50,000 for the manufacture of the Pathfinder.[94] The Pathfinder automobile, designed by Karl Felicke,[95] had three models available to the public: the Martha Washington coach, the armored roadster, and a touring car.[96]

The management of the Indianapolis Motor Speedway announced the running of the second Indianapolis 500 for Memorial Day 1912. In setting the date, management had checked with the manufacturers of the racers to determine their wishes. Seventy-five percent wanted to have a 500-mile contest, while a lower number was in favor of a 12-hour event.[97] The announcement of the race on Memorial Day was met with opposition from the Sons of Veterans of the United States. Newton J. McGuire, commander, issued the following statement:

> The selection of Memorial Day as the date to stage the Speedway races here is a blot upon the fair name of Indianapolis; it is a shameful disregard of state pride; it is a national disgrace that men claiming themselves to be public spirited should in this commercial age take advantage of the general public by using the most popular attraction of today to unwittingly lead the people to desecrate and debauch the most sacred of all holidays, Memorial Day, and all because it is thought that a few extra dollars could be made.[98]

With their eyes focused on bringing top-notch drivers to Indianapolis for the race, Speedway management announced $50,000 in prizes, with $20,000 going to the winner and cash prizes for the top 12 racers. With the inclusion of prizes from the accessory companies, the total purse was expected to be in the $100,000 range. There were changes to the specifications for the cars to be raced. The weight limitation was dropped from 2,300 pounds in 1911 to 2,000 pounds for the 1912 race. Management also announced a second two-day meet to be held over Labor Day weekend 1912. The Ideal Motor Car Company was the first to register for the Indianapolis 500. Piloting the Stutz car which bore the number 1 was Gil Andersen.[99]

Four Indianapolis racing teams planned to participate in the Savannah races in November; however, all but Marmon withdrew after the death of Sam Butler, the head of the AAA.[100] Marmon entered three cars in the Savannah Challenge Cup, two racers in the Vanderbilt Cup, and two racers in the Grand Prize. Fred J. Wagner visited Indianapolis in an attempt to get additional manufacturers interested in participating in the multiple days of racing but came away empty handed. Arthur Newby, pleased with the National racing team's victories in eight of the ten races in which it was entered in 1911, stated that the company did not want to go to any additional expense for the season-ending races. Cole also declined. With the departure of Bill Endicott from its team, Cole didn't have any drivers available to race. Replacement driver Johnny Jenkins was unfit for a grind as long as the various races, while the other drivers were suffering from minor injuries. Likewise, Stutz had closed out its 1911 racing campaign.[101]

In practice for the races, Dawson was seriously injured when riding in a car driven by Joe Nikrent that encountered a touring car. In an effort to avoid a collision, Nikrent plowed into a high bank of the road and Dawson was thrown about 50 feet from the vehicle.[102] With the injuries to Dawson, Howard Marmon engaged Louis Heinemann to drive the Marmon racer in the race for small cars if Dawson wasn't ready to go.[103] When the injuries to Dawson prohibited him from participating in the Grand Prize race, Bob Burman was contracted to drive the big Marmon racer. The Marmon racer driven by Louis Heinemann finished second in the Savannah Challenge Trophy race for small cars. His car was some three minutes behind the winner, Hughie Hughes.[104] However, like the earlier races, the Grand Prize race was a disappointment for the Marmon team as both Marmon racers were sidelined from the action. The racer driven by Bob Burman exited the race on the eighth lap when a stone punctured the gasoline tank, and the racer driven by Cyrus Patschke left the race on the ninth lap when an air pump failed, ending his day of racing.[105]

Late in 1911 American moved into new facilities located at Meridian Street and the Belt Railroad. The property's main building was 60 feet wide by 160 feet long with two wings. The wing on the south side of the building was dedicated to building motors and frames while the wing on the north side was used for finished stockroom. The property also had test sheds and a large storage building.[106]

The growth in auto shows paralleled the growth of the automobile. In 1900, there was one show, New York City, with a second being added shortly thereafter in Chicago. By the fall of 1911, there were 15 shows, with Indianapolis being the first on the calendar. New York hosted three automobile shows, one for importers and the other two for domestic cars. Other cities hosting shows included Chicago, Cincinnati, Detroit, Buffalo, Providence, St. Louis, Grand Rapids, Minneapolis, Newark, Binghamton, and Hartford.[107]

Harry Stutz, William Guy Wall, chief engineer of National, and Johnny Wood were part of a delegation of the Society for Automotive Engineers which traveled to England. Stutz noted that the English chassis designs were lighter and more complicated than the American designs. Filled with Yankee pride, Stutz wrote, "If we had a chassis on exhibit at the London show, it would have been the sensation of the display." Stutz was clearly not impressed with his foreign travels, as he wrote, "I wouldn't give $1,000.00 for all that I have seen on this trip, nor 15 cents to see any of it again."[108] While Stutz might not have been impressed with what he saw while in England, he brought home several ideas which he thought he might incorporate in the passenger and racing cars.[109]

Upon Harry Stutz's return from England, the Ideal Motor Car Company cancelled its order for the large four-cylinder motor it had planned to install in one of its race cars. Instead, Stutz decided to rebuild the car that had won the Fairmount Park road race in Philadelphia using the same motor. For the second racer, Stutz decided to use a four-cylinder Wisconsin motor with 398 cubic inches of displacement.[110]

Evansville, Indiana, sponsored a hill climb over the Thanksgiving weekend. A Cole piloted by Charlie French won the one-half-mile contest in 48.75 seconds. An Indianapolis-built American roadster finished the climb in 52 seconds. In the free-for-all contest, the Cole also won, beating other competitors including Stutz, Oldsmobile, American, Buick, Locomobile, and Pullman.[111]

At the end of 1911, National declared that it was the 1911 champion despite not winning the Indianapolis 500 or participating in the Vanderbilt or Savannah races. The company's claim to the title was based upon the success of the National 40, which had won the "stock car championship" and the "road race championship" in addition to other events including hill climbs, beach racing, motordrome races, and track meets. Based upon its record, National believed it would win four or five championships. Over the season, National had won nine road races, 21 beach races, 35 speedway and motordrome events, and 15 track meets. Overall, the company had won 84 firsts, 48 seconds, and 30 thirds.[112]

The Prest-O-Lite Company developed a self-starter for cars which Carl Fisher believed, like the lighting device, would revolutionize automobiles because it would eliminate the need and danger of cranking the car to get it to start. The Prest-O-Lite starter was tested on Cole, Stoddard-Dayton, National, Overland and Buick cars before being marketed. The first company to install the Prest-O-Lite starter was Cole on its 1912 models.[113] The Prest-O-Lite self-starter and one developed by Delco would introduce acetylene gas into the cylinders where it would mix with air causing the car to start. Those cars not equipped with acetylene-powered headlights could easily be modified with an acetylene tank.[114]

For 1912, American introduced the Scout, a two-passenger car, at the New York Auto Show. American also displayed a six-passenger Traveler and a four-passenger Tourist. National had four cars on exhibit at the auto show including a roadster, a five-passenger touring car of series S, a toy tonneau, and a series V touring car.[115]

6

National Leads the Way

By 1912, Indianapolis boasted 12 automobile manufacturers employing 7,000 workers with a payroll of $7 million. The estimated 10,300 cars produced each year had a value of $20 million with an average retail price of $2,000, which fell in the medium to high price category. The city was known for the quality of its automobiles. An article in the *Indianapolis Star* pointed this out:

> Lower priced cars are turned out by a number of the concerns, but the habit of doing everything well has taken so firm a hold upon the Indianapolis manufacturers that even these are characterized by good material and careful and honest workmanship. There is no attempt at wholesale flooding of the country by sacrificing quality to quantity.[1]

To help promote the Indianapolis automobile industry on a national basis, Joseph Cole proposed a general fund among the manufacturers for newspaper and magazine advertisements.[2] Various manufacturers including Premier, Marmon, Stutz, National, Cole, Henderson, Waverley, American, Pathfinder, Marion, Mais Motor Truck Company, and Empire banded together and purchased a two-page advertisement in a national weekly emphasizing Indianapolis as the "ultimate motor car hub of the world."[3]

In early January, National announced that two of its cars would participate in the Indianapolis 500 and named Wilcox and Herr as their drivers on the factory team. The West Coast team consisted of Merz and Herrick, who were employees of the Los Angeles dealership as a mechanic and salesman respectively. Aitken was the team captain.[4]

At the New York and Chicago auto shows, Marmon displayed a limousine featuring a ventilator in the roof in addition to one in the dashboard, resulting in the circulation of fresh air without a draft. The driver had an individual seat with an aisle. A folding seat could be folded down to provide for a second seat in the front. The back seat of the limousine could be folded down to provide additional space for packages. The body of the limousine was a combination of brown, gray, and English vermillion.[5]

National adopted central transmission control for all of its automobiles. Having the gear shift and brake levers in the middle of the car made the cars simpler to use and eliminated connecting links that sometimes broke. Additionally, having the controls in the middle made it possible to enter the car from either side. It also provided for better protection of the levers and made the automobiles simpler to construct.[6]

Joseph Cole proposed that the 20 largest Indiana automobile manufacturers should band together for a national tour. The tour would visit all of the major cities in the country for a day, with transportation by a special train. At each stop, the Indiana-built cars would be

In 1912, National moved its controls to the center of the car (*Horseless Age*, February 21, 1912).

displayed under a large tent-top.[7] Members of the proposed sponsor, the IATA, discussed the proposal. Although there was some support for it, a spring tour wasn't found to be attractive as it would conflict with the local automobile show. There was a possibility that a fall tour displaying the 1913 models could be arranged.[8] Convinced that Indianapolis needed to promote its automobiles on a national basis, and spurred on by the recent collaboration to promote Indianapolis' motor cars in a national magazine, Joseph Cole gave $5,000 as seed money for a $50,000 fund to promote Indianapolis automobiles in a variety of newspapers. Cole explained,

> Imbued with belief in Indianapolis' future as the recognized automobile center of the world, and impeded by the certain knowledge that there is not a single Indianapolis-built car which cannot endure the utmost publicity, I hereby propose, publically, in order that the public at large may realize the spirit of cooperation, fair-mindedness among Indianapolis makers of motor cars, that ten Indianapolis manufacturers create a fund of $50,000, each donating $5,000, to be used in whatsoever way they may see fit to exploit the merits of our city from the standpoint of the user of the gasoline-driven motor cars.[9]

Although negotiations were in progress, the news around town was that Cecil Gibson and B. W. Twyman were leading a syndicate of Detroit and Indianapolis businessmen planning to take over Empire, which had ceased operations in 1911, and build a small touring car priced at $850. Although they had an option on the Empire factory site, the syndicate members believed it was insufficient for their purposes and they planned to build a larger factory in Indianapolis.[10] In March 1912 the deal was completed. The new company, Empire Automobile Company (Empire), was capitalized at $100,000. Officers of the new company were A. Waldheim of St. Louis, president; David May of Cincinnati, vice president; Charles B. Sommers of Indianapolis, secretary/treasurer; and Cecil Gibson of Indianapolis, factory manager and general manager. Management planned to manufacture a four-cylinder, 25-horsepower car available in a five-passenger touring car and a two-passenger roadster.[11] A little more than a month later, the Empire 25 with five passengers on board was tested on the roads surrounding Indianapolis and reportedly achieved a speed of 45 miles per hour.[12] Although the purchase price for the business wasn't announced, it later became known that Allison, Fisher, and Newby had sold Empire's assets, with an estimated value of $200,000, to the syndicate for $80,000.[13] Within a month the Empire touring car was on display at the Indianapolis auto show.[14]

With demand for its products increasing, American expanded its plant with a 59,400 square foot three-story building at a cost of $12,000.[15]

Waverley introduced the Model 90, a sheltered roadster which had the appearance of a gasoline-powered car with a luggage compartment at the rear, a folding landau top, and a glass windshield and doors which could be folded out of the way when not in use.[16]

Cole was planning to introduce a medium-priced car in 1913. With a sales price between $1,200 and $1,500, the car would be called the Cole Junior. The company planned to build another wing on to its factory at a cost of $100,000. The new wing would manufacture the Cole Junior while the other wing would continue to manufacture the bigger 40-horsepower autos.[17]

In April, a reorganization by James I. Handley of the Marion Motor Car Company was announced. The capital stock of the company was increased from $100,000 to $1,125,000 with $625,000 in common stock and $500,000 in preferred stock. The majority of the stock was taken by John Willys of Willys-Overland and James Handley. They planned to produce $7 million worth of vehicles at the Marion plant in Indianapolis during the 1913 season, which began in July.[18] To support the production increase, the company planned to build a large plant in Indianapolis.[19]

The company produced three different models. At a price of $1,350, the Model 37 was a 40-horsepower five-passenger touring car on a 112-inch wheelbase. The Model 48 was a

1913 Cole 50. The engine was produced by Northway and the car featured a Delco lighting system (LeRoy Cole Collection, Gilmore Car Museum).

45-horsepower five-passenger touring car with a 120-inch wheelbase, priced at $1,750. The Model 36 Bobcat was a 40-horsepower two-passenger roadster built on a 112-inch wheelbase and priced at $1,350. All models featured a glass windshield, a Prest-O-Lite self-starter, a Prest-O-Lite tank, and five lamps as standard equipment.[20]

Handley, a Texas native (born in 1871), had become half owner and general manager of the Maxwell-Briscoe-Handley Company of Dallas, Texas, in 1907. Within a year, he had become responsible for the sales and finances of the Maxwell-Briscoe Company of New York. He was in charge of the Maxwell-Briscoe Company's reorganization. He subsequently was put in charge of the Maxwell-Briscoe St. Louis Company and the Maxwell-Briscoe Indianapolis Company. When the United States Motor Company was chartered, he became the vice president of that organization. In 1911, he moved to Indianapolis and took over the affairs of the American Motor Car Company, organizing the American Motors Company.[21]

When National unveiled its 1913 lineup of models in April 1912, all featured a left hand drive and a center console, which was gaining favor with the driving public. This was a change from having the driver sit on the right hand side of the car.[22]

If you were able to read the tea leaves, the departure of Marmon from the racing game should not have been a big surprise. In April, Walter Marmon said,

> The automobile that wins great races often builds up a reputation for being a fast, high powered car that leads women to prefer some car she believes is safer and easier to handle.
>
> The Marmon has built up an unequaled record in racing contests and holds the world's record for 400 and 500 miles. We have received great benefits from the great number of victories the Marmon has won in all parts of the country but many people who are not acquainted with the car have the idea that it is of exceptional high power.
>
> Practically all the victories won by the Marmon have been the result of the superior endurance and the ability to maintain a certain speed and economize in tires, fuel, and oil for 100 miles or more without a stop.

An ad in the *Indianapolis Star* made the decision perfectly clear. It also kept the Marmon name visible to the public as the Indianapolis 500 was gearing up, reminding the readers of the victories of the past:

> Victories of Marmon Cars in races are demonstrations of the better design and manufacture of *every* Marmon.
>
> It is needless to repeat the Marmon list of victories in the *world's greatest and most important* contests.
>
> A year ago the Marmon won the first 500-mile International Sweepstakes race, making world's records for 300, 400 and 500 miles. In that race it defeated 44 cars, among them the best and highest priced products of the greatest manufacturers of Europe and America, the largest and classiest list of entries *ever* started in any race.
>
> But "get behind the scenes" in this racing proposition—the cheers, the trophies, the glory. What do racing victories *mean to you* as a purchaser?
>
> The winning of all of the world's great races by one car could mean only this to you: that the manufacturer can design and construct a car that is superior in durability, easier on tires, that has the proper lubrication, that economizes fuel, that is well balanced.
>
> Nordyke & Marmon in its racing victories has proved it can design and construct such a car.[23]

When Marmon quit auto racing, its premier driver, Joe Dawson, reappeared in a big blue National racer on May 14, joining the team of Howdy Wilcox, David Bruce-Brown and Don Herr with Johnny Aitken as the team manager.[24]

The 1912 Indianapolis 500 was won by Joe Dawson piloting the National racer (# 8) with a time of 6 hours 21 minutes 6.03 seconds. The official AAA records reflected Teddy

Tetzlaff in the lead at the 100, 150, 200 and 250 mile marks. However, by the 300 mile mark Dawson had taken control of the race because the rules included the proviso that a car needed to finish the race for its results to be counted.[25]

Of course, National took the opportunity to publicize its win in the 500-mile race:

> 500 Miles in 381 minutes and 6 seconds
> Winning World's Fastest Long Distance Race
> Average 78.72 Miles Per Hour
>
> What did the International 500-mile race teach you? It told the story of Quality. Not only did the National have speed, but it had stamina, dependability, and longevity.[26]

The winning of the Indianapolis 500 and the advertising campaign resulted in increased demand for National products. B. M. Wylie, National's distributor for Indiana, made a tour of the state in a National V Series car and reported large demand for the movie of the 500-mile race as well as for the vehicles. National experienced the same phenomenon that Marmon had the prior year: people clamoring to see the National racer which had won the Indianapolis 500. The car was put on display at the Indiana State Fair.[27] Wylie said,

> Everywhere I go I am asked questions concerning this race. It is surprising how well educated people are on motor cars in general, and even specific details of a car's construction. Even at "cross-road towns" I have been stopped by farmers and village inhabitants who, noting that my car has a National name on the radiator, instantly want to ask questions about the race and about motor cars.[28]

In early June, Nordyke & Marmon announced an expansion to its manufacturing facilities. The company planned to add two additional stories to one of its buildings, bringing total manufacturing space to 25,300 square feet of floor space. It also planned to construct a new two-story office building with 13,300 square feet of floor space. The bottom floor would be for the executive offices while the second floor would be for drafting.[29]

In its continuing effort to reposition Marmon from the racing game to being a reliable automobile for regular people, Marmon published the following advertisement:

> Last May a Marmon 32, built in the autumn of 1908, which had been in service continually in the rough quarry region of Indiana, was sold second-hand to an Indianapolis man residing seven miles in the country. Last week was the anniversary of his purchase. It has carried him to and from his office in town every day and brought the family in every Sunday, besides making other trips back and forth almost daily—365 days of service, the coldest winter, the heaviest snows and the deepest mud known for thirty years. During the great blizzard, when steam roads, trolley lines, and city street cars were partially or wholly out of commission, the Marmon plowed its way through the drifts. There have been minor repairs and adjustments, of course, but the point we make is this Marmon, four years old, was staunch enough and sound enough to overcome difficulties which balked the railroads and traction lines.[30]

Around Indianapolis, residents had been seeing several new Marmon cars with unfinished bodies since early spring.[31] In June, after two years in development and testing,[32] an announcement was made about the Marmon Six, a new six-cylinder, 48-horsepower car incorporating many of the engineering advances first tried out on the Marmon Wasp racer, including a new axle design.[33] The car had shifted to a central control on the front axle, which made for safer reaction when a front tire burst.[34] It also allowed for easier turning of the car with its 145-inch wheelbase, as well as additional stability. The car was manufactured in seven-, five-, four- and two-passenger bodies as well as a limousine and landaulet. The aluminum body was finished in blue-black with nickel trim.[35]

The Henderson Motor Sales Company, exclusive sales agent for Cole, was absorbed by Cole Motor effective July 1. When Cole was originally formed, it was felt best to have the manufacturing and sales efforts remain separate. In the merger, Charles P. Henderson was named as the general sales manager of Cole.[36] The announcement indicated that the joining of the two forces had been contemplated since the organizations' beginning.

The Henderson Motor Car Company (Henderson) was formed to produce cars with a retail price of $1,200 by Ransom P. Henderson. In May, the company was incorporated with a capitalization of $100,000. The officers were L. Carter of Jessup, Georgia, president; Ransom Henderson, vice president; L. S. French, secretary and advertising director; and C. K. Snare, treasurer. The directors were L. Carter, Charles Henderson, Ransom Henderson, Chester Ricker, and E. E. Rogers.[37] Chester S. Ricker, a technical expert who was later closely associated with the Indianapolis 500, was named the chief engineer.[38] Carter was the second largest stockholder in the Cole Motor Car Company and had previously been the president of the Henderson Motor Car Sales Company.[39] Plans were made to construct a factory for the Henderson car, but until that was accomplished, the firm leased 13,000 square feet of space in the Industrial Building located at Tenth Street and the canal.[40]

Ransom Henderson explained the vision for the new car. It was expected to be in two models: a five-passenger model priced at $1,385 and a two-passenger roadster priced at $1,285.[41] Both cars would be powered by a 35-horsepower engine.

> We have ideas which will be embodied in a car bearing the Henderson name plate to cost in the neighborhood of $1,200, and in view of the long connection with the Cole, we are convinced that the public expects something unusual, if not sensational, and it is not our purpose to disappoint it. It is our intention to manufacture this car in Indianapolis if it is possible, and the first model will not be long in making its appearance.[42]

In a stroke of marketing brilliance, the first Henderson car produced was unveiled on the day before Memorial Day, when the eyes of the country were focused on Indianapolis with the running of the Indianapolis 500. A procession of about 50 automobiles escorted the Henderson automobile to Monument Circle, where Indianapolis Mayor Samuel Shank welcomed the car as a part of the Indianapolis automobile industry. Afterward the car was taken to Indianapolis' premier hotel, the Claypool, where it was put on display in the lobby.[43]

Cole occupied the bottom three floors of a new building under construction on Washington Street at Division Street. On April 25, 1912, a 30-foot section of the roof collapsed as the wooden braces were being removed from the structure; it went through the fourth floor with a portion ending up in a storeroom on the third floor. One man, Herman Johnson, was cleaning up the fourth floor as the collapse happened and was killed. The initial theory about the collapse was that the cement had not been properly cured due to cold weather prior to the removal of the bracing.[44]

Cole made several changes to its eight-cylinder car lineup, including the choice of three different chassis. The Cole 50 was a four-cylinder, 122-inch wheelbase automobile with five different body styles including a five-passenger touring car, a toy tonneau, a two-passenger roadster, a three-passenger coupe and the Berlin limousine. The company also brought out the Cole 40, a smaller four-cylinder car with a 115-inch wheelbase available in a roadster and five-passenger touring models. A six-cylinder car with a 132-inch wheelbase was also introduced to the marketplace with a five-passenger touring car, a toy tonneau, a two-passenger roadster, a three-passenger coupe, and the Berlin limousine. On all models, the front seat was divided and curved to give greater comfort to the passenger and the driver.[45]

To promote Indiana-built cars, a four-state tour through Ohio, West Virginia, Kentucky, and Indiana was planned. Two Marmons led the tour. Other Indianapolis manufacturers participating included Marion with two cars and American with three cars, while Cole and Premier supplied the press cars.[46] After successfully completing the four-state tour, John M. Maxwell, who followed the tour for the *Indianapolis Star*, proclaimed that the automobile had reached "approximate perfection." He also believed the buyer was safe in buying any Indiana-built car that had participated in the tour. Throughout the tour, the Marmon car was the only one not to need to replenish air in the tires.[47]

Walter Marmon believed the lack of need for additional air in the tires was another example of the soundness of the Marmon automobile. Not only had the car completed the four-state tour without the need for air, but it was also the only car participating in a 1,100-mile round trip endurance run between Minneapolis and Winnipeg which did not suffer a puncture or blowout over "some of the worst roads in the country." The previous year, a Marmon car had completed a 1,465-mile endurance run between Minneapolis and Helena, Montana, without a tire failure. He commented,

> There is one infallible means of determining whether or not a car is in perfect balance, and that is in its ease on tires. Good springs and shock absorbers often counteract defects in balance that would be apparent to the passengers and therefore the tires are the one means by which balance can be absolutely demonstrated.[48]

In August, Charles Henderson, Cole's sales manager, left to join Henderson,[49] where he would serve as president. About two weeks earlier, Cole had announced a new sales plan to divide the United States into five territories, each of which would be headed by a district sales manager. It was believed that this new setup would result in a more efficient selling force.[50]

A Pathfinder 40 delivery truck with the capacity to carry 1,500 pounds was developed by the Motor Car Manufacturing Company. The first two delivery trucks were sold to Charles Mayer and the A. Kiefer Drug Company of Indianapolis. Part of the company's plan was to expand the manufacture of delivery trucks as a part of its normal production.[51]

For 1913 the Motor Car Manufacturing Company planned to make six different car models, all on the same chassis. A five-passenger touring car and a five-passenger phaeton were available for $1,875, while a two-passenger speedster and a two-passenger armored roadster cost $2,000. The three-passenger Martha Washington coach was priced at $2,500 while the delivery wagon cost $2,000. The company also offered Gray & Davis starting and lighting systems as optional equipment at a cost of $175.[52] One of the advantages of the new starting system was that the driver couldn't choke his engine as it crossed railroad tracks. At the time, the crossing of railroad tracks was a significant problem and up to 90 percent of this type of accident was attributed to driver error.[53]

As part of the Good Roads movement, a Pathfinder 40 automobile was selected to make three transcontinental trips in search of a route for the country's first transcontinental highway on behalf of the AAA and the U.S. Government. Loaded with duffel bags, camping items and water bottles, the car left New York and within three weeks had crossed the country on the northern route from New York to Seattle. The trip included scaling 30 percent grades in the mountains and fording streams along the way. Of interest to the public was that the same air

Stutz Series B Includes a Six Cylinder Chassis.

Stutz Series B six-cylinder car introduced in 1912 (*Horseless Age*, October 22, 1912).

with which the car started in its journey in New York was still in the tires when the car reached Seattle. Using the success of the Pathfinder on the journey, the Motor Car Manufacturing Company issued advertisements.[54] After traveling down the west coast to San Francisco, the Pathfinder 40 began its second journey, traveling through Chicago to New York City where it arrived in late September.[55] On the third transcontinental trip, the Pathfinder stopped in Indianapolis, where its driver, A. L. Westgard, was feted at the Columbia Club.[56] After reaching San Francisco on the third leg of the trip, Westgard drove back to Indianapolis.[57] In all, the Pathfinder traveled 12,678 miles in a six-month period and averaged 13.5 miles per gallon of gasoline.[58]

With plans to produce 5,000 cars a year, Empire abandoned its plant in Indianapolis to manufacture cars in Connersville, Indiana, Knightstown, Indiana, and Greenville, Pennsylvania.[59]

For the 1913 season Marion announced the continuation of the three automobiles it had successfully produced over the past several years, with updated styling of the three models. The 37-A was a 30- to 40-horsepower five-passenger touring car. The other models were the 48-horsepower five-passenger 48-A and the Bobcat roadster.[60] Marion reduced the price of its models, with the 37-A being reduced to $1,175, the 48-A to $1,850, and the Bobcat roadster to $1,125.[61] Marion's management believed that the key to success in 1913 was the stylishness and equipment offered as part of the car. The latter included a Disco self-starter, a dynamo electric light system, Q. D. demountable rims, a Warner speedometer, a ventilated windshield, and an 80-hour auxiliary storage battery. The 48-A model also included an electric horn.[62]

The Ideal Motor Car Company introduced the Series B, a new six-cylinder Stutz model, to the market. The primary change was the T-head engine. The car was available in roadster and four- and six-passenger touring cars built on a wheelbase ranging from 124 to 130 inches. The company continued to offer the four-cylinder model that had premiered the prior year as Series A. The cars were available in Napier green or vermillion.[63]

Premier, which had manufactured four-cylinder and six-cylinder autos since 1907, announced that beginning with the 1913 model year it would produce only a six-cylinder automobile. With this announcement, the company also introduced the Premier Little Six, priced at $2,600 for the base model, which excluded the top and windshield, and $2,735 fully equipped. The transmission was a three speed mounted in the center of the car. The car had two sets of brakes, with the service brakes being activated by a pedal on the floor and the emergency brake being operated by a hand lever. The company's other car, the Big Six, was virtually the same as the model already on the market. Both of the Premier six-cylinder cars had a compressed air self-starting system activated by a starting switch on the dashboard. The bodies on all the cars were straight lined with the handles and hinges concealed.[64] The demand for Premier autos resulted in the company needing additional manufacturing space. The company planned an expansion of its manufacturing facility with two new two-story buildings. The first was 140 feet by 40 feet and the second was 148 feet by 40 feet.[65]

Recognizing that the Indiana State Fair had always been a gathering spot for Indiana's farmers, the auto companies decided to have an auto show as part of the Fair. In 1912, four automobile manufacturers (Marmon, Studebaker Corporation, Premier, and Cole), along with distributor Hearsey-Willis Company, banded together and used the Studebaker Building on the fairgrounds for the exhibit. In addition to displaying its cars, Marmon displayed its racing trophies and the Wasp that had won the 1911 Indianapolis 500. Premier displayed for the first time the new Little Six. Cole's exhibit included a stripped chassis so that the mechanically inclined could see how it worked.[66] The decision to have an auto show at the Fair appears to have been a good one. By the time the Fair was running, 20 different makes were on display. Additions included Indianapolis companies National, Marion, and American. The companies reported that they had more buyers than lookers and that they thought an auto show at the Fair should be a regular event.[67]

When automobiles were first built in the United States, they followed the pattern used in England of having the driver sit on the right hand side of the car. In 1912, National introduced the steering controls on the left side of the car. Believing that this was a superior placement, the company emphasized this feature in its advertisements:

> Advantages of the Left Side Drive and Center Control on National Cars are many:
> You not only have a clear vision of the road ahead and behind, but you are enabled to go around other vehicles with greater ease and safety. You can negotiate corners better. You have access to both front doors. The passenger in the front seat is always next to the curb and can get in and out of the car without disturbing the driver and without walking around the car in the street.
> The natural instinct of drivers to reach for control levers with the right hand is not lost, as these levers, being in the center, are at the driver's right.[68]

In August 1912 Marmon introduced a light truck with a carrying capacity between 1,200 and 1,500 pounds. To carry the heavier load, the truck was equipped with a heavy duty rear suspension and dual rear wheels. The truck utilized the same motor as was in the Marmon 32. An unusual aspect of the truck was that it had a speed governor limiting the top speed to 20 miles per hour.[69]

Cole claimed to be the first automobile company with a nameplate. Designed by the Cole advertising manager, Homer McKee, the nameplate consisted of an American eagle behind the Cole shield. Below the shield, which was adorned with the Cole name in large script letters, was "Bonus Est" which roughly translates to "it is good." The implication of the nameplate was that this was a good American car.[70]

Cole also departed from tradition and used the Sunday newspapers in major metropolitan areas to introduce its 1913 automobiles, which had three different chassis: a medium sized car with a 116-inch wheelbase retailing for $1,685; a large sized Four with a 122-inch wheel-base retailing for $1,985; and a large sized Six with a 132-inch wheel-base retailing for $2,465. For 1913, each model had the Delco electric starting, lighting, and ignition systems as regular equipment.[71]

The movement to start what would later be called the Lincoln Highway Association began in Indianapolis in the fertile mind of Carl Fisher. On the evening of September 11, 1912, Fisher and Allison hosted a banquet at the German House for automobile and accessory companies to unveil a plan to build a road from New York City to San Francisco by April 1, 1915. The road would be built of stone with the cost of the raw materials being funded by the Lincoln Highway group. The cost of construction would be borne by the cities and counties through which the road passed. The engineering and monitoring of the road would be overseen by the United States War Department. When the idea of a road across America was unveiled, there was immediate enthusiasm.

James Handley of American and Marion was the first to endorse the idea, saying, "I think the time for oratory has passed. All I can say is that I am heartedly in favor of the movement and wish to be the first to subscribe the one per cent required." Very quickly, others joined in making pledges. By the end of that night, $300,000 had been pledged to the movement.[72]

Joseph Cole held an informal meeting of the various automobile manufacturers at the Columbia Club to discuss a convention on advertising and salesmanship. His idea was to have a national meeting on October 7 and 8 in Indianapolis, where salesmen would be taught by national experts on the art of selling.[73] With little time before the convention, an executive committee was formed consisting of Joseph Cole, Howard Smith, James Handley (Marion), Howard Marmon, Henry Campbell (Stutz), George Dickson (National), D. M. Sommers, and Ransom Henderson.[74]

Premier president Howard Smith heartily endorsed the idea:

> The automobile started as a plaything. Now it is a business institution. What we must do today is to create a demand for the automobile. Make the business a real business, a businessman's business, not a "four flusher's." People do not know the economy of the machine. The salesman must show this. The automobile has created a field of its own. It has solved the question of transportation for the individual. We must

Henderson Six (*Horseless Age*, May 28, 1913).

not let the automobile salesman become dormant. We must keep him stirred up. We must till new soil in the field of prospects. To my mind it is only a question of time until the huckster will be bringing his products to market in a light delivery truck. His farm will be further from the city. His taxes and other expenses will be less—a possible solution of the high cost of living.

Plans for the national convention included demonstrations of driving skills at the Indianapolis Motor Speedway and a parade of automobiles.[75] An outgrowth of the convention was the General Automobile Sales Association to promote the automobile to even greater heights.[76] Although the convention was a success, was the brainchild of an Indianapolis man, and came to fruition due to the efforts of the Indianapolis automobile industry, the members of the newly organized Association decided to hold the 1913 convention in Detroit.[77]

From the various talks at the convention, Joseph Cole assembled a book outlining the methods dealers should use in the sale of automobiles, proper ways of advertising automobiles, and ways of working with a customer with the goal of the dealership being profitable.[78]

National and Henderson announced new models for 1913. National announced a five-passenger touring car with a left-hand drive and a center console.[79] Henderson announced two models, the Model 45 roadster and the Model 47 touring car, both available with wire wheels. When a change of tire was necessary, the entire wheel was dismounted from the hub.[80]

With a need for more space, the Motor Car Manufacturing Company, maker of Pathfinder automobiles, built a two-story building adjacent to its existing plant in West Indianapolis.[81]

For the 1913 model year, Marion expected to continue with the same three cars it had been producing: the Model 37-A, a 30- to 40-horsepower five passenger priced at $1,475; the Model 36-A, a 30- to 40-horsepower two-passenger roadster known as the Marion Bobcat selling for $1,425; and the Model 48-A, a five-passenger deluxe touring car retailing for $1,850. All of the Marion automobiles had four-cylinder engines with 30 to 40 horsepower. The Marion cars for 1913 also had a lower profile, being closer to the ground by 1¾ inches, and a concealed tool box. The Marion Bobcat was finished in bright red with bucket seats. The touring cars were available either in Brewster green or deep red. All accessories for the Marion automobiles were included in the purchase price of the car, including a self-starter, a dynamo electric lighting system, a Warner speedometer, and a plate glass windshield.[82]

Pathfinder five-passenger touring car (*Horseless Age*, **November 27, 1912**).

In response to customer and prospect demand for a roadster with up-to-date lines, Marion announced in late December a second roadster model, the 38-A, which was built upon the same chassis as the Marion 37-A. Its standard equipment included a self-starter, a Prest-O-Lite tank, a dynamo electric starting system, an 80-hour storage battery, and a Warner speedometer.[83] The car, available in Brewster green, a deep wine, or a cardinal red, had 30 to 40 horsepower.[84]

American unveiled its closed Traveler Limousine. It was built on the same chassis as the American Traveler, an open car with a 140-inch wheel-base.[85] In February 1913 the company changed the motor on the American Scout to a long stroke which had a four-inch bore and a five-inch stroke. V. A. Longaker, general manager of the company, called the motor the "ideal power plant of the year."[86]

7

Legislation Threatens the Indianapolis Auto Industry

Indianapolis was abuzz with rumors of something mysterious happening at the Marmon factory, with the doors being closed to everyone except for a select few. Speculation centered around Ray Harroun designing a new race car to be entered in the Indianapolis 500. Neither company officials nor the Speedway management commented on the rumors, adding further speculation.[1]

The Motor Car Manufacturing Company, maker of the Pathfinder, put the finishing touches on a new two-story plant located at Division and Morris Streets. Built of vitrified brick with a bilateral lighting system, the new facility doubled the floor space for production and its efficiency doubled production capacity. The company anticipated building 1,500 cars per year.[2]

As early as 1913 Premier's general manager, George Dickson, believed the history of the Indianapolis automobile industry should be preserved and suggested a museum. With pride in its automobiles, the Indianapolis automobile industry was supportive of Dickson's suggestion. The Motor Car Manufacturing Car Company offered the Pathfinder 40 which had made three cross-country trips over 147 days as part of the Good Roads movement. Indianapolis manufacturers also felt that Elwood Haynes' automobile should be in the museum along with the National and Marmon racers that had won the 1912 and 1911 Indianapolis 500. Wayne K. Bromley, secretary/treasurer of the Motor Car Manufacturing Company, said,

> Indianapolis cars, because of their remarkable success on speedway and track, on endurance tests and tours, should hold prominent places in the motor museum. The Pathfinder has made history on its transcontinental tour, the greatest pathfinding expedition of all time, a tour typical of the energy and progress of the American people.
>
> To show the highest art of the builder alongside the earlier models that paved the way to perfection should be the unselfish object of the proposed motor museum. The project would have a tremendous educational value—would benefit the schools and create interest in Indiana's biggest industry.[3]

The Pathfinder 40 that had crisscrossed the United States in 1912 was chosen as the automobile for the 1913 transcontinental search for three additional routes across America. The hope was by the end of the summer to have six routes available for those tourists who wanted to cross the country.[4]

Cole introduced a new six-cylinder, 60-horsepower, seven-passenger car built on a 132-inch wheelbase for 1913. The car had a clear rain vision windshield and was equipped with

Cole 6–60 (*Horseless Age*, January 1, 1913).

a Delco electric lighting, starting, and ignition system. The car was sleek in appearance with the running boards being free of tool boxes, extra tires, or any other projections. The interior trim on the dashboard was made with German silver.[5]

The Waverley Company had eight different models available to the public in 1913, ranging from the two-seat Victoria phaeton priced at $1,850 to the five-passenger limousine priced at $3,500.[6]

Although the Indianapolis Motor Speedway was originally envisioned as a place to improve the quality of automobiles in addition to racing, the idea of using it as a test track had not caught on. One of the issues in utilizing the Speedway for testing was that the cars needed to use city streets to get to the track. Nine of the local manufacturers used the city streets for testing each day, creating a backlash. Although every manufacturer in the city held the tester responsible for his driving, the testers frequently exceeded the speed limit and were occasionally involved in automobile accidents. A tester who was caught speeding was responsible for his own fine and frequently was dismissed by the firm.

Nevertheless, responding to the issues created by the testers, a bill was introduced in the Indiana legislature by S. J. Miller of Indianapolis to prohibit the use of city streets for "test" cars and motorcycles, with the exception of travel to the Indianapolis Motor Speedway. Originally this bill was written to include all of Indiana; however, pressure from the manufacturers outside Indianapolis resulted in the Indiana Senate modifying it to apply only to Marion County (Indianapolis). This brought great consternation to Indianapolis' burgeoning automobile industry. The bill listed fines ranging from $50 to $200, but the manufacturers' greatest concern was that, without the streets to test their cars, they would be uncompetitive. They believed that although they could test their cars at the Indianapolis Motor Speedway, that facility would be too small to test the volume of cars produced in the city. The manufacturers also believed that the laws on the books about speeding should be strictly enforced rather than used only to limit their ability to test their automobiles. The manufacturers' sentiments about the bill were very negative.[7] Howard Smith's comments were representative:

> The proposed law, if passed, will prove the death knell of the greatest industry in the United States in a state which is recognized as second in rank among the producers of motor cars. I believe in reasonable restrictions, but the proposed law would ruin the business in this state, as it would give the outside makers who are allowed the privilege of road tests a chance to prejudice the minds of prospective purchasers.[8]

Adjoining states seized the opportunity to try to induce auto manufacturers to leave Indianapolis. A rumor led the *Detroit Free Press* to run an article about automobile manufacturers, and Cole in particular, leaving Indiana. The article said in part,

> Due to the fact that it is reported that there are certain laws in Indianapolis and before the present Legislature that are not confined to help boost the automobile industry in Indiana, it is said that this might have some influence not only on the Cole organization but on other plants to move from Hoosierdom,[9]

The rumor that Cole was contemplating leaving Indianapolis was immediately refuted by Joseph Cole, who issued a statement categorically denying that the company was contemplating leaving Indianapolis and also providing an explanation of how this rumor might have started:

> The only explanation that I can advance to the appearance of this story is from the fact that when the recent bill passed the Legislature I dropped the remark that should we be forced off of the public highways, preventing us from testing our cars, I felt it might be the beginning of the Legislature enacting such laws opposing the automobile interest, and if such legislation was allowed to be enacted in this state the Cole Company might be compelled to seek a factory site elsewhere.[10]

Despite assurances from Joseph Cole that the company wasn't moving out of state, the work on an expansion of its factory was suspended until the fate of the bill was determined.[11]

Waverley Electric Victoria Phaeton, Model 96 (Indiana Historical Society, P0235).

Pathfinder Speedster with a special top (*Horseless Age*, December 10, 1913).

To the dismay of the automobile men, S. J. Miller's bill passed both houses of the Indiana legislature and headed to the desk of Governor Samuel Ralston for signature or veto. Hoping to influence the governor's decision, representatives of each of the automobile companies, led by James L. Gavin, president of the Hoosier Motor Club, visited the governor and explained why the bill should be vetoed.[12] Their efforts were successful.

American unveiled its 1914 models including an American Underslung 6 (also known as a 666), a six-cylinder touring car with a four-speed transmission retailing for $4,500. The company also introduced a smaller six-cylinder underslung car, the 644, and a four-cylinder model, known as the 422, which had three gears.[13]

Due to the success of the Pathfinder automobiles, the Motor Car Manufacturing Company reported a sales increase of 117 percent for the first five months of 1913 over a like period in 1912 and noted that it had sold out of the 1913 models.[14] For 1914, there were few changes to the Pathfinder car with the exception of bumpers and wide tires.[15] Like other automobile manufacturers, Pathfinder had gone to a more streamlined look for the body of the car. The company changed its strategy and determined that for 1914 all optional equipment would be included in the price of the car. The five-passenger touring car was priced at $2,185, the two-passenger roadster sold for $2,160, the two-passenger cruiser for $2,175, and the Martha Washington coach for $2,500.[16]

Pierce-Arrow objected to the Motor Car Manufacturing Company's trademark of an arrow as they believed it created confusion between the two brands. The Motor Car Manufacturing Company responded with a new trademark designed by H. H. Thomas of the Bastion Brothers' Indianapolis office. The new trademark depicted three generations of pathfinders ranging from the Indian to the prairie schooner and the automobile.[17]

Utilizing his engineering skill, Ray Harroun developed a new carburetor which could handle lower grade fuels. Harroun said of his invention,

> The latter years of development in the motor car industry have been devoted to the finish of details and fineness of construction in practically every part of the car except the carburetor. My unsuccessful efforts

to find a high-grade carburetor designed especially for high-grade cars and harmonious in construction with the car, inspired me to design this carburetor.

Although Harroun had established a separate corporation for the production of the new carburetor, he had a ready-made market with sales to Marmon.[18]

William Guy Wall of National was also experimenting with different types of fuels and announced following extensive testing that he believed kerosene would soon become the primary fuel used because it was cheaper and more abundant than gasoline. The one difficulty of using kerosene was starting the engine, which required a small amount of gasoline.[19]

During the New York Auto Show, Howard Marmon, secretary of Nordyke & Marmon, was elected by his peers to be the president of the Society of Automobile Engineers, the preeminent trade group of automobile men in the country. Also during the New York Auto Show, the Automobile Board of Trade and the National Association of Automobile Manufacturers decided to merge. Charles Hanch, National's treasurer and the vice president of the Automobile Board of Trade, said of the merger,

> The formation of the Automobile Chamber of Commerce is the realization of the dreams of every automobile man in the country who has looked forward to seeing the entire industry united under one head. The Automobile Board of Trade and the National Association of Automobile Manufacturers did a great and lasting work in bringing about complete organizations under two different heads, but both realized the immense advantage of unification, and when the time came, turned all their energies in that direction.
>
> With the new central controlling trade organization there are unlimited possibilities for good. Whatever is done in the future will be for the betterment of the industry as a whole.[20]

In March, Cole introduced a six-cylinder auto and adopted the use of the Delco lighting, starting and ignition system on all of its models. The six-cylinder car was very similar in appearance to the Cole four cylinder except that it was a little bigger.[21] Anticipating strong growth in sales, Joseph Cole announced a $150,000 expansion of the Cole factory on East Washington Street. Indianapolis architect Herbert L. Bass was hired to design the four-story building, to be located to the south of the existing plant on property formerly occupied by the Dell Coal Yard. The L-shaped building was designed with 100 feet of frontage on Washington Street, 232 feet on Market Street and a depth of 386 feet from Washington to Market Streets. Construction of the building, estimated at six months, was expected to be completed by October 1, 1913.[22]

Empire introduced the 31, a five-passenger touring car with the nickname of the Little Aristocrat. This was a bigger version of the 25 introduced in 1912 by the new owners of the company.[23] The Little Aristocrat was chosen as the pilot car for the Little Glidden Tour (also known as the Iowa State Tour) during 1913.[24]

In response to the public's demand for greater horsepower, Marmon introduced a new six-cylinder car in March 1913 with a variety of body styles ranging from a two-person roadster to the seven-passenger berline. The car was very similar to the popular Marmon 32 but had a larger engine, longer wheelbase, and larger wheels. The T-head engine was rated at 48.6 horsepower by the ALAM. Maximum horsepower was stated by the company to be 50 percent greater than the ALAM rating. Ignition was a two-point dual system, with the spark plugs located directly over the cylinders providing two sparks simultaneously. A redesign of the front fenders allowed for large boxes which cleared the running boards. The boxes on the left front fender allowed for tools and the storage battery while the space on the right front fender offered storage space for three suitcases. The roadster models had a retail price of $5,000 while the limousines sold for $6,250.[25]

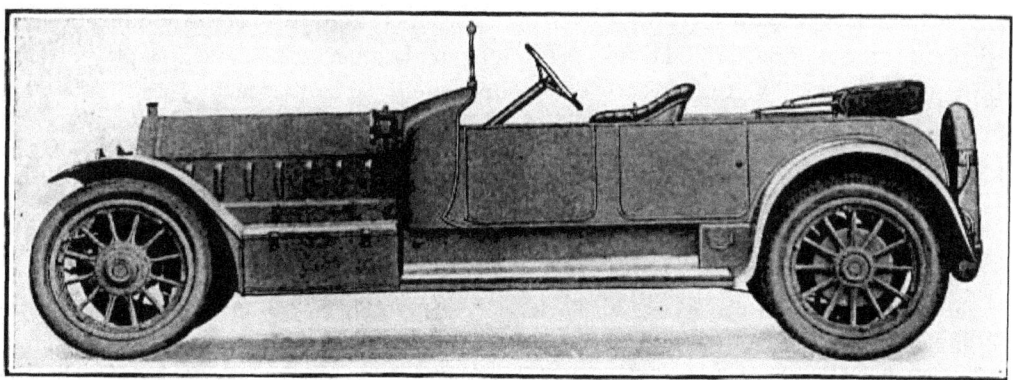

Marmon 48 roadster (*Horseless Age*, March 19, 1913).

Harry Stutz decided to change the name of Ideal Motor Car Company to Stutz Motor Car Company (Stutz) in order to have the name of the company identifiable with the automobiles produced.[26] Stutz also designed an electric self-starter operated by a floor pedal which threw an electrical current while simultaneously meshing the gears. The electric self-starter would be used first on the Series E cars.[27]

National expanded its facilities with the added benefit that the new space allowed for better flow inside the plant. The new facility was a 20,000 square foot, three-story building constructed of brick and cement. On the first floor, the company expanded its machine shop. The second floor was an expansion of the paint shop, while the third floor was used for an expansion of the trimming and upholstery operations.[28]

On the evening of March 25, 1913, the skies opened up and much of the Midwest, including Indianapolis, was deluged with rain. The Flood of 1913 was one of the worst natural disasters ever to hit Indianapolis and other points in the Midwest. Particularly hard hit was the west side of Indianapolis when the levees surrounding the White River broke. Estimates of damage in the city exceeded $25 million.

It was difficult getting around town. The Meridian Street Bridge over Fall Creek, which had cost $250,000 when built and was one of the most beautiful spans in the city, fell into the raging water and was carried downstream. The West Washington Street Bridge, a major east-west bridge, was threatened by the rising waters of the White River. At least two sections of the bridge were torn from the structure.[29]

In making an appeal for donations to help alleviate the suffering due to the storm, the Mayor of Indianapolis issued the following statement:

> The City is facing one of the gravest situations in its history, the flood having made hundreds of families homeless. The city is doing everything in its power to alleviate the condition of the suffering and the unfortunates, but it will be impossible for the city to care for all of those who have been made homeless.[30]

Marmon's automobile factory in West Indianapolis was submerged by the flood waters, with estimates of the depth of the water surrounding the building being between 20 and 30 feet.[31] The company avoided disaster by moving its completed cars out of danger while its chassis were moved to the American plant.[32]

The Indianapolis automobile industry responded to the Flood of 1913. Even though Marion had suffered from the flood waters, it opened its plant, located at the foot of the

Oliver Street bridge, to those who had been rescued. The second story of the building became a shelter for those impacted. Likewise, the American plant became an essential player in the effort to rescue flood victims. Nearly 200 people sheltered in that facility until they were transported to various relief stations in the city. Cole and National, whose factories on the east side of Indianapolis were far away from the flooding, provided cars to aid in the rescue efforts.

The IATA decided to hold its annual auto show the week before the 500-mile International Sweepstakes race. With thousands of visitors expected in town, it was a good time for the various manufacturers to show off their models. George Dickson explained,

> This auto show is not held under one roof but is held for days before the race and days after the race in Indianapolis factories and many of those over the state surrounding the city.
>
> Many motor car companies all over the country will take advantage of the race meet and come to the city to witness the contest and also do business with the many factories here. Likewise, there are private owners who will visit all of the many Indianapolis showrooms.[33]

While other Indianapolis automobile manufacturers displayed their cars at their showrooms, Henderson took advantage of the thousands of visitors to Indianapolis for the race by displaying its 1914 models in the lobby of the Claypool Hotel.[34]

From a high of seven Indianapolis-built cars entering the 500-mile International Sweepstakes race in 1911, only four cars were entered in the 1913 event: three Stutz cars and a Henderson entry driven by Billy Knipper.[35] Pressure continued to be placed upon National to enter the car that had won the 1912 race.[36]

With the 1913 Indianapolis race approaching, people were questioning why no Marmon was entered in the race. After all, the Marmon Wasp, piloted by Ray Harroun, had won the race in 1911, and Joe Dawson, a member of the Marmon staff, had piloted a National to victory in 1912. Herbert Rice provided the answer.

Foundry of Nordyke and Marmon wrecked by the 1913 flood (Indiana Historical Society, P0136).

> There are better reasons for the Marmon staying out of this race than there are for its entering. During 1909, 1910, and 1911, we were entered in practically all of the big races. We had something to prove out and we wanted to prove it by the best cars we could find and from the victories chalked up to the Marmon cars during that time I think we proved it.
>
> That something was not speed. It takes speed to win races, of course, but we were more anxious to prove consistent performance, efficiency, durability, economy of fuel and ease on tires.
>
> Marmon cars proved consistency. In the first Sweepstakes race we entered two cars. One finished first and the other fifth.
>
> Against the few reasons we should enter, there are better reasons why we should not go into a racing campaign this season.
>
> To make cars ready for races such as this takes the services of our best men in the spring when they are needed most on other important work. This spring we are employing more men, turning out more cars and doing more business than ever before and there is not a man or a car in the factory to be spared for racing.
>
> Nothing would give us more pleasure than to have two cars out in practice work at the track, and I believe the Marmon would be a serious factor to consider in naming the winner, but I would rather be tied up making and getting cars out into the hands of customers than getting them ready to race.[37]

After winning the 1912 Indianapolis 500, National had also decided not to continue racing. Additionally, Buick announced that it would not participate in the race. Without the presence of three of the stronger racing teams, the Speedway owners became concerned about the size and quality of the field. The Speedway partners thought that if they attracted some European drivers and cars, they could maintain interest in the race. C. A. Sedwick was sent to Europe to recruit teams.[38] Among those recruited for the race was Jules Goux, whose Peugeot racer was considered "the fastest car in Europe."[39] Goux dominated the race, crossing the finish line in 6 hours 35 minutes 5 seconds.[40]

The victory of Jules Goux in the race and the fact that Johnny Aitken had acted as the Peugeot team manager led to several rumors: that National had intentionally constrained the speed of the Peugeot so that the race results from 1912, when a National vehicle won, would not be beaten; that the National factory had worked to aid the Peugeot team against the American automobiles; and that betting by National employees on Goux led them to help him win the race. George Dickson, general manager, pointed out the absurdity of these charges. No American brand was able to take the lead away from Goux.[41]

Although National did not enter the Indianapolis 500, it provided assistance to eight different teams including the winning Peugeot team. In 1914, George Dickson recalled the company's efforts to help the Peugeot team:

> We must remember one thing, however. Before last year the foreign eligibles looked with suspicion upon the Speedway. They were not familiar with the actual facts. They had no definite idea of the track's size and the event's magnitude. Last year when the foreigners came over here it was pitiful how unprepared they were for the strenuous conflict. It looked like the drivers had sneaked out the back doors of their factories without letting their management know it. They did not have spare parts, and in a number of ways were poorly prepared for such a hard race.
>
> It was then that our company offered assistance to one and all. It is said that the Peugeot people give our factory's assistance great credit for getting their cars into shape to win the race. If this is true, it is equally true that our company gave help one way or another to seven other competing teams.[42]

Cole stockholders approved an increase in the firm's capitalization from $500,000 to $1 million at a meeting in late May and approved a doubling of the production goals to respond to the rapid growth in demand for the company's cars. At the time, Cole was one of four nationally recognized manufacturers of medium priced automobiles.[43]

On the evening of June 4, Joseph Cole was enjoying dinner at the Columbia Club in downtown Indianapolis when his Cole automobile was stolen from in front of the building. After notifying the Indianapolis police, Cole decided to take further action and wired the Cole agents in Indiana, Illinois, Ohio and Kentucky of the missing automobile. At 3:30 a.m. a report was received that the car was in Springfield, Ohio. Cole responded by sending telegrams to Cole agencies in Michigan, Pennsylvania, West Virginia, and New York. At noon, E. A. Green of the Cole Motor Company in Buffalo, New York, saw the car, flagged down a policeman and gave chase. The two young men who had stolen the car abandoned it and the car was returned to Indianapolis.[44] The thieves were later arrested.

On the same evening, another Cole automobile was stolen downtown, with the joyriders being found in Indianapolis a couple of hours later. With car thefts becoming a large problem, Joseph Cole responded by establishing a stolen vehicles bureau within Cole's national selling organization to aid in the recovery of stolen Cole automobiles and the arrest of the perpetrators. Cole also enlisted the aid of a national detective agency in this effort. If a Cole was stolen, the owner called Cole headquarters, which would then notify the various Cole dealerships throughout the nation. There were identifying numbers in a variety of places on the Cole automobile, and Cole instituted having a number concealed to prevent the car being disguised or the visible numbers taken off.[45]

Based upon the success of the Premier Little Six, 1913 was a very good year for Premier, which experienced an 83 percent growth in sales for the first five months of the year.[46]

On July 1, 1913, the Indiana Automobile Manufacturers Association tour to San Francisco, a distance of 3,580 miles, left Indianapolis following a parade through downtown.[47] Carl Fisher had proposed the tour to promote the National (Lincoln) Highway, which stretched from New York City to San Francisco.[48] The tour, also designed to promote Indiana-made automobiles, passed through eight states and was the first automobile tour to cross the Rocky Mountains.[49] Among those participating in the tour were two Marions, two Americans, two Hendersons, an Empire, two Premiers, a Stutz, a Pathfinder, and a Marmon representing the

Joseph J. Cole (LeRoy Cole Collection, Gilmore Car Museum).

7. *Legislation Threatens the Indianapolis Auto Industry* 115

The Cole participating in the 1914 Indiana Good Roads Tour (LeRoy Cole Collection, Gilmore Car Museum).

Prest-O-Lite Company.[50] On July 27 the tour reached the Pacific Ocean.[51] Upon leaving San Francisco, the tour headed south to Los Angeles. Fisher and C. A. Bookwalter did not travel to Los Angeles but returned to Indianapolis.[52]

The Pacific Coast highway tour was the perfect opportunity for Henderson to show off two new models, a six cylinder and a four cylinder. Both models were available in a variety of body styles including a five passenger, a roadster, a coupe and a sedan. The prices for the cars included $1,585 for a "light" four-cylinder car with 44 horsepower, $1,785 for a deluxe four-cylinder car, and $2,285 for a six-cylinder car. The deluxe four and the six-cylinder car had the option of a Harroun carburetor which could run on either gasoline or kerosene, with the adjustment for the different fuels being made from the dashboard. The cars also had the option of either wire wheels or traditional wooden wheels. If a customer selected the wooden wheel option, detachable rims were provided, including an extra rim. If a wire wheel was desired, the company provided an extra wheel. Henderson was the first American manufacturer to offer wire-wheeled models. The cars also came with large tires (35 × 4½ inches), resulting in a smoother ride.[53]

James Handley formed the J. I. Handley Company with capitalization of $1,250,000 to hold his various automobile interests with operations in Indianapolis, including Marion, American, the American Motors Realty Company, and the A and M Sales and Service Company. Also folded into the new company was the American-Marion Sales Company of New York and the American Motors California Company located in San Francisco. The new company became the sole sales agent for the American underslung and Marion cars. Handley believed the new structure would bring greater efficiencies to his various interests:

With the sales advertising and service work entirely removed from the manufacturing companies and thrown into another individual company, whose function will be the successful distribution of the product of both American Motors and Marion Motor Car Companies, we will be able to pursue a more concrete manufacturing program.

In other words, the American Motors Company will have nothing to do but build the famous American underslung. Similarly, the Marion Motor Car Company will concentrate entirely upon the production of the Marion Sixes and Marion Fours. Thus the new company will be able to specialize and concentrate all its efforts in distributing and promoting both products.

This amalgamation will not affect in any way the individuality of either of the manufacturing companies. The American Motors Company will do all of its own engineering, purchasing, financing and building. The board of directors and officers will be undisturbed. This also holds true for the Marion Motor Car Company. Under this new arrangement each manufacturer will have one big customer for its products instead of many and will look solely to one big customer for successful distribution. On the other hand, this one customer, the J. I. Handley Company, will come in direct contact with the many American dealers and Marion dealers.[54]

Joseph Cole believed a better car was produced by using standardized parts. Unfortunately for Cole, most people saw this as an "assembled" car which was less valuable than a car where the parts were manufactured by the automobile manufacturer. To change the public's perception, Cole started the "standardized" car movement and assembled a group of 200 men representing the automobile parts manufacturing businesses in Indianapolis for a conference in mid–July.[55]

For 1914, Cole announced that the Series Nine models would be made entirely from standardized parts. The line included four- and six-cylinder models with the engines provided by Northway Three Point Suspension Motor Manufacturing Company. The four-cylinder engine would have 41 horsepower and the six-cylinder engine 68 horsepower. The cars had a streamlined look with the hinges and latches being concealed and the running boards being free from obstruction. A notable feature of the cars was their wide doors, 24 inches for the front door and 26 inches for the back door, which made for easy entrance and exit. Built upon a 120-inch wheelbase, the four-cylinder car came in three body styles for two, four and five passengers. The six-cylinder car was built on a longer 136-inch wheelbase with different body styles for two, six, or seven passengers.[56] The cars had a six-volt Delco electric starting and lighting system which featured a circuit breaker rather than fuses. For the first time, Cole automobiles had a horn. The company also had switched to the left-hand drive and center control.[57]

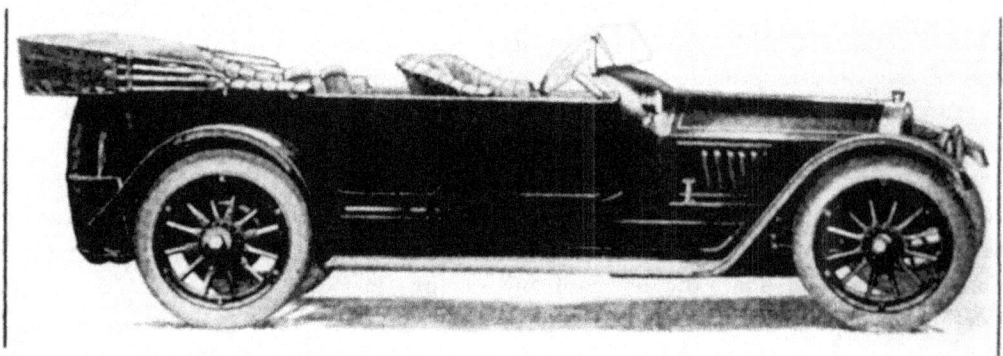

Cole Series Nine automobile (*Horseless Age,* July 23, 1913).

Marion Co. Out with a "Six."

Marion Six introduced in 1913 (*Horseless Age*, August 20, 1913).

In July 1913, National introduced the four-cylinder V-3 series which came in five different models ranging in price from $2,750 to $3,400.[58] Models included a semi-racing car, a speedway roadster, a toy tonneau, a five-passenger touring car and a seven-passenger touring car.[59]

Marion joined the growing list of companies producing a six-cylinder car with the introduction of the Marion 6 which was available in two models: the G5, a five-passenger touring car, and the G2, a two-passenger roadster. Both cars used the same 124-inch wheelbase chassis. The cars featured a Westinghouse electric starting and lighting system.[60] The roadster weighed 3,000 pounds and sold for $2,150 while the five-passenger touring car weighed 4,000 pounds and sold for $3,000.[61]

Marion began producing a closed car in the fall of 1913 with two models: a four-passenger coupe mounted on either the four-cylinder or six-cylinder chassis and a five-passenger sedan mounted on the larger six-cylinder chassis. The four-passenger coupe had a unique seating arrangement. Three could be seated side-by-side on the front seat. So as to not interfere with the driver, the driver's seat was set forward by six inches. The fourth passenger would be accommodated in a folding seat attached to the front panel of the car. The sedan accommodated the driver and another passenger in separate seats in the front while the rear seat could hold three passengers. The cars featured electric self-starters and lighting system and a dome light.[62]

Nordyke & Marmon expanded its capital base in July 1913 by issuing an additional $200,000 in common stock and $500,000 in preferred bonds to support the growing automobile business.[63]

That summer Bruce Keene tested a Marmon 32 Speedster at the Indianapolis Motor Speedway, going 82 miles per hour. This did not represent a return to racing for the company. It had a line of cars which were racy in appearance with the motors being built for speed. There was a pressure feed from the gasoline tank. The car featured a left hand drive and center control while its seats could be moved back and forth to provide more room if needed.[64]

While not part of the Stutz racing team, on the West Coast Earl Cooper was having great success with his Stutz racer. At the Tacoma race over the July 4 weekend, he won the Potlach Trophy, defeating Bob Burman by 16 minutes. His domination of the field continued when, two days later, he beat Dave Lewis driving a Fiat in the Montamarathon Trophy race. A month later, Cooper's winning ways continued when he beat Barney Oldfield in a 400-mile race at Santa Monica. In the September races at Corona, California, Cooper won not only the 250-mile race for his car's class, but also the free-for-all contest.[65]

With Harry Stutz directing the efforts of his team from the pits, Gil Andersen won the 301-mile Elgin Cup Trophy race and set a new course record with an average speed of 71.5 miles per hour. After taking the lead on the fourth lap, Andersen did not relinquish control through the remainder of the 36-lap race. In the first victory of his racing career, Andersen took home the $1,750 first prize. Before the race, Andersen said, "I have one of the best cars in the race and I am going to prove it."[66]

Encouraged by its performance in the Elgin Cup Trophy Race, Stutz was the first manufacturer to register a car for the 1914 Indianapolis 500, with two entries piloted by Gil Andersen and Earl Cooper. In 1913, the Stutz team of Andersen and Cooper won seven of the 11 races they entered.[67] Cooper was named the national champion for 1913 while Andersen finished sixth.[68]

1913 Stutz racing team including Merz (#2), Andersen (#3), and Herr (#8) (courtesy of Carl Jensen).

Pathfinder Announces a Six-Cylinder Model for 1914.

Pathfinder's six-cylinder Leather Stocking model (*Horseless Age*, October 22, 1913).

Herbert Rice, Marmon's sales manager, explained why the company wasn't making any major changes in its 1914 cars:

> While the motoring public seems to demand a yearly announcement from the manufacturer, we do not believe it is necessary to make radical changes in body lines and mechanical details merely to answer this demand. We believe the buyer would much prefer to see a car with every feature proven practically by years of service if he could be assured of one fact—that the car would be up to every requirement in a mechanical way as well as appearance.[69]

American announced a new car, the 646, a six-cylinder, 40-horsepower, six-passenger vehicle, for 1914. This car effectively replaced the American Traveler. It was a departure from the company's policy of limiting its lower priced cars to four passengers.[70]

Three new members, Franklin Vonnegut, Arthur R. Baxter, and A. R. Smith, were added to Henderson's board of directors at the September stockholder meeting and provided an additional $200,000 in capitalization to the company. Although the production of a lower-priced automobile using a kerosene carburetor was discussed, a decision wasn't made about its implementation.[71]

The Motor Car Manufacturing Company planned an unusual advertising campaign for its Pathfinder brand by tapping into satisfied owners. President W. C. Teasdale, Jr., explained the campaign.

> After all, there is only one thing that counts in the manufacture of a successful car and that thing is satisfied ownership. Indianapolis has long been known as a leader in the production of high-grade automobiles, and the reason for this splendid reputation is the general satisfaction that Indianapolis cars have been giving in the hands of private owners.[72]

An example of this advertising appeared in the *Indianapolis Star*:

> George A. Kuhn, an Indianapolis banker, has just returned from a trip to the East. He says his Pathfinder pulled through mud that three six-cylinder cars and another "four" were unable to pull through until the Pathfinder led the way.
>
> Dr. H. E. Mock, surgeon for Sears, Roebuck Co., Chicago, averages 27 miles per hour between Chicago and Muncie, a distance of 250 miles, with comfort and ease for himself and his family. The original tires on this car have run more than 6,000 miles.[73]

Gil Andersen relaxing after winning the Elgin Trophy Race (courtesy Carl Jensen).

Pathfinder introduced a new six-cylinder car for the 1914 model year. Nicknamed the Leather Stocking model, this car featured an eight-day clock, a motor-driven tire pump, and left-hand controls for $2,750.[74]

Premier's business doubled in 1913. To support the growth, the company arranged for an additional $500,000 in stock, increasing its capital base to $1,250,000. During model year 1913, the company doubled its production. Premier attributed its success to reducing the price of the Little Six while maintaining[75] the quality of the larger Six, as well as to the Pacific Coast tour during the summer.[76]

In addition to the 4–40 and the 6–60, Premier introduced a new six-cylinder model for the 1914 year. It featured a Weidley overhead valve motor which had a 31.5-horsepower rating from the Society for Automotive Engineers. With a 132-inch wheelbase, the car could accommodate seven passengers.

In December, National unveiled its new six model in a toy tonneau and a five-passenger model with a price of $2,375. The six-cylinder car had 33.75 horsepower.[77]

8

Adopting the Six-Cylinder Car

One hundred forty-five automobile manufacturers were manufacturing cars at the beginning of 1914. On a national basis, 45 percent of the manufacturers were producing a car on only one chassis. Included in the ranks of one-chassis manufacturers were most of the large quantity builders: Ford, Studebaker, Overland, and Buick. In 1913 approximately 50 percent of the cars had self-starters; by 1914 this had grown to an estimated 90 percent. Another feature which had become nearly universal was the driver sitting on the left hand side of the car. The average price of the automobile had declined to $2,347.[1]

Six-cylinder cars had become popular, with many companies introducing cars equipped with the higher powered engine. Marmon unveiled the Marmon 41, a smaller six-cylinder car built upon a 132-inch wheelbase, in January 1914. Five body styles were offered: a two-passenger roadster, a five-passenger touring car, a four-passenger touring car, a limousine and a landaulet.[2] The Marmon 41 was advertised as having "ample power, moderate size, and reasonable price." The five-passenger touring car, four-passenger touring car, two-passenger roadster, and the Speedster were all were priced at $3,250, while the limousine model was priced at $4,750.[3]

Empire surprised even its distributors when it unveiled two new offerings at the New York Auto Show.[4] One of the new cars was a streamlined roadster described as being "foreign in line and beauty,"[5] with a retail price of $900. The other was a five-passenger touring car equipped with a Remy electric starting and lighting system[6] and with a retail price of $1,025,[7] making Empire the only company in its price range to feature an electric system.[8]

Marion, which had been placed in the hands of a receiver on November 3, 1913, exited receivership prior to the Chicago Auto Show in February. The company's claims to be solvent when placed into receivership appeared to be valid given its quick exit.[9] Marion announced at the New York and Chicago Auto Shows a six-cylinder Bobcat built upon a larger chassis.[10]

Pathfinder unveiled two six-cylinder cars including the Daniel Boone model priced at $2,222[11] in addition to a four-cylinder model at the New York Auto Show, while Premier unveiled a car powered by a six-cylinder Weidley engine.[12]

Frederick E. Moscovics, who would later become closely associated with the Stutz car, joined Marmon as the commercial manager in January 1914.[13] Moscovics was well known in the automobile industry for his sales and engineering expertise. He had begun his career as an apprentice in the Daimler factory in Germany and was one of the founders of the Motor Racing Association of New York. Before joining Nordyke & Marmon, Moscovics was a principal in the Jones Electric Starter Company of Chicago. He would continue his ownership interest in that company as well as provide consulting services to it.[14]

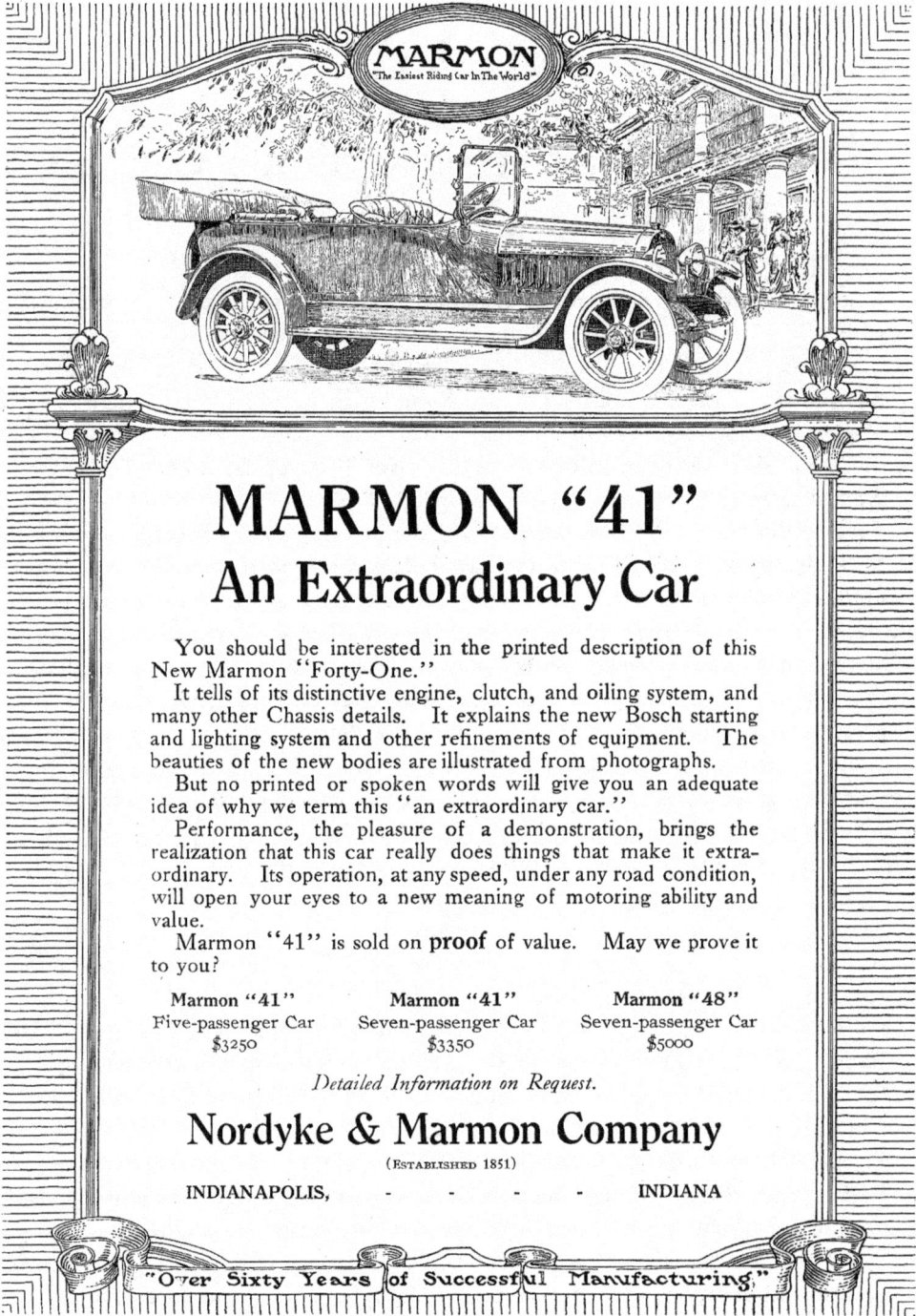

Marmon 41 automobile advertisement (Indiana Historical Society, P0143).

Experiencing strong sales growth, Cole again expanded its production facilities, adding a four-story 176,000-square-foot addition. While the building was made of concrete and reinforced steel, the exterior fronting Washington Street had a façade of white tile and columns with cut stone cornices which resembled the trademark for Cole's standardized car. Joseph Cole's desire to have all departments in the same building, including sales, was realized when the addition was completed.[15] The factory was provided with the latest equipment to save time and to improve the quality of the automobile: a pneumatic body hoist and traveling crane, a grease-cup filler, a linoleum-cutting machine, and a machine which would prevent the linoleum from warping when installed on the running boards. Before the adoption of the pneumatic hoist and traveling crane, it took eight or nine men to position a chassis on a seven-passenger car. With this piece of equipment, one man could perform the work. The linoleum-cutting machine lifted the 350-pound rolls of linoleum from the floor to the ceiling where they could be fed through the cutting machine. Previously, the cutting was done on the floor, where the rolls of linoleum were subject to damage.[16]

The end for American came in March 1914 when it went into receivership. The firm's assets were purchased by Samuel L. Wilternitz & Company of Chicago at a public auction for $110,000.[17]

In announcing Stutz's entry of two cars driven by Gil Andersen and Earl Cooper in the Vanderbilt and Grand Prize races in California, Harry Stutz said,

> We do not want to seem conceited or vainglorious because the Stutz has officially been proclaimed champion of the 1913 racing season, but we have entered our cars in these races in the sincere belief that our product has the merit to repeat in 1914 what they so well have accomplished in 1913.[18]

Although Herbert Rice declared that Marmon would not participate in any races, he left the window open for others. "However, we cannot keep private owners of fast Marmon cars from entering them in race meets."[19] Responding to a request by Wilbur D'Alene of Los Angeles, the Marmon factory sent a racer which D'Alene entered in the Vanderbilt Cup and Grand Prize races.[20] The Marmon sent to D'Alene had finished second in the Santa Monica races in 1911 and had participated in the Vanderbilt Cup and Grand Prize races in Savannah in the same year.[21]

Marmon 41 owned by Warren Witherell (courtesy Norma Arsenault).

The Vanderbilt Cup and Grand Prize races were disappointing for Indianapolis-built cars. Ralph DePalma in a Mercedes won the 294-mile Vanderbilt Cup, while Earl Cooper, driving an Indianapolis-made Stutz, finished fourth in the field, earning $1,000. Gil Andersen, piloting the second Stutz, left the race after experiencing a broken drive shaft. Of the 16 cars which entered the race, only five finished.[22] Two days later, Guy Ball, driving a privately owned Marmon, finished second. Andersen's car developed engine trouble only six laps from the finish when it looked like he would take home second place. The other Stutz entry driven by Earl Cooper finished its day of racing on the sixth lap.[23]

Stutz hoped to enter three cars in the Indianapolis 500. After the 1913 season, Earl Cooper joined the Stutz team and journeyed east to participate in the race. In addition to Andersen and Cooper, Stutz wished to add Barney Oldfield to the list of drivers. Although many thought Oldfield's best days were over, there was fierce competition for his services from Maxwell and Mercer. Ernie Moross, the former publicity director for the Indianapolis Motor Speedway, believed he had secured Oldfield's services for the Maxwell team but by early March did not have him under contract.[24] Another hurdle was crossed when Oldfield patched up his relationship with Carl Fisher. This became known when Oldfield told Harry Stutz that he would be driving one of the "ghosts" in the Indianapolis 500.[25]

C. E. Erbstine of Chicago entered his privately owned Marmon in the 1914 Indianapolis 500 to be driven by Joe Dawson. Dawson said of the car,

> The Marmon which I will drive in the 500-mile race this year is the same car I drove in the first five century race in 1911. In fact, I consider this the real test of a car's stamina.
>
> I think manufacturers sometimes make a mistake in putting new cars in these events, as the car that shows up to the best advantage is one that has been driven long enough to discover all weaknesses and correct and improve them.
>
> The six-cylinder Marmon Wasp with which Ray Harroun won the first 500-mile race had several important victories to its credit beforehand. On Decoration Day, 1910, the Wasp, with Ray Harroun driving, won the 200-mile event for the Wheeler & Schebler Trophy on the Speedway.
>
> The first race the Wasp was entered in was at Atlanta in May, 1910, when it won the 10- and 12-mile free-for-all with Harroun driving.
>
> To my mind, the fact a car has seen hard service is no reason it can't repeat if properly handled and provided luck doesn't break against it.[26]

On May 15, Dawson showed that the reconditioned Marmon would be competitive with the field for the 1914 Indianapolis 500 when he smashed the lap record going nearly 94 miles per hour in practice.[27] Many felt that Dawson's unofficial speed record couldn't be matched. They were proven wrong the next day when George Boillot, driving a Peugeot, recorded the same time.[28]

Just as in 1913, National offered its employees, machinery and equipment as assistance to the entries in the 1914 500-mile race. George Dickson said of the offer,

> While these drivers are coming here with the idea in mind to win the race and break the record for the distance that was established by the National, we feel it is our duty to do all we can to assist them. We want to make the race as good as possible. It has been our pleasure to help competitors in races where we had National cars entered. We hope no accidents will happen, but if they do we extend our facilities to the unfortunate drivers so they may repair their machines in the best possible way.[29]

Expecting 40 entries for the 1914 Indianapolis 500, management established a rule limiting the number of entries per team to two. Wanting to have three cars in the race, Stutz and Mercer responded by selling one of their racing autos to a private individual with a proviso in the contract requiring that the car be entered in the race. Bob Maypole from Chicago purchased the Stutz piloted by Barney Oldfield. Walter Almy purchased the Mercer piloted by Edward Pullen, the recent winner of the Grand Prize.[30] Several days later the Maxwell race cars constructed by Ray Harroun followed the same strategy. Two factory cars were entered, while a third car was entered by W. S. Bennett of Indianapolis.[31] AAA Contest Board rules prohibited more than three entries from any one brand.[32]

After Jules Goux won the 1913 Indianapolis 500, the Automobile Club of France had decided to grant competition licenses to all Europeans who participated in the 1914 race. This meant there would be an internal competition among the Europeans in addition to the race itself, as the finish for the European drivers would count in their points total.[33]

Taking advantage of the crowds gathered in Indianapolis for the race, the local dealership displayed the Empire No. 19, the smallest car to participate in the Indiana-Pacific Coast tour in the summer of 1913. This car, one of the few to return to Indianapolis after reaching the West Coast, traveled 19,000 miles on its journey.[34]

To help the sales effort of its moderately priced car, Empire adopted a financing strategy started on the West Coast. A down payment was made on the car with the balance being made in installments. H. M. McDermid, Empire's district manager, talked of the financing scheme:

> This arrangement marks the greatest volume of automobile selling in the history of the industry. By this method, the man who is desirous of owning an automobile, but because of limited capital has hesitated, now has the way open for him.
>
> Under our new arrangements all objections are overcome. A purchaser makes payments on a car at such intervals as may be convenient to him and he has the car immediately.[35]

With a fiscal year ending August 31, Cecil Gibson reported in late July that not only were sales of Empire automobiles 38 percent ahead of where they were in the previous year but the company had done more business in the ten months of 1913–1914 than it had for the entire 1912–1913 year. He talked about the factor driving the growth in sales of the Empire automobile.

> Eight out of every ten buyers in our experience prefer a car that cost less than $1,000, and dealers are finding it profitable to handle low-priced cars of quality along with the higher priced makes.
>
> The "consumer" of the automobile is studying costs. He finds that a low-cost car gives equal service for daily needs—and the man who can afford to invest in two cars keeps a small car for business and personal needs along with the family car that is used for touring and pleasure.[36]

George Weidley, Premier's chief engineer, designed a new engine which was first displayed at the 1914 New York Auto Show. The engine was revolutionary in that it had fewer parts, weighed less,[37] and reportedly used up to 75 percent less fuel. It could also operate with lower grades of fuel.[38] In May, Premier introduced the 6–49 roadster model designed by Weidley.[39] The company offered two variations of the six-cylinder car. The traditional T-head motor had a price tag of $2,395 while a car equipped with the Weidley engine retailed for $2,700.[40] With the introduction of the 6–49 automobile, Premier ceased production of four-cylinder automobiles.

Needing new facilities, Harry Stutz and Henry F. Campbell, the secretary and treasurer of the Stutz Motor Company, bought the home owned by Harry New on Capitol Avenue for $20,000 with plans to build a four-story building with a 90-foot frontage on Capitol and 204 feet on 10th Street.[41] In late April, a building permit was issued for the new Stutz factory with an estimated cost of $75,000.⁴² Stutz wasn't the only manufacturer expanding. Cole opened its new 160,000-square-foot building in May 1914. A newcomer to the automotive industry, Lyons-Atlas, was also based in Indianapolis. The successor to the Atlas Engine Works, the company produced the Lyons-Knight car in the old Atlas factory.⁴³

Cole's four-cylinder Ten-Four model was met with great enthusiasm by the buying public. Joseph Cole gave this explanation of why this car was so popular:

> As I see it, the market is calling for a quality five-passenger family touring car of light weight, easy on fuel consumption, and combining those qualities of durability and refinement that the American family of moderate wealth demands.⁴⁴

One of the factors driving the demand for the Cole Ten-Four automobile was the introduction of the Stewart-Warner vacuum control. Designed by former auto racer Webb Jay, this invention increased fuel efficiency, eliminating the need for an auxiliary air pump on the motor and the air pressure pump control on the dashboard.⁴⁵ Manufactured by the Stewart-Warner Speedometer Corporation, the system consisted of a small round tank with two chambers providing a steady feed of fuel from the gasoline tank to the engine. The upper chamber was connected to the intake manifold and to the gasoline tank. The lower chamber was connected to the carburetor. A float valve allowed gasoline to flow down into the lower chamber.⁴⁶ The Stewart Vacuum Gasoline System was tested at the Indianapolis Motor Speedway under the supervision of the AAA. A Cole test car experienced a 17 percent increase in mileage while another Cole test car recorded a gain of 22 percent.⁴⁷ Tests on the system were also conducted on a Buick 55-C, resulting in an increase of 12.75 percent in fuel efficiency. Tests on the Cole Ten-Four on Clifton Hill in Cincinnati showed that the adoption of the vacuum control mechanism improved the hill climbing ability of the car.⁴⁸ The system was adopted by various automobile manufacturers including Cole and Marmon. By December, 25 percent of cars being sold were equipped with the Stewart gasoline vacuum system.⁴⁹

While the Cole Ten-Four had the same equipment as the previous Cole four-cylinder model, it weighed three hundred pounds less, resulting in the car using less gasoline. Another benefit of the Cole Ten-Four was the lower price achieved through the standardization of parts. Prior to the adoption of the standardized car, a Cole would cost $1,925; standardization

Cole 10–4 automobile introduced in 1914 (*Horseless Age*, April 29, 1914).

dropped the price to $1,665.[50] The Cole factory was turning out 20 cars per day, and with its new facilities the company planned to increase the volume to 30 cars per day.[51] The Cole Ten-Four was available in Brewster green with black on the fenders, frame, splasher, wheel hubs, and moldings.[52]

The path Indianapolis took with the development of automobiles was always different from that of Detroit. Early on, Detroit adapted the mass production techniques of Henry Ford, and Detroit cars, by and large, were lower priced than those made in Indianapolis. On the other hand, Indianapolis was proud of the quality of its vehicles, which were usually more expensive than those made in Detroit. One of the trends noticed by Marmon was that the buyers of expensive automobiles wanted something unique. Fred Moscovics, commercial manager, talked about this trend:

> There seems to have been a decided change in the last two years of the demands of the owners of high-priced cars.
>
> They no longer simply buy a car on its price and past reputation and no longer like their cars "ready-made," so to speak, but insist that the cars not only be up to date mechanically but their coach and body work be distinctly "tailor-made" and different from their neighbors.
>
> Recognizing this, the Marmon company makes nearly every job a special one to meet the requirements of customers, and, as a result of this policy, is doing a tremendous business, besides setting the fashion in the high-priced field.[53]

After being on shaky financial ground for some time, Henderson was placed into receivership in late May 1914 by a suit brought by W. C. Mock of the Hydraulic Pressed Steel Company of Cleveland, Ohio. Ransom Henderson, vice president, announced a decision to liquidate the company rather than sustain further losses. Over a year before, a creditors' agreement had allowed the company to go on producing cars with the hope that it could return to viability. The following statement was issued by the company about its liquidation:

> Last September the Henderson company was seriously affected by the slump in the motor car business and the restricting financial conditions existing at that time. Since September, it has operated its business strictly on a cash basis and has a very credible record in that more than 85 percent of the number of its accounts have been paid cash in full. The remaining 15 percent have been paid two substantial payments and the present authority to sell the company's assets will make it possible for immediate additional payments to be made.[54]

In addition to his interests in Henderson Motor Car Company, Charles Henderson was also vice president of Regal Motor Car Company and for some time had maintained his office in Detroit. Ransom Henderson joined his brother at Regal Motor Car Company.

On the first day of qualifications for the 1914 Indianapolis 500, Joe Dawson in a Marmon broke the track record with a time of 1 minute 34.8 seconds for a lap. The new track record didn't last long as Teddy Tetzlaff, piloting a Harroun-designed Maxwell and running on a mixture of 50 percent kerosene and 50 percent gasoline, established a new record at 1 minute 33.4 seconds. Just minutes later, that record was broken by Jules Goux in a Peugeot, who lowered the track record for a lap to 1 minute 31.71 seconds.[55]

Although Marmon was out of the racing game, the company utilized the Indianapolis 500 as an entertainment opportunity, sponsoring two Marmon Days. More than a hundred people, including dealer representatives as well as customers, attended the first of the Marmon Days during which they could tour the factory. The company set up a special exhibit detailing the construction of the Marmon automobile, including sectional exhibits of various parts such as the wheels, spokes and radiator. The company also had special displays of the crank shaft and oiling system for the Marmon 41 and 48, which was unique to the brand. In addition to the Marmon Days, the company served boxed lunches to visiting newspapermen at the 500-mile race and held a dinner for its dealers at the German House following the race.[56]

National also devised a mechanism for promoting its brand at the race. General manager George Dickson developed a system for spectators to easily keep track of the racers, which could be picked up at the National sales office on North Capitol Avenue. He said, "It has been demonstrated as practically impossible for the average spectator to get full enjoyment from the race and keep accurate record of the 30 cars in their efforts to encircle the track 200 times."[57]

The Delage and Peugeot entries put on quite a battle for the estimated crowd of 110,000 at the 1914 Indianapolis 500. Rene Thomas, piloting a Delage, won the race with a time of 6 hours 3 minutes 45.99 seconds or 82.7 miles per hour. At the end of the race, he was three laps ahead of his nearest competitor, an underpowered Peugeot with 183 cubic inches of displacement driven by Duray. In his march to victory, Thomas took home the Wheeler-Schebler Trophy by being ahead at the 400-mile mark; the Prest-O-Lite Trophy valued at $2,750 for being ahead at the 300-mile mark; the Remy Grand Brassard valued at $2,500 for being in first place at the 200-mile mark; and the G & J Trophy worth $1,500 for being in the lead at the end of 100 miles. He also won the Rayfield Trophy and $1,000 in cash for using a Bosch magneto. Guyot finished third and the 1913 winner of the Indianapolis 500, Goux, finished fourth.[58]

Barney Oldfield in a Stutz started from the 27th position and finished at the top of the American drivers. Some say he drove the best race of his life. Bruce Keene and his riding mechanic, Rogers, had built the Beaver Bullet in an Indianapolis garage. Beginning the race in the 28th position, Keene finished in ninth place. Indianapolis favorite Dawson, the winner of the 1912 Indianapolis 500, was seriously injured in one of the few crashes of the day.[59] Driving a Marmon, he tried to avoid the Isotta driven by Ray Gilhooley after it bumped the concrete wall and was turning over and over in front of him on the 41st lap. As Dawson was trying to go around the Isotta, his wheel slipped off the track and the car overturned. Dawson's injuries included a broken collarbone and internal injuries including a hemorrhage of the kidneys. He begged the medical attendants, "Don't allow mother and father to know how badly I am hurt."[60] Stutz racers, piloted by Andersen and Cooper, failed to finish the race, with Andersen experiencing the failure of the timing gear while a blown-out tire finished Cooper's day.[61]

Although the French dominated the Indianapolis 500, Stutz took the opportunity to promote its car's performance in the race. In an advertisement, Stutz Motor Car crowed

> Now that the smoke and the noise of the International 500-mile race has died down, let us look at the important facts. The Sturdy Stutz proved its class in competition with the world's best speed cars. The performance of the Stutz in this race, crowning its many past demonstrations of superiority, indicate the long life and sturdy service your Stutz car will give in everyday use. Stutz racers and Stutz touring cars are built in the same Stutz factories by the same Stutz engineers with the same quality of materials, the same methods of manufacture, the same skill and workmanship and the same design.[62]

Dawson's next race was supposed to be the 300-mile Sioux City, Iowa, "mini" Indy race driving C. E. Erbstine's Marmon racer over the July 4 holiday. After his injuries kept him in the hospital for four weeks, Erbstine hired Cyrus Patschke, Harroun's relief driver for in his 1911 Indianapolis 500 victory.[63] Stutz announced that it was entering two racers in the Fourth of July 300-mile auto race, with Barney Oldfield piloting the car in which he had placed fifth in the Indianapolis 500 while Gil Andersen would be at the wheel of the racer in which he had won the 1913 Elgin race.[64] Andersen finished in fourth place while Patschke in the Marmon, with blood streaming from a cut over his eye caused by a flying rock, finished fifth.[65] Barney Oldfield, the favorite to win the race, dropped out with mechanical problems.[66]

Earl Cooper, driving a Stutz, won the 250-mile Montamarathon Trophy in Tacoma, Washington, with an average speed of 73.51 miles per hour, finishing 14 laps ahead of the second place finisher, Ruckstaller driving a Mercer. Ray Harroun was also at Tacoma with his specially built racer, which dropped out of the race because of mechanical issues.[67]

Harry Stutz added a second make of car to his stable. The H.C.S. was a smaller car built for the businessman. With a retail price of $1,475, it was powered by a Wisconsin engine and had Firestone tires.[68]

Premier introduced five-passenger, seven-passenger, and roadster models of the 6-49 at its Indianapolis showroom in mid–July 1915. Built upon a 132-inch wheelbase, the car's six-cylinder engine reportedly could produce between 49 and 70 horsepower. The car sported a three point suspension system and a Remy six volt electric starter and lighting system.[69]

In the first day of a two-day meet at Elgin, Illinois, Andersen driving a Stutz narrowly lost to Ralph DePalma in the Cobe Cup race. DePalma finished the 305-mile race with a time of 4 hours 5 minutes 0.1 seconds. Andersen crossed the finish line 44 seconds later.[70]

Given his victory in the Cobe Cup race, DePalma was the favorite to win the 305-mile Elgin Trophy race run the next day. DePalma did not disappoint, winning the race with an average speed of 73.5 miles per hour. Barney Oldfield, at the wheel of a Stutz racer, finished third in the Elgin Trophy race an average speed of 68.2 miles per hour.[71]

Cole introduced a Little Six at the Indiana State Fairgrounds in September 1914. With a 126-inch wheelbase, the car could comfortably carry seven passengers.[72] A four-cylinder Cole loaded with seven passengers set a new record for fuel economy in a test monitored by the AAA at the Indianapolis Motor Speedway, going 24⅛ miles on a gallon of gasoline. The car also set a record for autos under 300 cubic inches of displacement, going at an average of 55.6 miles per hour over a 30-minute period. Charles Henderson said of the test,

> What the automobile buyer of today is looking for is the car which will cover the most miles on the least quantity of gasoline. Every maker of motor cars in the country seeks to increase this mileage. In the tests just completed, the Cole has set a record which stamps it as the economical car.[73]

The Cole Sensible Six was also a fuel-efficient car. In a tour of Massachusetts, a Cole Sensible Six averaged more than 16 miles per gallon over a variety of roads. In another test of 500 miles over Indiana country roads, the Cole Sensible Six averaged 19 miles per gallon.[74]

Empire unveiled a five-passenger touring car complete with electric starter and lighting system for less than $1,000 at the Indiana State Fair. The Empire Model 31-40, priced at $975, carried a one year guarantee on all parts including the electrical system instead of the standard 90-day guarantee. Empire also offered a five-passenger touring car without the electric starting system with a retail price of $850 in addition to the roadster model.[75] Pathfinder also had an exhibit featuring its 1915 models at the Indiana State Fair. The exhibit included a five-passenger and seven-passenger Daniel Boone, a two-passenger and four-passenger roadster, and the six-cylinder, seven-passenger Leather Stocking touring car.[76]

The Speedway frequently opened the track when conventions were held in Indianapolis. Not only did this benefit the Speedway from the perspective of creating interest in auto racing but it also helped the Indianapolis automobile industry, which showed off its race cars. Canadian Shriners heading to Atlanta, Georgia, for a convention enjoyed an exhibition race staged by Gil Andersen and Barney Oldfield at the Indianapolis Motor Speedway on May 10.[77] Later in the year, the Wholesale Druggist Association's convention included a 25-mile meet at the Speedway with seven Cole racers taking to the field. There was also an exhibition run by Andersen in a Stutz racer and the famous Marmon Wasp.[78]

Although the United States didn't enter World War I until 1917, the hostilities in Europe had the Federal Government seeking to tax the automobile industry $1 for every unit of horsepower.[79] There was also a tax on the sale of gasoline at 2 cents per gallon. Although most thought the gas tax was acceptable, they felt the rate should be reduced to 1 cent per gallon.[80] After a meeting of the Indiana Automobile Manufacturer's Association, a telegram was sent to Lincoln Dixon, the chairman of the House Ways and Means Committee, protesting the tax. The attendees also decided to have petitions signed by their employees sent to Washington. Stutz was the first to respond to this appeal. It was also decided that representatives of the IATA should present their opposition of this proposed tax directly to the Indianapolis representatives and senators.[81]

Stutz entered the 7th annual Cactus Derby free-for-all race from Los Angeles to Phoenix with Barney Oldfield driving the car he had piloted to fifth place in the Indianapolis 500. Also driving a Stutz entry in the nearly 700-mile race was W. M. Brown.[82] Based upon elapsed time, Oldfield won this race, beating the second place car, a Paige 36 driven by Louis Nikrent, by 34 minutes 21 seconds.[83] At one point, with the help of a team of horses, Oldfield had to drag his racer from the swollen Aqua Fria River, and nine miles from the finish, engine trouble caused a brief delay.[84]

Marmon returned to the Indianapolis Motor Speedway in November 1914 for a special test of its 41. Although the company had been very successful with its racing automobiles, many car owners wanted to know about the performance of a touring car with its top and windshield raised. Howard Marmon commented on the results of the test:

> Today, on the Motor Speedway, electrically timed under AAA supervision, we have given a decisive answer to this question. The registered stock 1915 Marmon 41 touring car, with top and windshield up and carrying five passengers, has covered 62.891 miles in one hour's continuous running and set a new standard for automobile performance, which should appeal to every motorist.
>
> This means that the car must overcome the enormous wind pressure, the drag of the raised top, the weight of five men, and make close to 70 miles on the straight-aways to maintain this average for 60 minutes. It means a greater strain on the stock engine than a racing engine would encounter in a 500-mile race. It means greater strain than would come in the lifetime of any car in touring under even extraordinary circumstances.[85]

In a friendly sale, James Handley bought Marion, which had been operating for several months in bankruptcy, from its receivers.[86]

Meanwhile, Premier, one of Indianapolis' oldest automobile manufacturers, had become insolvent. Frank E. Smith was selected to head the company while in receivership.[87] Well known in the auto industry, Smith had been president of the Indiana Automobile Manufacturers' Association and was previously the trustee of Maxwell Motor Company located in New Castle, Indiana.[88] Under Smith's leadership, the company brought out the 650.[89] The new car at a lower price point was well received in the marketplace. After a tour of dealerships in the East, South and West, sales manager Walter M. Beiling said, "I am confident that we have struck the right chord in our manufacturing plans. The new Premier product at the new sales price of $1,985 has removed sales resistance."[90]

One of the strategies pursued by Frank Smith was to market to the funeral industry. The car's long wheelbase and the strength of its chassis made it particularly well suited for this industry. It also had the ability to run smoothly at low speeds. The company offered a hearse and casket wagon, an ambulance, or a berline-type passenger wagon which could carry eight people. The average price of a funeral auto was about $3,000.[91]

9

Stutz Named Car of the Year

Indiana was well represented among the 87 automobile exhibitors at the 1915 New York Auto Show. With a prized location on the first floor, National[1] displayed its new National Six, a parlor car with individual seats which could swivel and move forward and backward. This arrangement permitted passengers to face one another to engage in conversation and also allowed the driver to adjust the distance from the gas and brake pedals as well as the steering wheel.[2] George Dickson explained the changes in the look of the automobile:

> The title of streamlined, as applied to automobile bodies, is taken from the general line of boats, especially motor boats and racing craft. The design of motor car carriages is definitely nautical. Our new cars are all long and low, all lines blend into symmetrical units of beauty with nothing to break up and spoil the effect of the entire car. Automobiles used to look like a crazy quilt. A boxlike hood was put up against a boxlike body. Everything was stiff and angular. Nowadays we try to make the entire car look like it had been poured out of one mold. The hood, body, fenders and everything are so designed as to blend into a harmonious unit of grace and beauty.[3]

In addition to the National Six, the company also displayed a coupe, a roadster, and a polished chassis at the New York Auto Show. The focal point of the Marmon exhibit was a large painting of the Marmon 41 making its record breaking 62.89 miles in one hour at the Indianapolis Motor Speedway with its top and windshield raised. Howard Marmon was on location in New York promoting the Marmon four-passenger and seven-passenger touring cars and the Marmon limousine, which had a Moore and Munger body. Cole displayed a lineup of touring cars including the Model 440 Four, a new streamlined Cole Six, the Big Six model 660, and the Cole Sensible Six model 650. Pathfinder displayed the Daniel Boone, a seven-passenger touring car, and a Daniel Boone roadster. The Lyons-Atlas Company display consisted of the Lyons-Knight seven-passenger limousine, a seven-passenger touring car, and a two-passenger roadster.[4]

Cole introduced its new eight-cylinder car at the Chicago car show. The development of the car was kept under wraps until the show, resulting in it garnering a great deal of attention. Arranged in a V formation with a rating of 39.52 horsepower,[5] the Cole eight-cylinder was reportedly the most powerful of all eight-cylinder cars available on the market.[6] In unofficial testing, the engine obtained 70 horsepower.[7] Cole offered the eight-cylinder engine in a variety of body styles including a roadster, a cabriolet, and four-, five-, and seven-passenger touring cars.[8] It had a 126-inch wheelbase and the front seats were divided.[9] The price of the open car was $1,785.[10] Prior to releasing it to the public, Cole tested it at the Indianapolis Motor Speedway and also on the hills of Brown County, Indiana, Cincinnati, and Pittsburgh.[11]

Marmon car with tonneau (*Horseless Age*, February 24, 1915).

For the 1915 season, Premier introduced the Sextet, a six-cylinder car priced under $2,000. The Premier 6–50 was built upon a 135-inch wheelbase. Its engine reportedly developed 102 horsepower at 1,950 revolutions. At a lower 1,000 rpm, the engine developed 55 horsepower.[12]

J. Guy Monihan announced the addition of an eight-cylinder car with a 115-inch wheelbase priced at $1,500 to the Marion product lineup. Other offerings included a four-cylinder car with a 115-inch wheelbase priced at $1,250 and a larger six-cylinder car with a 122-inch wheelbase priced at $1,300. The Marion cars came with Timken axles, Bosch magnetos, Gray and Davis separate electric lighting and starting systems, and a Stewart vacuum gasoline system. The offering of the three different models fit in with Marion's slogan of "A complete line of popular-priced motor cars built of American standard units on a mutual motors plan of intensified specialization."[13]

The growth in demand for the automobile was explosive. Following the Chicago Auto Show, Indianapolis manufacturers saw a significant increase in demand for their product. Joseph Cole called his factory superintendent with orders to put on a second shift of workers to keep up with the demand. Demand was also strong for the Marmon and Premier automobiles and both companies increased production.[14]

The demand for the Cole Eight was so strong that Cole reportedly entered negotiations with its engine supplier, Northway, to dedicate Northway's entire factory to making the engine. The Northway plant was already running two shifts on many days and indicated a willingness to run three eight-hour shifts if Cole would promise to accept 1,000 eight-cylinder engines a month for the 1915 year.[15] The agreement reached with Northway was that Northway would supply ten engines per day until April 1, when the volume would increase to 20 engines per day—far below the desired 1,000 per month that Northway had requested to give Cole the exclusive supply of the eight-cylinder engine.[16] To meet the demand for the Cole Eight, the Cole factory began running two shifts on April 15.[17]

Shortly after the introduction of the Premier Sextet, Howard Smith, Premier's president, voluntarily filed for bankruptcy, listing assets of $122,584 and liabilities of $142,320. Of the assets listed by Smith, $121,430 was in Premier common and preferred stock, and $80,982 of Smith's liabilities were related to Premier.[18] By this point, Premier was already in the hands of a receiver.

With Premier's uncertain future, chief engineer George Weidley started Weidley Motors Company to manufacture the engines he designed. The company was capitalized initially with $350,000. Its officers were W. Edward Showers, president; George Weidley, vice president and general manager; and William Umphrey, secretary/treasurer.[19]

James Handley, Marion's president, announced the formation of Mutual Motors Company to operate an automobile manufacturing facility for the Marion and Imperial brands in Jackson, Michigan.[20] While Handley remained as president of both Mutual Motors Company and Marion Motor Car Company, he handed the day-to-day responsibility for the Marion operation to J. Guy Monihan. Monihan had previously been the advertising and sales manager for Premier and general sales manager for Cole.[21] Handley said of the new venture,

> The Mutual Motors Company is strictly a manufacturing concern and in no way interests itself in the sales or distribution of either Marion or Imperial cars or any other cars hereafter added to its manufacturing program. Each organization will remain independent and complete within itself, simply engaging the Mutual Motors Company to take care of the manufacturing end of its business.
>
> The idea of organizing a big, efficient manufacturing company for the sole purpose of building automobiles has appealed to some of the leading financiers of the country as being a decided step forward toward the final solution of the automobile problem. It is a commonplace that the consumer is constantly clamoring harder and harder for the best car it is possible to build, at the lowest possible retail price. In order to meet this demand, every device known to engineering and manufacturing efficiency must be brought into play. I regard the new idea expressed in the organization of the Mutual Motors

1915 Cole (LeRoy Cole Collection, Gilmore Car Museum).

Company as offering maximum help in this direction. That by concentrating a separate organization of specialists on each phase of motor car production and distribution and by combining in an indirect way the purchasing power of several separate automobile organizations, that these two steps will result in increased economies accepted by competent authorities as being obvious. The additional advantage in the direction of improved quality is equally obvious.[22]

It didn't take long for the manufacture of Marion cars to move to Jackson, Michigan, and vacate the factory in West Indianapolis. Along with the relocation of the manufacturing facilities, Handley and Monihan moved to Jackson and the sales office on Capitol Avenue closed.[23] All of the plant's equipment, valued at $100,000 was sold at a public auction.[24]

Indianapolis was represented with five entries in the 1915 294-mile Vanderbilt Cup and the 406-mile Grand Prix races. Held at the Panama-Pacific International Exposition in San Francisco, the races were run on a circuit that was asphalt except for a ¾ mile section of board track. The Vanderbilt Cup required cars to have an engine displacement of less than 600 cubic inches and be non-stock cars, while the Grand Prize race was a free-for-all. Total prize money for both races was about $25,000 including $8,000 in gold. Stutz entered a three-car team with Cooper, Andersen, and Wilcox as pilots.[25] Although Marmon had exited the racing game after winning the 1911 Indianapolis 500, two of its cars were entered and driven by their owners, A. A. Caldwell and Wilbur D'Alene.[26]

Wilcox finished in a second place seven minutes behind Dario Resta in a Peugeot in the Vanderbilt Cup race.[27] In an era before television brought happenings to the home, people would go to a theater to watch news events. A movie made of the Vanderbilt Cup was shown in Indianapolis in early May. One night was proclaimed Stutz Night, when members of the Stutz team including Andersen, Cooper, Wilcox, and their riding mechanics were seated in box seats for the viewing.[28]

The 406-mile American Grand Prize race was rain-soaked, which kept speeds down. Dario Resta crossed the finish line first, earning $3,000 with a time of 7 hours 7 minutes 57.5 seconds. Wilcox, driving a Stutz, finished second in the race, three laps behind Resta. Another Stutz car driven by Andersen finished fourth.[29] Stutz immediately took an ad in the *Indianapolis Star* proclaiming its second and fourth place finishes.[30]

Readers of the *Indianapolis Star* were probably shocked when they picked up the March 30 edition and read that Stutz did not anticipate entering the Indianapolis 500, although the three entry team of Cooper, Andersen, and Wilcox was scheduled to drive in the Chicago Speedway race on June 19. Meanwhile, across town, another intrigue was developing. Johnny Aitken, the mechanical supervisor for National, was building a special racer. He held great hope for it, saying, "If the National racer, which I am preparing especially for the track, isn't capable of circling the Speedway course in 1:35, I won't monkey with it much more this year."[31]

On the afternoon of April 9, 1915, a fire broke out in Premier's testing area. When the fire was discovered, it had already spread throughout the one-story building and flames were bursting through the roof. Fanned by strong winds, the fire spread across the adjoining property of Henry W. Klaussman, a builder, who had stored a large amount of lumber on the property. The damage was estimated at $5,000 to Premier's property and $3,000 to Klaussman's property.[32]

Two weeks later a second, larger fire broke out at the Premier plant, destroying the machine shop. The night watchman, Allen Cox, discovered the fire, which had started near the first floor office. He had difficulty reaching a fire alarm box and suffered burns in his effort.

Although the fire station was close by, by the time the firemen got their fire lines laid, the fire had engulfed the building and the second floor had collapsed. The fire, fanned by high winds, did an estimated $50,000 in damage.[33] However, Lady Luck smiled on Premier. As devastating as the fire was, it did not destroy the production plant. The next day, the company announced that the production of automobiles would continue as scheduled. A second portion of good fortune was that the plans for the various autos were stored in a vault and were protected from the flames.[34]

At the time Premier was just beginning the production of a six-cylinder car built upon a 132-inch wheelbase with three different body styles: a two-passenger roadster with a detachable top, the three-passenger Cloverleaf speedster priced at $2,385, and a seven-passenger touring car selling for $1,985.[35] Frank Smith described the Cloverleaf:

> The racy roadster of today is a happy blending of the extreme and the conventional type. Take, for instance, the Premier speedster as it is called and the Premier Cloverleaf, which carries comfortably three persons on three separate seats of regulation size.[36]

Unbelievably, a third fire hit Premier less than a month later. This fire started in a bale of excelsior in the pattern room. Due to the quick sounding of the alarm by the night watchman, Frank Johnson, damage was limited.[37]

When the entire production run of Empire automobiles for 1915 was sold out by the beginning of March, Empire announced the first of its 1916 automobiles, the Model 33 touring

Premier automobile, 1916 (Bass Photo Co. Collection, Indiana Historical Society, P0136).

Empire 33 touring model (*Horseless Age,* April 28, 1915).

car. The wheelbase on this car was lengthened by four inches to 112 inches, which made for more comfort for the five passengers. It featured a left-side drive with a center control area. An improved engine increased the power of the model by ten percent to 35 horsepower. One of the car's optional features was a detachable sedan roof which made the car a closed limousine for winter weather and a touring car for the summer months.[38] The standard finish of the car was Brewster green with black fenders.[39] The announcement of this new car led to a rush of orders—the largest in the history of the company.[40] The company also planned to produce a lightweight car on a 118-inch wheelbase priced at $750.

National unveiled the Newport model, a four-passenger, six-cylinder car, to the Indianapolis market in mid–April. While the car was constructed on the same chassis as the National Salon model, the rear seat had been moved forward so that it was near the center of the long and narrow car, giving the rear seat passengers the same level of comfort as those in the front seat. Another innovation was that every seat in the back was a separate unit with armrests to provide comfort. The center armrest contained a glove box accessible by raising the top of the box. The car also had a special luggage compartment in the rear of the car, giving the rear seat passengers better leg room.[41]

Stutz entered two racers driven by Dave Lewis and Earl Cooper in the 200-mile free-for-all Southwest Sweepstakes in Oklahoma City. Against strong competition including Bob Burman, Barney Oldfield, Billy Carlson, Louis Disbrow, and Eddie Hearne, Lewis finished in second place[42] in the car that Wilcox had piloted to second in the Grand Prize and Vanderbilt Cup races and Andersen had driven to second place in the Elgin road race.[43]

Rather than travel to Oklahoma City for the Southwest Sweepstakes, Howdy Wilcox tested a new 300-cubic-inch engine at the Indianapolis Motor Speedway. The Stutz team hoped this engine could break Rene Thomas' record speed of 82.47 miles per hour set in the 1914 Indianapolis 500. Taking to the course, he turned a lap at 93 miles per hour. Andersen took the wheel of the car and drove 50 miles at 87.1 miles per hour.[44]

The Indianapolis Chamber of Commerce sponsored a Know Your City tour to various factories around town and to the Indianapolis Motor Speedway. Five hundred people witnessed an exhibition run around the oval with an average speed of 87.5 miles per hour by Andersen and Wilcox in their Stutz racers. Each driver also did two laps around the track to show the speed of the cars. Wilcox's solo run had an average speed of 98 miles per hour, reaching speeds of about 105 miles per hour on the straightaway. Andersen's two-lap average was 90 miles per hour, reaching speeds of about 100 miles per hour on the straightaway.[45]

About two weeks later, the Stutz team put on an exhibition race for the annual convention of the Travelers' Protective Association. About 800 people witnessed an impromptu ten-mile race at the Speedway between Andersen, Wilcox, and Cooper. With an average speed of 86.5 miles per hour, it was a very close match, with Andersen crossing the finishing line first and Cooper nosing out Wilcox for second. Later in the day, Cooper drove sixty miles in a tire test averaging 87 miles per hour.[46]

Although Stutz had indicated that its racers wouldn't be part of the 1915 Indianapolis 500, by mid–April the cars had been entered.[47] By the end of the entry period, 40 entries had been received. Qualifying was done in reverse order with the most recent entry qualifying first, and drivers were given three opportunities to make the field. A minimum qualifying speed of 80 miles per hour was required. When the time trials for the 1915 Indianapolis 500 ended, 25 cars were in the field, including the three Stutz entries with Andersen, Wilcox, and Cooper at the wheel.[48] This was the smallest field ever entered in the contest as World War I kept many European cars from the field and changes in the engines mandated by the rules kept others away. Despite the low number of qualifiers, Carl Fisher believed that new speed records would be set.[49]

On May 6, 1915, Indianapolis native Edwin G. "Cannonball" Baker left San Diego for New York driving a Stutz Bearcat in an effort to break the world record. The previous year, he had set the record for riding an Indian motorcycle from coast to coast in 11 days 12 hours and 10 minutes, cutting the then-existing record by half.[50] Baker drove the distance of 3,728.4 miles in 11 days 7 hours and 15 minutes, with the final check-in point at 42nd Street and Park

National Newport model (*Horseless Age*, April 28, 1915).

Stutz ad in *The Automobile* after "Cannonball" Baker's record-setting cross-country run (courtesy Stutz Club).

Avenue. His average (running) speed was 25.2 miles per hour and he averaged 10.6 miles per gallon on the cross-country trip.[51] Harry Stutz greeted Baker on his arrival in New York. Wanting to ensure that the car got the praise it deserved, Stutz had the car examined by Herbert Chase, the Automobile Club of America's engineer.[52] Never one to let a good advertising opportunity go to waste, Stutz took out an ad proclaiming, "Another Record Smashed." The advertisement mentioned that the previous record for a coast-to-coast drive was by a six-cylinder, 60-horsepower car which took three teams of relief drivers 15 days 10 hours to cross the nation.[53] Over the years, Cannonball Baker would be called upon by many manufacturers to establish records.

When it was first established, the Motor Car Manufacturing Company didn't have a name for the company. After the Pathfinder automobile was well established, the firm changed its name to the Pathfinder Company (Pathfinder).[54] It was incorporated with $250,000 in capitalization by Charles W. Richards, George I. Lufkin, and Leo Kaminsky.[55] Shortly after the recapitalization of the company, it announced that it was going to introduce a 12-cylinder car with a 122-inch wheelbase to the market. The car would be priced at $1,975.[56]

In late May the development of a 12-cylinder engine (the Twin Six) was announced by the Packard Motor Company. Within days of Packard's announcement, National unveiled its 12-cylinder automobile built upon a 128-inch wheel base,[57] which had been under development for about a year. The car was priced at $1,990. The 12-cylinder car was an addition to the six-cylinder car, which had been on the market since 1905 with a retail price of $1,690, and the Newport model introduced in 1914 with a price of $2,375.[58] George Dickson talked about the advantage of a 12-cylinder engine to the consumer:

> We hear much talk about 12-cylinder automobiles and how the increased number of cylinders tends towards smoother running cars. However, one of the greatest assets in a 12-cylinder car is its longer life. The one thing above all else that has caused the automobile to depreciate is vibration. Now, if the 12-cylinder car did not run one bit better, but did eliminate vibration, which is the biggest handicap of a car's prolonged usefulness, it would be sufficient reason for adopting the twelve."[59]

Johnny Aitken joined Wilcox, Andersen, and Cooper on the Stutz racing team with Harry Stutz as team manager on May 8.[60] During qualifying for the Indianapolis 500, Harry Stutz promised Wilcox a $200 diamond stick pin if he could better Ralph DePalma's qualification time. With 8,000 spectators watching the qualification trials, Wilcox roared down the track with a recorded time of 1 minute 31 seconds, only 87/100 off the world record established by Georges Boillot in 1914. When he returned to the pits, Wilcox shouted to Stutz, "Give me that diamond pin." With that, Stutz pinned the brooch onto Wilcox's oil stained shirt.[61] Wilcox sat on the pole of the Indianapolis 500 with a time of 1 minute 31 seconds or 98 miles per hour. Ralph DePalma was in the number two slot with a time of 1 minute 31.3 seconds.[62]

As race day approached, Indianapolis was full of speculation about who might eventually win the 500-mile contest. Leading the pack of contenders was Dario Resta driving a Peugeot. Although he had never driven on the Indianapolis track before, he was one of the favorites following his victories in the Vanderbilt Cup and the Grand Prix. The 1914 champion Rene Thomas was back to see if he could put together another winning effort. Although Harroun, the winner of the first Indianapolis 500, wasn't driving, he was leading a team including a Harroun racing machine and three Maxwells.[63] The pick of the betting line to win the race was Ralph DePalma with odds of 2:1. The three Stutz racers were also highly rated with odds of 4:1 for Wilcox and 5:1 for Cooper.[64]

Because Memorial Day fell on a Sunday, the race was originally to be run on Saturday. When there was a massive rain storm between 2 a.m. and 4 a.m., and with the forecasters calling for more rain throughout the day, Carl Fisher and general manager Charles Sedwick postponed the race until Monday, May 31.[65]

The 1915 edition of the Indianapolis 500 saw four cars break the world record for 500 miles. Ralph DePalma in a Mercedes won the race with an average speed of 89.84 miles per hour. Dario Resta finished second with an average speed of 89.28 miles per hour. Indianapolis-made Stutzes also broke the record established by Rene Thomas the year before. Gil Andersen with Johnny Aitken as a substitute driver finished in third place at an average speed of 87.00 miles per hour while Earl Cooper and Johnny Aitken finished fourth with an average speed of 86.19 miles per hour. A third member of the Stutz team, Howdy Wilcox, finished seventh despite the failure of two cylinders on his car.[66]

Citing reduced overhead and increased factory efficiency, Pathfinder announced that the Fremont Six would be priced at $1,695.[67] The Fremont was rated by the Society of Automobile Engineers with 29.4 horsepower. For the 1916 model year, the company also introduced the LaSalle 12, nicknamed Pathfinder the Great and priced at $1,975.[68] The LaSalle 12 was powered by a Continental 12-cylinder aluminum-copper alloy engine with 430 cubic inches of displacement and 43.2 horsepower.[69] The popular six-cylinder Daniel Boone model continued to be priced at $2,222. The new motto for Pathfinder was "a quality car for a quantity price."[70] With a plan to produce 3,500 vehicles in 1916, Pathfinder planned a 400-foot by 60-foot expansion to its plant.[71]

Along with many other companies, Pathfinder believed that the six- and 12-cylinder engines were the wave of the future. W. E. Stalnaker, sales manager for Pathfinder, said,

> The Pathfinder Company is committed to multiple cylinder policy. In our contact with both dealers and users over the country the fact that everyone is ready for multiple cylinder luxury is strikingly demonstrated.
>
> If the multiple cylinder principle is right the manufacturer should lend himself to it whole-heartedly. We all know that a six-cylinder motor is more flexible, smoother, and more flexible than a four-cylinder motor.
>
> It is the Pathfinder company's contention that the six-cylinder motor therefore should be used as a working basis whereon to develop the ideal multiple cylinder power plant. The Pathfinder company is building both sixes and twin sixes. We believe these two lines belong logically together, and that the public demand, so far as we are concerned at least, is not for fours or twin fours.[72]

The naming of the new line of National autos as the Highway series was probably tied to the national highway system being championed by Fisher and Allison, close business associates of Newby, the president of National. In March 1916, George Dickson said,

> All over the United States there is a quickening in activity and pride in highways and posterity will even be indebted to the originators of the Lincoln and Dixie Highways. The year of 1916 promises to be a big year in cross-country touring. The amount of good roads work that has been done and the tremendous cars sales of this year means that the motoring public will live on the highways as never before.[73]

A certified test of a Marmon 41-C stock car was made in New York to verify both its ability to run on high gear in the city and its gas mileage in the city and on country roads. Monitored by the Automobile Club of America, the car drove 12.17 miles through the lower part of Manhattan, stopping 75 times in high gear, using one gallon of gasoline. When possible, the car was driven at 18 miles per hour through the city traffic. The second test of the car's performance was made on Coney Island Boulevard, where it went 16.07 miles on one gallon of gasoline. As in the previous test, the car's average speed was 18 miles per hour. This was significantly better than a previous test in the Chicago Loop area, where the car had averaged 7.75 miles per gallon in city traffic. In a country road test outside of Chicago, the car had averaged 15.75 miles per gallon. The company wasn't sure what caused the difference in performance between the two city tests, but thought it was probably a variety of factors including a more seasoned driver in the New York City test.[74]

Fisher, Allison, Frank Wheeler, Charles Sedwick, Theodore "Pop" Myers and Captain Carpenter (the track's guard force leader) were spectators at the Chicago Automobile Derby as Indianapolis-built Stutz cars finished fourth and sixth. Earl Cooper finished fourth with an average speed of 94.9 miles per hour, well behind the pacesetting pace of Dario Resta at 97.6 miles per hour. Andersen's average speed was 94.04 miles per hour. Both drivers' performance was hampered by numerous pit stops, with Andersen making 11 stops and having 13 new tires installed.[75]

In July, Stutz sold the racer that Wilcox had driven in the Indianapolis 500 and the Chicago race to Ralph DePalma and E. C. Patterson, who planned to enter it in the Elgin National Trophy Race. Hoping to put to rest any possible rumors that Stutz was getting out of the racing game, the company issued a press release:

> The Stutz company announces also that it has no intention of discontinuing racing, as it believes that only in this way has it been able to develop its product to its high state of development. The company considers and knows by experience that by racing weaknesses are developed and can be corrected immediately, which otherwise would take months and possibly years to eliminate, and with this knowledge and experience to guide it, it will continue its racing program as in the past.[76]

With significant success in the market place, Empire needed bigger facilities and relocated back to Indianapolis after taking possession of the Federal Motors Company plant on West Fifteenth Street. This was the same plant where Marion had previously had its operations. C. B. Sommers, Empire's secretary, talked about the decision to relocate the factory to Indianapolis:

> It became evident after planning our 1916 production on a larger scale than ever before that greater manufacturing facilities would have to be obtained, and in view of shipping conditions good railroad connections were demanded. The men interested in our company have other large financial interests in the city.
> We felt it only due Indianapolis that the large amount of money expended on payroll in producing Empire cars should be retained in this city. Furthermore, the financial transactions having to do with the buying of materials and sale of cars is justly due, and should be added to, the bank clearings of the city. These desires, taken in connection with the fact that Indianapolis has splendid railroad facilities, led to the decision to remove the plant to this city.[77]

The company expected to continue manufacturing the four-cylinder car at the Connersville, Indiana, plant through the remainder of 1915. At the time of announcing the relocation of the plant to Indianapolis, the company also announced the development of a six-cylinder automobile.[78] Louis Schweitzer, chief engineer for the company, had been at work developing this car for about a year and had been seen driving around town and performing tests on it at the Indianapolis Motor Speedway.[79] The six-cylinder car had a 120-inch wheelbase with the driver and front seat passenger enjoying separate parlor-type seats. Empire was the only automobile company in Indianapolis to produce a four-cylinder car with a retail price under $1,000 and a six-cylinder car with a retail price of $1,100.[80]

Marmon Model H roadster (courtesy New York Public Library).

Empire introduced a four-cylinder model, the 40,[81] priced at $895[82] in August. Although Empire's automobiles continued to be smaller and cheaper than those built by Marmon and Cole, they were gradually increasing in size. The Model 40 had greater leg room for the passengers and the 37-horsepower engine produced more power.[83]

In July, Marmon introduced some new body styles for its 41, including a three-passenger roadster and a two-passenger speedster. The three-passenger roadster used a center aisle from the front row.[84] Built upon a 132.5-inch wheelbase, the two-passenger speedster, the three-passenger roadster, and the four- and five-passenger touring cars were all priced at $3,250 while the seven-passenger touring car was available for $3,350.[85] Fred Moscovics commented on the popularity of the three-passenger roadster:

> We found a remarkable demand for this type of car. We had planned to make only a limited number because, as a rule, there is not a very brisk sale for high-priced roadsters. We soon found this to be different, as we had orders for the entire allotment before a single one had been delivered. Now we have increased the production of this type to what we feel will meet the demands.[86]

Cole also introduced a new seven-passenger, six-cylinder car, the 666, with a 136-inch wheelbase. The majority of the changes were on the interior of the car with a focus on luxury. It had soft upholstery on deep seats to give a cushioned ride.[87] The cost of the car was $2,385.[88]

The Chicago Speedway hosted a 100-mile challenge event involving only four of the top cars and drivers in the nation. Entering the race were Dario Resta, winner of the Vanderbilt Cup and Grand Prize races, in a Peugeot: Barney Oldfield in a new Delage racing car: Bob Burman in a Peugeot: and Earl Cooper in a Stutz racer.[89] The pace was set by Resta, who won the race averaging 102.85 miles per hour. After experiencing tire trouble while running neck-and-neck with Resta, Cooper finished second with an average speed of 101.41 miles per hour.[90]

The Stutz team of Cooper and Andersen placed first and second in the Chicago Auto Club Trophy Race, upsetting Ralph DePalma in a Mercedes who was favored to win. Cooper won the match with an average speed of 74.97 miles per hour. Hampered by engine trouble which required a pit stop, Andersen finished second with an average speed of 73.85 miles per hour. DePalma was forced out of the race when his engine failed at 175 miles.[91]

The next day, Stutz recorded another 1–2 finish with Andersen driving to victory with an average speed of 77.256 miles per hour. Both Andersen and Cooper, who finished second with an average speed of 76.25 miles per hour, drove the entire race without a tire change. Dropping out of the race on the 17th lap with a sticking valve was another Stutz driven by Andy Burt.[92]

As a preliminary to the races at the new Minneapolis two-mile speedway, Cooper and Andersen finished first and second in the 500-mile race at the Snelling Speedway in St. Paul, crossing the finish line 30 feet apart. Of the field of 14 racers, eight finished. The track had seating for 100,000 but fewer than 30,000 showed up for the races, much to the disappointment of the promoters.[93]

The highlight of Stutz's racing season was the 1915 Labor Day races on the new two-mile speedway in Minneapolis. Harry Stutz managed the two-car team with veteran drivers Andersen and Cooper.[94] Multiple cars succumbed to the track and toward the end of the race it became obvious that the race was a two-person match between the two Stutz drivers. When Harry Stutz learned that both of his drivers were on the same lap, he waited until the final lap of the race to hold up a sign that said, "Position." Cooper told the story of the finish of the race that saw him taking the checkered flag:

> As we neared the pit to start the last lap I read the sign and I reacted before Anderson [sic]. We both pushed our throttles to the floor and in that manner we completed the last lap. My initial momentum had given me a wheel-length advantage and I won the race, 500 miles at an average speed of 86 mph, 25 one-hundredths of a second in front of Gil.[95]

In order to insure there were cars to race at the Indianapolis Motor Speedway, Fisher and Allison started two racing teams in September. They selected Aitken to head the Speedway Team and purchased two Peugeots from Europe. They also commissioned Premier to build three new racers for the Speedway Team. Fisher and Allison also started the Prest-O-Lite Team with four Maxwells under the leadership of Eddie Rickenbacker. Only two of the four Maxwells would be raced at a time.[96]

The first races for the Speedway and the Prest-O-Lite teams were at a 350-mile event at the Sheepshead Bay race course in early October.[97] Eight cars with Indianapolis connections were in the starting field for the race, including three Stutzes piloted by Andersen, Cooper, and Tom Rooney, the Stutz owned by Ralph DePalma, two Peugeots owned by Speedway Team Company driven by Aitken and Wilcox, and two Maxwells driven by Rickenbacker and Tom Orr of the Prest-O-Lite Team.[98]

With 70,000 people watching, Andersen won the crash-marred 350-mile Sheepshead Bay race, setting a new world record speed of 102.6 miles per hour. He was compensated for his victory with $20,000 in cash and $80,000 in trophies including the Astor Cup. Andersen's teammate Rooney finished second in the race, collecting $10,000 in cash. Some of the best known names in racing were forced out by mechanical issues, including Ralph DePalma, Bob Burman, Johnny Aitken, Earl Cooper, Howdy Wilcox, Dario Resta, Barney Oldfield, and Ralph Mulford.[99] The Lyric Theater in downtown Indianapolis showed a film of Gil Andersen's victory in the Sheepshead Bay race as an extra feature of the vaudeville act.[100]

1915 was a wonderful year for Stutz racing. In 23 contests Stutz finished in the money 22 times, bringing home $62,000 in prize money. Stutz won races at San Diego; finished second in the Grand Prize and Vanderbilt Cup in San Francisco and in the Montamarathon and Potlach Trophy races in Tacoma; finished third, fourth and seventh in the Indianapolis 500;

took second in the 100-mile match race at Chicago; took first and second in the Chicago Automobile Club Trophy race and the Elgin National Race; and took first in Kalamazoo, second in Des Moines, and first and second at Minneapolis.[101] Topping off the wonderful year, Earl Cooper was named the Driver of the Year and Stutz the Car of the Year by *Motor Age* magazine. *Motor Age* used the Mason point scoring methodology which gave ten points for a win, six points for second, four points for third, three points for fourth, two points for fifth, one point for sixth, ⅞ point for seventh, ¾ point for eighth, ⅝ point for ninth, and ½ point for tenth. During the season, Cooper scored 51 points with three wins, three second place finishes, and two fourth place finishes. He was eliminated in three of the 11 races he entered. Cooper's teammate Andersen finished tied for second with Eddie O'Donnell in the point rankings but was named the second place finisher due to his two wins compared to O'Donnell's one victory.[102]

After the conclusion of the 1915 racing season, the Stutz team was feted with a dinner with 175 Indianapolis businessmen in attendance.[103] Among the people praising the Stutz organization was Richard Lieber, president of the Merchants and Manufacturers Insurance Bureau of Indianapolis,[104] who said,

> Their work stands today not as proof of luck, but a proof of genius, as the evidence not merely of a superb machine, but of a wonderful organization in which singleness of purpose, fidelity, and honesty are the outstanding marks. Mr. Haynes, A. C. Newby, Howard Marmon, and J. J. Cole, I am sure, will agree with what I say when I repeat that this year's races have established the superiority of the American cars over the pick of the world and the best drivers they could put up.[105]

Harry Stutz paid tribute to the Stutz organization: "What we have done is not the work of one man, but of a complete organization from the man at the bench to the head of the organization, all working hand in hand. We have enjoyed genuine cooperation."[106]

Through its racing victories, Stutz gained an international reputation. The company sent eight of its vehicles to Portugal, one to Spain and ten to Australia. Unlike today when cars are loaded onto transport vans, each of these automobiles had a special wood crate built to protect it on the long ocean voyage. The boxes were transported to the train station by horse-drawn carts.[107]

Toward the end of September, the Indianapolis manufacturers began to announce their 1916 models. Cole introduced the eight-cylinder berline limousine which had a six-passenger capacity. The car's capacity was due to the addition of three "disappearing" seats which when not in use were enclosed in an upholstered compartment. Cole also announced the option of a demountable sedan top which could be securely fastened to the car quickly and easily[108] for the Cole Eight sedan, as well as its three-passenger eight-cylinder Tuxedo roadster model that included a compartment for driving gloves and goggles and a separate compartment which could hold up to three sets of golf clubs.[109]

The demand for the National Highway cars, both sixes and 12s, had outstripped the ability of the company to produce them. The company addressed the issue by expanding its plant to take up an entire city block at an estimated cost of $100,000.[110] One of the buildings constructed was 400 feet long and 80 feet wide, fronting on Yandes Street and used for factory operations. The second building under construction faced 22nd Street and was 278 feet long. It was used for offices, the drafting and engineering departments, and the factory supervising department.[111]

After extensive testing, Pathfinder announced that the Weidley 12-cylinder engine would be used in its 1916 model cars and contracted for the full output of Weidley's factory. The

Weidley engine was constructed primarily of aluminum alloys and the company claimed to be the first to produce a 12-cylinder engine for regular automobile use.[112]

In November, National announced some new closed cars which featured a "drive-your-own-car" type of construction. While many people preferred to drive their own cars, driving in winter posed challenges with which many people didn't wish to deal. National offered both a four-passenger coupe and a five-passenger sedan with either a six- or a 12-cylinder engine. Among the features were automatic window raisers, increased window size, and special luggage compartments.[113]

In late November, Frank E. Smith announced that a consortium of Indianapolis businessmen planned to purchase the Premier plant for $125,000. While the Indianapolis businessmen did not buy Premier, creditors were given five days to oppose the plan for the firm, which was in bankruptcy.[114] A syndicate of businessmen from Joliet, Illinois, and Detroit, Michigan, organized the Premier Motor Car Company (Premier) with authorized capitalization of $2.5 million to manufacture 10,000 automobiles annually. The syndicate purchased all the assets of the old Premier Motor Manufacturing Company with the exception of the real estate. For a manufacturing facility, the syndicate purchased the former plant of T. B. Laycock Manufacturing Company[115] which made iron beds.[116] The syndicate planned to purchase $500,000 in new equipment for the new plant. The only Indianapolis resident involved with the new company was E. W. Steinhart, who was bullish on the future of the new company:

> Already the capital stock of $2,500,000 has been oversubscribed and within a year I confidently believe we will have 5,000 men at work in our new plant. This is the biggest business proposition that has ever come to Indianapolis.[117]

The president of the new firm, J. C. Flowers of Joliet, owned one of the largest color printing companies in the world. Steinhart, owner of the E. W. Steinhart Company, which distributed Dodge cars, and the Cadillac Automobile Company of Indiana, which distributed Cadillacs,[118] was named secretary. Joining Flowers in relocating to Indianapolis were F. W. Woodruff and George Woodruff who headed a national bank and trust company in Joliet.[119]

Flowers talked about the vision for the firm:

> Plans provide for the best car that the best men working under the best conditions can produce—under the most competent business management.
>
> The basic idea is volume which implies price and quality advantages obtained in no other way. The company and its product are to be conservatively and truthfully represented at all times. The car is to be honestly built and honestly sold. It will maintain a character distinctly its own. The organization is imbued with the idea of a large, permanent success founded on complete preparedness, highest efficiency, and absolute integrity.[120]

Shortly after forming Premier, the syndicate purchased Mais Motor Truck Company (Mais), which had developed the first American-made internal-gear-driven truck. Mais had been building these trucks in Indianapolis for the prior six years.[121]

A Cole Eight had an unusual test in traffic in Boston, Massachusetts. The shifting lever was removed and the car was locked in high gear. Additionally, to prevent the car from exceeding five miles per hour, the spark plugs and throttle levers were sealed and the suction and supply valves to the Stewart vacuum tank were removed. With two quarts of gasoline, the car was driven at an average speed of 3.675 miles per hour with an average gasoline consumption of 12¼ miles to the gallon.[122]

As the year ended, Marmon reported that its annual output of cars had increased in 1915. This was attributed to the Model 46 touring car costing up to $5,000 and the 41 models costing $3,250.

As 1915 was nearing an end, National was experiencing the best year of its 15-year existence. With a fiscal year of July 1, the company by the end of December had sales surpassing those for all of the prior fiscal year, which up until that point was the best ever.[123]

Empire was also expecting 1916 to be a banner year, with an anticipated production of 3,000 automobiles in the first six months of the year.[124] For 1916, Empire adopted the use of the Continental motor. Traditionally, moderately priced cars were produced in dark blue or dark green. Empire was promising that its cars would depart from this tradition and would become much more colorful.[125]

The Waverley Company introduced the Model 110, the Waverley Silent Light Four, a four-passenger car with a shorter wheelbase and a lighter weight than the four-passenger models previously offered by the company. The Light Four had two different seating options, including one with the driver's seat set slightly forward. With a lower manufacturing cost, the retail price of the Light Four was $2,000.[126]

At the end of 1915, Joseph Cole announced a $190 reduction in the price of Cole eight-cylinder cars from $1,785 to $1,595.[127] While the price of the car was being decreased, the construction and features of the car were better than those of the Cole Eight introduced the year before. The engine had a counterbalanced crankshaft and aluminum pistons. The wheelbase was lengthened to 127 inches, providing three more inches in the rear compartment. There was also an adjustment in the auxiliary seats that provided more foot room for the rear passengers. The car also had an improved spring suspension system providing a more comfortable ride.[128] Another feature of the car was a tire pump. Its hose, which was attached to the pump, was under the front seat of the car. When a tire needed to be inflated, a small knob on the floor of the car would align the tire pump with the engine and the power generated by the engine could inflate the tire.[129]

10

The Marvelous Marmon 34

The sensation of the 1916 New York and Chicago Auto Shows was the Marmon 34. It was the first car to have an aluminum engine, which weighed far less than the traditional cast iron engine.

Advertisements for a new car to be unveiled began appearing in various trade journals about two months before the New York Auto Show, but without an indication of the maker, creating great speculation. The advertisements promised that the new car was "a distinct innovation in automobile construction; that it marks a new method of construction and the more extensive use of lighter materials." It was a luxury car, yet weighed 1,000 pounds less than other cars in its class. The magazine *Automobile* described the new car:

> The light weight has been obtained by a highly scientific design in combination with a careful choice of materials. There is much aluminum employed and much high tensile steel in thin section. The new car is new from stem to stern; no single opportunity has been missed where there was a chance to increase efficiency and reduce weight.
>
> As a performer on the road its accelerative power of high gear is indicated by its ability to speed up from ten to 50 miles per hour in substantially less than 18 seconds. Its maximum speed is between 60 and 70 miles per hour; it seats seven passengers with the comfort which is expected of the most expensive cars and it has an unexcelled ease of steering and control.[1]

Fred Moscovics was amazed that Marmon had kept the development of the car under wraps for more than a year and a half. He talked about the development process:

> We began working the car out on the Indianapolis Speedway in 1913, although, of course, we had the motor sealed in one of our old chassis at that time. We worked on roads around Indianapolis for months until we had the motor and chassis perfected. Of course, the mystery surrounding the car was talked about. We couldn't evade that so we decided to ship it, new body and all, to the Arizona desert, where we were assured secrecy to a certain extent and road conditions which would test the durability of any car to the utmost.
>
> I suppose the secrecy with which we worked and the veil of mystery which surrounded the car and our unwillingness to discuss it with the Arizonians first excited the comment which later grew into the wildest sort of rumors.
>
> The car was generally taken from the garage at an early hour and returned after dark. Several times when on the desert traveling at racing speed wide-eyed natives watched us pass from their camps at the roadsides. Our men never traveled slowly, as our object was to break the car to bits if possible, so it became rumored that they were testing a racing motor mounted in a touring chassis. Our car has distinctive foreign lines. This no doubt gave rise to the report that we were testing a European machine with the view of duplicating it here in America.
>
> On our return home it was found that our new car was the object of discussion everywhere. No one knew it was our car, yet it was the fact that the 1916 season would bring forth a mysterious machine,

which combined some unheard of ideas, caused no end of comment. Some of the reports were grossly exaggerated.

We soon saw that, unless we regulated the gossip, the public would be led to expect a freak at show time, so we set a campaign of truth about the car, and if possible, still keep the company's name a secret. In this we have been successful. Few people, indeed, knew Nordyke & Marmon Company was back of the mystery campaign.[2]

The Marmon 34 was a great hit at the Chicago Auto Show in early 1916. Fred Moscovics exulted:

The crowds were really too great for the exhibit to be completely satisfactory. Our booth was overcrowded at all times. For that reason, we had to open up an auxiliary exhibit at the branch, and then make arrangements to continue the show during the next week. Many persons who came with the express desire of inspecting our newest construction were unable to get close to the car. Others gave up the struggle in the crowds and many more could not examine the exhibit in the detail which they desired.

We found that there was a manifest interest in the new light-weight construction. Motorists are commencing to realize more and more that pulling a lot of dead weight around is a serious and expensive matter, and the old fallacy that a car must be heavy to ride comfortably is smashed by the remarkable riding qualities of the new methods of obtaining perfect balance and perfect spring suspension.[3]

To form strong cylinder walls, the company used cast iron for the sleeve and cylinder heads. To further reduce the car's weight, Marmon made as much of it from aluminum as possible, including the radiator shell, body, fender, hood, transmission housing, and differential housing in addition to the engine. Also contributing to the reduction in weight, the car was constructed in three sections: the cowl containing the gasoline tank and instrument panel; the front seat containing a compartment for the extra seats; and the tonneau seats, with each section of the car being bolted separately to the frame. The car was available in four different passenger styles: a three-passenger roadster, a four-passenger roadster, a five-passenger touring car and a seven-passenger touring car. Both the three- and the four-passenger roadsters had an aisle between the front seats. The seven-passenger touring car sold for $2,750 while the other three models sold for $2,700.[4] Built upon a 136-inch wheelbase, the seven-passenger, six-cylinder touring car weighed 3,450 pounds.

Marmon Model H roadster (courtesy New York Public Library).

Marmon anticipated a strong increase in sales in 1916 with the introduction of the Marmon 34. The new car featured a greater use of Lynite aluminum in the cylinder castings and the upper half of the crankcase.[5] Another feature of the Marmon 34 was its upholstery, which could easily be removed for cleaning.[6] Overall, the weight of the car was lowered from 4,500 pounds to 3,300 pounds.

To keep up with the demand for its automobiles, the company expanded its manufacturing facilities with a new 37,500-square-foot building.[7] One of the people impressed with the Marmon 34 was Henry Ford, who purchased one for his son Edsel.[8]

In 1916 Empire unveiled its Model 45, a four-cylinder automobile that was built on a 116-inch wheelbase.[9]

Pathfinder was among the first American manufacturers to announce a 12-cylinder (twin six) automobile. The car was available in two models: a seven-passenger touring car priced at $2,475 and the Cloverleaf, a three-passenger roadster priced at $2,750. The cylinders with a 2⅞ inch bore by 5-inch stroke were cast in sets of three and arranged in two sets of six.[10]

After the marvelous 1915 racing season, Stutz, at least on a temporary basis, ceased its auto racing exploits. Harry Stutz explained at the New York Auto Show:

> The Stutz factory is not necessarily through with racing. We have established records that have never been equaled, for both speed and endurance. The first and second prizes we piled up crowned our product as the speed king. Somebody will go after our record, and when they equal it the Stutz crew will again be seen on the American race courses. How long that will be depends upon the other fellow, and in his attempts he is entitled to have the "spotlight."[11]

The task of building the three Premiers for the Speedway Team Company in 12 weeks for the 1916 Indianapolis race fell to John L. Yarian, the engineer for the company. Since the new Premier plant was not yet functional, the cars were built at the Mais Motor Truck plant.[12] The third Premier was completed just in time to participate in the elimination trials for the 300-mile race. The car was started at the plant and then driven to the Speedway for its trial run.[13]

As winter turned into spring, the war clouds were getting more threatening. The United

Marmon 34 automobile (Indiana Historical Society, P0143).

States' role in supplying the Allies (England and France) with armaments resulted in a February 8 German manifesto that submarines would target supply ships as they crossed the Atlantic Ocean. In response, President Woodrow Wilson demanded the cessation of the submarine warfare. If the Germans did not comply, it was widely believed the United States would be drawn into the hostilities.[14]

The war in Europe caused shortages of materials such as cast iron and steel, leading to the widespread use of Lynite aluminum in automobiles. It wasn't long before the demand for Lynite aluminum led to shortages of that material, too. The cost of other raw materials used in the production of automobiles also increased. In March 1916 Marmon increased the price of its Marmon 34 seven-passenger touring car to $2,950 and the price of the three-passenger and four-passenger touring cars to $2,900. Walter Marmon explained the price increase:

> This increase in price is caused by the actual increase in the cost of material and labor entering into the construction of the 34 car. As a matter of fact, this advance does not fully cover the increased cost. However, in view of the unprecedented sales of the car, and the fact that the sales resistance is so much less than anticipated, we believe we are justified in marketing the car at the new price rather than advance the full amount of the increased cost of material and labor.[15]

Empire introduced the Tourabout, a four-passenger, six-cylinder roadster very similar to the other Empire cars in profile. Most significant for the passengers was a roomier interior. The car had individual seats for the driver and the front passenger. In between the two seats was a ten-inch-wide aisle providing access to the back seat. The backseat was 36 inches wide with an 18-inch clearance from the front seat. The luggage area was accessed by lowering the back seat.[16] Not wanting to cheapen the materials used in the cars, Empire announced an increase in the price of its automobiles effective April 15.[17]

Pathfinder introduced a moderately priced six-cylinder model, the Dolly Madison.[18] Additionally, Pathfinder increased the price of its twin six automobiles. The touring car's new price was $2,750 while the twin six Cloverleaf roadster was increased to $2,900. W. E. Stalnaker, sales manager, explained the price increase:

> It has been plainly evident to every person who is at all informed on the market and manufacturing conditions prevailing for some time past that there has been a tremendous increase in the price of all material that is necessary in building high-grade automobiles.[19]

George Dickson talked about the value of a trademark in making an announcement that National had been granted a trademark for both "National" and "Highway," to be used in connection with automobiles in April 1916.

> A long established name and trade-mark is now considered to be a vital asset by some of the most reliable manufacturers of the country. Names and trade-marks are placed upon goods in order to identify them, thereby fixing their responsibility for their quality.
> Trade-marks make profits out of good will. That is why we have trade-marked the name "National," and why we now guard it so closely. [20]

National had good reason to trademark its name. The Highway 12 had been accepted by the public, with sales in 1916 increasing more than 300 percent over the record in 1915. To support the growth in automobile sales, the company expanded its factory. Before the introduction of the Highway 12, National had employed 500 people and shipped out four freight cars of automobiles daily. By April 1916, employment had grown to nearly 1,000 and the company was shipping ten freight cars daily.[21]

Despite increasing the size of its plant, Cole found itself out of room to meet the demand for its cars. The company responded by moving the factory service department to another location in downtown Indianapolis and by concreting a large court on which to store frames at the main plant. The success of the Model 860 Cole Eight, introduced in January, was responsible for production in March 1916 of four times the level of production in March 1915.[22]

Convinced of the superiority of its car to others in the same price range, Cole challenged its customers to design their own road test. Most Cole dealers adopted the slogan, "Pick out your own test; the harder it is, the better it suits us." What might seem pure folly to a consumer imparted confidence in the construction of the car. General Manager A. F. Knobloch said, "Of course, we feel sure that the Cole Eight will prove equal to any reasonable trial, or we would not allow our dealers to use a slogan of that nature."[23]

For companies like Empire which did not participate in the racing game, various long distance runs continued to be an important aspect of proving the sturdiness and worth of a car. Starting from San Francisco, Bobby Hammond established a new record[24] of 6 days 10 hours 58 minutes[25] driving to New York City. The previous record had been established several weeks before by Cadillac; Hammond beat it by 25 hours.[26]

In April 1916, it was announced that Johnny Aitken, the very successful race car driver associated with National who later headed the pit crew for National in 1912 and the French

Pathfinder introduced its 12-cylinder car in 1916 (*Horseless Age*, February 1, 1916).

1916 Cole (LeRoy Cole Collection, Gilmore Car Museum).

team in 1913, would drive a Speedway Team Company Peugeot in the 1916 International race in Indianapolis.[27]

Leading up to the Indianapolis race there was a day of racing at Sheepshead Bay, New York. Aitken in the Speedway Team Peugeot easily won the 20-mile Coney Island Cup race. In the 50-mile Queen's Trophy race, Aitken's car's connecting rod bearings burned out on the 42nd mile. In the 150-mile feature event, the Prest-O-Lite team scored a victory, with Eddie Rickenbacker in a Maxwell taking home the Metropolitan Trophy and a $15,000 purse at an average speed of 96.23 miles per hour. Proudly watching Rickenbacker and Aitken were Carl Fisher, Jim Allison, and Frank Wheeler.[28]

The Indianapolis Motor Speedway reduced the 1916 race to 300 miles for non-stock cars with a maximum engine displacement of 300 cubic inches and a weight not to exceed 2,500 pounds. The drivers battled for $30,000 in prize money and three trophies to be awarded: the Remy Brassard Trophy, the Prest-O-Lite Trophy, and the Wheeler-Schebler Trophy.[29] Traditionally the race was started at 10 a.m., but with a shorter 300-mile contest, Speedway management established the start time at 1:30 p.m.[30] Howard Marmon was named the race's official starter.[31]

When Stutz didn't enter the Indianapolis race, Gil Andersen initially decided he wasn't going to participate. But the pull of Indianapolis was too strong and Andersen was cleared by Stutz to drive any make he desired in the race. Harry Stutz said,

I do not feel it is fair to Gil to interfere with his taking part in racing simply because we have made up our minds to stay out of all speed contests until our world's record and past performances are tied or beaten. The best of feeling prevails between Mr. Anderson [sic] and the Stutz company, in fact, he is still connected with us. If Stutz cars ever need to race again, we all hope that Gil will be behind the wheel. We wish him the best of luck in all of his races and will all pull for him.[32]

Andersen found a ride with Premier as part of a three-car team. The other two cars would be piloted by Tom Rooney, another former Stutz mechanic and driver, and Harry Stillman.[33]

A week before the race, bookies had Dario Resta as the odds-on favorite to win. Eddie Rickenbacker, driving a Prest-O-Lite Maxwell, and Josef Christiaens, driving a Sunbeam, had odds of five to one, Aitken's odds were six to one, and Barney Oldfield's odds were eight to one.[34] Only 21 cars qualified to run in the race. Oldfield thrilled the crowd, estimated at 10,000, when he established a new record for the track, going 102.623 miles per hour for one lap during qualifying. After setting the new record, Oldfield took the old four-cylinder Premier built for Fisher around the track with an average speed of 63 miles per hour. The three Premier cars built by J. L. Yarian qualified for the race. Two of the Premiers had only two or three days' practice, while the one piloted by Howdy Wilcox had been driven only 25 miles before qualifying.[35]

As the countdown to the Indianapolis 300-mile race continued, the Hoosier Motor Club presented Harry Stutz with a bronze tablet on behalf of the citizens of Indianapolis for the fame his racing team had brought to the city. The tablet said, "The Citizens of Indianapolis present this token of their esteem to the Stutz Motor Car Co." The tablet listed all of the victories Stutz racers had achieved in 1915.[36]

Dario Resta won the 1916 Indianapolis race, averaging 84.05 miles per hour[37] and receiving $12,000[38] for his efforts. Resta took the lead at 50 miles and never relinquished it, winning the Remy Grand Brassard, the Prest-O-Lite Trophy, and the Wheeler-Schebler Trophy for being in the lead at 100, 200 and 250 miles respectively. Andersen, driving a Premier for Howdy Wilcox, placed seventh. Johnny Aitken, driving the Speedway Team's Peugeot, was in second place when a broken valve ended his day of racing at 175 miles.[39]

Needing more space, Stutz built a four-story building just north of its existing factory. With measurements of 204 feet long and 70 feet wide, this addition doubled the company's manufacturing space.[40]

While not participating in racing, Pathfinder found a way to promote its twin six automobile. The company drove a 12-cylinder stock car from coast to coast using only the high and reverse gears. The car was painted red, white and blue and bore the emblem of the Lincoln Highway Association on its side. Henie Scholler, pilot, and Walter Weidley left San Diego on July 1 and headed across the United States using the Lincoln Highway. The transmission of the car was sealed by a representative of the AAA.[41] The car finished its 4,889-mile journey across the United States on August 1 having averaged ten miles per gallon of gasoline. After arriving in New York City, the car was driven to Sheepshead Bay Speedway where it successfully attained a speed of 60 miles per hour.[42] This trip was not meant to establish any speed records, as W. E. Stalnaker, sales manager, explained.

> No attempt at excessive speed is being made on this trip. This is not a run to beat speed records, but is a test which we consider infinitely greater—a test of flexibility and endurance which will cause Pathfinder the Great to be proclaimed King of Twelves" without a dissenting voice.[43]

For the summer, Cole introduced a four-passenger Tuxedo roadster. Built upon a 127-

inch wheelbase, the car had a Northway eight-cylinder engine which produced between 70 and 75 horsepower. The car featured a dry and dust-free compartment for the storage area, which was accessible by tilting the back seat forward a few inches. The car also had side vanity pockets for the storage of things such as goggles or veils. A. F. Knobloch described the car:

> Our Tuxedo roadster is not only a dress car for city driving, it is an ideal recreation car for the doctor, sportsman, businessman, or woman, whether for long jaunts or short tours. When our designers were set at work on this model, they were told to produce something new and more efficient for general purposes.[44]

Although Marmon had always sold a limited number of closed automobiles, the company announced that the fall 1916 cars would all be closed and built upon the 34 chassis. The bodies would be built by specialty coach companies including Holbrook & Company of New York, New Haven Carriage Company, Kimball & Company of Chicago, and E. J. Thompson Company of Pittsburg. Depending upon the type of body selected, the car would weigh between 3,800 and 4,000 pounds. One of the features of the Marmon enclosed-body cars was the windows. Indianapolis Marmon branch manager A. B. Wagner explained:

> In the past these bodies have been constructed with hinged windows and uprights which folded down into the inside of the body and were covered by a sheet metal flap. This construction allowed for only two positions—either completely closed with no ventilation, or fully open with too much ventilation. However, in the new type of construction, such as used on the Marmon 34 bodies, the steel framed windows slide up and down and only the uprights fold to the inside. Quarter windows are removed and placed behind the upholstery of the rear seat. By having the windows slide rather than fold, the windows may be partially opened for ventilation. This is an important provision which will be found first in Marmon bodies.[45]

In June 1916, controlling interest in Stutz was sold to a New York consortium headed by Allan A. Ryan, a New York financier. Ryan pledged that Stutz operations would not be changed. The officers of the new corporation, Stutz Motor Car Company of America (Stutz), included Harry Stutz, president; Allan A. Ryan, vice president; and George H. Saylor of Chase Bank, secretary/treasurer.[46] In July, Stutz Motor Car Company of Indianapolis declared a dividend of $125,000 payable to its parent, Stutz Motor Car Company of America.[47]

In July, Cole introduced the eight-cylinder Cole-Springfield Toursedan, designed to give moderate priced buyers the advantages of a luxurious touring car and a limousine. The car was a year-round model with the roof being built as part of the car, unlike other cars which had a detachable top. Cole advertised that the switch from summer to winter driving could be done by a man, a woman, or a child. The windows at the sides and rear of the car could easily be removed and stored in padded cases. When winter weather returned, the car could become a closed car by lifting the windows from their padded cases and slipping them into place. Cole expected this innovation to revolutionize the car industry. The cost of the seven passenger Toursedan was $2,195.[48] The car's standard body color was American Flag Blue. The company offered an option for the interior finish of either a gray coach cloth or a French-plaited leather. Other features included lights that illuminated when the car was entered, push-button locks, a cigar lighter, and floor exhausts to keep feet warm during the cold winter months.[49] Cole also offered two other models using the Cole-Springfield body: the Tourcoupe, also selling for $2,195, and a Towncar with a retail price of $2,495.[50] Joseph Cole said,

> Any one at all acquainted with motor cars knows that the best running motor is the one that is worked consistently and given adequate attention. Disuse breeds depreciation just as surely as does misuse.

Therefore the only alternative is the construction of a car which will assure its owner of absolute comfort during the coldest and most disagreeable weather. No one cares to ride in a car half frozen, even for economical reasons.[51]

Although the United States wasn't directly involved with World War I, increases in the price of raw materials led National to increase the cost of the Highway 12 beginning in July 1916. George Dickson explained the increase in pricing:

It would be folly for the National Company to attempt to hold their present price by reducing the quality of materials that enters into the construction of the twelve-cylinder car.

Practically every piece of material that enters into the construction of the National 12-cylinder motors has increased in costs. Furthermore, our mechanics are receiving the highest wages in the history of our company. We build our own 12-cylinder motors and, regardless of cost, we do not allow the quality of the strict inspection to depreciate in the slightest degree.[52]

Indianapolis cars fared well at the races at Sioux City, Iowa. Howdy Wilcox, driving a Premier, won the 50-mile feature event, driving at an average speed of 72.57 miles per hour. In the ten-mile race, Wilbur D'Alene driving a Duesenberg set the pace at 79.64 miles per hour, followed by Charlie Merz driving a Peugeot. Howdy Wilcox in a Premier placed fourth. Wilcox won the 20-mile race with an average speed of 78.52 miles per hour, followed by D'Alene in a Duesenberg in second and Merz driving a Peugeot in third.[53]

In late July, a Marmon driven by millionaire sportsman Samuel B. Stevens of Rome, New York, set a new record traveling the Lincoln Highway from Columbus Circle in New York City to Third and Market Streets in San Francisco, a distance of 3,476 miles in 5 days 18 hours and 30 minutes. The previous record for the trip was lowered by 41 and ½ hours for 3,371 miles from Los Angeles to New York. The car was a standard Marmon 34 model with the tonneau removed and an auxiliary fuel tank added for the western part of the trip. Stevens, the head of the American Defense Society, made the trip to test the speed of motor transportation across the United States.[54] The AAA sealed the car prior to it leaving New York and certified that it had not been repaired, other than tires and wheels, in the dash across the country, adding another feather to the Marmon cap.[55] This car was featured in the Marmon exhibit at the Indiana State Fair along with a Marmon 34 with an enclosed body.[56]

Needing more room for its expanding operations, National announced the construction of a 68,400-square-foot, three-story concrete building at its facilities on 22nd Street at a cost of $60,000.[57] Less than a month later, the company bought a city block that had previously consisted of small one-story homes across Yandes Street from the original location. In addition to the previously announced three-story building, the company built a 45,920-square-foot single story structure[58] at a cost of $15,000.[59]

Just as Marmon released an auto reminiscent of the Marmon Wasp, National also played upon the success of its early racers. George Dickson explained,

The National car acquired the keynote of its character in its early racing days. Every individual National car is somewhat reminiscent of the race track. The lines of this latest National Highway Twelve are lines that bespeak good blue-blooded breeding. They give to the National car a look of strength and cleanliness and aggressiveness that no other car begins to possess.[60]

The introduction of the 1917 National Highway 12 included improvements to the one introduced the prior year. The 1917 model had a larger body with improved seating for the passengers, enough room for seven passengers, and folding seats which were covered when in a folded position, making them disappear. On the outside, the doors were flush with the body, giving the car a smooth exterior, and the windshield was set at an angle, decreasing wind resistance, eliminating glare, and giving the car a sleeker look.[61]

National tested the Highway 12 at the Indianapolis Motor Speedway. Wanting to get some hill work in, Aitken tested the car on Tabor Hill near Bloomington, Indiana, considered to be Indiana's toughest hill. Afterwards, seeking more difficulty, the company's engineers took six cars to Uniontown, Pennsylvania, which had a three-mile run with a grade between 8 and 10 percent. The results of the test at Uniontown were described as remarkable. The Highway 12's average speed was 34 miles per hour in high gear with seven passengers, a full tank of gas, and the windshield and top up. Some National Sixes were also tested on the hill, where they were able to start and maintain an average speed of ten miles per hour.[62]

Premier introduced a seven-passenger auto featuring an aluminum engine and a Cutler-Hammer magnetic gear shift as standard equipment. As with the Marmon car, Premier lined the cylinders with cast iron. The car was built upon a 125½-inch wheelbase and had a price of $1,685.[63] Premier was able to achieve this lower price point by using a combination of parts purchased from specialized manufacturers, such as Timken axles and Delco electric starters and lighting systems, and parts manufactured in house, such as the aluminum engine.[64]

Gil Andersen parted company with the Premier racing team and purchased the Stutz racer in which he had become the nation's speed king. As the private owner of the car, he could enter whatever races he desired. First on his list were a 300-mile Labor Day Weekend race in Cincinnati and the Harvest Auto Racing Classic at the Indianapolis Motor Speedway the following week.[65] The race at Cincinnati wasn't kind to Andersen, who suffered a broken leg when he was ejected from his car. Traveling at an estimated 100 miles per hour, Andersen was following a car whose tire blew and hit the right front of Andersen's racer, causing the machine to spin around. His riding mechanic, Bert Shields, sustained significant injuries including a broken back.[66]

Of the 29 cars which started the Labor Day race at Cincinnati, only seven finished, led by Aitken with an average speed of 97.06 miles per hour before an estimated 50,000 fans, including Arthur Newby who watched from the judge's stand. Five of the seven cars which completed the 300-mile drive had Duesenberg engines. Aitken's Speedway Team Peugeot was one of the two cars without a Duesenberg engine. Indianapolis-based drivers who dropped out of the race included Charlie Merz in a Speedway Team Peugeot on the 42nd lap, Howdy Wilcox on the 47th lap, Pete Henderson on the 71st lap, Dave Lewis on the 81st lap, and Eddie Rickenbacker, driving the Prest-O-Lite Maxwell, on the 108th lap.[67]

Stutz Bulldog Special (*Horseless Age*, August 21, 1916).

Management of the Indianapolis Motor Speedway held the Harvest Auto Racing Classic in the fall with three events—a 100-mile, a 50-mile, and a 25-mile race.[68] Aitken took home the honors in each of the races. In the 25-mile race, he averaged 95.08 miles per hour, and in the 50-mile race he averaged 91.85. The 100-mile event was the most exciting. Aitken drove the last eight miles with a broken steering arm, chasing down Eddie Rickenbacker. On the final lap, Rickenbacker went out when both rear wheels collapsed. Aitken's average speed was 89.44 miles per hour.[69]

Stutz introduced its Series R, which included a new four-cylinder car known as the Bulldog Special priced at $2,550. This car was available with either four- or six-passenger seating. The company continued to produce its popular roadster priced at $2,275. Unlike most automobile manufacturers, which had switched to the left-hand position for the driver, the Stutz cars continued to have the driver seated on the right side. Built on a 130-inch wheelbase, the cars were available in battleship gray and Mercedes red with a choice of interior finish of either hand-buffed black leather or hand-buffed Spanish brown.[70]

The National Motor Car & Vehicle Corporation (National) was established under the laws of New York in early November 1916 as a holding company for the National Motor Vehicle Company by a consortium of New York financiers. Capitalization consisted of 80,000 shares, of which 27,000 were for the existing stockholders while the remaining 53,000 were available for sale. The stock offering estimated the company would sell 6,000 cars during its current fiscal year ending July 1, 1917, with profits between $1 million and $1.1 million. The output for the fiscal year ended July 1, 1916, was 2,499 cars with a net profit of $425,000. The National Motor Vehicle Company had no mortgage, no bonds, and no preferred debt at the time of the stock offering. The new company hoped to be listed on the New York Stock

1917 Stutz Series R owned by Dave Marriner (courtesy Graeme Bristow).

Series Eight Cole roadster (Indiana Historical Society, P0555).

Exchange.⁷¹ While National's existing management was to remain in place, Indianapolis banker Stoughton A. Fletcher joined the board of directors. The stock issue was very successful, being over-subscribed by almost two thirds. The increase in capitalization was used to support the growth in sales.⁷²

With three championship races left in 1916, Johnny Aitken stood at the top of the racers, with Dario Resta in second place and Eddie Rickenbacker in third. When Rickenbacker's contract to head up the Prest-O-Lite Team expired, he left the team and entered the Vanderbilt Cup driving a Duesenberg.⁷³

As the 21 teams prepared to do battle in the Vanderbilt Cup, Johnny Aitken, who would start fifth in the race, was confident about his chances: "It is a tough bunch to go against. I will get all there is out of my Peugeot and, barring mishaps, should be out in front at the final lap."⁷⁴ The drivers were vying for $7,500 in gold to be divided among the top four finishers, plus 1,750 points in the driving championship.⁷⁵ Aitken didn't finish the Vanderbilt Cup race as he was sidelined with a broken crankshaft, lessening his chances to win the AAA championship. Dario Resta won the race, taking home $4,000 in prize money. Earl Cooper, driving a Stutz, finished second. Resta also ended up on top of the leaderboard with 4,100 points in the national championship, followed by Aitken with 3,440 points and Eddie Rickenbacker with 2,210 points.⁷⁶

Two days after running the Vanderbilt Cup on the Santa Monica Raceway, the racing teams got ready to do battle for the Grand Prize, a 403-mile race. The favorites to win the race and a prize totaling $13,500 were Resta in a Peugeot, Aitken in the Speedway Team's Peugeot, Rickenbacker and Weightman driving Duesenbergs, and Cooper driving a Stutz.

Both Aitken's and Rickenbacker's cars had been repaired from the broken parts which put them out of the Vanderbilt race. Jim Allison watched[77] as Wilcox and Aitken as the relief driver in the Speedway Team Company Peugeot won the Grand Prize race. Johnny Aitken was given credit for the win with an average speed of 85.59 miles per hour. Earl Cooper in his Stutz finished the race in second place.[78]

With the price of raw materials continuing to rise, another round of price increases was announced by the Indianapolis manufacturers. Marmon announced a second price increase of its Marmon 34 effective January 1, 1917, but didn't state the amount of the increase.[79] Cole announced a price increase on its eight-cylinder touring car and roadster by $100 on January 1. Although it was not announced, the other Cole models were expected to increase by $200.[80] Empire also announced a second price increase due to inflationary pressure.[81] Putting a positive spin on the price increase, the company advertised that it was the only car priced under $2,000 with a T-head engine. The four-cylinder 45 had a new sales price of $960.[82]

Empire unveiled its first closed car for the 1917 model year. The six-cylinder Model 70, constructed on a 120-inch wheelbase, could be converted in the summer to a convertible by removing the windows. The car had two doors situated about mid-way on the body, which gave access to the back seat. The front seats were accessed by a center aisle.[83]

National dealers were delighted with the announcement of a new body style for the Highway Six model in either a blue or a gray available in 1917 without additional cost. It was very similar to the body on the popular National 12 and had the same features, with a tilted windshield to reduce wind resistance and glare, an ignition lock, and doors that swung open with the curtains adjusted.[84]

Premier started producing automobiles in late November or early December, and by December 12 was producing seven vehicles per day. The company believed that production would grow to ten cars per day by the end of the month and 20 cars per day during January 1917. The production target for 1917 was 7,500 cars.[85]

Premier had issued $1 million in bonds for a period of five years with interest at 5 percent. The repayment schedule was $100,000 on November 1, 1918, $200,000 on November 1, 1919, $300,000 on November 1, 1920, and $400,000 on November 1, 1921. According to the bond prospectus, the company had orders for 2,600 cars by January 1, 1917, and 7,500 cars during 1917.[86] However, since the bond prospectus was dated from November 1916 and the company was just beginning production, there was no possibility of meeting the projected production of 2,600 cars by January 1, 1917. Premier also announced a price increase on all of its models because of the rise in the cost of raw materials.[87]

11

The War Years

After President Woodrow Wilson's administration racked up $300 million of debt, Treasury Secretary William G. McAdoo proposed a tax on automobiles of $1 per horsepower. Not only did the manufacturers oppose this tax, they also felt it singled out the automobile industry, like the proposed tax on horsepower in 1915. Indianapolis manufacturers joined in the widespread condemnation of this proposed tax. National's George Dickson commented,

> We are already paying double tax on automobiles. First, we are already paying tax on autos as personal property, and second, a tax to use the state highways. This third tax would be unjust and the ultimate consumer, as in all like cases, would have to pay the cost. It simply would cause the manufacturers to add to the cost of their product.[1]

Indianapolis manufacturers showed off their new models at the New York Auto Show in early January 1917. Stutz, along with White Motor Company, introduced a 16-valve engine. Following in the footsteps of Marmon, Premier introduced an aluminum engine, becoming the second manufacturer to use aluminum motors in its vehicles. The overhead six-cylinder engine, which weighed 225 pounds less than a similar cast iron engine, had 72 horsepower.[2] Use of the aluminum engine made the car more even in weight distribution and enabled Premier to use a heavier frame, resulting in the car being easier to drive.[3] Premier also introduced the Cutler-Hammer electric gearshift as a part of the standard equipment package.[4] This gearshift consisted of three buttons on the steering column with each controlling a gear speed, making shifting gears easy.[5]

National's Six included the Prest-O-Lite vacuum brake,[6] which through the use of a lever applied pressure from the intake manifold on the rear brakes. This invention was said to "relieve the driver of muscular effort under any conditions, by the employment of engine power."[7]

Empire displayed a new, longer six-cylinder car with a 120-inch wheelbase available in two color combinations: cobalt blue with a black interior or autumn brown with a Spanish brown interior. Auxiliary seats, which folded into the front seats when not in use, were optional on the five-person car.[8] The five-person, six-cylinder car had a price of $1,235 while the seven-person option retailed for $1,265.[9] The company also unveiled a new two-passenger speedster complete with wire wheels[10] for $1,165.[11] The speedster, available in vermillion red or canary yellow, was equipped with a 40-horsepower Teeter-Hartley T-head engine.[12]

The Lyons-Knight automobile had quietly faded from the automobile landscape. In February 1917, the Atlas-Lyons Company announced the purchase and relocation of the Hume Manufacturing Company, a well established tractor manufacturer, to Indianapolis to occupy the Lyons-Atlas plant. At the time of the purchase, Lyons-Atlas was primarily engaged in the manufacture of engines and employed about 1,200 people.[13]

Cole announced a doubling of its production in 1917. One of the keys that allowed Cole to meet this goal when there were multiple material shortages was that Cole had contracted with Northway for engines eight months earlier. Cole also made sure that Northway had enough raw materials to complete the contracts.[14] The doubling of production meant that Cole was the third most popular of all brands built in the United States at its price point or higher.[15]

A new entrant to the Indianapolis automobile manufacturing group was Robert H. Hassler, Inc., which unveiled its four-cylinder roadster at the Chicago Auto Show. The car had a proprietary spring suspension, which led to the tag line of "the restful riding car." The company was started by Robert Hassler, whose company produced shock absorbers for Ford Motor Company.[16] Designed by Charlie Merz, the former race car driver on the National team, the Hassler car reportedly produced 40 horsepower. The two-seat roadster sold for $1,650. Production was limited, and with the onset of the United States' involvement in World War I, the company ceased operations.[17]

There was a small mention in the *Indianapolis Star* of the formation of Federated Motors Company by a syndicate led by Broughton & Company of New York to take over the business of Pathfinder Company and another unnamed Indiana automobile manufacturer. The two companies would merge at the Indianapolis Pathfinder factory. Capitalization of the new company was reported to be $5 million. The announcement was anticipated on January 11, but no confirmation of the formation of Federated Motors Company appeared in the *Indianapolis Star*.[18]

Pathfinder Company building (Bass Photo Co. Collection, Indiana Historical Society).

Rather than becoming a part of Federated Motors, Pathfinder announced that its authorized capitalization had been increased to $5 million, consisting of $2 million in preferred stock and $3 million in capital stock. The increase in the capitalization of the company was driven by the strong demand for the Pathfinder. The company was producing three times the projected number of automobiles. The stock issue was underwritten by A. R. Sheffer & Company with offices in the Midwest, including Indianapolis.[19] The sale of Pathfinder stock must not have been well received in the market. In April, A. R. Sheffer & Company ran a long advertisement imploring Indianapolis residents to purchase the stock. In part, the advertisement said,

> The Pathfinder Company did a business last year of $2,000,000 on small capital, which they had to turn over ten times, or every five weeks.
>
> They have produced the best and most talked about car in the market today. Orders have been pouring in—more money is needed. We have put their new stock on sale all over the country. Ninety percent of this money is coming from outside of Indiana.
>
> Do you want the Pathfinder Company to stay in Indianapolis? They are asking no charity—your investment is a good, reliable one in an established business. Why is Detroit and Michigan growing so fast in automobile building? They support and invest in their home companies.[20]

In early May, A. R. Sheffer & Company ran another long advertisement promoting the 7 percent premium on the Pathfinder preferred stock. It also reassured investors that their money was safe. The preferred stock was secured by a first lien on the assets of the company and no

Ezra Meeker, who had traveled the Oregon Trail in an oxcart, took a trip across America in 1916 in a modified Pathfinder to memorialize the Oregon Trail (Bass Photo Co. Collection, Indiana Historical Society).

other preferred stock or debt instrument could be issued until the preferred stock was redeemed. The advertisement appealed to the local pride of Indianapolis residents and implored them to show their loyalty through investing in the Pathfinder equity issue.[21]

Compared with the companies operating out of Detroit, which produced cars by the hundreds, by mid–March 1917 National was producing 35 cars per day.[22] National was also bucking the national trend of using dynamometers to test its cars prior to shipping them to the automobile dealers, opting instead for the old fashioned method of using testers to drive the cars around town and at the Indianapolis Motor Speedway to discover any flaws in the vehicle. The testers were also used on the experimental models developed by the company.[23] One of the experimental models in 1917 was a four-passenger sport phaeton model available as either a six-cylinder or a 12-cylinder model. It was roomier than the National Cloverleaf model but not as spacious as the seven-passenger touring car.[24]

The National 12 was available in a seven-passenger touring car, a four-passenger sport phaeton, or a four-passenger roadster, with all three body styles being priced at $2,250. The company offered the choice of either pearl gray or blue for the exterior finish of the car.[25]

Premier introduced a four-passenger roadster, the Foursome, at the Indianapolis Auto Show. The car had four doors, a feature which was unique at the time in a roadster, enabling the backseat passengers to get into and out of the car easily. Access to the trunk of the car was through the hinged upholstered backseat cushion. This had the advantage of keeping the luggage area dry as well as eliminating clanging from the trunk.[26]

On the evening of March 9, a fire, believed to have been caused by spontaneous combustion, broke out in Cole's third floor finishing room, causing an estimated $15,000 in damage. The finishing room contained car bodies which were drying after having been finished and trimmed. The fire was spotted by some truckers, who noticed smoke coming from the east side of the building and sounded the alarm. As the Indianapolis Fire Department worked to extinguish the blaze, the salvage corps spread covers over the cars on the second floor, shielding them from the water cascading from the third floor.[27] After the fire was extinguished, another crew turned excess space on the fourth floor into a temporary finishing area. The workmen were successful, as a temporary finishing area was ready by 7 a.m. the next morning.

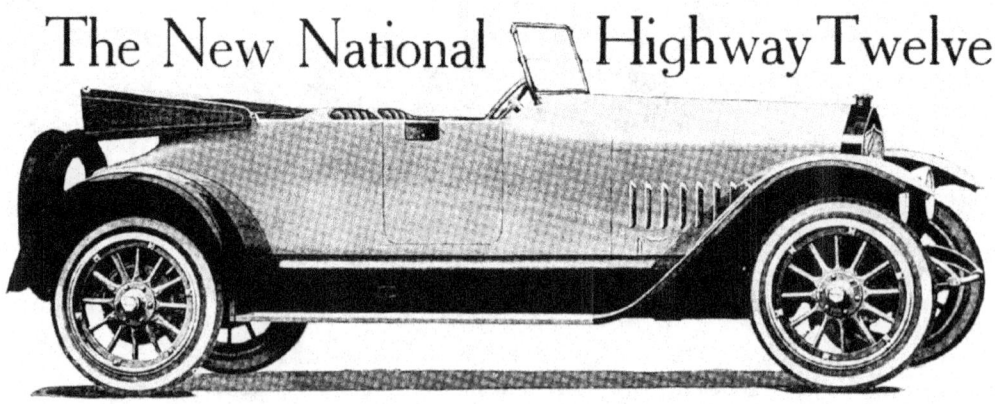

National Highway 12 model (*Horseless Age*, June 1, 1917).

Just as it is today, regular maintenance of a car was essential to keep a car in good running order. The Cole Sales Company of Indiana, the local distributors for Cole automobiles, established its "flying squadron" with this in mind. J. S. McFarland explained:

> This consists of a corps of expert mechanics who make it a point to visit every Cole eight owner on our list at intervals and simply look over the car. They are liable to drop in most any morning just as the owner is starting out for the day to look the car over—see that it starts properly and that everything is in adjustment. Further than that, if any minor adjustment is required, the mechanic calls it to the attention of the owner before it becomes serious.[28]

One of the plans considered by the Federal Government to support the war effort was to have the production of steel diverted for military use and the contracts between the steel mills and the automobile companies cancelled.[29] Developed by Bernard Baruch,[30] head of the War Industries Board, this plan was a direct and imminent danger to the auto industry. While some felt that the government would not take this draconian step, others felt that if it was enacted, the industry's survival was in peril. Harry Stutz planned to immediately buy $2 million in steel if the plan was implemented. Cole's Charles Henderson felt the proposed takeover of the steel industry would happen:

> We are preparing ourselves with the view that the government will assume control of the steel industry. If the supply is shut off to auto manufacturers it will be the worst thing that has come up in the industry.[31]

George Dickson of National had a more positive outlook:

> I suppose if the plan is really carried out in the manner which it is interpreted it will be a serious handicap to the industry, but very few of the steel men I have talked with seem to think that such drastic action will be necessary. The volume of steel used in the auto business is so small when compared to that used in other work that I am of the opinion that other industries will be shut off before the auto industry.[32]

As it became clearer that the United States would inevitably be pulled into World War I, one of the initiatives the government took was to increase the airpower of the United States. Howard Marmon was selected to lead a group of engineers to France to study airplane motor building on behalf of the government.[33]

After the United States declared war on Germany on April 17, 1917, the government started issuing Liberty Bonds to support the war needs. Throughout the country, peer pressure encouraged all to "do their full duty" and the government assigned a quota for counties to reach a certain level of participation. Marion County (Indianapolis area) was assigned to raise $11 million in Liberty Bonds. The Indianapolis community, including the automobile and related manufacturers, responded. Typical of the effort, Nordyke & Marmon canvassed its 2,000 employees. The company held group meetings where employees were invited to invest their savings in Liberty Bonds. To help spur saving, the company devised a payment plan for the purchase of bonds. Adding pressure for the purchase of the bonds were meetings with individual employees to help them choose the best payment plan and to fill out the application.[34] Within two weeks, Nordyke & Marmon had purchased $50,000 in Liberty Bonds and its employees had subscribed an additional $127,500 in bonds.[35]

Two months later, another effort to promote the sale of Liberty Bonds resulted in 1,000 Nordyke & Marmon employees investing in the bonds. Walter Marmon believed it was the patriotic duty of citizens to buy the bonds and purchased $100,000 worth of the bonds to be distributed to Nordyke & Marmon employees.[36]

After the United States entered World War I, companies across the country mobilized for the war effort. Nordyke & Marmon won a contract for 3,000 airplane engines valued at $2.7 million to be delivered by June 1, 1918. Reportedly, this was one of the largest airplane engine contracts awarded by the War Department.[37] Prior to the issuance of the Liberty engine contract, the company had agreed to build 2,500 Hall & Scott engines for use in training planes. After the company had built 1,000 Hall & Scott engines, the Federal Government urged it to switch to building the Liberty engines. This meant the company had to absorb the cost of the tooling for the Hall & Scott engines without having a full run.[38] To support the engine production, Nordyke & Marmon planned a 27,000-square-foot, one-story steel and glass expansion to its manufacturing facilities[39] at a cost of $400,000.[40] Although there were parallels between an automobile and an aircraft engine, it was necessary for the company to retool with additional machinery and equipment[41] at a cost of $1.5 million.[42] Walter Marmon discussed the company's desire to aid the government, which started about when diplomatic relations with Germany were severed in February 1917:

> We felt this meant war and like many other American industrial plants we at once began to figure how we could help. Our offers were accepted later and a program was laid down for us that was dumfounding in its magnitude.[43]

Nearby Allison Engineering, started by Jim Allison to maintain the race cars at the Indianapolis Motor Speedway, worked in concert with Nordyke & Marmon in development of the airplane engines. Allison also produced a variety of war machines. National built trucks as part of the mobilization.[44] Engine supplier Weidley Motors won a $20 million contract from Cleveland Tractor to build 15,000 motors in 1918, 25,000 in 1919, and 30,000 in 1920. To meet the need for additional working capital, Weidley Motors issued $400,000 in preferred stock. The company also planned a $150,000 expansion to its manufacturing facilities.[45]

Indianapolis automobile manufacturers lent some of their top engineers to the war effort. The engineers were called upon to advise the government on the development of aircraft engines, motors, motor trucks, and tractors as well as the building of factories for the war effort both in the United States and in France. William Guy Wall, National's vice president and engineer, was assigned to the motor equipment division in Washington, D.C., to motorize the artillery, which previously had been powered by horses. Howard Marmon, after serving in France, was stationed at the aviation station in Dayton, Ohio, where he was involved with the design of the Liberty aircraft engine. Cole's M. B. Morgan was assigned to Washington, D.C., to purchase equipment for the mobile machine shops which followed the Army. Earl G. Gunn, an engineer with Premier, served in the Signal Corps, as did Everett G. White, the purchasing agent for Empire.[46]

Just as they were in World War II and during the oil embargo of the 1970s, Americans were urged to conserve gasoline. The AAA joined the Bureau of Mines and the Council of National Defense to begin a "Don't Waste" campaign. The Bureau of Mines estimated that the nation wasted 1.5 million gallons of gasoline daily and identified multiple ways for the public to join in on the "Don't Waste" campaign. The primary waste of gasoline identified was needless use of passenger cars at 807,400 gallons per day. The second source of waste was poorly adjusted carburetors at 240,000 gallons per day, followed by motors running while idling at 150,000 gallons per day.[47]

Marmon used the "Don't Waste" campaign to promote the Marmon 34. Herbert Rice, sales manager, talked about the gasoline-efficient Marmon 34:

> Take, for instance, the gasoline savings effected by the eliminated weight of each Marmon 34. Through the use of aluminum, scientific design and other factors this car is 1,100 pounds lighter than comparable cars. This represents a comprehensible gasoline saving every time a car of this model is run a mile. That the owner of a Marmon 34 saves the gasoline it would take to propel an extra ton through the life of his car may seem to him a thing of small moment and in no-wise a public service. A little figuring nevertheless will prove to him that he is helping in a very important manner at the big task of the day.
>
> To date 5,500 Marmon 34s have been delivered. The 1,100 pounds of eliminated weight each of these cars represent mean that the 5,500 cars have saved the gasoline necessary for the transportation of some 6,050,000 pounds or 3,025 tons. The 3,025 tons converted into cars would mean 1,784 Marmon 34s and the gasoline these would consume in a year of average use may make the saving more tangible.[48]

The success of the Marmon 34 resulted in the need for expanded manufacturing facilities. Marmon responded with a one-story, 60,000-square-foot addition at a cost of approximately $150,000.[49] Later in the year, the company also made enhancements to its Marmon 34, including making the car "thief proof." Marmon engineers designed a special gear shift lock which, when engaged, would keep the car in neutral. Operation was through a Yale key which also secured the hinged tool shelf in the left front door and the spare tire in the rear of the car.[50]

On the day war was declared on Germany, Cole started affixing the national flag emblem to the windshield of every automobile leaving the factory. Cole also sent a supply of the stickers to its distributors for already owned Coles.[51] Cole was also a leader in the Liberty Bonds being sold to finance the war effort. One of the innovative ideas to help both the war effort and the consumer was the company's plan to accept Liberty Bonds for payment on the purchase of a Cole car. As an incentive, the company provided $102 for each $100 bond presented for the purchase of an auto. Any bonds garnered by Cole would be turned over to the banks, which were eager to hold them in their investment portfolios.[52]

In May Cole announced a new type of wheel for the Cole Eight. The company substituted a rolled steel felloe for the previously used bent wood felloe. The spokes of the new wheel were assembled alternately from opposite sides of the wheel. When they got to the felloe, they were forced together under 40 tons of pressure. The Goodrich steel felloe prevented the loosening of the felloe band and eliminated the need for a locking ring on the rim, giving the wheel a sleeker appearance.[53]

At the end of July, the Pathfinder Motor Company of America (Pathfinder) was organized in the state of Delaware with $2 million in capital stock and purchased the Pathfinder Company. In addition to the Pathfinder car, the company announced it would build trucks at the Indianapolis plant and would expand the manufacturing facilities. The officers of the new company included Charles McCutcheon, Indianapolis, president; Fred C. Dorn, Cleveland, Ohio, vice president; and Paul N. White, Indianapolis, secretary/treasurer. The directors included C. J. Root of Terre Haute, Indiana, as the chairman of the board, and Crawford Fairbanks of Terre Haute, Indiana, A. C. Brown of St. Louis, Missouri, William A. Umphrey of Indianapolis, Paul N. White of Indianapolis, and George Mosher of Los Angeles, California. The former officers of the firm were not part of the new organization.[54]

Empire showcased its automobile with a reliability run to Mackinaw City, Michigan. The six-cylinder car, loaded with five passengers and 200 pounds of luggage, made the 583-

mile trip in 21 hours 55 minutes. Traveling over heavily graveled roads, the car made the trip without a mechanical adjustment. Advertising of the run boasted that the car had "not one drop of water added to the radiator." After its return trip to Indianapolis, the advertisement went on to boast that the car "still [had] Indianapolis air in all four original tires."[55]

National's advertising wrapped itself in patriotism. With the development of the Liberty engine at Allison Engineering and production of the Liberty engine at Nordyke & Marmon, National used its development of the V-12 motor and low fuel consumption as its advertising hook.

> National—with airplane-type motor.
> For all of its elegance and comfort, there is no other thing in the National Touring Sedan that can compare with its 12-cylinder motor. Quick, competent and quiet, it has the airplane engine's staunchness as well as form. It makes this car as capable for cross-country driving as for city usage. Under all conditions, it is surprisingly economical of fuel.[56]

In a field of 27 racers, Earl Cooper driving a Stutz won the third annual 250-mile race at the Chicago Speedway with an average speed of 103.1 miles per hour. Cooper nosed out Ralph Mulford in a Hudson Super-Six, who had led the race at 100 and 200 miles.[57]

With prices of raw materials rising before the war and continuing to rise, an agreement was reached by President Woodrow Wilson and the steel companies for a 50 percent reduction in the price of raw steel. Many consumers believed there would be a corresponding reduction in the price of cars. The automobile companies were quick to quash this idea. Joseph Cole explained:

> Steel is just one of many contributing elements in automobile production. It is by no means the determining factor. Of course, without steel we cannot proceed. But there is so much difference between raw steel and steel as we automobile manufacturers use it that a cut in 50 percent of raw steel can bring little relief to us.
> For it is after the raw steel is bought and paid for that the automobile builder's expense begins. It must be refined; it must be made into suitable parts; it must be transported to our plants. These are all expensive operations that are increasing in cost from day to day. Furthermore, being compelled to buy our steel products months in advance, we are now operating and will continue to operate for months on materials purchased at the higher prices.[58]

In support of the war effort, Stutz offered to donate six chassis constructed especially for ambulance purposes to the Indiana National Guard. Upon hearing of the offer, the Parry Manufacturing Company, which was then building bodies, offered to build the bodies for the ambulances.[59] Cole was selected to provide a fleet of its eight-cylinder Toursedan to the United States Army for use by General Pershing's staff in France. The cars were modified for Army purposes and painted a "drab olive" with black interiors. The cars featured special lighting, heating and telephone equipment.[60]

Premier received good news with the awarding of a $10 million contract with the United States Government to build trucks for the war effort. With a shortage of men due to enlistments, Premier planned to hire and train between 300 and 400 women for the factory work.[61] Premier also planned to introduce a limousine-sedan which could be easily converted from a limousine to a touring car or a sedan.[62]

1917 was a very good year for Stutz. Production increased 43 percent, with 2,207 cars being built compared with 1,535 cars produced in 1916. The company announced a profit of $1,074,778, a growth of 65.6 percent over the profitability in 1916.[63]

The end for Pathfinder came quickly. After being acquired by Pathfinder Motor Company of America in late July, the Pathfinder jigs, dies, tools and blueprints were relocated to 430 North Capitol in January 1918. An announcement in the *Indianapolis Star* indicated that the same men who built the Pathfinder car were available to repair it.[64] The equipment, machinery, stock and finished cars of the Pathfinder was auctioned off on March 5, 1918.[65]

In an effort to ensure adequate fuel supplies, President Woodrow Wilson appointed Harry Garfield to head the newly established Federal Fuel Administration. This Administration imposed fuel controls, with an emphasis upon coal used by many industries for power and by homes for heating. Responding to shortages of coal in the Northeast caused by an unusually cold December 1917, the government took over the railroads, which were unable to keep up with the demand for coal. In January 1918, Garfield imposed an "idle Monday" order where all non-essential factories were shuttered for five consecutive days beginning January 18 and then every Monday through March 25.[66] This order, of course, impacted the auto industry in Indianapolis.

Some companies, including pharmaceutical manufacturer Eli Lilly & Company, agricultural pharmaceutical company Pitman-Moore Company, and Nordyke & Marmon got an exemption from the "idle Monday" order because of the critical need for their products. Nordyke & Marmon was granted an exemption for the building of aircraft engines, but this exemption did not apply to its milling equipment production. The manufacture of automobiles by Marmon, Premier, and other Indianapolis auto companies was affected. In one twist, office workers were able to continue working dressed in heavy clothing, as the order permitted the heating of buildings to a degree where pipes wouldn't freeze.[67] Premier was also exempted for the manufacture of government trucks.[68] The five-day mandated closing of the plants in January impacted National, Stutz, Empire, and Cole.[69]

Another aspect of the automobile industry impacted by the war effort was the shipment of cars, which had traditionally been done by the railroads. Instead of using freight cars to ship their cars throughout the United States, Marmon used "driveaways," where the cars would be driven to various dealerships.[70] With the cost of raw materials continuing to rise, Marmon announced a $200 price increase for its open automobiles. The new price for the four-passenger roadster and the seven-passenger touring car was $3,750; for the five-passenger touring car it was $3,700, and for a chassis with cowl it was $3,450.[71]

Despite the efforts to conserve fuel, the New York and Chicago auto shows went on. At the Chicago show National unveiled a new speedster, the Dispatch, with a 12-cylinder engine capable of obtaining speeds of up to 85 miles per hour.[72] Cole's exhibit included three Aero Eight models powered by aircraft engines with 80 horsepower, which joined its other offerings: a seven-passenger touring car, a four-passenger Tuxedo, the Tourcoupe, and the Toursedan. The Aero Eight was offered in roadster, speedster, and tourister models powered by a V-8 engine. The body style of the Cole roadster model resembled an aircraft with high cowls, low beveled panels, and large fenders to decrease air resistance.[73] The new streamlined design resulted in speeds being increased by ten miles per hour, and an improved radiator resulted in a 27 percent increase in cooling efficiency. Cole also improved the gasoline feed to the engine on long uphill climbs with a triple capacity vacuum tank[74]. Although it took a year to prove, the Aero Eight was also easy on tires, and the company began promoting that a Cole Aero Eight could get 15,000 miles in normal driving. Some customers had driven in excess of 21,000 miles on a set of tires.[75] J. S. McFarland, president of Lathrop-McFarland Company, sales agent for Cole, said of the design:

Few designers, it is said, have a real scientific foundation beyond the designs they conceive for automobile bodies. They simply endeavor to produce a body that is comfortable to ride in and pleasing to look at.

In the Aero-Eight the designers worked from an entirely new angle. Taking into account all that had been discovered by the engineers who have had the task of perfecting our war planes, they found that by adapting a similarly shaped and similarly constructed body to an automobile, they could add immeasurably to the performance of a car. The most equal balance was secured. The seating arrangement enabled them to place the passengers most advantageously so that the weight could be distributed over the entire frame instead of being concentrated at certain particular points.[76]

With the number of women drivers increasing due in part to men being called to serve in the armed forces, Cole adapted its automobiles with special equipment designed to appeal to women. Among these devices were long control and brake levers, an improved pedal arrangement, a place to rest the accelerator foot, and the easy and simple operation of the gears, emergency brake, foot brake and clutch.[77]

Late on the afternoon of January 13, one of the largest fires in Indianapolis history consumed the Industrial Building located on 10th street at the Central Canal. The building housed 23 different businesses, including some involved in the U.S. Government's war effort, raising immediate suspicions that German agents had set the fire. High winds sent sparks throughout the area, setting fire to adjoining buildings and destroying a church, a grocery store, a saloon, and six houses, in addition to causing smaller fires up to a mile away. The fire caused an estimated $2 million in damage. The building, which was a complete loss, had $500,000 in insurance. Hardest hit was the automobile industry. Empire had stored 400 autos worth $350,000 for the spring trade in the building. Federal had trucks valued at $50,000 and Cole Sales Company had 35 Maxwells stored in the building.[78]

The cause of the fire was a mystery. There was no heat on in the building because of a shortage of coal. The automatic sprinklers had been drained of water to prevent the pipes from bursting. The flames were first seen on the western side of the second floor, which was used by Empire. Two Empire employees had left the facility about 45 minutes before the fire was discovered, but they stated that there was no evidence of fire before they departed.[79]

In February, National announced an increase in the retail price for all six- and 12-cylinder models with the exception of the convertible sedan. The seven-passenger touring car, four-passenger phaeton, and four-passenger roadster were increased by $125. In a six-cylinder car, the new price was $2,150, while for the 12-cylinder cars the new price was $2,750. The two-passenger Dispatch roadster price was increased by $100 to $2,850. The six-cylinder sedan remained with a price of $2,820 while the 12-cylinder convertible sedan price was $3,420. The increase in the retail price of the cars was attributable to the increase in raw materials caused by the war effort.[80]

Although few changes were made in the 1918 Marmon models, the company raised the price of the five-person touring car to $3,500 and the limousine to $5,250.[81] In early April, it raised the price of the Marmon 34 roadster and the seven-passenger touring car to $3,750, the four-passenger to $3,700, and a chassis with a cowl to $3,450.[82]

Stutz introduced four new 16-cylinder models for the 1918 model year, including the Bearcat, a roadster, a four-passenger car, and a six-passenger car. The Bearcat and the roadster retailed for $2,550 while the four-passenger car sold for $2,650 and the six-passenger car for $2,750.[83]

Nordyke & Marmon's aviation department employees were delighted with the visit of Lieutenant Georges Flashaire, a French aviator credited with making over 500 flights and downing 14 German planes. He and Major Joseph Tulasne, chief of the French aviation mission to the United States, were in Indianapolis to see the building of the Liberty engine. The employees were captivated by Flashaire's heroic tales and took pride when Major Tulasne conveyed that the key to victory over Germany was air power. Having flown airplanes in combat, Lieutenant Flashaire emphasized to those present the need for quality of construction, as one of his planes had failed because of an oversight.[84]

All did not go smoothly for Nordyke & Marmon in the building of the Liberty engine. Behind schedule, the first Liberty engine produced was finally ready for 50 hours of testing in June 1918. The company was criticized by Federal officials for being far behind its production schedule. Gathering 300 employees in the assembly room, Walter Marmon addressed the criticism of the company, which he believed to be unfair to the company and its workers. The crowd heard that the government's criticism ignored that the company had been asked to undertake the production of the Liberty engine because the anticipated need exceeded the capacity of the other suppliers. The company agreed to help even though it was in the midst of fulfilling the contract for 2,500 Hall-Scott engines. Marmon told the workers,

> The country was at war and we felt we should accept the schedules and complete them if it was humanly possible to do it. I am proud of what the organization has done and I know that when we begin to turn out the Liberty motor in quantity that the best made to be delivered to the government will be from our plant and our organization. The article was not fair in its implication that we were behind. It did not say that practically all other plants under contract to deliver the Liberty motors were also behind. And the other factories have not, as we did, turned out the Hall-Scott or other engines.[85]

Four months later, the company was vindicated when the Bureau of Aircraft Production awarded Nordyke & Marmon a pennant for the largest percentage in excess of the quota for production of Liberty motors of the 20 plants producing the engines. With a quota of 125 engines for October, the company turned out a total of 306 engines. This production record was stunning, as at the end of September the plant was 40 percent below its quota. Celebrating this achievement, Indianapolis held a parade. Thousands lined the parade route of more than a mile and a half. During the parade, two airplanes powered by Liberty engines flew over the city and dropped "bombs" containing messages to the Liberty motor workers and patriotic messages. One of the officials attending the celebration was Archer A. Landon, the chief production official for the aircraft board. He told the Nordyke & Marmon employees that the government needed 750 engines per month to reach a goal of sending 50,000 airplanes to Europe by the spring. The employees responded with much cheering and a commitment to meet this goal. Landon also said, "Don't kid yourself into thinking peace is coming soon. With the tanks and the infantry the American forces can go to the Rhine, but after that it is up to the airplanes."[86] A mere week and a half later, the armistice was signed.

The AAA ran an economy test from Los Angeles to Yosemite National Park, a distance of 382 miles. A Marmon 34 with a full complement of passengers and luggage scored the best fuel mileage at 15½ miles per gallon.[87]

Nordyke & Marmon expanded again, with a triangular shaped three-story office building costing $50,000 at the corner of Kentucky Avenue and Morris Streets.[88] The company also moved its showroom from New York and Meridian Streets to a new three-story building at the corner of Eleventh and Meridian Street, about a mile north of the previous location.[89]

The first floor of the building provided a showroom for new cars on Meridian Street and an entrance for used cars on Eleventh Street. The second floor contained a paint department as well as the accounting function, while the third floor was the service department. The building was equipped with two large elevators for the transport of vehicles.[90] During the auto show in the spring of 1919, the company showed movies on the building of the Liberty engines.[91]

For the winter of 1918-1919, Cole announced that it would build an enclosed car using the same design as the popular Aero Eight models. The offerings would be a seven-passenger Toursedan, a four-passenger Tourcoupe with a collapsible front seat, and a town car built by special order. The Toursedans would be with or without a permanent glass partition between the front and back seats.[92]

Before the war's conclusion, the French government placed an order for 350 Marmon 34s. Despite the Armistice, the order was reconfirmed.[93] Marmon used this purchase as part of an advertising campaign:

> In the hour of peril when the French motor car companies were engaged in war work, France, the birthplace of the modern motorcar, turned to America for help to supply her great army staff with means of reliable transportation. France knew what she wanted—reliability, endurance, speed, and ease of riding.
>
> We consider it a signal honor that in this crucial time the French government motor experts chose the Marmon 34 as the American product suited to their needs.
>
> Every Marmon owner may well consider this a tribute to his judgment.[94]

When the country went to a wartime basis, due to the combination of the Federal Government's restrictions on the production of automobiles and the automobile industry producing war implements in addition to automobiles,[95] there was a marked decrease in the number of cars produced. In 1918, the production of autos dropped by 703,000 to 1,170,000.[96] After the Armistice on November 11, the automobile companies started refocusing on peacetime production. Understandably, it would take a while before production would reach prewar levels. George Dickson of National believed it would take nine to 12 months for National to gear up its production levels. Bruce M. Wylie, sales manager for the Indianapolis National distributor, explained:

> The readjustment period in the automobile industry will be longer than the average layman anticipates. This is due primarily to the fact that the world war ended eight months sooner than the most optimistic of the American military authorities expected.[97]

Cole announced the doubling of the number of cars to be produced for 1919. Additionally, the company planned to implement pre-war pricing on its product line,[98] with all models having a $300 price reduction. The new price for the Model 871 roadster, the Model 872 four-passenger touring car, and the Model 870 seven-passenger touring car was $2,595. Other prices included the sedan at $3,595, the limousine at $3,695, and the coupe and town car at $3,795.[99]

The William Small Company, distributor for Monroe automobiles nationwide since 1914, purchased the assets of the Monroe Motor Company's plant in Pontiac, Michigan. Relocating production to Indianapolis, the company anticipated building 20 cars per day.[100] The Monroe automobile was available as either a touring car or a roadster.[101] The company was incorporated in November 1917 with a capitalization of $1 million. William Small said of the purchase,

> In buying and moving the Monroe factory to this city I am making a deal that gives me a known quantity to work on. The Monroe car is a proven result. I have always been an enthusiastic believer in the Monroe principle and construction.[102]

When Stutz announced its earnings for 1918, they were down from the previous year, with earnings of $594,047 in fiscal year 1918 as compared to $1,074,778 in fiscal year 1917. The decrease in profitability was partially attributable to a decrease in sales from $4,448,315 in 1917 to $3,536,537 in 1918. Also contributing to the decline in profitability was a decrease in gross profit from 24.7 percent in 1917 to 18.2 percent in 1918, primarily reflecting the increase in the cost of raw materials.[103]

The close of the war also meant that the Indianapolis Motor Speedway would once again be hosting races. Fisher, Allison, and Newby, all of whom were wintering in Florida, decided to hold the race on May 31, 1919, and applied to the AAA Contest Board to sanction the $50,000 Victor Sweepstakes. The owners did not want the race to conflict with any Memorial Day celebrations.[104]

12

Peace Brings Significant Growth

After the war's conclusion, the United States issued Victory bonds to pay off the debt incurred during the conflict. Nordyke & Marmon fully supported subscription to this effort and purchased $250,000 in bonds. They also encouraged their employees to buy Liberty bonds and guaranteed the employees they would not lose money on the bonds. At a meeting of the company's 2,500 employees, Walter Marmon said,

> I believe it is our duty to subscribe to the limit of our ability, and the company wants every one of its employees to have the opportunity. We are going over 100 percent and we hope that every person in the plant will subscribe at least $100.[1]

At the end of December 1918, Empire ceased production. When the lease on the company's three-story manufacturing facility expired, management decided not to renew. Rather, management indicated that the company would look for or construct a new facility better suited to its manufacturing needs.[2] That never happened.

In March, an executive committee was formed to manage the affairs of Premier because J. C. Flowers, the company's president, didn't have the time to devote to the business. Members of the executive committee included Charles S. Crawford, F. P. Nehrbas, and E. F. Schaeffer.[3]

After having set a new standard with its comparably lightweight Marmon 34, Marmon announced in March 1919 that it was going to build a "post-war" car utilizing some of the knowledge gleaned during the building of the Liberty engine. Fred Moscovics talked about car construction after World War I:

> Briefly, these cars will be much lighter than our current ones; they will use more aluminum and pressed steel parts, they will have better bodies, be more comfortable, be more economical, cheaper in price and show a general refinement in detail all through.[4]

By May, production in Indianapolis was 80 cars per day, which exceeded pre-war production even though there were fewer manufacturers. The demand for Indianapolis manufacturers' automobiles exceeded the supply. Marmon, which had produced 12 cars per day before the war, increased its production by 50 percent to 18 cars per day. Cole was producing 25 cars per day and had plans to substantially increase production to 5,000 per year. National was producing 15 cars per day while Stutz was producing 12 cars daily. Premier, negatively impacted by difficulty in procuring materials, was building only 10 cars per day.[5]

When racing returned to the Indianapolis Motor Speedway in 1919, 33 cars were chasing $50,000 in prize money put up by the organizers. Of the 33 drivers, 17 were new to racing at Indianapolis. The expectation of those going to the race was that speed records would be broken. Four Frontenacs, designed by Louis Chevrolet, all exceeded 100 miles per hour in qualifications, and Rene Thomas, the 1914 winner of the Indianapolis 500, turned a lap at 104.7 miles per hour.[6] While most of the cars entered in the race utilized the four-cylinder engine, including the Peugeots, Stutz, Chevrolet, Durant, Roamer, Premier and Frontenac,[7] some used engines based upon aircraft engines. A Ballot car used two eight-cylinder engines arranged in a row, and five cars used a Duesenberg engine which was based upon the 16-valve training plane engine,[8] while the Packard Company entered a 12-cylinder car based upon the Liberty engine.[9]

At the beginning the race, Rene Thomas was in the pole position with a qualifying speed of 104.7 miles per hour. Next to Thomas was Indianapolis driver Wilcox driving a pre-war Peugeot owned by Allison. His qualifying speed was much slower at 100.1 miles per hour. In an era when the racers were lined up in rows of four, a Stutz driven by Earl Cooper was on the third row. Given the speed shown during practice, the Frontenacs were tightly bunched, with one on the third row and the remaining three on the fourth row.[10]

Having expanded to handle the war time production of aviation engines while continuing the production of automobiles and milling equipment, Nordyke & Marmon ran the risk of having too much manufacturing space when the war-related activities ceased. This was not the case. In fact, the demand for Nordyke & Marmon's products continued to exceed the company's available production space. In June 1919, the company announced the expansion of its manufacturing facilities with two additional buildings, which would make the plant one of the biggest in the Midwest. Made of reinforced concrete, one building was five stories tall with 270,000 square feet and was used for the construction of five different types of automobile bodies. The second building, with 80,000 square feet, was used for the final assembly of automobiles[11] and was built at a cost of $90,000.[12] The expansion enabled the company to double both the number of cars manufactured and the production of flour mill machinery. Walter Marmon said of the expansion,

> When we finally took a mental inventory we found we had large machine shop facilities, but not sufficient body and wood working facilities. These had to be furnished, or we would be in the position of having an unbalanced plant. This, and the fact that the officers of the plant felt it a splendid time to insure our financial position for the future to enable us to occupy that position in the automobile industry which we appear destined to fill, impelled us to consider adding to the financial strength of the company.
>
> The demand on our milling department, too, is growing by leaps and bounds. Last year was the greatest in the history of the business, and with the necessity of feeding the world we felt that American flour mill manufacturers will be pressed in the next decade more than ever. To meet this condition, it was necessary to give additional room to our flour milling machinery business.[13]

Nordyke & Marmon obtained bond financing for this expansion and working capital from Fletcher American National Bank in the amount of $2.5 million. The bonds had an interest rate of 6 percent with ten annual payments of $250,000 beginning in July 1921. An advertising prospectus indicated that the company's average profit for the four years ended June 30 was $903,646, more than adequate for the annual debt service of $400,000. The prospectus also indicated the company had paid over $1.8 million in federal income tax over the prior three years. Total assets were $9.4 million while total liabilities, including the proceeds from the bond offering, were $4.3 million.[14] This bond issue sold out in less than six hours.[15]

Cole announced a $155 price increase for open cars at the end of July. The new price was $2,750 for a four-passenger touring car, a seven-passenger touring car, a two-person roadster, and the Sportster. The closed car pricing remained the same. The Sportscoupe was priced at $3,795, the Sportsedan and Towncar at $3,895, and the Tourosine, Sportosine and Toursedan were $3,995.[16]

With plans to build a factory with production capabilities of up to 250 automobiles per day, the William Small Company, manufacturer of the Monroe automobile, purchased 18 acres at the intersection of Washington Street and Belmont Avenue for $54,000. At the time of the purchase, the manufacture of Monroe automobiles was located at 701–707 Fulton Street.[17] The company announced the hiring of Louis Chevrolet as a consulting engineer in September. In addition to designing race cars for the 1920 campaign, Chevrolet would help with engineering problems with the Monroe car being produced.[18]

In August, Stutz announced a significant expansion to its production facilities. Plant managers planned for a doubling in the number of automobiles produced from 3,000 to 6,000 cars annually. The addition to the motor plant was a one-story building at the corner of Tenth Street and Senate Avenue. Two additional four-story buildings were also erected. One of the new buildings was erected at 11th and Capitol while the other building was erected on Senate Avenue. The additions to the facilities would result in floor space of 450,000 square feet at a cost, including machinery, of $800,000. The company also announced the issuance of an additional 25,000 shares of stock, bringing the total stock issued to 100,000 shares.[19] The additional shares were offered at the rate of one new share for every three shares currently owned for $100 per share purchased. The company used the proceeds from the stock issuance to support its expansion.[20]

Harry Stutz announced his resignation from Stutz effective July 1, perhaps driven by the significant growth planned for the company. Stutz had a personal creed about his automobiles:

> I believe, first of all, that the real business of anything mechanical is to work well and to wear well. Therefore, I hold simplicity, strength and serviceability above all else.
>
> I believe, on the other hand, that an engineered product can be both strong and well designed. Then beauty can be built around these features.
>
> I hold that true beauty is always simple and so avoid all unnecessary embellishments. Real beauty, too, is based on genuineness, and it cannot be obtained by using cheap or imitative materials. I insist on the best of everything and never tolerate substitutes or "seconds."
>
> Having strength and beauty, I bear in mind the point of economy and insist on applying the very limit of practical engineering to the motor, so that it can get the last ounce of power out of every drop of fuel.
>
> A motor car can never be any better than the shop in which it is built and the men who built it. You can't get quality except in a rigidly disciplined shop from which all workmen except the most conscientious and expert are barred.
>
> Finally, I believe there is a point in any factory's expansion where the penalty for increased production may become decreased quality, and I will never build any more cars than I can build well.[21]

Replacing Stutz as president was Allan Ryan, the New York financier. Stutz told the newspaper he planned to retire from business activities and pursue personal interests.[22]

The Cole Aero Eight received an endorsement from Howdy Wilcox, who purchased one:

> I have been watching the Aero Eight ever since it was first introduced in 1918. From the standpoint of appearance I believe it a finished and symmetrical car. But, of course, the mechanism was of vital concern to me.

I believe in confining one's speeding to the race track, but I can say frankly that I make a car give me all that it has to deliver. The light weight of the Aero Eight, its splendid balance, its easy riding qualities appealed to me from the start. I found by inquiry that Aero Eights in service were averaging better than 15,000 miles on tires.[23]

Cole announced three new all-season models: the Tourosine, the Toursedan, and the Sportosine. By eliminating the overlapping of the upper body, the models had a sleeker appearance and a stronger body. The Sportosine combined the fun of a sport model with the luxury of a touring car. There was a glass partition between the front and rear seats which when raised would convert the car into a limousine or sedan. The rear compartment could accommodate four passengers: two on the seat and an additional two on cab seats which, when not in use, folded into the back of the front seat. The Tourosine, a seven-passenger automobile, featured Cole's proprietary clear-vision, storm-proof windshield.[24] The windshield consisted of two distinct sections which joined each other at the roof and were separated by about ten inches at the cowl. The outer section was comprised of two panes of glass while the inner section was one pane of glass. The windshield could be adjusted so that when there was a storm the lower pane of the outer section was turned out until it was level with the upper edge of the interior pane and the top pane was adjusted out until an open space of about two inches was between its lower edge and the upper edge of the lower section.[25]

Projecting an annual production of 12,000 automobiles in 1920, Cole purchased a large tract of land to the north adjacent to the existing plant and made plans to double the plant's size. The new brick and steel five-story structure had approximately 150,000 square feet of floor space. Cole also constructed a private rail yard which would connect with an existing rail line to facilitate the shipment of materials and cars. The first floor of the new building was used for storage of the company's fleet of cars plus those of the executives. The final test area and the shipping and receiving departments were located on the second floor. The third floor contained the offices for the service department and the supplies and parts department. The two upper floors were utilized by the paint shop and the service repair shop.[26]

Cole wasn't the only Indianapolis manufacturer with big plans for the 1920 model year. Marmon planned to produce 5,000 automobiles and was increasing its manufacturing facilities by 350,000 square feet. National planned to build 6,000 cars, an increase of 50 percent. William Small Company, the manufacturer of the Monroe automobile, planned to build a new facility with the goal of producing 10,000 automobiles in 1920 and ultimately producing 30,000 cars a year. Stutz planned to double the number of cars it produced to 6,000 and was expanding its manufacturing facilities. Premier anticipated building between 4,000 and 5,000 automobiles in 1920.[27]

In September controlling interest in Premier was sold to L. S. Skelton, an Oklahoma capitalist, who was immediately named as general manager of the plant. Skelton had Hoosier roots, having been born in Princeton, Indiana. He was a pioneer in the Oklahoma oil industry with operations beginning in 1898, and he owned the Security Motor Company with dis-tributorships in Kansas City, Omaha, Los Angeles, San Francisco, and Dallas for a variety of cars including Premier. He also had mining interests, including zinc and lead, as well as glass interests. Upon taking control of the plant, he announced an expansion of the facilities. The company reportedly manufactured 1,000 automobiles from January 1 through August. Skelton expected to increase the volume of cars produced and double the workforce to 2,000.[28]

With the purchase of Premier by Skelton, both J. C. Flowers and E. W. Steinhart retired from the business. Skelton announced plans to build 3,000 automobiles during 1920. The company planned to erect a 50,000 square foot building for the storage of materials. Additionally, it planned a garage in which to store employees' vehicles.[29] Skelton immediately put the company on a stronger financial basis with the repayment of all liabilities incurred by the former owners, with the proviso that all interest be forgiven. Skelton sent a letter to the various creditors as follows:

> As you recall, the creditors' agreement calls for the repayment of your accounts through monies received from government contract for trucks. These contracts for some time have been completed, but final settlement with the government has been indefinitely delayed, due to many causes incident to the settlement of government claims.
> Dr. Skelton has made the proposition that he will provide the necessary money to pay all creditors 100 percent immediately, merely suggesting the waiving of the interest on the balance of these claims.[30]

The Premier plant, in the location of the former T. B. Laycock Company, had 500,000 square feet and was the third largest plant in Indianapolis. For 1920 Premier introduced a new car with an aluminum motor and magnetic gear shifting.[31]

The Greater Indianapolis Industrial Association was overjoyed when it attracted the newly formed LaFayette Motors Company (LaFayette) to the Mars Hill area where the Association owned 202 acres. The Association had negotiated for some time with a consortium

LaFayette Motors Company building in the Mars Hill section of Indianapolis (Indiana Historical Society, P0555).

of out-of-town businessmen to locate a new automobile company in Mars Hill. With an approved capitalization of $6 million, LaFayette purchased a 15-acre tract of land which included a building formerly occupied by the Stenotype Company plant.[32] Indianapolis was selected because of the clustering of automobile companies in the town. The company's capitalization of $6 million included $4 million in preferred stock, which was oversubscribed in four days. The remainder consisted of 40,000 shares of common stock, including 10,000 shares which were distributed with the purchase of the preferred stock.[33]

The company's president, Charles W. Nash, was also the president of Nash Motors of Kenosha, Wisconsin. Other officers of the company included D. McCall White and Earle C. Howard, who would lead the company on a day-to-day basis. Howard was formerly the sales manager for Cadillac Motor Car Company. White, the designer, was known as the designer of the English Daimler and Napier engines and Cadillac 8 in America, as well as for having played a significant role in the development of the Liberty engine which powered many of the United States aircraft during World War I.[34]

By December, LaFayette was making plans for the expansion of the factory. The proposed one-story brick and concrete building, 100 feet wide and 1,000 feet long, would be one of the longest buildings in Marion County.[35] The company was also planning to debut a car in New York City in the lobby of the Commodore Hotel while the New York Auto Show was going on. The car to be displayed was an experimental, hand-built chassis with a sedan body.[36]

Responding to requests by employees for help with the high cost of living, Nordyke & Marmon opened a co-operative grocery store for its employees. Managed by shop and office employees, the store sold goods to employees at cost. For the first week of its operation, the store sold $1,700 worth of goods. It was anticipated that the store would sell $1,000 worth of goods daily.[37]

Within months after announcing his retirement from business, Harry Stutz founded the H. C. S. Motor Corporation (HCS).[38] The company was organized in Indianapolis with a capital base of $1 million, and Stutz was the primary shareholder and president of the firm. Other corporate officers were Samuel T. Murdock, vice president; Henry F. Campbell, treasurer; and A. Gordon Murdock, secretary.[39]

As the winter of 1919 approached, coal production was off by 30 to 50 percent in some mines, which the mine operators attributed to a lack of coal cars to transport the coal.[40] The production decline was expected to affect both industry and residential homes. Industry responded by switching part of the supply for its electrical needs to gasoline and oil. Nordyke & Marmon utilized six International Harvesters, six Fordson tractors,[41] and 30 Marmon 34 engines in this effort, cutting its coal usage by 50 percent during December 1919.[42] National used seven National motors, including the engine to car No. 8, which had powered Dawson's National to victory in the 1912 Indianapolis 500, to augment its power production.[43] Stutz used 16 Stutz motors to supplement the power.[44]

National anticipated production of 5,000 units of its new Sextet model, introduced in late 1919.[45] The company unveiled the four-passenger Sextet Coupe at the New York Auto Show. The car featured an all-aluminum body on a 130-inch wheel base.[46] The striking feature of the car was that it was 3⅜ inches lower to the ground than other models, which was achieved through the body wrapping the chassis frame rather than sitting upon it. This provided the car with additional stability.[47] The company also announced a $140 price increase for the open Sextet models. The seven-passenger Sextet, four-passenger phaeton, and two-passenger roadster would retail for $3,290, while the four-passenger coupe would sell for $4,200 and the seven-passenger sedan for $4,250.[48]

For 1920, Marmon anticipated a doubling of its production of automobiles. The assembly building was anticipated to be completed in November 1919 while the five-story production plant would be finished in early 1920. The top floor of the production plant was dedicated to the building of bodies. Previously the production of the closed bodies had been outsourced. The plant, which had been built in 1917 to produce aviation motors, had been converted into a machine shop for the production of motors and chassis.[49]

In 1919, Stutz had revenues of approximately $7.5 million and profits of $1 million. This was an improvement from 1918, when the company had sales of $3.5 million.[50]

13

Overcapacity and an Economic Recession

Three Indianapolis brands were displayed in salon showings during the 1920 New York Auto Show. The LaFayette car, designed by D. McCall White whose reputation for engineering design spanned both sides of the Atlantic, had many people focusing on the design of the eight-cylinder engine while the car was displayed at the Commodore Hotel. The engine, influenced in design by aircraft engines, could produce 90 horsepower while having fewer parts than the normal eight-cylinder engine then prevalent in the industry. Among other features, the valves were set at an angle of nine degrees with the cylinders, making the engine more efficient, while the crankshaft had 16 cams rather than the more traditional eight.[1]

An HCS automobile was shown in the east dining room of the Astor Hotel. What was amazing about the HCS was that on September 22, 1919, the car existed only in blueprint form. Within two months, there were two models ready to be displayed at the auto show.[2]

The Commodore Hotel also had a private exhibit of a Marmon 34[3] which had numerous changes for 1920, the most significant of which was the substitution of aluminum instead of cast iron for the cylinders, achieved by casting the cylinders in blocks of three. Additionally, the car had a two-piece iron and aluminum piston. The new engine construction saved three inches under the hood, allowing a two-inch increase in the tonneau and a one-inch increase in the front compartment.[4]

An advertisement touted Marmon's newest motor:

> Under the stress and strain of the necessities of war, the scientist, the engineer and the manufacturer were compelled to win victories of mental and productive effort to adequately back up the great men on the fighting fronts.
>
> The battles of the laboratory and factory were as insistent and tremendous in their way as the operations on the battle-fields of France.
>
> Keyed to this tremendous mental pressure, men did the impossible as a routine of the day's work. Under these conditions the new Marmon high efficiency motor was born.
>
> It was freely predicted that the world's truly great motor car would eventually be made by one of those few motor car manufacturers who were honored by being called to Washington in 1917 to devote their factories, their capital and their brains to the building of aircraft motors. Because they, and only they, learned the mighty lessons which mean much to you, a lesson of heretofore unknown production difficulties overcome, heretofore unknown engineering feats accomplished. It is from the accumulated knowledge of this experience prefaced by 67 years of manufacturing experience that we present the new Marmon.[5]

Marmon arranged for a test of the Marmon seven-passenger touring car's acceleration and speed at the Indianapolis Motor Speedway and of its hill climbing ability at Centennial Hill in Mooresville, Indiana, which had a grade of 6.11 percent. Observers for the tests were Chester A. Ricker, technical observer for the Indianapolis Motor Speedway, and Jay Edward Schnipper, representative for several automobile trade magazines. Joe Dawson and C. E. Jeffers, the chief engineer for Marmon, drove the cars during the tests. One of the cars accelerated from 10 to 50 miles per hour in 18.8 seconds with a gear ratio of 3.75 and traveled a half mile averaging a little better than 60 miles per hour. Starting at five miles per hour, the car reached the 1,000-foot mark with an average speed of 24 miles per hour in the hill climb. In the test to the top of the 1,775-foot hill, the car averaged 40 miles per hour. The second car, with a gear ratio of 4:1, accelerated from 10 to 50 miles per hour in 15.8 seconds and traveled the half-mile distance with a speed of about 65 miles per hour. In the hill climb, the second car traveled to the 1,000-foot mark with an average speed of 27 miles per hour and to the top of the hill starting at 4 miles per hour with an average speed of 43 miles per hour.[6]

After World War I, the auto industry assumed there would be a large demand for its automobiles. In both 1916 and 1919, the demand exceeded the supply.[7] The industry responded, increasing its production capacity from 2 million cars in 1919 to 3 million in 1920.[8] Unfortunately for the industry, the buyer was being squeezed by higher costs and lower wages. Not only were there multiple strikes, including in the steel and coal industries,[9] but the anticipated demand for the automobile shrank in 1920.

In early February, Marmon raised the price of its cars by $350. The four- and seven-passenger touring cars and the four-passenger roadster were priced at $5,000, while the coupe was priced at $6,100. The sedan was priced at $6,600 and the town car and the limousine at $6,800.[10]

The William Small Company, maker of the Monroe automobile, increased its capitalization by $2 million to support the erection of a large, modern factory on West Washington Street and to provide working capital.[11]

Looking to expand its product line to include trucks, National entered into negotiations with George A. Steinle to purchase the Four Lakes Ordnance Company plant used for the manufacturer of guns during World War I. Included in the company's plans was a three-story, 54,000-square-foot expansion of the 75,000-square-foot plant.[12] This potential acquisition was never accomplished.

Anticipating an increased demand for Indianapolis automobiles and related products, there was a building boom. In addition to the Nordyke & Marmon expansion, which included a four-story office building, a five-story production plant and a one-story plant with an estimated cost of $1 million, the Wheeler-Schebler Carburetor Company added a two-story concrete-reinforced factory at a cost of $100,000.[13] With plans to double production of the Aero Eight to 12,000 cars,[14] Cole also built a five-story factory at an estimated cost of $300,000.[15]

Not only was there a building boom in Indianapolis to support the manufacture of automobiles, there was also a need for housing to support the factory workers. Partially owned by LaFayette, the LaFayette Building Company planned to erect between 100 and 150 modern houses near the plant and claimed to be the first to address the desperate need for housing stock in Indianapolis. To support the initiative, LaFayette Building Company had authorized capitalization of $1 million equally split between common and preferred stock with a seven percent premium. The initial common stock issuance was $300,000. Of that amount, LaFayette subscribed $100,000 and Indianapolis businessmen the remaining $200,000.[16]

With big plans for their planned community, LaFayette Building Company purchased 110 acres just a short walk west of the LaFayette plant. The entrance to the subdivision on LaFayette Drive had a park for the enjoyment of the homeowners. Adjoining the park and facing LaFayette Avenue, two acres were set aside for a school to consist of eight classrooms and a large assembly hall, which would also serve as a community center for the Mars Hill and Maywood areas of greater Indianapolis. As a special feature, the company planned to build a plaza at the intersection of Sixth Avenue and LaFayette Drive with a large fountain in the center. Most of the building lots were 50 feet by 110 feet. Home styles ranged from a two-bedroom bungalow to a two-story four-bedroom home, with the majority of the homes being one and one-half stories with three bedrooms. The company boasted that although there were 14 different housing plans, no two homes would be identical, the difference being color and design (primarily porches and room layout). The exteriors were to be stucco with concrete tile roofs and the houses were equipped with electricity and telephone, with water supplied by a community water system. The homes were sold on an installment basis. The company planned to incorporate the Mars Hill area as a separate town. Maurice J. Moore, president of LaFayette Building Company and secretary/treasurer of LaFayette, said, "It is the biggest building project ever started in Indianapolis and we intend to make it distinctive in the quality of house construction as well as one of the prettiest sections of the city."[17] By July, 60 of the planned 200 homes were under construction by Bedford Stone and Construction Company.[18]

Stutz stock experienced a meteoric rise from $123.50 per share at the close of business on March 8 to $391 per share at the close of business on March 31. Rumors around Wall Street were that a "steel man" went short on the stock by some 200 points and that he was being squeezed. Another rumor surrounding the stock was that the automobile concerns controlled by the Allan Ryan group were to be consolidated into one company.[19] The Governors of the New York Stock Exchange responded by suspending the trading of Stutz stock on March 31, 1920. The action was unprecedented in the history of the stock exchange, since it prohibited trading on the floor of the Exchange as well as among members outside of the Exchange.[20]

Several days later, the situation became clearer when New York Stock Exchange officials ruled that the failure to deliver the shares of stock which had been sold short would not be considered a breach of contract. At the time, Allan Ryan and his associates controlled roughly 80 percent of the 100,000 shares outstanding. The stock had been loaned and re-loaned to traders, who sold it short in the open market. Ryan and his associates had begun buying back the stock until the number of shares held by Ryan et al. and the short sale contracts exceeded the total number of shares issued, which had caused the price to increase dramatically. The Ryan group also declared two dividends, one of 20 percent and the second of 80 percent. Under the Exchange rules, a trader buying a stock short was liable for any cash or share dividends declared. Through his actions, Ryan was able to manipulate the market, resulting in the meteoric rise in the stock price.[21]

Not surprisingly, Ryan protested that the short in Stutz stock was not of his making:

> The Stutz situation was not designed or created by me. It was the result of persistent attacks on the stock by persons having absolutely no interest in the Stutz company, who were determined to profit by hammering down the Stutz stock and deliberately promoting a campaign for selling that which they did not own. They hoped to force down the stock so as to buy the stock at ridiculous figures, in order thereby to

reap a great profit at the expense of every stockholder as indeed they would have done but for my ability to protect the company and its stockholders.[22]

Ryan subsequently resigned as president of Stutz and was succeeded by William N. Thompson, the company's general manager.[23] In his letter of resignation, Ryan charged that the "members of the Governing Committee were members of houses, which either for themselves or for their customers, were short of Stutz stock, and hence were sitting as judge and jury in a case in which they were financially interested."[24] In mid–June, charges were filed against Ryan for his actions on the Stutz stock. In summary, the allegations were:

> When said stock had been stricken from the list of the New York stock exchange, and the stock of said company had been increased by a stock dividend on April 15, 1920, he did in fact exact from the parties liable upon contracts liable for delivery of said stock, arbitrary, excessive, and unreasonable amounts in settlement of said contracts; to wit, more than $500 for each share which said parties were liable to deliver before the stock of said company was increased by the stock dividend of April 15, 1920; all of which constituted conduct of proceeding inconsistent with just and equitable principles of trade.

Ryan immediately declared that the charges were "ridiculous on their face" and accused the exchange officials of "defiance of public opinion and autocratic disregard of the public interest."[25]

After selling his Stutz stock, Harry Stutz founded HCS and Stutz Fire Engine Company. The first HCS cars were constructed inside the Stutz Fire Engine Company factory located

HCS Motor Car Company building, which appears to be very similar to the Stutz building with the exception of the logo on top of the building (Bass Photo Co. Collection, Indiana Historical Society).

at 1411 North Capitol. The demand for the Stutz Fire Engine increased after one of its vehicles recorded a perfect score in a 12-hour test, resulting in the need for the entire factory to be used for the building of fire engines. As a result, Harry Stutz announced there would be a new four-story factory for the production of HCS automobiles located at the corner of 14th Street and Capitol Avenue. The factory would consist of two buildings, each with a 60-foot frontage on Capitol and a depth of 200 feet, constructed of steel and concrete with a brick façade. The estimated cost for both buildings was $500,000. It was hoped the business could occupy the first building in less than 60 days.[26]

Indianapolis was hit with an unauthorized switchman's strike in April 1920. This strike had the potential of closing automobile factories and other Indianapolis industries. Although this was long before the just-in-time method of inventory control, the automobile companies didn't have a great supply of inventory. Particularly hard hit were National, Stutz, Weidley Motors, and LaFayette, all of whom faced being shut down if the strike wasn't settled. Marmon was the best prepared with inventories that would last between two and three weeks.[27]

National introduced a new phaeton model noted for its extreme narrowness, with the rear seat at 40 inches being no wider than the front of the car. The car was also elongated with the cowl being longer than the regular touring car.[28]

For the 1920 racing season, the AAA Contest Board lowered the engine capacity to 183 cubic inches of displacement. Fred Duesenberg responded by developing a smaller version of the successful 300-cubic-inch engine.[29] In 1920, Duesenberg would build four of these 183-cubic-inch engines.[30] The 1920 racing season started with a Duesenberg victory in a 250-mile race in Los Angeles, won by Jimmy Murphy with an average speed of 103 miles per hour.[31]

Harry Miller, Fred Duesenberg, and Louis Chevrolet were busy designing racers to compete in the Indianapolis 500 race.[32] The Duesenbergs were favored to win. Tommy Milton, who had earned the title of "speed king" for driving a Duesenberg car on the white sands of Daytona Beach, covering a mile with an average speed of 156.04 miles per hour, and who held the world's record for 300 miles,[33] signed a contract on May 20 to drive an eight-cylinder Fred Duesenberg-designed car. He joined the stable of Duesenberg racers that included Eddie Hearne, Jimmy Murphy, and Eddie O'Donnell. Just two days before, Milton had announced that he would be driving a Monroe. He had been in Indianapolis waiting for the arrival of his Duesenberg when the announcement was made.[34] The Eight-in-a-Row Duesenberg which Milton drove to the world records was put on display in the lobby of the Claypool Hotel.[35] Additionally, a Duesenberg eight-cylinder engine was also in the ReVere entry driven by Tom Rooney and the Mulford Special piloted by Ralph Mulford. Many believed this would give the Duesenberg entries an excellent chance of taking home a portion of the $70,000 in prize money being offered by the Speedway.[36]

Also sponsoring a team in the Indianapolis 500 was Monroe. Joining Louis Chevrolet, captain of the team, were Gaston Chevrolet, Roscoe Sarles, and Joe Thomas.[37]

After selling their Elizabeth, New Jersey engine plant to John Willys[38] in May 1920, Frederic (Fred) and August (Augie) Duesenberg purchased a 16½ acre parcel at the corner of West Washington and Harding streets for a factory site[39] where they would build "a car designed and built for the connoisseur" using the Eight-in-a-Row Duesenberg engine.[40] Duesenberg Automobile & Motors Company (Duesenberg) was incorporated in New Jersey with authorized capital stock totaling $5,000,000. The officers of the company were Newton VanZandt, president; L. M. Rankin, vice president and general manager; F. A. Riley, secretary;

Jacob Shaefer, treasurer; Fred Duesenberg, chief engineer; and Augie Duesenberg, assistant engineer.[41] The automobile, which was anticipated to weigh 400 pounds less than similar cars, featured four-wheel brakes and a new type of axle designed by Fred Duesenberg[42] and had a retail price of approximately $6,000.[43] The company anticipated producing 2,400 cars in the first year.[44] At the time of this announcement, Indianapolis ranked as second in the United States in the production of automobiles.[45] Later in May, the company opened an office in the Lemcke building in downtown Indianapolis.[46]

Even though the Duesenberg entries for the Indianapolis 500 were built in New Jersey, the final touches were being made in Indianapolis, giving the race cars, at least to some extent, a hometown appeal.[47] Duesenberg had been making racing engines for ten years, and for the past three years, cars equipped with a Duesenberg engine had won 60 percent of all the authorized races entered.[48]

The Apperson Brothers Automobile Company of Kokomo, Indiana, filed a suit for $219,620 against the Wisconsin Motors Manufacturing Company for labor performed and materials furnished, and named Premier Motor Corporation as a co-defendant. Premier allegedly owed Wisconsin Motors Manufacturing over $350,000.[49]

Barney Oldfield was practicing on the track, this time not as a competitor but as the driver of the pace car, a Marmon six cylinder. Clipping off laps at 90 miles per hour, Barney remarked, "Don't tinker with this job any more—it's fast enough for me."[50]

August (Augie) and Frederic (Fred) Duesenberg (Auburn Cord Duesenberg Automobile Museum).

Getting the cars ready for the Indianapolis 500, always a challenge for the Duesenberg team, was particularly difficult in 1920. Duesenberg used a foundry in Chicago for the engine castings, which were ready to be shipped to the Duesenberg factory in New Jersey about a month before the race when a freight strike occurred. Fred Duesenberg sent Eddie Miller to Chicago to pick up the parts and deliver them to New Jersey. Upon arriving in Chicago, Miller was met by Ernie Olson, who was on his way to the Duesenberg plant to construct the Philbrin Special. Using their ingenuity, Miller and Olson packed the engine parts in foot lockers, which they then succeeded in getting on board the first class cabin as their luggage. Arriving at the New Jersey factory, the engines were built and installed in the cars, which were then shipped to Indianapolis without the axles, which were then machined. The four Duesenberg racers took to the track for qualifications without having been tested.[51]

On the first day of qualifications, Ralph DePalma won the pole with an average speed of 99.65 miles per hour. A Duesenberg driven by Eddie Hearne earned a starting spot on the third row with an average speed of 88.05 miles per hour.[52] On May 28, Tommy Milton qualified his Duesenberg for the race with a qualifying speed of 90.20 miles per hour.[53]

On race day, the bookies favored Ralph DePalma to win with 4:1 odds. The odds on the Duesenbergs were Milton, 10 to 1; Murphy, 20 to 1; O'Donnell, 15 to 1; and Hearne, 20 to 1.[54] The bookies were wrong. Ralph DePalma finished fifth in the race with an average speed of 82.12 miles per hour.[55] He was leading with a two lap edge when on the 187th lap he ran out of gas. His riding mechanic, Pete DePaolo, ran one-half mile to the pits to get some fuel, but despite this gallant effort, the race was lost. Shortly after getting more fuel, his car appeared to catch fire. Taking the lead was Gaston Chevrolet in a Monroe with an average speed of 88.55 miles per hour. He was lucky to have won. He, too, ran out of gas on the 197th lap but coasted into the pits to pick up enough fuel to finish the race.[56] The next nearest competitor, Rene Thomas, crossed the finish line almost three minutes later. Two of the Duesenbergs finished third (Tommy Milton) and fourth (Jimmy Murphy). The Monroe car was designed by Louis Chevrolet and built by the William Small Company at its factory in Indianapolis.[57] At the banquet the next evening, a total of $93,550 was presented to those participating in the race.[58]

The William Small Company took the opportunity to capitalize on the Monroe car victory in the 1920 Indianapolis 500 with an advertisement. Simple and straight to the point, it simply said "Monroe Wins." The advertisement indicated that the company planned to produce 7,500 cars in the next year and that they built all of their own axles and motors.[59]

In mid–June, Duesenberg announced the sale of the remaining $5,000,000 in preferred stock, offering as a bonus 50 percent in common stock. The preferred stock had a dividend rate of 8 percent payable semi-annually.[60]

In July, a Duesenberg piloted by Tommy Milton won the 225-mile race at Tacoma, Washington with an average speed of 85 miles per hour. A ReVere with a Duesenberg engine driven by Eddie Hearne finished third, while Jimmy Murphy and Eddie O'Donnell in Duesenberg Eight-in-a-Row cars finished sixth and eighth.[61]

The Universal Trophy races at Uniontown, New Jersey, showed the strength of the Duesenberg cars, as they finished in the top four positions with Tommy Milton finishing first, Jimmy Murphy finishing second, Eddie O'Donnell finishing third, and Isaac Fetterman finishing fourth. In fifth place was Ralph Mulford in his Mulford Special, which had a Duesenberg engine.[62]

Cole put three of its Aero Eight cars to a test at the Indianapolis Motor Speedway in late July 1920. The cars, picked at random from Indianapolis Cole dealerships by the AAA, were subjected to 36 different tests of engine performance, including acceleration tests and running at more than 60 miles per hour for an extended period. After the pistons on the cars were changed, the tests were repeated without any diminishment of performance. Chester Ricker, who performed the tests on behalf of AAA, said,

> I know of no other car made which could be taken right out of the showroom with less than 50 miles of use and run at maximum speed for one-half mile. The new piston is a real mechanical achievement, especially as respects the interchangeability of the pistons, the uniformity of operation and the solution it offers for the car service problem.[63]

In August, William Small asked the courts to appoint a receiver for the William Small Company. In the filing, the indebtedness of the company was listed as $900,000 and there weren't enough assets to cover the indebtedness. Two weeks previously, the company had borrowed $200,000 secured by its property.[64] In response to the request, the court appointed J. W. Fesler as receiver for the company. The company returned to court in March 1921, requesting $70,000 for the purchase of materials to construct automobiles, which was approved. The court anticipated the company would be on a more solid financial footing in two or three months.[65]

In the fall of 1920, an economic slump caused a tightening of the money supply. A survey by the Indianapolis Auto Trade Association of its membership showed that although there was slightly lower production at the plants, the economic slump did not represent a significant issue and the members anticipated plenty of demand for the automobile by the public.[66] Premier's general manager, F. P. Nehrbas, talked about the downturn:

> We feel that the business has struck its lowest point at this time and the point is not so low as to cause any uneasiness. At present, we are frank to say, we are running a little under normal, but not because of any lack of demand or financial stringency.[67]

The factories expected to be running at capacity during the winter months. A trade association report said,

> What is more indicative of the sound condition of the industry in Indianapolis than anything else is the fact that two new factories are going right ahead with their building operations, one upon a $1,000,000 scale. None sees a slackening of the normal demand.[68]

The $1 million expansion was by LaFayette, which was building a plant and homes for its workers in the Mars Hill area of Indianapolis.[69]

Despite the positive talk, the economic slump extended well into 1921. When the Indianapolis manufacturers attended the New York Auto Show in January 1921 they were encouraged by the interest in the cars and the numerous orders. Based upon this, the manufacturers believed there would be a resurgence of sales.[70] They would be disappointed.

The 1920–1921 economic slump was the precursor to difficult times in the industry. The high price of commodities from food to housing lessened the demand by consumers for automobiles. The short-term result was an oversupply of automobiles being produced. Henry Ford was the first to take action in an attempt to move inventory when in September 1920 he reduced the price of his cars.[71] Most automobile manufacturers did not follow in Ford's footsteps—they just shuttered their factories for several weeks or operated on a limited production schedule of two or three days per week.[72] This, obviously, would reduce the supply of automobiles over time but it also had the impact of reducing the wages available to workers.

13. Overcapacity and an Economic Recession

1920 Duesenberg Touring Car (Auburn Cord Duesenberg Automobile Museum).

In this difficult market, HCS introduced the HCS Roadster, "the car that was demanded." The roadster was priced at $2,925 while a five-passenger model was priced at $2,975.[73]

The economy failed to improve in the fall, resulting in downward pressure on pricing. LaFayette did not reduce its pricing structure despite being in the upper tier. The prices of the LaFayette included the chassis for $4,750, the touring car and torpedo for $5,625, the Coupe for $7,200, the sedan for $7,400 and the limousine for $7,500.[74] E. C. Howard, vice president of LaFayette, talked about the company's decision:

> LaFayette prices of course will not be reduced. In establishing our present prices we speculated on a downward trend in our costs and assumed that six or eight months from now we shall be operating under improved conditions. These prices reflect an average estimated basis of cost over a period of several months. If they were based on costs today they would be considerably higher. If our premise is not substantiated and our production costs remain at their present high level, a price increase will be necessary.[75]

Fighting the trend in the industry, Cole also did not cut its prices. J. E. Roberts, Cole's sales general manager, explained:

> Cole prices have always been kept on a reasonable plane. Increases have been made only when they have been deemed necessary due to advances in material and labor, or the cost of improvements to the car itself. It is not the intention of this company to let anything stand in the way of the development of our product, and we will not hesitate to advance the price of our car, if by so doing we are able to add to its refinement and efficiency.[76]

Duesenberg unveiled its first luxury passenger car, the Model A, at the Sixteenth Automobile Salon at the Commodore Hotel in New York in November 1920. Until the appearance of the Duesenberg, which rivaled the top European brands of Bugatti, Rolls Royce, and Mercedes, Americans wanting a luxury automobile did not have a domestic brand from which to choose. Always acting at the last minute, Fred Duesenberg had to bribe a hotel employee to get the car on the floor of the Commodore Hotel. *Automotive Industries* reported:

> In the design of the new chassis, it has been Duesenberg's aim to produce a car that should embody the most up-to-date features in automotive engineering; a car that, having all the liveliness and speed that the fastidious owner demands, yet would be economical to operate. Fuel economy has been achieved by the use of an engine of moderate engine displacement (260 cu. in.) and capable of running at very high speed, and tire economy by the use of cord tires of liberal size and the reduction of all unsprung weight to a minimum to eliminate bouncing of the wheels and consequent slipping and wear of the tires.[77]

The article continued with a description of the engine, which was adapted from the famed Duesenberg racing engine:

> In the engine shown at the Salon, the well-known Duesenberg arrangement of valves is used, the inlet and exhaust valves being arranged in the cylinder head horizontally and operated by means of rocker levers extending up the sides of the cylinders. However, owing to the very satisfactory results obtained with the racing engines, which have inclined valves in the head, operated by an overhead camshaft, it has been decided to adopted this construction in the stock cars, and this feature will be introduced in the next lot of engines to be built.[78]

To raise additional working capital, National's stockholders voted to increase the capital stock of the company from 80,000 shares to 140,000 shares and to issue 10,000 shares in preferred stock with an 8 percent interest rate which would be sold.[79]

By December, a consortium of banks had taken conservatorship of Allan Ryan's assets. Ryan's liabilities approximated $16 million, most of which were loans to provide financing for his various companies including Stutz. It was believed that Ryan's assets exceeded his total liabilities. Despite Ryan's financial difficulties, Stutz continued under the banks. A brief visit to the Stutz plant by Ryan and Charles Schwab led to speculation that Schwab might buy Ryan's interest in the company.[80]

14

The Duesenberg Brothers Unveil Their Automobile

To introduce the Duesenberg automobile to its new hometown, the company displayed a 1921 roadster and the chassis for a touring car in the lobby of the Claypool Hotel. The roadster's straight-eight motor produced up to 75 horsepower. Equipped with four wheel brakes, a new innovation, the car also had a new design with a tubular front axle and an aluminum body with a total weight of 2,900 pounds.[1] Eventually Duesenberg would equip the car with balloon tires, the first manufacturer to use such tires on an American passenger car.[2] The car came with an option of either the cast iron pistons favored by most consumers or aluminum pistons, which the Duesenbergs traditionally used in their racing machines.[3]

Duesenberg hired the Mead Construction Company to build a new factory and separate office building on West Washington Street for a total cost of $125,000.[4] By the end of May, the Indianapolis plant had built its first three cars, with the shipment to sales agents expected on July 1. In addition to the consumer cars, the plant also built four racing cars to participate in the Grand Prix in Le Mans, France.[5]

In May, the stockholders of the William Small Company, makers of the Monroe automobile, decided to advance the company $200,000 in non-interest-bearing notes due in one, two, three and four years. The money would allow the company to pay its existing creditors and exit from receivership.[6] The company also decided to reduce the price of a Monroe car from $1,440 to $1,295 for either the touring model or the roadster.[7] Despite the willingness of the shareholders to lend the company more money, the company was liquidated by a receiver at the end of December.[8]

After complaining of not feeling well at the National Auto Show in New York City, Dr. Leslie S. Skelton, who had purchased Premier in October 1919, died at age 56 in late January. Leaving early from the auto show, he continued his business trip with stops in Cleveland and Chicago before returning to the Kansas City area, where he was hospitalized.[9] This placed Premier's future in question. The board of directors indicated the company would continue and hired George W. Goethal & Company to provide recommendations on the future path for the company and its reorganization. The board's reorganization committee members were Ivan F. Schaefer as chairman, Newton P. Hutchinson, S. Follansbee, J. D. Sutherland, and a representative from the Fletcher American National Bank.[10] The reorganization of Premier occurred on March 30, 1921, with capitalization of $1 million. Representatives of creditors, minority stockholders, Premier dealers, and company officers were elected as directors.[11]

Part of the company's path forward might have been the proceeds from a $200,000 life insurance policy purchased on May 28, 1920, by Dr. Skelton. In the application, Skelton stated he was not afflicted with disease nor had he had surgery. The life insurance policy was pledged to Fletcher American National Bank as security for a loan. Wanting to collect the life insurance proceeds, the bank filed against Premier, the American Central Life Insurance Company and the Traveler's Insurance Company. The Traveler's Insurance Company filed a cross-complaint against the company, Fletcher American National Bank, and the estate of Leslie S. Skelton alleging that Dr. Skelton's health was misrepresented at the time of the issuance of the policy.[12]

The severity of the economic slump of 1920 was lessening. Despite the protestations that demand for cars was off in the previous fall, comments by various manufacturers gave insight into the depth of the problem. William Thompson, Stutz president, said, "We are running at about 80 percent of full capacity and have orders booked that will assure operations at the present rate until early May." Premier, Marmon and National also all reported an increase in activity.[13]

Despite the increase in activity, Marmon announced a 20 percent decrease in the price of its cars to eliminate excess inventory. The new pricing included a four-person or seven-person touring car for $3,985, a speedster for $4,185, a coupe for $4,875, a sedan for $5,275, and a town car or limousine for $5,400. Moscovics talked about the rationale for the reduction in prices:

> Material can now be purchased for less than was the case a year ago. Present inventories are worth their reproduction value. So we have disregarded prices paid for present inventories and figured instead what materials and labor can be purchased for now or in the immediate future. We believe the public is entitled to purchase its needs at present day valuations and my company is willing to sell its motor cars regardless of the necessary sacrifices.[14]

Marmon wasn't alone in reducing its prices. Jordan was the first auto company to reduce its prices, followed by Marmon.[15] Shortly thereafter, Chevrolet and Oakland announced price reductions and it was anticipated that General Motors would follow.[16] The strategy of the price reductions worked well for Marmon. Within two weeks, the entire stock with the exception of three closed cars had been sold and the company experienced strong demand for its products.[17]

When fire struck the third floor of the Stutz plant in May, water caused significant damage to inventories. The company estimated that it had lost approximately $100,000 in materials and it would take six weeks for the plant to resume normal production levels.[18]

Recognizing the engineering strength of the HCS roadster and promoting its Indianapolis manufacturer, race organizers named the car as the 1921 Indianapolis 500 pace car with Harry Stutz at the wheel. Stutz practiced with his Stutz racer on the track for several days before the Indianapolis 500, obtaining a speed of roughly 60 miles per hour.[19]

For the 1921 Indianapolis 500, Fred Duesenberg registered six cars. Just as in 1920, the arrival of some of the Duesenbergs from New Jersey happened at the last minute, including one piloted by Eddie Pullen that arrived just four days before the race.[20] The Duesenbergs piloted by Joe Boyer and Roscoe Sarles joined pole sitter Ralph DePalma on the front row. Other members of the Duesenberg team ended up further back in the pack, with Eddie Hearne on the third row, Albert Guyot and Benny Hill on the fifth row, Jimmy Murphy on the seventh row, and Eddie Pullen on the eighth row.[21]

The winner of the race would be awarded $20,000 from the Speedway with additional

14. The Duesenberg Brothers Unveil Their Automobile

Harry Stutz with Barney Oldfield in the 1921 HCS pace car at the Indianapolis 500 (courtesy Stutz Club).

prize money awarded to the top ten finishers. Just as in 1920, a lap fund was put up by the citizens of Indianapolis. The fund would award $100 to the leader of each of the first 150 laps and then to the leader of alternating laps for the remainder of the race.[22] To improve his chances to win the race, Sarles had 300 gallons "of especially fine quality" gasoline shipped to him from Los Angeles at a cost of $1,100. The gasoline, shipped in one-gallon containers, cost $3.62 per gallon including delivery charges.[23]

Driving a Louis Chevrolet-designed Frontenac, Tommy Milton won the 1921 Indianapolis 500, setting a new speed record of 89.62 miles per hour for cars with 183 cubic inches of displacement. The citizens of Indianapolis took pride in the fact that Indianapolis-built race cars took home the vast majority of the prize money. The Frontenacs finished first, third (Percy Ford, Burke, and Ellingboe), and ninth (Ralph Mulford), while the Duesenberg entries finished second (Sarles), fourth (Eddie Miller), sixth (Guyot, Boyer, and Miller), and eighth (Benny Hill and Underlick).[24] Of the 23 entries, only nine were running at the conclusion of the race. For the first time in the history of the Indianapolis 500, a car designed by the same person (Louis Chevrolet) won back-to-back races.[25]

The Indianapolis 500 set up a clash between two Indianapolis manufacturers at the 225-mile Universal Trophy race at Uniontown, New Jersey in mid–June. In the Duesenberg camp were Jimmy Murphy (captain), Roscoe Sarles, Eddie Miller, and Eddie Pullen or Joe Boyer, who would face off against the Frontenac group which included Tommy Milton, Ralph Mulford, and Jules Ellingboe. Adding particular interest to the race was the fact that Milton had been part of the Duesenberg camp and set a world record at Daytona Beach prior to 1921.[26] The Duesenberg team dominated the Universal Trophy race, with Sarles winning with an average speed of 97.75 miles per hour and Miller finishing third. Milton, who was favored to win the race, finished eighth (last).[27]

Having watched others benefit from lower pricing, by the end of June other car companies announced price reductions. Cole reduced the prices of its Aero Eight models by amounts ranging from $455 to $700. The company attributed this reduction in price to the greater buying power it had with the increased number of cars being manufactured.[28] Premier, which had offered a guarantee that prices would not be cut, joined the throng, reducing prices on its automobiles on the day the guarantee expired. The new pricing for its cars ranged from a $710 reduction for a seven-passenger open car or a seven-passenger art craft top car to a $1,000 reduction for a four-passenger sedan.[29] Despite these significant price decreases, the Premier models remained as medium priced cars. National also announced significant price reductions, ranging from $760 on the four passenger touring car, seven passenger touring car, and the roadster to $990 on the four-passenger coupe and the seven-passenger sedan.[30] Stutz Motor Car Company also announced a price reduction of $650 on all models. The Bearcat and roadster models were cut from $3,900 to $3,250 while the four- and six-passenger open cars were reduced from $4,000 to $3,350.[31] LaFayette also joined the crowd, reducing the price on its cars by amounts ranging from $750 to $950. The touring car and roadster were reduced by $775 to $4,850, the four-door coupe was reduced by $950 to $6,250, the sedan was reduced by $950 to $6,500, and the limousine was reduced by $750 to $6,750.[32]

HCS also announced a price reduction of $200 on all of its cars effective August 1. The new prices were a roadster at $2,725, a four-passenger touring car at $2,775, and a coupe at $3,450. The just introduced four-passenger sedan continued with its introductory price of $3,650. The company explained the rationale for the price reduction as well as reassured the buying public that the quality of the HCS would remain:

> When the HCS was first introduced in 1919 it was considered one of the fairest-priced cars on the market and this reduction, which is possible because of a decrease in the price of raw materials and labor savings, expresses Mr. Stutz's policy of always giving the public a square deal. The same high standard of workmanship and materials which Mr. Stutz has set will be strictly adhered to.[33]

Duesenberg Straight Eight Coupe (Bass Photo Co. Collection, Indiana Historical Society).

For the French Grand Prix race, Fred Duesenberg entered four specially made racers but failed to send in the entry money.[34] That was provided by Albert Champion, an émigré to America who had become a multimillionaire after founding Champion Spark Plugs with W. S. Durant.[35] The four-member Duesenberg team included Jimmy Murphy, Joe Boyer, Albert Guyot, and Louis Inghibert.

While practicing on the Grand Prix course, Jimmy Murphy and his riding mechanic, Louis Inghibert, were injured when a horse jumped over a fence and stopped in the middle of the track. In an attempt to miss the horse, Murphy swerved sharply and ended up in a ditch, where the car overturned.[36] On race day, despite being taped from his hips to his arm pits, Murphy took the checkered flag. The Duesenberg piloted by Dubonnet, who replaced Inghibert, finished fourth and Guyot finished sixth. Boyer's Duesenberg exited the race when a connecting rod broke on lap 18.[37]

After the Uniontown and French Grand Prix races, Duesenberg announced that it was going to exit the racing game to concentrate on the building of stock cars. The cars, priced between $5,000 and $8,000,[38] featured straight-eight engines and four-wheel hydraulic brakes. J. Edward Schipper, writing for *Automotive Industries*, described the Duesenberg car:

> This car is one of the most direct interpretations of racing experience which has ever been offered to the public. Its engine is identical in many respects with the 183 cu. in. engine of the Duesenberg racer which recently won the French Grand Prix race.[39]

In September, Marmon announced three new closed-body styles for the Marmon 34: a coupe, a suburban, and a sedan which could accommodate seven passengers with five in the back and two in the front of the car.[40]

The idea of a creating a $50 million company composed of auto parts and auto manufacturers was bandied about by the creditors' group of the Jackson Motors Company. In addition to Jackson Motors, the idea included National and Cole as part of the new corporation along with the Traffic Truck Company of St. Louis, the Covert Gear Company of Lockport, New York, the Herschell-Spillman Company of North Tonowanda, New York, the Liberty Motor Car Company of Detroit, the Mitchell Motor Car Company of Racine, Wisconsin, and the Gardner Motor Company of St. Louis. This idea was not seriously considered by either National or Cole officials. Joseph Cole indicated he had not heard of the plan, while George Dickson of National said he had been contacted:

> About 60 days ago, I believe it was in July, one of our directors said someone had mentioned to him that such a merger was being discussed. Soon after that we received a communication mentioning the proposed merger and asking us to attend a meeting to discuss it. We immediately replied we were not the least interested.[41]

The Indianapolis Motor Speedway hosted a special 100-mile race among six of the "speed kings" on September 21, 1921, as part of the American Society for Steel Treating convention in Indianapolis. Pitting the Frontenac race cars against Duesenberg race cars, the race included Tommy Milton, winner of the Indianapolis 500, Howdy Wilcox, winner of the 1919 Indianapolis 500, Benny Hill, and Eddie Hearne on the Frontenac team, and Jimmy Murphy, winner of the French Grand Prix, and Roscoe Sarles for the Duesenberg team.[42] The race received the AAA sanction, meaning that any speed records would be official. The night before the race, Tommy Milton's car arrived from Syracuse, New York, where he had participated in a race.[43] On race day after a rain delay, it was decided that the race would be shortened to 50 miles long instead of the previously announced 100 miles. Wilcox won the race with an average speed of 97.5 miles per hour. Placing second was Jimmy Murphy, who led the entire race until the last lap, when he developed engine trouble and had to limp across the finish line. Benny Hill and his riding mechanic were injured when his Frontenac, going about 85 miles per hour, jumped the retaining wall on the south turn. The Wilcox Peugeot had 274 cubic inches of displacement as compared to the other car's 183 cubic inches of displacement.[44]

In a field of five racers in another special race at the Speedway in November, Eddie Hearne, driving a Duesenberg, won a 25-mile race in honor of Marshal Ferdinand Foch, the commander of Allied Forces during World War I, with an average speed of 97.5 miles per hour. Finishing one second behind Hearne was Wilcox, also driving a Duesenberg. Hearne passed Wilcox on the backstretch of the final lap to win the race. Mort Roberts, driving a Duesenberg, finished third. Both Frontenac entries failed to finish the race. Benny Hill suffered a broken connecting rod while Cornelius Van Ranst failed to finish.[45]

In October Cole introduced a new model, the 890, with a price tag of $2,485. This new model was priced approximately $110 lower than the Aero Eight model first introduced in 1918.[46]

Change was afoot at LaFayette when D. McCall White, vice president and chief engineer, resigned, stating that he no longer felt that the company needed his design services. The firm had no plans for a replacement.[47]

1921 was not a good year for Stutz, which announced a loss of $632,370. In his report to shareholders, president William Thompson attributed the loss to production problems and sales inefficiency.[48]

One of Indianapolis' original automobile firms, Premier, was in the process of reorganizing when Hiram A. Whitman, holder of four $1,000 past due notes, petitioned the court to appoint a receiver for the company. The company had assets of $2 million in excess of its liabilities.[49] Trying to put the company in better financial health, the board obtained a $60,000 loan from Fletcher American National Bank. The financial stress on the company was underscored by the comments of M. A. Whipple, the firm's vice president and general manager:

> In order not to deplete the cash reserves necessary to the operation of this company's business, the board of directors, by and with the approval of several committees representing the creditors of Premier Motor Corporation, found it expedient and necessary to borrow the sum of $60,000 on a secured basis, viz, a temporary bond or note issued secured by a deed of trust to the Fletcher American National Bank as trustee.
>
> The obtaining of this amount of money was required in order that the company could pay its taxes due to the county of Marion, the state of Indiana, and the United States; and by doing so, avoid having imposed oppressive penalties.[50]

15

Industry Under Stress

A Louis Chevrolet-designed Frontenac automobile premiered at the Hotel Commodore during the 1922 New York Auto Show. Frontenac had been organized by financier Allan A. Ryan[1] as a Delaware Corporation with authorized capital of $1 million[2]; the Frontenac car was expected to cost between $2,000 and $2,200.[3] Shortly after the incorporation of Frontenac, Ryan resigned from the Stutz Motor Car Company board, although his stock in Stutz Motor Car Company was in the hands of a trustee.[4]

At the New York Auto Show there was talk about how car prices were likely to rise. Perhaps this was wishful thinking on the part of the automobile manufacturers, as multiple companies including Stutz announced a decrease in the price of their automobiles.[5] Stutz also introduced the option of either a right-hand or a left-hand drive. Until 1922, drivers had occupied the right-hand side of all Stutz cars.[6]

Joining the ranks of automobile companies reducing the price of their automobiles was Marmon in early January.[7] While the January price reduction was relatively small, over the prior year, Marmon's aggregate price reduction ranged from a low of $1,300 to a high of $1,500. Despite the price decreases, Walter Marmon thought the industry outlook was improving:

> We do not expect any enormous increase in production during the coming year but we do expect a substantial increase, say 20 percent, over last year, and we have very good reasons for believing that this recovery is well on its way. The national automobile show held recently at New York was productive of a better business than was generally expected and there is no reason to believe that production of cars will not be larger by a good margin than during 1921.[8]

Likewise, LaFayette Motors announced significant price cuts ranging from $700 to $1,350. When added together with a price cut about 12 months before, the price of a LaFayette car was reduced, on average, by 30 percent. After the price cut, the cost of an open LaFayette car ranged from $3,085 to $4,000.[9]

Concerned over the price cutting in the automobile industry, B. A. Worthington, president of Duesenberg Motors, warned of the dangers of further cuts in a speech to the Indianapolis Chamber of Commerce:

> I would sound an admonition to the automobile trade in opposition to the wholesale price cutting that has been rampant throughout the country. In fact, this fever has gone so far that many high grade cars today are sold for less than their actual cost, probably for the purpose of gaining temporary financial assistance that cannot be gained in any other way.
>
> It is highly necessary to the welfare of the automobile industry that manufacturers realize a reasonable profit from the sale of each car. Any other policy is short-sighted and absolutely ruinous to the trade.

There ought to be some means evolved by those who are vitally interested in getting together and stabilizing profits.[10]

The property belonging to the William Small Company, manufacturer of the Monroe automobile, was sold at a receiver's sale to the Fletcher American National Bank for $175,000. Although the company had approximately $900,000 in undisputed claims and $200,000 in disputed claims by an estimated 450 creditors, a reorganization of the company was anticipated.[11]

Needing funds to sustain it after the prolonged downturn, in January National filed for $750,000 in bonds to be secured by its plant and equipment. Only a portion of the 8 percent bond notes to be issued in increments of $100, $500, and $1,000 would be drawn at the time, with the remainder being available as necessary. The maturity date of the bonds was January 1, 1927.[12]

National's need for funds was highlighted in March when the Columbia Axle Company of Cleveland, Ohio, filed a claim for $12,305 and sought a receiver for the company. The company protested that it was not insolvent and had liquid assets in excess of $12,305.[13] Columbia Axle agreed to withdraw the receivership suit when National arranged for an additional $450,000 in financing. With the additional funding, the company planned to increase the volume of cars being produced.[14]

Stutz made numerous changes in its 1922 models. The most significant was increasing the fuel efficiency of the engine while providing a 50 percent increase in power, resulting in better hill climbing ability and higher maximum speeds. The speed of the car was increased from 60 miles per hour to 75 miles per hour.[15]

New York financier Allan Ryan, chairman of Frontenac Motors, visited the Indianapolis Motor Speedway to watch the trials of the first Frontenac car. Louis Chevrolet, the firm's vice president, made several laps around the track averaging more than 70 miles per hour.[16] The test was one of those crucial landmarks, as six Frontenacs were entered by Louis Chevrolet in the 1922 Indianapolis 500. Chevrolet planned to have four cars with four-cylinder engines in the race, including the car which Gaston Chevrolet had driven to victory in 1920. The two remaining cars had eight-cylinder engines, including the car driven by Tommy Milton in the 1921 Indianapolis 500.[17]

Ryan was in town not only to witness the car trials, but also to search for a location for the Frontenac production facility, as the prototype and the first few models were being produced in a temporary facility on West Tenth Street. He said,

> I have investigated several industrial properties here, but at the moment I cannot say definitely just what will be done. This much is certain, however. We are going to acquire one of the finest plants that it is possible for us to obtain for the manufacture of the Frontenac, and we are making every effort to make a decision just as quickly as possible."[18]

Eventually Frontenac identified the old Empire/Federal Motor Works site on 15th Street with 100,000 square feet of factory floor space as a site for purchase. Frontenac Motor Corporation of America, Inc., which was listed on the stock exchange, planned to employ up to 1,500 people in the plant. The company planned to offer three different models: a four-passenger touring model, a two-passenger roadster, and a four-passenger enclosed car.[19] William Thompson, Stutz president, who served on the Frontenac board, explained the plans for the company:

15. Industry Under Stress

Stutz D-H engine advertisement (courtesy Stutz Club).

Though other cities made a bid for the Frontenac plant, we are glad to say we are able to keep the enterprise here in Indianapolis, and our selection of the ex-Empire plant came after we had investigated numerous other active properties. The new Frontenac factory site is ideally located so far as rail connections are concerned and is so centrally situated as to be accessible from all parts of the city.

It is our intention to waste no time in getting started. Work will proceed at once to put the factory in readiness and we have no doubt that all equipment and machinery will be installed for production within 30 days. We plan to have our first sample cars ready by the latter part of May. We should be in production in a limited way by June.[20]

With the expansion of its manufacturing facilities completed, Stutz had 400,000 square feet of production facilities. The company equipped the plant with tools and equipment specifically designed for the D-H model which was under development. The *Indianapolis Star* reported that technical experts proclaimed that the manufacturing standards at the plant ranked with those of the leading producers of automobiles. Among the equipment used at the plant were dynamometers to test engines before they affixed in the chassis and axometers for the testing of rear axles.[21]

News reports in April, confirmed by LaFayette officials, indicated that LaFayette and the Pierce-Arrow Motor Company of Buffalo, New York, had agreed in principle to merge. Charles Nash, president of Nash Motors Company and LaFayette, would become the head of the new organization. Both plants would continue with their existing nameplates.[22] The merger negotiations subsequently failed because one of the smaller banks held out for a higher interest rate on the indebtedness than others thought should be paid.[23]

With the merger of LaFayette and Pierce-Arrow called off, the LaFayette stockholders approved the recapitalization of the company with an additional $2 million in working capital and the establishment of LaFayette Motors Corporation (LaFayette) to buy the assets of the current company.[24] Nash Motors had loaned LaFayette Motors Company approximately $500,000 and had endorsed $1 million in bank loans. In return, about 80 percent of the stock in the original LaFayette Motors Company had been transferred to Charles Nash.[25] In conjunction with the recapitalization, Nash, who would become more involved with the company,[26] explained,

> It must not be thought that simply because $2,000,000 of additional money has been put into this company we will immediately double or treble our production. Rather, what is have in mind is a gradual, orderly development which will insure continuity of operations and under which the quality of the car may be consistently be made. Every detail of manufacture is of so much importance, and labor of the most skilled and intelligent type is so essential, that an increase in production is necessarily slow.[27]

Less than two months after the recapitalization of LaFayette Motors, Nash announced that the company would move to Milwaukee, Wisconsin. Land had already been acquired adjacent to the Nash Motors Company and a plant would be built. Nash said of the decision to relocate the company,

> LaFayette has been greatly hampered for space in its present plant at Mars Hill, Indianapolis, and this handicap will become much more serious as the company's production increases, thus making necessary an increased capacity either here or elsewhere. In view of these conditions and the growing desirability of a closer geographic co-ordination of all Nash activities, it seemed logical to establish the LaFayette in a new plant in Milwaukee, even at the sacrifice of the many advantages which have been found in Indianapolis. The new Milwaukee plant will triple the present manufacturing capacity of the company.[28]

By the end of 1922, operations at the Indianapolis LaFayette Motors plant had ended. Over a six-week period during November and December, equipment from the plant was loaded onto train cars and shipped to Milwaukee.[29]

An advertisement placed by H. B. MacAlpine Corporation[30] attempted to raise an additional $3 million[31] in capital for Duesenberg in January 1922, proclaiming that the Duesenberg factory had $12,000,000 in orders and was working 13 hours per day. The sale of preferred shares with an 8 percent premium at $100 per share also offered a bonus of a one-half share of common stock for each share of preferred stock purchased.[32]

Premier, which had struggled financially for years, was placed into receivership as a result of a friendly petition by the American Foundry Company, a number of other creditors, and stockholders including James A. Price of Okmulgee, Oklahoma, Newton P. Hutchinson of Providence, Rhode Island, B. L. Craig of Detroit, Michigan, and H. M. Hottel of Indianapolis. The suit indicated that Premier owed more than $1 million to creditors, but its assets were believed to be adequate for the repayment.

A refinancing plan was formulated to raise an estimated $500,000 in funds. The reorganization plan was conditioned upon transferring the assets of the Premier Motor Corporation, a Delaware company, to the Premier Motor Corporation, an Indiana corporation. Capital of the new company would be $1 million divided equally between common and preferred stock.[33] Hutchinson discussed the reorganization of the company:

> Under date of March 1, 1922, there was submitted to the creditors of Premier Motor Corporation a plan and an agreement for the reorganization of the company. This plan and agreement has since received the acceptance of 95 per cent of the creditors in amount.
>
> The reorganization committee, after a further conference with a view of completing the plan of reorganization and particularly to satisfy any of the financial interests willing to purchase the bonds with reference to the title to the assets on which the bonds will be secured by a first mortgage, have concluded, under advice of counsel, that it will be necessary to have a judicial sale of all the assets, in order to clear the titles properly. The fact that even as small as 5 percent in amount of the creditors have failed to accept the plan, presents a legal objection.[34]

The receiver for Premier, the Indianapolis-based Fletcher Savings and Trust Company, agreed to provide financing to continue the operations of the business.[35] The assets of Premier were sold on the courthouse steps in order to obtain clear title for a reorganization.[36]

In April, the William Small Company, the maker of the Monroe automobile, was reorganized as the Monroe Automobile Company with capitalization of $500,000. The board of directors included William Small, president and general manager; J. H. O'Brien, vice president and executive manager; and F. A. King, J. C. F. Martin, and H. A. Alexander. Alexander, who had been the sales manager of William Small Company and the Indianapolis branch of Buick, introduced a new method for the sale of automobiles to consumers. People would purchase an automobile directly from the factory, which would eliminate both the distributor and the sales agent and thus result in a lower sales price. Alexander said of the plan,

> The sales plan is, perhaps, revolutionary as compared with old sales methods but the interest shown in it on the part of automobile dealers, garage men, service station owners and purchasers indicates that Small, when he conceived of this method of sales, was getting rather close to something which a big part of the public was thinking about. We know that our new plan makes economies which are worthwhile. Out of these economies, coupled with production savings, the Monroe touring and roadster has been priced at $875.[37]

When Fred Duesenberg sold his racing team, one of the first buyers was Harry Hartz, who began his racing career when he won the boys' speed championship of the West Coast driving a miniature race car outfitted with a motorcycle engine. After finishing third in a March race at the Los Angeles Speedway, Hartz decided to enter the Indianapolis 500.[38]

By May, the economic recession appeared to be over. Businesses across Indianapolis were improving, including the automobile industry. The various plants reported that they were running between 60 percent and 80 percent of capacity. Since most of the Indianapolis automobile manufacturers expanded their plants during the war or in 1919, expecting an after-war boom in demand, production was ahead of the level before the war.[39]

Hope grew for a new speed record at the Indianapolis Motor Speedway when Jimmy Murphy set a new unofficial record at the Beverly Hills Speedway with a speed of 120.3 miles per hour in mid–May. It was the first time a car had been clocked going two miles per minute.[40]

A week before the 1922 Indianapolis 500, there was a special race at the Indianapolis Motor Speedway as part of the B'nai B'rith district convention. A field of five—a Monroe driven by Wilbur D'Alene, a Ballot driven by Eddie Hearne, a Fronty-Ford driven by C. Glenn Howard, and two Frontenacs driven by Art Klein and Ralph Mulford—answered the call for a 15-mile race. Hearne won the race, followed by Klein and Mulford.[41]

On the first day of qualifications, held just five days before the Indianapolis 500, Jimmy Murphy took the pole position with an average speed of 100.5 miles per hour in the Murphy Special.[42] The Murphy Special was the Duesenberg racer modified with a Miller engine in which Murphy had won the 1921 French Grand Prix.[43] Sitting next to Murphy on the starting row were Duesenbergs driven by Harry Hartz with an average speed of 99.99 miles per hour and Ralph DePalma with an average speed of 99.55 miles per hour.[44]

Indianapolis was well represented, with 18 cars in the field of 27 racers for the 1922 Indianapolis 500. Duesenberg racers were piloted by Ralph DePalma, Jules Ellingboe, Jerry Wonderlich, Isaac Fetterman, Ora Haibe, Joe Thomas, Ira Vail, and Harry Hartz. Frontenac racers designed by Louis Chevrolet were driven by Roscoe Sarles, Pete DePaolo, Leon Duray, Ralph Mulford, E. G. "Cannonball" Baker, and Art Klein, with the cars driven by Mulford and Sarles being newly built for the race.[45] One of the innovations Chevrolet planned to use during the Indianapolis 500 was a radio in the racer to receive instructions from the pit crew. The pit crew would telephone Hatfield Electric, located about two miles from the track, with the information they wanted conveyed to the drivers. The information would then be sent by radio back to the race cars. Louis Chevrolet came up with this idea as he felt the manual signals were often misunderstood or misconstrued by the drivers.[46] Monroe had three participants in the race, including Tom Alley, L. L. Corum, and Wilbur D'Alene.[47] The three Monroes were cars that had participated in the 1920 race, including the winner of the Indianapolis 500. For the 1921 racing season, all three cars had been mothballed. As part of the reconditioning process, one of the cars was equipped with a wireless system for messages from the pits.[48]

Jimmy Murphy, driving the Murphy Special, was the first driver to win both the pole and the Indianapolis 500. In doing so, Murphy set a new record for speed at 94.48 miles per hour, shattering the record set by Ralph DePalma in 1915 of 89.62 miles per hour. Four other racers—Hartz, Hearne, DePalma, and Haibe—joined Murphy in shattering DePalma's record. For his efforts, Murphy took home $20,000 in prize money from the Speedway and $6,100 in special prizes.

It was a wonderful day for the Indianapolis-produced cars, with eight finishing in the top ten excluding the Murphy Special. Duesenberg-built racers finished second (Hartz),

1922 Cole by Willoughby (LeRoy Cole Collection, Gilmore Car Museum).

fourth (DePalma), fifth (Haibe), sixth (Wonderlich), seventh (Fetterman), eighth (Vail), and tenth (Thomas). The Monroe driven by Alley finished ninth.[49] The results for the other Indianapolis-built racers who were still running when the race was called were Cannonball Baker (11th) and Wilbur D'Alene (15th). While the day was worthy of much celebration by the Duesenberg teams, it was a day of disappointment for the Frontenac teams. Corum had a piston failure on the 169th lap, Mulford had a valve failure on the 161st lap, DePaolo crashed on the 110th lap, Klein had a connecting rod failure on the 108th lap, Duray had a broken axle rod on the 94th lap, Sarles had a connecting rod failure on the 88th lap, and Ellingboe crashed on the 25th lap.[50]

Jimmy Murphy followed up his win of the Indianapolis 500 by winning the 225-mile Universal Trophy race in mid–June, setting a new speed record for the Uniontown, Pennsylvania track at 102.2 miles per hour. It was another strong day of performance for Indianapolis-built racers, with Mulford in a Frontenac finishing second, Wonderlich driving a Duesenberg finishing third, Fetterman in a Duesenberg finishing fourth, and Haibe in a Frontenac finishing fifth.[51]

In June 1922 Indianapolis ranked third in the country behind Detroit and Cleveland in the production of automobiles. The Indianapolis automobile manufacturers included HCS, Cole, Premier, Stutz, National, Marmon, a branch plant of Ford Motor Company, Monroe, Duesenberg, and Frontenac. Total output was in excess of $75 million annually, and the car companies employed 11,000 with a payroll of $10.5 million.[52]

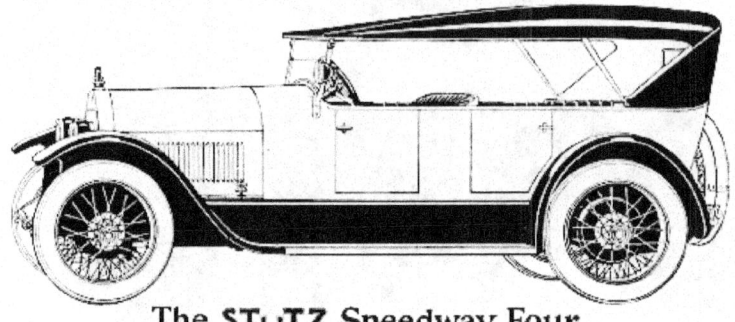

THE SATURDAY EVENING POST

Announcement
COMPANY of AMERICA Inc.

Price Announced
New York Auto Show
or upon Application

The STUTZ Speedway Four

Empowered with an engine so advanced that it reaches far into the future for comparisons in principle as well as in performance—

Developing more than 75 HP with surpassing economy; equally capable of less than a mile or more than 70 m. p. h. on high; with wind-swift acceleration and never a trace of periodic vibration—

From its finely tailored permanent top to the last small detail in appointments, the Stutz Six inspires the highest appraisal.

Here, indeed, is a product worthy of the enviable Stutz trademark —a real advancement, as impressive as is its renowned contemporary—the Stutz Speedway Four.

Stutz Speedway Four

For more than eleven years the Stutz has ranked among the world's automotive masterpieces.

Track, road and thoroughfare have seen it prove its undeniable supremacy. Experience and facilities such as only the Stutz company commands have been lavished upon it.

To its inherent speed, power and stamina now is added an ease of handling comparable only with its gratifying riding composure.

Epitomizing the sportsman's preference in a motor car, the Stutz Speedway Four makes available for refined private ownership the vigor and spirit of champion ability.

* * *

The Stutz line for 1923 offers dominating value. Never has the distinction of Stutz ownership been available to so many. Never have automobile merchants been given so great an opportunity to take advantage of the compelling prestige of the Stutz.

STUTZ MOTOR CAR COMPANY OF AMERICA, Inc.
Indianapolis, Indiana, U. S. A.

Special Displays during Automobile Shows at
Commodore Hotel, New York — Congress Hotel, Chicago
New York show space B-4 — Chicago show space M-2

Speedway Four advertisement (courtesy Stutz Club).

Supporting the lively automobile manufacturing companies were approximately 50 suppliers, the most important of which were Robert H. Hassler, Inc. (spring shocks, stabilizers, and shock absorbers), Martin-Parry Corporation (bodies), Zenite Metal Company, Robbins Body Corporation, Oakes Company (auto parts), Parker Tire and Rubber Company, Wheeler-Schebler Carburetor Company, Sanders and Barth, Weidley Motors Company, and Prest-O-Lite Company.[53]

At a special meeting in June, the stockholders of National Motor Car & Vehicle Company agreed to merge with the newly formed Associated Motor Industries, a consolidation of eight firms with a valued of $80 million. The terms of the transaction were $125,000 in cash and $1,050,000 in stocks and bonds of the company. The creditors of National were asked to accept ten percent in cash, 25 percent in one-year notes, 15 percent in bonds, and 50 percent in preferred stock.[54]

Will I. Ohmer, chairman of Associated Motors, explained the transaction and how it would be competitive in the marketplace:

> This merger is unique in that it has purchased outright all its plants. Instead of being a holding corporation and separate operating corporations, with the holding company holding the majority of the stock with a full set of officers and each operating corporation having a full set of officers and staff, Associated Motor Industries eliminates all of that duplication. The executive officers of the consolidation are the only executive officers of the merger. All the plants will be operated as a unit from the central offices. It is not an imitation of any organization that has gone before it.[55]

In July, Cole introduced the Model 890. Designed by Joseph Cole, the car had new exclusive features including the Ultramite frame, a streamlined Etruscan body, an envelope manifold, and the hydro-cushion spring action.[56]

Stutz shareholders were asked to approve $1.5 million in 7½ percent gold debentures to be repaid over 15 years, as well as 63,000 additional shares, of which 30,000 would be offered to the shareholders at $20 per share with the remainder being set aside for a possible conversion of the bonds. The new stock was offered to the existing shareholders on the basis of three new shares for 20 shares currently owned. The potential issuance of stock in a conversion of the bonds would be 33 shares of stock for every $1,000 in bonds held.[57]

Stutz seven-passenger auto with California top (Indiana Historical Society, P0555).

Stutz announced the Speedway Four Series with eight different body styles, including a seven-passenger phaeton, a four-passenger sportster, a two-passenger roadster, a Deluxe Bearcat Roadster, a seven-passenger car with a California top, a four-passenger car with a California top, a four-passenger coupe, and a five-passenger Sportsedan.[58]

Expecting a 200 percent increase in production within the next six months, Duesenberg announced a $30,000 addition to its manufacturing facilities in August 1922.[59] The company decided to use an existing 200 foot by 60 foot steel building in Scottsburg, Indiana, for the plant addition. The company arranged to have the building torn down and the pieces moved to Indianapolis where the building would be reassembled.[60]

The construction of the new building was not without intrigue. J. R. Skinner, superintendent of the construction company, sought police protection after two conversations with John J. McNamara, the business agent for the Bridge and Structural Iron Workers Union No. 22, who warned that the company might "expect some contention on the job"[61] unless union members were employed. On the night of September 20, 1922, a fire at the Farmer's Terminal Feed and Grain Company adjacent to the Duesenburg plant was raging when the iron framework of the Duesenberg plant collapsed. Prior to the fire, the side columns of the Duesenberg building were in place and an iron truss connected the two side columns. A jin pole used for hoisting trusses and other framework was on the south side. After a night watchman in a nearby building reported seeing the ironwork on the building sway and fall, investigators found that bolts had been removed from the bottom of the west side columns and the guy wires holding the jin pole in place had been cut, causing the jin pole to fail and the framework to collapse. Suspicion grew when the police were unable to find McNamara, who had previously served 5½ years in a California prison for dynamiting the Llewellyn Iron Works[62] and bombing the *Los Angeles Times* building where 22 died.[63] The fire, which caused $100,000 in damage, was believed to have been arson.[64]

It took several years, but McNamara was found guilty of blackmail. The case involved the $1 million construction project at the Elks Club building in 1924. Although it was the Elks Club case on which McNamara was convicted, he was also at the center of several other high profile cases of blackmail and vandalism in Indianapolis, including vandalism at the American Legion headquarters.[65]

Marmon began production of a new seven-passenger phaeton priced at $3,185 which featured a reduction of the height of the car by four inches and a lengthening of the body by one inch. It also had a "panorama" type top.[66]

Allan Ryan, the financier who had engineered the cornering of Stutz stock, filed for bankruptcy in August 1922. The bankruptcy filing reflected $18 million in liabilities, of which $14 million were secured liabilities, and assets of $643,533. The primary creditors were the banks which had taken over the management of Ryan's financial affairs after the Stutz stock corner. Included in the assets were 130,000 shares of Stutz stock securing the banks' loans.[67] To protect the banks from loss, there was a move to relist Stutz stock on the New York Stock Exchange. The bank with the largest exposure was the Guaranty Trust Company, which had 120,614 shares pledged.[68] In the bankruptcy sale, Guaranty Trust bought 132,914 shares at $20 per share for $2,686,286. The remaining 15,000 shares were purchased by the Empire Trust Company for $30,000. With the purchase of the stock, Guaranty Trust gained control of the Stutz Motor Car Company.[69]

Subsequently, Charles Schwab and Eugene V. R. Thayer gained control of Stutz in August when they purchased the Stutz Motor Car shares from the Guaranty Trust Company for $20 per share. One of the Stutz directors had been working on the deal ever since Guaranty Trust bought the shares at the bankruptcy sale.[70] Upon taking control, Schwab announced a price cut ranging from $200 to $500 on the Stutz cars. Additionally, anticipating an increase in production, an expansion of the Stutz plant was planned.[71]

Schwab's controlling interest in the Stutz organization included Ryan's interest in Frontenac Motors. Schwab also made the decision to shutter Frontenac Motors. The company had produced just a few automobiles on a trial basis. The planned purchase of the former Empire Automobile factory by Frontenac was never consummated.[72]

For the first time in its history, Stutz began producing closed cars in late 1922, offering two models to the public. A four-passenger coupe was priced at $3,490 while a four-passenger touring sedan was priced at $4,450. The touring sedan's front doors hinged forward and the tonneau doors hinged backward, giving the car a drawing room effect when the doors were opened. The coupe had two doors which opened at the back. The driver's seat was forward of the front passenger's seat. The passenger's seat folded under the instrument board when not in use.[73]

Anticipating doubling its output in 1923, Cole filed for an increase in its approved capital stock from $1 million to $2 million.[74] At the New York Auto Show in January 1923, Cole announced a reduction in the prices of its models.[75]

Taking advantage of the reputation of the National brand, Associated Motors Corporation changed its name to National Motors Corporation (National) in January 1923 and moved its corporate headquarters to Chicago.[76] National was incorporated in Delaware with 800,000 shares of stock.[77] The company unveiled the National 631, a new model designed by H. L. Holbrook, with a six-cylinder engine producing 35 horsepower and a 112-inch wheelbase. National announced a production schedule of 30,000 of these small six models. Also part of the National lineup were the 671 with a 130-inch wheelbase and the 651 with a 121-inch wheelbase.[78]

Despite its financial difficulties, Premier displayed four models at the New York Auto Show.[79] Also at the show, HCS introduced its first six-cylinder car, the Series 4 Model 6, which had 80 horsepower and was built upon a 126-inch wheelbase.[80] The car's engine was produced by Midwest. While offering the car in blue, gray, and carmine, HCS would do special paint work on a special order basis. The interior of the car offered hand-buffed leather in shades to match the paint. The price of the six-cylinder phaeton was $2,650. The company continued to offer its four-cylinder cars and had reduced the price of the four-cylinder phaeton and roadster from $2,475 to $2,250.[81]

Stutz also introduced a moderately priced six-cylinder car with three models, a roadster, a phaeton, and a sedan. The phaeton and roadster were priced at $1,995 while the five-passenger sedan sold for $2,550. The Stutz Special engine produced 70 horsepower. The car had left-hand steering. For the year, Stutz planned to produce 10,000 automobiles, with 8,000 being six-cylinder models. The company believed the demand for the four-cylinder car would be stronger in 1923 than the 1,200 cars sold in 1922 and revived the Bulldog model, a four-passenger car retailing for $3,115. The remainder of the four-cylinder cars were a phaeton, $2,640; a roadster, $2,450; a standard sportster, $2,790; a Bearcat deluxe speedster, $2,765; and a four-passenger coupe, $3,490.[82] To finance the expansion of the business, Stutz offered $1 million in 15-year 7.5 percent convertible gold debenture bonds maturing October 1, 1937. The bonds were convertible into Stutz stock on the basis of 33 shares for each $1,000 bond.[83]

Duesenberg announced price reductions in early February including $300 for the sedan, $550 for the coupe, $850 for the seven-passenger phaeton, and $1,000 for the two-passenger roadster and the five-passenger phaeton. The company also announced a new sport model to be priced at $5,750.[84]

National had an aggressive goal to produce 55,000 autos and trucks in 1923. Part of the plan was to take over a large unidentified manufacturing facility in Detroit.[85] Following a trend in the industry toward vertical integration, National announced that it would manufacture practically all of the parts for the six-cylinder chassis. This was a benefit of the purchase of various parts suppliers.[86] To support the volume increase, the company arranged for a ten-year bond issue of $3,000,000 at a 7.5 percent interest rate in March 1923, secured by the various plants.[87]

When the AAA Contest Board reduced the engine size requirement to 122 cubic inches of displacement, resulting in a lighter race car, Louis Chevrolet, who had designed and built the winning entries for the 1920 and 1921 Indianapolis 500, designed three new race cars for the May classic using a rotary valve for the first time. The cars, with an estimated 5,000 rpm, would be raced as Scheel-Frontenac autos. Chevrolet anticipated that the 122-cubic-inch engine would generate the same amount of power as the 183-cubic-inch engine.[88]

As the racing year began, Murphy, the racing champion for 1922, continued his winning ways at a 250-mile race in Los Angeles with an average speed of 115.8 miles per hour. For his efforts, Murphy, driving the Durant Special, won the top prize of $9,000. Benny Hill, driving a McDonald Special, finished five yards behind Murphy in second place. DePalma, in a Duesenberg special, finished third.[89]

Stratton Motors Corporation was formed with capital stock of $500,000 as a sales organization in March 1923 by a group of investors including Edward Gates, an Indianapolis attorney, and New Yorkers Frederick Barrows and Frank A. Kateley. The incorporators planned to enter the manufacture of automobiles. Frederick Van Nuys, the attorney for the incorporators, said:

> The company expects to enter the manufacturing field just as quickly as negotiations can be closed for the purchase of manufacturing plants. I can say that deals are pending for two Indianapolis automobile plants but I cannot say what plants they are.[90]

While Van Nuys might not have been at liberty to discuss what Indianapolis plants were under consideration, automobile men in Indianapolis believed the targets were Premier and Monroe, both of whom had been operating on a limited scale for several months. Monroe had been sold to Fletcher American National Bank about a year before. Monroe superintendent J. H. O'Brien confirmed that negotiations with Stratton Motors had occurred but did not release any details. Likewise, Ivan Schaeffer, secretary/treasurer of Premier, confirmed that the company had been in negotiations.[91]

Within days, the *Indianapolis Star* announced the asset purchase of Monroe by Stratton Motors (Stratton). The company had been formed by Frank S. Stratton to manufacture a car of his design which he drove from Cleveland to Indianapolis, as well as to continue the manufacture of Monroe automobiles. Officers and directors of the firm included Frank S. Stratton, president; Frederick I. Barrows, Connersville, Indiana, vice president; Frank A. Kateley, Toledo, Ohio, secretary-treasurer; Alwin A. Gloetzner, New York; and Edward E. Gates, Indianapolis. To support operations, Stratton intended to issue $500,000 in preferred bonds with interest at 6 percent.[92] By June, the production of Monroe cars had ceased so that Stratton could concentrate on its Stratton car, which had a retail price of $695.[93]

In May, a bid made by Frederick I. Barrows of Connersville, Indiana, for Premier was accepted by Fletcher Savings Bank and Trust and ratified by the court. Barrows organized Premier Motors, Inc. (Premier), putting $225,000 in cash into the transaction, and provided lien notes to the receivers secured by 25,000 shares of stock in the new company distributed among the creditors. Barrows was named president of the new Premier, while Ivan F. Schaeffer, who had operated the plant while the company was in receivership,[94] was named vice president and continued to be the active head.[95] The directors included Barrows, Arthur Dixon, J. D. Sutherland, and Blaine H. Miller. Dixon was the president of American Bearing Corporation of Indianapolis and had previously been with the McFarlan Motor Corporation and vice president and manager of Ansted Engine Company, both located in Connersville. Sutherland was the sales manager of the Wyman-Gordon Company of Cleveland, Ohio, a maker of crankshafts as well as numerous aircraft parts including engines, propellers, airframes and landing gear. Miller was the president of the American Foundry Company.[96]

Barrows was no stranger to the automobile industry. He was the vice president and treasurer of the Lexington Motor Company, located in nearby Connersville, Indiana. When Lexington went into receivership in early 1923, Barrows, along with the majority of management, left the company.[97] He also had been president of the Teeter-Hartley Corporation of Hagerstown, Indiana.[98]

Ivan Schaeffer spoke of the future of Premier:

> Approximately 8,000 Premiers are in use in America and in almost every country in the world. The present capacity of the plant is 25 cars a day. The plant has been operating during the receivership and cars have been manufactured and sold. The service has been maintained and selling agencies, in the main, have been kept going. We have in prospect large orders for a taxicab that has already been developed at the plant and we are now equipped and in position to produce these taxicabs in quantities, in addition to the regular line of Premier passenger cars. A sample taxicab has been submitted to interested parties and has been approved by them after being subjected to rigorous tests. With the addition of this commercial factor to the already well-developed passenger car business of the company, it would seem that the future of Premier Motors, Inc. as one of the strong Indianapolis automobile producing companies, is definitely assured.[99]

As part of its strategy for survival, Premier negotiated a five-year agreement with a New York taxicab company to supply taxicabs, with 1,000 being supplied for the first year, increasing by 10 percent each succeeding year. The first shipment of taxicabs was expected in July 1923.[100]

The sale of Premier was blocked by the United States government in June. The government claimed Premier had been overpaid on contracts dating back to November 20, 1917, and wanted Fletcher Savings Bank and Trust, as receiver, to show why all monies held after payment of the priority claims should not be held in escrow and why the 25,000 shares of stock should not be held in abeyance until the government claims were satisfied.[101]

Shortly after Stratton announced that it would not be producing the Monroe car, Barrows announced the organization of Monroe Motors, Inc. (Monroe) to continue production of the Monroe. Space was leased in a portion of the Premier factory. Barrows said of the plans:

> The officials of the Monroe institution announce that experimental work is well underway for the production of other models than those now offered by the Monroe line. Two eminent consulting engineers have been invited to make reports on the models and every progress is being made in the presentation of

a light, quality production job at an economical cost. These plans absolutely require more space than the old Monroe plants offer and hence the lease of a part of the larger Premier plant.[102]

The stockholders of Elgin Motors, Inc. selected Indianapolis for the relocation of their manufacturing plant and purchased the old Empire/Federal Motor Works building. They planned to use the equipment from the old Elgin Motor Car Company and had it shipped to Indianapolis. The company, having bought the patents and name of a car which had been under development for five years, planned to make a six-cylinder car retailing for less than $1,500 with production beginning in September. Estimated employment was 500 men.[103]

One of the problems facing the auto industry was the supply of used automobiles. The industry produced 3.6 million new cars in 1923. To sell the new cars, dealers took 2.8 million cars in trade.[104] So, in reality, to break even the industry needed to sell 6.4 million cars during 1923. It wasn't only the increased sales volume that needed to be supported. According to the Automobile Dealers Association, the average trade-in allowance was $322 but the average resale price of the autos was $308, resulting in the dealer losing $14 on each used car, not including the costs incurred in reconditioning and reselling the car.[105]

Breaking with tradition, Cole announced that it would no longer accept used cars as trade-ins for new vehicles. Instead, buyers of the Cole Aero Eight were given a lower price, reflecting the elimination of the used car inventory.[106] The discount to the dealer was $800 on the seven-passenger car, the four-passenger sport car, and the two-passenger roadster; $300 on the coupe; and $1,000 on the sedan.[107] This followed 18 months of analysis which indicated that the used car business threatened the stability of the automobile industry. Joseph Cole commented on the difficulties of accepting used cars in trade:

> Bankers refused to make adequate loans to assist in carrying used car inventories. In some sections, they refused to make any loans at all.
>
> The reason is not far to seek. Simple analysis of a dealer's statement over a season will reveal that considerably more than half of a dealer's supposed profit margin is consumed in maintaining a used car department. There are interest charges, commissions, rent, light, heat, labor, clerical hire, advertising, etc, to say nothing of the eventual loss which comes when the used car is sold that is below the allowance made to the buyer of a new car.[108]

Cole's assessment was on target. Used car inventory had become a terrible problem for the automobile industry. A March 15, 1923, report by the National Automobile Dealers' Association based upon a survey of 3,333 dealers in 18 states estimated that there were 400,000 used cars in the stock of automobile dealers, representing an investment of $152.2 million. It was believed that the loss on used cars totaled $23 million during the first three months of 1923.[109]

Cole dealers agreed to abandon the practice of trading in used cars and closed their used car departments. Several dealers reported an increase in sales after the announcement of the no-trade-in policy.[110]

Between 1922 and 1923, 1,450,000 cars were sold for scrap and another 700,000 were exported. Basically, the industry was saturated. The industry's years of expansion were over, leading to increased competition. This gave those manufacturers who were teetering two options: consolidate or go out of business. The early to mid–1920s saw many old companies fade from the landscape, including several Indianapolis manufacturers.[111]

In April 1923, Peter A. Pfisterer filed a petition for the receivership of Duesenberg, claiming the company was insolvent and charging its officers with mismanagement and an internal feud with the engineers. Duesenberg reacted by claiming to have more than $1 million in assets and no liabilities. Pfisterer was the owner of one share of Duesenberg stock and was an officer with Western Wrecking Company.[112] The case was heard by Judge James M. Leathers of the Indiana Superior Court. In the hearing, Chester Ricker, general manager of Duesenberg, acknowledged tension between the company engineers and management but denied it was anything out of the ordinary, saying under oath,

> There was some dissention between automotive engineers. Dissention between automotive engineers is natural. They usually disagree as to the qualifications of the motor. Such was the case between me and Fred S. and August Duesenberg, chief engineer and assistant, respectively of the Duesenberg Company.[113]

While the company had spent $50,000 on racing activities in 1922, Ricker denied the charges that the company was a part owner of the Duesenberg racing cars being assembled for participation in the Indianapolis 500 at a location other than the manufacturing facility. While neither Fred or August owned any Duesenberg stock, each received royalties on the cars manufactured.[114] Under oath, Pfisterer admitted that he had no proof of the insolvency of the company. The information he relied upon was from a confidential informant. Judge Leathers denied the petition for the appointment of a receiver for Duesenberg, stating, "Pfisterer's charges of gross mismanagement, dissention, extravagance and insolvency against the officers of Duesenberg Company are unfounded." He continued, "Pfisterer's allegations are not proved by a preponderance of evidence. His charges that Duesenberg officers were dishonest; that they misappropriate proceeds of stock sales; that they quarreled, and that the company is hopelessly insolvent, are not borne out by the evidence." He pointed to the fact that the company was organized in 1920 and that the past three years had been spent in development of the car.[115]

Frontenac submitted a voluntary petition for bankruptcy in April 1923, claiming assets of $425 and liabilities of $88,163. The company had produced only one car, which was shown to Indianapolis visitors in late May 1922.[116]

Duesenberg used the Indianapolis Motor Speedway as a test track in late April 1923. Wanting to duplicate a trip across the United States, Duesenberg ran one of its autos for 3,155 miles at an average speed of 62.63 miles per hour. The engines ran for 2 days 2 hours 45 minutes without stopping as gasoline, oil and water were supplied from another Duesenberg driven by a stock supply car as well as during the car's three stops for new tires. When a change of drivers was needed, it was accomplished with the supply car running at about 50 miles per hour.[117]

For years, Marmon had touted its superior engineering. In 1923 the company commissioned a national study of Marmon owners about the cost of maintenance for those cars serviced by Marmon service centers. The average cost of repairs on the 1922–1923 series Marmons was $4.71 per month. Fred Moscovics said,

> The difference of a few cents or a few dollars per month is not a primary consideration to a man who wants a car of maximum performance and comfort, but the reliability of the car is of permanent importance. A reliable car is one which will keep on running and stay out of the shop. The real significance of average monthly maintenance figures, therefore, is not the actual savings in dollars and cents, but the fact that the car with the lowest maintenance costs is also the car most constantly in service.[118]

Marmon announced a new four-passenger speedster featuring a collapsible top in the spring of 1923.[119]

Cole Royal Sedan advertisement (Indiana Historical Society, P0143).

With operations expanding, Stutz was out of production space and negotiated a lease of the three-story building at the corner of Tenth and Roanoke streets where it had first begun operations. Ideally located across the street from the Stutz location on Capitol Avenue, this 15,000-square-foot facility was used for the storage of raw materials.[120]

As time kept ticking down toward the big race, Indianapolis residents wondered where the three Duesenbergs entered in the race were. As late as May 25, the first day of qualifications, they had not yet appeared at the Speedway and reportedly weren't yet ready. The Duesenberg racers weren't the only cars missing from the field. The four Louis Chevrolet-designed Scheel-Frontenacs with rotary valves were withdrawn from the race as they weren't ready.[121]

It would be the first time that a Louis Chevrolet-designed car had not been a part of the race since 1916. Chevrolet explained the decision:

> The rotary valve principle has great possibilities and there is no question but that it will be used successfully on the race course in the future. We started building too late, and when some new and radical ideas in bearing construction, which we incorporated, proved unsuccessful, we did not have sufficient time to reconstruct the cars.

He also promised future participation in auto racing, saying, "We will go right on with the cars and will have these in future races."[122]

Race day dawned with 23 cars having qualified for the race.[123] Unlike the previous year when Indianapolis-made cars dominated the starting field, only two Indianapolis-made cars were in the field. An HCS Special with Milton at the wheel held the pole position with a qualifying speed of 108.17 miles per hour, while a second HCS car was on the third row with Howdy Wilcox as the pilot.[124] Although the Duesenbergs were not ready during the last qualifying period the day before the race, a special ruling allowed them to qualify early on race day. Despite that, only one of the Duesenbergs made it to the track for the trial; it arrived unpainted, while the other two were unable to get through the crowd for the qualification run.[125] Ironically, Fred Duesenberg drove a Model A Duesenberg phaeton as the pace car that year.[126]

In front of an estimated crowd of 150,000, Milton in the HCS Special won the Indianapolis 500 with an average speed of 90.95 miles per hour, becoming the first driver to have two victories.[127] Harry Stutz attributed the win to two chief factors: the teamwork of the mechanics and drivers on the HCS team and the care given to preparing the cars for the race. The winning car had been rebuilt three times prior to the race to insure it was the best it could be, with Harry Stutz commenting, "Absolutely nothing has been overlooked to make the machine as mechanically perfect as possible."[128]

Stutz, who hadn't participated in racing for several years, was thrilled with the victory and believed it placed the manufacturers of motor cars in the limelight instead of the drivers and racing teams, which he believed had converted the race into a commercial sporting event rather than maintaining the Speedway's historical roots in the improvement of the American automobile. He commented,

> One of my primary reasons in entering cars in the race yesterday was to attempt to interest manufacturers of motor cars in the racing business as a means of promoting engineering development in automobiles.[129]

Harkening back to an earlier time, HCS took the victory at the Indianapolis 500 as an advertising opportunity:

H.C. S. Special Wins 500-Mile Race
  The present Series of H.C.S. are now the only cars Harry C. Stutz builds and are the best ones he *ever* built.
  H.C.S. cars are as far in advance of present-day design and construction as the former winners built by Harry C. Stutz in their day.
  If you want a car in either a Four or Six-Cylinder type, with long, sturdy life built into it, plus speed, plus economy, plus good looks, plus perfect balance and driving ease, come in and see the H.C.S. right away. Why not drive a winner?[130]

In June, Cole held an open house at its new factory showroom to unveil its new Master Models.[131] The eight-cylinder Master Models were available in six body styles: two open cars, the four-passenger Volante and the seven-passenger Westchester, retailing for $2,175; an Imperial coupe for $2,750; a Royal Limousine for $3,175; and a seven-passenger Royal Sedan and a four-passenger Brouette for $3,075. The new Master Model series was built upon a 127.5-inch wheelbase. The company also continued to manufacture the cheaper Model 890, with the seven-passenger phaeton, four-passenger phaeton, and two-passenger roadster being priced at $1,885.[132]

Cole employed Edwin "Cannonball" Baker as the driver in several road tests. Baker set new speed records between Indianapolis and Cincinnati,[133] Chicago and St. Louis,[134] Sioux City and Moville, Iowa, and between Lincoln, Nebraska and Omaha, Nebraska.[135] Baker also drove a series of fuel economy tests on behalf of Cole, including one between Sioux City and Des Moines, Iowa, averaging 18.64 miles per gallon, and one between Lincoln, Nebraska, and Sioux City, Iowa, averaging 15.8 miles per gallon for the 150.17-mile run.[136]

Premier was more than delighted to promote the fact that a Premier automobile had completed a round-trip run from Cincinnati to Indianapolis three minutes faster than the run by "Cannonball" Baker in the Cole. The Premier was driven by William F. Troescher in his personal automobile, which had 12,000 miles on the odometer prior to the run. A Premier advertisement said of the accomplishment,

> The record made by Mr. Troescher, himself an amateur driver, proves what every other Premier owner has always known—that the Premier knows no equal in stamina and reliability. The magnificent Premier motor responded evenly and smoothly for the call to continuous high speed—as splendidly as it responds to the slightest touch in every day service.[137]

There was a flurry of new car announcements during July. HCS added a five-passenger sedan to its six-cylinder models. Duesenberg added a three-passenger roadster with a body by Rubay built upon a 134-inch wheelbase.[138]

Charles Schwab believed that the main Stutz plant should be producing as many of the items used in the cars as possible, resulting in Stutz's announcement that it would begin building its own six-cylinder engines at the end of July with a target of 10,000 motors in 1924. Stutz was a seasoned engine builder, as it was already producing the four-cylinder D-H motor in house.[139]

W. H. Duval & Son sought a reorganization of National after the company refused to pay a $10,987.35 judgment for a shipment of consigned materials. The predecessor company, National Motor Car & Vehicle Company, had rejected the materials.[140] George Dickson explained National's position:

> The suit and the judgment against the company grew out of a disputed claim for velour trimming materials bought by the old company during 1920 and later found to be defective. Further shipments of the materials were ordered stopped and acceptance refused.
>
> Materials were shipped to this city and put in storage by those acting for the sales agents. Later the Duval concern, financial agents of the sales agents and material factory, brought suit in New York and obtained judgment.[141]

Weeks later, another creditor of National Motor Car & Vehicle Company, Polson Manufacturing Co., a manufacturer of windshields, filed a suit against the successor company asking for a judgment of $900.[142]

In July 1923, C.A. Earl, president, announced that National had been put on a "sound financial basis" following the approval by stockholders, bondholders, banks and other creditors of the merged organization of a revolving line of credit to support the operations of the firm.[143] As part of the plan, a Revolving Fund Corporation was to be established to provide working capital for a two-year period. The Revolving Fund would make all purchases of materials and pay for all labor incident to assembling the material into finished products. Proceeds from the sale of the cars would be applied first to repayment of advances made by the Revolving Fund and the remainder divided among the present creditors. An arrangement was made for the funding for a period of five years of obligations totaling $5,1043,100, which would have to be paid in cash. These items included a $500,000 yearly sinking fund, $637,500 in interest coupons on the collateral trust gold notes, and $1,656,000 in collateral gold notes.[144] The plan also included centralization of essential functions. George Dickson talked about the role of the Indianapolis plant:

> The Indianapolis division will manufacture the higher priced cars in the line, as in the past, and will probably assist in the production of parts and units for use in other plants located at Louisville, Ky., St. Louis, Mo., Jackson, Mich., Saginaw, Mich., Lockport, N.Y., Dayton, O, Atlantic, Mass., and Houston, Tex.
>
> It is the intention to make the Indianapolis plant one of the most active in the entire organization, as the plant is particularly well equipped for the manufacture of a thoroughly reliable and high-grade motor car.[145]

In August National again found it necessary to seek more financing, this time totaling $5,750,000 in debenture trust notes with interest at 7 percent. The financing was provided by M. E. Elstum, Walter M. Anthony, and A. A. Gloetzner, all of whom were officers and directors of the firm. The purpose of the financing was another reorganization of the company.[146]

Weidley Motors was placed into a friendly receivership in August in an attempt to protect the company from a downturn in business. One of the company's clients had advised Weidley to hold up shipments of engines until new releases were ordered, causing the company to not have sufficient cash to meet its obligations. The company had total assets of $1,270,940 and liabilities of $851,924. Since January 1, 1923, the company had built more than $1 million in motors. The company maintained that had it received the contractual 60-day notice, it would have managed through the downturn.[147]

To celebrate the first batch of Premier taxicabs, the company arranged for a parade through Indianapolis in August. Led by a military band and a police escort, the parade included ten Premier taxicabs, several Premier cars filled with management, and several Monroe cars, including the Monroe No. 28 which had been the pride of the Monroe racing team. The taxis were on their final test runs prior to being shipped to New York City where they would become part of the Premier Cab Association. The bodies, built by Indianapolis firm Millspaugh & Irish, were painted brown, while the hoods and fenders were painted black.[148]

One of the ways Premier cut costs was to share its factory with Monroe. The superintendent of Monroe, Ezra Brown, had roots in Connersville, Indiana, where he had been the superintendent at McFarlan Motor Car Company and Lexington Motor Car Company.[149] Not long after the two companies started sharing factory space, they started sharing the same general sales manager, Fred Leeds, who had been hired by Premier. He was previously the sales manager of Lexington Motor Car Company of Connersville, Indiana.[150]

Premier announced the building of a seven-passenger sedan with a McFarlan body to retail for $3,385. The company's line also included a seven-passenger phaeton priced at $2,585, a five-passenger phaeton for $2,535, a five-passenger sport model for $2,635, and a roadster for $2,535. The Premier taxicab sold for $2,400.[151]

In October H. H. Woodsmall & Company filed for receivership of Premier over the failure to pay $557 in insurance premiums.[152] The suit was settled out of court when Premier paid the premium.[153]

Marmon started offering front-wheel brakes as an option for an additional $125. One of the goals of Marmon with the design of the front-wheel brakes was to minimize the foot pressure required to apply the brakes. In most designs, there was a trade-off between the long pedal travel and the foot pressure required.[154]

In September 1923 Cole was the first large scale automobile manufacturer to adopt the balloon tire that had been developed by Firestone Rubber & Tire Company. The balloon tires were optional equipment on all of the Cole models with the exception of the Volante, where they were standard equipment. An outgrowth of World War I, balloon tires were first used on airplanes. The tires at low inflation were able to withstand the pressure of landing on rough terrain. Joseph Cole explained the advantages of the balloon tire:

> Before adopting the balloon tires, we made the most thorough investigation, including actual road tests aggregating thousands upon thousands of miles—as did also the Firestone Rubber and Tire Company. We find that balloon tires give an improved degree of riding comfort that you never conceived possible, softness and smoothness even over the roughest roads obtained in no other way.
>
> They give you more than double the brake efficiency and without locking the front wheels or endangering the lives of your passengers. They greatly reduce the likelihood of skidding—another great safety factor.[155]

It wasn't long before others adopted balloon tires. In December, HCS announced that the tires were optional on its automobiles.[156]

At the Indianapolis Auto Show held at the State Fairgrounds, Cole showed off the balloon tires on the Volante model. Other cars shown by Cole included the Brouette; the Royal Sedan, a seven-passenger auto; the Westchester, a seven-passenger open car; and the Imperial sports coupe, which was an enclosed car. All the cars had a new design that included a multiple disc clutch, specially designed brakes, and a new method of insulating the car.[157]

In October 1923, Duesenberg leased additional space for testing so that the company could increase the space for production of enclosed cars. Chester Ricker explained the decision: "The ever-increasing popularity of the Duesenberg straight eight with its three years of owner proof to back it up is very gratifying to company officials." He continued, "Just at present the demand for Duesenberg inclosed [sic] cars is considerably beyond our output, but with the new space gained for the production of inclosed [sic] types we will be in splendid shape within the month."[158]

Duesenberg experienced a fire at the Central Storage Warehouse where it had stored automobile bodies. Duesenberg believed the bodies could be refinished, as the majority of the damage was smoke related. The company had been carrying about two months' worth of bodies in case there was an unexpected delay. The company indicated that the loss was fully covered by insurance.[159]

Duesenberg returned to its winning ways at the Beverley Hills Speedway on Thanksgiving Day when Benny Hill won a 250-mile race with an average speed of 112.44 miles per hour. Other Indianapolis-built cars in the race included Phil Shafer in a Duesenberg Special, who finished sixth, and Joe Boyer in a Duesenberg Special, who finished eighth. Cooper's HCS Special continued to be snake-bit, as it went out of the race with valve trouble. Milton's HCS Special was leading the race when it spun out of control on the 134th lap. Hearne, driving a Durant Special, finished third in the race but won the 1923 driving championship.[160]

Despite its financial difficulties, Premier was able to obtain an additional $500,000 in financing. The proceeds were used to increase the company's taxicab business and passenger cars.[161]

Entered by a Zurich dealer, a Marmon stock touring car won the prestigious 1923 International Mountain race on the Klausen Hill before 40,000 people. The race, called the "Grand Prix of the Alps," was second in importance only to the French Grand Prix. The track was 20.5 kilometers in length with 24 turns. *Motor*, the official publication of the Automobile Club of Switzerland, said of the Marmon victory,

> The victory of the splendid Marmon cars was complete in the greatest and most spectacular race ever held in Europe. The three Marmons made almost identical time in the straightaway kilometer, proving the dependability and even performance of this make. And, we recognize this performance even more, when we realize the Marmons were carrying standard equipment and were not specially geared for the race while most of the close competitors in the race were geared for higher than standard speed. The length of the course and the difference in altitude make it one of the best tests to be found in the mountain country.[162]

In late 1922, Stutz introduced the Speedway Six series to complement the Special Six. Built on a 130-inch wheelbase, the Speedway Six was produced in five models including five- and seven-passenger phaetons, a five-passenger sport brougham, a seven-passenger berline, and a five-passenger Suburban. The company offered four-wheel brakes and balloon tires as optional equipment. The car had 80 horsepower with a speed in excess of 70 miles per hour when fully loaded.[163]

16

Duesenberg Dominates Racing

At the National Automobile Chamber of Commerce dinner in New York City in early January 1924 Charles Schwab, the head of Bethlehem Steel, predicted the continued consolidation of the automobile industry. The pace of consolidation was escalating as several smaller automobile firms had failed. Schwab said,

> In not many years from now, the number of automobile manufacturing companies will be reduced to about ten. These ten will be making a total of about 15 makes of cars. Public demand for better prices and the subsequent intense competition among manufacturers to supply this demand will cause some of the smaller and weaker concerns to drop by the wayside and get some of the better known firms together.[1]

With the Indianapolis automobile industry focusing on higher quality, more expensive automobiles, this viewpoint could not have been comforting. Despite an improving economy, at least two Indianapolis manufacturers were financially stressed, and within the year they would be reorganized with people from outside of Indianapolis taking control.

Compounding issues for the auto industry was an economic downturn in late 1923 which stretched into 1924. The industry responded by reducing production levels,[2] but this wasn't enough to counteract the stresses of the past few years. The pace of companies going out of business or joining forces with other companies continued. By the end of 1924, Indianapolis would lose two of its earliest companies: National and Premier.

On January 2, 1924, William T. Rasmussen, a real estate dealer, was appointed the receiver for Duesenberg by Probate Judge Mahlon E. Bash. The petition to appoint a receiver was filed by Acme Works, Inc. of Indianapolis for a $2,638.99 bill for automobile castings unpaid since November 1923. The petition stated that the company was indebted to a large number of creditors with debts of $150,000. Chester Ricker, Duesenberg's general manager, said the petition was a friendly one and would allow the company to reorganize.[3]

Later in January, the United States Patent Office notified Duesenberg that its application for the trademark of "Straight Eight" had been granted. The Straight Eight had been in use continually since November 1, 1920.[4]

National was also in distress. In mid–January, the executive officers of the corporation resigned, including Clarence A. Earl, president; Walter M. Anthony, vice president; and Walter J. Mery, secretary. William Guy Wall, chief engineer of National Motor, gave insight into the operations of the company at the plant on East 22nd Street. "The Indianapolis company is operating with a limited crew of workmen. I am informed that some of the plants are making money."[5] The end for the company came quickly, with National "withdrawing" from Indiana in early February.[6]

A reorganization of Weidley Motors, which had ceased operations after an automobile manufacturer suddenly stopped shipments of its engines, was approved by Circuit Court Judge Harry L. Chamberlin. With a plan in place to resume operations, the company's assets were sold for approximately $300,000 to the majority bondholders, W. Edward Showers and W. A. Humphrey, treasurer and general manager of the company.[7]

One of the cars drawing attention at the New York Auto Show was the Stutz Speedway Six, which featured balloon tires and four-wheel brakes as optional equipment. The prices on this model ranged from a low of $2,650 to a high of $3,600 for the standard edition. The optional equipment increased the price by $185.[8] The Stutz cars were well received at both the New York and the Philadelphia auto shows, with orders increasing demand by an estimated 500 percent.[9]

The 1924 Marmon also featured balloon tires and four-wheel brakes as optional equipment.[10] Balloon tires had been mounted on Gaston Chevrolet's winning car in the 1920 Indianapolis 500. In early 1924, Barney Oldfield made a 2,120 mile cross-country trip from Akron, Ohio, to Los Angeles, California, in a car using balloon tires equipped with 30 pounds of air pressure in the front tires and 35 pounds in the rear tires. In letters to Howard Marmon and Harvey S. Firestone (Firestone Tire & Rubber Company), he gave a ringing endorsement of balloon tires: "I can heartily recommend balloon tires after their marvelous performance on this trip."[11]

In a town that embraced the Indianapolis 500 and race drivers, Marmon management was frequently asked why so many race drivers chose a Marmon for their personal vehicle. It was another selling point differentiating Marmon from other brands. Marmon sent a questionnaire to Barney Oldfield; Tommy Milton, who had won the past two Indianapolis 500 races; Jimmy Murphy, who had won the 1921 French Grand Prix; Eddie Hearne, who had won the 1923 racing championship; Benny Hill, who had won the Thanksgiving race at the Beverly Hill Speedway in Los Angeles; and Joe Boyer, the millionaire driver. All of them responded that the safety features including the strength of the frame, the wide running boards which acted as "side bumpers," and the four-wheel brakes of the Marmon were important to them. Eddie Hearne wrote, "I suppose every man in my line of business unconsciously sets up an ideal of what he thinks is perfection in an automobile. We are so concerned with performance and safety in our racing jobs that we automatically learn to appreciate these qualities in other cars."[12]

At the Indianapolis Auto Show, H. L. Peterson, the local Marmon branch manager, talked about the enhancements to the Marmon:

> The fundamental design and construction remains the same, including the frame with running boards integral, the six-cylinder, high efficiency power plant, the 110-pound balanced crankshaft, and two-piece pistons. The 16 refinements which have been added to the basic elements of the car contribute not only to its mechanical efficiency and dependability but to the appearance as well.[13]

Some of the 16 improvements to the car included the four-wheel braking system, a folding trunk rack for the four- and seven-passenger phaetons, and plate glass windshield wings for the two- and four-passenger speedsters.[14] Marmon was among three different automobile companies to announce a price increase on the 1924 models.[15]

In May, a significant portion of the stock in Nordyke & Marmon was sold to George M. Williams. Williams had begun his career as an assistant engineer with the H. E. Talbot

Company of Dayton, Ohio, an industrial contractor specializing in hydroelectric power plants. Between 1915 and 1917, he was the second vice president of Dayton Metal Products. Beginning in 1917, he was the general manager of the Wright Airplane Company of Dayton. Williams was the president of Wire Wheel Corporation of America for a year before becoming involved with Nordyke & Marmon.[16] With the sale, Walter Marmon stepped down as president of the organization which had been in the family for 75 years. While Walter Marmon remained as the board chair, Williams became the new president. Howard Marmon stayed on as the chief engineer and vice president.[17]

Premier announced a price increase of between $350 and $590 per car. The newspaper noted that Wall Street had just about decided that prices of cars would be decreasing.[18] The problem for Premier was that it based its pricing upon the cost to produce the cars. Unfortunately, with limited production, overhead was spread over fewer cars and the company didn't benefit from volume buying of materials. It was a vicious cycle. The more the company raised prices to cover its costs, the fewer cars were sold.

In May 1924 Indianapolis Motor Speedway management announced that, in addition to the $50,000 in prize money to be divided among the top ten finishers, the remaining starters would share $10,000 based upon the number of laps raced.[19] They also picked the Cole V8 to be the pace car for the Indianapolis 500.[20]

Qualification trials for the Indianapolis 500 began on May 26. To make the field, a racer had to drive ten miles at an average speed of 80 miles per hour. On the first day of qualifying, Jimmy Murphy, the winner of the 1922 Indianapolis 500, roared around the track with an average speed of 108.01 miles per hour. Joining Murphy on the front row were Harry Hartz with an average speed of 107.16 and Tommy Milton with an average speed of 105.20 miles per hour. Three of the four Duesenbergs registered for the race made the field. Joe Boyer sat on the inside of the third row with an average speed of 104.85 miles per hour. Indianapolis 500 rookie Ernie Ansterberg was on the fourth row with an average speed of 99.40 miles per hour.[21] Ansterberg cut his racing teeth as the riding mechanic to Joe Boyer, Louis Chevrolet, and Roscoe Sarles. His first speedway championship race was Thanksgiving Day 1923 at the Beverly Hills Speedway.[22] The third Duesenberg racer to make the field was piloted by Peter DePaolo with an average speed of 99.3 miles per hour.[23] Two days before the race, the final Duesenberg entry, piloted by L. L. Corum with an average speed of 93.07 miles per hour, qualified for the race.[24]

Carl Fisher, Jim Allison, and Arthur Newby were presented with embossed testimonials of their contributions to the city and the nation at a Chamber of Commerce "smoker" the night before the 1924 Indianapolis 500. On behalf of the Chamber of Commerce and Indianapolis' automotive industries, Homer MeKee said in part,

> Greater to us even than our beloved James Whitcomb Riley, and even more conducive to us of honor, is this Motor Speedway of ours. The poetry of Riley has found the heart strings of the world, and on them, played the sweetest music. But the Indianapolis Motor Speedway has taught the world its most practical lessons in human transportation. It has saved more lives than any antitoxin ever devised by science. Without the lessons learned on the Indianapolis Motor Speedway, traffic today would be a deadly shambles—an inconceivable inhumanity. We are too prone to look upon the great motor classic as a mere sporting event.[25]

As part of his acceptance of the honor bestowed upon the three founders, Fisher said,

L. L. Corum, winner of the 1924 Indianapolis 500 (Auburn Cord Duesenberg Automobile Museum).

I think the Speedway has played a part in the development of the automobile. We have seen the piston displacement reduced. The test of cars in races has shown flaws, and demonstrated the value of improvements. I think the time shall come when we will have motors even smaller than the ones in use in the racing cars today—and today's motor, remember, is only about three times the size of a coffee pot, while the motors in the earliest 500-mile races were about the size of a bathtub. These little motors use about as much gas in a week as the old ones used in an hour.[26]

The odds-on favorites to win the Indianapolis 500 race were the 14 Harry Miller cars in the field of 22. Blaine Patton, sports editor for the *Indianapolis Star*, said, "The odds on one of Harry Miller's jobs being returned the victor in this afternoon's strenuous grind figure 14 to 4—the four representing the four Duesies, the only four serious contenders against the California engineer." Patton believed that Murphy, Benny Hill or Harry Hartz had the best opportunity to win the race.[27]

Remarkably, one of the Millers did not win the race. Rather, it was the Indianapolis-made Duesenberg piloted by L. L. Corum. Team captain Joe Boyer took the wheel of the winning car on the 106th lap when it appeared his own machine did not have the speed to remain competitive. The Corum/Boyer combination crossed the finish line with an average speed of 98.23 miles per hour.[28] For their efforts, Corum and Boyer split $30,000 of the $86,850.50 in total prizes, while Fred Duesenberg received a silver tea service from Indianapolis clothier L. Strauss & Company.[29]

Throughout the race, Fred Duesenberg had been in the pits with his team. He was somewhat short of words about the victory:

> I really haven't much to say; I don't know what to say, except that I am very proud that one of my cars finished first. I have always wanted to win this race. I have put good cars into it, but we just had one streak of bad luck after another until today. A lot of credit goes to my brother, August.[30]

After the race, Fred Duesenberg said, "These are the last racing cars I expect to build; I have achieved my greatest ambition in winning the Indianapolis 500-mile race and no one can hope for more than that."[31]

The engine of the winning car was a straight eight made of aluminum with case-hardened steel sleeves. The pistons were also aluminum, with hard rubber gaskets used in the sleeves. The engine also had a new type of cooling system, with water coming into direct contact with the steel sleeves. The car's frame was also made of aluminum.

On the west side of town, George Williams started guiding Nordyke & Marmon on a new course. He wanted to increase the production of automobiles by 50 percent over the previous year. To accomplish the higher level of production, Williams planned to increase the work force by 1,000 men. He also realigned the factory flow to make it faster[32] and hired Robert K. Mitchell, formerly Maxwell-Chrysler Corporation's production superintendent.[33]

Elgin Motor, which had begun operations in Indianapolis in 1923, was put into receivership in June 1924 when Merton S. Black, the works manager, filed for the payment of $300 in salary. Black alleged that the company owed in excess of $40,000. At the time of the filing, the plant was inactive.[34]

After studying the market, HCS entered the production of taxicabs. HCS Cab Manufacturing Company was incorporated with capitalization of $1 million by Harry Stutz, Henry Campbell, A. G. Murdock, H.K. Grubb, A. V. Clifford, E. R. Raub, Jr., and F. E. Matson. The new company planned to make and sell taxicabs, motor cars and other automotive vehicles. It shared the HCS plant for manufacturing.[35] Harry Stutz talked about the decision-making process:

> For some time we have realized the necessity of a broader field of manufacture and distribution than we could obtain in building practically custom made passenger cars. Our dealers, too, have needed a more complete line of cars in order to profitably operate their business.
> We have made a study of the marvelous growth of the taxicab industry. The congested condition of the streets of every city of the United States, together with a lowering of taxi cab operations, has greatly increased the use of taxicabs as a means of city transportation.
> The principal objection to the use of cabs now in the market is the fact that their heavy weight and consequent operating costs have made them unprofitable to their owners except at a high rate of fare.
> We have designed an unusually attractive cab, of the lighter weight, yet sturdy of construction, and one which can be maintained at a low operating cost. The price, too, will be considerably less than the standard cabs now on the market.[36]

By late August, the first HCS taxicabs rolled off the production line. The cab was built on a 110-inch wheelbase but had a tight turning radius. It featured a Ricardo type of engine and a special transmission. The introduction of the taxicab resulted in numerous orders for the company.[37]

Frontenac Motors Corporation (Frontenac) was incorporated in August 1923 by E. L. Jacoby, president, and Louis Chevrolet, vice president and engineer. Chevrolet designed a new car using an eight-in-line Burt single sleeve valve engine with 80 horsepower. There was no expectation that this company's cars would be mass produced, but rather that it would make custom-built cars. The company bought the patent rights to the Burt engine and anticipated building both closed and open cars with production to begin in early 1925.[38]

After the Duesenberg victory in the Indianapolis 500, the racing team went to Altoona, Pennsylvania, to participate in a 250-mile race but was disappointed by its performance. Peter DePaolo's car exited the race on the 59th lap with carburetor trouble, and the carburetor failed on Joe Boyer's Duesenberg after 225 miles. This race was won by Jimmy Murphy.[39]

The Duesenberg racers returned to the Indianapolis Motor Speedway in September for a 50-mile exhibition race sponsored by Eli Lilly & Company as part of the entertainment for a wholesale druggist convention. Included in the race was the car that had won the 1924 Indianapolis 500.[40] Later in the month, during a 250-mile race on the Altoona, Pennsylvania, track, Joe Boyer's Duesenberg racer crashed through a guard rail. At the time of the crash, Boyer was in second place, trying to overtake the leader with the race nearing a conclusion. Severely injured, he was taken to the hospital, where doctors amputated his two crushed legs. Fred Duesenberg, who was at the race, told his wife he thought Boyer would recover. Sadly, Boyer died later that evening.[41]

Jimmy Murphy, the winner of the 1922 Indianapolis 500 who was on his way to becoming the racing champion for 1924, died at a 150-mile race on a dirt track at the Syracuse, New York, fairgrounds when he crashed through a wooden fence on a curve on the 138th lap. He was valiantly trying to close the distance with front runner Phil Shafer, who had led throughout the race and at the 100-mile mark was two laps ahead. Shafer, driving a Duesenberg, went on to win the race with a time of 1 hour 54 minutes 28.2 seconds.[42]

In October, Marmon unveiled the Marmon 74, its first new model since the introduction of the Marmon 34 in 1916. The company introduced three new open car models: a seven-passenger touring car, a five-passenger phaeton, and a roadster that retailed for $3,165. The closed cars included a five-passenger sedan and four-door brougham coupe retailing for $3,295. The company also introduced a deluxe line which included a coupe priced at $3,455, a five- passenger sedan priced at $3,775, a five-passenger sedan-limousine deluxe priced at $3,900, a seven-passenger sedan priced at $3,850, and a seven-passenger sedan-limousine deluxe priced at $3,975.[43] The new car featured a better oiling system, a design of the steering to work well with balloon tires, extra heavy gears and rear axle, a larger radiator, and placement of the gasoline tank in the rear of the auto.[44]

In a time when all other manufacturers were mass producing cars using parts sourced from multiple vendors, Duesenberg was producing one car per day. Ed Updyke, whose company represented Duesenberg in Indiana, said of the company's product, "Practically every part used in the making of the Duesenberg is machined and built at the local plant, a fact which means everything in the custom-built motor carriage." B. K. Harding, works manager at Duesenberg, explained that quality was the primary consideration: "We employ only the highest-priced labor that money will buy. Every man in the Duesenberg factory is a thorough mechanic and comes highly recommended."[45]

Duesenberg entered a race at a new Charlotte, North Carolina, board track in October. During a practice session, Eddie Ansterberg was piloting his car around the oval at 106 miles per hour when he lost control, striking the guard rail. Ansterberg, a member of the Duesenberg racing team for about a year, was killed in the crash. At the time of his death, he held the world speed record for a mile and a quarter. It was the second death in two months for the Duesenberg team.[46]

The *Indianapolis Star* reported that Premier's taxicabs were in use on a large scale in New York, Chicago, Philadelphia, Baltimore, and St. Louis, with many other cities anxious to have franchises. The article claimed that the taxis on the streets had a value of $6 million and there were 5,000 men employed driving the cabs. The company also announced its newest taxicab model, known as the 4B. Barrows, president of the company, indicated that 1925 would be the biggest in the company's history.[47] In December, Premier began production of a new model taxicab with four-wheel brakes. The cab, priced at $2,400 FOB Indianapolis, was built on a 112-wheelbase.[48]

To support an expansion of the production of taxicabs from 150 per month to 300 per month, Premier issued $2,000,000 in preferred stock with a 7 percent dividend in addition to the $500,000 in bonds outstanding with interest at 6 percent with a maturity date of 1932.[49] Even though Premier planned to increase the number of taxicabs produced, the gigantic plant still had plenty of space. The company leased half of the plant to Rub-Tex Products Company, which formerly had its facilities in New Castle, Indiana.[50]

After Duesenberg had been in bankruptcy for nearly two years, Marion County Probate Court Judge Mahlon E. Bash ordered the sale of the Duesenberg plant with a minimum price of $375,000. William T. Rasmussen, Duesenberg's receiver, was directed to give five weeks' notice of the sale of the plant.[51]

In 1925, Marmon decided to bring the production of its automobile bodies in house and built a state-of-the-art facility.[52] The choice of a body designer was easy. W. E. Pierce, president of the Hume Body Corporation, was hired as the company's chief body engineer.[53] The relationship with Pierce had begun in the late teens when the Boston sales agent, F. E. Wing, hired Hume Body to craft some custom bodies. Between 1920 and 1925, Hume Body

Peter DePaolo in the Duesenberg racer in which he won the 1925 Indianapolis 500 (Auburn Cord Duesenberg Automobile Museum).

built hundreds of bodies for Marmon from its production facilities in Massachusetts, including designing the Marmon 74 coachwork.[54]

Weidley Motors sued Stutz for $750,000 alleging a breach of contract that had caused the company's failure when Stutz failed to take delivery of the engines ordered. Weidley Motors maintained that the contract between the two companies called for the production of 5,000 engines. At the time the contract was halted, only 2,191 motors had been accepted by Stutz. William Thompson, Stutz president, attributed the discontinuation of the contract to a clause requiring Weidley to keep its finances up to a certain standard, which was not done.[55]

In 1923 Fred Moscovics left Nordyke & Marmon to join H. H. Franklin Manufacturing Company as the sales manager.[56] His tenure with Franklin was fairly short. In late 1924 he sued the company for failure to pay his salary. In an out-of-court settlement, Moscovics was awarded $100,000.[57] In February Moscovics returned to Indianapolis as president of Stutz, replacing William Thompson, who had resigned.[58] By June Stutz had introduced a new sedan, the 6–94, with a retail price of $3,050. Among the features of this five-passenger car were more room for the front seat occupants and a special windshield construction that provided improved vision.[59]

On February 21, 1925, articles of incorporation were filed with the Indiana Secretary of State for Duesenberg Motors Company with authorized capital of $500,000. The stockholders had raised the capital in fewer than 30 days. Joining Fred S. Duesenberg as president and general manager were James H. Dunn of Uniontown, Pennsylvania as vice president, Edward Wildman as secretary, and Harry B. Mahan as treasurer. The firm was reportedly in sound financial condition with total liabilities of $327,000 while inventory was more than $1 million. Upon the incorporation of the firm, Fred Duesenberg said,

> The operation of our plant during the last year under the direction of William T. Rasmussen, receiver, has been very satisfactory. We manufactured and delivered more than 100 cars in that time, with an average value of $7,000 each.[60]

Under the new management, production of new cars was anticipated to double.[61] Judge Bash approved the sale of Duesenberg for $375,000 to the Security Trust Company as trustee for the creditors and a number of large stockholders.[62] Of the $375,000 sales price, $130,912.36 was paid in cash, with the balance of the indebtedness to be in bonds representing about 60 percent of the creditors.[63]

The suit by the U.S. Government for a $361,000 overpayment to Premier was set aside by Judge Linn Hay in April. The company had issued a notice that all claims against the company should be filed by October 22, 1922, but the government attempted to file a large claim on December 5, 1923.[64] The judge allowed the payment of $45,000 to the receiver (Fletcher Savings Bank & Trust) and attorneys representing Premier in the case.[65] The court found that the previous settlement of the government with the company was binding in the absence of fraud.[66] The U.S. Attorney indicated he would appeal this decision.[67] Judge Hay also approved the issuance of stock in the new company to about 300 creditors of the old copany.[68]

Marmon added two new models to its Marmon 74 Series: a five-passenger club phaeton and a seven-passenger touring car, both selling for $3,465. The finish on both models was Duco, an automotive paint made by DuPont, with a choice of three colors.[69]

In May Marmon announced that the prices on parts would be standardized and reflected in a parts manual. Previously, the distributors set the price of the parts, which caused a wide variation. The prices on the West Coast were 10 percent higher than those east of the Rocky Mountains.[70]

When the deadline for submitting entries to the 1925 Indianapolis 500 passed, the largest field since 1919 was entered, including five foreign entries. Although after winning the 1924 Indianapolis 500 Fred Duesenberg had said that it would be his last race, the entry list included four Duesenberg Specials by the Duesenberg Bros. Three of the drivers were identified as Peter DePaolo, Phil Shafer, and Peter Kreis.[71] The fourth driver, Antoine Mourre, was added later.[72]

On the first day of qualifications, 18 cars made the lineup for the Indianapolis 500, with six cars beating the speed record of 108.17 miles per hour set by Tommy Milton in an HCS on the first day of qualifications. Sitting on the pole was Leon Duray in a Miller Special with an average speed of 113.196 miles per hour. Others beating Milton's record included Peter DePaolo in a Duesenberg, Harry Hartz in a Miller Special, Earl Cooper in a Junior Eight, Dave Lewis in a Junior Eight, and Ralph Hepburn in a Miller Special.[73] Phil Shafer qualified his Duesenberg racer the day before the race in the car which had won the 1924 Indianapolis 500.[74]

When the dust settled, 22 cars took to the starting line for the Indianapolis 500. In front of a crowd estimated at 150,000, Pete DePaolo, relieved by Norman Batten, won with an average speed of 101.13 miles per hour—the first time the average speed had exceeded the century mark—in his Indianapolis-built Duesenberg. Second place was won by Dave Lewis piloting a Miller Special, while third place was won by Phil Shafer in a Duesenberg. Shafer was relieved by Wade Morton, who crashed his Duesenberg on the 400th mile. Peter Kreis, the final Duesenberg entry, finished eighth.[75] It was a good payday for the Duesenberg team, with DePaolo taking home $36,150 in prizes, Shafer $8,550, and Kreis $1,600. The total purse for the 1925 Indianapolis 500 was $87,750.[76]

Two weeks later, DePaolo placed second to Tommy Milton in a very close 250-mile race at Altoona with an average speed of 115.9 miles per hour. Milton's margin of victory was a mere second or two.[77] Following the race, Frank Elliott filed a protest. A review by the AAA Contest Board discovered that a lap by Elliott had not been recorded. The victor in the race was then declared to be DePaolo, with Elliott finishing second and Milton third. The back-to-back victories at Indianapolis and Altoona put DePaolo in the driver's seat to win the 1925 driver's championship.[78]

DePaolo considered entering the Grand Prix race at Vernair, Belgium, in early July. However, being in the hunt for the 1925 driving championship, he decided against participating in the race as he would be unable to return in time to participate in an upcoming race at Laurel, Maryland. The rules required a driver to participate in all championship events to qualify for the driving championship.[79] It was a good decision. Although Bob McDonough took the checkered flag at the inaugural race at the Baltimore-Washington Speedway in Laurel, Maryland, DePaolo questioned officials who then discovered that two laps had not been counted in his run, ultimately handing DePaolo the victory in the 250-mile race.[80]

Duesenberg added a new five-passenger sedan retailing for $7,700 to its product line in May 1925. The company also announced a price increase on the remainder of the line with the exception of a four-passenger coupe. The new prices were $6,850 for a three-person roadster, a four-person phaeton, and a seven-person phaeton, $6,500 for a five-person phaeton, $7,500 for a four-person coupe, and $8,300 for a seven-person sedan.[81]

WHEN THE YOUNG PEOPLE OF A GREAT NATION ENTHUSIASTICALLY APPLAUD, THERE MUST INEVITABLY FOLLOW AN EVEN MORE THOUGHTFUL SCRUTINY OF A CAR THAT SO ALLURES ITS AGE WITH OUT-RANKING SPEED, SAFETY AND BEAUTY.

THE
SPLENDID
STUTZ

THE SAFEST CAR HAS THE RIGHT TO BE THE FASTEST

Safety Stutz advertisement. The tag line is, "The safest car has the right to be the fastest" (courtesy Stutz Club).

Nordyke & Marmon shareholders were undoubtedly delighted to learn of the company's earnings of $1,174,198 for the six-month period ending June 30, 1925. President Williams attributed the growth in earnings to a higher level of sales, a strengthened dealer network, and a more efficient production system. Shipments of Marmon cars had doubled over the level for the six-month period ending June 30, 1924, while the dealer network had increased 20 percent. Williams reported that dealers were finding the Marmon 74 easily sold.[82]

Indianapolis residents awoke on the morning of August 8 to the news that Joseph Cole had died of heart disease at age 56. He had been in declining health for the previous two years and had been gravely ill for three days before his death.[83]

A Duesenberg team including Peter DePaolo, Tommy Milton, and Peter Kreis was selected to represent America in the 1925 Italian Grand Prix at Monza in September. When the team announcement was made, DePaolo already had enough championship points with wins at Fresno, Indianapolis, Altoona, and Laurel to win the 1925 driver championship. Also scheduled to participate in the race was Antoine Ascari of the Alfa-Romeo team, who was the leading European driver.[84] When Ascari was killed in a race at the Montlhéry track in July, the Alfa-Romeo factory sought out Peter DePaolo to drive one of its racers in the Italian Grand Prix, and he accepted.[85]

During practice, the Duesenberg driven by Peter Kreis set the fastest lap at 101.5 miles per hour.[86] The Italian Grand Prix was won by Gaston Brilli-Peri with an average speed of 94.82 miles per hour.[87] Hampered by a gear box failure necessitating finishing the race in top gear,[88] Tommy Milton in a Duesenberg took fourth place, finishing 32 minutes after Brilli-Peri. Fifth place went to DePaolo driving for the Alfa-Romeo team. Kreis, driving the second Duesenberg entry, was eliminated by a crash.[89]

Back in America, DePaolo in a Duesenberg won the inaugural 250-mile race at the Rockingham Speedway, a board track in Salem, New Hampshire, with an average speed of 128 miles per hour. The previous record had been set by Tommy Milton at 126.85 miles per hour.[90]

In December, Stutz introduced the New Vertical Eight built upon a 121-inch wheelbase and featuring four-wheel brakes. What distinguished this car was its height of 70 inches. A man of ordinary height standing over the curb could see over the top of the car. The low profile of the car led to it being safer than the normal height cars, leading to the moniker of the "Safety Stutz." Despite the lowness of the car, it had 39 inches of headroom. The maximum output for the eight-cylinder engine was 92 horsepower. The car was tested at the Indianapolis Motor Speedway, where it made several laps at 75 miles per hour. An additional feature of the car was the shockproof windshield, in which horizontal wires about 2½ inches apart were placed in the glass as it was manufactured. This meant that stones or other ordinary obstacles would not easily pass through the glass.

The car was available in six body styles priced at $2,995. Wire wheels were optional equipment for an additional cost. A two-passenger speedster was fitted with a rumble seat for two passengers and golf equipment. The four-passenger speedster was similar to the two-passenger speedster except that it did not have a rumble seat or space for golf equipment. The Victoria coupe was a four-passenger car with an individual driver's seat and an auxiliary seat which folded under the instrument panel. There was room for golf clubs on the rear deck. The two-passenger coupe had a single cross seat which could accommodate three people. It also had a rumble seat which could accommodate two extra passengers.[91]

17

E. L. Cord Buys Duesenberg

The 1926 New York Auto Show featured four new models: the Chrysler Imperial Eighty, the Pontiac by General Motors, the Willys-Knight Six, and the Stutz Vertical Eight.[1]

Marmon now had 15 various models for sale to the public. One of the goals of the company was to stay six months ahead of the current motor car styles and engineering improvements. One of the enhancements to the 1926 Marmon was the double-fire ignition system where each cylinder had two spark plugs firing simultaneously to ignite the gases in the combustion chamber. The Marmon cars also had improved acceleration and gasoline economy. Another innovation introduced by Marmon was the self-lubricating chassis. Instead of having to hand lubricate, the driver merely had to push a plunger in the driving compartment. The third improvement to the 1926 Marmon was the "three-way" oil purifier which would decrease the need for oil changes.[2]

In February 1926 Nordyke & Marmon changed its name to the Marmon Motor Car Company (Marmon) with the Indiana Secretary of State. After 1925 became the largest sales year in Marmon's history, the company anticipated a 20 percent increase in sales during 1926.[3] The company also filed articles of incorporation for Nordyke & Marmon, Inc. with 1,200 shares; this company would serve as a "foundry" to continue the milling operations.[4] After the separation of the automobile business, the company continued to operate Nordyke & Marmon as a separate entity until November 1926, when the flour mill operations were sold to Allis-Chalmers of Wisconsin.[5]

In a field of 18, Peter DePaolo, driving a Duesenberg, continued his winning ways by winning the inaugural 300-mile race at the Fulford-by-the-Sea racetrack with an average speed of 129.29 miles per hour. DePaolo was awarded the Carl G. Fisher Cup plus a portion of the $30,000 in prizes. In winning the race, DePaolo shattered the former world record for 100 miles set by Tommy Milton in 1922 at Kansas City. This new board track was built by Carl Fisher as another attraction for Miami Beach, where he was heavily involved in development.[6]

DePaolo was scheduled to defend his 1925 Indianapolis 500 championship. His Duesenberg racer was identical to that of the prior year except that the engine size had been reduced to conform with the new, lower limit of 91.5 cubic inches.[7] As time neared for the race, DePaolo muddied the waters of his ride when he also registered a Miller racer. Fred Duesenberg signed speedway veteran Ralph Mulford to pilot one of his cars.

The 1926 Indianapolis 500 was dominated by Harry Miller-designed racers which took nine of the top ten finishes. Winning the rain-soaked race, which was called off after 400 miles, was Frank Lockhart, age 23, with an average speed of 94.63 miles per hour. Lockhart, a rookie in the race, had come to Indianapolis as a relief driver for Benny Hill.[8] The only racer in the top 10 not driving a Miller car was Pete DePaolo, who ultimately made the decision to drive a Duesenberg and placed fifth in the race. The other Duesenberg entry, driven by Ben Jones, skidded into the wall on the 53rd lap. The racer driven by Jones had a controversial, innovative two-cycle engine with small piston displacement that had been developed by Fred Duesenberg.[9]

In April 1926 Duesenberg purchased a group life insurance policy covering 132 employees with a benefit of $180,000 from the Aetna Life Insurance Company. The policy not only insured the life of each employee but also provided coverage for permanent and total disability before age 60. The requirement for physicals on the employees covered was waived. Employees in the shop could obtain coverage up to $1,000 while foremen could obtain coverage up to $2,500.[10]

Duesenberg was positioned against other luxury cars including Mercedes and Rolls Royce, and its advertising focused on the company's primary demographic:

> When a Duesenberg Stops—A Person Of Note Steps Out.
> There is no better proof of Duesenberg supremacy than its owner group. Men who have "arrived." Level headed and distinguished ... outstanding successes. Women who are leaders ... in activities, clubs, and social prominence. Families of faultless taste and judgment.[11]

The Indianapolis 500 continued to have an impact on the passenger car. Fred Duesenberg and Harry Miller told a gathering of the Society for Automotive Engineers at French Lick, Indiana, that the size of the engine in passenger cars would continue to get smaller as the technology improved. They anticipated the introduction of a two-cycle automobile to the driving public along with front-wheel drive, both of which were in use in the 1926 Indianapolis 500. Harry Miller told the gathered crowd, "Our stock-car company is already considering introducing the front-wheel drive on touring cars and limousines. It leads to safe driving on dirt roads and easier steering." Fred Duesenberg told the engineers of the improvement to the engine: "Touring car speeds will be increased by 25 to 50 percent, principally by valve and valve mechanism improvement, similar to that developed in two-cycle racing motors. We have not yet made this new type do all it can. It gives the promise of being speedier than the present four-cycle motor and it is more economical."[12]

While the Miller automobiles dominated the 1926 Indianapolis 500, Fred Duesenberg's fighting spirit continued. Intending to refine the two-cycle engine, Duesenberg challenged Miller for the race, promising an improved version of the two-cycle engine. Duesenberg explained,

> It's my guess against the other fellow's. We work hard, applying our "hunches" to racing car construction. But only the big race proves whose hunch is right. However, I believe the winning racer of the future will be a two-cycle car, and I believe the principle of the two-cycle motor will be applied to automobiles for everyday use making them 25 percent faster.[13]

In June 1926 Marmon leased its 400,000 square foot Plant #3 to the Murray Body Corporation of Detroit, Michigan, which expected to employ 2,000 people.[14] Plant #3 had been built when the company was building the Marmon 34. The Murray Body Corporation had negotiated a deal with Marmon to produce all of its bodies. At the time, the Murray Body Corporation was in bankruptcy, but it would exit in 1927.[15]

With the increase in sales and a more efficient plant, Marmon announced a profit of $1.8 million for the year ended June 30, 1926. Additionally, the company had paid off its bank debt totaling $1,888,000.¹⁶ Further pointing to the rosy future for Marmon was the declaration of a dividend of $1 per share of common stock, to be paid on December 1.¹⁷

By 1926, installment plans for the purchase of automobiles had become standard in the industry, allowing millions of people to purchase automobiles. Consumer debt for the purchase of automobiles in July 1926 was estimated at $1.5 billion. H. L. Purdy, Marmon vice president, explained:

> We are told that more than 70 percent of the cars turned out by the factories are sold on the new budget plan. This plan has the additional advantage of encouraging thrift and productiveness. The average man will save and economize to meet certain payments due and with a definite end in view, when he might find it not so easy to save for more accumulation.

Installment buying also benefited the industry. Purdy continued,

> Installment buying, by eliminating peak periods and keeping the plant busy at all seasons of the year, makes for lower prices. A lowered factory production means high prices.[18]

Marmon introduced the Marmon 75 car in October 1926. Although the car had the standard Marmon features, it was priced lower than other Marmon cars.[19] Improvements in the Marmon 75 included four-wheel mechanical brakes, a sturdier front axle, and an improved steering system to prevent the car from "shimmying."[20]

In October 1926, E. L. Cord, owner of the Auburn Automobile Company, purchased the Duesenberg plant in Indianapolis, including all equipment. Cord established a new corporation, Duesenberg, Inc. (Duesenberg), with a capitalization of $1 million. Fred Duesenberg continued with the new entity as vice president. The deal was put together by Manning & Company of Chicago. Cord planned to have a stock issue with 150,000 shares of "B" stock and 75,000 shares of "A" stock with no par value.[21]

Cord discussed his plans for the brand:

> Duesenberg cars will be strictly custom built, the owners selecting their own body styles, their own body makers and selecting their own colors. The price will probably be $18,000 no matter what model, from racer to limousine. We will give the buyer 120 miles an hour speed if desired. Naturally, the production of this type of automobile, which carries a warranty of 15 years, will be limited and we are now taking orders for delivery within six months.[22]

Essential to Cord's plans was the engineering genius of Fred Duesenberg, whom he held in high esteem:

> The list of his inventions and his mechanical creations and perfections speaks for itself. The undisputed dominance that his creations have maintained on the race tracks on both continents is of record.
>
> Mr. Duesenberg built the first American car to win the famous Grand Prix at Le Mans, France, driven by Jimmy Murphy, and establishing a new road record in outdistancing the entire field by 14 minutes. This was in 1921, and it was not only the first American-made car to win, but the first ever to place in a foreign event.
>
> Duesenberg was America's first straight-eight, and that term belongs to no other company. Likewise Duesenberg was the first American car with four-wheel brakes.
>
> Known in both America and Europe as "the master gasoline engine designer," Fred Duesenberg's record is a living exposition of Rudyard Kipling's "They copied all they could follow, but they couldn't copy my mind. And I left 'em sweating and stealing a year and a half behind."
>
> Mr. Duesenberg's leadership is all the more pronounced because it has been achieved in an industry for having developed so many exceptional men. Way back when Elwood Haynes, Elmer Apperson, and R. E. Olds were still experimenting, Fred S. Duesenberg in Rockford, Iowa, was making with his own

hands his first gasoline motor. He has always pioneered. He was scoffed at in 1912, when he entered the Indianapolis race with a motor of 239 cubic inches as against 450 cubic inches of the other cars. However, his success caused the trend to smaller piston displacement engines.

Mr. Duesenberg's engineering supremacy has been equally marked in marine and airplane engines. During the war he was responsible for the success of many high speed submarine chasers. From 1919 to 1926 the victories of Duesenberg designed racing cars is the greatest ever compiled, affording the pedigree of the present Duesenberg automobile, for out of the crucible of racing has come commercial excellence.[23]

Not surprisingly, later that month, it was announced that the Duesenberg would have the highest priced automobile in the world.[24]

George Williams, Marmon president, believed American manufacturers would follow the example of European ones and produce smaller cars. The smaller car would be supplemental to the larger family car. He explained,

> I regard it as highly important that the industry guard against being swept into extreme measures by all this small car agitation, bearing in mind always that the big, luxurious car has become an inherent part of our transportation system, and utterly indispensable to the type of family of means which loves to go places and do things. So far as Marmon is concerned, we have become, during the course of years, so inseparably identified with this large car field that nothing could induce us to even consider departing from it or in any way temporizing with our present large car program.
>
> However, it is a fact that Marmon engineers and executives have recently spent much time abroad, making an exhaustive study of the engineering phases of European motor cars, which have found such favor with Americans of means and discrimination. Concurrently, our engineers have considered the possibility of adapting European engine practice to American manufacture, arriving at the conclusion that the low engine powers prevailing in Europe would be distasteful to the impetuous and more dynamic American temperament.
>
> It seem that the logical solution is a combination of the best elements of European body design with tried American engine practice. Unquestionably, this country is realizing the necessity for a small, beautiful, high-powered type of car that will go far toward at least temporarily relieving our traffic congestion and solving the parking problem. Beauty, speed, safety and power in miniature seem to be the next call in prospect for the American manufacturer.[25]

Marmon's entry into the small car market was the Little Marmon, an eight-in-line cylinder car producing 65 horsepower, more power per cubic inch than any other production engine.[26]

Before being unveiled to the public, in November 1926 the Little Marmon was tested at the Indianapolis Motor Speedway and also on Pumpkin Vine hill near Martinsville, Indiana, for the benefit of automobile journalists.[27] Thomas J. Litle, Jr., Marmon's chief engineer, explained the value of testing cars at the Indianapolis Motor Speedway:

> In tests made at the Indianapolis Speedway, which is paved with brick, it frequently has been observed that more parts failures occur than when driving over similar distances on either board or dirt tracks. For this reason, a track of this type is particularly useful in checking up on an automobile from an endurance standpoint.
>
> For instance, making one lap of this track a car must pass over 50,000 joints or grooves between bricks and, in the course of a day, 13,000,000 vibrations can be set up in the entire structure in consequence. It is apparent, therefore, that if high speeds are maintained over such a course for a prolonged period, parts may be fatigued to an extent never encountered on smooth road courses.[28]

With anticipated sales of 24,000 cars for the first year, production was already underway. The car, unveiled to the public at the 1927 New York Auto Show, was the first car priced under $2,000 to maintain the qualities of a "fine" car. It featured an eight-cylinder in-line engine.[29]

18

Then There Were Three

By 1927, there was a trend toward two-car families. Marmon officials believed they were well positioned to take advantage of this trend with both their large Marmon 75 and the Little Marmon. The smaller cars were desired for negotiating through traffic. Marmon sales manager H. H. Brooks explained,

> Many families have not owned two cars because it was not possible to obtain a small automobile that retained the advantages and quality feature of the large car. The new Little Marmon eight has been accepted as the car the public has been waiting for to bring the two-car-per-family into a prominent place in the automobile picture.[1]

By early 1927 Marmon was producing 100 cars per day and anticipating a 50 percent increase to 150 cars per day with the introduction of the Little Marmon and the conversion of Plant #1 from the manufacture of milling machinery to automobile production.[2] Growth was rapid, particularly for the Little Marmon. Company officials believed they would ship 750 Marmon 75s and 2,500 Little Marmons during a four-week period spanning March and April. The company was manufacturing cars in 27 different body styles, not including the custom-built bodies.[3] The Little Marmon custom-built bodies included a two-window sedan priced at $2,595, a three-window sedan priced at $2,595, a Victoria priced at $2,595, and a town cabriolet priced at $3,125. The prices were established to be midway between the pricing for the standard Little Marmon and the standard Series 75.[4]

The Indianapolis Auto Trade Association sponsored the annual auto show featuring cars ranging in price from $300 to $11,500. Included in the show were six Marmon 75s and seven Little Marmons. Within 15 minutes of the show opening, one of the Little Marmons" was bought by George M. Binger, the advertising manager for William H. Block Company, an Indianapolis clothier. The most expensive car shown was a Duesenberg straight-eight which had a guaranteed speed of 110 miles per hour. Also displayed by Duesenberg was a sport phaeton with a price tag of $10,500. The Stutz display included a Cabriolet 70, Cabriolet 80, and a five-passenger 80 sedan. The show wasn't limited to Indianapolis brands but included others such as Ford, Buick, and Losey-Nash.[5]

Duesenberg set itself aside from other mass-produced automobiles by handcrafting. Its facilities didn't have the look of those of other automobile factories. The machinery was highly polished and the workers wore white uniforms. Duesenberg also had specialized tools normally found only in European shops. E. L. Cord proudly explained,

> The methods, the procedures, and in fact every step of operation in the Duesenberg plants are as foreign to ordinary automobile factories as though they were actually built in the "hands" method of Europe.

This kind of experience, methods, and ideals are indispensible to originate and create the particular type of car Duesenberg builds.⁶

The New York Auto Show had 43 separate makes of automobiles on display, of which eight were from Indiana, including Indianapolis brands Marmon and Stutz. Duesenberg was not included in the list as it did not participate in the New York show but rather had salon viewings at various hotels.⁷

In January 1927 Lionel D. Edie, director of Bureau of Research at Indiana University's School of Commerce and Finance, predicted great things for the Indiana and Indianapolis automobile industry. Confident of the continued growth in automobiles, Professor Edie believed that output in Indiana in 1927 should exceed that of 1926. He stated, "Certainly no automobile depression is in sight, and the general tone in automobile circles is one of confidence and conservative optimism."⁸

Duesenberg introduced the Model X in 1927. It was equipped with the straight-eight engine generating 100 horsepower and capable of going 90 miles per hour. A supercharger was also available on the car, with which the car could reach up to 110 miles per hour. The sporty car featured one of the strongest chassis on the market. With a body built by Locke, the car had a 136-inch wheelbase with an eight-inch chrome and nickel steel frame with five tubular cross members.⁹ Only 12 chassis for the Model X were built.¹⁰

Marmon engineers introduced an anti-scuff valve on the Little Marmon to protect the engine when starting in the harsh winter weather. To ensure proper lubrication, this valve would deposit a small quantity of oil on each cylinder when the car was started.¹¹

Samuel B. Stevens of Rome, New York, offered the Stevens Challenge Trophy as an incentive for stock closed cars of American manufacture. To win the trophy, a car had to

Duesenberg building in Indianapolis (Auburn Cord Duesenberg Automobile Museum).

George Souders, 1927 Indianapolis 500 winner (Auburn Cord Duesenberg Automobile Museum).

maintain an average speed in excess of 60 miles per hour for 24 consecutive hours. Despite alternating snow and rain, Stutz won the Stevens Challenge Cup at the Indianapolis Motor Speedway, averaging 68.44 miles per hour with a stock five-passenger auto. For the 24 hours, 1,642 miles were driven. Close behind the pace-setting car was a second five-passenger Stutz equipped with a Weymann body averaging 67.176 miles per hour for the 24-hour grind.[12] Stutz retained the trophy until a Marmon drove 1,634.2 miles in October 1931.[13]

In May, Stutz again took to the track, this time in a 75-mile stock car race at the Atlantic City Motor Speedway. Tom Rooney won the race with an average speed of 86.249 miles per hour. Following closely behind was an Auburn 8–88 roadster driven by Wade Morton, which finished the race just 0.23 second behind Rooney.[14]

As an incentive to buy a Safety Stutz, the Stutz company gave a free one-year insurance policy to each buyer of the car. The policy covered physician, hospital and similar fees up to $1,200 in case of bodily injury while riding in the Safety Stutz. The policies were underwritten by Lloyd's of London. Stutz also offered a "loss of use" policy that paid the owner $5 a day if the car was stolen.[15]

Six Duesenbergs were among the 41 entries in the 1927 Indianapolis 500. The high hopes of the Duesenbergs were dashed on the first day of qualifying when the only Duesenberg to qualify was the slowest of the day. L. L. Corum had an average speed of 94.601 miles per hour, way off the pace set by the other drivers, including Frank Lockhart, winner of the 1926 Indianapolis 500, who held the pole position with an average speed of 120.100 miles per hour.[16] Four additional Duesenbergs qualified on the second day, including George Souders on the eighth row, Babe Stapp and Wade Morton on the ninth row, and Dave Evans on the tenth row. On the final day of qualifications Corum was eliminated but another Duesenberg driven by Ben Shoaff was added to the field.[17]

Souders, who has been described as "the darkest of dark horses," pulled off an upset, winning the Indianapolis 500 with an average speed of 97.451 miles per hour. The second-place finisher, Earl Devore, was well behind the pace set by Souders with an average speed of 93.867 miles per hour. The Duesenberg piloted by Evans finished fifth. The Duesenbergs came very close to having a one-two finish. Ben Shoaff's Perfect Circle racer was on its way to a second place finish when its drive shaft broke on mile 495. Babe Stapp's Duesenberg went out of the race on the 25th lap with a broken universal drive.[18]

Following his victory in Indianapolis, Souders was entered as the pilot of his Duesenberg in the Grand Prix at Monza, Italy. To run in the Grand Prix, Souders had to get permission from the AAA Contest Board as he was leading in the 1927 driver's championship. Other American drivers entered in the Grand Prix race were Peter Kreis and Earl Cooper.[19] Souders was offered $5,000 to drive in the race by the Italian government. About a week before the Grand Prix, he was injured when his car crashed through a fence. Despite having a dislocated left shoulder and cuts to his back, he took to the wheel of his Duesenberg and was leading when the car developed fuel issues, causing him to drop out of the race. He was also scheduled to drive the Duesenberg in the British Grand Prix, but withdrew from the race when his injuries did not heal.[20]

Marmon adopted the "just in time" manufacturing strategy in June 1927, lowering its cost of production. Carl J. Sherer, treasurer, explained the strategy to a meeting of the American Management Association in Detroit:

> Its whole aim and purpose is to accomplish economy in manufacturing by efficient purchase and production methods and its principal advantage is the elimination of storerooms with many incidental savings.
> Our scheme is briefly an arrangement of the manufacturing equipment in parallel lines at right angles to the line of assembly so that raw material of any description entering one side of the plant by means of a single delivery aisle progresses in parallel lines to the assembly stations. These machine lines are arranged to produce parts in the sequence of their assembly into the motor on one side of the plant and into the chassis on the other side, the motor and chassis meeting at the end of their respective travels through the assembly operations.[21]

The Little Marmon Eight had a significant impact upon Marmon. In fewer than six months of having the Little Marmon on the market, the company experienced a 51 percent increase in revenues. For fiscal year 1926 the company recorded sales of 5,701 units, which doubled to 10,366 units for the fiscal year ending June 30, 1927.[22] General sales manager H. H. Brooks commented, "The strong financial position of the Marmon company is a direct result of the introduction of the Marmon eight and the record sales so far this year." Marmon's net worth increased by nearly $2 million to $10 million.[23]

At the end of 1927 Marmon introduced the Marmon 78 at the Indianapolis showroom a month before the car would be introduced nationally at the New York Auto Show. Priced at $1,895, the Marmon 78 featured a straight-eight motor producing 86 horsepower with six different body styles. As with other Marmon cars, the 78 was tested at the Indianapolis Motor Speedway where it obtained speeds of 70 to 80 miles per hour and acceleration from 10 miles per hour to 50 miles per hour in 15 seconds. The car was also tested at the Uniontown, Pennsylvania, hill, where it reached 43 miles per hour in high gear from a standing start.[24]

18. Then There Were Three

In September, Stutz won a 150-mile race for stock cars at the Atlantic City track with an average speed of 96.308 miles per hour, establishing a new record for the distance. The car was piloted by Tom Rooney. Entries included three Stutz Black Hawks, two Auburn 8–88s, a Duesenberg, a Chrysler 80, a Chrysler 72, a Packard eight, a Packard six, a LaSalle, a Nash Advanced Six and a Buick Master Six. The other Stutz entries finished second and third.[25]

Although Marmon had been a company that didn't believe in bringing out new models every year, that changed under Williams' leadership. Marmon was the first auto company to introduce a low-priced car with a straight-eight engine when it unveiled the Marmon 68 at the 1929 New York Auto Show. With piston displacement of 201.9 cubic inches, the 68 had a top speed of 65 to 70 miles per hour. Like other Marmon cars, the 68 was tested at the Indianapolis Motor Speedway, on hill climbs, and on cross-country road trips. The car also had some features for the convenience and comfort of the driver. The steering wheel could be tilted and was ribbed for gripping. It also had a lighted central instrument panel which included a speedometer, oil pressure and gasoline gauges, and an engine heat indicator.[26] There were four body styles in the 68 including a five-passenger sedan, a coupe with a rumble seat, a Victoria coupe and a roadster with a rumble seat. The five-passenger sedan and the coupe with rumble seat sold for $1,465 in the 68 model, while the Victoria coupe sold for $1,520 and the roadster with rumble seat sold for $1,565. At the time of the Marmon 68's introduction, Marmon claimed to be the largest producer of cars equipped with straight-eight engines.[27] In addition to the 68 the company also produced six body styles of its 78s and the higher priced 75 series, a six-cylinder car.[28]

Marmon was thrilled with the reception given the 68 and 78 models. H. H. Brooks, general sales manager, commented on the new cars:

> Introduction of the two new lines by Marmon bears twofold importance since it marks the entrance into volume production of one of the oldest manufacturers in the industry, and, moreover, establishes the modern straight-eight motor car as a leading factor in both the low and medium-priced fields.[29]

Based upon the feedback from the auto show, Marmon projected producing 45,000 cars in 1928.[30]

Marmon's production had an impact upon Indianapolis beyond the walls of the Marmon factory. Many of materials for the cars were sourced through Indianapolis businesses at an estimated cost of $18 million. The largest supplier was the Murray Body Company, which employed between 1,100 and 1,200 men. Additionally, the company anticipated increasing its employment rolls to 3,400 with a total expenditure of $4.5 million.[31] The growth in Marmon production (98 percent) far exceeded the average growth for the industry (27 percent) for the first 2½ months of 1928.[32]

For 1928 Stutz instituted a program where no two cars would have the same color combination. The Safety Stutz was being produced in 12 different models and those with the Weymann body were produced in 11 different models.[33]

Rumors were floating around Indianapolis that Duesenberg was going to introduce a new car. Although the details of the new car were carefully guarded by company officials, test cars had been clocked at the Indianapolis Motor Speedway at more than 100 miles per hour.[34] E. L. Cord, president, confirmed the rumors and promised the new car would soon be released:

During the intervening months, many motors and many automobiles have been built at the Indianapolis factory and the new Duesenbergs have been driven many, many thousands of miles on Speedway and country road, over desert and mountain, during hottest summer and zero winter. Many problems were met and mastered by a corps of learned engineers headed by the master, Duesenberg. Unheard of power and speed made necessary the development of new carburetors, ignition units, pistons, in fact every part had to excel all predecessors to qualify for this super automobile.

Clever artists and prominent designers from all over the world were consulted with regard to individual appearance and most luxurious bodies. Competent metallurgists perfected formulas to ensure large margins of safety. Rubber engineers designed tires to withstand acceleration and speed unknown until the advent of this new Duesenberg.

And now, we have the most perfect car, more powerful, more speed, instantaneous acceleration, luxurious, different, excelling all others. We are busy getting delivery on material, rearranging our factory to insure accurate workmanship and making ready for production. In a very few weeks, we will place before those who appreciate the best in life, the motor carriage they have always wished for.[35]

In March Marmon hired Earl Cooper, the famed auto racer and member of the Marmon racing teams in 1909–1911, for its experimental engineering staff. Following his retirement from auto racing, Cooper had entered four cars of his own design in the Indianapolis 500, three of which had front wheel drive. He had also consulted with Marmon on the development of the straight-eight motor used in the 78 and 68 models.[36] Shortly after Cooper's hiring, Marmon added fellow auto racer Pete Kreis to its engineering staff.[37]

With the announcement of Cooper's hiring, there was no mention that he and Howard Marmon had designed a car to participate in the Indianapolis 500. In April, the company announced the entry of two Marmon 68 Specials for the race, with Cooper as the team captain.[38] The cars were numbered as 32, in honor of the car which won the 1911 Indianapolis 500, and 34, commemorating the model 34, the long-time product of the company. Built on a 100-inch wheelbase, the cars had two forward and one reverse speed[39] and were equipped with a straight-eight engine and front wheel drive. Just as in 1910 with the introduction of the Marmon Wasp, Howard Marmon explained that the entries were to test new engineering principles:

> Changes in the future design of passenger automobiles are coming so fast that we decided to take some of our advanced engineering ideas to the race course for a trial. We are entering the Indianapolis race, not so much from a competitive standpoint, but rather because Marmon engineering research has developed many innovations which will revolutionize the passenger car as we know it today. Therefore, we are taking these new ideas to the track in Indianapolis to ascertain, in a 500-mile race with the best and fastest automobiles in the world, just how near a state of perfection these innovations have progressed.[40]

When entries for the 1928 Indianapolis 500 closed, the 36 hopefuls included the Marmons[41] painted in the company's racing colors of yellow with black trim, harking back to the days of the Wasp.[42] Four Duesenbergs were entered, including two by the Duesenberg brothers plus entries by A. S. Kirkely and Henry Maley, while two Stutz Specials were entered by the estate of Frank Lockhart.

The first day of qualifying found 19 cars in the lineup, including a Stutz Special driven by Tony Gullotta on the second row and a Marmon Special driven by Johnny Seymour on the fourth row.[43] On the second day of qualifying, five additional cars were added to the lineup, including Peter Kreis in a Marmon Special on the seventh row and Russell Snowberger in a Marmon Special and Jimmy Gleason in a Duesenberg on the eighth row.[44] On the third day of qualifying, which occurred three days before the race, four additional cars made the field, including two Duesenbergs driven by 1924 winner L. L. Corum and Dutch Bauman.[45] Both of the Duesenbergs were subsequently eliminated by crashes during practice.[46]

The starting grid of 31 cars also included the last two qualifiers: Duesenbergs driven by Ben Shoaff and Ira Hall on the tenth row.[47] Leading the pace lap was a Marmon 78 driven by Joe Dawson.[48] The race was a real heart breaker for Jimmy Gleason in his Duesenberg. Leading the race on the 195th lap, he came into the pits with a broken water hose that caused water to run onto the spark plugs and distributor. Although his team fixed the water hose and restarted the engine, Gleason reentered the race in 13th place. The stop cost him $20,000 in earnings.[49]

The race was won by Louis Meyer in a Miller Special with an average speed of 99.482 miles per hour. Indianapolis-built racers finished eighth and tenth. Fred Frame in the S.A.M.I. Special, the Duesenberg with which George Souders had won the 1927 race, finished eighth, while Tony Gullotta in a Stutz Special finished tenth.[50]

Stutz introduced a two-door coupe to its product line. The car was built on a 131-inch wheelbase and priced at $3,990. The front seat was divided and tilted forward. The body was of aluminum.[51]

In October 1928, Marmon changed its body supplier from the Murray Body Corporation to the Hayes Body Corporation of Grand Rapids, Michigan, which also supplied bodies to Reo and Chrysler. In this transaction, Marmon leased Plant #3, which had previously been occupied by Murray Body, to Hayes. Except for the plant manager, the personnel employed

Duesenberg J231 (Auburn Cord Duesenberg Automobile Museum).

at the factory, estimated at 1,000, remained the same. Marmon's president, George Williams, said of the change,

> The Hayes company is familiar with and accustomed to the Marmon standards of body quality, having previously made some of our custom bodies in their Grand Rapids plant. We feel that this new connection constitutes an important step in Marmon's progressive program of expansion. All Marmon bodies will continue to be built to our own design and specifications under our direct supervision and inspection.[52]

Marmon introduced two new body styles, a collapsible coupe and a touring speedster, for its 68s and 78s to Indianapolis residents prior to introducing them at the 1929 New York Auto Show. The collapsible coupe was what we today would call a convertible. Raising the top resulted in a standard coupe, while lowering it resulted in a racy open car. To insure the snugness of the roof, Marmon utilized zipper fasteners rather than the standard snaps on the sides, which also made for ease of operation. Both lines had a rumble seat for two additional passengers.[53] Both the 68 and the 78 speedster could seat six, with three on the front seat and three on the back seat. The front seats on both models could be adjusted to meet the needs of the driver for increased or decreased leg room. Additionally, at the back of the speedsters was a compartment to store side curtains and arm rests.[54]

After being in development for two years,[55] the straight-eight Duesenberg Model J with 265 horsepower was revealed at a New York salon in early December.[56] While no maximum speed had been established on a long straightaway before the car show, the car unofficially went 117 miles per hour with a standard touring body and the top and windshield up and fenders on. The engine, with 420 cubic inches of displacement, was similar in design to the Duesenberg eights except for the adoption of four valves per cylinder. Another unusual feature of the car was the aluminum dashboard, which included a 150 mph speedometer, a tachometer, a water temperature gauge, a brake pressure gauge, an ammeter, and a gasoline gauge. Two wheelbases were offered: 142.5 inches for cars seating five passengers or fewer, and 153.5 inches for seven-passenger cars.[57] After receiving 102 orders at the show, the company expected to manufacture 300 of the cars in 1929[58] with the sales price of the chassis alone set at $8,500 FOB Indianapolis.[59] Three other body types were available for an additional $3,000.[60]

Stutz also modified its cars for the 1929 auto show. Changes to the engine included an increase in the valve diameter and improvements in the intake manifold, resulting in an increase to 115 horsepower. The cars had adjustable European-type front seats as regular equipment on all models except for the Victoria coupe and the two-passenger coupe, which had adjustable seat backs.[61]

Stutz added another optional feature to its cars: a six-tube radio. The company tested the radios for two years before their introduction. Based upon the test results, the company added special shielding so that neither the operation of the generator nor the distributor was affected by the reception. The set was built into the instrument board and was entirely hidden except for the dials and controls, which were grouped on the instrument panel. A miniature loudspeaker was located on the top of the windshield and the antenna was concealed in the top. The radio operated from the car's storage battery using about 1½ amp.-hrs.[62]

As 1928 came to a close, the outlook for the Indianapolis automobile industry was bright. Marmon announced a major expansion of its factory to take care of expanded sales.[63] In a special meeting, the Marmon board of directors voted to increase the company's common stock from 200,000 shares to 400,000 shares. The existing shareholders were offered an option to buy an aggregate 60,000 shares of stock at $55 per share in proportion to holdings on January 7, 1929. Three-tenths of one new share could be bought for one share of existing owned shares. George Williams, president, anticipated that the funds raised by the new stock offering would total more than $3 million and would be used for working capital to support the anticipated doubling of production in 1929. In addition to the Marmon 68 and Marmon 78, the company was planning to start a new car line, the Roosevelt, named after President Teddy Roosevelt. The Roosevelt would feature a straight-eight engine and would be priced at less than $1,000.[64]

Likewise, Stutz was also planning an expansion of its manufacturing facilities and anticipated financing of the expansion through a $1 million stock offering. When the Stutz announcement was made, the company's stock was selling at twice the price of a year before ($18). Marmon's stock had also had a large increase in value, from $48 per share the year before to $85 per share.[65]

The Stutz Blackhawk introduced at the 1929 New York Car Show garnered a lot of attention. The car had new features including four forward speeds, the "noback" and Ryan-lites. Ryan-lites, used on the Stutz Bearcat as well as the Blackhawk,[66] were new to the market and promised the "safest and most satisfactory illumination ever invented. A long, low forward beam and wide, bright sidewise fans that light the whole road."[67] The "noback" was a device which prevented cars from rolling backward on hills.[68]

Marmon also had a very successful New York Auto Show, displaying 40 of its cars in five different displays, two at Grand Central Palace and the remainder at the Belmont and Commodore hotels and at the company's New York branch office. While at the New York Auto Show, president George Williams talked about the vision for the company:

> Opening the New York show marked another step in our plans to offer a full line of eights in all price classes—cars that are the result of years of development by the most capable engineering and manufacturing staff possible to assemble under a single roof.[69]

At a board meeting on January 24, Fred Moscovics, Stutz's president, resigned in order "to have more time to attend to his personal affairs." The board of directors immediately elevated E. S. Gorrell, vice president, to president. Gorrell, a graduate of West Point and the Massachusetts Institute of Technology, had begun his automobile career in the Northeast as a distributor. His tenure in Indianapolis began in the sales department with Marmon; he joined Stutz as a vice president in September 1925.[70]

On the day Marmon set a new single-day record of producing 250 automobiles, the company also introduced the Roosevelt. With a base factory price of $995, it was equipped with a straight-eight engine[71] with 70 horsepower. The car had some unique features, including the "single button control." The button, situated in the middle of the steering wheel, would sound a horn if it was pressed, start the car when it was pulled, and turned the lights on when the button was turned.[72] The Roosevelt came in three different body styles: a two-passenger standard coupe with rumble seat; a collapsible coupe with rumble seat; and a four-passenger Victoria coupe.[73]

Management attributed Marmon's ability to sell an automobile equipped with an eight-cylinder engine at a price below $1,000 to the company's expertise and operations in the eight-cylinder field. Thomas Jarrard, general sales director, explained Marmon's ability to produce the car:

Not only is the Roosevelt an example of concentrated eight-cylinder development, but the Marmon 68 and 78 as well show how broad research and practical experience has enabled Marmon to make available to all buyers the advantages of straight-eights. As a matter of fact, when the Marmon 68 was introduced in the $1,500 price class, it created comment of the same sort that has greeted the Roosevelt, but continued record-breaking sales and outstanding performance records of this model have shown the value of intensive development and quantity production.[74]

The initial reception of the Roosevelt car was very encouraging. Within the first two days, reports filtered back to Indianapolis that 500,000 people nationwide had visited Marmon/Roosevelt showrooms to see the new car.[75]

Stutz was able to lower the cost of the Blackhawk because of larger production facilities and increased demand for the automobile.[76] The prices on the six- and eight-cylinder Blackhawk cars were the same and ranged from a low of $2,395 for a five-passenger sedan or a five-passenger coupe to a high of $2,735 for a four-passenger Speedster with tonneau cowl.[77] In July, Stutz announced a further reduction in the base price of the Blackhawk to $1,995, as well as some enhancements to the car including increased headroom, a visor adjustable from the inside, and a new instrument panel.[78]

Historically, Marmon engineers were only responsible for the design of the automobiles, including testing, experimental work and running the research laboratories. In April, the company announced a new strategy, putting the engineering staff in charge of the inspection of the cars while they were being assembled. Management hoped this would put the engineers closer to the process and provide direct feedback on the practicality of the design. Another

1929 Roosevelt (courtesy Dennis Breeden).

Advertisement for 1929 Duesenberg, "The World's Finest Motor Car" (Indiana Historical Society, P0143).

benefit of the change was that the engineers could interpret the blueprints if the production staff needed guidance. Although engineering inspection was used by other industries, Marmon was an early adopter of the practice in the automobile industry.[79]

While Duesenberg was not part of the New York Auto Show, it displayed the highest priced auto in the United States, a 265-horsepower phaeton, at a salon in a New York City hotel.[80]

For the fiscal year ending February 28, 1929, Marmon announced earnings of $1,447,920 on revenues of $23.9 million (16,551 cars). The financials included $168,900 in expenses related to the introduction of the Roosevelt in late February. From profits the company paid $70,000 in dividends.[81]

Part of the success of the Marmon cars was due to the ability of the consumer to finance car purchases. While this had become commonplace in the industry, a Marmon advertisement promised a new twist to financing—no down payment with a trade-in. This program allowed a buyer to own a new Marmon 68 for $65 per month, which included fire and theft insurance and all finance charges. A similar plan for the Marmon 78 was available at a "slightly higher monthly rate."[82]

In June, Marmon announced record sales for the first quarter ending May 31, 1929. The company had shipped 14,847 Marmon and Roosevelt cars, an increase of 115 percent from the like period in 1928. Although it didn't announce earnings in early June, the company

Marmon 68 advertisement in the *Saturday Evening Post* (Indiana Historical Society, P0143).

stated that the net earnings would be "considerably in excess of our total dividend requirement for the year."[83]

With a history of continually being late for the Indianapolis 500, the Duesenberg brothers promised their cars would be finished in time to be broken in prior to qualifications for the 1929 race. Chuckling, Fred Duesenberg told the *Indianapolis Star*,

18. Then There Were Three

You see, Augie and I always divide the work of building cars. When we were late for a race or when anything went wrong, we used to blame each other. It's different now. I am so busy with other endeavors that I have turned over the racing division to Augie. Now all I have to do is to see that he does it. And I will, too. I don't forget the times he blamed me for not having my part of the work done. He will have all the cars on the track by May 1 or we'll all know the reason why not.[84]

While Augie failed to have the cars ready for the May 1 date, they were finished by May 5, much earlier than normal.[85]

Forty-five cars were on the entry list when the application period for participation in the Indianapolis 500 ended. The list included six Duesenbergs: three by Augie Duesenberg, a privately owned Duesenberg by C. H. Cunard (Buckeye-Duesenberg), and Duesenberg Specials owned by Ray Keech and Tommy Milton.[86] On race day, 33 cars lined up for a chance at the estimated $100,000 in prizes. The Duesenbergs in the race were Bill Spence on the fourth row, Ernie Triplett and Freddy Winnai on the seventh row, and Jimmy Gleason on the eighth row.[87]

Despite hope for another championship, the Duesenberg cars weren't successful. On the eighth lap of the race, Spence slid into the wall at high speed, causing the car to overturn multiple times. Spence was ejected from the car and died of a skull fracture.[88] The highest finisher was Jimmy Gleason, who finished third with an average speed of 93.699 miles per hour—nearly four miles per hour slower than the winner of the race, Keech. The only other Duesenberg to finish in the top ten was the car piloted by Winnai, which took home the sixth place honors.[89] A check of the race tape resulted in Winnai's finish being restated as fifth.[90] The Duesenberg driven by Triplett suffered a broken connecting rod on lap 48.[91]

With all but one car in the Indianapolis 500 being powered by a straight-eight engine, Marmon took the opportunity to promote its straight-eight lineup in the *Indianapolis Star* on race day:

Straight-eight Leadership On The Speedway
Since 1924, every place in every race has been won by a straight-eight. So pronounced has become this supremacy that all cars except one were straight-eights.
Straight-Eight Leadership By Marmon
Marmon, following straight-eight development on the Speedway, has incorporated in its products all proved engineering advances. Marmon is the first of all manufacturers to make the straight-eight available in all price fields. Roosevelt, $995; Marmon 68, $1,465; Marmon 78, $1,965. Priced at factory. Group equipment extra.[92]

After the 1929 Indianapolis 500, the Speedway was used for an endurance run by three Roosevelt automobiles chosen at random from the production line at Marmon. To keep the cars running, Marmon had teams of drivers and mechanics working in eight hour shifts.[93] Hundreds witnessed the three Roosevelt cars circling the track as the Speedway was open to anyone who wished to see the test in progress.[94]

Not surprisingly, Marmon used the test of the Roosevelt at the Indianapolis Motor Speedway as a way to tout its cars:

IT'S STILL RUNNING!
Bulletin.
Indianapolis Motor Speedway, June 25, 1929.
At 9 o'clock tonight the Marmon built Roosevelt eight, which has been running continuously since 10 A.M., June 12, has been rolling along just as smoothly as it did the first day, having completed 323 hours (13 days, 11 hours), without stopping either engine or car. This is a stock car in every mechanical detail,

fully equipped with shock absorbers, bumpers front and rear, trunk rack and two extra wire wheels, tires, tubes and covers, completely ready for the road.[95]

The test of the Roosevelt car was stopped after 440 hours 31 minutes,[96] smashing the previous best non-stop run on the Speedway of 50 hours 21 minutes 1 second.[97] The test was called off when a fierce thunderstorm blew through the area, ripping the roofs from the grandstands with the debris blocking the track.[98] Afterwards, the car was taken to the Marmon factory where it was disassembled and found to be in perfect working order after inspection by Louis Chevrolet, AAA representative Charlie Merz, and S. E. Rowe, chassis engineer for the Stutz.[99] The Roosevelt car was then put on display at the Marmon showroom in Indianapolis along with the car used for refilling of the Roosevelt cars participating in the test.[100]

Not only was the Roosevelt automobile the first car priced under $1,000 to be equipped with a straight-eight engine, it was also among the first eight-cylinder cars in the new market of rental agencies. At the time, cars could be rented by the mile or by the hour.[101]

In the Pike's Peak Hill Climb, a Roosevelt collapsible coupe won first prize in the light car class, which was open to all cars with a factory price of less than $1,000. The car was entered by the Colorado Springs, Colorado, service manager, William P. Bentrup. The car made the 12-mile trip in 26 minutes 56.2 seconds. At the time, an average driver took an hour to complete the journey.[102]

Just days before the stock market crash of 1929, Marmon announced the best six months in the company's history, having earned $1,150,282. During the period, the company had shipped 21,841 Roosevelt and Marmon cars, an increase of about 110 percent over the same period in 1928.[103]

The stock market crash of 1929, which started the Great Depression, rattled markets. As a response, the Marmon board of directors voted the payment of the dividend with the hope of inspiring public confidence at a special meeting. The dividend was $1 per share of common stock payable on December 1. Combined with the earlier dividend, Marmon paid out approximately 60 percent of its earnings to its stockholders.[104]

With the design of a new automobile taking months prior to its release, Marmon had decided to re-enter the large car luxury market months before the stock market collapse. The new car had a straight-eight engine producing 125 horsepower[105] and a four-speed transmission with a factory base price of $3,000, FOB Indianapolis.[106] President George Williams commented about the new line,

> The new Big Eight will serve to reestablish Marmon in the field in which it has been noted in the past, and in which it has a large clientele of owners. It will have such advanced features as a 125 hp engine and four-speed transmission, in addition to incorporating numerous innovations in appearance, luxury, comfort and performance.[107]

Four models of the new Big Eight, including a coupe, a seven-passenger sedan, a four-door club sedan, and a four-door brougham, were unveiled in Indianapolis in mid–December 1929. Although they were not shown at the dealership, the company also offered as part of the Big Eight line a five-passenger sedan, a two-passenger coupe, and a seven-passenger limousine. The length of the car was 202 inches. The car also featured shatterproof plate glass, another new invention. The front seats were adjustable and the steering wheel could tilt for the comfort of the driver. In an innovation taken from the aircraft industry, the car also featured a dual carburetor system.[108]

Stutz introduced the Chateau Series featuring Weymann flexible bodies. Expert coach builders were brought from Europe to duplicate the famous models owned by nobility including the Prince of Wales, the Duke of York and Lord Louis Mountbatten. The Monte Carlo Coupe won first place honors for beauty at the International Concours d'Elegance at Monte Carlo. As with all cars featuring a Weymann body, the frame was made of ash, with every joint having a steel pivot allowing for the flexibility of the cars. One of the items touted was the safety of a Weymann body because it was not as top heavy as a metal body. The Chateau line was available as a Versailles, a five-passenger, four-door sedan; and the Longchamps, a closed-coupled two-door sedan for four people. Both the Versailles and the Longchamps were built on a 134.5-inch wheelbase. The Chaumont, a five-passenger sedan, and the Monte Carlo, a close-coupled four-door coupe, were built on a longer 145-inch wheel base. The cars retailed from $3,945 to $4,495 FOB Indianapolis.[109]

Stutz also had a special production run of 25 cars equipped with a supercharging system. The company planned to be selective in selling the car only to "purchasers who understand the mechanism." Use of the supercharger reportedly increased engine power by 20 to 25 percent, with car speed being increased proportionally. Tests showed that a car traveling at 60 miles per hour would achieve a speed of 72 to 75 miles per hour when the supercharger was used. The price of this optional equipment was $1,500 FOB Indianapolis.[110]

The three Indianapolis manufacturers planned to be at the New York Auto Show in January 1930. Marmon had the largest group of vehicles, ranging from the low-priced Roosevelt ($1,000) to the high-priced Big Eight ($3,000). Stutz showed its Blackhawk model with a sales price of $2,000 to $3,000 for regular Stutzes or, if custom coach work was involved, $4,000 to $5,000. Although Duesenberg wasn't at the New York Auto Show, the company had a display at the Commodore Hotel featuring a 265-horsepower engine car with a cost of over $10,000.[111]

19

The End Comes

As 1930 began, automobile manufacturers were filled with optimism because of the swarming crowds at the Grand Central Palace, scene of the main exhibits. They undoubtedly remembered the significant economic downturn in 1920–21 from which the economy had rebounded. Marmon exhibited the Eight-69 and the Eight-79 models along with a Roosevelt automobile.[1] The Eight-69 was a moderately priced car in the $1,500 range while the Eight-79 was somewhat higher in the $2,000 range. Marmon also displayed its new Big Eight, which had been introduced at the end of 1929.[2] Stutz exhibited Stutz and Blackhawk cars with Weymann bodies, and Duesenberg had its 265-horsepower Model J on exhibit at a salon.[3]

Underscoring his belief in the future, G. M. Williams, Marmon president, told the Marmon-Roosevelt distributors,

> This great American public which has moved from downtown homes to the suburbs, depending upon the motor car for transportation, may have met reverses but these people are not going to stick to the subway long. High hats have been discarded and America has gone back to work. We are all only a generation or so removed from the shirt-sleeve period, anyway, and if all will follow in the movement back to work there will be no sales problem in 1930.[4]

Williams was so convinced of the upturn in business that Marmon increased the capacity of the plant.[5] Williams said,

> The outlook for Marmon is exceedingly bright, and we are preparing to operate our factory on an increasing scale during the coming months. After a careful analysis we feel that substantial improvements are being effected monthly in the general business situation throughout the country. This opinion is concurred in by leading industrial and financial authorities.[6]

Across town, Stutz was in dire financial condition. The company had been in merger discussions with an undisclosed automobile company when receivership and bankruptcy suits were filed. The company maintained that the suits amounted to one month of business while the company had quick assets (inventory and accounts receivable) of $2.5 million and total assets of $4 million. The bankruptcy petition was filed by Indianapolis companies E. C. Atkins & Company, Hide, Leather, & Belting Company, and Vonnegut Company with total owed of $2,176. The three companies also maintained that Stutz had made preferential payments to another party. The receivership action was filed by the Standard Automotive Equipment Company, which was owed $753, and Faires Manufacturing Company for $1,399.[7] As a result of the bankruptcy petition, shares of Stutz stock dropped to $1.[8] Edgar Gorrell, Stutz president, talked about the damage to the company:

> The news was carried on the tickers. Negotiations were broken off, of course. You couldn't blame the

other side, when the credit of one of the companies in the proposed consolidation had been attacked in this way.[9]

Stutz responded to the bankruptcy petition by asking that it be dismissed due to a technicality. The petition stated that the company was incorporated in New Jersey, when in fact it was a New York corporation.[10] Stutz also filed suit to recover $30,000 from the Internal Revenue Service for overpayment of taxes in 1920. In the tax filing, Stutz had reported an investment of $2.5 million in fixtures, furniture, and equipment when it should have reported an investment of $3.5 million.[11] Earlier in the month, Stutz had recovered $28,906 from the Internal Revenue Service for overpayment of 1919 taxes.[12]

To generate sales, Marmon offered to credit a buyer of a 1930 Roosevelt automobile with the purchase price of a 1929 Ford or 1929 Chevrolet from January 17 until February 15.[13]

At the February board of directors meeting, Williams announced that Marmon had had its best January ever, with sales of the Marmon and Roosevelt automobiles exceeding those for January 1929. Confident of the company's future, the board approved a 50 cent per share dividend payment.[14]

The Roosevelt cars displayed at the Indianapolis auto show in 1930 had numerous improvements over the models introduced in 1929. The spring and axle systems had been improved, allowing the car to be lowered one inch. The cars also sported a larger radiator than was usually found on Marmon automobiles. The company increased the size of the passenger compartment, allowing for greater comfort. The car was available in four body styles, including a five-passenger sedan, a two-passenger coupe with rumble seat, a four-passenger Victoria coupe, and a convertible coupe with rumble seat.[15] With continued faith in the future, Marmon introduced three new models in May: a seven-passenger touring car with a body by LeBaron in the Big Eight line, and five-passenger phaeton speedsters in the 69 and 79 lines.[16]

Later in the month, Marmon announced a 12,000-mile or one-year guarantee on each of its 1930 straight eight models, describing the guarantee as revolutionary. The new policy replaced a guarantee of 90 days. G. M. Williams, president, said of the guarantee:

> We realize that the Marmon company is making an important departure in agreeing to guaranty the material and workmanship of its automobiles for a 12-month period or its average equivalent in actual mileage. However, the Marmon company has been manufacturing straight eights for some four years and we firmly believe our manufacturing, inspection, and purchasing standards have reach a point where it is actually possible to know the dependability and stability of our cars in the hands of owners.[17]

Marmon added a car radio as an accessory for all of its 1930 straight-eight models. The controls for the radio were located on the dashboard and the radio had a 90-day guaranty.[18]

By March, merger negotiations were back on for Stutz to merge with the Gardner Motor Car Company and the Moon Motor Car Company, both of St. Louis, Missouri. It was anticipated that an announcement would be made shortly and that the Stutz operations would relocate to St. Louis.[19] However, Gorrell denied that the company was planning to leave Indianapolis:

> I am much surprised to find that the residents of Indianapolis are not only giving credence to, but actually circulating the rumor that the Stutz Motor Car Company of America is to be moved to St. Louis, Missouri. This rumor is absolutely incorrect.

Gorrell also denied rumors that the company was closed and selling its product at cut-rate prices. He acknowledged that during the winter months the company had been shuttered, as had many others in the country, but stated that operations had resumed after the Chicago Auto Show. To show the strength of the firm, he commented that in the past year, the company had paid off bank loans totaling more than $1.3 million and that quick assets had increased by $189,311. Frustrated with the rumor mill causing damage to the firm, he asked that unsubstantiated rumors about the firm be discontinued.[20] In May, Gorrell reported that unfilled orders were 25 percent greater than they had been prior to the stock market crash.[21]

The early favorite to win the Indianapolis 500 was one of the Duesenbergs entered. Those entering Duesenbergs included Pete DePaolo with two entries, A. S. Duesenberg with two, Bill Alberti with one, and Henry Maley with one to be driven by Deacon Litz.[22] DePaolo, the 1925 and 1927 American racing champion, qualified his Duesenberg racer with an average speed of 99.956 miles per hour.[23] The next day, DePaolo was taking the second Duesenberg from the factory where it was built to the track for a qualification attempt by Bill Cummings just before the close of business. Near the Big Four railroad tracks, he accelerated his racer just as a train was approaching. To avoid crashing into the train, he slammed on his brakes, spun around twice and ended up in a ditch. The undamaged racer was taken to the track, where Cummings recorded a qualifying speed of 106.173 miles per hour.[24] Deacon Litz qualified his Duesenberg racer just two days before the race with an average speed of 105.755 miles per hour, while Babe Stapp qualified with a speed of 104.950 miles per hour.[25] Other qualifiers in Duesenberg racers were Joe Caccia and Cy Marshall on the fourth row with an average speed of 100.846 miles per hour. L. L. Corum in a Stutz racer qualified with an average speed of 94.130 miles per hour.[26]

The race was not good for the Indianapolis-built racers. Of the eight Duesenberg entries, Cummings finished the race in fifth place and L. L. Corum in 10th place. The others were sidelined by crashes. After taking the lead on the third lap, Billy Arnold never relinquished it.[27]

Car sales, which had decreased after the stock market crash, bottomed out in March 1930 in Indianapolis. However, despite slow improvement in sales, registrations of new cars continued to be significantly lower than in the previous year; in September 1930 they were 45 percent lower than they had been in September 1929.[28] Marmon responded to the economic downturn by cutting back production and the workforce.[29] In mid–June, Marmon announced a price reduction of up to $180 for its Roosevelt car.[30] There was a ray of hope that perhaps the economic downturn was easing, as Marmon experienced strong demand for its automobiles in August based largely upon this reduction in pricing.[31]

In June Stutz's creditors agreed to a repayment plan for open accounts at 35 cents per dollar of debt.[32] To fund the debt repayment and provide additional working capital, Stutz announced a new stock issue in October, hoping to raise $600,000 in cash. The company also planned a reverse stock split where ten shares of the existing stock would become one share of the newly issued stock.[33] After extensive due diligence, investment bankers from the house of L. L. Harr & Company purchased the $1,130,000 stock issue. A spokesman from Harr talked about the company's confidence in Stutz:

> We consider that Stutz has able management that has practically accomplished the superhuman during the past year. It is the first time, to our knowledge, that an automobile factory could ever live through the unfortunate and regrettable obstacles placed in the way of Stutz during this past year. Not only did Stutz live through this period, but made progress all the time, in spite of the obstacles.[34]

The new stock issue would allow Stutz stock to be listed on the Chicago exchange.[35] In May 1931, L. L. Harr & Company purchased an additional $700,000 of Stutz stock.[36]

19. The End Comes

In celebration of its 20th anniversary, Stutz unveiled its 1931 models designed with safety in mind. A double drop frame, steel running boards and a lower center of gravity were keys to the safety factors of the car. Stutz was the only American company to integrate the steel running boards with the frame. The company spent a half million dollars on engineering, tools, dies, jigs, and fixtures for the new models. The LA model with a cost of $1,795 to $1,985, the lowest cost ever for a Stutz car, was built on a 127½-inch wheelbase. The MA model cost between $3,445 and $3,795 and was built on a 134½-inch wheelbase. The top of the line MB ranged from a low of $3,885 to a high of $10,800 and was built on a 145-inch wheelbase. The cars retailing in the $10,000 range had the DV-32 engine capable of going 100 miles per hour. All cars sported a custom body.[37]

Cannonball Baker set a new record for a transcontinental drive from New York to Los Angeles with a time of 60 hours 51 minutes in a Stutz. Baker, who made the trip as the sole driver, took 6 hours 47 minutes off the previous record, set in 1929 by a relay team.[38]

By 1931, four of every five cars produced were by one of the big three: Ford (Ford and Lincoln), General Motors (Cadillac, LaSalle, Buick, Pontiac, Oakland, and Chevrolet), and Chrysler (Chrysler, DeSoto, Dodge, and Plymouth). General Motors and Chrysler offered models throughout all price ranges while Ford offered models at the low end and upper end.[39] The Indianapolis manufacturers, who historically had favored high quality, high cost automobiles, had always had an uphill battle. But the economic downturn, which was entering its second year, would provide more challenges to the companies.[40]

The severe economic downturn took a toll upon Marmon, which reported a loss of $1.9 million for the nine months ended November 30, 1930, as compared to a profit of $727,010 for the nine months ending November 30, 1929. The impact of the economic downturn was clearly visible in the three-month results, with a loss of $423,271 for the quarter ending September 30, 1929, increasing to $1,120,861 for the quarter ending September 30, 1930.

Marmon introduced the Marmon16, an automobile powered by a 16-cylinder engine producing 200 horsepower. The engine, originally designed by Howard Marmon in 1926, had undergone four years of refinement and testing.[41] Built upon a 145-inch wheelbase, the car retailed for less than $5,000. The company also introduced two new eight-cylinder automobiles—the Marmon 88 with 125 horsepower selling in the $2,000 classification, and the Marmon 70 with 84 horsepower selling in the $1,000 classification. The Marmon 88 had was built upon two different wheelbases, a 130-inch for the two- and five-passenger bodies, and a 136-inch for seven-passenger and custom bodies.[42] Howard Marmon received an award from the Society of Automotive Engineers for the most noteworthy achievement in automobiles in the prior year.[43]

A Marmon 16 won the Samuel B. Stephens Trophy with an average speed of 76.425 miles per hour over a 24-hour period. Driven by a tester from the factory, the car traveled 1,834.214 miles. AAA officials picked two Marmon 16s at random for the test. The second car, a five-passenger closed coupe, completed the 24-hour trial with an average speed of 75.07 miles per hour. The two cars had the challenge of rain for an hour overnight.[44]

In March 1931 Marmon started a subsidiary, Marmon-Herrington, to build commercial vehicles. Williams was named president with Colonel Arthur W. Herrington as vice president and chief engineer. Fred Moscovics was chairman of the board and Walter Marmon served on the board. Manufacture of the commercial vehicles would be in a dedicated portion of the Marmon factory.[45] The establishment of Marmon-Herrington was, in part, in keeping with President Hoover's policy of maintaining industrial output during the economic slump. Among the first orders for Marmon-Herrington was one from the U.S. Army for 33 heavy duty trucks, which were delivered in June 1931.[46]

Among the 71 entries for the 1931 Indianapolis 500 was L. L. Corum in a Stutz Bearcat[47] and Leon Duray and Phil Pardee in Duesenbergs.[48] Fred Duesenberg, who announced this was his last year in auto racing, had two entries in the field, one piloted by his son, Denny, and the other by Jimmy Gleason.[49] Three Duesenbergs finished in the top 10 in the race. Fred Frame finished second with an average speed of 96.406 miles per hour, while Gleason finished sixth with an average speed of 94.026 miles per hour and Triplett in the Buckeye Duesenberg Special finished seventh with an average speed of 93.041 miles per hour.[50] The second Fred Duesenberg car, driven by Phil Pardee, exited the race when the relief driver, Wilbur Shaw, hopped the wall on the 59th lap.[51]

Things were looking up for Stutz, which recorded a net income of $38,000 for May 1931 and indicated that it had been profitable for the past six months.[52] In July Charles Schwab, who had been Stutz's largest stockholder before divesting his shares, purchased Stutz stock and again became the largest stockholder. Through this purchase, Schwab and his associates controlled 70 percent of the company's stock.[53]

The Commodore Hotel auto salon in New York City had all three Indianapolis manufacturers displaying their vehicles in addition to displays by Rolls-Royce, Chrysler Imperial, Delange, Franklin, Isotta-Fraschini, Lancia, Lincoln, Maybach, Minerva, and Pierce-Arrow. Duesenberg displayed a town limousine, informally called the "Madam's car," which retailed for $16,500.[54]

Marmon's losses in the fiscal year ending in February 1932 were significant. The company had a net operating loss of $1.4 million. Additionally, the company took a writedown of $2.3 million to reflect the current value of its assets.[55] Williams went to work on a plan to right-size the company. In early January, Marmon realigned its production facilities into Plant #2, enabling it to become more efficient. Williams said of the space,

> We have selected the largest, newest and most economical of all our plants to house all manufacturing operations as well as administrative offices and the various departments of the business. General offices are joined with engineering and factory offices in this plant. This makes for better cars at less cost. It provides a close to the product set-up that could not be accomplished otherwise.

With one million square feet of excess space, Marmon established the Marmon Industrial Center to be leased to third parties.[56]

By May Williams had arranged the refinance of $2,427,829 of debt. Half of the debt restructure was in five-year notes with interest at 5 percent. The remainder of the debt was exchanged for Marmon common stock. Despite the financial difficulties, Williams remained confident of the firm's future:

> The 200-horsepower Sixteen in particular has been acknowledged as one of the outstanding cars on the market. Throughout the country, this model is enjoying definite favor and we believe that we will realize an even greater volume of business in the high-priced field during the remainder of the year.
>
> Our entire manufacturing, sales, and executive operations have been consolidated in the most modern of all the company's several plants and all other activities have otherwise been coordinated for maximum efficiency and economy. The dealer and distributor body is being constantly augmented by the addition of new representation in important centers.
>
> Therefore, we feel confident that the company is now in a position to show a favorable operating result even under existing adverse conditions.[57]

19. The End Comes

Stutz was encouraged by an increase in orders with the return of spring.[58] In May the company introduced its 1933 models, which included the Challenger models available in both a single valve and a double valve eight-cylinder engine. The company also announced price reductions which President Gorrell called the "lowest price" ever offered for a Stutz eight-cylinder car. Stutz offered cars ranging from a low of $1,500 to models suited for the luxury market. Engineering improvements to the cars included a new camshaft design, improved cooling, and a more comfortable ride.[59]

A Duesenberg Special driven by Fred Frame won the 1932 Indianapolis 500 with an average speed of 104.144 miles per hour. Duesenberg Specials also finished seventh and ninth, driven by Ira Hall and Billy Winn respectively.[60] This would be the last time Fred Duesenberg saw one of his cars participate in the race. He was killed in an auto accident later in the year.

Marmon-Herrington won a contract for a truck-tractor and trailer equipment to be used to construct a 1,200-mile pipeline in Iraq. The equipment, weighing about 20 tons and 100 feet in length, was designed to pull steel pipe weighing about 40 tons over the desert and unimproved roads. The massive truck-tractor and trailer was tested at the Indianapolis Motor Speedway under AAA supervision.[61] In the test, the truck-tractor averaged 28.68 miles per hour for the 100-mile test.[62]

Improvements to the Marmon 16 focusing on the internal and external appearance of the car were introduced in October 1932. With the introduction of the 1933 16, the company made the decision to concentrate exclusively on the ultrafine market. George C. Tennet explained the decision:

> It has been in this field in the past that Marmon has achieved its greatest success from the standpoint of prestige and recognition as well as financial progress. The remarkable success of the Marmon 16 during the past year and a half, particularly emphasized by the sharp uptrend in owner demand in the last few weeks, has added tremendously to the quality car reputation which has been the heritage of the company since long before the historic days of the Glidden tours.[63]

Despite the engineering success of the car, Marmon quietly faded from the auto industry. Marmon-Herrington, the former subsidiary, continues to produce drivetrain products today.

Stutz successfully negotiated for the rights to manufacture the Pak-Age-Car, a light delivery vehicle which was a cheaper alternative to the horse-drawn dray.[64] While attending the New York Auto Show, Charles Schwab gave a speech introducing 15 of the Stutz models and the Pak-Age-Car, which were displayed on the showroom floor.[65] Sensing that the Pak-Age-Car was the key to its future, Stutz put the vehicle into production in early March.[66] Later in the year, Stutz stopped the production of automobiles.[67]

Following a call to action by President Franklin D. Roosevelt, E. L. Cord Corporation gave all of its 10,000 employees, including those at the Duesenberg operation in Indianapolis, a five percent raise. The raise was announced within 12 hours of Roosevelt's speech.[68]

In July 1933, Stutz issued an additional 50,223 shares of stock, of which 40,000 were sold to New York bankers. The proceeds of the stock sale to the New York bankers provided additional working capital to support the purchase of inventory for the Pak-Age-Car. The remainder of the shares (10,223) were used to convert outstanding bond issues into common stock. The conversion rate was 33 shares of stock for each $1,000 bond.[69]

Both Duesenberg and Stutz had displays at the 1934 New York Auto Show. In general, the price of cars increased, but this was offset by an increase in efficiency and comfort. Duesenberg displayed a five-passenger sport convertible phaeton. The top was hinged so that it could disappear into the rear deck of the automobile. Stutz's display consisted of both eight- and sixteen-cylinder cars with two chassis lengths.[70]

In April Stutz president Colonel Edgar Gorrell was appointed by George H. Dern, Secretary of War, to a national committee to investigate the state of the United States' aviation preparedness. Gorrell was a member of the "Early Birds," a national organization of pioneer flyers. A graduate of West Point, at one point he was the joint holder of a cross-country non-stop flying record.[71]

One of the challenges facing the drivers in the 1934 Indianapolis 500 was a limit of 45 gallons of fuel to be used during the race, which would require an average in excess of 11 miles per gallon to go the 500 miles.[72] Cummins Corporation, the manufacturer of diesel engines, entered two cars in the race. On the eighth row were two Duesenbergs: a Miller-Duesenberg driven by Rex Mays and a Duesenberg driven by Joe Russo.[73] Russo finished the race in fifth place while Mays went out of the race on the 53rd lap with a broken axle.[74]

In early 1935 Stutz stockholders were asked to approve a $500,000 loan from the Reconstruction Finance Corporation (RFC). The RFC was established in 1932 by the United States government to provide financing to banks, railroads, and other businesses to help the banking industry resume normal operations.[75]

Although the numbers weren't nearly as impressive as those of 1920, manipulations of Stutz stock happened again in 1935. Stutz stock was traded on the New York curb market. On January 2, the stock traded at $2 per share. In the manipulation, the stock rose to 3⅞ until April 10, when J. J. Burke & Company stopped buying the stock. Then it suddenly fell to 1¼. James Connolly, an investigator for the Securities & Exchange Commission (SEC), indicated that 57 percent of the trading in Stutz stock was done by J. J. Burke & Company. Joseph Mendelson and Leon Sutterman were central to the manipulation. Mendelson, an employee of Burke, withdrew $24,000 from the company.[76] In June, the SEC charged a half dozen brokerage houses with a "giant interstate stock swindle" in Stutz stock. The SEC believed that the brokerage houses sold many times the available amount of Stutz stock on a partial payment basis. Losses to investors were estimated at $800,000. The brokerage houses involved were McCormick & Company, Kenyon & Company, Kopald, Quinn & Company, H. J. Levitt & Company of Philadelphia, L. L. Harr & Company, Gould & Company, and John J. Burke & Company.[77]

In September, Joseph Mendelson, Leonard Sutterman, Joseph Sherman, John J. Burke, and John J. Burke & Company were charged with conspiring to sell 150,000 shares of Stutz stock. There were only 134,000 shares issued and outstanding at the time. John J. Flynn, trial attorney for the SEC, said that in the prior two years, the four had made between $3 million and $5 million in profits in the trading of various stocks including Stutz.[78]

The final time a Duesenberg appeared in the lineup for the Indianapolis 500 was in 1935. Fred Winnai in the Duesenberg Special exited the race on the 16th lap due to a broken connecting rod.[79]

A supercharged 325-horsepower Duesenberg set a new speed record at the Bonneville Salt Flats in September 1935. Ab Jenkins averaged 135.47 miles per hour in a 24-hour run. Throughout the majority of the run, the car averaged over 150 miles per hour. Decreasing the average time were the stops for oil, gasoline, and tires, as well as a fire caused by the heat of the desert and the driving of the car. Although this Duesenberg had a special racing body and a second carburetor, the car was essentially the same car that was produced for the consumer.[80]

19. The End Comes

Indianapolis received good news in November 1935 when Marvin E. Hamilton, president of Stutz, announced the hiring of additional employees to support anticipated growth of the Pak-Age-Cars.[81] Stutz had re-engineered the Pak-Age-Car with a focus on the ratio of load to dead weight of the vehicle, low gasoline and oil consumption, and easiness on the tires. Central to the improvement was the power unit which included the engine, clutch, transmission, and final drive. If necessary, the power unit could easily be removed from the vehicle and replaced.[82] In June 1936 Stutz received an order for 340 Pak-Age-Cars from California.[83] At the national bakery exposition in September 1936, Stutz unveiled a larger Pak-Age-Car to be used for the delivery of bulky items. This new model provided for either the stand-drive option found on the original truck or a seat for the driver.[84]

Providing a much-needed lifeline, Stutz received a federal income tax refund including interest of approximately $200,000 in June 1936. The company had overpaid $101,000 in Federal taxes in 1917.[85]

In August 1936, E. L. Cord transferred his ownership interests in Cord Corporation to a group of New York financiers including Schroeder, Rockefeller & Company. Cord Corporation was a holding company for a variety of automotive and aviation companies including Cord, 28½ percent of Auburn and its subsidiary Duesenberg, 33 percent of Checkered Cab Manufacturing, 29 percent of Aviation Corporation, and 29 percent of New York Shipbuilding.[86] At the time of the acquisition of shares by the New York group, the Duesenberg factory was primarily involved with the rebuilding and servicing of existing automobiles rather than the production of new ones.[87] It didn't take long for the new owners of the Cord interests to shutter the Duesenberg factory. In October 1937, the factory was sold to Marmon-Herrington Company, the manufacturer of heavy duty trucks and all-wheel-drive motor vehicles.[88]

Stutz filed for bankruptcy in April 1937, listing assets of $1,179,077 and liabilities of $732,933. Although the company couldn't meet the required debt repayments, it was believed that, with additional financial support, it could return to profitability with the Pak-Age-Car.[89] Arnet B. Cronk was named the bankruptcy trustee.[90] As the creditors attempted to reorganize the firm, Cronk petitioned the court in September to have the trading of Stutz stock on both the Chicago and New York curb markets suspended.[91] The bankruptcy court also approved the manufacture of 100 Pak-Age-Cars in late October.[92]

Numerous bankruptcy plans were filed for the company's future, most of which were centered around trying to utilize the Pak-Age-Car as a path forward. In mid–November Cronk, Homer Davidson, and Charles Thomas were appointed to the management board with the authority to operate, negotiate the sale or lease of, or liquidate the company. It was believed the November plan, if implemented, would provide a better return to the creditors than earlier versions. The expectation was that the company would be liquidated but the manufacture of the small delivery cars would continue under a different organization.[93]

Although the company continued to operate while in bankruptcy, the creditors were unable to agree upon a plan, and in April 1939, the firm was ordered to be liquidated.[94] The Auburn Automobile Company established the Pak-Age-Car Corporation of Connersville as a wholly-owned subsidiary to manufacture the delivery vehicles, and the related equipment moved to Connersville.[95]

With the bankruptcy of Stutz, the Indianapolis automobile industry came to an end.

Chapter Notes

Introduction

1. Delancy, *The History of the Cole Motor Car Company*, p 62.
2. *Ibid.*, p 63.
3. *Ibid.*, p 62.
4. *Ibid.*, p 64.
5. Kimes, *Standard Catalog of American Cars*, p 128.
6. *Ibid.*, p 424.
7. *Ibid.*, p 682.
8. "Parry Manufacturing," Coachbuilt.com, http://www.coachbuilt.com/bui/p/parry/parry.htm. Accessed March 4, 2016.
9. "Motordome's Chiefs Acclaim Debt to Speedway Founders," *Indianapolis Star*, May 30, 1924, p 2.

Chapter 1

1. Kennedy, *The Automobile Industry*, p 6.
2. Flanaghan, untitled manuscript, April 15, 1937. (Manuscript is at the Indiana State Library.)
3. Blakely, "On Motor Row," *Indianapolis Star*, March 19, 1913, p 9.
4. "Ends Another Good 'Indiana-Made' Year," *Indianapolis Star*, December 7, 1913, p 20.
5. "Minor Mention," *Horseless Age*, May 30, 1900, p 23.
6. Delancy, *The History of the Cole Motor Car Company*, p 40.
7. *Ibid.*, p 53.
8. Kennedy, *The Automobile Industry*, p 17.
9. *Ibid.*, p 16.
10. "National Gains Financing," *Indianapolis Star*, April 8, 1922, p 15.
11. Horvath, "Recycling the National Motor Vehicle Company Site," http://historicindianapolis.com/recycling-the-national-motor-vehicle-company-site/. Accessed October 31, 2016.
12. "Minor Mention," *Horseless Age*, June 30, 1900, p 29.
13. "New York Trap of the National Automobile and Electric Co.," *Horseless Age*, September 19, 1900, p 84.
14. Heldt, "Electric Vehicles at the Madison Square Garden Show," *Horseless Age*, November 7, 1900, p 42–45.
15. "New York Trap of the National Automobile and Electric Co.," *Horseless Age*, September 19, 1900, p 84.
16. "Indiana Is Third," *Indianapolis Star*, June 30, 1907, p 59.
17. "Minor Mention," *Horseless Age*, July 3, 1901, p 323.
18. Edenburg, "Indiana Is Home of Automobile," *Indianapolis Star*, March 23, 1913, p 18.
19. "Minor Mention," *Horseless Age*, August 7, 1901, p 408.
20. "The Madison Square Garden Show," *Horseless Age*, October 30, 1901, p 408.
21. "The Waverley Electric Vehicle," *Horseless Age*, May 14, 1902, p 576–578.
22. "Electric," *Horseless Age*, March 12, 1902, p 328.
23. Borgeson, *The Golden Age*, p 36.
24. "No Noise And Ever Ready To Go," *Indianapolis Star*, February 5, 1905, p 24.
25. Horvath, "Disappearing Indy Auto Landmarks," September 24, 2012, http://historicindianapolis.com/disappearing-indy-auto-landmarks/. Accessed December 11, 2015.
26. "The Premier Motor Car," *Horseless Age*, June 3, 1903, p 650.
27. "Overland," http://www.earlyamericanautomobiles.com/americanautomobiles12.htm. Accessed December 17, 2015.
28. Standard Wheel Company, *The Overland Runabout*, p 2.
29. "Overland," http://www.earlyamericanautomobiles.com/americanautomobiles12.htm. Accessed December 17, 2015.
30. Martin, *Indiana: An Interpretation*, p 123.
31. "Charles A. Bookwalter," *Indianapolis Star*, April 30, 1905, p 38.
32. "Crawfordsville To Have Smokeless Fuel," *Indianapolis Star*, December 27, 1903, p 12.
33. "City News In Brief," *Indianapolis Star*, November 5, 1904, p 7.
34. "National Motor Vehicle Company," *Horseless Age*, February 25, 1903, p 288.
35. "Some Electric Mileage Records," *Horseless Age*, September 16, 1903, p 304.
36. Hendry, "Marmon a Quest for Perfection," *Automobile Quarterly*, Vol. 7, No. 2, p 117.
37. *Ibid.*
38. "Nordyke & Marmon," *Horseless Age*, April 17, 1907, Vol. 19, No. 16, p 541–542.
39. Hendry, "Marmon a Quest for Perfection," p 119.
40. "Nordyke & Marmon," *Horseless Age*, April 17, 1907, p 541–542.
41. Hendry, "Marmon a Quest for Perfection," p 121.
42. "Nordyke & Marmon May Enter New Field," *Indianapolis Star*, July 15, 1903, p 8.
43. *Ibid.*
44. "Building a New Auto at Nordyke, Marmons," *Indianapolis Star*, August 21, 1904, p 12.
45. Hendry, "Marmon a Quest for Perfection," p 121.
46. "The Providence Races," *Horseless Age*, September 23, 1903, p 340.
47. "The National Motor Vehicle Company," *Horseless Age*, January 20, 1904, p 77.
48. *Ibid.*, p 81.
49. "The Pope Waverley Surrey," *Indianapolis Star*, September 19, 1904, p 7.
50. "Pope-Waverley Electric," *Indianapolis Star*, September 28, 1904, p 7.
51. "Employers of Indianapolis to Organize," *Indianapolis Star*, January 2, 1904, p 10.
52. "Strike of Machinists Will Affect Few Men," *Indianapolis Star*, June 6, 1904, p 8.
53. "Quiet Prevails in Local Labor World," *Indianapolis Star*, June 13, 1904, p 5.
54. "No Noise And Ever Ready To Go," *Indianapolis Star*, February 5, 1905, p 24.

55. Borgeson, *The Golden Age*, p 37–38
56. Kimes, *Standard Catalog of American Cars*, p 366.
57. "Fisher May Drive in Big Auto Meet," *Indianapolis Star*, October 25, 1904, p 7.
58. Borgeson, *The Golden Age*, 37–38.
59. Fisher, *The Pacesetter*, p 24.

Chapter 2

1. "No Noise And Ever Ready To Go," *Indianapolis Star*, February 5, 1905, p 24.
2. "Auto Makers Are Organized," *Indianapolis Star*, February 26, 1905, p 6.
3. "The National Model C," *Horseless Age*, January 4, 1905, p 18.
4. "Greatest of Auto Shows Is Opened," *Indianapolis Star*, February 5, 1905, p 15.
5. "A Mechanical Masterpiece," *Indianapolis Star*, February 5, 1905, p 23.
6. Hendry, "Marmon a Quest for Perfection," p 121.
7. "Up-to-Date Vehicle Made 'A Mechanical Masterpiece'," *Indianapolis Star*, February 5, 1905, p 23. Hendry, "Marmon a quest By Local Firm," *Indianapolis Star*, March 29, 1905, p 2.
8. "Indianapolis Daily Traffic," *Indianapolis Star*, May 5, 1904, p 8.
9. "Pope-Waverley Electric Truck," *Horseless Age*, June 28, 1905, p 707.
10. Fisher, *The Pacesetter*, p 39.
11. Ibid., p 40.
12. Ibid., p 41.
13. "Farmers See Autos," *Indianapolis Star*, September 14, 1905, p 3, and "The Marion," *Indianapolis Star*, September 17, 1905, p 6.
14. "Carl Fisher Gives Up Track Racing," *Indianapolis Star*, August 6, 1905, p 14.
15. Fisher, *The Pacesetter*, p 42.
16. Ibid.
17. "Fisher to Compete in a Big Auto Race," *Indianapolis Star*, September 24, 1904, p 7.
18. Fisher, *The Pacesetter*, 24.
19. "Pope-Toledo Car First Across Line," *Indianapolis Star*, September 24, 1905, p 21.
20. "Course Will Include Automobile Study," *Indianapolis Star*, October 10, 1906, p 3.
21. Catlin, "The Harry Stutz Era," *Automobile Quarterly*, Winter 1970, Vol. 8, No. 3, p 230.
22. "Incorporations," *Indianapolis Star*, May 15, 1905, p 11.
23. "Plans Being Made for Big Auto Race," *Indianapolis Star*, October 1, 1905, p 11.
24. "Auto Race Meet to Be Held Here Oct. 21," *Indianapolis Star*, October 8, 1905, p 22.
25. "Clemens Sets New 100-Mile Record," *Indianapolis Star*, November 5, 1905, p 18.
26. "Clemens Sets New 150-Mile Record," *Indianapolis Star*, November 17, 1905, p 6.
27. Ibid.
28. "Many New Records Set in 24-Hour Run," *Indianapolis Morning Star*, November 18, 1905, p 7.
29. Fisher, *The Pacesetter*, p 43 & 44.
30. "National Entered in Ormond Races," *Indianapolis Star*, December 5, 1905, p 6.
31. "Indianapolis Now Called Auto City," *Indianapolis Star*, December 17, 1905, p 14.
32. Horvath, "The American Underslung—'The safest car on earth.'" HistoricIndianapolis.com, http://historicindianapolis.com/the-american-underslung-the-safest-car-on-earth/. Accessed March 12, 2016.
33. "The 'American' Touring Car," *Automobile Quarterly*, January 24, 1906, Vol. 17, No. 4, p 182.
34. "National Motor Vehicle Company," *Automobile Quarterly*, January 17, 1906, Vol. 17, No. 4, p 130.
35. "Premier 1906 Models," *Horseless Age*, January 24, 1906, p 175–177.
36. "Premier Motor Manufacturing Company," *Horseless Age*, January 24, 1906, p 163–164.
37. "Indianapolis Now Called Auto City," *Indianapolis Star*, December 17, 1905, p 14.
38. "New Vehicles and Parts," *Horseless Age*, May 2, 1906, p 636.
39. "Apperson Car First," *Indianapolis Star*, May 25, 1906, p 7.
40. "Auto Races Today; Good Entry List," *Indianapolis Star*, May 30, 1906, p 7.
41. "Oldfield Breaks Record for Mile," *Indianapolis Star*, May 31, 1906, p 7.
42. "Contract for Airship," *Indianapolis Star*, March 8, 1906, p 15.
43. "Indianapolis to Have Auto Show," *Indianapolis Star*, February 18, 1906, p 17.
44. "Pope-Waverley Electrics," *Indianapolis Star*, January 27, 1907, p 10.
45. "Premier Car Is in the Lead," *Indianapolis Star*, July 21, 1906, p 7.
46. "Thomas Hurled from Auto," *Indianapolis Star*, September 4, 1906, p 11.
47. "Premier Runabout," *Horseless Age*, July 18, 1906, p 86, and "New Incorporations," *Horseless Age*, July 25, 1906, p 127.
48. "New Incorporations," *Horseless Age*, July 25, 1906, p 127.
49. "Hunting Good Auto Roads," *Indianapolis Star*, July 13, 1906, p 7.
50. "The Hassler Transmission," *Horseless Age*, August 29, 1906, p 269–271.
51. "Entries for the Russell Relief Fund," *Indianapolis Star*, October 20, 1906, p 7.
52. "Oldfield's Record Broken by Webb," *Indianapolis Star*, October 21, 1906, p 34.
53. "Hats Off to the Buick," *Indianapolis Star*, October 21, 1906, p 11.
54. "Premier Machine Is Entered in Big Run," *Indianapolis Star*, January 1, 1909, p 10
55. "Premier Car First," *Indianapolis Star*, November 18, 1906, p 34.
56. "Premier Runabout," *Horseless Age*, December 26, 1906, p 929.
57. "Marmon 1907 Models," *Horseless Age*, November 21, 1906, p 715–717.
58. "National 1907 Models," *Horseless Age*, January 9, 1907, p 48–49.
59. "The National Motor Vehicle Company," *Horseless Age*, February 13, 1907, p 240.
60. "Capital Auto Co.," *Indianapolis Star*, January 27, 1907, p 15.
61. "New Incorporations," *Horseless Age*, March 6, 1907, p 355.
62. "D. M. Parry Erects Shops," *Indianapolis Star*, July 27, 1907, p 8.
63. "Pope Automobiles," *Indianapolis Star*, February 3, 1907, p 30.
64. "The National Motor Vehicle Company," *Horseless Age*, December 5, 1906, p 794.
65. "The American Motor Company's 1907 Line," *Horseless Age*, December 5, 1906, p 829.
66. "Incorporations," *Indianapolis Star*, July 23, 1907, p 10.
67. "Nordyke & Marmon Company," *Horseless Age*, December 5, 1906, p 788.
68. "Premier Interchangeable Air and Water Cooled 1907 Models," *Horseless Age*, August 22, 1906, p 238.
69. "Hoosiers In Front," *Indianapolis Star*, April 8, 1907, p 7.
70. "Propose Three Day Race of Stock Cars," *Indianapolis Star*, June 16, 1907, p 34.
71. Ibid.
72. Ibid.
73. "To Meet A. A. Board," *Indianapolis Morning Star*, May 17, 1907, p 7.
74. "Ready for Auto Tour," *Indianapolis Star*, July 10, 1907, p 7.
75. "Big Array of Autos to Visit Our City, *Indianapolis Star*, July 7, 1907, p 32.
76. "City Pays Tribute to Glidden Tourists," *Indianapolis Star*, July 17, 1907, p 7.
77. "Glidden Tourists Have Pleasant Trip," *Indianapolis Star*, July 13, 1907, p 7.
78. "City Pays Tribute to Glidden Tourists," *Indianapolis Star*, July 17, 1907, p 7.
79. Ibid.
80. "Entry List Closes," *Indianapolis Star*, July 6, 1907, p 6.

81. "Glidden Tourists Climb Three Ranges," *Indianapolis Star*, July 21, 1907, p 45.
82. "Local Autoists Find National Road Best," *Indianapolis Star*, July 28, 1907, p 10.
83. "Premier Cars Perform Consistently," *Indianapolis Star*, July 28, 1907, p 29.
84. "Premier Roadster or Touring Car $2,250," *Indianapolis Star*, June 23, 1907, p 34.
85. "Premier Six Pulls Three Autos Out of Mud," *Indianapolis Star*, September 22, 1907, p 26.
86. "Eyes of Auto World Focused on New York," *Indianapolis Star*, October 20, 1907, p 12.
87. "1908 National Cars," *Horseless Age*, October 23, 1907, p 619.
88. "The Marmon Line for 1908," *Horseless Age*, September 25, 1907, p 399–400.
89. "The Marion Flyer," *Horseless Age*, October 9, 1907, p 556.
90. "The Marion Motor Car Company," *Horseless Age*, October 30, 1907, p 637.
91. "Premier '45'—Six Cylinders," *Horseless Age*, October 16, 1907, p 589.
92. "Hoosier Clips Mark," *Indianapolis Star*, November 3, 1907, p 16.
93. "Two Scores Perfect," *Indianapolis Star*, November 27, 1907, p 5.
94. "Auto Concern Opens Office," *Indianapolis Star*, November 21, 1907, p 8.
95. "Two Local Men Honored by American Auto Assn.," *Indianapolis Star*, December 8, 1907, p 29.
96. "Chicago Auto Show Throws Open Doors," *Indianapolis Star*, December 1, 1907, p 10.
97. "Curtain Goes Down on Big Auto Show," *Indianapolis Star*, December 8, 1907, p 29.
98. "Enthuse over Big Race," *Indianapolis Star*, December 6, 1908, p 6.
99. "Perfect Score by the Marmon in New England," *Indianapolis Star*, February 24, 1908, p 8.
100. "The Overland Automobile Company Affairs," *Horseless Age*, February 5, 1908, p 158.
101. "Auto Show Excites Interest of State," *Indianapolis Star*, February 16, 1908, p 32.
102. "Incorporations," *Indianapolis Star*, February 7, 1908, p 12.
103. "To Increase Overland Plant," *Indianapolis Star*, May 31, 1908, p 20.
104. "Trade Personals," *Horseless Age*, February 5, 1908, p 159.
105. "Auto Show Excites Interest of State," *Indianapolis Star*, February 16, 1908, p 32.
106. "Auto Show Week Complete Success," *Indianapolis Star*, March 29, 1908, p 10.
107. "Local Happenings in the Local Auto World," *Indianapolis Star*, March 15, 1908, p 40.
108. "Other Cities Seeking Indianapolis Factory," *Indianapolis Star*, July 24, 1908, p 8.
109. "Auto Show Excites Interest of State," *Indianapolis Star*, February 16, 1908, p 32.
110. "Autoists to Wager," *Indianapolis Star*, February 15, 1908, p 32.
111. "Grand Parade, Hill Climb, and Novelty Contests Arranged for This Week," *Indianapolis Star*, March 22, 1908, p 41.
112. "Parade of Autos Is a Record Breaker," *Indianapolis Star*, March 26, 1907, p 7.
113. "Auto Show Opens in Blaze of Glory," *Indianapolis Star*, March 24, 1908, p 7.
114. "Entries in Hill Climb Today," *Indianapolis Star*, March 24, 1908, p 7; "Auto Show Week Complete Success," *Indianapolis Star*, March 29, 1908, p 10.; and "How They Finished in the Hill Climbing Contest," *Indianapolis Star*, March 25, 1908, p 7.
115. "A Clean Sweep of the Stoddard-Dayton," *Indianapolis Star*, March 25, 1908, p 6.
116. "Auto Show Week Complete Success," *Indianapolis Star*, March 29, 1908, p 10.
117. Ibid.
118. "Overland Cars Meet with Success at Philadelphia," *Indianapolis Star*, June 14, 1908, p 10.
119. Horvath, "Disappearing Indy Auto Landmarks," September 24, 2012, http://historicindianapolis.com/disappearing-indy-auto-landmarks/. Accessed December 11, 2015.
120. "Make Plans for Run," *Indianapolis Star*, April 16, 1908, p 6.
121. "Route for Big Auto Contest Given Out," *Indianapolis Star*, May 17, 1908, p 10.
122. "Thirty-Seven Cars to Go in Contest, *Indianapolis Star*, May 20, 1908, p 8.
123. "Start of One of the 'Perfect-Score' Marmons," *Indianapolis Star*, May 22, 1908, p 9.
124. "Premier in New Test," *Indianapolis Star*, May 26, 1908, p 9.
125. "Laying Out Route," *Indianapolis Star*, May 17, 1908, p 10.
126. "Premier Car Stands Test," *Indianapolis Star*, May 8, 1908, p 9.
127. "Glidden Tour Will Start on Thursday," *Indianapolis Star*, July 5, 1908, p 17.
128. "Marmons Hold Own," *Indianapolis Star*, July 19, 1908, p 18.
129. "Autos Keep Perfect Scores," *Indianapolis Star*, July 28, 1909, p 9.
130. "Hower Contest Called Off," *Indianapolis Star*, July 29, 1908, p 8.
131. "Great Arrow Wins," *Indianapolis Star*, July 30, 1908, p 3.
132. "Hower Contest Called Off," *Indianapolis Star*, July 29, 1908, p 8.
133. "Plan Big Contest," *Indianapolis Star*, August 12, 1908, p 4.
134. "Endurance Contest to Start October 1," *Indianapolis Star*, August 23, 1908, p 28.
135. "Will Hold Big Auto Races at Fair Grounds," *Indianapolis Star*, September 15, 1908, p 5.
136. "Auto Speed Fiends Hope to Set Records," *Indianapolis Star*, September 18, 1908, p 8.
137. "Christie Betters Mark for Mile," *Indianapolis Star*, September 20, 1908, p 11.
138. "Marmon Has Clean Record," *Indianapolis Star*, September 26, 1908, p 27.
139. "Ray McNamara Driving Premier in Hard Run," *Indianapolis Star*, September 27, 1908, p 14.
140. "New Auto Company Formed," *Indianapolis Star*, September 26, 1908, p 8.
141. "See Waverley Boom," *Indianapolis Star*, September 27, 1908, p 15.
142. "The New Waverley Electric," *Indianapolis Star*, January 31, 1909, p 8.
143. "Honors to Premier," *Indianapolis Star*, October 12, 1908, p 6.
144. "Marmon Models Out," *Indianapolis Star*, October 25, 1908, p 15.
145. "Hoosier Auto Is Admired," *Indianapolis Star*, January 17, 1909, p 19.
146. "Overland 1909 Models," *Horseless Age*, October 14, 1909, p 524–525.
147. "Marion Plant Purchased by President Willys, of the Overland Automobile Company," *Horseless Age*, October 28, 1908, p 595.
148. "New Mail Automobiles Make Their Trial Trips," *Indianapolis Star*, December 4, 1908, p 9.
149. "Century Car on Trip," *Indianapolis Star*, December 13, 1908, p 28.
150. "Like Premier Motor System," *Indianapolis Star*, December 27, 1908, p 26.

Chapter 3

1. "Auto Show Opens in New York Palace," *Indianapolis Star*, January 3, 1909, p 23.
2. "Premier Machine Is Entered in Big Run," *Indianapolis Star*, January 1, 1909, p 10.
3. "Premier Lays Case Before the A.A.A.," *Indianapolis Star*, January 11, 1909, p 9.
4. "Substitute Glass Hood," *Indianapolis Star*, February 7, 1909, p 22.
5. "Medium Autos Favorites," *Indianapolis Star*, February 14, 1909, p 44.
6. Delancy, *The History of the Cole Motor Car Company*, p 29.

7. *Ibid.*, p 30.
8. *Ibid.*, p 33.
9. *Ibid.*, p 35.
10. *Ibid.*, p 36.
11. "Cole Solid Tire Automobile," *Indianapolis Star*, March 21, 1909, p 19.
12. Delancy, *The History of the Cole Motor Car Company*, p 37.
13. *Ibid.*, p 36.
14. Delancy, *The History of the Cole Motor Car Company*, p 84.
15. "Incorporations," *Indianapolis Star*, June 23, 1909, p 11.
16. "New Auto Firm Expects to Have Enormous Output," *Indianapolis Star*, July 28, 1909, p 14.
17. "Indianapolis Home of New Motor Car Concern," *Indianapolis Star*, August 15, 1909, p 45.
18. "Auto Dealers Turn Towards Show Week," *Indianapolis Star*, February 21, 1909, p 16.
19. "Auto Show Begins in Medley Honks," *Indianapolis Star*, March 23, 1909, p 8.
20. "Women Add Spice to Gala Auto Day," *Indianapolis Star*, March 24, 1909, p 11.
21. "Marmon to Be Shown," *Indianapolis Star*, March 14, 1909, p 19.
22. "Premier Branches Out," *Indianapolis Star*, March 14, 1909, p 18.
23. "Improvements Are Pushed," *Indianapolis Star*, March 21, 1909, p 8.
24. Trask, "On Railroad Row," *Indianapolis Star*, March 20, 1909, p 10.
25. "Local Driver Races," *Indianapolis Star*, March 21, 1909, p 14.
26. Seeds, Russel. "Fisher's Vision and Allison's Brass Tacks Gave Premier Speedway of World to City," *Indianapolis Star*, May 30, 1924, p 1.
27. "Motor Speedway to Be Best in World," *Indianapolis Star*, February 7, 1909, p 34.
28. "Incorporations," *Indianapolis Star*, March 21, 1909, p 38.
29. "Motor Speedway to Be Best in World," *Indianapolis Star*, February 7, 1909, p 34.
30. "Rays of Auto Light from Show Machines," *Indianapolis Star*, February 26, 1909, p 17.
31. "Contract Let for Motor Speedway," *Indianapolis Star*, March 16, 1909, p 9.
32. *Ibid.*
33. "Motor Cup Offered Is Finest in World," *Indianapolis Star*, March 18, 1909, p 7.
34. "Honks Heard Among the Auto Show Fans," *Indianapolis Star*, March 24, 1909, p 11.
35. "Hassler," *History of the Early American Automobiles*, http://www.earlyamericanautomobiles.com/americanautomobiles20.htm. Accessed February 24, 2016.
36. Kimes, "The Rise & Fall of the Empire," *Automobile Quarterly*, Summer 1974, Vol. 12, No. 1, p. 68.
37. "New Auto Plant Launched," *Indianapolis Star*, April 23, 1909, p 10.
38. "First Cars Are Entered," *Indianapolis Star*, July 13, 1909, p 9.
39. "Increases Overland Cars," *Indianapolis Star*, March 21, 1908, p 10.
40. "Overland Puts Taxicab on Market," *Indianapolis Star*, March 7, 1909, p 19.
41. "Auto Committees Hold a Meeting," *Indianapolis Star*, March 20, 1909, p 9.
42. "Motor Cup Offered Is Finest in World," *Indianapolis Star*, March 18, 1909, p 7.
43. "Automobile Company to Buy New Factory Site," *Indianapolis Star*, April 2, 1909, p 16.
44. "Overland Procures Pope-Toledo Plant," *Indianapolis Star*, April 7, 1909, p 9.
45. "Three Factories May Go," *Indianapolis Star*, April 7, 1909, p 9.
46. "Will Close Pope Option," *Indianapolis Star*, April 25, 1909, p 29.
47. "Auto Factory Enlarged," *Indianapolis Star*, June 11, 1909, p 12, and "Overland to Spend $40,000," *Indianapolis Star*, July 24, 1909, p 3.
48. "Indianapolis Cars Get Perfect Score," *Indianapolis Star*, April 29, 1909, p 9.
49. *Ibid.*
50. "National Makes Records," *Indianapolis Star*, April 27, 1909, p 9.
51. "Hoosier Road Race to Cost $60,000," *Indianapolis Star*, May 1, 1909, p 9.
52. "Premier Endures Trials at Pittsburg Auto Run," *Indianapolis Star*, May 4, 1909, p 9.
53. "Hoosiers Will Dot Big Glidden Tour," *Indianapolis Star*, April 1, 1909, p 1.
54. "Marmon Glidden Entries Are Like Two Peas," *Indianapolis Star*, July 11, 1909, p 29.
55. "Hoosiers Will Dot Big Glidden Tour," *Indianapolis Star*, April 1, 1909, p 1.
56. "Premiers Depart Today for Detroit," *Indianapolis Star*, July 6, 1909, p 11.
57. "Motor Fans Bow to Local Autos," *Indianapolis Star*, August 1, 1909, p 20.
58. Horvath, "Disappearing Indy Auto Landmarks," September 24, 2012, http://historicindianapolis.com/disappearing-indy-auto-landmarks/. Accessed December 11, 2015.
59. "Hoosiers Will Dot Big Glidden Tour," *Indianapolis Star*, April 1, 1909, p 1.
60. "Marmons Test Course," *Indianapolis Star*, May 9, 1909, p 17.
61. "Picks Balloon Officers," *Indianapolis Star*, May 20, 1909, p 9.
62. "Fine Cobe Race Stretch," *Indianapolis Star*, May 30, 1909, p 41.
63. "Stutz Enters Marions," *Indianapolis Star*, May 15, 1909, p 8.
64. "Mechanics Get Little Honors," *Indianapolis Star*, May 28, 1911, p 24.
65. "Summary of Indiana Cup Race Shows No Auto Headed Monson in Marion Car," *Indianapolis Star*, June 19, 1909, p 9.
66. "Premiers Depart Today for Detroit," *Indianapolis Star*, July 6, 1909, p 11.
67. "Nationals Lead Racers," *Indianapolis Star*, June 1, 1909, p 11.
68. "Marion Leads Up Hill," *Indianapolis Star*, July 8, 1909, p 9.
69. "Waverley Exhibits Its New Driving System," *Indianapolis Star*, June 2, 1909, p 8.
70. "Marion Leads Up Hill," *Indianapolis Star*, July 8, 1909, p 9.
71. "Atlanta Builds Track," *Indianapolis Star*, July 9, 1909, p 9.
72. "Death Nearly Wins Motorcycle Races," *Indianapolis Star*, August 15, 1909, p 37.
73. "Racing Auto Runs Over Mechanician," *Indianapolis Star*, August 18, 1909, p 1.
74. "Ziengal Makes a Record Trial Spin," *Indianapolis Star*, August 16, 1909, p 9.
75. Bloemker, *Five Hundred Miles to Go*, p 60.
76. Scott and Gray, *Indy Racing Before the 500*, p 47 and 49.
77. Bloemker, *Five Hundred Miles to Go*. p 63.
78. Scott and Gray, *Indy Racing Before the 500*, p 65, 66, and 70.
79. Fisher, *The Pacesetter*, p 52.
80. "Motor Plants Enlarge," *Indianapolis Star*, August 25, 1909, p 12.
81. "Auto Makers Join Big Association," *Indianapolis Star*, October 24, 1909, p 36.
82. "National 1910 Models," *Horseless Age*, October 6, 1909, p 371–373.
83. "The National Motor Vehicle Company," *Horseless Age*, November 19, 1909, p 518.
84. "Local Cars in Big Race," *Indianapolis Star*, October 18, 1909, p 9.
85. "Vanderbilt Sees Fastest Cup Race," *Indianapolis Star*, October 28, 1909, p 8.
86. "Cars Make Fast Time," *Indianapolis Star*, October 25, 1909, p 9.
87. "Drivers of Indianapolis Cars in Eastern Auto Race," October 31, 1909, p 21.
88. "Brand Cup Event As Mere Mockery," *Indianapolis Star*, October 31, 1909, p 19.
89. "Moross Gives Up Post," *Indianapolis Star*, October 28, 1909, p 8.
90. "Waverley Models Changed," *Indianapolis Star*, October 24, 1909, p 36.
91. "Chevrolet Winner In 200-Mile

Race," *Indianapolis Star*, November 10, 1909, p 9.
92. "Aitken Sets New Auto Track Mark," *Indianapolis Star*, November 12, 1909, p 9.
93. "Marmon Trophies Here," *Indianapolis Star*, November 21, 1909, p 17.
94. "Aitken Sets New Auto Track Mark," *Indianapolis Star*, November 12, 1909, p 9.
95. "Fifty Mile Record Broken at Atlanta," *Indianapolis Star*, November 13, 1909, p 8.
96. "Marmon Trophies Here," *Indianapolis Star*, November 21, 1909, p 17.
97. "Return with Trophies," *Indianapolis Star*, November 17, 1909, p 8.
98. "Date Set for the Speedway Trials," *Indianapolis Star*, November 18, 1909, p 9.
99. "Marmon Wins Long Races at New Orleans," *Indianapolis Star*, November 23, 1909, p 8.
100. "Oldfield Lowers Marks," *Indianapolis Star*, November 22, 1909, p 4.
101. "Marmon Wins Long Races at New Orleans," *Indianapolis Star*, November 23, 1909, p 8.
102. "Speedway to Hold Six Meets in 1910," *Indianapolis Star*, November 21, 1909, p 23.
103. "Dates Announced for Auto Meeting," *Indianapolis Star*, December 8, 1909, p 10.
104. "Record Trials to Be Next Feature," *Indianapolis Star*, October 24, 1909, p 36.
105. "Champion Jeffries Falls from Curzon's Flying Machine," *Indianapolis Star*, November 27, 1909, p 8.
106. "Dates Announced for Auto Meeting," *Indianapolis Star*, December 8, 1909, p 10.
107. "Speedway to Hold Six Meets in 1910," *Indianapolis Star*, November 21, 1909, p 23.
108. "Champion Jeffries Falls from Curzon's Flying Machine," *Indianapolis Star*, November 27, 1909, p 8.
109. "Incorporations," *Indianapolis Star*, November 30, 1909, p 3.
110. Rothermel, "The Stutz Motor Car Company—The Car That Made Good in a Day," http://www.classiccarclub.org/info_garage/car_profiles/stutz.html. Accessed March 12, 2016.
111. "Gossip of Wide Awake Motor Devotees," *Indianapolis Star*, January 9, 1910, p 33.
112. "Harry C. Stutz," *Horseless Age*, July 13, 1910, p 65.
113. "The American 1910 Models," *Horseless Age*, December 13, 1909, p 697.
114. "The Marion Motor Car Company," *Horseless Age*, November 10, 1909, p 516.
115. "Say Record Will Fall on New Track," *Indianapolis Star*, December 12, 1909, p 1.
116. "Speedway Almost Ready for Races," *Indianapolis Star*, November 28, 1909, p 22.
117. "Say Record Will Fall on New Track," *Indianapolis Star*, December 12, 1909, p 1.
118. "Two Entries for Speedway Trials," *Indianapolis Star*, December 5, 1909, p 31.
119. "Say Record Will Fall on New Track," *Indianapolis Star*, December 12, 1909, p 1.
120. "Motor Car Company Now Occupies Two Big Plants," *Indianapolis Star*, December 12, 1909, p 4.
121. "Cole 30," *Indianapolis Star*, December 12, 1909, p 3.
122. "Speedway Trials Will Start Today," *Indianapolis Star*, December 17, 1909, p 8.
123. *Ibid.*
124. Bloemker, *Five Hundred Miles To Go*, p 71.
125. "Five-Mile Record Takes a Tumble," *Indianapolis Star*, December 19, 1909, p 29.
126. "Speedway Trials Will Start Today," *Indianapolis Star*, December 17, 1909, p 8.
127. "Five-Mile Record Takes a Tumble," *Indianapolis Star*, December 19, 1909, p 29.
128. "Speed Defies Cold in Race for Marks," *Indianapolis Star*, December 18, 1909, p 1.
129. "Five Mile Record Takes a Tumble," *Indianapolis Star*, December 19, 1909, p 29.
130. *Ibid.*
131. "Indianapolis Now Big Motor Center," *Indianapolis Star*, December 5, 1909, p 21.
132. "Indianapolis Cars Will Cut Figure," *Indianapolis Star*, November 21, 1909, p 9.

Chapter 4

1. "Leads All in Racers," *Indianapolis Star*, January 26, 1910, p 8.
2. "Licensed Ranks Grow," *Indianapolis Star*, January 6, 1910, p 8.
3. "Seeks Sanctions for Motor Races," *Indianapolis Star*, January 4, 1910, p 8.
4. "Licensed Ranks Grow," *Indianapolis Star*, January 6, 1910, p 8.
5. "Big Show Ends Tonight," *Indianapolis Star*, January 7, 1910, p 8.
6. "Parry Says Patent Suit Is Filed As Scarecrow," *Indianapolis Star*, April 28, 1910, p 14.
7. "Seeks Sanctions for Motor Races," *Indianapolis Star*, January 4, 1910, p 8.
8. "English Propose Race," *Indianapolis Star*, January 12, 1910, p 8.
9. "Seeks Sanctions for Motor Races," *Indianapolis Star*, January 4, 1910, p 8.
10. *Ibid.*
11. "Kokomo Motorist Talks to Devotees At Y.M.C.A.," *Indianapolis Star*, January 5, 1910, p 10.
12. "Gossip Concerning Honk, Honk Devotees," *Indianapolis Star*, January 23, 1910, p 33.
13. "Prepares for Season," *Indianapolis Star*, January 25, 1910, p 8.
14. "Builds Speedy Auto," *Indianapolis Star*, January 30, 1910, p 36.
15. Delancy, *The History of the Cole Motor Car Company*, p 87.
16. "Enters Marmon Racer," *Indianapolis Star*, January 13, 1910, p 8.
17. "Auto Officer Here on Secret Mission," *Indianapolis Star*, February 12, 1910, p 10.
18. "Enters Marmon Racer," *Indianapolis Star*, January 13, 1910, p 8.
19. "Quits Racing Game," *Indianapolis Star*, February 17, 1910, p 9.
20. "Second Day Crowd Pleases Show Men," *Indianapolis Star*, March 30, 1910, p 9.
21. "Stutz Wins Races," *Indianapolis Star*, April 9, 1910, p 8.
22. "Wins Motor Car Plant," *Indianapolis Star*, February 28, 1910, p 4.
23. "Auto Plant Not to Move; Lafayette Bankers Balk," *Indianapolis Star*, May 21, 1910, p 4.
24. "Auto Officer Here on Secret Mission," *Indianapolis Star*, February 12, 1910, p 10.
25. *Ibid.*
26. Catlin, "The Harry Stutz Era," *Automobile Quarterly*, Winter 1970, Vol. 8, No 3, p 231.
27. "Trophy Question Rises," *Indianapolis Star*, February 20, 1910, p 48.
28. "Tries New Auto Racer," *Indianapolis Star*, March 17, 1910, p 9.
29. Moross, "Marmon Racer Is Built," *Indianapolis Star*, March 20, 1910, p 18.
30. Marmon, "Marmon Follows New Speed Theory," *Indianapolis Star*, March 20, 1910, p 8.
31. "Local Cars Lead In 'Piepani Races," *Indianapolis Star*, April 8, 1910, p 25.
32. "Apperson Car Is Wrecked on Track," *Indianapolis Star*, April 11, 1910, p 8.
33. "Marmon a 'Yellow Peril,'" *Indianapolis Star*, April 11, 1910, p 9.
34. "Tire Loss Halts Marmon Car," *Indianapolis Star*, April 12, 1910, p 35.
35. "Mishaps Feature Motordrome Meet," *Indianapolis Star*, April 16, 1910, p 8.
36. "Drives Two Hours Without One Stop," *Indianapolis Star*, April 17, 1910, p 42.
37. "Harroun Wins Feature," *Indianapolis Star*, April 18, 1910, p 9.

38. "The Marmon," *Indianapolis Star*, March 20, 1910, p 18.
39. "Cole 30," *Indianapolis Star*, April 10, 1910, p 34.
40. "For Glidden Tour," *Indianapolis Star*, May 29, 1910, p 32.
41. "Premiers Head Glidden," *Indianapolis Star*, June 19, 1910, p 35.
42. Smith, "Asks Better Route For Next Glidden," *Indianapolis Star*, July 10, 1910, p 22.
43. "Premier Named Victor," *Indianapolis Star*, July 3, 1910, p 31.
44. "Premier Gets Law's Aid," *Indianapolis Star*, July 26, 1910, p 9.
45. "Will Contest Decision," *Indianapolis Star*, July 26, 1910, p 9.
46. "Premier Gets Law's Aid," *Indianapolis Star*, July 26, 1910, p 9.
47. "A.A.A. Disqualifies Premier Company," *Indianapolis Star*, July 28, 1910, p 3.
48. "Demands Court Hearing," *Indianapolis Star*, July 28, 1910, p 3.
49. "Glidden Trophy Awarded," *Indianapolis Star*, September 12, 1910, p 8.
50. "Marion," *Horseless Age*, July 27, 1910, p 123.
51. "New Building for National," *Horseless Age*, March 23, 1910, p 456.
52. "Premier Plant Is Setting Fast Pace," *Indianapolis Star*, April 3, 1910, p 28.
53. "National Torpedo Body Car," *Horseless Age*, April 13, 1910, p 548.
54. "American Traveler Torpedo Cars Rakish," *Horseless Age*, March 23, 1910, p 446.
55. "Waverley Electric Gentleman's Roadster," *Horseless Age*, April 13, 1910, p 549.
56. "Local Design for Auto Fire Wagon," *Indianapolis Star*, May 4, 1910, p 9.
57. "Enter Speedway Races," *Indianapolis Star*, April 12, 1910, p 34.
58. Moross, "Marmon Car Surprises," *Indianapolis Star*, April 17, 1910, p 47.
59. "Enter Speedway Races," *Indianapolis Star*, April 12, 1910, p 34.
60. "Harroun Departing for Atlanta Tells Plans for Coming Season," *Indianapolis Star*, May 2, 1910, p 9.
61. Ibid.
62. "After Atlanta Winners," *Indianapolis Star*, May 4, 1910, p 9.
63. "Indiana Pilots in Sweep at Atlanta," *Indianapolis Star*, May 6, 1910, p 9.
64. "Indianapolis Cars Take Every Event," *Indianapolis Star*, May 7, 1910, p 11.
65. "Indianapolis Pilots and Cars Return With Bulk of Trophies," *Indianapolis Star*, May 8, 1910, p 20.
66. "What Motor Folk Are Doing," *Indianapolis Star*, May 15, 1910, p 48.
67. "Pay Race Pilots Well," *Indianapolis Star*, June 19, 1910, p 32.
68. "Races Place Cars Before Public Eye," *Indianapolis Star*, May 8, 1910, p 34.
69. "The Marmon," *Indianapolis Star*, May 15, 1910, p 46.
70. "Auto World's Eye on Indiana Course," *Indianapolis Star*, May 8, 1910, p 52.
71. "Cole Wins Fuel Contest," *Indianapolis Star*, May 22, 1910, p 17.
72. "Strang to Pilot Marion," *Indianapolis Star*, May 5, 1910, p 9.
73. "Death Takes Toll at Brighton Beach," *Indianapolis Star*, May 14, 1910, p 1.
74. "Indiana Auto Pilots Condemn Brighton Beach Racing Course," *Indianapolis Star*, May 16, 1910, p 21.
75. "Simplex Car Wins in Eastern Grind," *Indianapolis Star*, May 15, 1910, p 32.
76. "Indiana Auto Pilots Condemn Brighton Beach Racing Course," *Indianapolis Star*, May 16, 1910, p 21.
77. "Auto Maker Sees Sport in Contests," *Indianapolis Star*, May 15, 1910, p 47.
78. "Auto Race Entries Fill Events Well," *Indianapolis Star*, May 25, 1910, p 23.
79. Shuart, "Auto Pilots Set Marks in Safety," *Indianapolis Star*, May 28, 1910, p 1.
80. Shuart, "Victor Shatters Records in Race," *Indianapolis Star*, May 29, 1910, p 16.
81. "Winner Tells Reasons," *Indianapolis Star*, June 5, 1910, p 24.
82. Shuart, "Victor Shatters Records in Race," *Indianapolis Star*, May 29, 1910, p 16.
83. Willis, "Thousands Wonder As Men Defy Time," *Indianapolis Star*, May 29, 1910, p 24.
84. "Marmon Wins the Crowning Event," *Indianapolis Star*, May 29, 1910, p 26.
85. "Oldfield to Cut Record," *Indianapolis Star*, May 29, 1910, p 24.
86. Shuart, "Crowds and Autos Set New Records," *Indianapolis Star*, May 31, 1910, p 1.
87. Ibid.
88. Deupree, "Records Fall in Speedway Races," *Indianapolis Star*, May 31, 1910, p 7.
89. "Local Cars Show Big Race Records," *Indianapolis Star*, June 5, 1910, p 23.
90. "The Marvel of Motordome," *Indianapolis Star*, June 12, 1910, p 28.
91. "Local Cars Show Big Race Records," *Indianapolis Star*, June 5, 1910, p 23.
92. Moross, "July Auto Racing Gives Big Promise," *Indianapolis Star*, June 12, 1910, p 29.
93. "Circuit Auto Races On," *Indianapolis Star*, July 9, 1910, p 4.
94. "Ready for Hill Climb," *Indianapolis Star*, June 10, 1910, p 23.
95. "Knox and Marmon Cars Take Prizes," *Indianapolis Star*, June 15, 1910, p 11.
96. "Finishes Reliability Tour," *Indianapolis Star*, June 15, 1910, p 11.
97. "Harroun Memphis Star," *Indianapolis Star*, June 18, 1910, p 14.
98. "The Marmon," *Indianapolis Star*, June 19, 1910, p 33.
99. "Ray Harroun Wins Twice; Oldfield Lowers Record," *Indianapolis Star*, June 24, 1910, p 8.
100. "Cars Burn Air in Speedway Workouts," *Indianapolis Star*, June 29, 1910, p 5.
101. "Overland Reorganization Planned," *Horseless Age*, June 8, 1910, p 868.
102. "Receivership Suit Against Sales Company," *Horseless Age*, May 25, 1910, p 808.
103. "Overland Reorganization Planned," *Horseless Age*, June 8, 1910, p 868.
104. "Empire '20' For 1911," *Horseless Age*, June 29, 1910, p 962.
105. Willis, "Motor Races Test Cars and Drivers," *Indianapolis Star*, July 2, 1910, p 5.
106. Behr, "Big Fields Meet in Speedway Races," *Indianapolis Star*, July 2, 1910, p 1.
107. "Heat Prostrates Two," *Indianapolis Star*, July 2, 1910, p 1.
108. Behr, "Big Fields Meet in Speedway Races," *Indianapolis Star*, July 2, 1910, p 1 & 2.
109. Willis, "Motor Races Test Cars and Drivers," *Indianapolis Star*, July 2, 1910, p 5.
110. Behr, "Big Fields Meet in Speedway Races," *Indianapolis Star*, July 2, 1910, p 1 & 2.
111. Deupree, "New Marks Crown Efforts of Pilots," *Indianapolis Star*, July 3, 1910, p 31.
112. "Many Come for Races," *Indianapolis Star*, July 4, 1910, p 1.
113. Behr, "Cobe Trophy Lure for Races Today," *Indianapolis Star*, July 4, 1910, p 4.
114. Behr, "Boy Wins Brilliant Cobe Trophy Race," *Indianapolis Star*, July 5, 1910, p 6.
115. Ibid.
116. "Circuit Auto Races On," *Indianapolis Star*, July 9, 1910, p 4.
117. "Indiana Cars Win Latonia Races," *Indianapolis Star*, July 11, 1910, p 7.
118. "Dashes to Death 80 Miles Per Hour," *Indianapolis Star*, July 7, 1910, p 1 & 5.
119. "Bill Endicott and Hughes Star in Dayton Auto Meet," *Indianapolis Star*, July 16, 1910, p 9.
120. "'Hughie' Hughes in Parry Star in Columbus Races," *Indianapolis Star*, July 31, 1910, p 45.
121. "Endicott Victor in Exciting

Race," *Indianapolis Star*, July 24, 1910, p 49.
122. "May Take Up Racing," *Indianapolis Star*, July 10, 1910, p 23.
123. "The Marmon," *Indianapolis Star*, July 3, 1910, p 34.
124. "Marvel at Feats of City's Racers," *Indianapolis Star*, July 24, 1910, p 38.
125. Ibid.
126. "Local Cars Show Big Race Records," *Indianapolis Star*, June 5, 1910, p 23.
127. Ibid.
128. "Remy Will Pay Both," *Indianapolis Star*, July 29, 1910, p 9.
129. "Local Cars Gain with Buick Barred," *Indianapolis Star*, July 29, 1910, p 9.
130. "Endicott in 24-Hour Race," *Indianapolis Star*, August 19, 1910, p 8.
131. "Stearns Cuts Record in 24-Hour Race; Cole Star," *Indianapolis Star*, August 21, 1910, p 42.
132. "Elgin Entries All In," *Indianapolis Star*, August 21, 1910, p 42, and "Elgin Races National," *Indianapolis Star*, August 7, 1910, p 27.
133. "Harroun Likes Elgin Course," *Indianapolis Star*, August 10, 1910, p 4.
134. Deupree, "Local Cars Grab Honors at Elgin," *Indianapolis Star*, August 27, 1910, p 5.
135. Deupree, "Lozier Wins with Nationals Behind," *Indianapolis Star*, August 28, 1910, p 23.
136. "1911 American Line," *Horseless Age*, September 7, 1910, p 329.
137. "Marmon Enters Race," *Indianapolis Star*, August 4, 1910, p 4.
138. "DePalma Here to Enter," *Indianapolis Star*, August 31, 1910, p 4.
139. "Marmon Will Be Busy," *Indianapolis Star*, September 4, 1910, p 31.
140. "Flying Nationals Grab Remy Honors," *Indianapolis Star*, September 4, 1910, p 18.
141. Behr, "Westcott Trails Benz in Big Race," *Indianapolis Star*, September 4, 1910, p 15 & 22.
142. Behr, "Nationals First in Speedway Feature," *Indianapolis Star*, September 6, 1910, p 12.
143. Deupree, "Benz Wins Great Free-For-All Race," *Indianapolis Star*, September 6, 1910, p 14.
144. Deupree, "Vanderbilt Racers Hit Trail at Dawn," *Indianapolis Star*, October 1, 1910, p 6.
145. Deupree, "Four Killed, Many Hurt Is Race Toll," *Indianapolis Star*, October 2, 1910, p 23 & 27.
146. "Dawson Shades Grant," *Indianapolis Star*, October 9, 1910, p 41.
147. Deupree, "Four Killed, Many Hurt Is Race Toll," *Indianapolis Star*, October 2, 1910, p 23 & 27.
148. "Dawson Shades Grant," *Indianapolis Star*, October 9, 1910, p 41.
149. "The Marmon," *Indianapolis Star*, October 2, 1910, p 39.
150. Deupree, "Four Killed, Many Hurt Is Race Toll," *Indianapolis Star*, October 2, 1910, p 23 & 27.
151. Ibid.
152. "Calls Race Course Deadly," *Indianapolis Star*, October 16, 1910, p 41.
153. "Driver Escapes Death," *Indianapolis Star*, October 6, 1910, p 11.
154. Deupree, "Len Zengel Pilots Chadwick to Front," *Indianapolis Star*, October 9, 1910, p 37.
155. "Dawson Risks Neck to Win Auto Race," *Indianapolis Star*, November 5, 1910, p 1.
156. "'13' Figures Big in Race Lozier Wins," *Indianapolis Star*, November 8, 1910, p 10.
157. "The Original Savannah Races," *North American Motorsports Journal*, http://www.na-motorsports.com/Journal/1997/3/RussellJ.html. Accessed February 6, 2016.
158. "Savannah Is Ready for Big Auto Race," *Indianapolis Star*, November 7, 1910, p 10.
159. "Auto Racing Pilot Meets Tragic End," *Indianapolis Star*, November 2, 1910, p 1.
160. "National Ends Season," *Indianapolis Star*, November 8, 1910, p 10.
161. "Marmon Driver Is Victor," *Indianapolis Star*, November 12, 1910, p 9.
162. "Race Signals Are Vital," *Indianapolis Star*, October 16, 1910, p 41.
163. "Marmon 1911 Cars," *Horseless Age*, August 17, 1910, p 230–231.
164. "Premier Auto Company Makes Few Changes," *Indianapolis Star*, November 13, 1910, p 32.
165. "Premier Line for 1911," *Horseless Age*, October 12, 1910, p 500–502.
166. "Frame of Premier Assures Great Strength," *Indianapolis Star*, February 26, 1911, p 19.
167. "Cole Changes for 1911," *Horseless Age*, August 10, 1910, p 204.
168. "Cole 1911 Plans," *Horseless Age*, September 28, 1910, p 448.
169. "New Electric Is Luxurious," *Indianapolis Star*, September 11, 1910, p 36.
170. "Speed King Harroun Quits Motor Strife," *Indianapolis Star*, November 20, 1910, p 44.
171. "Local Flyers to Race in France?" *Indianapolis Star*, December 25, 1910, p 30.
172. "1911 Motor Racing Will Be Best Yet," *Indianapolis Star*, December 4, 1910, p 42.
173. "Writes City's Name in Motor Archives," *Indianapolis Star*, February 26, 1911, p 17.
174. "Receiver for Auto Firm," *Indianapolis Star*, December 4, 1910, p 64.
175. "Wishes to Operate Factory," *Indianapolis Star*, December 20, 1910, p 3.
176. "Auto Plant Ordered Sold," *Indianapolis Star*, December 30, 1910, p 10.
177. "Syndicate Gets Parry Plant on $150,000 Bid," *Indianapolis Star*, January 11, 1911, p 16.
178. "Parry to Make 1,000 Cars," *Indianapolis Star*, January 15, 1911, p 15.

Chapter 5

1. "A.A.A. Ready to Meet," *Indianapolis Star*, January 10, 1911, p 10.
2. "Contemplates Few Changes in Laws," *Indianapolis Star*, January 22, 1911, p 23.
3. "Rules Committee Meets in Chicago," *Indianapolis Star*, January 29, 1911, p 28.
4. Ibid.
5. "Will Build Cole Racer for the Trade," *Indianapolis Star*, January 15, 1911, p 17.
6. "Cole Uses One Chassis," *Indianapolis Star*, January 1, 1911, p 16.
7. "Racing Campaign Aid to Customer," *Indianapolis Star*, March 12, 1911, p 22.
8. "DePalma to Race in National Cars," *Indianapolis Star*, February 21, 1911, p 10.
9. "National Names Three Cars for Big Contest," *Indianapolis Star*, March 5, 1911, p 40.
10. "DePalma to Race in National Cars," *Indianapolis Star*, February 21, 1911, p 10.
11. "National Names Three Cars for Big Contest," *Indianapolis Star*, March 5, 1911, p 40.
12. "Heads Million Dollar Company," *Indianapolis Star*, January 22, 1911, p 20.
13. "New American Car," *Horseless Age*, March 8, 1911, p 422.
14. "Auto Move Is Announced," *Indianapolis Star*, March 16, 1911, p 1.
15. "Long Speed Battle Draws Big Winners," *Indianapolis Star*, March 5, 1911, p 29.
16. "Prepares for Big Speedway Contest," *Indianapolis Star*, March 26, 1911, p 36.
17. "Long Speed Battle Draws Big Winners," *Indianapolis Star*, March 5, 1911, p 29.
18. Catlin, "The Harry Stutz Era," *Automobile Quarterly* Winter 1970, Vol. 8, no 3, p 231.
19. "H. C. Stutz," *Horseless Age*, March 8, 1911, p 472.
20. "Long Speed Battle Draws Big Winners," *Indianapolis Star*, March 5, 1911, p 29.
21. "Racing Campaign Aid to Customer," *Indianapolis Star*, March 12, 1911, p 22.
22. "Barney Oldfield Quits Racing Game," *Indianapolis Star*, March 2, 1911, p 10.

23. "Imports Monarch of Foreign Races," *Indianapolis Star*, March 9, 1911, p 13.
24. "Harroun Announces Final Retirement from Big Ring," *Indianapolis Star*, March 23, 1911, p 9.
25. "Famous Drivers to Pilot Speedy Cars," *Indianapolis Star*, March 26, 1911, p 42.
26. Ibid.
27. Ibid..
28. Deupree, "Wilcox Cuts Mile Mark In National," *Indianapolis Star*, March 30, 1910, p 10.
29. "Famous Glidden Contest Will Be Decided June 7," *Indianapolis Star*, April 17, 1910, p 8.
30. "Stops Glidden Litigation," *Indianapolis Star*, June 28, 1911, p 9.
31. "Premier Is Reinstated," *Indianapolis Star*, January 16, 1912, p 9.
32. "Ty Cobb Reels Off Fast Mile in Auto," *Indianapolis Star*, April 5, 1911, p 10.
33. "Real Estate Transfers," *Indianapolis Star*, April 6, 1911, p 14.
34. "To Stop Price Cutting," *Horseless Age*. April 19, 1911, p 668.
35. "Alleged Brass Thieves Rounded up by Police," *Indianapolis Star*, April 16, 1911, p 34.
36. "Sets New World Record Mark for 24-Hours," *Indianapolis Star*, April 10, 1911, p 9.
37. "Harroun Yields to Lure of High Speed," *Indianapolis Star*, April 23, 1911, p 37.
38. "Morgan Seeks Cars for Foreign Race," *Indianapolis Star*, April 26, 1911, p 10.
39. "The History of the French Grand Prix," http://uniquecarsandparts.com/formula_one.htm. Accessed September 12, 2016.
40. "New Cole Speedster," *Horseless Age*, April 26, 1911, p 710.
41. "Field of 44 Cars in 500-Mile Race," *Indianapolis Star*, May 3, 1911, p 9.
42. "Racers Start Tuning Up for Big Race," *Indianapolis Star*, April 8, 1911, p 11.
43. "Stang Brings Case Team to Tune Motors for Big Race," *Indianapolis Star*, May 10, 1911, p 9.
44. "Racers Start Tuning Up for Big Race," *Indianapolis Star*, April 8, 1911, p 11.
45. "Motor Pilots to Begin Workouts," *Indianapolis Star*, April 16, 1911, p 42.
46. "Cole Presents Reasons," *Indianapolis Star*, May 28, 1911, p 25.
47. Edenburn, "'Bill' Endicott Is Hero of Wreck," *Indianapolis Star*, May 14, 1911, p 42.
48. Harroun, "Tells Why He Uses Wasp," *Indianapolis Star*, May 28, 1911, p 17.
49. "Harroun Rules Favorite," *Indianapolis Star*, May 30, 1911, p 6.
50. Deupree, "Smoking Monsters Thrill from Start," *Indianapolis Star*, May 31, 1911, p 1.
51. Willis, "Queen of Tragedy Hovers over Race," *Indianapolis Star*, May 31, 1911, p 1.
52. "Stutz Will Build Racer Duplicates," *Indianapolis Star*, June 11, 1911, p 31.
53. Catlin, "The Harry Stutz Era," *Automobile Quarterly* Winter 1970, Vol. 8, no. 3, p 231.
54. "Joe Dawson Gets Fifth in Big Race," *Indianapolis Star*, June 1, 1911, p 9.
55. Ibid.
56. "Long Island's Loss Is Savannah's Gain," *Indianapolis Star*, August 6, 1911, p 29.
57. "Crowds Throng Building to Examine Marmon Cars," *Indianapolis Star*, June 2, 1911, p 11.
58. "The Marmon," *Indianapolis Star*, May 31, 1911, p 5.
59. "Famous Pilots to Compete in Races," *Indianapolis Star*, June 4, 1911, p 36.
60. "One Death Mars Hawthorne Races," *Indianapolis Star*, June 11, 1911, p 41.
61. "Local Cars Win Four Events," *Indianapolis Star*, July 30, 1911, p 43.
62. "Cole Company to Build New Plant," *Indianapolis Star*, June 4, 1911, p 34.
63. "Real Estate Transfer Record," *Indianapolis Star*, July 19, 1911, p 11.
64. "Real Estate Transfer Record," *Indianapolis Star*, July 20, 1911, p 11.
65. "American Cars in New Models," *Indianapolis Star*, June 11, 1911, p 30.
66. "Four-States Tour Will Start July 12," *Indianapolis Star*, May 10, 1911, p 9.
67. Edenburn, "Interstate Tour Held Hoosier Ad," *Indianapolis Star*, April 9, 1911, p 43.
68. "Waverley Completes Four-States Run," *Indianapolis Star*, July 28, 1911, p 9.
69. "Dickson Endorses Hill Climb Events," *Indianapolis Star*, August 27, 1911, p 31.
70. "National Wins Hill Climb," *Indianapolis Star*, September 10, 1911, p 37.
71. "Jenkins Stars in Fernbank Races," *Indianapolis Star*, September 10, 1911, p 37.
72. "Stutz Will Build Racer Duplicates," *Indianapolis Star*, June 11, 1911, p 31.
73. "The Stutz Car—A Newcomer In High Powered Class," *Horseless Age*, June 14, 1911, p 1014.
74. "Stutz Will Build Racer Duplicates," *Indianapolis Star*, June 11, 1911, p 31.
75. "Will Market New Autos," *Indianapolis Star*, September 3, 1911, p 33.
76. "Cole Company Will Make Seven Models," *Indianapolis Star*, August 13, 1911, p 26.
77. "Cole London Limousine," *Indianapolis Star*, October 29, 1911, p 35.
78. "Waverley Will Build Bigger 1912 Electric," *Indianapolis Star*, August 20, 1911, p 30.
79. "'Full-View-Ahead' Auto Well Liked by Purchasers," *Indianapolis Star*, February 11, 1911, p 29.
80. "Three New Pilots to Drive Marmons," *Indianapolis Star*, September 23, 1911, p 9.
81. "Two More Racing Cars Add Entries," *Indianapolis Star*, September 24, 1911, p 35.
82. Ibid.
83. "Wilcox and Merz to Drive on Coast," *Indianapolis Star*, September 22, 1911, p 9.
84. "Thirteen Pilots on Edge for Frays," *Indianapolis Star*, October 1, 1911, p 20.
85. "Local Pilot Will Drive in Farimont," *Indianapolis Star*, September 3, 1911, p 31.
86. "Amateur Pilot Is Winner in Big Race," *Indianapolis Star*, October 10, 1911, p 8.
87. "Describes New Marmon Racer," *Indianapolis Star*, October 11, 1911, p 10.
88. "J. Dawson Smashes Coast Course Mark," *Indianapolis Star*, October 13, 1911, p 7.
89. "'Howdy' Wilcox, Disappointment in Santa Monica Road Race, Gave up His Chance in Eliminating Fiat," *Indianapolis Star*, October 21, 1911, p 11.
90. "World Marks Twice Go on Coast Course," *Indianapolis Star*, October 15, p 41.
91. "'Howdy' Wilcox, Disappointment in Santa Monica Road Race, Gave up His Chance in Eliminating Fiat," *Indianapolis Star*, October 21, 1911, p 11.
92. "Twelve Lots Purchased," *Indianapolis Star*, September 30, 1911, p 7.
93. "American Cars in New Models," *Indianapolis Star*, June 11, 1911, p 30.
94. "Motor Notes and Gossip Picked up from Garage and Factory," *Indianapolis Star*, October 15, 1911, p 36.
95. "Pathfinder Designer Sails," *Indianapolis Star*, November 5, 1911, p 38.
96. "Hoosier Motor Club Lays Plans for Membership Campaign, Wide in Scope," *Indianapolis Star*, December 22, 1911, p 9.
97. "Two Speedway Race Dates Set," *Indianapolis Star*, November 1, 1911, p 8.
98. "Opposes Auto Racing on Patriotic Holiday," *Indianapolis Star*, November 1, 1911, p 8.
99. "Two Speedway Race Dates Set," *Indianapolis Star*, November 1, 1911, p 8.

100. "Shy at Entry in Final Race," *Indianapolis Star*, October 29, 1911, p 36.
101. "Wagner's Visit Here Fruitless," *Indianapolis Star*, November 7, 1911, p 11.
102. "Pilot Killed on Savannah Track," *Indianapolis Star*, November 21, 1911, p 9.
103. "Heinemann May Drive Marmon," *Indianapolis Star*, November 22, 1911, p 11.
104. "Mulford Wins Vanderbilt Cup," *Indianapolis Star*, November 28, 1911, p 10.
105. "Bruce Brown's Big Fiat Winner of Grand Prize," *Indianapolis Star*, December 1, 1911, p 11.
106. "New American Motors Large," *Indianapolis Star*, November 6, 1911, p 9.
107. "Hoosier Display Is First Event," *Indianapolis Star*, November 12, 1911, p 29.
108. "Stutz Writes About Trip Abroad," *Indianapolis Star*, December 3, 1911, p 36.
109. "Burman Is Here for Speed Tests," *Indianapolis Star*, December 15, 1911, p 11.
110. *Ibid.*
111. "Cole Takes Climb Honors," *Indianapolis Star*, December 1, 1911, p 11.
112. "National Car Claims 1911 Championship," *Indianapolis Star*, December 18, 1911, p 8.
113. "Self-Starter Added to Cole Equipment," *Indianapolis Star*, November 12, 1911, p 30.
114. Ricker, "Three Starter Types Defined," *Indianapolis Star*, December 3, 1911, p 36.
115. "National to Exhibit Four Cars in Gotham," *Indianapolis Star*, December 28, 1911, p 9.

Chapter 6

1. "Indianapolis Hub of Motor World," *Indianapolis Star*, June 24, 1912, p 16.
2. *Ibid.*
3. "Indianapolis Becomes 'Unit Power Plant' in Advertising Automobiles," *Indianapolis Star*, May 17, 1912, p 11.
4. "National Enters Cars in Big Race," *Indianapolis Star*, January 21, 1912, p 17.
5. "Marmon Torpedo Limousine," *Horseless Age*, February 7, 1912, p 316.
6. "National Adopts Centre Controls," *Horseless Age*, February 21, 1912, p 387.
7. "Proposes National Tour in Big Tent of Auto Show," *Indianapolis Star*, March 28, 1912, p 10.
8. "Traveling Auto Show Is Boomed," *Indianapolis Star*, April 2, 1912, p 11.
9. "Seeks Unity in Advertising," *Indianapolis Star*, May 29, 1912, p 7.
10. "Company Plans to Build Touring Car," *Indianapolis Star*, February 9, 1912, p 10.
11. "Reorganize Empire Motor Company," *Horseless Age*, March 6, 1912, p 481.
12. "The New Empire '25,'" *Horseless Age*, April 17, 1912, p 710.
13. "City Notes," *Indianapolis Star*, September 24, 1913, p 6.
14. "Holds Motor Center Here," *Indianapolis Star*, March 24, 1912, p 68.
15. "Realty Transfers in Marion County," *Indianapolis Star*, April 12, 1912, p 13.
16. "Waverley Electric Looks Like Gasoline Roadster," *Indianapolis Star*, March 10, 1912, p 39.
17. "Cole to Introduce Medium Priced Cars," *Indianapolis Star*, May 15, 1912, p 11.
18. "Marion Company Deal Completed," *Indianapolis Star*, May 5, 1912, p 35.
19. "Marion Co. Reorganizes," *Horseless Age*, May 8, 1912, p 838.
20. "Marion," *Indianapolis Star*, June 2, 1912, p 36.
21. "Marion Company Deal Completed," *Indianapolis Star*, May 5, 1912, p 35.
22. "Change to Left-Hand Drive," *Indianapolis Star*, April 26, 1912, p 10.
23. "Marmon," *Indianapolis Star*, May 26, 1912, p 50.
24. "Tetzlaff Here with Big Fiat," *Indianapolis Star*, May 15, 1912, p 11.
25. "A.A.A. Contest Board Announces Records," *Indianapolis Star*, June 29, 1912, p 11.
26. "National," *Indianapolis Star*, June 9, 1912, p 35.
27. "National," *Indianapolis Star*, September 3, 1912, p 7.
28. "Picture Shows Seek Winner," *Indianapolis Star*, August 4, 1912, p 29.
29. "Nordyke & Marmon Factory Is Enlarged," *Indianapolis Star*, June 1, 1912, p 14.
30. "Marmon," *Indianapolis Star*, June 2, 1912, p 37.
31. "Two-Year Test Ushers in Car," *Indianapolis Star*, June 16, 1912, p 35.
32. "Marmon Brings out a Six," *Horseless Age*, June 26, 1912, p 1116.
33. "Two-Year Test Ushers in Car," *Indianapolis Star*, June 16, 1912, p 35.
34. "Marmon Brings out a Six," *Horseless Age*, June 26, 1912, p 1116.
35. "Two-Year Test Ushers in Car," *Indianapolis Star*, June 16, 1912, p 35.
36. "Cole and Henderson Forces Are Merged," *Indianapolis Star*, March 28, 1912, p 7.
37. "Business Men Form New Motor Company," *Indianapolis Star*, May 7, 1912, p 11.
38. "Outlines Plans for New Henderson Car," *Indianapolis Star*, April 7, 1912, p 36.
39. "Business Men Form New Motor Company," *Indianapolis Star*, May 7, 1912, p 11.
40. "Demand for 1913 Models Keeps Local Plant Busy," *Indianapolis Star*, October 27, 1912, p 40.
41. "Henderson Debut May 30," *Horseless Age*, May 22, 1912, p 919.
42. "Outlines Plans for New Henderson Car," *Indianapolis Star*, April 7, 1912, p 36.
43. "New Henderson Car Christened," *Horseless Age*, June 5, 1912, p 987.
44. "Building Collapses; One Man Killed," *Indianapolis Star*, April 16, 1912, p 3.
45. "Cole Departs from Yearly Model—Brings out Series Eight," *Horseless Age*, September 18, 1912, p 434–436.
46. "Autoists Start Long Tour Today," *Indianapolis Star*, July 9, 1912, p 9.
47. Maxwell, "Automobile Is Held Practically Perfect," *Indianapolis Star*, July 28, 1912, p 45.
48. "Tire Effect Is Proof of Perfect Balance," *Indianapolis Star*, August 25, 1912, p 18.
49. "Change Announced in Local Motor Plants," *Indianapolis Star*, September 27, 1912, p 11.
50. "New Sales Plan Adopted by Cole," *Indianapolis Star*, September 15, 1912, p 36.
51. "New Commercial Car," *Indianapolis Star*, August 18, 1912, p 22.
52. "The Pathfinder 40," *Indianapolis Star*, September 8, 1912, p 37.
53. "Electric System for Pathfinder," *Indianapolis Star*, September 8, 1912, p 38.
54. "Pathfinder Reaches Goal," *Indianapolis Star*, August 11, 1912, p 20.
55. "Pathfinder Is Now in Gotham" *Indianapolis Star*, September 22, 1912, p 37.
56. Blakely, "Offer to Aid Rock Road Path," *Indianapolis Star*, October 8, 1912, p 7.
57. "Well Known Tourist to Arrive Today," *Indianapolis Star*, December 14, 1912, p 10.
58. "Pathfinder '40' Ends Triple Transcontinental Tour," *Horseless Age*, December 11, 1912, p 882.
59. "For Drivers and Owners," *Indianapolis Star*, September 26, 1912, p 11.
60. "Few Changes on Marion Models," *Indianapolis Star*, September 22, 1912, p 34.
61. Handley, "Harmony Is Seen in Lines of Auto," *Indianapolis Star*, March 23, 1913, p 29.
62. "Few Changes on Marion Models," *Indianapolis Star*, September 22, 1912, p 34.
63. "Stutz Series B Includes a Six Cylinder Chassis," *Horseless Age*, October 22, 1912, p 517–518.

64. "Premier Sixes Only for 1913—A New Model Introduced," *Horseless Age*, October 2, 1912, p 512–514.
65. "Additions to Premier Plant," *Horseless Age*, October 2, 1912, p 492.
66. "Auto Dealers Ready for Fair This Week," *Indianapolis Star*, September 1, 1912, p 15.
67. "Auto Show at Fair Proves Big Success," *Indianapolis Star*, September 7, 1912, p 7.
68. "National," *Indianapolis Star*, July 28, 1912, p 45.
69. "Builds Commercial Car," *Indianapolis Star*, August 14, 1912, p 9.
70. "Adopts Auto Name Plate," *Indianapolis Star*, August 18, 1912, p 20.
71. "Automobile Company Gets Results in Sunday Papers," *Indianapolis Star*, August 25, 1912, p 26.
72. Blakely, "Road Across U.S. Proposed by Auto Men," *Indianapolis Star*, September 11, 1912, p 1 & 9.
73. "Auto Convention Plan Is Indorsed," *Indianapolis Star*, September 15, 1912, p 20.
74. "Committees Named for Auto Convention," *Indianapolis Star*, September 17, 1912, p 7.
75. "Propose Parade of 2,000 Autos," *Indianapolis Star*, September 16, 1912, p 9.
76. Blakely, "Motor Industry Given Big Boost," *Indianapolis Star*, October 13, 1912, p 34.
77. Blakely, "Auto Men Close Big Convention," *Indianapolis Star*, October 10, 1912, p 13.
78. "Issues Book on Auto Convention," *Indianapolis Star*, December 22, 1912, p 35.
79. "New Model Completed by Local Plant," *Indianapolis Star*, November 17, 1912, p 27.
80. "Henderson Wire Wheel Models," *Horseless Age*, November 27, 1912, p 819.
81. "Enlarging Pathfinder Plant," *Horseless Age*, November 6, 1912, p 689.
82. "Marion Company's Tenth Announcement," *Horseless Age*, November 13, 1912, p 735.
83. "New Marion Car Announced," *Indianapolis Star*, December 22, 1912, p 35.
84. "A New Marion Model," *Horseless Age*, December 25, 1912, p 976.
85. "New Type Inclosed Car Placed on Market," *Indianapolis Star*, December 1, 1912, p 22.
86. "Long-Stroke Motor Is Used," *Indianapolis Star*, February 9, 1913, p 30.

Chapter 7

1. Blakely, "Harroun May Enter Next 500-Mile Race," *Indianapolis Star*, January 20, 1913, p 8.
2. "Pathfinder Will Hold Open House," *Indianapolis Star*, February 2, 1913, p 28.
3. "Local Maker Favors Motor Museum Plan," *Indianapolis Star*, February 23, 1913, p 32.
4. "Westgard to Make Three Other Tours," *Indianapolis Star*, April 27, 1913, p 34.
5. "New Cole Six-60 on the Market," *Horseless Age*, January 1, 1913, p 25.
6. "Eight Models Described in 1913 Waverley Year Book," *Indianapolis Star*, February 9, 1913, p 31.
7. Blakely, "Auto Test Car Bill Put Through Senate," *Indianapolis Star*, February 12, 1913, p 9.
8. Blakely, "Auto Men's Ire Aroused by Bill," *Indianapolis Star*, January 31, 1913, p 11.
9. "Rumor Has Cole To Move To Detroit." *Detroit Free Press*, February 9, 1913, p 60.
10. Blakely, "Refutes Rumor of Cole Change," *Indianapolis Star*, February 16, 1913, p 28.
11. Blakely, "On Motor Row," *Indianapolis Star*, February 20, 1913, p 10.
12. "On Motor Row," *Indianapolis Star*, February 21, 1913, p 10.
13. "American Plant Announces Cars," *Indianapolis Star*, April 20, 1913, p 36.
14. "Pathfinder New Series," *Horseless Age*, July 16, 1913, p 103.
15. "No Radical Changes in New Pathfinder," *Indianapolis Star*, June 29, 1913, p 34.
16. "The Pathfinder for 1914," *Horseless Age*, September 10, 1913, p 428.
17. "No Radical Changes in New Pathfinder," *Indianapolis Star*, June 29, 1913, p 34.
18. "Harroun Designs New Carburetor," *Indianapolis Star*, February 9, 1913, p 34.
19. "Kerosene Used to Run National Car," *Indianapolis Star*, February 23, 1913, p 28.
20. "Local Auto Men Get High Offices," *Indianapolis Star*, February 2, 1913, p 29.
21. "Cole Line Adopts New Car Model and Delco Lighting," *Indianapolis Star*, March 30, 1913, p 26.
22. "Big Addition for Cole Auto Plant," *Indianapolis Star*, April 13, 1913, p 41.
23. "Empire Car Is Dubbed 'The Little Aristocrat,'" *Indianapolis Star*, March 23, 1913, p 32.
24. "'Little Aristocrat' Gains Honored Post," *Indianapolis Star*, May 18, 1913, p 31.
25. "The New Marmon Six Cylinder Car," *Horseless Age*, March 19, 1913, p 537–539.
26. "Ideal Is Now Stutz Motor Car Co," *Horseless Age*, May 14, 1913, p 889.
27. "Electric Self Starter on Stutz Cars" *Horseless Age*, July 16, 1913, p 91.
28. "National's Factory Enlarged," *Horseless Age*, March 5, 1913, p 444.
29. "Two Bridges Wrecked, Boulevard Is Broken," *Indianapolis Star*, March 26, 1913, p 5.
30. "Mayor Issues Flood Fund Appeal; The Star Will Receive Donations," *Indianapolis Star*, March 26, 1913, p 1.
31. "Fight Waged to Save Homeless Thousands," *Indianapolis Star*, March 26, 1913, p 1 & 5.
32. "Auto Makers Aid Work of Rescue," *Indianapolis Star*, March 27, 1913, p 10.
33. "Sees Great Benefit to City in Big Race," *Indianapolis Star*, April 27, 1913, p 36.
34. "Henderson Exhibit During 500 Mile Race," *Horseless Age*, June 18, 1913, p 1096.
35. "27 Cars Race Await Battle on Brick Oval," *Indianapolis Star*, May 30, 1913, p 14.
36. "Sees Great Benefit to City In Big Race," *Indianapolis Star*, April 27, 1913, p 36.
37. "Tells Why Cars Are Not in Race," *Indianapolis Star*, May 25, 1913, p 70.
38. Bloemker, *500 Miles To Go*, p 118.
39. Clymer, *Indianapolis 500 Mile Race History*, p 47.
40. *Ibid.*, p 60.
41. "Dickson Asserts Charges Unfair," *Indianapolis Star*, June 29, 1913, p 33.
42. "Speedway Race Can't Be 'Doped Out' Now," *Indianapolis Star*, March 22 1914, p 9.
43. "Local Company Doubles Capital," *Indianapolis Star*, May 25, 1913, p 78.
44. "Auto Manufacturer Proves His Ability As Detective," *Indianapolis Star*, June 5, 1913, p 14.
45. "On the Trail of Motor Thieves," *Indianapolis Star*, June 8, 1913, p 35.
46. "Increase in Premier Business," *Horseless Age*, June 18, 1913, p 1105.
47. Blakely, "State Autoists Leave Today on Tour to Pacific," *Indianapolis Star*, July 1, 1913, p 1.
48. Blakely, "Hearty Welcome Given Hoosiers," *Indianapolis Star*, July 29, 1913, p 1 & 5.
49. "Coast Tour to Aid Good Roads," *Indianapolis Star*, January 26, 1913, p 30.
50. Blakely, "State Autoists Leave Today on Tour to Pacific," *Indianapolis Star*, July 1, 1913, p 1.
51. "Glimpse Pacific for First Time," *Indianapolis Star*, July 28, 1913, p 3.
52. Blakely, "Autoists Enjoy Views in Frisco," *Indianapolis Star*, July 30, 1913, p 2.
53. "Henderson Adds a Six to Their Line," *Horseless Age*, May 28, 1913, p 982.

54. "Handley Welds Auto Interests," *Indianapolis Star*, July 27, 1913, p 28.
55. "Auto Meeting Convenes Here," *Indianapolis Star*, July 13, 1913, p 20.
56. "Stream-lined Bodies and Left Hand Drive Characterize New Cole Models," *Horseless Age*, July 23, 1913, p 142–146.
57. "Announces New Cars for 1914," *Indianapolis Star*, August 17, 1913, p 31.
58. "National," *Indianapolis Star*, July 13, 1913, p 20.
59. "National Firm Announces Six," *Indianapolis Star*, December 21, 1913, p 20.
60. "Marion Company out with a 'Six,'" *Horseless Age*, August 20, 1913, p 306–307.
61. "Marion Motor Car Co., Indianapolis," *Horseless Age*, October 13, 1913, p 617.
62. "Two Closed Types Marions Announced," *Indianapolis Star*, September 28, 1913, p 33.
63. "Nordyke & Marmon Increase Capital," *Horseless Age*, July 23, 1913, p 137.
64. "New Marmon Speedway Type 'Speedster,'" *Indianapolis Star*, July 20, 1913, p 27.
65. Catlin, "The Harry Stutz Era," p 234.
66. Blakely, "Gil Anderson in Stutz Car Wins Elgin Road Race," *Indianapolis Star*, August 31, 1913, p 17 & 19.
67. Blakely, "First Entries For 500-Mile Race Received," *Indianapolis Star*, September 21, 1913, p 32.
68. Catlin, "The Harry Stutz Era," p 234.
69. "1914 Marmon Is Not Radically Changed," *Indianapolis Star*, September 28, 1913, p 32.
70. "'Type 646' Is Latest Car Announced by American Co.," *Indianapolis Star*, September 7, 1913, p 18.
71. "Henderson to Bring Out Lower Priced Cars," *Horseless Age*, September 24, 1913, p 1.
72. "Pathfinder Firm Plans Campaign," *Indianapolis Star*, October 5, 1913, p 19.
73. "Pathfinder," *Indianapolis Star*, October 19, 1913, p 20.
74. "Pathfinder Announces a Six-Cylinder Model for 1914," *Horseless Age*, October 22, 1913, p 687–688.
75. "A New Premier Model with an Overhead Valve Motor," *Horseless Age*, December 24, 1913, p 1079–1081.
76. "Premier Increases Its Capitalization to $1,250,000," *Horseless Age*, June 18, 1913, p 1.
77. "National Firm Announces Six," *Indianapolis Star*, December 21, 1913, p 20.

Chapter 8

1. "Decrease Shown in Auto Price," *Indianapolis Star*, January 4, 1914, p 31.
2. "Light Six Added to Marmon Line," *Horseless Age*, January 7, 1914, p 37–39.
3. "Announcing the Marmon 'Forty-One,'" *Indianapolis Star*, January 4, 1914, p 31.
4. "Empire Surprises Staff," *Indianapolis Star*, January 11, 1914, p 17.
5. "Empire Exhibits New Creations," *Indianapolis Star*, February 22, 1914, p 51.
6. Ibid.
7. "Empire," *Indianapolis Star*, February 22, 1914, p 47.
8. "Empire Exhibits New Creations," *Indianapolis Star*, February 22, 1914, p 51.
9. "Marion Receivership Lifted; Finances Adjusted," *Horseless Age*, January 28, 1914, p 1.
10. "Marion Announcing the Bobcat," *Indianapolis Star*, February 26, 1914, p 28.
11. "Pathfinder Six $2222," *Indianapolis Star*, February 22, 1914, p 51.
12. "Decrease Shown in Auto Prices," *Indianapolis Star*, January 4, 1914, p 31.
13. "Chicago Society Visits Big Show," *Indianapolis Star*, January 29, 1914, p 11.
14. "F. E. Moskovics Comes to Join Marmon Staff," *Indianapolis Star*, February 1, 1914, p 20.
15. "New Cole Factory Finished in Spring," *Indianapolis Star*, January 18, 1914, p 42.
16. Blankenbaker, "Cole Company Uses Four Labor Saving Devices," *Indianapolis Star*, April 26, 1914, p 54.
17. Blankenbaker, "On Motor Row," *Indianapolis Star*, March 31, 1914, p 11.
18. "Enters Stutz at Los Angeles," *Indianapolis Star*, January 25, 1914, p 18.
19. "Local Race Pilot Departs Today for Pacific Coast to Prepare for Race Events," *Indianapolis Star*, February 8, 1914, p 20.
20. Ibid.
21. "Los Angeles Owner Has Winning Marmon," *Indianapolis Star*, March 8, 1914, p 20.
22. "DePalma Is Winner of Vanderbilt," *Indianapolis Star*, February 27, 1914, p 10.
23. "Pullen Wins Grand Prix; Ball Second," *Indianapolis Star*, March 1, 1914, p 45.
24. Blankenbaker, "Three Companies Bid for Oldfield," *Indianapolis Star*, March 17, 1914, p 14.
25. Blankenbaker, "On Motor Row," *Indianapolis Star*, March 31, 1914, p 11.
26. "Dawson Says Old Car Is Best," *Indianapolis Star*, April 26, 1914, p 56.
27. Blankenbaker, "Joe Dawson Smashes the Lap Record," *Indianapolis Star*, May 16, 1914, p 7.
28. Blankenbaker, "Dawson's Record Is Endangered," *Indianapolis Star*, May 17, 1914, p 45.
29. Blankenbaker, "Bugatti Will Be in 500-Mile Race," April 29, 1914, p 12.
30. "Private Owners Enter Big Race," *Indianapolis Star*, April 8, 1914, p 8.
31. "Ray Harroun Cars Entered at Speedway," *Indianapolis Star*, April 21, 1914, p 7.
32. "Private Owners Enter Big Race," *Indianapolis Star*, April 8, 1914, p 8.
33. Blankenbaker, "French Stamp 500-Mile Race Biggest Event," *Indianapolis Star*, April 26, 1914, p 47.
34. "Empire No. 19 Is Still in Service," *Indianapolis Star*, May 31, 1914, p 30.
35. "Empire District Manager Makes Auto Buying Simple," *Indianapolis Star*, June 21, 1914, p 19.
36. "Optimism Holds Sway As Buyers Throng 'the Row,'" *Indianapolis Star*, July 28, 1914, p 7.
37. "Engineers Praise New Weidley Motor," *Indianapolis Star*, January 18, 1914, p 43.
38. "Weidley Motor on Display," *Indianapolis Star*, February 25, 1914, p 11.
39. "This Car Is Expected to Be a Winner," *Indianapolis Star*, May 17, 1914, p 54.
40. "Sees Auto Boom in Spite of War," *Indianapolis Star*, September 4, 1914, p 6.
41. "Stutz Factory Is Planned," *Indianapolis Star*, March 1, 1914, p 3, and "Boulevard Boom Given New Boost," *Indianapolis Star*, January 18, 1914, p 31.
42. "Building Permits," *Indianapolis Star*, April 7, 1914, p 10.
43. Daniels, "All Roads Lead to Indianapolis," *Indianapolis Star*, May 24, 1914, p 56.
44. "New Cole Model a Big Success," *Indianapolis Star*, May 17, 1914, p 54.
45. "Cole Improves As Hill Climber," *Indianapolis Star*, August 2, 1914, p 17.
46. "Stewart Vacuum Tank," *Motor Age*, Vol. 31, p 92. https://books.google.com/books?id=xFYfAQAAMAAJ&pg=RA1-PA92&dq=stewart+vacuum+gasoline+system&hl=en&sa=X&ved=0ahUKEwiQ2pOSl4TLAhXFNT4KHb4LDcOQ6AEIQjAD#v=onepage&q=stewart%20vacuum%20gasoline%20system&f=false. Accessed February 19, 2016.
47. "Saves from 15% to 30% of Your Gasoline Bills," *Indianapolis Star*, November 29, 1914, p 22.
48. "Cole Improves As Hill Climber," *Indianapolis Star*, August 2, 1914, p 17.
49. "Vacuum System Proves Popular," *Indianapolis Star*, December 6, 1914, p 23.

50. "New Cole Model Uses Little Gas," *Indianapolis Star*, May 3, 1914, p 5.
51. "New Cole Model a Big Success," *Indianapolis Star*, May 17, 1914, p 54.
52. "Series 10–4 Cole Announced," *Horseless Age*, April 29, 1914, p 671–673.
53. "Smart Set Demands Tailor-Made Bodies," *Indianapolis Star*, May 10, 1914, p 46.
54. "Friendly Receivership to End Henderson Company," *Horseless Age*, May 27, 1914, p 1.
55. Blankenbaker, "Three Racers Break Marks at Speedway," *Indianapolis Star*, May 27, 1914, p 5.
56. "Marmon Factory Mecca for Visitors," *Indianapolis Star*, May 29, 1914, p 6.
57. "Scoring System Devised for the Speedway Race," *Indianapolis Star*, May 29, 1914, p 6.
58. Blakely, "Foreign Pilots Are First Four in Auto Classic," *Indianapolis Star*, May 31, 1914, p 1 & 6.
59. *Ibid*.
60. Watkins, "Dawson, Injured, Fights For Life," *Indianapolis Star*, May 31, 1914, p 1 & 7.
61. Blakely, "Foreign Pilots Are First Four in Auto Classic," *Indianapolis Star*, May 31, 1914, p 1 & 6.
62. "Consistent Service Wins Again for the Sturdy Stutz," *Indianapolis Star*, June 7, 1914, p 21.
63. "Marmon in Sioux City Sweepstakes," *Indianapolis Star*, June 28, 1914, p 15.
64. Glenn, "On Motor Row," *Indianapolis Star*, June 25, 1914, p 10.
65. "Rickenbacker Wins Thrilling Race of 300 Miles," *Indianapolis Star*, July 5, 1914, p 23.
66. Sioux City's Mini Indy, http://www.siouxcityhistory.org/art-a-leisure/123-sioux-citys-mini-indy-sports-and-competition-have-been-an-important-part-of-sioux-citys-history-si. Accessed February 20, 2016.
67. Bradfield, "Cooper in Stutz Wins at Tacoma," *Indianapolis Star*, July 5, 1914, p 23.
68. "New Car for Busy Business Man," *Indianapolis Star*, July 19, 1914, p 17.
69. "1915 Premier on Display July 6–11," *Indianapolis Star*, July 5, 1914, p 14.
70. "Gil Anderson, in a Stutz, Pushes DePalma That Record Is Broken in Race for the Cobe Trophy over Elgin Road Course," *Indianapolis Star*, August 22, 1914, p 6.
71. "Elgin Trophy Is Won by De-Palma," *Indianapolis Star*, August 23, 1914, p 41.
72. "Plans New Surprise at Automobile Show," *Indianapolis Star*, September 6, 1914, p 13 & 23.
73. "Cole Sets Gas Economy Mark," *Indianapolis Star*, October 11, 1914, p 20.
74. "Gasoline Saved by Sensible-Six," *Indianapolis Star*, November 8, 1914, p 19.
75. "Empire," *Indianapolis Star*, September 6, 1914, p 21.
76. "Pathfinder Builder to Have Exhibit at Fair," *Indianapolis Star*, 6, 1914, p 14.
77. Blankenbaker, "French Drivers Come in Today," *Indianapolis Star*, May 10, 1914, p 40.
78. "Cole Testers Treat Druggists to Race," *Indianapolis Star*, September 27, 1914, p 34.
79. "Auto Firms Send Formal Protest," *Indianapolis Star*, October 7, 1914, p 14.
80. "Local Auto Men Oppose War Tax," *Indianapolis Star*, October 5, 1914, p 5.
81. "Auto Firms Send Formal Protest," *Indianapolis Star*, October 7, 1914, p 14.
82. "Eighteen Drivers Entered in Western Auto Classic," *Indianapolis Star*, October 25, 1914, p 23.
83. "Paiges Strong in Cactus Derby," *Indianapolis Star*, November 22, 1914, p 22.
84. "Oldfield Wins Big Road Race," *Indianapolis Star*, November 12, 1914, p 8.
85. "Thinks Question Fully Answered," *Indianapolis Star*, November 15, 1914, p 25.
86. "Marion Motor Company Bought by J. I. Handley," *Indianapolis Star*, November 6, 1914, p 16.
87. "Frank E. Smith Elected Premier Company Trustee," *Indianapolis Star*, December 15, 1914, p 10.
88. "Reorganized Premier Motor Corporation Ready to Set New Mark in Industry," *Indianapolis Star*, April 2, 1916, p 22.
89. "Throng Attends Great Auto Show," *Indianapolis Star*, January 6, 1915, p 5.
90. "Big Spring Seen by Premier Head," *Indianapolis Star*, March 21, 1915, p 22.
91. "Yes, Indeed, It's Nice to 'Enjoy' Funeral in Comfortable Autos," *Indianapolis Star*, March 7, 1915, p 69.

Chapter 9

1. Willis, "New York Auto Show Is Opened," *Indianapolis Star*, January 3, 1915, p 19.
2. "National Parlor Car Delights Women," *Indianapolis Star*, February 7, 1915, p 18.
3. "Simplicity in New National," *Indianapolis Star*, March 21, 1915, p 16.
4. Willis, "New York Auto Show Is Opened," *Indianapolis Star*, January 3, 1915, p 19.
5. "Cole Announces New 8-Cylinder," *Indianapolis Star*, January 21, 1915, p 11.
6. "New Cole Eight Show Headliner," *Indianapolis Star*, January 24, 1915, p 13.
7. "Cole Announces New 8-Cylinder," *Indianapolis Star*, January 21, 1915, p 11.
8. "Cole Introduces Eight Cylinder Model," *Horseless Age*, January 20, 1915, p 95.
9. "New Cole Eight Show Headliner," *Indianapolis Star*, January 24, 1915, p 13.
10. "Cole Introduces Eight Cylinder Model," *Horseless Age*, January 20, 1915, p 95.
11. "Cole Eight Soon to Go on Market," *Indianapolis Star*, January 31, 1915, p 21.
12. "New Premier Sextet with Timken Axles and Worm Bevel Drive," *Horseless Age*, January 6, 1915, p 34–35.
13. "Contract Made at Auto Show," *Indianapolis Star*, January 26, 1915, p 9.
14. "Auto Factories Profit by Show," *Indianapolis Star*, January 29, 1915, p 9.
15. "Eight Cylinder in Demand," *Indianapolis Star*, February 28, 1915, p 21.
16. "Ten Motors Per Day for Cole Motor Car Company," *Indianapolis Star*, March 7, 1915, p 58.
17. "Day and Night Shift for Cole," *Indianapolis Star*, March 28, 1915, p 19.
18. "H. O. Smith Files Bankruptcy Petition," *Horseless Age*, February 10, 1915, p 193.
19. "Weidley Motors Capitalized at $350,000," *Horseless Age*, January 15, 1916, p 95.
20. "J. I Handley Chosen Head of Mutual Motors Company," *Indianapolis Star*, January 3, 1915, p 19.
21. "John Guy Monihan Named Marion Company Manager," *Indianapolis Star*, January 6, 1915, p 11.
22. "J. I Handley Chosen Head of Mutual Motors Company," *Indianapolis Star*, January 3, 1915, p 19.
23. "J. G. Monihan Guest at Farewell Dinner," *Indianapolis Star*, February 13, 1915, p 13.
24. "Public Auction Sale," *Indianapolis Star*, March 10, 1915, p 13.
25. "Plans Complete for Frisco Race," *Indianapolis Star*, February 21, 1915, p 17.
26. "Entries Numerous for Big Auto Races," *Indianapolis Star*, February 14, 1915, p 14.
27. "Resta Wins and Wilcox Comes Next," *Indianapolis Star*, March 7, 1915, p 45.
28. "Films at Colonial Theater to Show Famous Cup Race at Exposition," *Indianapolis Star*, May 1, 1915, p 17.
29. "Resta Captures Grand Prix in

Peugeot," *Indianapolis Star*, February 28, 1915, p 45.

30. "The Sturdy Stutz Wins Again," *Indianapolis Star*, February 28, 1915, p 22.

31. "Stutz Racers May Not Be in the 500-Mile Speedway Race," *Indianapolis Star*, March 30, 1915, p 10.

32. "2 Firemen Hurt in $8,000 Blaze at Motor Plant," *Indianapolis Star*, April 10, 1915, p 1 & 14.

33. "Blaze Loss Estimated at $50,000," *Indianapolis Star*, April 25, 1915, p 1 & 8.

34. "Business Is Not Marred by Fire," *Indianapolis Star*, April 26, 1915, p 14.

35. "Some Features of the New Premier," *Horseless Age*, April 28, 1915, p 569.

36. "Speed Is Mania in America, Says a Well-Known Auto Man," *Indianapolis Star*, May 30, 1915, p 36.

37. "Fire Again Hits Premier," *Indianapolis Star*, May 6, 1915, p 1.

38. "Empire Reveals First 1916 Type," *Indianapolis Star*, April 11, 1915, p 24.

39. "The New Premier Model 33," *Horseless Age*, April 28, 1915, p 570–571.

40. "Empire Reports Record Business," *Indianapolis Star*, May 2, 1915, p 55.

41. "National Newport Model," *Horseless Age*, April 28, 1915, p 572.

42. "Speed Demons in Oklahoma Race," *Indianapolis Star*, April 4, 1915, p 26.

43. "Stutz Scores Again," *Indianapolis Star*, April 30, 1915, p 12.

44. "Stutz Racing Team Makes High Speed in Time Trial," *Indianapolis Star*, April 22, 1915, p 3.

45. "Civic Tourist Visit Speedway," *Indianapolis Star*, May 1, 1915, p 18.

46. Farrington, "Crowd Sees Cars in Tune-Up at Speedway," *Indianapolis Star*, May 14, 1915, p 13.

47. "Fisher Mentioned As Head of Circuit," *Indianapolis Star*, April 13, 1915, p 10.

48. "Official Trials on for Race Cars Today," *Indianapolis Star*, May 20, 1915, p 10.

49. "Twenty-Five Are Eligible for Classic," *Indianapolis Star*, May 25, 1915, p 11.

50. "Baker Breaks Record," *Indianapolis Star*, May 19, 1915, p 10.

51. "A.C.A. Tests Stutz Transcontinental Car," *Horseless Age*, May 26, 1915, p 697.

52. "Baker Coast-to-Coast Run Remarkable Stutz Record," *Indianapolis Star*, May 23, 1915, p 58.

53. "Another Record Smashed," *Indianapolis Star*, May 23, 1915, p 57.

54. "Motor Car Mfg. Co. Is Now the Pathfinder Company," *Indianapolis Star*, May 26, 1915, p 16.

55. "Incorporations," *Indianapolis Star*, May 22, 1915, p 17.

56. "Two More 'Twelves' and a New 'Eight,'" *Horseless Age*, June 23, 1915, p 838.

57. "Twelve Cylinder Announcements Startle Industry," *Horseless Age*, May 26, 1915, p 1.

58. "National Twelve to Appear Soon," *Indianapolis Star*, May 28, 1915, p 8.

59. "Feature of Twelve Is Its Longer Life," *Indianapolis Star*, July 18, 1915, p 14.

60. "Johnny Aitken to Be Member of the Stutz Racing Team," *Indianapolis Star*, May 9, 1915, p 37.

61. "Stutz Car, Wilcox Up, Sets Mark," *Indianapolis Star*, May 24, 1915, p 10.

62. Tibbetts, "Howdy Wilcox Record for Lap Would Mean 500 Miles in 5:03:20 Should This Speed Be Possible in Race," *Indianapolis Star*, May 31, 1915, p 11.

63. Willis, "Stars of Racing May Shatter Records," *Indianapolis Star*, May 23, 1915, p 49.

64. Jackson, "Ralph DePalma Is Favorite in Betting on 500-Mile Race," *Indianapolis Star*, May 28, 1915, p 12.

65. Rankin, "Lauds Decision Postponing Race," *Indianapolis Star*, May 30, 1915, p 1.

66. Farrington, "Four Cars Break Records in Race DePalma Wins," *Indianapolis Star*, June 1, 1915, p 7.

67. "Quantity Price Pathfinder Policy," *Indianapolis Star*, June 6, 1915, p 18.

68. "Knows Demands of Car Buyers," *Indianapolis Star*, July 18, 1915, p 16.

69. "LaSalle Twelve New Pathfinder," *Indianapolis Star*, July 4, 1915, p 13.

70. "Quantity Price Pathfinder Policy," *Indianapolis Star*, June 6, 1915, p 18.

71. "Addition to Pathfinder Plant," *Horseless Age*, August 1, 1915, p 160.

72. "Shows Vantage of 'Twin Six,'" *Indianapolis Star*, August 15, 1915, p 18.

73. "Epitomizes 1916 Auto Season," *Indianapolis Star*, March 5, 1916, p 20.

74. "Official High Gear Test of Marmon Car," *Horseless Age*, May 5, 1915, p 591.

75. Willis, "Resta Sets New Record at Chicago," *Indianapolis Star*, June 27, 1915, p 1 & 11.

76. Goodman, "Ralph DePalma Visits Here and Purchases Stutz Racer," *Indianapolis Star*, July 16, 1915, p 14.

77. "Empire Expects Big Production," *Indianapolis Star*, December 31, 1915, p 24.

78. "Empire Car Factory Is Moved Here," *Indianapolis Star*, July 1, 1915, p 1 & 3.

79. "Dame Rumor Predicts an Empire 'Six' Soon," *Indianapolis Star*, June 27, 1915, p 19.

80. "Empire Car Factory Is Moved Here," *Indianapolis Star*, July 1, 1915, p 1 & 3.

81. "New Four Added to Empire Line," *Indianapolis Star*, August 15, 1915, p 18.

82. "At the Fair This Week," *Indianapolis Star*, September 5, 1915, p 43.

83. "New Four Added to Empire Line," *Indianapolis Star*, August 15, 1915, p 18.

84. "New Cars Added to '41,'" *Indianapolis Star*, June 25, 1915, p 20.

85. "New Series Marmon 41 with Body," *Horseless Age*, July 23, 1915, p 842–843.

86. "Club Roadster Grows Popular," *Indianapolis Star*, August 1, 1915, p 23.

87. "Cole Producing New Six Model," *Indianapolis Star*, July 11, 1915, p 17.

88. "Cole Announces a Big New Six," *Horseless Age*, July 14, 1915, Vol. 36, p 40.

89. Rankin, "Resta Favorite in Speed Battle," *Indianapolis Star*, August 7, 1915, p 11.

90. "Cooper, in Stutz, Throws Scare into Resta," *Indianapolis Star*, August 8, 1915, p 41.

91. Rankin, "Cooper Is First at Road Race in Elgin," *Indianapolis Star*, August 21, 1915, p 8.

92. "Stutz Driven to Another Victory," *Indianapolis Star*, August 22, 1915, p 41 & 42.

93. "Indianapolis Cars Driven to First and Second in Race," *Indianapolis Star*, September 5, 1915, p 29.

94. "Stutz Goes to Mill City," *Indianapolis Star*, August 29, 1915, p 43.

95. Catlin, "The Harry Stutz Era," *Automobile Quarterly* 3 no. 8, p 236.

96. Blakely, "Peugeot Racer Ready for Tuesday," *Indianapolis Star*, March 26, 1916, p 56.

97. "Stutz Racers to Be Called in after Sheepshead Event," *Indianapolis Star*, September 21, 1915, p 12.

98. "Stage All Set for N. Y. Auto Race Today," *Indianapolis Star*, October 9, 1915, p 10.

99. "Anderson Sheepshead Speed King," *Indianapolis Star*, October 10, 1915, p 17.

100. "Motion Pictures of Race," *Indianapolis Star*, October 18, 1915, p 10.

101. "Stutz Racers Set Wonderful Record," *Indianapolis Star*, September 12, 1915, p 22.

102. "Horseless Age Picks Stutz and Cooper as Champions," *Indianapolis Star*, October 31, 1915, p 17.

103. "Stutz Victory Is Celebrated," *Indianapolis Star*, October 17, 1915, p 12.

104. Bodenhamer and Barrows, *Encyclopedia of Indianapolis*, p 907.

105. "Stutz Victory Is Celebrated," *Indianapolis Star*, October 12, 1915, p 27.

106. *Ibid.*

107. "Europe and Australia Buy Stutz Car," *Indianapolis Star*, December 31, 1915, p 24.
108. "Limousine New Cole '8' Model," *Indianapolis Star*, August 22, 1915, p 15.
109. "Cole Roadster Makes Friends," *Indianapolis Star*, October 31, 1915, p 21.
110. "New Additions Almost Ready," *Indianapolis Star*, October 24, 1915, p 28.
111. "Work on New National Buildings Is Being Rushed to the Limit," *Indianapolis Star*, November 28, 1915, p 22.
112. "Weidley Motor Now Used Here," *Indianapolis Star*, September 5, 1915, p 47.
113. "Believe Owners Desire to Drive," *Indianapolis Star*, November 21, 1915, p 33.
114. "Premier Plant to Be Sold," *Indianapolis Star*, November 28, 1915, p 10.
115. "Premier Motor Company Formed," *Indianapolis Star*, December 8, 1915, p 2.
116. Browne, "Industrial Building—Home of T. B. Laycock Manufacturing," Historic Indianapolis. http://historicindianapolis.com/industrial-building-former-home-of-tb-laycock-manufacturing/. Accessed April 24, 2016.
117. "Premier Motor Company Formed," *Indianapolis Star*, December 8, 1915, p 2.
118. "New Premier Vice President Appoints Private Secretary," *Indianapolis Star*, December 12, 1915, p 32.
119. "Premier Motor Company Formed," *Indianapolis Star*, December 8, 1915, p 2.
120. "Reorganized Premier Motor Corporation Ready to Set New Mark in Industry," *Indianapolis Star*, April 2, 1916, p 22.
121. "Mais Truck Stands High in Auto Field," *Indianapolis Star*, January 16, 1916, p 6.
122. "Cole Eight Makes Strong Record," *Indianapolis Star*, December 19, 1915, p 21.
123. "Predict Great New York Show," *Indianapolis Star*, December 19, 1915, p 23.
124. "Empire Expects Big Production," *Indianapolis Star*, December 31, 1915, p 24.
125. "Empire Features Striking Colors," *Indianapolis Star*, February 27, 1916, p 57.
126. "Waverley Co. Ready with a New Electric," *Indianapolis Star*, December 31, 1915, p 23.
127. "Cole Company Announces Reduction in Price of '8,'" *Indianapolis Star*, December 31, 1915, p 43.
128. "New Cole '8,' Cut $190, Now Here," *Indianapolis Star*, January 23, 1916, p 20.
129. "Cole Tire Pump Handy," *Indianapolis Star*, February 27, 1916, p 57.

Chapter 10

1. "Mystery Car Is Solved at Last," *Indianapolis Star*, December 26, 1915, p 18.
2. "Local Factory Has Hard Time Keeping Plans Under Cover," *Indianapolis Star*, February 27, 1916, p 63.
3. "Marmon Booth Holds Interest," *Indianapolis Star*, January 30, 1916, p 21.
4. "The Unconventional Marmon," *Horseless Age*, January 1, 1916, p 14 & 15.
5. "Mystery Car Is Solved at Last," *Indianapolis Star*, December 26, 1915, p 18.
6. "Marmon 34 Is Unique Car," *Indianapolis Star*, January 30, 1916, p 19.
7. "Local Company Adds to Output," *Indianapolis Star*, December 31, 1915, p 27.
8. "Crowds Throng N.Y. Auto Show," *Indianapolis Star*, January 4, 1916, p 2.
9. "New Empire to Be Shown," *Indianapolis Star*, February 13, 1916, p 21.
10. "The Twelve Cylinder Pathfinder," *Horseless Age*, February 1, 1916, p 104–105.
11. Bull, "Auto Exhibitors See Sales Boom," *Indianapolis Star*, January 5, 1916, p 2.
12. "Wilcox to Drive Third Premier," *Indianapolis Star*, May 28, 1916, p 68.
13. Blakely, "Third Premier Ready to Race," *Indianapolis Star*, May 27, 1916, p 13.
14. "U.S. at Brink of War with Germany Is Belief of Officials at Washington," *Indianapolis Star*, May 5, 1916, p 14.
15. "Discusses Increases in Marmon Prices," *Indianapolis Star*, March 26, 1916, p 28.
16. "Empire Company Has New Roadsters," *Indianapolis Star*, April 16, 1916, p 23.
17. "Empire Announces Increase in Price," *Indianapolis Star*, April 2, 1916, p 24.
18. Bull, "Gasoline Cost Is Cut Down by Care in Use of Machine," *Indianapolis Star*, April 2, 1916, p 23.
19. "Price Rise Necessary for Pathfinder Twin Six Cars," *Indianapolis Star*, April 2, 1916, p 25.
20. "Gets Protection of Trade-Mark," *Indianapolis Star*, April 30, 1916, p 27.
21. "New National Is Big Success," *Indianapolis Star*, April 23, 1916, p 18.
22. "Cole Company Branches Out," *Indianapolis Star*, April 23, 1916, p 20.
23. "Cole Firm Invites Any Difficult Task," *Indianapolis Star*, May 14, 1916, p 22.
24. "Record Breaking Indianapolis Car," *Indianapolis Star*, May 24, 1916, p 12.
25. "Bales Puncture Plugger Saves Time," *Indianapolis Star*, May 28, 1916, p 41.
26. "Record Breaking Indianapolis Car," *Indianapolis Star*, May 24, 1916, p 12.
27. "Aitken, with Peugeot, Heads Speedway Team," *Indianapolis Star*, April 2, 1916, p 23.
28. "Two Die in New York Feature Race Won by Eddie Rickenbacker," *Indianapolis Star*, May 14, 1916, p 62 & 63.
29. "Speedway Pilots to Strive for Prizes Totaling $30,000," *Indianapolis Star*, May 8, 1916, p 10.
30. Blakely, "Big Speedway Race on May 30 Starts at 1:30 in the Afternoon," *Indianapolis Star*, April 27, 1916, p 15.
31. "Howard Marmon Asked to Officiate as Starter," *Indianapolis Star*, April 27, 1916, p 15.
32. Blakely, "Gil Anderson Free to Chose Mount for Local Race in May," *Indianapolis Star*, April 16, 1916, p 58.
33. "Race Germ Hits Restaurant Man," *Indianapolis Star*, May 1, 1913, p 13.
34. Blakely, "Rickenbacker and Sunbeam Pilot Are Second in List," *Indianapolis Star*, May 23, 1916, p 14.
35. Blakely, "New Track Record Set by Oldfield," *Indianapolis Star*, May 29, 1916, p 1 & 14.
36. "Tablet Presented to Harry C. Stutz as Token of Esteem of Local Citizens," *Indianapolis Star*, May 24, 1916, p 3.
37. Blakely, "Driver for Peugeot Victor at Average of 84 Miles an Hour," *Indianapolis Star*, May 31, 1916, p 1.
38. "Speedway Pilots to Strive for Prizes Totaling $30,000," *Indianapolis Star*, May 8, 1916, p 10.
39. Blakely, "Driver for Peugeot Victor at Average of 84 Miles an Hour," *Indianapolis Star*, May 31, 1916, p 1.
40. "Four-Story Addition for Stutz," *Horseless Age*, February 15, 1916, p 166.
41. "Pathfinder to Try Coast-to-Coast Trip," *Indianapolis Star*, June 18, 1916, p 22.
42. "Feat of Pathfinder Should Add Interest," *Indianapolis Star*, August 13, 1916, p 21.
43. "High Gear Coast-to-Coast Pathfinder Headed East," *Indianapolis Star*, July 23, 1916, p 22.
44. "Cole Roadster Sets New Style," *Indianapolis Star*, June 25, 1916, p 20.
45. "Marmon Turns to Closed Cars," *Indianapolis Star*, June 18, 1916, p 20.
46. "New York Capitalists Buy Interest in Stutz Company," *Indianapolis Star*, June 22, 1916, p 12.
47. "Stutz Declares Dividend," *Indianapolis Star*, July 11, 1916, p 21.
48. "Cole Announces All-Year Eight," *Indianapolis Star*, July 9, 1916, p 16.

49. "New Cole Convertible Bodies," *Horseless Age*, October 15, 1916, p 259.
50. "Cole Announces All-Year Eight," *Indianapolis Star*, July 9, 1916, p 16.
51. "All-Year Car Here to Stay," *Indianapolis Star*, December 3, 1916, p 21.
52. "National Twelve Price Increased," *Indianapolis Star*, June 18, 1916, p 16.
53. "Wilcox Takes Two Sioux City Events," *Indianapolis Star*, July 9, 1916, p 57.
54. "Coast-to-Coast Record Smashed," *Indianapolis Star*, August 13, 1916, p 19.
55. "Marmon 34 Sealed for Long Test Trip," *Indianapolis Star*, August 20, 1916, p 17.
56. "Marmon to Show at State Fair," *Indianapolis Star*, September 3, 1916, p 21.
57. "Realty Board Wants Farm Loan Bank Here," *Indianapolis Star*, August 10, 1916, p 12.
58. "Additions Begun," *Indianapolis Star*, September 3, 1916, p 28.
59. "Real Estate News," *Indianapolis Star*, September 1, 1916, p 21.
60. "National Exhibit to Be Preserved," *Indianapolis Star*, September 10, 1916, p 18.
61. *Ibid.*
62. "National Twelve Mounts Big Hill," *Indianapolis Star*, October 1, 1916, p 14.
63. "The New Premier Aluminum Six," *Horseless Age*, Vol. 38, p 188–189.
64. "Premier Adopts New Gear Shift," *Indianapolis Star*, August 20, 1916, p 17.
65. "Anderson Enters Stutz in Races," *Indianapolis Star*, August 22, 1916, p 10.
66. Blakely, "Aitken Wins Race and $13,000 at Cincinnati," *Indianapolis Star*, September 5, 1916, p 12.
67. *Ibid.*, p 12 & 16.
68. Blakely, "Thirteen Racers in Short Events," *Indianapolis Star*, August 29, 1916, p 10.
69. Blakely, "Aitken Wins Every Race—Indians Gain on the Clymers," *Indianapolis Star*, September 10, 1916, p 45.
70. "The New Series 1917 Stutz Car," *Horseless Age*, August 21, 1916, p 122–123.
71. "National Motor Car & Vehicle Corporation," *Indianapolis Star*, November 7, 1916, p 15.
72. "National's Name Is Widely Known," *Indianapolis Star*, November 5, 1916, p 21.
73. "Rickenbacker to Drive Duesenberg in Vanderbilt," *Indianapolis Star*, November 1, 1916, p 11.
74. Whitney, "Aitken Confident at Being There at the Finish," *Indianapolis Star*, November 16, 1916, p 10.
75. *Ibid.*
76. "Resta Wins with Cooper Next at Santa Monica," *Indianapolis Star*, November 17, 1916, p 10.
77. Whitney, "Speed Kings Set for the Grand Prize Event," *Indianapolis Star*, November 18, 1916, p 4.
78. "4 Dead in Race Won by Aitken," *Indianapolis Star*, November 19, 1916, p 33.
79. "Marmon Announces Price Increase to Be Effective Jan. 1," *Indianapolis Star*, November 19, 1916, p 23.
80. "Advance of $100 in Price of Coles," *Indianapolis Star*, November 19, 1916, p 23.
81. "Empire Will Boost Price Before Jan. 1; High Cost Is Cause," *Indianapolis Star*, November 5, 1916, p 23.
82. "Empire," *Indianapolis Star*, March 4, 1917, p 22.
83. "Empire Announces Attractive Sedan, Ready About Dec. 1," *Indianapolis Star*, November 19, 1916, p 23.
84. "National Announces New Body Without Additional Cost," *Indianapolis Star*, December 10, 1916, p 20.
85. "Wake Up, Indianapolis," *Indianapolis Star*, December 19, 1916, p 10.
86. "$1,000,000, Premier Motor Corporation," *Indianapolis Star*, December 7, 1916, p 14.
87. "More Companies Raise Prices," *Horseless Age*, December 15, 1916, p 424.

Chapter 11

1. "Auto Men Take Fling at M'Adoo," *Indianapolis Star*, January 5, 1917, p 11.
2. Base, "Premier Offers Aluminum Six," *Indianapolis Star*, January 7, 1917, p 20.
3. Base, "Motor Truck Is Coming into Own," *Indianapolis Star*, October 7, 1917, p 19.
4. Bull, "Great Variety of Machines Offered at National Show," *Indianapolis Star*, January 7, 1917, p 19.
5. Bull, "Rotarians Show Guests Thursday," *Indianapolis Star*, February 7, 1917, p 7.
6. "Auto Show Notes," *Indianapolis Star*, January 14, 1917, p 17.
7. "The Prest-O-Lite Vacuum Brake," *Automobile Trade Journal*, Sept 1916, p 271. https://books.google.com/books?id=PnBIAQAAMAAJ&pg=RA3-PA271&lpg=RA3-PA271&dq=prest-o-lite+vacuum+brake&source=bl&ots=lJVXe21K7A&sig=zM-EPVsSayPAKllUj70T_BnY6nM&hl=en&sa=X&ved=0ahUKEwjGt6H1JDLAhXKOz4KHeSbDH4Q6AEIHzAB#v=onepage&q=prest-o-lite%20vacuum%20brake&f=false. Accessed February 24, 2016.
8. "New Empire Six Model Is Larger," *Indianapolis Star*, February 4, 1917, p 75.
9. "Empire," *Indianapolis Star*, April 22, 1917, p 16.
10. "Auto Truck Taking Place in Indianapolis Concerns," *Indianapolis Star*, April 8, 1917, p 16.
11. "Empire," *Indianapolis Star*, April 22, 1917, p 16.
12. "The Aristocrat of the Road," *Indianapolis Star*, May 6, 1917, p 22.
13. "City to Obtain Tractor Plant," *Indianapolis Star*, February 24, 1917, p 2.
14. "Cole Begins New Expansion Plan," *Indianapolis Star*, January 16, 1917, p 17.
15. Base, "Heavy Increase in Ford Demand," *Indianapolis Star*, February 25, 1917, p 19.
16. "Hassler Car to Appear at Home," *Indianapolis Star*, February 4, 1917, p 59.
17. Hassler, "History of the Early American Automobiles," http://www.earlyamericanautomobiles.com/americanautomobiles20.htm. Accessed February 24, 2016.
18. Bull, "Indiana Leading in Auto Display," *Indianapolis Star*, January 10, 1917, p 11.
19. "Pathfinder Capital Now $5,000,000," *Indianapolis Star*, March 19, 1917, p 9.
20. "What's the Answer?" *Indianapolis Star*, April 22, 1917, p 18.
21. "Investing and Loyalty," *Indianapolis Star*, May 6, 1917, p 11.
22. Bull, "National Making 35 Cars Each Day," *Indianapolis Star*, March 4, 1917, p 21.
23. Base, "Motordome Needs Its Tester Still," *Indianapolis Star*, April 1, 1917, p 16.
24. Bull, "Auto Engineers of Indiana Hold Recruiting Party," *Indianapolis Star*, March 25, 1917, p 18.
25. "The New National Highway Twelve," *Horseless Age*, June 1, 1917, p 23.
26. Bull, "Service Feature Attracts Buyers," *Indianapolis Star*, February 9, 1917, p 5.
27. "Flames Damage Cole Auto Plant," *Indianapolis Star*, March 9, 1917, p 16.
28. Base, "Sterling Firm Betters Service," *Indianapolis Star*, April 8, 1917, p 17.
29. "Steel Scarcity Threatens Auto," *Indianapolis Star*, May 12, 1917, p 8.
30. Kennedy, *The Automobile Industry*, p 102.
31. "Steel Scarcity Threatens Auto," *Indianapolis Star*, May 12, 1917, p 8.
32. *Ibid.*
33. Bull, "Auto Engineers to Hear Airplane Expert Friday," *Indianapolis Star*, June 10, 1917, p 19.
34. "State Pours Out $2,000,000 More," *Indianapolis Star*, June 1, 1917, p 1.
35. "Bond Laggards Shy

$10,000,000," *Indianapolis Star*, June 14, 1917, p 6.
36. "40,000 to Be Visited for Bonds," *Indianapolis Star*, October 7, 1917, p 1.
37. "$2,700,000 Airplane Contract Awarded Here," *Indianapolis Star*, June 9, 1917, p 23.
38. "Coffin Resigns from Aircraft Board; Refuses Post in Reorganization," *Automotive Industries, the Automobile*, April 25, 1918, p 809.
39. "Recent Trade Developments," *Horseless Age*, September 15, 1917, p 46.
40. "Marmon Enlarging Plant," *Automotive Industries, the Automobile*, January 21, 1918, p 251.
41. "Marmon Tells of War Motor," *Indianapolis Star*, July 24, 1918, p 14.
42. "Marmon Enlarging Plant," *Automotive Industries, the Automobile*, January 21, 1918, p 251.
43. *Ibid*.
44. Base, "Utility, Slogan of Auto Show," *Indianapolis Star*, January 6, 1918, p 10.
45. "$20 Million Contract for Weidely Motors Company," *Automotive Industries, the Automobile*, January 21, 1918, p 251.
46. "Indiana Genius in Big Demand," *Indianapolis Star*, January 6, 1918, p 23.
47. "Gasoline Must Be Conserved," *Indianapolis Star*, October 28, 1917, p 19.
48. Bull, "Don't Speed Car down to Office," *Indianapolis Star*, October 28, 1917, p 19.
49. "Factory Begins Large Addition," *Indianapolis Star*, June 28, 1917, p 11.
50. Base, "Motor Truck Is Blessing," *Indianapolis Star*, December 9, 1917, p 18.
51. Base, "Signal Advent of Motor Truck," *Indianapolis Star*, April 15, 1917, p 17.
52. "Cole Plan of Floating Liberty Bonds Taken Before U.S. Officials," *Indianapolis Star*, May 23, 1917, p 10.
53. Bull, "Something New in Wheels for Cole Eight This Year," *Indianapolis Star*, May 9, 1917, p 9.
54. "City Gets New Auto Industry," *Indianapolis Star*, July 29, 1917, p 1.
55. "Empire," *Indianapolis Star*, August 26, 1917, p 20.
56. "National—with Airplane Type Motor," *Indianapolis Star*, November 11, 1917, p 18.
57. Johnson, "Earl Cooper, with a Stutz, Is Victor in Chicago Event," *Indianapolis Star*, June 17, 1917, p 45.
58. Base, "Motor Truck Is Coming into Own," *Indianapolis Star*, October 7, 1917, p 19.
59. "Stutz and Parry Donate Motor Ambulances," *Horseless Age*, May 1, 1917, p 48.
60. "Cole Company to Supply Autos for Pershing Staff," *Indianapolis Star*, November 2, 1917, p 13.

61. "Auto Company to Employ Girls on Big War Contract," *Indianapolis Star*, December 22, 1917, p 3.
62. "Recent Trade Developments," *Horseless Age*, August 1, 1917, p 56.
63. "Stutz Earns $1,074, 778," *Automotive Industries, the Automobile*, January 24, 1918, p 245.
64. "Pathfinder the Great," *Indianapolis Star*, January 13, 1918, p 9.
65. "To Auction Pathfinder and Springfield Body Plants," *Automotive Industries, the Automobile*, February 28, 1918, p 483.
66. Wikipedia, "Harry Augustus Garfield," https://en.wikipedia.org/wiki/Harry_Augustus_Garfield. Accessed February 26, 2016.
67. "Manufacturers More Optimistic," *Indianapolis Star*, January 19, 1918, p 10.
68. "Plants Calling Workers Back," *Indianapolis Star*, January 20, 1918, p 12.
69. "Indianapolis Industry Suspends," *Automotive Industries*, January 21, 1918, p 202.
70. "Forty-Two Marmons Start Overland for New York," *Indianapolis Star*, March 17, 1918, p 21.
71. "Marmon Price Increase," *Automotive Industries, the Automobile*, March 21, 1918, p 613.
72. "Motor Exhibit On in Chicago," *Indianapolis Star*, January 27, 1918, p 7.
73. "Cole Aero-Eight Wins Approval," *Indianapolis Star*, February 25, 1918, p 9.
74. "Changes in Cole Eights Add to Car's Efficiency," *Indianapolis Star*, March 24, 1918, p 21.
75. "Cole Aero-Eight Is Easy on Tires," *Indianapolis Star*, March 9, 1919, p 55.
76. "Cole Aero-Eight New in Body and Power," *Indianapolis Star*, March 10, 1918, p 21.
77. "More Women Driving Autos," *Indianapolis Star*, March 1, 1918, p 12.
78. "Industrial Building, Five Houses, Church, and Store Burned," *Indianapolis Star*, January 14, 1918, p 1 & 4.
79. "No Evidence Obtained to Fix Blame for Big Fire," *Indianapolis Star*, February 4, 1918, p 18.
80. "National Raises Prices," *Indianapolis Star*, February 10, 1918, p 5.
81. "Marmon," *Horseless Age*, January 1, 1918, p 36.
82. "Nordyke & Marmon," *Horseless Age*, April 1, 1918, p 47.
83. "Stutz," *Horseless Age*, January 1, 1918, p 38.
84. "Ace Entertains Plant Workers," *Indianapolis Star*, May 9, 1918, p 8.
85. "Stamp Pledge Given As War Work Buzzes," *Indianapolis Star*, June 26, 1918, p 1.
86. "Marmon Glory Is Lauded in Fitting Style," *Indianapolis Star*, November 3, 1918, p 37.

87. "Marmon Finishes Economy Test in Perfect Condition," *Indianapolis Star*, June 23, 1918, p 15.
88. "$50,000 Office Block Planned," *Indianapolis Star*, June 28, 1918, p 18.
89. "Wacker Completes New Power Complex," *Indianapolis Star*, July 29, 1918, p 5.
90. "New Marmon Branch Is Best," *Indianapolis Star*, August 11, 1918, p 18.
91. "Money's Worth in Seeing Autos," *Indianapolis Star*, March 11, 1919, p 8.
92. "Cole Company to Make Aero Type As Specialty," *Indianapolis Star*, November 3, 1918, p 23.
93. "French Government Buys 350 Marmon 34 Cars," *Indianapolis Star*, November 17, 1918, p 32.
94. "Marmon 34," *Indianapolis Star*, January 12, 1919, p 21.
95. "Auto Adjustment Period Is Put at Nine Months," *Indianapolis Star*, December 22, 1918, p 20.
96. Kennedy, *The Automobile Industry*, p 103.
97. "Auto Adjustment Period Is Put at Nine Months," *Indianapolis Star*, December 22, 1918, p 20.
98. "Cole Speeds Production and Lowers List Prices," *Indianapolis Star*, December 1, 1918, p 22.
99. "Cole Price Reduction of $300," *Automotive Industries, the Automobile*, December 19, 1918, p 1068.
100. "Monroe Plant Is Moved Here," *Indianapolis Star*, December 8, 1918, p 4.
101. "Monroe Sales Are Increasing," *Indianapolis Star*, March 9, 1919, p 20.
102. "Monroe Plant Is Moved Here," *Indianapolis Star*, December 8, 1918, p 4.
103. "Stutz Profits Drop," *Automotive Industries, the Automobile*, February 20, 1919, p 442.
104. Head, "Date of Auto Classic Here Changed to May 31," *Indianapolis Star*, December 15, 1918, p 45.

Chapter 12

1. "Local Firm Stages Victory Drive," *Indianapolis Star*, April 30, 1919, p 11.
2. "No Empire 1919 Models," *Automotive Industries*, January 9, 1919, p 78.
3. "Premier Motor Corp. Appoints Executive Committee," *Automotive Industries*, March 20, 1919, p 670.
4. "Post War Car to Be Lighter," *Indianapolis Star*, March 9, 1919, p 64.
5. "Indianapolis Picking up on Production," *Automotive Industries*, May 22, 1919, p 1141.
6. "33 of Fastest Cars in History Ready for Dash," *Indianapolis Star*, May 31, 1919, p 1.

7. Bull, "Race to Reveal War's Changes," *Indianapolis Star*, May 30, 1919, p 20.
8. Borgeson, *The Golden Age*, p 118.
9. Bull, "Race to Reveal War's Changes," *Indianapolis Star*, May 30, 1919, p 20.
10. "Official List of Drivers, Mechanicians, and Relief Men in Race at Speedway Today," *Indianapolis Star*, May 31, 1919, p 20.
11. "Marmon Plans Big Expansion," *Indianapolis Star*, June 24, 1919, p 1 & 8.
12. "Story Added from Bottom," *Indianapolis Star*, July 24, 1919, p 19.
13. "Marmon Plans Big Expansion," *Indianapolis Star*, June 24, 1919, p 1 & 8.
14. "$2,500,000 Nordyke & Marmon 6% Serial Gold Notes," *Indianapolis Star*, July 2, 1919, p 15.
15. "Huge Serial Note Issue Sold Out in Six Hours," *Indianapolis Star*, July 3, 1919, p 21.
16. "More Cars Announce an Advance in Price," *Automotive Industries*, August 21, 1919, p 394.
17. "Woolling Plans Big Apartment," *Indianapolis Star*, June 6, 1919, p 9.
18. "Louis Chevrolet Will Design for Monroe," *Automotive Industries*, September 18, 1919, p 589.
19. "Stutz Company Will Double Local Plant," *Indianapolis Star*, August 8, 1919, p 1.
20. "Approve Stutz Expansion," *Automotive Industries*, September 4, 1919, p 498.
21. "Stutz Named H.C.S. Dealer," *Indianapolis Star*, January 11, 1920, p 22.
22. "Harry C. Stutz Resigns As Head of Motor Plant," *Indianapolis Star*, June 21, 1919, p 1.
23. "Two Winners in Already Great Auto History of Indianapolis," *Indianapolis Star*, June 22, 1919, p 52.
24. "All Season Models Out," *Indianapolis Star*, August 3, 1919, p 53.
25. "New Windshield Is Storm Proof," *Indianapolis Star*, August 31, 1919, p 60.
26. "Cole Company Doubles Plant," *Indianapolis Star*, September 27, 1919, p 1 & 5.
27. "Push Production in Indiana Plants," *Automotive Industries*, October 2, 1919, p 695.
28. "Buys Premier Motor Control," *Indianapolis Star*, September 19, 1919, p 1 & 5.
29. "Skelton Takes Premier Helm," *Indianapolis Star*, October 15, 1919, p 13.
30. "Creditors Paid in Full," *Indianapolis Star*, November 14, 1919, p 10.
31. Ibid.
32. "Assure Future for Mars Hill," *Indianapolis Star*, October 14, 1919, p 12.
33. "Stock Is Oversubscribed," *Indianapolis Star*, October 26, 1919, p 67.
34. "Will Produce LaFayette Cars," *Indianapolis Star*, October 7, 1919, p 1.
35. "Plans Factory Addition," *Indianapolis Star*, December 28, 1919, p 10.
36. "Lafayette Debut at Commodore Hotel," *Automotive Industries*, December 11, 1919, p 1189.
37. "Co-Operative Store Opens," *Indianapolis Star*, October 18, 1919, p 13.
38. "City Leader in Fine Cars," *Indianapolis Star*, December 14, 1919, p 78.
39. "Harry E. Stutz to Make New Car," *Automotive Industries*, October 16, 1919, p 800.
40. "Coal Shortage Sure to Appear During Winter," *Chicago Tribune*, September 1, 1919, p 7.
41. "Ready to Push Coal Embargo," *Indianapolis Star*, December 3, 1919, p 1.
42. "Gasoline Engines Supply Automobile's Plant During Coal Shortage," *Indianapolis Star*, December 14, 1919, p 3.
43. "Famous Racing Motor Put to Work in Auto Factory," *Indianapolis Star*, December 7, 1919, p 35.
44. "Automobile Motors and Tractors Maintain Car Production," *Indianapolis Star*, December 7, 1919, p 63.
45. "News and Views of the Auto Trade," *Indianapolis Star*, October 19, 1919, p 64.
46. "Sextet Coupe at Auto Show," *Indianapolis Star*, December 14, 1919, p 76.
47. "Much Praise for Sextets," *Indianapolis Star*, October 26, 1919, p 71.
48. "National Price Increase," *Automotive Industries*, October 16, 1919, p 788.
49. "Marmon Output to Be Doubled," *Indianapolis Star*, September 2, 1919, p 9.
50. "Stutz Company Plans Production of 5,000 in 1920," *Automotive Industries*, February 5, 1920, p 430.

Chapter 13

1. "Gotham Sees Hoosier Car," *Indianapolis Star*, January 4, 1920, p 60.
2. Bull, "Indiana Cars Loom at Show," *Indianapolis Star*, January 4, 1920, p 1.
3. Ibid.
4. Schipper, "Heavy Crankshaft Features New Marmon Engine," *Automotive Industries*, January 29, 1920, p 347.
5. "The New Marmon," *Indianapolis Star*, January 4, 1920, p 6.
6. "Marmon Sets New Records," *Indianapolis Star*, January 25, 1920, p 62.
7. Kennedy, *The Automobile Industry*, 138.
8. Ibid., 106.
9. Ibid., 114.
10. "Prices on Marmon Models Raised $350," *Automotive Industries*, February 5, 1920, p 442.
11. "Boost Stock to $3,000,000," *Indianapolis Star*, February 29, 1920, p 13.
12. "Report National to Enter Truck Field," *Automotive Industries*, January 15, 1920, p 287.
13. "Construction Company Reports New Building Equaling War Record," *Indianapolis Star*, January 5, 1920, p 4.
14. "Cole Plans Double Output This Year," *Automotive Industries*, January 8, 1920, p 101.
15. "Construction Company Reports New Building Equaling War Record," *Indianapolis Star*, January 5, 1920, p 4.
16. "LaFayette Building Company," *Indianapolis Star*, March 17, 1920, p 11.
17. "City of Model Homes Rises for Motor Company Employees," *Indianapolis Star*, August 13, 1920, p 10 & 11.
18. "Bedford Company Has Busy Season," *Indianapolis Star*, July 12, 1920, p 8.
19. "Stop Put to Stutz Trading," *Indianapolis Star*, April 1, 1920, p 4.
20. "Ryan to Start War on Banks," *Indianapolis Star*, November 28, 1920, p 2.
21. "Stutz 'Corners' Stirs Interest," *Indianapolis Star*, April 12, 1920, p 5.
22. "Ryan Resigns Seat on Stock Exchange," *Automotive Industries*, April 15, 1920, p 942.
23. "Heads Stutz Company," *Indianapolis Star*, April 6, 1920, p 5.
24. "Ryan Resigns Seat On Stock Exchange," *Automotive Industries*, April 15, 1920, p 942.
25. "Charges Made Against Ryan," *Indianapolis Star*, April 11, 1920, p 2.
26. "H.C.S. Motors Company Builds Factory," *Indianapolis Star*, April 11, 1920, p 13.
27. "Indiana Factories Hard Hit by Strike," *Automotive Industries*, April 22, 1920, p 982.
28. "National Develops New Touring Model," *Automotive Industries*, May 20, 1920, p 1178.
29. Borgeson, *The Golden Age*, p 122.
30. Wolff, "Duesenberg," *Automobile Quarterly*, Vol. 4, No. 4, p 355.
31. "The Duesenberg—The Speedway Racing Sensation of 1920," *Indianapolis Star*, July 8, 1920, p 17.
32. "Foreign Entry List Expected to Prove Fast," *Indianapolis Star*, March 28, 1920, p 25.
33. "Duesenberg Locates Here," *Indianapolis Star*, May 14, 1920, p 8.
34. "Tommy Milton to Pilot Monroe in Auto Classic," *Indianapolis Star*, May 19, 1920, p 11.

35. "Milton's Car Will Arrive in Town Today," *Indianapolis Star*, May 22, 1920, p 11.
36. "Monroe Cars Take to Track," *Indianapolis Star*, May 21, 1920, p 8.
37. "Monroe Drivers Out to Give City a Victory," *Indianapolis Star*, May 30, 1920, p 30.
38. Wolff, "Duesenberg: It's A Grand Old Name," *Automobile Quarterly*, Spring 1966, Vol. 4, No. 4, p 53.
39. "Duesenberg Locates Here," *Indianapolis Star*, May 14, 1920, p 8.
40. Duesenberg Stock Subscription Ad, *Indianapolis Star*, May 21, 1920, p 14.
41. "Duesenberg Locates Here," *Indianapolis Star*, May 14, 1920, p 8.
42. "Duesenberg Designs Special Axle for Car," *Automotive Industries*, May 20, 1920, p 1191.
43. "Duesenberg Buys Indianapolis Site," *Automotive Industries*, May 12, 1920, p 1135.
44. "Duesenberg Designs Special Axle for Car," *Automotive Industries*, May 20, 1920, p 1191.
45. "One More Indianapolis Made Car," *Indianapolis Star*, May 14, 1920, p 6.
46. Duesenberg Stock Subscription Ad, *Indianapolis Star*, May 29, 1920, p 19.
47. "Duesenberg Given Great Chance for Slice of $50,000," *Indianapolis Star*, May 23, 1920, p 27.
48. Duesenberg Stock Subscription Ad, *Indianapolis Star*, May 29, 1920, p 19.
49. "Automobile Firm Sues," *Indianapolis Star*, May 21, 1920, p 6.
50. "Monroe Cars Take To Track." *Indianapolis Star*, May 21, 1920, p 8.
51. Borgeson, *The Golden Age*, p 22.
52. "DePalma Gets the Pole at Start of Big Race," *Indianapolis Star*, May 27, 1920, p 14.
53. "Four More Qualify for Big Speedway Classic," *Indianapolis Star*, May 29, 1920, p 9.
54. "DePalma Big Favorite to Win Classic," *Indianapolis Star*, May 31, 1920, p 11.
55. "Monroe Wins," *Indianapolis Star*, June 1, 1920, p 10.
56. Feightner, "Gaston Chevrolet Wins," *Indianapolis Star*, June 1, 1920, p 1.
57. "Monroe Wins," *Indianapolis Star*, June 1, 1920, p 10.
58. "Race Winners Given Prizes," *Indianapolis Star*, June 2, 1920, p 1.
59. "Monroe Wins," *Indianapolis Star*, June 1, 1920, p 10.
60. Duesenberg Automobile & Motors Co., Inc. stock offering, *Indianapolis Star*, June 14, 1920, p 15.
61. "The Duesenberg—The Speedway Racing Sensation of 1920," *Indianapolis Star*, July 8, 1920, p 17.
62. "Duesenberg Sweeps the Field at Uniontown," *Indianapolis Star*, June 23, 1920, p 14.
63. "Record Set by Cole Cars," *Indianapolis Star*, August 1, 1920, p 8.
64. "City News in Brief," *Indianapolis Star*, August 24, 1920, p 5.
65. "End of Receivership Seen in Rush of Auto Orders," *Indianapolis Star*, March 11, 1921, p 15.
66. "Auto Industry Booming Here," *Indianapolis Star*, September 4, 1920, p 18.
67. Ibid.
68. Ibid.
69. "Survey Shows Gain," *Indianapolis Star*, January 24, 1921, p 5.
70. Kennedy, *The Automobile Industry*, p 119.
71. Ibid., p 120.
72. "HCS," *Indianapolis Star*, October 17, 1920, p 22.
73. "Eight Cylinder Automobile Has Light Weight Feature," *Automotive Industries*, August 19, 1920, p 362.
74. "Auto Price Is Unchanged," *Indianapolis Star*, October 16, 1920, p 20.
75. "No Cut in Cole Price," *Indianapolis Star*, October 9, 1920, p 10.
76. Heldt, "Duesenberg Car Has 'Straight-Eight' Engine and Four Wheel Brakes," *Automotive Industries*, November 18, 1920, p 1007.
77. Heldt, "Duesenberg Car Has 'Straight-Eight' Engine and Four Wheel Brakes," *Automotive Industries*, November 18, 1920, p 1007.
78. Ibid.
79. "National to Increase Stock," *Automotive Industries*, December 9, 1920, p 1196.
80. "Ryan's Difficulties Not Serious to Stutz," *Automotive Industries*, December 2, 1920, p 1147.

Chapter 14

1. "Duesenbergs Catch Eye," *Indianapolis Star*, February 17, 1921, p 11.
2. Steinwedel and Newport, *The Duesenberg*, p 25.
3. Ibid., p 21.
4. "Companies Obtain Permits for $175,000 Projects," *Indianapolis Star*, January 27, 1921, p 5.
5. "Duesenberg Plant Turns Out First Cars for Trade," *Indianapolis Star*, May 28, 1921, p 3.
6. "Small Stockholders to Advance $200,000," *Automotive Industries*, May 5, 1921, p 979.
7. "Monroe," *Indianapolis Star*, May 25, 1921, p 5.
8. "Small Property to Be Sold," *Automotive Industries*, December 22, 1921, p 1242.
9. "Dr. L. S. Skelton Dies in West," *Indianapolis Star*, January 29, 1921, p 20.
10. "Premier Directors Plan to Reorganize Company," *Indianapolis Star*, February 10, 1921, p 8.
11. "Premier Motor Files New Incorporation," *Automotive Industries*, April 7, 1921, p 783.
12. "Sues to Annul Skelton Policy," *Indianapolis Star*, May 18, 1921, p 18.
13. "Industry Here Gaining," *Indianapolis Star*, March 18, 1921, p 5.
14. "Marmon Cuts Price to New Cost Basis," *Automotive Industries*, May 5, 1921, p 978.
15. Kennedy, *The Automobile Industry*, p 130.
16. "Wall Street Gossip," *Indianapolis Star*, May 11, 1921, p 16.
17. "Sales Slump Hits Lines Not Reduced," *Automotive Industries*, May 19, 1921, p 1076.
18. "Fire Damages Stutz Plant," *Automotive Industries*, May 19, 1921, p 1086.
19. Schleppey, "Thirteen Drivers Will Make Elimination Trial Today," *Indianapolis Star*, May 27, 1921, p 1.
20. Ibid.
21. "How the Drivers Will Line Up at Speedway," *Indianapolis Star*, May 29, 1921, p 13.
22. Schleppey, "Thirteen Drivers Will Make Elimination Trial Today," *Indianapolis Star*, May 27, 1921, p 1.
23. "World's Best Ready," *Indianapolis Star*, May 30, 1921, p 13.
24. "Seven Indianapolis Machines Capture Most of Prize Money," *Indianapolis Star*, May 31, 1921, p 1.
25. "Milton Wins 500-Mile Race," *Indianapolis Star*, May 31, 1921, p 1.
26. "Frontenacs and 'Duesies' Clash," *Indianapolis Star*, June 12, 1921, p 36.
27. "Sarles Winner at Uniontown," *Indianapolis Star*, June 19, 1921, p 25.
28. "Cole Aero-Eight Prices Come Down $455 to $700," *Indianapolis Star*, June 29, 1921, p 5.
29. "Premier Motor Company Cuts Prices $710 to $910," *Indianapolis Star*, July 1, 1921, p 18.
30. "National Makes Big Cut," *Automotive Industries*, June 30, 1921, p 1457.
31. "Stutz Prices Down $650," *Automotive Industries*, June 30, 1921, p 1457.
32. "Lafayette Prices Cut Ranging $750 to $950," *Automotive Industries*, June 2, 1921, p 1184.
33. "H.C.S. Motor Car Company Cuts Prices Tomorrow," *Indianapolis Star*, July 31, 1921, p 24.
34. Borgeson, *The Golden Age*, p 140.
35. "Champion, Spark Plug Maker, Dies," *Indianapolis Star*, October 28, 1927, p 12.
36. "Joe Murphy Hurt When Duesenberg Racer Turns Over," *Indianapolis Star*, July 16, 1921, p 10.

37. Borgeson, *The Golden Age*, p 144 & 146.
38. "Duesenberg Quits Racing to Build Stock Cars," *Automotive Industries*, June 16, 1921, p 1360.
39. Schipper, "New Duesenberg Reflects Experience Gained with Racing Cars," *Automotive Industries*, November 3, 1921, p 854 & 858.
40. "New Closed Body Types Introduced by Marmon," *Indianapolis Star*, September 18, 1921, p 64.
41. "Motor Heads Deny Merger," *Indianapolis Star*, September 29, 1921, p 5.
42. "Speed Kings in Big Race Here," *Indianapolis Star*, September 12, 1921, p 14.
43. "Milton Enters Speedway Race," *Indianapolis Star*, September 21, 1921, p 10.
44. "Wilcox's Peugeot Wins Invitational Speed Race," *Indianapolis Star*, September 22, 1921, p 13.
45. "Hearne Is Winner of Foch Race at Motor Speedway," *Indianapolis Star*, November 5, 1921, p 11.
46. "Cole Aero-Eight Model Is Reduced to $2,485," *Indianapolis Star*, October 27, 1921, p 3.
47. "Engineer of LaFayette Motors Company Resigns," *Indianapolis Star*, October 14, 1921, p 8.
48. "Stutz Reports Net Loss of $632,370 at End of 1921," *Automotive Industries*, May 25, 1922, p 1145.
49. "Petition Asks Receiver for Premier Motor Firm," *Indianapolis Star*, December 11, 1921, p 8.
50. "Premier Takes Steps Toward Refinancing," *Indianapolis Star*, January 21, 1922, p 16.

Chapter 15

1. "Ryan Heads Company Producing Frontenac," *Automotive Industries*, January 5, 1922, p 40.
2. "Stutz Head Mentioned As Frontenac President," *Automotive Industries*, January 12, 1922, p 90.
3. "Ryan Heads Company Producing Frontenac," *Automotive Industries*, January 5, 1922, p 40.
4. "Allan A. Ryan Resigns from Stutz Directorate," *Automotive Industries*, January 19, 1922, p 155.
5. "Stutz Makes Revisions," *Automotive Industries*, January 5, 1922, p 37.
6. Hannagan, "Indiana Cars Center of Show," *Indianapolis Star*, January 8, 1922, p 11.
7. "Marmon Automobiles Reduced in Price," *Indianapolis Star*, January 4, 1922, p 3.
8. "Business Men Optimistic," *Indianapolis Star*, January 16, 1922, p 16.
9. "LaFayette Motors Shows Second Cut in Prices," *Indianapolis Star*, January 8, 1922, p 59.
10. "Carnival Reigns at Show," *Indianapolis Star*, March 11, 1922, p 5.
11. "Small Property Sold to Bank for $175,000," *Automotive Industries*, January 5, 1922, p 36.
12. "National Motor to Issue Bonds," *Indianapolis Star*, January 24, 1922, p 1.
13. "Denies Need of Receiver," *Indianapolis Star*, March 23, 1922, p 9.
14. "National Gains Financing," *Indianapolis Star*, April 8, 1922, p 15, and "New Working Funds Provided National," *Automotive Industries*, April 22, 1922, p 836.
15. Schipper, "Powerplant in New Stutz Model Incorporates Many Changes," *Automotive Industries*, April 6, 1922, p 750–751.
16. "May Buy Frontenac Site," *Indianapolis Star*, March 10, 1922, p 1 & 21.
17. "Six Frontenacs Enter Big Race," *Indianapolis Star*, February 12, 1922, p 23.
18. "May Buy Frontenac Site," *Indianapolis Star*, March 10, 1922, p 1 & 21.
19. "Frontenac Company Buys Site Here," *Indianapolis Star*, April 12, 1922, p 1 & 19.
20. Ibid.
21. "Stutz Factory Well Equipped," *Indianapolis Star*, April 9, 1922, p 54.
22. "Confirm Motor Merger," *Indianapolis Star*, April 15, 1922, p 3.
23. "Pierce-Lafayette Merger Announced," *Automotive Industries*, p 1090.
24. "Announce Reorganization of LaFayette Motors," *Indianapolis Star*, June 3, 1922, p 12.
25. "Plan Would Put Nash Closer to Lafayette," *Automotive Industries*, June 8, 1922, p 1294.
26. "Approves Recapitalization," *Indianapolis Star*, June 22, 1922, p 3.
27. "Kenosha Auto Magnate Finances LaFayette Motors," *Indianapolis Star*, June 6, 1922, p 16.
28. "LaFayette Motors to Quit Indianapolis," *Indianapolis Star*, July 30, 1922, p 12.
29. "Skinner Tells of Increase in 1922," *Indianapolis Star*, January 8, 1923, p 10.
30. "A 'Going Concern'—and Going Good," *Indianapolis Star*, January 22, 1922, p 34.
31. "Duesenberg Automobile & Motors Co., Inc.," *Automotive Industries*, June 15, 1922, p 1356.
32. "A 'Going Concern'—and Going Good," *Indianapolis Star*, January 22, 1922, p 34.
33. "Majority Creditors Accept Premier Plan," *Automotive Industries*, March 23, 1922, p 692.
34. "Bank Receiver for Premier Company," *Indianapolis Star*, July 2, 1922, p 12.
35. Ibid.
36. "Premier to Be Sold As Part of New Plan," *Automotive Industries*, October 12, 1922, Vol. 47, p 738.
37. "Alexander Heads Monroe Sales; New Idea in Selling," *Indianapolis Star*, April 16, 1922, p 63.
38. "Milton," *Indianapolis Star*, March 6, 1922, p 16.
39. "Auto Industry Shows Trend Toward Normal," *Indianapolis Star*, May 22, 1922, p 10.
40. "Murphy Goes 120.3 on Beverley Hills Track," *Indianapolis Star*, May 18, 1922, p 14.
41. Patton, "Hearne in Ballot Wins 15-Mile Race," *Indianapolis Star*, May 23, 1922, p 13.
42. Patton, "Nineteen Cars Qualify for Speedway Marathon," *Indianapolis Star*, May 26, 1922, p 14.
43. Patton, "Murphy Drives Record Race," *Indianapolis Star*, May 31, 1922, p 1.
44. Patton, "Nineteen Cars Qualify for Speedway Marathon," *Indianapolis Star*, May 26, 1922, p 14.
45. Patton, "Speedway Race Occupies Spotlight of Sportdom with 26 Cars Ready," *Indianapolis Star*, May 30, 1922, p 1 & 3.
46. "Racing Autoists to Be Directed by Radio 'Phone,'" *Indianapolis Star*, April 8, 1922, p 1.
47. Patton, "Speedway Race Occupies Spotlight of Sportdom with 26 Cars Ready," *Indianapolis Star*, May 30, 1922, p 1 & 3.
48. "Three Monroes to Be in Race," *Indianapolis Star*, April 30, 1922, p 22.
49. Patton, "Murphy Drives Record Race," *Indianapolis Star*, May 31, 1922, p 1.
50. RacingReference.info. http://racing-reference.info/race/1922–01/X. Accessed January 18, 2016.
51. "Murphy Winner in Race at Uniontown," *Indianapolis Star*, June 18, 1922, p 25.
52. "Indianapolis Is Third City in Country in Automobile," *Indianapolis Star*, June 19, 1922, p 8.
53. Ibid.
54. "National Will Join Associated Motors," *Automotive Industries*, June 22, 1922, p 1402.
55. "$80,000,000 in Motor Merger," *Indianapolis Star*, July 2, 1922, p 1 & 6.
56. "New Series Cole Is Distinctive in Feature Creations," *Indianapolis Star*, July 25, 1922, p 16.
57. "New Capital to Aid Stutz Development," *Automotive Industries*, October 19, 1922, p 789.
58. "Dealers Meet Schwab at Stutz Meeting," *Automotive Industries*, November 16, 1922, p 1003.
59. "Duesenberg Adds $30,000 Building to Factory Here," *Indianapolis Star*, August 16, 1922, p 8.
60. "Heavy Transfer Work Im-

proves," *Indianapolis Star*, November 27, 1922, p 9.
61. "Believe Fire Screened Work of Iron Wreckers," *Indianapolis Star*, September 21, p 1 & 3.
62. *Ibid*.
63. "John J. M'Namara Convicted of Blackmail Charge; Judge to Pass Sentence Next Week," *Indianapolis Star*, September 23, 1925, p 1 & 2.
64. "Believe Fire Screened Work of Iron Wreckers," *Indianapolis Star*, September 21, p 1 & 3.
65. "John J. M'Namara Convicted of Blackmail Charge; Judge to Pass Sentence Next Week," *Indianapolis Star*, September 23, 1925, p 1 & 2.
66. "Marmon Changes Phaeton," *Automotive Industries*, August 17, 1922, p 339.
67. "Allan Ryan Files Bankruptcy Papers," *Automotive Industries*, July 27, 1922, p 194.
68. "May Relist Stutz to Protect Banks," *Indianapolis Star*, July 25, 1922, p 3.
69. "Stutz Control Goes to Guaranty," *Automotive Industries*, August 3, 1922, p 247.
70. "Stutz Control Goes to Schwab Interests," *Automotive Industries*, August 10, 1922, p 296.
71. "No Changes Planned in Stutz Personnel," *Automotive Industries*, August 17, 1922, p 338.
72. "Schwab Plans to Put More Money in Stutz Plant and Enlarge Operations," *Indianapolis Star*, August 12, 1922, p 12.
73. "Stutz Produces Closed Models As Part of Line," *Automotive Industries*, November 30, 1922, p 1098.
74. "Price of Cole to Be Reduced Soon; Capital Doubled," *Indianapolis Star*, December 30, 1922, p 5.
75. "Hoosier Cars Draw Interest at New York Motor Show," *Indianapolis Star*, January 7, 1923, p 52.
76. "Associated Motors Under New Name," *Indianapolis Star*, January 21, 1923, p 61.
77. "Incorporations," *Indianapolis Star*, January 25, 1922, p 17.
78. "Associated Motors Under New Name," *Indianapolis Star*, January 21, 1923, p 61.
79. "Hoosier Cars Draw Interest at New York Motor Show," *Indianapolis Star*, January 7, 1923, p 32.
80. "H.C.S. Six-Cylinder Model," *Indianapolis Star*, January 6, 1923, p 8.
81. "H.C.S. Produces New Six-Cylinder Model," *Automotive Industries*, January 4, 1923, p 42.
82. "Stutz Has Six-Cylinder; Conference with Schwab," *Automotive Industries*, January 4, 1923, p 43 & 46.
83. "Stutz Motor Car. Co. of America," *Automotive Industries*, January 18, 1923, p 156.

84. "Duesenberg Cuts List and Adds Sport Model," *Automotive Industries*, February 8, 1923, p 303.
85. "Spring Automobile Industry in Prosperous Condition," *Indianapolis Star*, March 18, 1923, p 60.
86. "National Will Make All Its Own Parts," *Automotive Industries*, January 11, 1923, p 94.
87. "National Issues Bonds," *Indianapolis Star*, March 30, 1923, p 20.
88. "Lighter Cars Being Built for 1923 Race," *Indianapolis Star*, January 7, 1923, p 35.
89. "Murphy Winner in Los Angeles Race," *Indianapolis Star*, February 26, 1923, p 14.
90. "New Automobile Selling Corporation Is Formed," *Indianapolis Star*, March 24, 1923, p 1 & 5.
91. *Ibid*.
92. "Stratton Company Seeks Third Plant to Make New Car," *Indianapolis Star*, March 25, 1923, p 19.
93. "Interest in Monroe Car Disposed of by Stratton," *Automotive Industries*, June 21, 1923, p 1353.
94. "Reorganization of Premier Motors Is Accepted by Court," *Indianapolis Star*, May 22, 1923, p 1 & 3.
95. "Premier Purchaser to Operate Factory," *Automotive Industries*, May 24, 1923, p 1146.
96. "Reorganization of Premier Motors Is Accepted by Court," *Indianapolis Star*, May 22, 1923, p 1 & 3.
97. Stanley, *Custom Built by McFarlan*, p 163.
98. "Reorganization of Premier Motors Is Accepted by Court," *Indianapolis Star*, May 22, 1923, p 1 & 3.
99. *Ibid*.
100. "Premier Plans to Ship First Taxicab in July," *Automotive Industries*, June 21, 1923, p 1351.
101. "U.S. Stops Sale of Premier Assets," *Indianapolis Star*, June 22, 1923, p 24.
102. "Barrows of Premier Also Heads Monroe," *Automotive Industries*, June 28, 1923, p 1440.
103. "Indianapolis Plant Bought for New Elgin," *Automotive Industries*, June 7, 1923, p 1250.
104. Kennedy, *The Automobile Industry*, p 139.
105. *Ibid.*, p 140.
106. "Cole Takes Lead in New Sales Plan," *Indianapolis Star*, February 4, 1923, p 12.
107. "Cole Discount Plan Is Aimed at Trading," *Automotive Industries*, January 11, 1923, p 98.
108. "Cole Takes Lead in New Sales Plan," *Indianapolis Star*, February 4, 1923, p 12.
109. "Huge Sums Invested in Used Motor Cars," *Indianapolis Star*, May 6, 1923, p 24.
110. "Cole Dealers Agree to Quit

All Trading," *Automotive Industries*, January 25, 1923, p 196.
111. Kennedy, *The Automobile Industry*, p 146.
112. "Asks Receivership for Duesenberg Co," *Indianapolis Star*, April 13, 1923, p 9.
113. "Duesenberg Case Draws near Close," *Indianapolis Star*, April 19, 1923, p 19.
114. *Ibid*.
115. "Court Declines to Name Receiver for Duesenberg Car Co.," *Indianapolis Star*, April 20, 1923, p 11.
116. "Frontenac Bankrupt with $88,163 Debts," *Automotive Industries*, April 19, 1923, p 896.
117. "Stock Duesenberg Makes Record Run," *Indianapolis Star*, April 30, 1923, p 3.
118. "Marmon Announces National Survey of Upkeep Costs," *Indianapolis Star*, March 4, 1923, p 64.
119. "Marmon Displays Speedster Model," *Indianapolis Star*, April 22, 1922, p 63.
120. "Stutz Outgrows Quarters; Leases Old 'Birthplace,'" *Indianapolis Star*, May 22, 1923, p 9.
121. Patton, "Observed from the Speedway Pits," *Indianapolis Star*, May 26, 1923, p 12 & 15.
122. *Ibid*.
123. Haynes, "Indianapolis Made Car Wins Laurels in Classic," *Indianapolis Star*, May 31, 1924, p 8.
124. Patton, "3 Duesenbergs Get Chance to Meet Test This Morning," *Indianapolis Star*, May 30, 1923, p 1.
125. Haynes, "Indianapolis Made Car Wins Laurels in Classic," *Indianapolis Star*, May 31, 1923, p 8.
126. Borgeson, *The Golden Age*, p 126.
127. "Milton Wins; Hartz 2nd; Murphy 3rd," *Indianapolis Star*, May 31, 1923, p 1.
128. "'Stutz of Old' Comes Back in Spectacular H.C.S. Victory," *Indianapolis Star*, May 31, 1923, p 10.
129. *Ibid*.
130. "H.C.S. Special Wins 500-Mile Race," *Indianapolis Star*, May 31, 1923, p 15.
131. "Cole Company Sets June 10 As New Model Day at Plant," *Indianapolis Star*, June 10, 1923, p 33.
132. "Cole Is Producing New Master Series," *Automotive Industries*, June 14, 1923, p 1303.
133. "Drives Cole 101.5 Miles in One Hour, 57 Minutes," *Indianapolis Star*, May 26, 1923, p 23.
134. "E. G. 'Cannonball' Baker in a Cole," *Indianapolis Star*, July 22, 1923, p 25.
135. "Baker Establishes Five Speed and Five Economy Records in Cole Master Model," *Indianapolis Star*, August 19, 1923, p 32.

136. *Ibid.*
137. "Premier Sets Another Remarkable Record," *Indianapolis Star*, June 17, 1923, p 72.
138. "New Duesenberg Roadster Equipped with Rubay Body," *Automotive Industries*, July 19, 1923, p 147.
139. "Stutz to Build Its Own Six-Cylinder Power Plants," *Automotive Industries*, August 2, 1923, p 246.
140. "Receivership Hearing of Motor Firm Continued," *Indianapolis Star*, July 19, 1923, p 18.
141. "Suit for Receivership Filed Against National," *Automotive Industries*, July 12, 1923, p 94.
142. "National Sued on Notes of Company It Succeeded," *Automotive Industries*, November 1, 1923, p 927.
143. "The Motors Is Put on Sound Basis," *Indianapolis Star*, July 28, 1923, p 1.
144. "National Reports New Finance Plan," *Automotive Industries*, August 2, 1923, p 252.
145. "National Motors Is Put on Sound Basis," *Indianapolis Star*, July 28, 1923, p 1.
146. "National Motors Is Mortgaged for Sum of $5,750,000," *Indianapolis Star*, August 7, 1923, p 18.
147. "Receiver Appointed for Weidley Motors," *Automotive Industries*, August 2, 1923, p 250.
148. "Premier Taxicabs Driven in Parade," *Indianapolis Star*, August 12, 1923, p 8.
149. "Monroe Factory Head," *Indianapolis Star*, August 12, 1923, p 32.
150. "Leeds to Direct Sale of Premier and Monroe Cars," *Indianapolis Star*, November 11, 1923, p 44.
151. "Premier Will Build 7-Passenger Sedan," *Automotive Industries*, September 20, 1923, p 606.
152. "Suit for Receivership Filed Against Premier," *Automotive Industries*, November 1, 1923, p 923.
153. "Premier Suit Settled," *Indianapolis Star*, November 3, 1923, p 13.
154. "Marmon Adopts Front-Wheel Brakes As Optional Equipment," *Automotive Industries*, September 27, 1923, p 632.
155. "Cole Adopts Balloon Tires As Equipment on 1924 Models," *Indianapolis Star*, September 2, 1923, p 45.
156. "Balloon Tires on H.C.S. Motor Cars," *Indianapolis Star*, December 9, 1923, p 77.
157. "1924 Cole Master Model on Display at Show This Week," *Indianapolis Star*, September 2, 1923, p 42.
158. "Duesenberg Leases Additional Space," *Indianapolis Star*, October 21, 1923, p 49.
159. "Warehouse Fire Damages Bodies for Duesenberg," *Automotive Industries*, November 29, 1923, p 1121.
160. "Hill Wins 250-Mile Race in Duesenberg; Averages 112.44 Miles Per Hour," *Indianapolis Star*, November 30, 1923, p 15.
161. "$500,000 New Money Obtained by Premier," *Automotive Industries*, December 13, 1923, p 1224.
162. "Marmon Stock Touring Car Triumphs by Winning the 'Grand Prix of the Alps,'" *Indianapolis Star*, October 28, 1923, p 47.
163. "Stutz to Build Engine for New Model in Its Own Plant," *Automotive Industries*, December 27, 1923, p 1296–1300.

Chapter 16

1. Haynes, "Motor Dust and Scissor Thrust," *Indianapolis Star*, December 7, 1924, p 69.
2. Kennedy, *The Automobile Industry*, p 161 & 162.
3. "Names Receiver for Duesenberg Automobile Firm," *Indianapolis Star*, January 4, 1924, p 15.
4. "Grants Duesenberg Trade Mark of Straight Eight," *Indianapolis Star*, January 13, 1924, p 59.
5. "Chief Officers Quit National Motors," *Indianapolis Star*, January 20, 1924, p 10.
6. "Incorporations," *Indianapolis Star*, February 9, 1924, p 21.
7. "Weidley Sale Approved; Will Resume Operations," *Automotive Industries*, January 24, 1924, p 204.
8. "Auto Show Is Tribute to Last Year's Models," *Indianapolis Star*, January 7, 1924, p 9.
9. "Stutz Production Increased to Meet Demand," *Indianapolis Star*, January 27, 1924, p 55.
10. "Balloon Tires on Marmon," *Indianapolis Star*, January 6, 1924, p 57.
11. "Barney Oldfield Gives Estimate of Balloon Tires," *Indianapolis Star*, February 17, 1924, p 59.
12. "Racing Engineers Select Marmons for Private Use," *Indianapolis Star*, March 6, 1924, p 12.
13. "Marmon Announces Sixteen Distinct New Refinements," *Indianapolis Star*, March 2, 1924, p 72.
14. *Ibid.*
15. "Three Factories Increase Prices," *Indianapolis Star*, April 13, 1924, p 75.
16. "Marmon Official on Trust Board," *Indianapolis Star*, April 14, 1926, p 1.
17. "G. M. Williams New Marmon Head," *Indianapolis Star*, May 16, 1924, p 16.
18. "Work in New York Scarce, Is Report," *Indianapolis Star*, May 8, 1924, p 21.
19. Patton, "Observed from the Speedway Pits," *Indianapolis Star*, May 25, 1924, p 23.
20. Bostwick, "Pilgrims Stop at Cleveland," *Indianapolis Star*, May 1, 1924, p 24.
21. Patton, "Observed from the Speedway Pits," *Indianapolis Star*, May 27, 1924, p 42.
22. "At the Two Speedways," *Indianapolis Star*, April 25, 1924, p 18.
23. Patton, "Observed from the Speedway Pits," *Indianapolis Star*, May 27, 1924, p 14.
24. Patton, "Cars Qualified in Speedway Race Pass Speed Mark," *Indianapolis Star*, May 29, 1924, p 1.
25. "Speedway Founders Honored at Smoker," *Indianapolis Star*, May 30, 1924, p 13 & 15.
26. *Ibid.*
27. Patton, "22 Street Chariots to Start in Speed Classic," *Indianapolis Star*, May 30, 1924, p 1 & 29.
28. Patton, "Speedway Victor Smashes Record," *Indianapolis Star*, May 31, 1924, p 1.
29. "Winners of Speed Classic Rewarded," *Indianapolis Star*, June 1, 1924, p 1.
30. Haynes, "Indianapolis Made Car Wins Laurels in Classic," *Indianapolis Star*, May 31, 1923, p 8.
31. *Ibid.*
32. "Plant Enlarges Working Force 100 Men Daily," *Indianapolis Star*, August 22, 1924, p 18.
33. "Mitchell Controls Marmon Outturn," *Indianapolis Star*, September 28, 1924, p 60.
34. "Elgin Sued for Salary; Receiver Is Appointed," *Automotive Industries*, July 3, 1924, p 76.
35. "Stutz Is President of New Cab Company," *Automotive Industries*, October 16, 1924, p 700.
36. "H.C.S. Firm Enters Taxi Cab Field to Broaden Industry," *Indianapolis Star*, June 29, 1924, p 67.
37. "New H.C.S. Taxicab Meets High Favor in U.S. Cities," *Indianapolis Star*, September 21, 1924, p 62.
38. "Frontenac to Build New Straight Eight," *Automotive Industries*, July 21, 1924, p 260.
39. "Murphy Wins 250-Mile Race on Altoona Track," *Indianapolis Star*, June 15, 1924, p 25.
40. "Lilly Convention Sees Auto Race," *Indianapolis Star*, August 19, 1924, p 9.
41. "Crash Is Fatal to Joe Boyer," *Indianapolis Star*, September 2, 1924, p 1.
42. "Jimmy Murphy Drives Race to Death," *Indianapolis Star*, September 16, 1924, p 1, and Borgeson, *The Golden Age*, p 126.
43. "Latest Marmon Model Has 10 Body Styles," *Automotive Industries*, October 30, 1924, p 789.
44. "Announce New Marmon 74 Line," *Indianapolis Star*, October 26, 1924, p 61 & 66.

45. "Duesenberg Motor Sales Go Upward," *Indianapolis Star,* October 12, 1924, p 67.
46. "Speed Car Crash Kills Ansterberg," *Indianapolis Star,* October 17, 1924, p 1.
47. "Premier Taxicabs Gain in Popularity," *Indianapolis Star,* December 31, 1924, p 10.
48. "Premier Produces Taxicab with Four Wheel Brakes," *Automotive Industries,* December 18, 1924, p 1067.
49. Henley, "Business and Comment," *Indianapolis Star,* February 26, 1925, p 20.
50. "Plans to Bring Plant Unit Here," *Indianapolis Star,* March 1, 1925, p 17.
51. "Court Orders Sale of Duesenberg Plant," *Indianapolis Star,* January 1, 1925, p 13.
52. "Hume Body Corp," Coachbuilt. com. http://www.coachbuilt.com/bui/h/hume/hume.htm. Accessed March 5, 2016.
53. "Marmon Employs New Body Chief," *Indianapolis Star,* February 20, 1925, p 12.
54. "Hume Body Corp," Coachbuilt. com. http://www.coachbuilt.com/bui/h/hume/hume.htm. Accessed March 5, 2016.
55. "Weidley Motors Sues Stutz for $750,000," *Automotive Industries,* January 29, 1925, p 210.
56. "Moscovics Plays Important Role in Auto Industry," *Indianapolis Star,* December 19, 1928, p 23.
57. "Franklin Settles in Moscovics Suit," *Automotive Industries,* March 5, 1925, p 484.
58. "New Head for Stutz Named," *Indianapolis Star,* February 19, 1924, p 1 & 6.
59. "Stutz Announces New 6–84 Sedan at $3,050," *Automotive Industries,* June 4, 1925, p 998.
60. "Duesenberg Company Will Continue Here," *Indianapolis Star,* February 22, 1925, p 1 & 8.
61. Ibid.
62. "Duesenberg Auto Plant Sold to Trust Company," *Indianapolis Star,* February 26, 1925, p 3.
63. "Duesenberg Sale Approved by Court," *Automotive Industries,* March 5, 1925, p 484.
64. "U.S. Government Loses on Appeal," *Indianapolis Star,* April 22, 1925, p 13.
65. "$45,000 Allowed, Fee to Premier Motors Receiver," *Indianapolis Star,* May 6, 1925, p 3.
66. "U.S. Government Loses on Appeal," *Indianapolis Star,* April 22, 1925, p 13.
67. "$45,000 Allowed, Fee to Premier Motors Receiver," *Indianapolis Star,* May 6, 1925, p 3.
68. "Creditors to Receive Premier Cab Stock," *Automotive Industries,* May 14, 1925, p 879.
69. "Two New Open Models Added to Marmon Line," *Automotive Industries,* April 23, 1925, p 757.
70. "Marmon Adopts Uniform Price Plan for Parts," *Indianapolis Star,* May 3, 1925, p 64.
71. "Thirty-Four Cars Entered in International Race at Speedway," *Indianapolis Star,* May 3, 1925, p 25.
72. Patton, "Observed from the Speedway Pits," *Indianapolis Star,* May 25, 1925, p 12.
73. Patton, "Duray Smashes Track Record and Wins Pole Position by Showing 113 Miles an Hour," *Indianapolis Star,* May 27, 1925, p 1.
74. Patton, "Gasoline Derby of Nation to Be Run Off at Speedway," *Indianapolis Star,* May 30, 1925, p 1 & 12.
75. Patton, "DePaolo Wins Sweepstakes in Indianapolis–Made Car at Dazzling Speed of 101.13," *Indianapolis Star,* May 31, 1925, p 1.
76. "$87,750 in Prizes Given Race Pilots," *Indianapolis Star,* June 2, 1925, p 1.
77. "Tommy Milton Victor in 250-Mile Altoona Race," *Indianapolis Star,* June 14, 1925, p 25.
78. "Altoona Checkup Gives Pete First," *Indianapolis Star,* June 14, 1925, p 13.
79. "DePaolo Not to Enter Grand Prix," *Indianapolis Star,* June 16, 1925, p 12.
80. "Recheck Shows DePaolo Wins First Laurel Race," *Indianapolis Star,* July 12, 1925, p 23.
81. "Duesenberg Makes Revision in Prices," *Automotive Industries,* May 7, 1925, p 842.
82. "Marmon Reports Larger Earnings," *Indianapolis Star,* July 5, 1925, p 45.
83. "Joseph J. Cole, Pioneer Auto Manufacturer Here, Is Dead," *Indianapolis Star,* August 8, 1925, p 1 & 8.
84. "Pete Going Home to Make Try for Grand Prix Prize," *Indianapolis Star,* July 26, 1925, p 26.
85. "Eyes of Racing Fans Are Turned to Monza Event," *Indianapolis Star,* September 6, 1925, p 26.
86. Borgeson, *The Golden Age,* p 127.
87. "Champions Add New Laurels to Impressive List," *Indianapolis Star,* September 20, 1925, p 74.
88. Borgeson, *The Golden Age,* p 127.
89. "Champions Add New Laurels to Impressive List," *Indianapolis Star,* September 20, 1925, p 74.
90. "DePaolo Sets New Record for 250 Miles at Salem's New Board Speedway," *Indianapolis Star,* November 1, 1925, p 27.
91. Carver, "Many Original Features in Design of New Stutz Vertical Eight," *Automotive Industries,* December 31, 1925, p 1090–1097.

Chapter 17

1. Goodman, "Stutz Creation Newest of New in Gotham Show," *Indianapolis Star,* January 10, 1926, p 25.
2. "Marmon Display at Show Strikes Responsive Chord," *Indianapolis Star,* February 17, 1926, p 10.
3. "Marmon Files for New Name," *Indianapolis Star,* February 3, 1926, p 12.
4. "Incorporations," *Indianapolis Star,* February 18, 1926, p 23.
5. "Nordyke-Marmon Mill Plant Sold," *Indianapolis Star,* November 27, 1926, p 1.
6. "DePaolo Makes New Record to Win at Fulford," *Indianapolis Star,* February 23, 1926, p 15.
7. "DePaolo Will Again Try for Speedway Honors This Year," *Indianapolis Star,* April 18, 1926, p 35.
8. Patton, "Lockhart Wins Speedway Race," *Indianapolis Star,* June 1, 1926, p 1.
9. Patrick, "Miller Cars Win in Race Classic," *Indianapolis Star,* June 1, 1926, p 8.
10. "Life Policies by Bushel," *Indianapolis Star,* April 19, 1926, p 7.
11. "When a Duesenberg Stops—A Person of Note Steps Out," *Indianapolis Star,* April 19, 1926, p 9.
12. "Smaller, Speedier Autos Predicted," *Indianapolis Star,* June 4, 1926, p 1.
13. "Forecast Fastest Things on Wheels," *Indianapolis Star,* June 27, 1926, p 53.
14. "Marmon Leases Plant #3 to Body Builders," *Indianapolis Star,* June 24, 1926, p 12.
15. "Murray Body Corp./Murray Corp. of America," http://www.coachbuilt.com/bui/m/murray/murray. htm. Accessed March 7, 2016.
16. "Marmon to Show $1,800,000 Profit," *Indianapolis Star,* July 8, 1926, p 10.
17. "Marmon Directors Declare Dividend," *Indianapolis Star,* October 15, 1926, p 1.
18. "Purdy Declares Payment Plan Reduces Automobile Costs," *Indianapolis Star,* July 25, 1926, p 57.
19. Patrick, "Marmon '75' Models Are Now Ready for Local Motor Buyer," *Indianapolis Star,* October 10, 1926, p 58.
20. "New Body Styles Feature Marmon," *Indianapolis Star,* October 17, 1926, p 72.
21. "Buys Duesenberg Motors Plant," *Indianapolis Star,* October 6, 1926, p 1.

22. *Ibid.*
23. *Ibid.*
24. "America Will Have Highest Priced Car in New Duesenberg," *Indianapolis Star*, October 17, 1926, p 69.
25. "Marmon Head Finds Small Cars Nearing," *Automotive Industries*, June 17, 1926, p 1075.
26. "Marmon Eight-In-Line Represents Entirely New Mode of Transportation," *Indianapolis Star*, January 16, 1927 p 55.
27. Patrick, "New Little Marmon Given First Formal Demonstration Here," *Indianapolis Star*, December 5, 1926, p 69 & 71.
28. "Marmon Receives 13 Million Jolts in 24-Hour Test," *Indianapolis Star*, August 28, 1927, p 62.
29. Patrick, "New Little Marmon Given First Formal Demonstration Here," *Indianapolis Star*, December 5, 1926, p 69 & 71.

Chapter 18

1. "2-Car-a-Family Trend of Today," *Indianapolis Star*, March 13, 1927, p 55.
2. "Annual Meeting Will Inaugurate New Car Series," *Indianapolis Star*, January 3, 1927, p 1.
3. "Marmon Expects New Sales Mark," *Indianapolis Star*, April 10, 1927, p 68.
4. "Little Marmon Has 4 Custom Bodies," *Automotive Industries*, January 29, 1927, p 141.
5. "Wide Range of Prices Offered at Motor Show," *Indianapolis Star*, February 16, 1927, p 1 & 9.
6. "Local Factory Method Unique in Car Building," *Indianapolis Star*, January 9, 1927, p 56.
7. Edie, "Predicts More Auto Sales by Indiana Manufacturers," *Indianapolis Star*, January 16, 1927, p 1 & 7.
8. *Ibid.*
9. "Presents New Duesenberg," *Indianapolis Star*, Mar 20, 1927, p 57 & 59.
10. Wolff, "Duesenberg: It's a Grand Old Name," *Automobile Quarterly*, Spring 1966, p 358.
11. "Antiscuff Valve Insures Starting Oil for Marmon," *Indianapolis Star*, February 27, 1927, p 57.
12. "Stutz Holds 68 mph to Win Stevens Cup," *Automotive Industries*, April 30, 1927, p 676.
13. "Stock Trophy Event Won by Marmon 16," *Indianapolis Star*, October 16, 1931, p 1 & 5.
14. "Stutz Takes First in Stock Car Races," *Automotive Industries*, May 14, 1927, p 747.
15. "Stutz Gives Buyers Insurance for Year," *Automotive Industries*, June 18, 1927, p 950.
16. "How They Qualified First Day," *Indianapolis Star*, May 27, 1927, p 1.
17. Patton, "33 Cars Are Ready for 500-Mile Whirl at Speedway Today," *Indianapolis Star*, May 30, 1927, p 1.
18. Patton, "Souders, in Duesenberg, Is Race Victor," *Indianapolis Star*, May 31, 1927, p 1 & 9.
19. "Duesenberg Entered in European Classic," *Indianapolis Star*, August 9, 1927, p 3.
20. "Race Driver Home from Foreign Trip," *Indianapolis Star*, September 28, 1927, p 20.
21. "Marmon Plant Abolishes Storerooms," *Indianapolis Star*, June 5, 1927, p 70.
22. "Marmon Output Gains 51 Percent in Year 1926-27," *Indianapolis Star*, August 14, 1927, p 52.
23. "Marmon Financial Position Strong Statement Shows," *Indianapolis Star*, August 21, 1927, p 55.
24. "New Marmon 78 Goes on Display," *Indianapolis Star*, December 8, 1927, p 1.
25. "Stutz Wins Classic at Atlantic City," *Automotive Industries*, September 10, 1927, p 395.
26. "Marmon Attains Volume Basis on New 68 and 78," *Indianapolis Star*, January 15, 1928, p 61.
27. "68 and 78 Series of Straight 8's Much Improved," *Indianapolis Star*, July 29, 1928, p 59 & 61.
28. "Nation Told of State's Success in Motor Field," *Indianapolis Star*, January 15, 1928, p 23.
29. "New Marmon 68 and 78 Models Star at Shows," *Indianapolis Star*, January 22, 1928, p 53.
30. Goodman, "1928 Auto Show Setting Records," *Indianapolis Star*, January 10, 1928, p 3.
31. Mushlitz, "Marmon to Put 45,000 Cars in Market in 1928," *Indianapolis Star*, February 1, 1928, p 1.
32. "Demand for Marmon Keeps Production Up," *Indianapolis Star*, March 18, 1928, p 63.
33. "Nation Told of State's Success in Motor Field," *Indianapolis Star*, January 15, 1928, p 23.
34. "New Duesenberg Soon to Appear," *Indianapolis Star*, January 15, 1928, p 1.
35. "New Duesenberg Progress Cited," *Indianapolis Star*, February 19, 1928, p 60.
36. "Veteran of Race Track on Marmon Technical Staff," *Indianapolis Star*, March 4, 1928, p 55 & 61.
37. "Two Past Presidents of S.A.E. on Engineering Staff at Marmon," *Indianapolis Star*, April 1, 1928, p 62.
38. "Marmon Enters Two Speed Cars in 500-Mile Race," *Indianapolis Star*, April 10, 1928, p 1.
39. "Marmon Enters Indianapolis Race with Front-Drive Specials," *Automotive Industries*, May 5, 1928, Vol. 58, p 686-687.
40. "Marmon Enters Two Speed Cars in 500-Mile Race," *Indianapolis Star*, April 10, 1928, p 1.
41. "Thirty-Six Speed Creations Entered in 16th Annual 500-Mile Race," *Indianapolis Star*, May 2, 1928, p 13.
42. "Marmon at Brick Oval," *Indianapolis Star*, May 20, 1928, p 39.
43. Patton, "Nineteen Pilots Qualify Cars for Long Grind," *Indianapolis Star*, May 27, 1928, p 33.
44. Patton, "List of Qualifiers Mounts to 24 As Five Speed Pilots Complete Four Fast Laps," *Indianapolis Star*, May 28, 1928, p 1.
45. Patton, "28 Qualified for Race; 5 to Try Today," *Indianapolis Star*, May 29, 1928, p 1.
46. "Meyer Victorious in 500-Mile Race," *Indianapolis Star*, May 31, 1928, p 8.
47. Patton, "31 Cars Await Start of 500 Mile Race," *Indianapolis Star*, May 30, 1928, p 1.
48. "Marmon to Pace Race," *Indianapolis Star*, May 20, 1928, p 66.
49. Borgeson, *The Golden Age*, p 129.
50. Patton, "Meyer Wins 500-Mile Speedway Classic," *Indianapolis Star*, May 31, 1928, p 1.
51. "Stutz Adds Coupe at $3,990," *Automotive Industries*, August 4, 1928, p 179.
52. "Marmon Leases Its Body Plant," *Indianapolis Star*, October 3, 1928, p 3.
53. "New Car Shown in Marmon Line," *Indianapolis Star*, December 23, 1928, p 46.
54. "Marmon Offers New Speedsters," *Indianapolis Star*, December 9, 1928, p 68.
55. "265 hp Duesenberg Eight Costs $8,500," *Automotive Industries*, December 1, 1928, p 790-794.
56. Henley, "Earnings," *Indianapolis Star*, December 5, 1928, p 18.
57. "265 hp Duesenberg Eight Costs $8,500," *Automotive Industries*, December 1, 1928, p 790-794.
58. Henley, "Earnings," *Indianapolis Star*, December 5, 1928, p 18.
59. Baker, "265 hp Duesenberg Eight Costs $8,500," *Automotive Industries*, December 1, 1928, p 790-794.
60. Priest, "Auto Industry Reaching Radio and Air Fields," *Indianapolis Star*, December 9, 1928, p 65.
61. "Stutz Increases Power and Makes Body Refinements," *Automotive Industries*, September 22, 1928, p 404-405.
62. "Stutz Makes Radio Optional on Cars," *Automotive Industries*, October 6, 1928, p 496.
63. "Indianapolis-Made Motor Cars," *Indianapolis Star*, December 14, 1928, p 6.
64. "Marmon Stock Issue Is Voted,"

Indianapolis Star, December 28, 1928, p 14.
65. "Indianapolis-Made Motor Cars," *Indianapolis Star,* December 14, 1928, p 6.
66. "New Stutz Auto Winning Acclaim," *Indianapolis Star,* January 6, 1929, p 8.
67. "Ryan-Lites," *Montreal Gazette.* March 9, 1929.
68. "New Stutz Auto Winning Acclaim," *Indianapolis Star,* January 6, 1929, p 8.
69. "Marmon Obtains Peak of Success," *Indianapolis Star,* January 20, 1929, p 51.
70. "Moscovics Resigns As Head of Stutz; Gorrell Elected," *Indianapolis Star,* January 25, 1910, p 1 & 10.
71. "Roosevelt Auto Put on Display," *Indianapolis Star,* March 29, 1929, p 12.
72. "These Interesting Roosevelt Features," *Indianapolis Star,* March 31, 1929, p 70.
73. "Body Styles and Features of Roosevelt 8," *Indianapolis Star,* March 31, 1929, p 57.
74. "Roosevelts Are Made Possible by Concentrating on Eights," *Indianapolis Star,* April 28, 1929, p 59.
75. "Roosevelt Gets Great Reception," *Indianapolis Star,* April 7, 1929, p 62.
76. "Blackhawk Cars Reduced in Price," *Indianapolis Star,* March 31, 1929, p 57.
77. "Added Stutz Facilities Permit Price Reduction," *Automotive Industries,* April 6, 1929, p 570.
78. "Stutz Prices Lower on New Series Cars," *Automotive Industries,* July 13, 1929, p 66.
79. "New Inspection System Is Used," *Indianapolis Star,* April 21, 1929, p 69.
80. "Duesenberg Racy and Rakish," *Indianapolis Star,* January 13, 1929, p 57.
81. "Annual Marmon Statement Reflects Strong Position," *Indianapolis Star,* April 20, 1929, p 16.
82. "Marmon," *Indianapolis Star,* May 19, 1929, p 68.
83. "Marmon Sets Record in Fiscal Quarter," *Automotive Industries,* June 8, 1929, p 892.
84. "Tardy Cars of Racing Game Will Be on Time This Year," *Indianapolis Star,* April 7, 1929, p 33.
85. "Sport Kaleidoscope," *Indianapolis Star,* May 12, 1929, p 37.
86. "Forty-Three Cars Form Entry List for International Speed Classic," *Indianapolis Star,* May 2, 1929, p 14 & 18.
87. Patton, "33 Cars Await Start of Speed Classic," *Indianapolis Star,* May 30, 1929, p 1.
88. Clifford, "Death of Spence First Since 1926," *Indianapolis Star,* May 31, 1929, p 10.
89. Patton, "160,000 Cheer As Ray Keech Wins Race," *Indianapolis Star,* May 31, 1929, p 1.
90. "Speedway Prize Melon Split at Driver's Dinner," *Indianapolis Star,* June 1, 1929, p 1.
91. "Keech, Woodbury Veterans of Racing," *Indianapolis Star,* June 16, 1929, p 3.
92. "The Greatest Proving Ground in the World," *Indianapolis Star,* May 30, 1929, p 9.
93. "Roosevelts Smash All Marks; Continue Toward 250 Hour," *Indianapolis Star,* June 21, 1929, p 12.
94. "Roosevelt No. 2 Nears 3rd Week," *Indianapolis Star,* June 26, 1929, p 24.
95. "It's Still Running!" *Indianapolis Star,* June 26, 1929, p 9.
96. "Display Record Roosevelt Sedan," *Indianapolis Star,* July 3, 1929, p 7.
97. "Every Nonstop Endurance Mark," *Indianapolis Star,* June 20, 1929, p 1.
98. "Display Record Roosevelt Sedan," *Indianapolis Star,* July 3, 1929, p 7.
99. "Engineers Inspect Motor Car After 440-Hour Test Ends," *Indianapolis Star,* July 7, 1929, p 52.
100. "See It at Our Salesroom," *Indianapolis Star,* July 3, 1929, p 12.
101. "Roosevelt Earns Public Approval," *Indianapolis Star,* June 16, 1929, p 58.
102. "Marmon-Built Roosevelt Car Proves Ability on Pike's Peak," *Indianapolis Star,* September 22, 1929, p 64.
103. "Marmon's Half Year Is Best in History," *Automotive Industries,* September 28, 1929, p 463.
104. "Marmon Company Votes Regular Dividend Early to Strengthen Market," *Indianapolis Star,* October 31, 1929, p 1.
105. "Marmon Re-Enters High Price Field Displaying First of the Big Eight Models at Local Salesroom," *Indianapolis Star,* December 1, 1929, p 61.
106. "Marmon Announces Big Eight Line with Four-Speed Transmission," *Automotive Industries,* November 2, 1929, p 642.
107. "Marmon Will Bring Out Straight-Eight," *Automotive Industries,* October 5, 1929, p 497.
108. "Marmon Re-Enters High Price Field Displaying First of the Big Eight Models at Local Salesroom," *Indianapolis Star,* December 1, 1929, p 61.
109. "Stutz Offers Chateau Series with Weymann Bodies," *Automotive Industries,* October 19, 1929, p 589.
110. "Stutz Offers Supercharge on Stock Model," *Automotive Industries,* November 2, 1929, p 645–646.
111. "Factories Here to Display Cars," *Indianapolis Star,* December 29, 1929, p 19.

Chapter 19

1. "Indiana Autos Feature New York Show," *Indianapolis Star,* January 5, 1930, p 1.
2. "Marmon Eights Get Good Start," *Indianapolis Star,* January 19, 1930, p 26.
3. "Indiana Autos Feature New York Show," *Indianapolis Star,* January 5, 1930, p 1.
4. Buck, "Marmon Leader Voices Optimism," *Indianapolis Star,* January 9, 1930, p 1.
5. Buck, "Increase in Auto Output Foreseen," *Indianapolis Star,* January 30, 1930, p 1.
6. "Marmon Expects Larger Output," *Indianapolis Star,* February 10, 1930, p 1.
7. "Litigation Halts Merger of Stutz," *Indianapolis Star,* January 1, 1930, p 1 & 2.
8. "New York Curb Market," *Indianapolis Star,* January 1, 1930, p 16.
9. "Litigation Halts Merger of Stutz," *Indianapolis Star,* January 1, 1930, p 1 & 2.
10. "Bankruptcy Act Fought by Stutz," *Indianapolis Star,* January 4, 1930, p 10.
11. "Stutz Files Suit to Recover $30,000," *Indianapolis Star,* January 27, 1930, p 14.
12. "$28,906 Tax Sum Returned to Stutz," *Indianapolis Star,* January 16, 1930, p 18.
13. "Big News for Owners of 1929 Fords and Chevrolets," *Indianapolis Star,* January 17, 1930, p 7.
14. "Marmon Sales Advance," *Indianapolis Star,* February 5, 1930, p 9.
15. "Many Improvements in Body and Motor," *Indianapolis Star,* February 16, 1930, p 38.
16. "Marmon Adds Three Open Cars," *Indianapolis Star,* May 11, 1930, p 33.
17. "Marmon Introduces Revolutionary Service Policy," *Indianapolis Star,* May 18, 1930, p 27.
18. "Radio Is Available for Marmon Cars," *Indianapolis Star,* June 15, 1930, p 29.
19. "Stutz in 3-Way Merger, Is Report," *Indianapolis Star,* March 20, 1930, p 3.
20. "Gorrell Denies Stutz Removal," *Indianapolis Star,* March 30, 1930, p 4.
21. "Go Indianapolis," *Indianapolis Star,* May 9, 1930, p 17.
22. Patton, "Speedway Gossip," *Indianapolis Star,* May 14, 1930, p 13.
23. "Peter DePaolo, Gulotta Qualify for Speed Grind," *Indianapolis Star,* May 26, 1930, p 1.
24. Patton, "DePaolo Escapes Death Under Train," *Indianapolis Star,* May 27, 1930, p 1.
25. "38 Cars to Start in 500-Mile

Classic," *Indianapolis Star*, May 29, 1930, p 1.
26. Patton, "170,000 Will See Speedway Derby Today," *Indianapolis Star*, May 30, 1930, p 1.
27. Patton, "Arnold Wins 500-Mile Speedway Classic," *Indianapolis Star*, May 31, 1930, p 11.
28. Bull, "Monthly New Car Totals in County Bottom Out in September," *Indianapolis Star*, October 5, 1930, p 27.
29. "Marmon Car Sales Increase in Month," *Indianapolis Star*, September 19, 1930, p 13.
30. "Marmon Roosevelt Price List Lower," *Indianapolis Star*, June 25, 1930, p 24.
31. "Marmon Car Sales Increase in Month," *Indianapolis Star*, September 19, 1930, p 13.
32. "Railroad Earnings Make Unfair Comparison," *Indianapolis Star*, June 25, 1930, p 19.
33. "Stutz Announces New Stock Plan," *Indianapolis Star*, October 20, 1930, p 1.
34. "New Stutz Auto Stock Purchased," *Indianapolis Star*, December 1, 1930, p 1.
35. "Stutz Stock Listed," *Indianapolis Star*, November 19, 1930, p 17.
36. "Eastern Bank Buys More Stutz Stock," *Indianapolis Star*, June 9, 1931, p 13.
37. "Stutz, Celebrating 20th Anniversary, Announces '31 Models in Three Lines," *Indianapolis Star*, October 26, 1930, p 29.
38. "Baker Sets Trans-U.S. Speed Record in Stutz," *Indianapolis Star*, November 7, 1930, p 3.
39. "Talk of Merger Gains Credence," *Indianapolis Star*, March 22, 1931, p 28.
40. "Income Shrinks," *Indianapolis Star*, January 23, 1931, p 19.
41. "Marmon 16 and Two New Eights Will Be Presented," *Indianapolis Star*, February 15, 1931, p 64.
42. Ibid.
43. "First of Marmon Sixteens, Winner of S.A.E. Medal, Is off the Line," *Indianapolis Star*, April 19, 1931, p 29.
44. "Stock Trophy Event Won by Marmon 16," *Indianapolis Star*, October 16, 1931, p 1 & 5.
45. "Marmon Starts Subsidiary Unit," *Indianapolis Star*, March 14, 1931, p 1.
46. "Big Truck Order Keeps up Policy," *Indianapolis Star*, June 29, 1931, p 18.
47. "71 Cars Entered in 500-Mile Race at Local Course," *Indianapolis Star*, May 3, 1931, p 1.
48. Patton, "Speedway Action Picks up with Many Pilots on Track," *Indianapolis Star*, May 15, 1931, p 16.
49. Patton, "Five More Qualify for Speedway Race," *Indianapolis Star*, May 26, 1931, p 1.
50. Patton, "Schneider Wins Race; Rain Cuts Speed," *Indianapolis Star*, May 31, 1931, p 1.
51. "Hard Luck Forces Many Drivers Out," *Indianapolis Star*, May 31, 1931, p 2.
52. "Stutz Net Income for May $38,000," *Indianapolis Star*, May 22, 1931, p 21.
53. "Schwab Again Buys Stutz Motor Control," *Indianapolis Star*, July 8, 1931, p 18.
54. "Three Indianapolis Firms Have Models in Gotham Show of Quality Models," *Indianapolis Star*, November 30, 1931, p 8.
55. "Marmon Enters New Motor Era," *Indianapolis Star*, May 10, 1932, p 1 & 2.
56. "Marmon Begins New Plant Plan," *Indianapolis Star*, February 22, 1932, p 11.
57. Marmon Enters New Motor Era," *Indianapolis Star*, May 10, 1932, p 1 & 2.
58. "Stutz Orders Gain," *Indianapolis Star*, March 6, 1932, p 27.
59. "1933 Stutz Line Lower in Price," *Indianapolis Star*, May 22, 1932, p 13.
60. Patton, "Frame Wins, Sets New Speedway Record," *Indianapolis Star*, May 31, 1932, p 1.
61. "Truck Test Run to Begin Today," *Indianapolis Star*, August 18, 1932, p 13.
62. "Huge Marmon-Herrington Passes Test," *Indianapolis Star*, August 19, 1932, p 11.
63. "1933 Marmon Sixteen Announced," *Indianapolis Star*, October 30, 1932, p 25.
64. "Stutz to Start on Pak-Age-Car," *Indianapolis Star*, November 29, 1932, p 9.
65. "New York Views 1933 Stutz Models," *Indianapolis Star*, January 6, 1933, p 12.
66. "Reports Stutz Car Production," *Indianapolis Star*, March 18, 1932, p 20.
67. "Stutz Firm Asks Bankruptcy Act," *Indianapolis Star*, April 3, 1937, p 3.
68. "Cord Increases Employees' Wages," *Indianapolis Star*, May 9, 1933, p 17.
69. "Stutz Company Issues 50,223 Shares of Stock," *Indianapolis Star*, July 19, 1933, p 16.
70. "Autos Convince Show Visitors," *Indianapolis Star*, January 8, 1934, p 3.
71. "Dern Appoints Col. Gorrell to Army Air Service Investigating Committee," *Indianapolis Star*, April 12, 1934, p 5.
72. Patton, "33 Cars Await $100,000 Speedway Race," *Indianapolis Star*, May 30, 1934, p 1.
73. Patton, "33 Cars Qualified for Speedway Grind," *Indianapolis Star*, May 29, 1934, p 1.
74. Buck, "Limited Gasoline Supply Doesn't Prove Hoodoo to Racers," *Indianapolis Star*, May 31, 1934, p 19.
75. "Reconstruction Finance Corporation," Wikipedia, https://en.wikipedia.org/wiki/Reconstruction_Finance_Corporation. Accessed October 22, 2016.
76. "Denies Connections to 2 Stutz Brokers," *Indianapolis Star*, July 26, 1935, p 2.
77. "Dealings in Stutz Stock Under Fire," *Indianapolis Star*, July 25, 1935, p 14.
78. "4 Warrants Issued in Stock Swindle," *Indianapolis Star*, September 1, 1935, p 5.
79. "17 Race Autos Forced to Quit," *Indianapolis Star*, May 31, 1935, p 11.
80. "Jenkins Again Claims Record," *Indianapolis Star*, September 22, 1935, p 18.
81. "Stutz Announces Production Boost," *Indianapolis Star*, November 6, 1935, p 22.
82. "Stutz Shows Pak-Age-Car," *Indianapolis Star*, November 10, 1935, p 57.
83. "Order Received for 340 Stutz Pak-Age-Cars," *Indianapolis Star*, June 14, 1936, p 21.
84. "Stutz Will Exhibit Larger Pak-Age-Car to U.S. Bakers," *Indianapolis Star*, September 27, 1936, p 23.
85. "Income Tax Refund of $101,000 Entered," *Indianapolis Star*, June 21, 1936, p 16.
86. "Cord Will Sell Stocks, Report," *Indianapolis Star*, August 6, 1937, p 1.
87. "Study Local Effect," *Indianapolis Star*, August 6, 1937, p 4.
88. "Marmon Acquires Duesenberg Plant," *Indianapolis Star*, October 23, 1937, p 1.
89. "Stutz Firm Asks Bankruptcy Act," *Indianapolis Star*, April 3, 1937, p 3.
90. "A. B. Cronk Named Trustee of Stutz," *Indianapolis Star*, May 2, 1937, p 24.
91. "Asks Suspension of Stutz Stocks," *Indianapolis Star*, October 24, 1937, p 12.
92. "Manufacture of 100 Cars by Stutz Is Approved," *Indianapolis Star*, October 29, 1937, p 5.
93. "Substitute Plan Filed for Stutz," *Indianapolis Star*, November 14, 1937, p 3.
94. "Liquidate, Stutz Order by U.S.," *Indianapolis Star*, April 26, 1939, p 13.
95. "Plans to Start on Pak-Age-Car," *Indianapolis Star*, August 25, 1939, p 24.

Bibliography

Books

Bloemker, Al. *500 Miles to Go: The History of the Indianapolis Motor Speedway.* New York: Coward-McCann, 1961.

Bodenhamer, David J., Robert G. Barrows, and David Gordon Vandersteel, Editors. *The Encyclopedia of Indianapolis.* Bloomington: Indiana University Press, 1994.

Borgeson, Griffith. *The Golden Age of the American Racing Car.* New York: Bonanza Books, 1966.

Clymer, Floyd. *Indianapolis 500 Mile Race History: A Complete Detailed History of Every Indianapolis Race Since 1909.* Los Angeles: Floyd Clymer, 1946.

Epstein, Ralph C. *The Automobile Industry, Its Economic and Commercial Development.* Chicago & New York: A. W. Shaw Company, 1928.

Fisher, Jerry M. *The Pacesetter: The Untold Story of Carl G. Fisher.* Ft. Bragg, CA: Lost Coast, 1998.

Kennedy, E. D. *The Automobile Industry: The Coming of Age of Capitalism's Favorite Child.* New York: Reynal & Hitchcock, 1941.

Kimes, Beverly Rae. *Standard Catalog of American Cars, 1805–1942.* Iola, Wisconsin: Krause Publications, 1996.

Martin, John Bartlow. *Indiana: An Interpretation.* Bloomington: Indiana University Press, 1942.

Scott, D. Bruce, and Hetty Gray. *Indy Racing Before the 500.* Batesville, IN: Indiana Reflections, 2005.

Stanley, Richard A. *Custom Built by McFarlan: A History of the Carriage and Automobile Manufacturer, 1856–1928.* Jefferson, N.C.; McFarland, 2012

Steinwedel, Louis William, and J. Herbert Newport. *The Duesenberg.* Philadelphia: Chilton Book Company, 1970.

Periodical Articles

"A.C.A. Tests Stutz Transcontinental Car." *Horseless Age*, May 26, 1915, Vol. 35, p 697.

"Added Stutz Facilities Permit Price Reduction." *Automotive Industries*, April 6, 1929, Vol. 60, p 570.

"Addition to Pathfinder Plant." *Horseless Age*, August 1, 1915, Vol. 35, p 160.

"Additions to Premier Plant." *Horseless Age*, October 2, 1912, Vol. 30, No. 14, p 492.

"Allan A. Ryan Resigns from Stutz Directorate." *Automotive Industries*, January 19, 1922, Vol. 46, p 155.

"Allan Ryan Files Bankruptcy Papers." *Automotive Industries*, July 27, 1922, Vol. 47, p 194.

"The American Motor Company's 1907 Line." *Horseless Age*, December 5, 1906, Vol. 18, No. 23, p 829.

"The American 1910 Models." *Horseless Age*, December 13, 1909, Vol. 24, No. 24, p 697.

"The 'American' Touring Car." *Automobile Quarterly*, January 24, 1906, Vol. 17, No. 4, p 182.

"American Traveler Torpedo Cars Rakish." *Horseless Age*, March 23, 1910, Vol. 25, No. 12, p 446.

"Approve Stutz Expansion." *Automotive Industries*. September 4, 1919, Vol. 41, p 498.

"Barrows of Premier Also Heads Monroe." *Automotive Industries*, June 28, 1923, p 1440.

Carver, Walter L. "Many Original Features in Design of New Stutz Vertical Eight." *Automotive Industries*, December 31, 1925, Vol. 53, p 1090–1097.

Catlin, Russ. "The Harry Stutz Era." *Automobile Quarterly*, Spring 1970, No. 8 Vol. 3, p 230.

"Coffin Resigns from Aircraft Board; Refuses Post in Reorganization." *Automotive Industries, the Automobile*, April 25, 1918, p 809.

"Cole Announces a Big New Six." *Horseless Age*, July 14, 1915, Vol. 36, p 40.

"Cole Changes for 1911." *Horseless Age*, August 10, 1910, Vol. 26, No. 6, p 204.

"Cole Dealers Agree to Quit All Trading." *Automotive Industries*, January 25, 1923, p 196.

"Cole Departs from Yearly Model—Brings Out Series Eight.," *Horseless Age*, September 18, 1912, Vol. 30, No. 12, p 434–436.

"Cole Discount Plan Is Aimed at Trading." *Automotive Industries*, January 11, 1923, p 98.

"Cole Introduces Eight Cylinder Model." *Horseless Age*, January 20, 1915, Vol. 35, No. 3, p 95.

"Cole Is Producing New Master Series." *Automotive Industries*, June 14, 1923, p 1303.

"Cole 1911 Plans." *Horseless Age*, September 28, 1910, Vol. 26, No. 13, p 448.

"Cole Plans Double Output This Year." *Automotive Industries*, January 8, 1920, Vol. 42, p 101.

"Cole Price Reduction of $300." *Automotive Industries, the automobile*, December 19, 1918, p 1068.

"Cole 30." *Indianapolis Star*, December 12, 1909, p 3.

"Creditors to Receive Premier Cab Stock." *Automotive Industries*, May 14, 1925, Vol. 52, p 879.

"Dealers Meet Schwab at Stutz Meeting." *Automotive Industries*, November 16, 1922, p 1003.

"Duesenberg Automobile & Motors Co., Inc." *Automotive Industries*, June 15, 1922, p 1356.

"Duesenberg Buys Indianapolis Site." *Automotive Industries*, May 12, 1920, Vol. 42, p 1135.

"Duesenberg Cuts List and Adds Sport Model." *Automotive Industries*, February 8, 1923, p 303.

"Duesenberg Designs Special Axle for Car." *Automotive Industries*, May 20, 1920, Vol. 42, p 1191.

"Duesenberg Makes Revision in Prices." *Automotive Industries,* May 7, 1925, Vol. 52, p 842.

"Duesenberg Quits Racing to Build Stock Cars." *Automotive Industries,* June 16, 1921, Vol. 44, p 1360.

"Duesenberg Sale Approved by Court." *Automotive Industries,* March 5, 1925, Vol. 52, p 484.

"Eight Cylinder Automobile Has Light Weight Feature." *Automotive Industries,* August 19, 1920, Vol. 43, p 362.

"Electric." *Horseless Age,* Vol. 9, No. 11, March 12, 1902, p 328.

"Electric Self Starter on Stutz Cars." *Horseless Age,* July 16, 1913, Vol. 32, No. 3, p 91.

"Elgin Sued for Salary; Receiver Is Appointed." *Automotive Industries,* July 3, 1924, Vol. 51, p 76.

"Empire '20' For 1911." *Horseless Age,* June 29, 1910, Vol. 25, No. 26, p 962.

"Enlarging Pathfinder Plant." *Horseless Age,* November 6, 1912, Vol. 30, No 19, p 689.

"Fire Damages Stutz Plant." *Automotive Industries,* May 19, 1921, Vol. 44, p 1086.

"$500,000 New Money Obtained by Premier." *Automotive Industries,* December 13, 1923, p 1224.

"Four More Qualify for Big Speedway Classic." *Indianapolis Star,* May 29, 1920, p 9

"Four-Story Addition for Stutz." *Horseless Age,* February 15, 1916, Vol. 37, p 166.

"Franklin Settles in Moscovics Suit." *Automotive Industries,* March 5, 1925, Vol. 52, p 484.

"Friendly Receivership to End Henderson Company." *Horseless Age,* May 27, 1914, Vol. 33, No. 21, p 1.

"Frontenac Bankrupt with $88,163 Debts." *Automotive Industries,* April 19, 1923, p 896.

"Frontenac to Build New Straight Eight." *Automotive Industries,* July 21, 1924, Vol. 51, p 260.

"Harry E. Stutz to Make New Car." *Automotive Industries,* October 16, 1919, Vol. 41, p 800.

"Harry O. Stutz." *Horseless Age,* July 13, 1910, Vol. 26, No. 2, p 65.

"The Hassler Transmission." *Horseless Age,* August 29, 1906, Vol. 18, No. 9, p 269–271.

"H.C.S. Produces New Six-Cylinder Model." *Automotive Industries,* January 4, 1923, p 42.

"H. C. Stutz." *Horseless Age,* March 8, 1911, Vol. 27, No. 10, p 472

Heldt. P. M. "Duesenberg Car Has 'Straight-Eight' Engine and Four Wheel Brakes." *Automotive Industries,* November 18, 1920, Vol. 43, p 1007.

_____. "Electric Vehicles at the Madison Square Garden Show." *Horseless Age,* Vol. 7, No 6, November 7, 1900, p 42–45.

"Henderson Adds a Six to Their Line." *Horseless Age,* May 28, 1913, Vol. 31, No. 22, p 982.

"Henderson Debut May 30." *Horseless Age,* May 22, 1912, Vol. 29, No. 21, p 919.

"Henderson Exhibit During 500 Mile Race." *Horseless Age,* June 18, 1913, Vol. 31, No. 25, p 1096.

"Henderson to Bring Out Lower Priced Cars." *Horseless Age,* September 24, 1913, Vol. 32, No. 13, p 1.

"Henderson Wire Wheel Models." *Horseless Age,* November 27, 1912, Vol. 30, No. 22, p 819.

Hendry, Maurice D. "Marmon: A Quest for Perfection." *Automobile Quarterly,* Vol. 7, No. 2, p 117–121.

"H. O. Smith Files Bankruptcy Petition." *Horseless Age,* February 10, 1915, Vol. 35, No. 6, p 193.

"Ideal Is Now Stutz Motor Car Co." *Horseless Age,* May 14, 1913, Vol. 31, No. 20, p 889.

"Increase in Premier Business." *Horseless Age,* June 18, 1913, Vol. 31, No. 25, p 1105.

"Indiana Factories Hard Hit by Strike." *Automotive Industries,* April 22, 1920, Vol. 42, p 982.

"Indianapolis Industry Suspends." *Automotive Industries,* January 21, 1918, p 202.

"Indianapolis Picking Up on Production." *Automobile Industries,* May 22, 1919, Vol. 40, p 1141.

"Indianapolis Plant Bought for New Elgin." *Automotive Industries,* June 7, 1923, p 1250.

"Interest in Monroe Car Disposed of by Stratton." *Automotive Industries,* June 21, 1923, p 1353.

Kimes, Beverly Rae. "The Rise & Fall of the Empire." *Automobile Quarterly,* Summer 1974, Vol. 12, No. 1, p 68–77.

"Lafayette Debut at Commodore Hotel." *Automotive Industries,* December 11, 1919, Vol. 41, p 1189.

"Lafayette Prices Cut Ranging $750 to $950." *Automotive Industries,* June 2, 1921, Vol. 44, p 1184.

"Latest Marmon Model Has 10 Body Styles." *Automotive Industries,* October 30, 1924, Vol. 51, p 789.

"Light Six Added to Marmon Line." *Horseless Age,* January 7, 1914, Vol. 33, No. 1, p 37–39.

"Louis Chevrolet Will Design for Monroe." *Automotive Industries,* September 18, 1919, Vol. 41, p 589.

"The Madison Square Garden Show." *Horseless Age,* Vol. 8, No. 31, October 30, 1901, p 408.

"Majority Creditors Accept Premier Plan." *Automotive Industries,* March 23, 1922, Vol. 46, p 692.

"Marion." *Horseless Age,* July 27, 1910, Vol. 26, No. 4, p 123.

"Marion Company Out with a 'Six.'" *Horseless Age,* August 20, 1913, Vol. 31, No. 20, p 306–307.

"Marion Co. Reorganizes." *Horseless Age,* May 8, 1912, Vol. 29, No. 19, p 838.

"Marion Company's Tenth Announcement." *Horseless Age,* November 13, 1912, Vol. 30, Vol. 20, p 735.

"The Marion Flyer." *Horseless Age,* October 9, 1907, Vol. 20, No. 15, p 556.

"The Marion Motor Car Company." *Horseless Age,* October 30, 1907, Vol. 20, No. 18, p 637.

"The Marion Motor Car Company." *Horseless Age,* November 10, 1909, Vol. 24, No. 19, p 516.

"Marion Motor Car Co., Indianapolis." *Horseless Age,* October 13, 1913, Vol. 31, No. 16, p 617.

"Marion Plant Purchased by President Willys, of the Overland Automobile Company." *Horseless Age,* October 28, 1908, Vol. 22, No. 18, p 595.

"Marion Receivership Lifted; Finances Adjusted." *Horseless Age,* January 28, 1914, Vol. 33, No. 4, p 1.

"Marmon." *Horseless Age,* January 1, 1918, Vol. 43, p 36.

"Marmon Adopts Front-Wheel Brakes As Optional Equipment." *Automotive Industries,* September 27, 1923, p 632.

"Marmon Announces Big Eight Line with Four-Speed Transmission." *Automotive Industries,* November 2, 1929, Vol. 61, p 642.

"Marmon Brings Out a Six." *Horseless Age.* June 26, 1912, Vol. 29, No. 26, p 1116.

"Marmon Car Sales Increase in Month." *Indianapolis Star,* September 19, 1930, p 13.

"Marmon Changes Phaeton." *Automotive Industries,* August 17, 1922, Vol. 47, p 339.

"Marmon Cuts Price to New Cost Basis." *Automotive Industries,* May 5, 1921, p 978.

"Marmon Enlarging Plant." *Automotive Industries, the Automobile,* January 21, 1918, p 251.

"Marmon Enters Indianapolis Race with Front-Drive Specials." *Automotive Industries,* May 5, 1928, Vol. 58, p 686–687.

"Marmon Head Finds Small Cars Nearing." *Automotive Industries,* June 17, 1926, Vol. 54, p 1075.

"The Marmon Line for 1908." *Horseless Age,* September 25, 1907, Vol. 20, No. 13, p 399–400.

"Marmon 1907 Models." *Horseless Age,* November 21, 1906, Vol. 18, No. 22, p 715–717.

"Marmon 1911 Cars." *Horseless Age,* August 17, 1910, Vol. 26, No. 7, p 230–231.

"Marmon Price Increase." *Automotive Industries, the Automobile,* March 21, 1918, p 613.

"Marmon Roosevelt Price List Lower." *Indianapolis Star,* June 25, 1930, p 24.

"Marmon Sets Record in Fiscal Quarter." *Automotive Industries,* June 8, 1929, Vol. 60, p 892.

"Marmon Showing Lighter Eight to Sell for $1,395." *Automotive Industries,* January 7, 1928, Vol. 58, p 16–17.

"Marmon Torpedo Limousine." *Horseless Age,* February 7, 1912, Vol. 29, No 6, p 316.

"Marmon Will Bring Out Straight-Eight." *Automotive Industries,* October 5, 1929, Vol. 61, p 497.

"Marmon's Half Year Is Best in History." *Automotive Industries,* September 28, 1929, Vol. 61, p 463.

"Minor Mention." *Horseless Age,* May 30, 1900, Vol. 6, No. 9, p 23.

"Minor Mention." *Horseless Age,* June 30, 1900, Vol. 6, No. 18, p 29.

"More Cars Announce an Advance in Price." *Automotive Industries,* August 21, 1919, Vol. 41, p 394.

"More Companies Raise Prices." *Horseless Age,* December 15, 1916, Vol. 38, p 424.

"National Adopts Centre Controls." *Horseless Age,* February 21, 1912, Vol. 29, No. 8, p 387.

"National Develops New Touring Model." *Automotive Industries,* May 20, 1920, Vol. 42, p 1178.

"National Makes Big Cut." *Automotive Industries,* June 30, 1921, Vol. 44, p 1457.

"The National Model C." *Horseless Age,* January 4, 1905, Vol. 15, No. 1, p 18.

"National Motor Car & Vehicle Corp." *Automotive Industries,* April 7, 1921, Vol. 44, p 786.

"National Motor Vehicle Company." *Automobile Quarterly,* January 17, 1906, Vol. 17, No. 4, p 130.

"National Motor Vehicle Company." *Horseless Age,* February 25, 1903, Vol. 11, No. 8, p 288.

"The National Motor Vehicle Company." *Horseless Age,* January 20, 1904, Vol. 13, No. 3, p 77.

"The National Motor Vehicle Company." *Horseless Age,* January 20, 1904, Vol. 13, No. 3, p 81.

"The National Motor Vehicle Company." *Horseless Age,* December 5, 1906, Vol. 18, No. 23, p 794.

"The National Motor Vehicle Company." *Horseless Age,* February 13, 1907, Vol. 19, No. 7, p 240.

"The National Motor Vehicle Company." *Horseless Age,* November 19, 1909, Vol. 24, No. 19, p 518.

"National Newport Model." *Horseless Age,* April 28, 1915, Vol. 35, No. 17, p 572.

"National 1907 Models." *Horseless Age.* January 9, 1907, Vol. 19, No. 2, p 48–49.

"National 1910 Models." *Horseless Age,* October 6, 1909, Vol. 24, No. 14, p 371–373.

"National Price Increase." *Automotive Industries,* October 16, 1919, p 788.

"National Reports New Finance Plan." *Automotive Industries,* August 2, 1923, p 252.

"National Sued on Notes of Company It Succeeded." *Automotive Industries,* November 1, 1923, p 927.

"National to Increase Stock." *Automotive Industries,* December 9, 1920, p 1196.

"National Torpedo Body Car." *Horseless Age,* April 13, 1910, Vol. 25, No. 15, p 548.

"National Will Join Associated Motors." *Automotive Industries,* June 22, 1922, Vol. 46, p 1402.

"National Will Make All Its Own Parts." *Automotive Industries,* January 11, 1923, p 94.

"National's Factory Enlarged." *Horseless Age,* March 5, 1913, Vol. 31, No. 10, p 444.

"New American Car." *Horseless Age,* March 8, 1911, Vol. 27, No. 10, p 422.

"New Building for National." *Horseless Age,* March 23, 1910, Vol. 25, No.12, p 456.

"New Capital to Aid Stutz Development." *Automotive Industries,* October 19, 1922, Vol. 47, p 789.

"New Cole Convertible Bodies." *Horseless Age,* October 15, 1916, Vol. 38, p 259.

"New Cole Six-60 on the Market." *Horseless Age,* January 1, 1913, Vol. 31, No. 1, p 25.

"New Cole Speedster." *Horseless Age,* April 26, 1911, Vol. 27, No. 17, p 710.

"New Duesenberg Roadster Equipped with Rubay Body." *Automotive Industries,* July 19, 1923, p 147.

"The New Empire '25.'" *Horseless Age,* April 17, 1912, Vol. 29, No. 16, p 710.

"New Henderson Car Christened." *Horseless Age,* June 5, 1912, Vol. 29, No. 23, p 987.

"New Incorporations." *Horseless Age,* July 25, 1906, Vol. 18, No. 4, p 127.

"New Incorporations." *Horseless Age,* March 6, 1907, Vol. 19, No. 10, p 355.

"A New Marion Model." *Horseless Age,* December 25, 1912, Vol. 30, No. 25, p 976.

"The New Marmon Six Cylinder Car." *Horseless Age,* March 19, 1913, Vol. 31, No. 12, p 537–539.

"The New National Highway Twelve." *Horseless Age,* June 1, 1917, Vol. 40, p 23.

"The New Premier Aluminum Six." *Horseless Age,* Vol. 38, p 188–189.

"The New Premier Model 33." *Horseless Age,* April 28, 1915, Vol. 35, No. 17, p 570–571.

"A New Premier Model with an Overhead Valve Motor." *Horseless Age,* December 24, 1913, Vol. 31, No 26, p 1079–1081.

"The Premier Motor Car." *Horseless Age,* June 3, 1903, Vol. 11, No. 22, p 650.

"New Premier Sextet with Timken Axles and Worm Bevel Drive." *Horseless Age,* January 6, 1915, Vol. 35, No. 1, p 34–35.

"New Series Marmon 41 with Body." *Horseless Age,* July 23, 1915, Vol. 35, p 842–843.

"The New Series 1917 Stutz Car." *Horseless Age,* August 21, 1916, p 122–123.

"New Vehicles and Parts." *Horseless Age,* May 2, 1906, Vol. 17, No. 18, p 636.

"New Working Funds Provided National." *Automotive Industries,* April 22, 1922, Vol. 46, p 836.

"New York Trap of the National Automobile and Electric Co." *Horseless Age,* Vol. 6, p 84.

"1908 National Cars." *Horseless Age,* October 23, 1907, Vol. 20, No. 17, p 619.

"1911 American Line." *Horseless Age,* September 7, 1910, Vol. 26, No. 10, p 329.

"No Changes Planned in Stutz Personnel." *Automotive Industries,* August17, 1922, Vol. 47, p 338.

"No Empire 1919 Models." *Automotive Industries,* January 9, 1919, p 78.

"Nordyke & Marmon." *Horseless Age,* April 17, 1907, Vol. 19, No. 16, p 541–542.

"Nordyke & Marmon." *Horseless Age,* April 1, 1918, Vol. 44, p 47.

"Nordyke & Marmon Company." *Horseless Age,* December 5, 1906, Vol. 18, No. 23, p 788.

"Nordyke & Marmon Increase Capital." *Horseless Age,* July 23, 1913, Vol. 32, No. 4, p 137.

"Official High Gear Test of Marmon Car." *Horseless Age,* May 5, 1915, Vol. 35, No. 18, p 591.

"The Overland Automobile Company Affairs." *Horseless Age,* February 5, 1908, Vol. 21, No. 6, p 158.

"Overland 1909 Models." *Horseless Age,* October 14, 1909, Vol. 22, No. 16, p 524–525.

"Overland Reorganization Planned." *Horseless Age,* June 8, 1910, Vol. 25, No. 23, p 868.

"Pathfinder Announces a Six-Cylinder Model for 1914." *Horseless Age,* October 22, 1913, Vol. 32, No. 18, p 687–688.

"The Pathfinder for 1914." *Horseless Age,* September 10, 1913, Vol. 32, No. 11, p 428.

"Pathfinder '40' Ends Triple Transcontinental Tour." *Horseless Age,* December 11, 1912, Vol. 30, No. 24, p 882.

"Pathfinder New Series." *Horseless Age,* July 16, 1913, Vol. 32, No. 3, p 103.

"Pierce-Lafayette Merger Announced." *Automotive Industries,* Vol. 46, p 1090.

"Plan Would Put Nash Closer to Lafayette." *Automotive Industries,* June 8, 1922, Vol. 46, p 1294.

"Pope-Waverley Electric Truck." *Horseless Age,* June 28, 1905, Vol. 15, No. 26, p 707.

"Premier '45'—Six Cylinders." *Horseless Age,* October 16, 1907, Vol. 20, No 16, p 589.

"Premier Increases Its Capitalization to $1,250,000." *Horseless Age,* June 18, 1913, Vol. 31, No. 25, p 1.

"Premier Interchangeable Air and Water Cooled 1907 Models." *Horseless Age,* August 22, 1906, Vol. 18, No. 8, p 238.

"Premier 1906 Models." *Horseless Age,* January 24, 1906, Vol. 17, No. 4, p 175–177.

"Premier Line for 1911." *Horseless Age,* October 12, 1910, Vol. 26, No. 15, p 500–502.

"The Premier Motor Car." *Horseless Age,* June 3, 1903, Vol. 11, No. 22, p 650.

"Premier Motor Corp. Appoints Executive Committee." *Automotive Industries,* March 20, 1919, p 670.

"Premier Motor Files New Incorporation." *Automotive Industries,* April 7, 1921, Vol. 44, p 783.

"Premier Motor Manufacturing Company." *Horseless Age,* January 24, 1906, Vol. 17, No. 4, p 163–164.

"Premier Plans to Ship First Taxicab in July." *Automotive Industries,* June 21, 1923, p 1351.

"Premier Produces Taxicab with Four Wheel Brakes." *Automotive Industries,* December 18, 1924, Vol. 51, p 1067.

"Premier Purchaser to Operate Factory." *Automotive Industries,* May 24, 1923, p 1146.

"Premier Runabout." *Horseless Age,* July 18, 1906, Vol. 18, No. 3, p 86.

"Premier Runabout." *Horseless Age,* December 26, 1906, Vol. 18, No. 26, p 929.

"Premier Six Pulls Three Autos out of Mud." *Indianapolis Star,* September 22, 1907, p 26.

"Premier Sixes Only for 1913—A New Model Introduced." *Horseless Age,* October 2, 1912, Vol. 30, No. 14, p 512–514.

"Premier to Be Sold As Part of New Plan." *Automotive Industries,* October 12, 1922, Vol. 47, p 738.

"Premier Will Build 7-Passenger Sedan." *Automotive Industries,* September 20, 1923, p 606.

"Prices on Marmon Models Raised $350." *Automotive Industries,* February 5, 1920, Vol. 42, p 442.

"The Providence Races." *Horseless Age,* September 23, 1903, Vol. 12, No. 14, p 340.

"Push Production in Indiana Plants." *Automotive Industries,* October 2, 1919, p 695.

"Receiver Appointed for Weidley Motors." *Automotive Industries,* August 2, 1923, p 250.

"Receivership Suit Against Sales Company." *Horseless Age,* May 25, 1910, Vol. 25, No. 21, p 808.

"Recent Trade Developments." *Horseless Age,* September 15, 1917, Vol. 41, p 46.

"Recent Trade Developments." *Horseless Age,* August 1, 1917, Vol. 41, p 56.

"Reorganize Empire Motor Company." *Horseless Age,* March 6, 1912, Vol. 29, No. 10, p 481.

"Report National to Enter Truck Field." *Automotive Industries,* January 15, 1920, Vol. 42, p 287.

"Ryan Heads Company Producing Frontenac." *Automotive Industries,* January 5, 1922, Vol. 46, p 40.

"Ryan Resigns Seat on Stock Exchange." *Automotive Industries,* April 15, 1920, Vol. 42, p 942.

"Ryan's Difficulties Not Serious to Stutz." *Automotive Industries,* December 2, 1920, Vol. 43, p 1147.

"Sales Slump Hits Lines Not Reduced." *Automotive Industries,* May 19, 1921, Vol. 44, p 1076.

Schipper, J. Edward. "Eight Cylinder Automobile Has Light Weight Feature." *Automotive Industries,* August 19, 1920, Vol. 43, p 362.

_____. "Heavy Crankshaft Features New Marmon Engine." *Automotive Industries,* January 29, 1920, Vol. 42, p 347.

_____. "New Duesenberg Reflects Experience Gained with Racing Cars." *Automotive Industries,* November 3, 1921, Vol. 44, p 854 & 858.

_____. "New Four-Cylinder Car Has Brakes on All Wheels." *Automotive Industries,* January 5, 1922, Vol. 46, p 5.

_____. "Powerplant in New Stutz Model Incorporates Many Changes." *Automotive Industries,* April 6, 1922, Vol. 46, p 750–751.

"Series 10-4 Cole Announced." *Horseless Age,* April 29, 1914, Vol. 33, No. 17, p 671–673.

"Small Property Sold to Bank For $175,000." *Automotive Industries,* January 5, 1922, Vol. 46, p 36.

"Small Stockholders to Advance $200,000." *Automotive Industries,* May 5, 1921, Vol. 44, p 979.

"Some Electric Mileage Records." *Horseless Age,* September 16, 1903, Vol. 12, No. 12, p 304.

"Some Features of the New Premier." *Horseless Age,* April 28, 1915, Vol. 35, No. 17, p 569.

"Stream-lined Bodies and Left Hand Drive Characterize New Cole Models." *Horseless Age,* July 23, 1913, Vol. 32, No. 4, p 142–146.

"Stutz." *Horseless Age,* January 1, 1918, Vol. 43, p 38.

"Stutz Adds Coupe at $3,990." *Automotive Industries,* August 4, 1928, Vol. 59, p 179.

"Stutz and Parry Donate Motor Ambulances." *Horseless Age,* May 1, 1917, Vol. 40, p 48.

"Stutz Announces New 6-84 Sedan at $3,050." *Automotive Industries,* June 4, 1925, Vol. 52, p 998.

"The Stutz Car—A Newcomer in High Powered Class." *Horseless Age,* June 14, 1911, Vol. 27, No. 24, p 1014.

"Stutz Company Plans Production of 5,000 in 1920." *Automotive Industries,* February 5, 1920, Vol. 42, p 430.

"Stutz Control Goes to Guaranty." *Automotive Industries,* August 3, 1922, Vol. 47, p 247.

"Stutz Control Goes to Schwab Interests." *Automotive Industries,* August 10, 1922, Vol. 47, p 296.

"Stutz Earns $1,074,778." *Automotive Industries, the Automobile,* January 24, 1918, p 245.

"Stutz Gives Buyers Insurance for Year." *Automotive Industries,* June 18, 1927, Vol. 56, p 950.

"Stutz Head Mentioned As Frontenac President." *Automotive Industries,* January 12, 1922, Vol. 46, p 90.

"Stutz Holds 68 mph to Win Stevens Cup." *Automotive Industries*, April 30, 1927, Vol. 56, p 676.
"Stutz Increases Power and Makes Body Refinements." *Automotive Industries*, September 22, 1928, Vol. 59, p 404–405.
"Stutz Is President of New Cab Company." *Automotive Industries*, October 16, 1924, Vol. 51, p 700.
"Stutz Makes Radio Optional on Cars." *Automotive Industries*, October 6, 1928, Vol. 59, p 496.
"Stutz Makes Revisions." *Automotive Industries*, January 5, 1922, Vol. 46, p 37.
"Stutz Offers Chateau Series with Weymann Bodies." *Automotive Industries*, October 19, 1929, Vol. 61, p 589.
"Stutz Offers Supercharge on Stock Model." *Automotive Industries*, November 2, 1929, Vol. 61, p 645–646.
"Stutz Prices Down $650." *Automotive Industries*, June 30, 1921, Vol. 44, p 1457.
"Stutz Prices Lower on New Series Cars." *Automotive Industries*, July 13, 1929, Vol. 61, p 66.
"Stutz Produces Closed Models As Part of Line." *Automotive Industries*, November 30, 1922, p 1098.
"Stutz Profits Drop." *Automotive Industries*, February 20, 1919, Vol. 40, p 442.
"Stutz Reports Net Loss of $632,370 at End of 1921." *Automotive Industries*, May 25, 1922, Vol. 46, p 1145.
"Stutz Series B Includes a Six Cylinder Chassis." *Horseless Age*, October 22, 1912, Vol. 30, No. 14, p 517–518.
"Stutz Takes First in Stock Car Races." *Automotive Industries*, May 14, 1927, Vol. 56, p 747.
"Stutz to Build Engine for New Model in Its Own Plant." *Automotive Industries*, December 27, 1923, p 1296–1300.
"Stutz to Build Its Own Six-Cylinder Power Plants." *Automotive Industries*, August 2, 1923, p 246.
"Suit for Receivership Filed Against National." *Automotive Industries*, July 12, 1923, p 94.
"Suit for Receivership Filed Against Premier." *Automotive Industries*, November 1, 1923, p 923.
"Stutz Wins Classic at Atlantic City." *Automotive Industries*, September 10, 1927, Vol. 57, p 395.
"To Auction Pathfinder and Springfield Body Plants." *Automotive Industries, the Automobile*, February 28, 1918, p 483.
"To Stop Price Cutting." *Horseless Age*, April 19, 1911, Vol. 27, No. 16, p 668.
"Trade Personals." *Horseless Age*, February 5, 1908, Vol. 21, No. 6, p 159.
"Twelve Cylinder Announcements Startle Industry." *Horseless Age*, May 26, 1915, Vol. 35, No. 21, p 1.
"The Twelve Cylinder Pathfinder." *Horseless Age*, February 1, 1916, Vol. 37, p 104–105.
"$20 Million Contract for Weidley Motors Company." *Automotive Industries, the Automobile*, January 21, 1918, p 251.
"265 hp Duesenberg Eight Costs $8,500." *Automotive Industries*, December 1, 1928, Vol. 59, p 790–794.
"Two More 'Twelves' and a New 'Eight.'" *Horseless Age*, June 23, 1915, Vol. 35, p 838.
"Two New Open Models Added to Marmon Line." *Automotive Industries*, April 23, 1925, Vol. 52, p 757.
"The Unconventional Marmon." *Horseless Age*, January 1, 1916, Vol. 37, p 14 & 15.
"Warehouse Fire Damages Bodies for Duesenberg." *Automotive Industries*, November 29, 1923, p 1121.
"Waverley Electric Gentleman's Roadster." *Horseless Age*, April 13, 1910, Vol. 25, No. 15, p 549.
"The Waverley Electric Vehicle." *Horseless Age*, May 14, 1902, Vol. 9, No. 20, p 576–578.
"Weidley Motors Sues Stutz for $750,000." *Automotive Industries*, January 29, 1925, Vol. 52, p 210.
"Weidley Sale Approved; Will Resume Operations." *Automotive Industries*, January 24, 1924, Vol. 50, p 204.
Wolff, Raymond A. "Duesenberg: It's a Grand Old Name." *Automobile Quarterly*, Spring 1966, Vol. 4, No. 4, p 348–355.

Newspaper Articles

"A.A.A. Contest Board Announces Records." *Indianapolis Star*, June 29, 1912, p 11.
"A.A.A. Disqualifies Premier Company." *Indianapolis Star*, July 28, 1910, p 3.
"A.A.A. Ready to Meet." *Indianapolis Star*, January 10, 1911, p 10.
"A. B. Cronk Named Trustee of Stutz." *Indianapolis Star*, May 2, 1937, p 24.
"Ace Entertains Plant Workers." *Indianapolis Star*, May 9, 1918, p 8.
"Additions Begun." *Indianapolis Star*, September 3, 1916, p 28.
"Adopts Auto Name Plate." *Indianapolis Star*, August 18, 1912, p 20.
"Advance of $100 in Price of Coles." *Indianapolis Star*, November 19, 1916, p 23.
"After Atlanta Winners." *Indianapolis Star*, May 4, 1910, p 9.
"Aitken Sets New Auto Track Mark." *Indianapolis Star*, November 12, 1909, p 9.
"Aitken, with Peugeot, Heads Speedway Team." *Indianapolis Star*, April 2, 1916, p 23.
"Alexander Heads Monroe Sales; New Idea in Selling." *Indianapolis Star*, April 16, 1922, p 63.
"All Season Models Out." *Indianapolis Star*, August 3, 1919, p 53.
"All-Year Car Here to Stay." *Indianapolis Star*, December 3, 1916, p 21.
"Alleged Brass Thieves Rounded Up by Police." *Indianapolis Star*, April 16, 1911, p 34.
"Altoona Checkup Gives Pete First." *Indianapolis Star*, June 14, 1925, p 13.
"Amateur Pilot Is Winner in Big Race." *Indianapolis Star*, October 10, 1911, p 8.
"America Will Have Highest Priced Car in New Duesenberg." *Indianapolis Star*, October 17, 1926, p 69.
"American Cars in New Models." *Indianapolis Star*, June 11, 1911, p 30.
"American Plant Announces Cars." *Indianapolis Star*, April 20, 1913, p 36.
"Anderson Enters Stutz in Races." *Indianapolis Star*, August 22, 1916, p 10.
"Anderson Sheepshead Speed King." *Indianapolis Star*, October 10, 1915, p 17.
"Announce New Marmon 74 Line." *Indianapolis Star*, October 26, 1924, p 61 & 66.
"Announce Reorganization of LaFayette Motors." *Indianapolis Star*, June 3, 1922, p 12.
"Announces New Cars for 1914." *Indianapolis Star*, August 17, 1913, p 31.
"Announcing the Marmon 'Forty-One.'" *Indianapolis Star*, January 4, 1914, p 31.
"Annual Marmon Statement Reflects Strong Position." *Indianapolis Star*, April 20, 1929, p 16.
"Annual Meeting Will Inaugurate New Car Series." *Indianapolis Star*, January 3, 1927, p 1.
"Another Record Smashed." *Indianapolis Star*, May 23, 1915, p 57.
"Antiscuff Valve Insures Starting Oil for Marmon." *Indianapolis Star*, February 27, 1927, p 57.
"Apperson Car First." *Indianapolis Star*, May 25, 1906, p 7.
"Apperson Car Is Wrecked on Track." *Indianapolis Star*, April 11, 1910, p 8.

"Approves Recapitalization." *Indianapolis Star,* June 22, 1922, p 3.

"The Aristocrat of the Road." *Indianapolis Star,* May 6, 1917, p 22.

"Asks Receivership for Duesenberg Co." *Indianapolis Star,* April 13, 1923, p 9.

"Asks Suspension of Stutz Stocks." *Indianapolis Star,* October 24, 1937, p 12.

"Associated Motors Under New Name." *Indianapolis Star,* January 21, 1923, p 61.

"Assure Future for Mars Hill." *Indianapolis Star,* October 14, 1919, p 12.

"At the Fair This Week." *Indianapolis Star,* September 5, 1915, p 43.

"At the Two Speedways." *Indianapolis Star,* April 25, 1924, p 18.

"Atlanta Builds Track." *Indianapolis Star,* July 9, 1909, 9.

"Attracts Attention at Auto Show." *Indianapolis Star,* December 16, 1906, p 12.

"Auto Adjustment Period Is Put at Nine Months." *Indianapolis Star,* December 22, 1918, p 20.

"Auto Committees Hold a Meeting." *Indianapolis Star,* March 20, 1909, p 9.

"Auto Company to Employ Girls on Big War Contract." *Indianapolis Star,* December 22, 1917, p 3.

"Auto Concern Opens Office." *Indianapolis Star,* November 21, 1907, p 8.

"Auto Convention Plan Is Indorsed." *Indianapolis Star,* September 15, 1912, p 20.

"Auto Dealers Ready for Fair This Week." *Indianapolis Star,* September 1, 1912, p 15.

"Auto Dealers Turn Towards Show Week." *Indianapolis Star,* February 21, 1909, p 16.

"Auto Factories Profit by Show." *Indianapolis Star,* January 29, 1915, p 9.

"Auto Factory Enlarged." *Indianapolis Star,* June 11, 1909, p 12.

"Auto Firms Send Formal Protest." *Indianapolis Star,* October 7, 1914, p 14.

"Auto Industry Booming Here." *Indianapolis Star,* September 4, 1920, p 18.

"Auto Industry Shows Trend Toward Normal." *Indianapolis Star,* May 22, 1922, p 10.

"Auto Maker Sees Sport in Contests." *Indianapolis Star,* May 15, 1910, p 47.

"Auto Makers Aid Work of Rescue." *Indianapolis Star,* March 27, 1913, p 10.

"Auto Makers Are Organized." *Indianapolis Star,* February 26, 1905, p 6.

"Auto Makers Join Big Association." *Indianapolis Star,* October 24, 1909, p 36.

"Auto Manufacturer Proves His Ability As Detective." *Indianapolis Star,* June 5, 1913, p 14.

"Auto Meeting Convenes Here." *Indianapolis Star,* July 13, 1913, p 20.

"Auto Men Take Fling at M'Adoo." *Indianapolis Star,* January 5, 1917, p 11.

"Auto Move Is Announced." *Indianapolis Star,* March 16, 1911, p 1.

"Auto Officer Here on Secret Mission." *Indianapolis Star,* February 12, 1910, p 10.

"Auto Plant Not to Move; Lafayette Bankers Balk." *Indianapolis Star,* May 21, 1910, p 4.

"Auto Plant Ordered Sold." *Indianapolis Star,* December 30, 1910, p 10.

"Auto Price Is Unchanged." *Indianapolis Star,* October 16, 1920, p 9.

"Auto Race Entries Fill Events Well." *Indianapolis Star,* May 25, 1910, p 23.

"Auto Race Meet to Be Held Here Oct. 21." *Indianapolis Star,* October 8, 1905, p 22.

"Auto Races Today; Good Entry List." *Indianapolis Star,* May 30, 1906, p 7.

"Auto Racing Pilot Meets Tragic End." *Indianapolis Star,* November 2, 1910, p 1.

"Auto Show at Fair Proves Big Success." *Indianapolis Star,* September 7, 1912, p 7.

"Auto Show Begins in Medley Honks." *Indianapolis Star,* March 23, 1909, p 8.

"Auto Show Excites Interest of State." *Indianapolis Star,* February 16, 1908, p 32.

"Auto Show Is Tribute to Last Year's Models." *Indianapolis Star,* January 7, 1924, p 9.

"Auto Show Notes." *Indianapolis Star,* January 14, 1917, p 17.

"Auto Show Opens in Blaze of Glory." *Indianapolis Star,* March 24, 1908, p 7.

"Auto Show Opens in New York Palace." *Indianapolis Star,* January 3, 1909, p 23.

"Auto Show Week Complete Success." *Indianapolis Star,* March 29, 1908, p 10.

"Auto Speed Fiends Hope to Set Records." *Indianapolis Star,* September 18, 1908, p 8.

"Auto Truck Taking Place in Indianapolis Concerns." *Indianapolis Star,* April 8, 1917, p 16.

"Auto World's Eye on Indiana Course." *Indianapolis Star,* May 8, 1910, p 52.

"Autoists Start Long Tour Today." *Indianapolis Star,* July 9, 1912, p 9.

"Autoists to Wager." *Indianapolis Star,* February 15, 1908, p 32.

"Automobile Company Gets Results in Sunday Papers." *Indianapolis Star,* August 25, 1912, p 26.

"Automobile Company to Buy New Factory Site." *Indianapolis Star,* April 2, 1909, p 16.

"Automobile Firm Sues." *Indianapolis Star,* May 21, 1920, p 6.

"Autos Convince Show Visitors." *Indianapolis Star,* January 8, 1934, p 3.

"Autos Keep Perfect Scores." *Indianapolis Star,* July 28, 1909, p 9.

"Baker Breaks Record." *Indianapolis Star,* May 19, 1915, p 10.

"Baker Coast-to-Coast Run Remarkable Stutz Record." *Indianapolis Star,* May 23, 1915, p 58.

"Baker Establishes Five Speed and Five Economy Records in Cole Master Model." *Indianapolis Star,* August 19, 1923, p 32.

"Baker Sets Trans–U.S. Speed Record in Stutz." *Indianapolis Star,* November 7, 1930, p 3.

"Bales Puncture Plugger Saves Time." *Indianapolis Star,* May 28, 1916, p 41.

"Balloon Tires on H.C.S. Motor Cars." *Indianapolis Star,* December 9, 1923, p 77.

"Balloon Tires on Marmon." *Indianapolis Star,* January 6, 1924, p 57.

"Bank Receiver for Premier Company." *Indianapolis Star,* July 2, 1922, p 12.

"Bankruptcy Act Fought by Stutz." *Indianapolis Star,* January 4, 1930, p 10.

"Barney Oldfield Gives Estimate of Balloon Tires." *Indianapolis Star,* February 17, 1924, p 59.

"Barney Oldfield Quits Racing Game." *Indianapolis Star,* March 2, 1911, p 10.

Base, W. H. "Heavy Increase in Ford Demand." *Indianapolis Star,* February 25, 1917, p 19.

_____. "Motordome Needs Its Tester Still." *Indianapolis Star,* April 1, 1917, p 16.

_____. "Motor Truck Is Blessing." *Indianapolis Star*, December 9, 1917, p 18.

_____. "Motor Truck Is Coming into Own." *Indianapolis Star*, October 7, 1917, p 19.

_____. "Premier Offers Aluminum Six." *Indianapolis Star*, January 7, 1917, p 20.

_____. "Signal Advent of Motor Truck." *Indianapolis Star*, April 15, 1917, p 17.

_____. "Sterling Firm Betters Service." *Indianapolis Star*, April 8, 1917, p 17.

_____. "Utility, Slogan of Auto Show." *Indianapolis Star*, January 6, 1918, p 10.

"Bedford Company Has Busy Season." *Indianapolis Star*, July 12, 1920, p 8.

Behr, Julian J. "Big Fields Meet in Speedway Races." *Indianapolis Star*, July 2, 1910, p 1.

_____. "Boy Wins Brilliant Cobe Trophy Race." *Indianapolis Star*, July 5, 1910, p 6.

_____. "Cobe Trophy Lure for Races Today." *Indianapolis Star*, July 4, 1910, p 4.

_____. "Nationals First in Speedway Feature." *Indianapolis Star*, September 6, 1910, p 12.

_____. "Westcott Trails Benz in Big Race." *Indianapolis Star*, September 4, 1910, p 15 & 22.

"Believe Fire Screened Work of Iron Wreckers." *Indianapolis Star*, September 21, p 1 & 3.

"Believe Owners Desire to Drive." *Indianapolis Star*, November 21, 1915, p 33.

"Big Addition for Cole Auto Plant." *Indianapolis Star*, April 13, 1913, p 41.

"Big Array of Autos to Visit Our City." *Indianapolis Star*, July 7, 1907, p 32.

"Big Show Ends Tonight." *Indianapolis Star*, January 7, 1910, p 8.

"Big Spring Seen by Premier Head." *Indianapolis Star*, March 21, 1915, p 22.

"Big Truck Order Keeps up Policy." *Indianapolis Star*, June 29, 1931, p 18.

"Bill Endicott and Hughes Star in Dayton Auto Meet." *Indianapolis Star*, July 16, 1910, p 9.

"Blackhawk Cars Reduced in Price." *Indianapolis Star*, March 31, 1929, p 57.

Blakely, A. S. "Aitken Wins Every Race—Indians Gain on the Clymers." *Indianapolis Star*, September 10, 1916, p 45.

_____, "Aitken Wins Race and $13,000 at Cincinnati." *Indianapolis Star*, September 5, 1916, p 12 & 16.

_____. "Auto Men Close Big Convention." *Indianapolis Star*, October 10, 1912, p 13.

_____. "Auto Men's Ire Aroused by Bill." *Indianapolis Star*, January 31, 1913, p 13.

_____. "Auto Test Car Bill Put Through Senate." *Indianapolis Star*, February 12, 1913, p 9.

_____. "Autoists Enjoy Views in Frisco." *Indianapolis Star*, July 30, 1913, p 2.

_____. "Big Speedway Race on May 30 Starts at 1:30 in the Afternoon." *Indianapolis Star*, April 27, 1916, p 15.

_____. "DePalma Wins Cobe Trophy; Dawson Second." *Indianapolis Star*, August 30, 1913, p 5.

_____. "Driver for Peugeot Victor at Average of 84 Miles an Hour." *Indianapolis Star*, May 31, 1916, p 1.

_____. "First Entries for 500-Mile Race Received." *Indianapolis Star*, September 21, 1913, p 32.

_____. "Foreign Pilots Are First Four in Auto Classic." *Indianapolis Star*, May 31, 1914, p 1 & 6.

_____. "Gil Anderson Free to Choose Mount for Local Race in May." *Indianapolis Star*, April 16, 1916, p 58.

_____. "Harroun May Enter Next 500-Mile Race." *Indianapolis Star*, January 20, 1913, p 8.

_____. "Hearty Welcome Given Hoosier." *Indianapolis Star*, July 29, 1913, p 1 & 5.

_____. "Motor Industry Given Big Boost." *Indianapolis Star*, October 13, 1912, p 34.

_____. "New Track Record Set by Oldfield." *Indianapolis Star*, May 29, 1916, p 1 & 14.

_____. "Offer to Aid Rock Road Path." *Indianapolis Star*, October 8, 1912, p 7.

_____. "On Motor Row." *Indianapolis Star*, February 20, 1913, p 10.

_____. "On Motor Row." *Indianapolis Star*, March 9, 1913, p 9.

_____. "Peugeot Racer Ready for Tuesday." *Indianapolis Star*, March 26, 1916, p 56.

_____. "Refutes Rumor of Cole Change." *Indianapolis Star*, February 16, 1913, p 28.

_____. "Rickenbacker and Sunbeam Pilot Are Second in List." *Indianapolis Star*, May 23, 1916, p 14.

_____. "Road Across U.S. Proposed by Auto Men." *Indianapolis Star*, September 11, 1912, p 1 & 9.

_____. "State Autoists Leave Today on Tour to Pacific." *Indianapolis Star*, July 1, 1913, p 1.

_____. "Third Premier Ready to Race." *Indianapolis Star*, May 27, 1916, p 13.

_____. "Thirteen Racers in Short Events." *Indianapolis Star*, August 29, 1916, p 10.

Blankenbaker, R. M. "Bugatti Will Be in 500-Mile Race." *Indianapolis Star*, April 29, 1914, p 12.

_____. "Cole Company Uses Four Labor Saving Devices." *Indianapolis Star*, April 26, 1914, p 54.

_____. "Dawson's Record Is Endangered." *Indianapolis Star*, May 17, 1914, p 45.

_____. "French Drivers Come in Today." *Indianapolis Star*, May 10, 1914, p 40.

_____. "French Stamp 500-Mile Race Biggest Event." *Indianapolis Star*, April 26, 1914, p 47.

_____. "On Motor Row." *Indianapolis Star*, March 31, 1914, p 11.

_____. "Three Companies Bid for Oldfield." *Indianapolis Star*, March 17, 1914, p 14.

_____. "Three Racers Break Marks at Speedway." *Indianapolis Star*, May 27, 1914, p 5.

"Blaze Loss Estimated at $50,000." *Indianapolis Star*, April 25, 1915, p 1 & 8.

"Body Styles and Features of Roosevelt 8." *Indianapolis Star*, March 31, 1929, p 57.

"Bond Laggards Shy $10,000,000." *Indianapolis Star*, June 14, 1917, p 6.

"Boost Stock to $3,000,000." *Indianapolis Star*, February 29, 1920, p 13.

Bostwick, Mary E. "Pilgrims Stop at Cleveland." *Indianapolis Star*, May 1, 1924, p 24.

"Boulevard Boom Given New Boost." *Indianapolis Star*, January 18, 1914, p 31.

Bradfield, H. C. "Cooper in Stutz Wins at Tacoma." *Indianapolis Star*, July 5, 1914, p 23.

"Brand Cup Event As Mere Mockery." *Indianapolis Star*, October 31, 1909, p 19.

"Bruce Brown's Big Fiat Winner of Grand Prize." *Indianapolis Star*, December 1, 1911, p 11.

Buck, Arthur C. "Increase in Auto Output Foreseen." *Indianapolis Star*, January 30, 1930, p 1.

_____, "Limited Gasoline Supply Doesn't Prove Hoodoo to Racers." *Indianapolis Star*, May 31, 1934, p 19.

_____. "Marmon Leader Voices Optimism." *Indianapolis Star*, January 9, 1930, p 1.

"Building a New Auto at Nordyke, Marmons." *Indianapolis Star*, August 21, 1904, p 12.

"Building Collapses; One Man Killed." *Indianapolis Star,* April 16, 1912, p 3.

"Building Permits." *Indianapolis Star,* April 7, 1914, p 10.

"Builds Commercial Car." *Indianapolis Star,* August 14, 1912, p 9.

"Builds Speedy Auto." *Indianapolis Star,* January 30, 1910, p 36.

Bull, Frank R. "Auto Engineers of Indiana Hold Recruiting Party." *Indianapolis Star,* March 25, 1917, p 18.

_____. "Auto Engineers to Hear Airplane Expert Friday." *Indianapolis Star,* June 10, 1917, p 19.

_____. "Auto Exhibitors See Sales Boom." *Indianapolis Star,* January 5, 1916, p 2.

_____. "Don't Speed Car Down to Office." *Indianapolis Star,* October 28, 1917, p 19.

_____. "Gasoline Cost Is Cut Down by Care in Use of Machine." *Indianapolis Star,* April 2, 1916, p 23.

_____. "Great Variety of Machines Offered at National Show." *Indianapolis Star,* January 7, 1917, p 19.

_____. "Indiana Cars Loom at Show." *Indianapolis Star,* January 4, 1920, p 1.

_____. "Indiana Leading in Auto Display." *Indianapolis Star,* January 10, 1917, p 11.

_____. "Monthly New Car Totals in County Bottom Out in September." *Indianapolis Star,* October 5, 1930, p 27.

_____. "National Making 35 Cars Each Day." *Indianapolis Star,* March 4, 1917, p 21.

_____. "Race to Reveal War's Changes." *Indianapolis Star,* May 30, 1919, p 20.

_____. "Rotarians Show Guests Thursday." *Indianapolis Star,* February 7, 1917, p 7.

_____. "Service Feature Attracts Buyers." *Indianapolis Star,* February 9, 1917, p 5.

_____. "Something New in Wheels for Cole Eight This Year." *Indianapolis Star,* May 9, 1917, p 9.

"Burman Is Here for Speed Tests." *Indianapolis Star,* December 15, 1911, p 11.

"Business Is Not Marred by Fire." *Indianapolis Star,* April 26. 1915, p 14.

"Business Men Form New Motor Company." *Indianapolis Star,* May 7, 1912, p 11.

"Business Men Optimistic." *Indianapolis Star,* January 16, 1922, p 16.

"Buys Duesenberg Motors Plant." *Indianapolis Star,* October 6, 1926, p 1.

"Buys Premier Motor Control." *Indianapolis Star,* September 19, 1919, p 1 & 5.

"Cab Concern Buys Local Auto Plant." *Indianapolis Star,* October 10, 1924, p 1.

"Calls Race Course Deadly." *Indianapolis Star,* October 16, 1910, p 41.

"Capital Auto Co." *Indianapolis Star,* January 27, 1907, p 15.

"Carl Fisher Gives Up Track Racing." *Indianapolis Star,* August 6, 1905, p 14.

"Carnival Reigns at Show." *Indianapolis Star,* March 11, 1922, p 5.

"Cars Burn Air in Speedway Workouts." *Indianapolis Star,* June 29, 1910, p 5.

"Cars Make Fast Time." *Indianapolis Star,* October 25, 1909, p 9.

"Century Car on Trip." *Indianapolis Star,* December 13, 1908, p 28.

"Champion Jeffries Falls from Curzon's Flying Machine." *Indianapolis Star,* November 27, 1909, p 8.

"Champion, Spark Plug Maker, Dies." *Indianapolis Star,* October 28, 1927, p 12.

"Champions Add New Laurels to Impressive List." *Indianapolis Star,* September 20, 1925, p 74.

"Change Announced in Local Motor Plants." *Indianapolis Star,* September 27, 1912, p 11.

"Change to Left-Hand Drive." *Indianapolis Star,* April 26, 1912, p 10.

"Changes in Cole Eights Add to Car's Efficiency." *Indianapolis Star,* March 24, 1918, p 21.

"Charges Made Against Ryan." *Indianapolis Star,* April 11, 1920, p 2.

"Charles A. Bookwalter." *Indianapolis Star,* April 30, 1905, p 38.

"Chevrolet Winner in 200-Mile Race." *Indianapolis Star,* November 10, 1909, p 9.

"Chicago Auto Show Throws Open Doors." *Indianapolis Star,* December 1, 1907, p 10.

"Chicago Society Visits Big Show." *Indianapolis Star,* January 29, 1914, p 11.

"Chief Officers Quit National Motors." *Indianapolis Star,* January 20, 1924, p 10.

"Christie Betters Mark for Mile." *Indianapolis Star,* September 20, 1908, p 11.

"Circuit Auto Races On." *Indianapolis Star,* July 9, 1910, p 4.

"City Gets New Auto Industry." *Indianapolis Star,* July 29, 1917, p 1.

"City Leader in Fine Cars." *Indianapolis Star,* December 14, 1919, p 78.

"City News in Brief." *Indianapolis Star,* November 5, 1904, p 7.

"City News in Brief." *Indianapolis Star,* August 24, 1920, p 5.

"City Notes." *Indianapolis Star,* September 24, 1913, p 6.

"City of Model Homes Rises for Motor Company Employees." *Indianapolis Star,* August 13, 1920, p 10 & 11.

"City Pays Tribute to Glidden Tourists." *Indianapolis Star,* July 17, 1907, p 7.

"City to Obtain Tractor Plant." *Indianapolis Star,* February 24, 1917, p 2.

"Civic Tourists Visit Speedway." *Indianapolis Star,* May 1, 1915, p 18.

"A Clean Sweep of the Stoddard-Dayton." *Indianapolis Star,* March 25, 1908, p 6.

"Clemens Sets New 100-Mile Record." *Indianapolis Star,* November 5, 1905, p 18.

Clifford, Eugene R. "Death of Spence First Since 1926." *Indianapolis Star,* May 31, 1929, p 10.

"Club Roadster Grows Popular." *Indianapolis Star,* August 1, 1915, p 2.

"Coast-to-Coast Record Smashed." *Indianapolis Star,* August 13, 1916, p 19.

"Coast Tour to Aid Good Roads." *Indianapolis Star,* January 26, 1913, p 30.

"Cole Adopts Balloon Tires As Equipment on 1924 Models." *Indianapolis Star,* September 2, 1923, p 45.

"Cole Aero-Eight Is Easy on Tires." *Indianapolis Star,* March 9, 1919, p 55.

"Cole Aero-Eight Model Is Reduced to $2,485." *Indianapolis Star,* October 27, 1921, p 3.

"Cole Aero-Eight New in Body and Power." *Indianapolis Star,* March 10, 1918, p 21.

"Cole Aero-Eight Prices Come Down $455 to $700." *Indianapolis Star,* June 29, 1921, p 5.

"Cole Aero-Eight Wins Approval." *Indianapolis Star,* February 25, 1918, p 9.

"Cole and Henderson Forces Are Merged." *Indianapolis Star,* March 28, 1912, p 7.

"Cole Announces All-Year Eight." *Indianapolis Star,* July 9, 1916, p 16.

"Cole Announces New 8-Cylinder." *Indianapolis Star*, January 21, 1915, p 11.
"Cole Begins New Expansion Plan." *Indianapolis Star*, January 16, 1917, p 17.
"Cole Company Announces Reduction in Price of '8.'" *Indianapolis Star*, December 31, 1915, p 43.
"Cole Company Branches Out." *Indianapolis Star*, April 23, 1916, p 20.
"Cole Company Doubles Plant." *Indianapolis Star*, September 27, 1919, p 1 & 5.
"Cole Company Sets June 10 As New Model Day at Plant." *Indianapolis Star*, June 10, 1923, p 33.
"Cole Company to Build New Plant." *Indianapolis Star*, June 4, 1911, p 34.
"Cole Company to Make Aero Type As Specialty." *Indianapolis Star*, November 3, 1918, p 23.
"Cole Company to Supply Autos for Pershing Staff." *Indianapolis Star*, November 2, 1917, p 13.
"Cole Company Will Make Seven Models." *Indianapolis Star*, August 13, 1911, p 26.
"Cole Eight Makes Strong Record." *Indianapolis Star*, December 19, 1915, p 21.
"Cole Eight Soon to Go on Market." *Indianapolis Star*, January 31, 1915, p 21.
"Cole Firm Invites Any Difficult Task." *Indianapolis Star*, May 14, 1916, p 22.
"Cole Improves As Hill Climber." *Indianapolis Star*, August 2, 1914, p 17.
"Cole Line Adopts New Car Model and Delco Lighting." *Indianapolis Star*, March 30, 1913, p 26.
"Cole London Limousine." *Indianapolis Star*, October 29, 1911, p 35.
"Cole Plan of Floating Liberty Bonds Taken Before U.S. Officials." *Indianapolis Star*, May 23, 1917, p 10.
"Cole Presents Reasons." *Indianapolis Star*, May 28, 1911, p 25.
"Cole Producing New Six Model." *Indianapolis Star*, July 11, 1915, p 17.
"Cole Roadster Makes Friends." *Indianapolis Star*, October 31, 1915, p 21.
"Cole Roadster Sets New Style." *Indianapolis Star*, June 25, 1916, p 20.
"Cole Sets Gas Economy Mark." *Indianapolis Star*, October 11, 1914, p 20.
"Cole Solid Tire Automobile." *Indianapolis Star*, March 21, 1909, p 19.
"Cole Speeds Production and Lowers List Prices." *Indianapolis Star*, December 1, 1918, p 22.
"Cole Takes Climb Honors." *Indianapolis Star*, December 1, 1911, p 11.
"Cole Takes Lead in New Sales Plan." *Indianapolis Star*, February 4, 1923, p 12.
"Cole Testers Treat Druggists to Race." *Indianapolis Star*, September 27, 1914, p 34.
"Cole 30." *Indianapolis Star*, April 10, 1910, p 34.
"Cole Tire Pump Handy." *Indianapolis Star*, February 27, 1916, p 57.
"Cole to Introduce Medium Priced Cars." *Indianapolis Star*, May 15, 1912, p 11.
"Cole Uses One Chassis." *Indianapolis Star*, January 1, 1911, p 16.
"Cole Wins Fuel Contest." *Indianapolis Star*, May 22, 1910, p 17.
"Committees Named for Auto Convention." *Indianapolis Star*, September 17, 1912, p 7.
"Companies Obtain Permits for $175,000 Projects." *Indianapolis Star*, January 27, 1921, p 5.
"Company Plans to Build Touring Car." *Indianapolis Star*, February 9, 1912, p 10.
Conduitt & Company Ad. *Indianapolis Star*, May 28, 1916, p 23.
"Confirm Motor Merger." *Indianapolis Star*, April 15, 1922, p 3.
"Contemplates Few Changes in Laws." *Indianapolis Star*, January 22, 1911, p 23.
"Consistent Service Wins Again for the Sturdy Stutz." *Indianapolis Star*, June 7, 1914, p 21.
"Construction Company Reports New Building Equaling War Record." *Indianapolis Star*, January 5, 1920, p 4.
"Contract for Airship." *Indianapolis Star*, March 8, 1906, p 15.
"Contract Let for Motor Speedway." *Indianapolis Star*, March 16, 1909, p 9.
"Contract Made at Auto Show." *Indianapolis Star*, January 26, 1915, p 9.
"Cooper, in Stutz, Throws Scare into Resta." *Indianapolis Star*, August 8, 1915, p 41.
"Co-Operative Store Opens." *Indianapolis Star*, October 18, 1919, p 13.
"Cord Increases Employees' Wages." *Indianapolis Star*, May 9, 1933, p 17.
"Cord Will Sell Stocks, Report." *Indianapolis Star*, August 6, 1937, p 1.
"Course Will Include Automobile Study." *Indianapolis Star*, October 10, 1906, p 3.
"Court Declines to Name Receiver for Duesenberg Car Co." *Indianapolis Star*, April 20, 1923, p 11.
"Court Orders Sale of Duesenberg Plant." *Indianapolis Star*, January 1, 1925, p 13.
"Crash Is Fatal to Joe Boyer." *Indianapolis Star*, September 2, 1924, p 1.
"Crawfordsville to Have Smokeless Fuel." *Indianapolis Star*, December 27, 1903, p 12.
"Creditors Paid in Full." *Indianapolis Star*, November 14, 1919, p 10.
"Crowds Throng Building to Examine Marmon Cars." *Indianapolis Star*, June 2, 1911, p 11.
"Crowds Throng N.Y. Auto Show." *Indianapolis Star*, January 4, 1916, p 2.
"Curtain Goes Down on Big Auto Show." *Indianapolis Star*, December 8, 1907, p 29.
"D. M. Parry Erects Shops." *Indianapolis Star*, July 27, 1907, p 8.
"Dame Rumor Predicts an Empire 'Six' Soon." *Indianapolis Star*, June 27, 1915, p 19.
Daniels, Bruce. "All Roads Lead to Indianapolis." *Indianapolis Star*, May 24, 1914, p 56.
"Dashes to Death 80 Miles Per Hour." *Indianapolis Star*, July 7, 1910, p 1 & 5.
"Date Set for the Speedway Trials." *Indianapolis Star*, November 18, 1909, p 9.
"Dates Announced for Auto Meeting." *Indianapolis Star*, December 8, 1909, p 10.
"Dawson Risks Neck to Win Auto Race." *Indianapolis Star*, November 5, 1910, p 1.
"Dawson Says Old Car Is Best." *Indianapolis Star*, April 26, 1914, p 56.
"Dawson Shades Grant." *Indianapolis Star*, October 9, 1910, p 41.
"Day and Night Shift for Cole." *Indianapolis Star*, March 28, 1915, p 19.
"Dealings in Stutz Stock Under Fire." *Indianapolis Star*, July 25, 1935, p 14.
"Death Nearly Wins Motorcycle Races." *Indianapolis Star*, August 15, 1909, p 37.
"Death Takes Toll at Brighton Beach." *Indianapolis Star*, May 14, 1910, p 1.

"Decrease Shown in Auto Prices." *Indianapolis Star,* January 4, p 31.

"Demand for Marmon Keeps Production Up." *Indianapolis Star,* March 18, 1928, p 63.

"Demands Court Hearing." *Indianapolis Star,* July 28, 1910, p 3.

"Denies Connections to 2 Stutz Brokers." *Indianapolis Star,* July 26, 1935, p 2.

"Denies Need of Receiver." *Indianapolis Star,* March 23, 1922, p 9.

"DePalma Big Favorite to Win Classic." *Indianapolis Star,* May 31, 1920, p 11.

"DePalma Gets the Pole at Start of Big Race." *Indianapolis Star,* May 27, 1920, p 14.

"DePalma Here to Enter." *Indianapolis Star,* August 31, 1910, p 4.

"DePalma Is Winner of Vanderbilt." *Indianapolis Star,* February 27, 1914, p 10.

"DePalma to Race in National Cars." *Indianapolis Star,* February 21, 1911, p 10.

"DePaolo Makes New Record to Win at Fulford." *Indianapolis Star,* February 23, 1926, p 15.

"DePaolo Not to Enter Grand Prix." *Indianapolis Star,* June 16, 1925, p 12.

"DePaolo Sets New Record for 250 Miles at Salem's New Board Speedway." *Indianapolis Star,* November 1, 1925, p 27.

"DePaolo Will Again Try for Speedway Honors This Year." *Indianapolis Star,* April 18, 1926, p 35.

"Dern Appoints Col. Gorrell to Army Air Service Investigating Committee." *Indianapolis Star,* April 12, 1934, p 5.

"Describes New Marmon Racer." *Indianapolis Star,* October 11, 1911, p 10.

Deupree, H. G. "Benz Wins Great Free-for-All Race." *Indianapolis Star,* September 6, 1910, p 14.

_____. Four Killed, Many Hurt Is Race Toll." *Indianapolis Star,* October 2, 1910, p 23 & 27.

_____. "Len Zengel Pilots Chadwick to Front." *Indianapolis Star,* October 9, 1910, p 37.

_____. "Local Cars Grab Honors at Elgin." *Indianapolis Star,* August 27, 1910, p 5.

_____. "Lozier Wins with Nationals Behind." *Indianapolis Star,* August 28, 1910, p 23.

_____. "New Marks Crown Efforts of Pilots." *Indianapolis Star,* July 3, 1910, p 31.

_____. "Records Fall in Speedway Races." *Indianapolis Star,* May 31, 1910, p 7.

_____. "Smoking Monsters Thrill from Start." *Indianapolis Star,* May 31, 1911, p 1.

_____. "Vanderbilt Racers Hit Trail at Dawn." *Indianapolis Star,* October 1, 1910, p 6.

_____. "Wilcox Cuts Mile Mark in National." *Indianapolis Star,* March 30, 1910, p 10.

"Dickson Asserts Charges Unfair." *Indianapolis Star,* June 29, 1913, p 33.

"Dickson Endorses Hill Climb Events." *Indianapolis Star,* August 27, 1911, p 31.

"Discusses Increases in Marmon Prices." *Indianapolis Star,* March 26, 1916, p 28.

"Display Record Roosevelt Sedan." *Indianapolis Star,* July 3, 1929, p 7.

"Dr. L. S. Skelton Dies in West." *Indianapolis Star,* January 29, 1921, p 20.

"Driver Escapes Death." *Indianapolis Star,* October 6, 1910, p 11.

"Drivers of Indianapolis Cars in Eastern Auto Race." October 31, 1909, p 21.

"Drives Cole 101.5 Miles in One Hour, 57 Minutes." *Indianapolis Star,* May 26, 1923, p 23.

"Drives Two Hours Without One Stop." *Indianapolis Star,* April 17, 1910, p 42.

"Duesenberg Adds $30,000 Building to Factory Here." *Indianapolis Star,* August 16, 1922, p 8.

"Duesenberg Auto Plant Sold to Trust Company." *Indianapolis Star,* February 26, 1925, p 3.

Duesenberg Automobile & Motors Co., Inc. stock offering. *Indianapolis Star,* June 14, 1920, p 15.

"Duesenberg Case Draws near Close." *Indianapolis Star,* April 19, 1923, p 19.

"Duesenberg Company Will Continue Here." *Indianapolis Star,* February 22, 1925, p 1 & 8.

"Duesenberg Entered in European Classic." *Indianapolis Star,* August 9, 1927, p 3.

"Duesenberg Firm to Continue Here." *Indianapolis Star,* February 22, 1925, p 1.

"Duesenberg Given Great Chance for Slice Of $50,000." *Indianapolis Star,* May 23, 1920, p 27.

"Duesenberg Leases Additional Space." *Indianapolis Star,* October 21, 1923, p 49.

"Duesenberg Locates Here." *Indianapolis Star,* May 14, 1920, p 8.

"Duesenberg Motor Sales Go Upward." *Indianapolis Star,* October 12, 1924, p 67.

"Duesenberg Plant Turns Out First Cars for Trade." *Indianapolis Star,* May 28, 1921, p 3.

"Duesenberg Racy and Rakish." *Indianapolis Star,* January 13, 1929, p 57.

"Duesenberg Salon Sales Ranked High." *Indianapolis Star,* November 16, 1930, p 30.

Duesenberg Stock Subscription Ad. *Indianapolis Star,* May 21, 1920, p 14.

_____. *Indianapolis Star,* May 29, 1920, p 19.

"Duesenberg Sweeps the Field at Uniontown." *Indianapolis Star,* June 23, 1920, p 14.

"The Duesenberg—The Speedway Racing Sensation of 1920." *Indianapolis Star,* July 8, 1920, p 17.

"Duesenbergs Catch Eye." *Indianapolis Star,* February 17, 1921, p 11.

Edenburn, W. D. "'Bill' Endicott Is Hero of Wreck." *Indianapolis Star,* May 14, 1911, p 42.

_____. "Indiana Is Home of Automobile." *Indianapolis Star,* March 23, 1913, p 18.

_____. "Interstate Tour Held Hoosier Ad." *Indianapolis Star,* April 9, 1911, p 43.

"E. G. 'Cannonball' Baker in a Cole." *Indianapolis Star,* July 22, 1923, p 25.

"Eight Cylinder in Demand." *Indianapolis Star,* February 28, 1915, p 21.

"Eight Models Described in 1913 Waverley Year Book." *Indianapolis Star,* February 9, 1913, p 31.

"Eighteen Drivers Entered in Western Auto Classic." *Indianapolis Star,* October 25, 1914, p 23.

"$80,000,000 in Motor Merger." *Indianapolis Star,* July 2, 1922, p 1 & 6.

"$87,750 in Prizes Given Race Pilots." *Indianapolis Star,* June 2, 1925, p 1.

"Electric System for Pathfinder." *Indianapolis Star,* September 8, 1912, p 38.

"Elgin Entries All In." *Indianapolis Star,* August 21, 1910, p 42.

"Elgin Races National." *Indianapolis Star,* August 7, 1910, p 27.

"Elgin Trophy Is Won by DePalma." *Indianapolis Star,* August 23, 1914, p 41.

"Empire." *Indianapolis Star,* February 22, 1914, p 47.

"Empire." *Indianapolis Star,* September 6, 1914, p 21.

"Empire." *Indianapolis Star,* March 4, 1917, p 22.

"Empire." *Indianapolis Star,* April 22, 1917, p 16.

"Empire." *Indianapolis Star*, August 26, 1917, p 20.

"Empire Announces Attractive Sedan, Ready About Dec. 1." *Indianapolis Star*, November 19, 1916, p 23.

"Empire Announces Increase in Price." *Indianapolis Star*, April 2, 1916, p 24.

"Empire Car Factory Is Moved Here." *Indianapolis Star*, July 1, 1915, p 1 & 3.

"Empire Car Is Dubbed 'The Little Aristocrat.'" *Indianapolis Star*, March 23, 1913, p 32.

"Empire Company Has New Roadsters." *Indianapolis Star*, April 16, 1916, p 23.

"Empire District Manager Makes Auto Buying Simple." *Indianapolis Star*, June 21, 1914, p 19.

"Empire Exhibits New Creations." *Indianapolis Star*, February 22, 1914, p 51.

"Empire Expects Big Production." *Indianapolis Star*, December 31, 1915, p 24.

"Empire Features Striking Colors." *Indianapolis Star*, February 27, 1916, p 57.

"Empire No. 19 Is Still in Service." *Indianapolis Star*, May 31, 1914, p 30.

"Empire Reports Record Business." *Indianapolis Star*, May 2, 1915, p 55.

"Empire Reveals First 1916 Type." *Indianapolis Star*, April 11, 1915, p 24.

"Empire Surprises Staff." *Indianapolis Star*, January 11, 1914, p 17.

"Empire Will Boost Price Before Jan. 1; High Cost Is Cause." *Indianapolis Star*, November 5, 1916, p 23.

"Employers of Indianapolis to Organize." *Indianapolis Star*, January 2, 1904, p 10.

"End of Receivership Seen in Rush of Auto Orders." *Indianapolis Star*, March 11, 1921, p 15.

"Endicott in 24-Hour Race." *Indianapolis Star*, August 19, 1910, p 8.

"Endicott Victor in Exciting Race." *Indianapolis Star*, July 24, 1910, p 49.

"Ends Another Good 'Indiana-Made' Year." *Indianapolis Star*, December 7, 1913, p 20.

"Endurance Contest to Start October 1." *Indianapolis Star*, August 23, 1908, p 28.

"Engineer of LaFayette Motors Company Resigns." *Indianapolis Star*, October 14, 1921, p 8.

"Engineers Inspect Motor Car After 440-Hour Test Ends." *Indianapolis Star*, July 7, 1929, p 52.

"Engineers Praise New Weidley Motor." *Indianapolis Star*, January 18, 1914, p 43.

"English Propose Race." *Indianapolis Star*, January 12, 1910, p 8.

"Enter Speedway Races." *Indianapolis Star*, April 12, 1910, p 34.

"Enters Marmon Racer." *Indianapolis Star*, January 13, 1910, p 8.

"Enters Stutz at Los Angeles." *Indianapolis Star*, January 25, 1914, p 18.

"Enthuse over Big Race." *Indianapolis Star*, December 6, 1908, p 6.

"Entries in Hill Climb Today." *Indianapolis Star*, March 24, 1908, p 7.

"Entries for the Russell Relief Fund." *Indianapolis Star*, October 20, 1905, p 7.

"Entries Numerous for Big Auto Races." *Indianapolis Star*, February 14, 1915, p 14.

"Entry List Closes." *Indianapolis Star*, July 6, 1907, p 6.

"Epitomizes 1916 Auto Season." *Indianapolis Star*, March 5, 1916, p 20.

"Europe and Australia Buy Stutz Car." *Indianapolis Star*, December 31, 1915, p 24.

"Every Nonstop Endurance Mark." *Indianapolis Star*, June 20, 1929, p 1.

"Eyes of Auto World Are Focused on Chicago." *Indianapolis Star*, January 25, 1931, p 24.

"Eyes of Auto World Focused on New York." *Indianapolis Star*, October 20, 1907, p 12.

"Eyes of Racing Fans Are Turned to Monza Event." *Indianapolis Star*, September 6, 1925, p 26.

"Factories Here to Display Cars." *Indianapolis Star*, December 29, 1929, p 19.

"Factory Begins Large Addition." *Indianapolis Star*, June 28, 1917, p 11.

"Famous Drivers to Pilot Speedy Cars." *Indianapolis Star*, March 26, 1911, p 42.

"Famous Glidden Contest Will Be Decided June 7." *Indianapolis Star*, April 17, 1910, p 8.

"Famous Pilots to Compete in Races." *Indianapolis Star*, June 4, 1911, p 36.

Farrington, Dick. "Crowd Sees Cars in Tune-Up at Speedway." *Indianapolis Star*, May 14, 1915, p 13.

_____. "Four Cars Break Records in Race DePalma Wins." *Indianapolis Star*, June 1, 1915, p 7.

"Farmers See Autos." *Indianapolis Star*, September 14, 1905, p 3.

"F. E. Moskovics Comes to Join Marmon Staff." *Indianapolis Star*, February 1, 1914, p 20.

"Feat of Pathfinder Should Add Interest." *Indianapolis Star*, August 13, 1916, p 21.

"Feature of Twelve Is Its Longer Life." *Indianapolis Star*, July 18, 1915, p 14.

Feightner, Harold C. "Gaston Chevrolet Wins." *Indianapolis Star*, June 1, 1920, p 1.

"Few Changes on Marion Models." *Indianapolis Star*, September 22, 1912, p 34.

"Field of 44 Cars in 500-Mile Race." *Indianapolis Star*, May 3, 1911, p 9.

"Fifty Mile Record Broken at Atlanta." *Indianapolis Star*, November 13, 1909, p 8.

"$50,000 Office Block Planned." *Indianapolis Star*, June 28, 1918, p 18.

"Fight Waged to Save Homeless Thousands." *Indianapolis Star*, March 26, 1913, p 1 & 5.

"Films at Colonial Theater to Show Famous Cup Race at Exposition." *Indianapolis Star*, May 1, 1915, p 17.

"Fine Cobe Race Stretch." *Indianapolis Star*, May 30, 1909, p 41.

"Finishes Reliability Tour." *Indianapolis Star*, June 15, 1910, p 11.

"Fire Again Hits Premier." *Indianapolis Star*, May 6, 1915, p 1.

"First Cars Are Entered." *Indianapolis Star*, July 13, 1909, p 9.

"First of Marmon Sixteens, Winner of S.A.E. Medal, Is off the Line." *Indianapolis Star*, April 19, 1931, p 29.

"Fisher May Drive in Big Auto Meet." *Indianapolis Star*, October 25, 1904, p 7.

"Fisher Mentioned As Head of Circuit." *Indianapolis Star*, April 13, 1915, p 10.

"Fisher to Compete in a Big Auto Race." *Indianapolis Star*, September 24, 1904, p 7.

"Five-Mile Record Takes a Tumble." *Indianapolis Star*, December 19, 1909, p 29.

"Flames Damage Cole Auto Plant." *Indianapolis Star*, March 9, 1917, p 16.

"Flying Nationals Grab Remy Honors." *Indianapolis Star*, September 4, 1910, p 18.

"For Drivers and Owners." *Indianapolis Star*, September 26, 1912, p 11.

"For Glidden Tour." *Indianapolis Star*, May 29, 1910, p 32.

"Forecast Fastest Things on Wheels." *Indianapolis Star,* June 27, 1926, p 53.
"Foreign Entry List Expected to Prove Fast." *Indianapolis Star,* March 28, 1920, p 25.
"$45,000 Allowed, Fee to Premier Motors Receiver." *Indianapolis Star,* May 6, 1925, p 3.
"40,000 to Be Visited for Bonds." *Indianapolis Star,* October 7, 1917, p 1.
"Forty-Three Cars Form Entry List for International Speed Classic." *Indianapolis Star,* May 2, 1929, p 14 & 18.
"Forty-Two Marmons Start Overland for New York." *Indianapolis Star,* March 17, 1918, p 21.
"4 Dead in Race Won by Aitken." *Indianapolis Star,* November 19, 1916, p 33.
"Four-States Tour Will Start July 12." *Indianapolis Star,* May 10, 1911, p 9.
"4 Warrants Issued in Stock Swindle," *Indianapolis Star,* September 1, 1935, p 5.
"Frame of Premier Assures Great Strength." *Indianapolis Star,* February 26, 1911, p 19.
"Frank E. Smith Elected Premier Company Trustee." *Indianapolis Star,* December 15, 1914, p 10.
"French Government Buys 350 Marmon 34 Cars." *Indianapolis Star,* November 17, 1918, p 32.
"Frontenac Company Buys Site Here." *Indianapolis Star,* April 12, 1922, p 1 & 19.
"Frontenacs and 'Duesies' Clash." *Indianapolis Star,* June 12, 1921, p 36.
"'Full-View-Ahead' Auto Well Liked by Purchasers." *Indianapolis Star,* February 11, 1911, p 29.
"G. M. Williams New Marmon Head." *Indianapolis Star,* May 16, 1924, p 16.
"Gasoline Must Be Conserved." *Indianapolis Star,* October 28, 1917, p 19.
"Gasoline Saved by Sensible-Six." *Indianapolis Star,* November 8, 1914, p 19.
"Gets Protection of Trade-Mark." *Indianapolis Star,* April 30, 1916, p 27.
"Gil Anderson, in a Stutz, Pushes DePalma That Record Is Broken in Race for the Cobe Trophy over Elgin Road Course." *Indianapolis Star,* August 22, 1914, p 6.
Glenn, W. M. "On Motor Row." *Indianapolis Star,* June 25, 1914, p 10.
"Glidden Tour Will Start on Thursday." *Indianapolis Star,* July 5, 1908, p 17.
"Glidden Tourists Climb Three Ranges." *Indianapolis Star,* July 21, 1907, p 45.
"Glidden Tourists Have Pleasant Trip." *Indianapolis Star,* July 13, 1907, p 7.
"Glidden Trophy Awarded." *Indianapolis Star,* September 12, 1910, p 8.
"Glimpse Pacific for First Time." *Indianapolis Star,* July 28, 1913, p 3.
"Go Indianapolis." *Indianapolis Star,* May 9, 1930, p 17.
"A 'Going Concern'—And Going Good." *Indianapolis Star,* January 22, 1922, p 34.
Goodman, Dan V. "1928 Auto Show Setting Records." *Indianapolis Star,* January 10, 1928, p 3.
_____. "Ralph DePalma Visits Here and Purchases Stutz Racer." *Indianapolis Star,* July 16, 1915, p 14.
_____. "Stutz Creation Newest of New in Gotham Show." *Indianapolis Star,* January 10, 1926, p 25.
"Gorrell Denies Stutz Removal." *Indianapolis Star,* March 30, 1930, p 4.
"Gossip of Wide Awake Motor Devotees." *Indianapolis Star,* January 9, 1910, p 33.
"Gotham Sees Hoosier Car." *Indianapolis Star,* January 4, 1920, p 60.
"Grand Parade, Hill Climb, and Novelty Contests Arranged for This Week." *Indianapolis Star,* March 22, 1908, p 41.
"Grants Duesenberg Trade Mark of Straight Eight." *Indianapolis Star,* January 13, 1924, p 59.
"Great Arrow Wins." *Indianapolis Star,* July 30, 1908, p 3.
"Greatest of Auto Shows Is Opened." *Indianapolis Star,* February 5, 1905, p 15.
"The Greatest Proving Ground in the World." *Indianapolis Star,* May 30, 1929, p 9.
"H.C.S." *Indianapolis Star,* October 17, 1920, p 22.
"H.C.S. Firm Enters Taxi Cab Field to Broaden Industry." *Indianapolis Star,* June 29, 1924, p 67.
"H.C.S. Motor Car Company Cuts Prices Tomorrow." *Indianapolis Star,* July 31, 1921, p 24.
"H.C.S. Motors Company Builds Factory." *Indianapolis Star,* April 11, 1920, p 13.
"H.C.S. Special Wins 500-Mile Race." *Indianapolis Star,* May 31, 1923, p 15.
Handley, J. I. "Harmony Is Seen in Lines of Auto." *Indianapolis Star,* March 23, 1913, p 29.
"Handley Welds Auto Interests." *Indianapolis Star,* July 27, 1913, p 28.
Hannagan. "Indiana Cars Center of Show." *Indianapolis Star,* January 8, 1922, p 11.
"Hard Luck Forces Many Drivers Out." *Indianapolis Star,* May 31, 1931, p 2.
"Harroun Announces Final Retirement from Big Ring." *Indianapolis Star,* March 23, 1911, p 9.
"Harroun Departing for Atlanta Tells Plans for Coming Season." *Indianapolis Star,* May 2, 1910, p 9.
"Harroun Designs New Carburetor." *Indianapolis Star,* February 9, 1913, p 34.
"Harroun Likes Elgin Course." *Indianapolis Star,* August 10, 1910, p 4.
"Harroun Memphis Star." *Indianapolis Star,* June 18, 1910, p 14.
Harroun, Ray. "Tells Why He Uses Wasp." *Indianapolis Star,* May 28, 1911, p 17.
"Harroun Rules Favorite." *Indianapolis Star,* May 30, 1911, p 6.
"Harroun Wins Feature." *Indianapolis Star,* April 18, 1910, p 9.
"Harroun Yields to Lure of High Speed." *Indianapolis Star,* April 23, 1911, p 37.
"Harroun's Car Leads." *Indianapolis Star,* March 6, 1910, p 38.
"Harry C. Stutz Resigns As Head of Motor Plant." *Indianapolis Star,* June 21, 1919, p 1.
"Hassler Car to Appear at Home." *Indianapolis Star,* February 4, 1917, p 59.
"Hats Off to the Buick." *Indianapolis Star,* October 21, 1906, p 11.
Haynes, Gene. "Indianapolis Made Car Wins Laurels in Classic." *Indianapolis Star,* May 31, 1924, p 8.
_____. "Motor Dust and Scissor Thrust." *Indianapolis Star,* December 7, 1924, p 69.
"H.C.S. Six-Cylinder Model." *Indianapolis Star,* January 6, 1923, p 8.
Head, John W. "Date of Auto Classic Here Changed to May 31." *Indianapolis Star,* December 15, 1918, p 45.
"Heads Million Dollar Company." *Indianapolis Star,* January 22, 1911, p 20.
"Heads Stutz Company." *Indianapolis Star,* April 6, 1920, p 5.
"Hearne Is Winner of Foch Race at Motor Speedway." *Indianapolis Star,* November 5, 1921, p 11.
"Heat Prostrates Two." *Indianapolis Star,* July 2, 1910, p 1 & 2.
"Heavy Transfer Work Improves." *Indianapolis Star,* November 27, 1922, p 9.
"Heinemann May Drive Marmon." *Indianapolis Star,* November 22, 1911, p 11.

Henley, Bert. "Business and Comment." *Indianapolis Star*, February 26, 1925, p 20.

———. "Earnings." *Indianapolis Star*, December 5, 1928, p 18.

"High Gear Coast-to-Coast Pathfinder Headed East." *Indianapolis Star*, July 23, 1916, p 22.

"Hill Wins 250-Mile Race in Duesenberg; Averages 112.44 Miles Per Hour." *Indianapolis Star*, November 30, 1923, p 15.

"Holds Motor Center Here." *Indianapolis Star*, March 24, 1912, p 68.

"Honks Heard Among the Auto Show Fans." *Indianapolis Star*, March 24, 1909, p 11.

"Honors to Premier." *Indianapolis Star*, October 12, 1908, p 6.

"Hoosier Auto Is Admired." *Indianapolis Star*, January 17, 1909, p 19.

"Hoosier Cars Draw Interest at New York Motor Show." *Indianapolis Star*, January 7, 1923, p 52.

"Hoosier Clips Mark." *Indianapolis Star*, November 3, 1907, p 16.

"Hoosier Display Is First Event." *Indianapolis Star*, November 12, 1911, p 29.

"Hoosier Motor Club Lays Plans for Membership Campaign, Wide in Scope." *Indianapolis Star*, December 22, 1911, p 9.

"Hoosier Road Race to Cost $60,000." *Indianapolis Star*, May 1, 1909, p 9.

"Hoosiers in Front." *Indianapolis Star*, April 8, 1907, p 7.

"Hoosiers Will Dot Big Glidden Tour." *Indianapolis Star*, April 1, 1909, p 1.

"Horseless Age Picks Stutz and Cooper As Champions." *Indianapolis Star*, October 31, 1915, p 17.

"How the Drivers Will Line Up at Speedway." *Indianapolis Star*, May 29, 1921, p 13.

"How They Finished in the Hill Climbing Contest." *Indianapolis Star*, March 25, 1908, p 7.

"How They Qualified First Day." *Indianapolis Star*, May 27, 1927, p 1.

Howard Marmon Asked to Officiate As Starter." *Indianapolis Star*, April 27, 1916, p 15.

"'Howdy' Wilcox, Disappointment in Santa Monica Road Race, Gave Up His Chance in Eliminating Fiat." *Indianapolis Star*, October 21, 1911, p 11.

"Hower Contest Called Off." *Indianapolis Star*, July 29, 1908, p 8.

"Huge Serial Note Issue Sold Out in Six Hours." *Indianapolis Star*, July 3, 1919, p 21.

"Huge Sums Invested in Used Motor Cars." *Indianapolis Star*, May 6, 1923, p 24.

"Huge Marmon-Herrington Passes Test." *Indianapolis Star*, August 19, 1932, p 11.

"'Hughie' Hughes in Parry Star in Columbus Races. *Indianapolis Star*, July 31, 1910, p 45.

"Hunting Good Auto Roads." *Indianapolis Star*, July 13, 1906, p 7.

"Imports Monarch of Foreign Races." *Indianapolis Star*, March 9, 1911, p 13.

"Improvements Are Pushed." *Indianapolis Star*, March 21, 1909, p 8.

"Income Shrinks." *Indianapolis Star*, January 23, 1931, p 19.

"Income Tax Refund of $101,000 Entered." *Indianapolis Star*, June 21, 1936, p 16.

"Incorporations." *Indianapolis Star*, May 15, 1905, p 11.

"Incorporations." *Indianapolis Star*, July 23, 1907, p 10.

"Incorporations." *Indianapolis Star*, February 7, 1908, p 12.

"Incorporations." *Indianapolis Star*, March 21, 1909, p 38.

"Incorporations." *Indianapolis Star*, June 23, 1909, p 11.

"Incorporations." *Indianapolis Star*, November 30, 1909, p 3.

"Incorporations." *Indianapolis Star*, November 25, 1914, p 10.

"Incorporations," *Indianapolis Star*, May 22, 1915, p 17.

"Incorporations." *Indianapolis Star*, March 31, 1921, p 13.

"Incorporations." *Indianapolis Star*, January 25, 1922, p 17.

"Incorporations." *Indianapolis Star*, February 9, 1924, p 21.

"Incorporations." *Indianapolis Star*, February 18, 1926, p 23.

"Increases Overland Cars." *Indianapolis Star*, March 21, 1908, p 10.

"Indiana Auto Pilots Condemn Brighton Beach Racing Course." *Indianapolis Star*, May 16, 1910, p 21.

"Indiana Autos Feature New York Show." *Indianapolis Star*, January 5, 1930, p 1.

"Indiana Cars Win Latonia Races." *Indianapolis Star*, July 11, 1910, p 7.

"Indiana Genius in Big Demand." *Indianapolis Star*, January 6, 1918, p 23.

"Indiana Is Third." *Indianapolis Star*, June 30, 1907, p 59.

"Indiana Pilots in Sweep at Atlanta." *Indianapolis Star*, May 6, 1910, p 9.

"Indianapolis Becomes 'Unit Power Plant' in Advertising Automobiles." *Indianapolis Star*, May 17, 1912, p 11.

"Indianapolis Cars Driven to First and Second in Race," *Indianapolis Star*, September 5, 1915, p 29.

"Indianapolis Cars Get Perfect Score." *Indianapolis Star*, April 29, 1909, p 9.

"Indianapolis Cars Take Every Event." *Indianapolis Star*, May 7, 1910, p 11.

"Indianapolis Cars Will Cut Figure." *Indianapolis Star*, November 21, 1909, p 9.

"Indianapolis Daily Traffic." *Indianapolis Star*, May 5, 1904, p 8.

"Indianapolis Home of New Motor Car Concern." *Indianapolis Star*, August 15, 1909, p 45.

"Indianapolis Hub of Motor World." *Indianapolis Star*, June 23, 1912, p 58.

"Indianapolis Is Third City in Country in Automobile." *Indianapolis Star*, June 19, 1922, p 8.

"Indianapolis-Made Motor Cars." *Indianapolis Star*, December 14, 1928, p 6.

"Indianapolis Now Big Motor Center." *Indianapolis Star*, December 5, 1909, p 21.

"Indianapolis Now Called Auto City." *Indianapolis Star*, December 17, 1905, p 14.

"Indianapolis Pilots and Cars Return with Bulk of Trophies." *Indianapolis Star*, May 8, 1910, p 20.

"Indianapolis to Have Auto Show." *Indianapolis Star*, February 18, 1906, p 17.

"Industrial Building, Five Houses, Church, and Store Burned." *Indianapolis Star*, January 14, 1918, p 1 & 4.

"Industry Here Gaining." *Indianapolis Star*, March 18, 1921, p 5.

"Investing and Loyalty." *Indianapolis Star*, May 6, 1917, p 11.

"Issues Book on Auto Convention." *Indianapolis Star*, December 22, 1912, p 35.

"It's Still Running!" *Indianapolis Star*, June 26, 1929, p 9.

"J. Dawson Smashes Coast Course Mark." *Indianapolis Star*, October 13, 1911, p 7.

"J. G. Monihan Guest at Farewell Dinner." *Indianapolis Star*, February 13, 1915, p 13.

"J. I. Handley Chosen Head of Mutual Motors Company." *Indianapolis Star*, January 3, 1915, p 19.

Jackson, Stewart. "Ralph DePalma Is Favorite in Betting on 500-Mile Race." *Indianapolis Star*, May 28, 1915, p 12.

"Jenkins Again Claims Record." *Indianapolis Star*, September 22, 1935, p 18.

"Jenkins Stars in Fernbank Races." *Indianapolis Star*, September 10, 1911, p 37.

"Jimmy Murphy Drives Race to Death." *Indianapolis Star*, September 16, 1924, p 1.
"Joe Dawson Gets Fifth in Big Race." *Indianapolis Star*, June 1, 1911, p 9.
"Joe Murphy Hurt When Duesenberg Racer Turns Over." *Indianapolis Star*, July 16, 1921, p 10.
"John Guy Monihan Named Marion Company Manager." *Indianapolis Star*, January 6, 1915, p 11.
"John J. M'Namara Convicted of Blackmail Charge; Judge to Pass Sentence Next Week." *Indianapolis Star*, September 23, 1925, p 1 & 2.
"Johnny Aitken to Be Member of the Stutz Racing Team." *Indianapolis Star*, May 9, 1915, p 37.
Johnson, Harold. "Earl Cooper, with a Stutz, Is Victor in Chicago Event." *Indianapolis Star*, June 17, 1917, p 45.
"Joseph J. Cole, Pioneer Auto Manufacturer Here, Is Dead." *Indianapolis Star*, August 8, 1925, p 1 & 8.
"Keech, Woodbury Veterans of Racing." *Indianapolis Star*, June 16, 1929, p 3.
"Kenosha Auto Magnate Finances LaFayette Motors." *Indianapolis Star*, June 6, 1922, p 16.
"Kerosene Used to Run National Car." *Indianapolis Star*, February 23, 1913, p 28.
"Knows Demands of Car Buyers." *Indianapolis Star*, July 18, 1915, p 16.
"Knox and Marmon Cars Take Prizes." *Indianapolis Star*, June 15, 1910, p 11.
"Kokomo Motorist Talks to Devotees at Y.M.C.A." *Indianapolis Star*, January 5, 1910, p 10.
"LaFayette Building Company." *Indianapolis Star*, March 17, 1920, p 11.
"LaFayette Motors Shows Second Cut in Prices." *Indianapolis Star*, January 8, 1922, p 59.
"LaFayette Motors to Quit Indianapolis." *Indianapolis Star*, July 30, 1922, p 12.
"LaSalle Twelve New Pathfinder." *Indianapolis Star*, July 4, 1915, p 13.
"Laying Out Route." *Indianapolis Star*, May 17, 1908, p 10.
"Leads All in Racers." *Indianapolis Star*, January 26, 1910, p 8.
"Leeds to Direct Sale of Premier and Monroe Cars." *Indianapolis Star*, November 11, 1923, p 44.
"Licensed Ranks Grow." *Indianapolis Star*, January 6, 1910, p 8.
"Life Policies by Bushel." *Indianapolis Star*, April 19, 1926, p 7.
"Lighter Cars Being Built for 1923 Race." *Indianapolis Star*, January 7, 1923, p 35.
"Like Premier Motor System." *Indianapolis Star*, December 27, 1908, p 26.
"Lilly Convention Sees Auto Race." *Indianapolis Star*, August 19, 1924, p 9.
"Limousine New Cole '8' Model." *Indianapolis Star*, August 22, 1915, p 15.
"Liquidate, Stutz Order by U.S.," *Indianapolis Star*, April 26, 1939, p 13.
"Litigation Halts Merger of Stutz." *Indianapolis Star*, January 1, 1930, p 1 & 2.
"'Little Aristocrat' Gains Honored Post." *Indianapolis Star*, May 18, 1913, p 31.
"Local Auto Men Get High Offices." *Indianapolis Star*, February 2, 1913, p 29.
"Local Auto Men Oppose War Tax." *Indianapolis Star*, October 5, 1914, p 5.
"Local Autoists Find National Road Best." *Indianapolis Star*, July 28, 1907, p 10.
"Local Cars Gain with Buick Barred." *Indianapolis Star*, July 29, 1910, p 9.
"Local Cars in Big Race." *Indianapolis Star*, October 18, 1909, p 9.
"Local Cars Lead in 'Piepan' Races." *Indianapolis Star*, April 8, 1910, p 25.
"Local Cars Show Big Race Records." *Indianapolis Star*, June 5, 1910, p 23.
"Local Cars Win Four Events." *Indianapolis Star*, July 30, 1911, p 43.
"Local Company Adds to Output." *Indianapolis Star*, December 31, 1915, p 27.
"Local Company Doubles Capital." *Indianapolis Star*, May 25, 1913, p 78.
"Local Design for Auto Fire Wagon." *Indianapolis Star*, May 4, 1910, p 9.
"Local Driver Races." *Indianapolis Star*, March 21, 1909, p 14.
"Local Factory Has Hard Time Keeping Plans Under Cover." *Indianapolis Star*, February 27, 1916, p 63.
"Local Factory Method Unique in Car Building." *Indianapolis Star*. January 9, 1927, p 56.
"Local Firm Stages Victory Drive." *Indianapolis Star*, April 30, 1919, p 11.
"Local Flyers to Race in France?" *Indianapolis Star*, December 25, 1910, p 30.
"Local Happenings in the Local Auto World." *Indianapolis Star*, March 15, 1908, p 40.
"Local Maker Favors Motor Museum Plan." *Indianapolis Star*, February 23, 1913, p 32.
"Local Race Pilot Departs Today for Pacific Coast to Prepare for Race Events." *Indianapolis Star*, February 8, 1914, p 20.
"Long Island's Loss Is Savannah's Gain." *Indianapolis Star*, August 6, 1911, p 29.
"Long Speed Battle Draws Big Winners." *Indianapolis Star*, March 5, 1911, p 29.
"Long-Stroke Motor Is Used." *Indianapolis Star*, February 9, 1913, p 30.
"Los Angeles Owner Has Winning Marmon." *Indianapolis Star*, March 8, 1914, p 20.
"Louisville Plans Motor Speedway." *Indianapolis Star*, December 27, 1910, p 9.
"Mais Truck Stands High in Auto Field." *Indianapolis Star*, January 16, 1916, p 6.
"Make Plans for Run." *Indianapolis Star*, April 16, 1908, p 6.
"Manufacture of 100 Cars by Stutz Is Approved." *Indianapolis Star*, October 29, 1937, p 5.
"Manufacturers More Optimistic." *Indianapolis Star*, January 19, 1918, p 10.
"Many Come for Races." *Indianapolis Star*, July 4, 1910, p 4.
"Many Improvements in Body and Motor." *Indianapolis Star*, February 16, 1930, p 38.
"Many New Records Set in 24-Hour Run." *Indianapolis Morning Star*, November 18, 1905, p 7.
"Marion." *Indianapolis Star*, June 2, 1912, p 36.
"Marion Announcing the Bobcat." *Indianapolis Star*, February 26, 1914, p 28.
"Marion Company Deal Completed." *Indianapolis Star*, May 5, 1912, p 35.
"Marion Leads up Hill." *Indianapolis Star*, July 8, 1909, p 9.
"Marion Motor Car Plant Damaged by Explosion." *Indianapolis Star*, March 14, 1909, p 8.
"Marion Motor Company Bought by J. I. Handley." *Indianapolis Star*, November 6, 1914, p 16.
Marmon, Howard. "Marmon Follows New Speed Theory." *Indianapolis Star*, March 20, 1910, p 8.
"The Marmon." *Indianapolis Star*, March 20, 1910, p 18.
"The Marmon." *Indianapolis Star*, May 15, 1910, p 46.
"The Marmon." *Indianapolis Star*, June 19, 1910, p 33.

"The Marmon." *Indianapolis Star,* July 3, 1910, p 34.
"The Marmon." *Indianapolis Star,* October 2, 1910, p 39.
"The Marmon." *Indianapolis Star,* May 31, 1911, p 5.
"Marmon." *Indianapolis Star,* May 26, 1912, p 50.
"Marmon." *Indianapolis Star,* June 2, 1912, p 37.
"Marmon." *Indianapolis Star,* May 19, 1929, p 68.
"Marmon a 'Yellow Peril.'" *Indianapolis Star,* April 11, 1910, p 9.
"Marmon Adds Three Open Cars." *Indianapolis Star,* May 11, 1930, p 33.
"Marmon Adopts Uniform Price Plan for Parts." *Indianapolis Star,* May 3, 1925, p 64.
"Marmon Announces National Survey of Upkeep Costs." *Indianapolis Star,* March 4, 1923, p 64.
"Marmon Announces Price Increase to Be Effective Jan. 1." *Indianapolis Star,* November 19, 1916, p 23.
"Marmon Announces Sixteen Distinct New Refinements." *Indianapolis Star,* March 2, 1924, p 72.
"Marmon at Brick Oval." *Indianapolis Star,* May 20, 1928, p 39.
"Marmon Attains Volume Basis on New 68 and 78." *Indianapolis Star,* January 15, 1928, p 61.
"Marmon Automobiles Reduced in Price." *Indianapolis Star,* January 4, 1922, p 3.
"Marmon Begins New Plant Plan." *Indianapolis Star,* February 22, 1932, p 11.
"Marmon Booth Holds Interest." *Indianapolis Star,* January 30, 1916, p 21.
"Marmon-Built Roosevelt Car Proves Ability on Pike's Peak." *Indianapolis Star,* September 22, 1929, p 64.
"Marmon Company Votes Regular Dividend Early to Strengthen Market." *Indianapolis Star,* October 31, 1929, p 1.
"Marmon Directors Declare Dividend." *Indianapolis Star,* October 15, 1926, p 1.
"Marmon Display at Show Strikes Responsive Chord." *Indianapolis Star,* February 17, 1926, p 10.
"Marmon Displays Speedster Model." *Indianapolis Star,* April 22, 1922, p 63.
"Marmon Driver Is Victor." *Indianapolis Star,* November 12, 1910, p 9.
"Marmon Eights Get Good Start." *Indianapolis Star,* January 19, 1930, p 26.
"Marmon Employs New Body Chief." *Indianapolis Star,* February 20, 1925, p 12.
"Marmon Enters New Motor Era." *Indianapolis Star,* May 10, 1932, p 1 & 2.
"Marmon Enters Races." *Indianapolis Star,* August 4, 1910, p 4.
"Marmon Enters Two Speed Cars in 500-Mile Race." *Indianapolis Star,* April 10, 1928, p 1.
"Marmon Expects Larger Output." *Indianapolis Star,* February 10, 1930, p 1.
"Marmon Expects New Sales Mark." *Indianapolis Star,* April 10, 1927, p 68.
"Marmon Factory Mecca for Visitors." *Indianapolis Star,* May 29, 1914, p 6.
"Marmon Files for New Name." *Indianapolis Star,* February 3, 1926, p 12.
"Marmon Financial Position Strong Statement Shows." *Indianapolis Star,* August 21, 1927, p 55.
"Marmon Finishes Economy Test in Perfect Condition." *Indianapolis Star,* June 23, 1918, p 15.
"Marmon Glidden Entries Are Like Two Peas." *Indianapolis Star,* July 11, 1909, p 29.
"Marmon Glory Is Lauded in Fitting Style." *Indianapolis Star,* November 3, 1918, p 37.
"Marmon Has Clean Record." *Indianapolis Star,* September 26, 1908, p 27.
"Marmon in Sioux City Sweepstakes." *Indianapolis Star,* June 28, 1914, p 15.
"Marmon Introduces Revolutionary Service Policy." *Indianapolis Star,* May 18, 1930, p 27.
"Marmon Leases Its Body Plant." *Indianapolis Star,* October 3, 1928, p 3.
"Marmon Leases Plant #3 to Body Builders." *Indianapolis Star,* June 24, 1926, p 12.
"Marmon Models Out." *Indianapolis Star,* October 25, 1908, p 15.
"Marmon Obtains Peak of Success." *Indianapolis Star,* January 20, 1929, p 51.
"Marmon Offers New Speedsters." *Indianapolis Star,* December 9, 1928, p 68.
"Marmon Official on Trust Board." *Indianapolis Star,* April 14, 1926, p 1.
"Marmon Output Gains 51 Percent in Year 1926–27." *Indianapolis Star,* August 14, 1927, p 52.
"Marmon Output to Be Doubled." *Indianapolis Star,* September 2, 1919, p 9.
"Marmon Plans Big Expansion." *Indianapolis Star,* June 24, 1919, p 1 & 8.
"Marmon Plant Abolishes Storerooms." *Indianapolis Star,* June 5, 1927, p 70.
"Marmon Receives 13 Million Jolts in 24-Hour Test." *Indianapolis Star,* August 28, 1927, p 62.
"Marmon Re-Enters High Price Field Displaying First of the Big Eight Models at Local Salesroom." *Indianapolis Star,* December 1, 1929, p 61.
"Marmon Reports Larger Earnings." *Indianapolis Star,* July 5, 1925, p 45.
"Marmon Sales Advance." *Indianapolis Star,* February 5, 1930, p 9.
"Marmon Sets New Records." *Indianapolis Star,* January 25, 1920, p 62.
"Marmon 16 and Two New Eights Will Be Presented." *Indianapolis Star,* February 15, 1931, p 64.
"Marmon Starts Subsidiary Unit." *Indianapolis Star,* March 14, 1931, p 1.
"Marmon Stock Issue Is Voted." *Indianapolis Star,* December 28, 1928, p 14.
"Marmon Stock Touring Car Triumphs by Winning the 'Grand Prix of the Alps.'" *Indianapolis Star,* October 28, 1923, p 47.
"Marmon Tells of War Motor." *Indianapolis Star,* July 24, 1918, p 14.
"Marmon 34." *Indianapolis Star,* January 12, 1919, p 21.
"Marmon 34 Is Unique Car." *Indianapolis Star,* January 30, 1916, p 19.
"Marmon 34 Sealed for Long Test Trip." *Indianapolis Star,* August 20, 1916, p 17.
"Marmon to Be Shown." *Indianapolis Star,* March 14, 1909, p 19.
"Marmon to Pace Race." *Indianapolis Star,* May 20, 1928, p 66.
"Marmon to Show at State Fair." *Indianapolis Star,* September 3, 1916, p 21.
"Marmon Trophies Here." *Indianapolis Star,* November 21, 1909, p 17.
"Marmon Turns to Closed Cars." *Indianapolis Star,* June 18, 1916, p 20.
"Marmon Will Be Busy." *Indianapolis Star,* September 4, 1910, p 31.
"Marmon Wins Long Races at New Orleans." *Indianapolis Star,* November 23, 1909, p 8.
"Marmon Wins the Crowning Event." *Indianapolis Star,* May 29, 1910, p 26.
"Marmons Hold Own." *Indianapolis Star,* July 19, 1908, p 18.

"Marmons Test Course." *Indianapolis Star*, May 9, 1909, p 17.

"Marvel at Feats of City's Racers." *Indianapolis Star*, July 24, 1910, p 38.

"The Marvel of Motordome." *Indianapolis Star*, June 12 1910, p 28.

Maxwell. "Automobile Is Held Practically Perfect." *Indianapolis Star*, July 28, 1912, p 45.

"May Buy Frontenac Site." *Indianapolis Star*, March 10, 1922, p 1 & 21.

"May Relist Stutz to Protect Banks." *Indianapolis Star*, July 25, 1922, p 3.

"May Take Up Racing." *Indianapolis Star*, July 10, 1910, p 23.

"Mayor Issues Flood Fund Appeal; The Star Will Receive Donations." *Indianapolis Star*, March 26, 1913, p 1.

"A Mechanical Masterpiece." *Indianapolis Star*, February 5, 1905, p 23.

"Mechanics Get Little Honors." *Indianapolis Star*, May 28, 1911, p 24.

"Medium Autos Favorites." *Indianapolis Star*, February 14, 1909, p 44.

"Meyer Victorious in 500-Mile Race." *Indianapolis Star*, May 31, 1928, p 8.

"Milton." *Indianapolis Star*, March 6, 1922, p 16.

"Milton Enters Speedway Race." *Indianapolis Star*, September 21, 1921, p 10.

"Milton Wins 500-Mile Race." *Indianapolis Star*, May 31, 1921, p 1.

"Milton Wins; Hartz 2nd; Murphy 3rd." *Indianapolis Star*, May 31, 1923, p 1.

"Milton's Car Will Arrive in Town Today." *Indianapolis Star*, May 22, 1920, p 11.

"Mishaps Feature Motordrome Meet." *Indianapolis Star*, April 16, 1910, p 8.

"Mitchell Controls Marmon Outturn." *Indianapolis Star*, September 28, 1924, p 60.

"Money's Worth in Seeing Autos." *Indianapolis Star*, March 11, 1919, p 8.

"Monroe." *Indianapolis Star*, May 25,1921, p 5.

"Monroe Cars Take to Track." *Indianapolis Star*, May 21, 1920, p 8.

"Monroe Drivers Out to Give City a Victory." *Indianapolis Star*, May 30, 1920, p 30.

"Monroe Factory Head." *Indianapolis Star*, August 12, 1923, p 32.

"Monroe Plant Is Moved Here." *Indianapolis Star*, December 8, 1918, p 4.

"Monroe Sales Are Increasing." *Indianapolis Star*, March 9, 1919, p 20.

"Monroe Wins." *Indianapolis Star*, June 1, 1920, p 10.

"More Women Driving Autos." *Indianapolis Star*, March 1, 1918, p 12.

"More Working Capital Provided Marmon Company." *Indianapolis Star*, June 16, 1931, p 20.

"Morgan Seeks Cars for Foreign Race." *Indianapolis Star*, April 26, 1911, p 10.

Moross, E. A. "July Auto Racing Gives Big Promise." *Indianapolis Star*, June 12, 1910, p 29.

_____. "Marmon Car Surprises." *Indianapolis Star*, April 17, 1910, p 47.

_____. "Marmon Racer Is Built." *Indianapolis Star*, March 20, 1910, p 18.

"Moross Gives Up Post." *Indianapolis Star*, October 28, 1909, p 8.

"Moscovics Plays Important Role in Auto Industry." *Indianapolis Star*, December 19, 1928, p 23.

"Moscovics Resigns As Head of Stutz; Gorrell Elected." *Indianapolis Star*, January 25, 1910, p 1 & 10.

"Motion Pictures of Race." *Indianapolis Star*, October 18, 1915, p 10.

"Motor Car Company Now Occupies Two Big Plants." *Indianapolis Star*, December 12, 1909, p 4.

"Motor Car Mfg. Co. Is Now the Pathfinder Company." *Indianapolis Star*, May 26, 1915, p 16.

"Motor Cup Offered Is Finest in World." *Indianapolis Star*, March 18, 1909, p 7.

"Motor Exhibit On in Chicago." *Indianapolis Star*, January 27, 1918, p 7.

"Motor Fans Bow to Local Autos." *Indianapolis Star*, August 1, 1909, p 20.

"Motor Heads Deny Merger." *Indianapolis Star*, September 29, 1921, p 5.

"Motor Notes and Gossip Picked Up from Garage and Factory." *Indianapolis Star*, October 15, 1911, p 36.

"Motor Pilots to Begin Workouts." *Indianapolis Star*, April 16, 1911, p 42.

"Motor Plants Enlarge." *Indianapolis Star*, August 25, 1909, p 12.

"Motor Speedway to Be Best in World." *Indianapolis Star*, February 7, 1909, p 34.

"Motordome's Chiefs Acclaim Debt to Speedway Founders." *Indianapolis Star*, May 30, 1924, p 2.

"Much Praise for Sextets." *Indianapolis Star*, October 26, 1919, p 71.

"Mulford Wins Vanderbilt Cup." *Indianapolis Star*, November 28, 1911, p 10.

"Murphy Goes 120.3 on Beverley Hills Track." *Indianapolis Star*, May 18, 1922, p 14.

"Murphy Winner in Los Angeles Race." *Indianapolis Star*, February 26, 1923, p 14.

"Murphy Winner in Race at Uniontown." *Indianapolis Star*, June 18, 1922, p 25.

"Murphy Wins 250-Mile Race on Altoona Track." *Indianapolis Star*, June 15, 1924, p 25.

Mushlitz, Earl. "Marmon to Put 45,000 Cars in Market in 1928." *Indianapolis Star*, February 1, 1928, p 1.

"Mystery Car Is Solved at Last." *Indianapolis Star*, December 26, 1915, p 18.

"Names Receiver for Duesenberg Automobile Firm." *Indianapolis Star*, January 4, 1924, p 15.

"Nation Told of State's Success in Motor Field." *Indianapolis Star*, January 15, 1928, p 23.

"National." *Indianapolis Star*, June 9, 1912, p 35.

"National" *Indianapolis Star*, July 28, 1912, p 45.

"National." *Indianapolis Star*, September 3, 1912, p 7.

"National." *Indianapolis Star*, July 13, 1913, p 20.

"National Announces New Body Without Additional Cost." *Indianapolis Star*, December 10, 1916, p 20.

"National Car Claims 1911 Championship." *Indianapolis Star*, December 18, 1911, p 8.

"National Ends Season." *Indianapolis Star*, November 8, 1910, p 10.

"National Entered in Ormond Races." *Indianapolis Star*, December 5, 1905, p 6.

"National Enters Cars in Big Race." *Indianapolis Star*, January 21, 1912, p 17.

"National Exhibit to Be Preserved." *Indianapolis Star*, September 10, 1916, p 18.

"National Firm Announces Six." *Indianapolis Star*, December 21, 1913, p 20.

"National Gains Financing." *Indianapolis Star*, April 8, 1922, p 15.

"National Issues Bonds." *Indianapolis Star*, March 30, 1923, p 20.

"National Makes Records." *Indianapolis Star*, April 27, 1909, p 9.

"National Motor Car & Vehicle Corporation." *Indianapolis Star*, November 7, 1916, p 15.

"National Motors Is Mortgaged for Sum of $5,750,000." *Indianapolis Star*, August 7, 1923, p 18.

"National Motors Is Put on Sound Basis." *Indianapolis Star*, July 28, 1923, p 1.

"National Names Three Cars for Big Contest." *Indianapolis Star*, March 5, 1911, p 40.

"National Parlor Car Delights Women." *Indianapolis Star*, February 7, 1915, p 18.

"National Raises Prices." *Indianapolis Star*, February 10, 1918, p 5.

"National to Exhibit Four Cars in Gotham." *Indianapolis Star*, December 28, 1911, p 9.

"National Twelve Mounts Big Hill." *Indianapolis Star*, October 1, 1916, p 14.

"National Twelve Price Increased." *Indianapolis Star*, June 18, 1916, p 16.

"National Twelve to Appear Soon." *Indianapolis Star*, May 28, 1915, p 8.

"National Wins Hill Climb." *Indianapolis Star*, September 10, 1911, p 37.

"National—with Airplane Type Motor." *Indianapolis Star*, November 11, 1917, p 18.

"Nationals Lead Racers." *Indianapolis Star*, June 1, 1909, p 11.

"National's Name Is Widely Known." *Indianapolis Star*, November 5, 1916, p 21.

"New Additions Almost Ready." *Indianapolis Star*, October 24, 1915, p 28.

"New American Motors Large." *Indianapolis Star*, November 6, 1911, p 9.

"New Auto Company Formed." *Indianapolis Star*, September 26, 1908, p 8.

"New Auto Firm Expects to Have Enormous Output." *Indianapolis Star*, July 28, 1909, p 14.

"New Auto Plant Launched." *Indianapolis Star*, April 23, 1909, p 10.

"New Automobile Selling Corporation Is Formed." *Indianapolis Star*, March 24, 1923, p 1 & 5.

"New Body Styles Feature Marmon." *Indianapolis Star*, October 17, 1926, p 72.

"New Car for Busy Business Man." *Indianapolis Star*, July 19, 1914, p 17.

"New Car Shown in Marmon Line." *Indianapolis Star*, December 23, 1928, p 46.

"New Cars Added to '41.'" *Indianapolis Star*, June 25, 1915, p 20.

"New Closed Body Types Introduced by Marmon." *Indianapolis Star*, September 18, 1921, p 64.

"New Cole '8,' Cut $190, Now Here." *Indianapolis Star*, January 23, 1916, p 20.

"New Cole Eight Show Headliner." *Indianapolis Star*, January 24, 1915, p 13.

"New Cole Factory Finished in Spring." *Indianapolis Star*, January 18, 1914, p 42.

"New Cole Model a Big Success." *Indianapolis Star*, May 17, 1914, p 54.

"New Cole Model Uses Little Gas." *Indianapolis Star*, May 3, 1914, p 5.

"New Commercial Car." *Indianapolis Star*, August 18, 1912, p 22.

"New Duesenberg Progress Cited." *Indianapolis Star*, February 19, 1928, p 60.

"New Duesenberg Soon to Appear." *Indianapolis Star*, January 15, 1928, p 61.

"New Electric Is Luxurious." *Indianapolis Star*, September 11, 1910, p 36.

"New Empire Six Model Is Larger." *Indianapolis Star*, February 4, 1917, p 75.

"New Empire to Be Shown." *Indianapolis Star*, February 13, 1916, p 21.

"New Four Added to Empire Line." *Indianapolis Star*, August 15, 1915, p 18.

"New H.C.S. Taxicab Meets High Favor in U.S. Cities." *Indianapolis Star*, September 21, 1924, p 62.

"New Head for Stutz Named." *Indianapolis Star*, February 19, 1924, p 1 & 6.

"New Home Bought by Engraving Firm." *Indianapolis Star*, September 27, 1924, p 1.

"New Inspection System Is Used." *Indianapolis Star*, April 21, 1929, p 69.

"New Mail Automobiles Make Their Trial Trips." *Indianapolis Star*, December 4, 1908, p 9.

"New Marion Car Announced." *Indianapolis Star*, December 22, 1912, p 35.

"The New Marmon." *Indianapolis Star*, January 4, 1920, p 6.

"New Marmon Branch Is Best." *Indianapolis Star*, August 11, 1918, p 18.

"New Marmon 78 Goes on Display." *Indianapolis Star*, December 8, 1927, p 1.

"New Marmon 68 and 78 Models Star at Shows." *Indianapolis Star*, January 22, 1928, p 53.

"New Marmon Speedway Type 'Speedster.'" *Indianapolis Star*, July 20, 1913, p 27.

"New Model Completed by Local Plant." *Indianapolis Star*, November 17, 1912, p 27.

"New National Is Big Success." *Indianapolis Star*, April 23, 1916, p 18.

"New Premier Vice President Appoints Private Secretary." *Indianapolis Star*, December 12, 1915, p 32.

"New Sales Plan Adopted by Cole." *Indianapolis Star*, September 15, 1912, p 36.

"New Series Cole Is Distinctive in Feature Creations." *Indianapolis Star*, July 25, 1922, p 16.

"New Stutz Auto Stock Purchased." *Indianapolis Star*, December 1, 1930, p 1.

"New Stutz Auto Winning Acclaim." *Indianapolis Star*, January 6, 1929, p 8.

"New Type Inclosed Car Placed on Market." *Indianapolis Star*, December 1, 1912, p 22.

"The New Waverley Electric." *Indianapolis Star*, January 31, 1909, p 8.

"New Windshield Is Storm Proof." *Indianapolis Star*, August 31, 1919, p 60.

"New York Capitalists Buy Interest in Stutz Company." *Indianapolis Star*, June 22, 1916, p 12.

"New York Curb Market." *Indianapolis Star*, January 1, 1930, p 16.

"New York Views 1933 Stutz Models." *Indianapolis Star*, January 6, 1933, p 12.

"1911 Motor Racing Will Be Best Yet." *Indianapolis Star*, December 4, 1910, p 42.

"1914 Marmon Is Not Radically Changed." *Indianapolis Star*, September 28, 1913, p 32.

"1915 Premier on Display July 6–11." *Indianapolis Star*, July 5, 1914, p 14.

"1924 Cole Master Model on Display at Show This Week." *Indianapolis Star*, September 2, 1923, p 42.

"1933 Marmon Sixteen Announced." *Indianapolis Star*, October 30, 1932, p 25.

"1933 Stutz Line Lower in Price." *Indianapolis Star*, May 22, 1932, p 13.

"No Cut in Cole Prices." *Indianapolis Star*, October 9, 1920, p 10.

"No Evidence Obtained to Fix Blame for Big Fire." *Indianapolis Star*, February 4, 1918, p 18.

"No Noise and Ever Ready to Go." *Indianapolis Star*, February 5, 1905, p 24.

"No Radical Changes in New Pathfinder." *Indianapolis Star*, June 29, 1913, p 34.

"Nordyke & Marmon Factory Is Enlarged." *Indianapolis Star*, June 1, 1912, p 14.

"Nordyke & Marmon May Enter New Field." *Indianapolis Star*, July 15, 1903, p 8.

"Nordyke-Marmon Mill Plant Sold." *Indianapolis Star*, November 27, 1926, p 1.

"Official List of Drivers, Mechanicians, and Relief Men in Race at Speedway Today." *Indianapolis Star*, May 31, 1919, p 20.

"Official Trials on for Race Cars Today." *Indianapolis Star*, May 20, 1915, p 10.

"Oldfield in New Field." *Indianapolis Star*, May 29, 1906, p 6.

"Oldfield Kills Man at Detroit Track." *Indianapolis Star*, September 10, 1903, p 1.

"Oldfield Lowers Marks." *Indianapolis Star*, November 22, 1909, p 4.

"Oldfield to Cut Record." *Indianapolis Star*, May 29, 1910, p 24.

"Oldfield Wins Big Road Race." *Indianapolis Star*, November 12, 1914, p 8.

"Oldfield's Record Broken by Webb." *Indianapolis Star*, October 21, 1906, p 34.

"On Motor Row." *Indianapolis Star*, February 21, 1913, p 10.

"On the Trail of Motor Thieves." *Indianapolis Star*, June 8, 1913, p 35.

"One Death Mars Hawthorne Races." *Indianapolis Star*, June 11, 1911, p 41.

"$1,000,000, Premier Motor Corporation." *Indianapolis Star*, December 7, 1916, p 14.

"Opposes Auto Racing on Patriotic Holiday." *Indianapolis Star*, November 1, 1911, p 8.

"Optimism Holds Sway As Buyers Throng 'the Row.'" *Indianapolis Star*, July 28, 1914, p 7.

"Order Received for 340 Stutz Pak-Age-Cars." *Indianapolis Star*, June 14, 1936, p 21.

"Other Cities Seeking Indianapolis Factory." *Indianapolis Star*, July 24, 1908, p 8.

"Outlines Plans for New Henderson Car." *Indianapolis Star*, April 7, 1912, p 36.

"Overland Car Second." *Indianapolis Star*, April 11, 1908, p 7.

"Overland Cars Meet with Success at Philadelphia." *Indianapolis Star*, June 14, 1908, p 10.

"Overland Procures Pope-Toledo Plant." *Indianapolis Star*, April 7, 1909, p 9.

"Overland Puts Taxicab on Market." *Indianapolis Star*, March 7, 1909, p 19.

"Overland to Spend $40,000." *Indianapolis Star*, July 24, 1909, p 3.

"Paiges Strong in Cactus Derby." *Indianapolis Star*, November 22, 1914, p 22.

"Parade of Autos Is a Record Breaker." *Indianapolis Star*, March 26, 1907, p 7.

"Parry Says Patent Suit Is Filed As Scarecrow." *Indianapolis Star*, April 28, 1910, p 14.

"Parry to Make 1,000 Cars." *Indianapolis Star*, January 15, 1911, p 15.

"Pathfinder." *Indianapolis Star*, October 19, 1913, p 20.

"Pathfinder Builder to Have Exhibit at Fair." *Indianapolis Star*, June 6, 1914, p 14.

"Pathfinder Capital Now $5,000,000." *Indianapolis Star*, March 19, 1917, p 9.

"Pathfinder Designer Sails." *Indianapolis Star*, November 5, 1911, p 38.

"Pathfinder Firm Plans Campaign." *Indianapolis Star*, October 5, 1913, p 19.

"The Pathfinder 40." *Indianapolis Star*, September 8, 1912, p 37.

"Pathfinder Is Now in Gotham." *Indianapolis Star*, September 22, 1912, p 37.

"Pathfinder Reaches Goal." *Indianapolis Star*, August 11, 1912, p 20.

"Pathfinder Six $2222." *Indianapolis Star*, February 22, 1914, p 51.

"Pathfinder the Great." *Indianapolis Star*, January 13, 1918, p 9.

"Pathfinder to Try Coast-to-Coast Trip." *Indianapolis Star*, June 18, 1916, p 22.

"Pathfinder Will Hold Open House." *Indianapolis Star*, February 2, 1913, p 28.

Patrick, Corbin. "Marmon '75' Models Are Now Ready for Local Motor Buyer." *Indianapolis Star*, October 10, 1926, p 58.

_____. "Miller Cars Win in Race Classic." *Indianapolis Star*, June 1, 1926, p 8.

_____. "New Little Marmon Given First Formal Demonstration Here." *Indianapolis Star*, December 5, 1926, p 69 & 71.

Patton, W. Blaine. "Arnold Wins 500-Mile Speedway Classic." *Indianapolis Star*, May 31, 1930, p 11.

_____. "Cars Qualified in Speedway Race Pass Speed Mark." *Indianapolis Star*, May 29, 1924, p 1.

_____. "DePaolo Escapes Death Under Train." *Indianapolis Star*, May 27, 1930, p 1.

_____. "DePaolo Wins Sweepstakes in Indianapolis-Made Car at Dazzling Speed of 101.13." *Indianapolis Star*, May 31, 1925, p 1.

_____. "Duray Smashes Track Record and Wins Pole Position by Showing 113 Miles an Hour." *Indianapolis Star*, May 27, 1925, p 1.

_____. "Five More Qualify for Speedway Race." *Indianapolis Star*, May 26, 1931, p 1.

_____. "Frame Wins, Sets New Speedway Record." *Indianapolis Star*, May 31, 1932, p 1.

_____. "Gasoline Derby of Nation to Be Run Off at Speedway." *Indianapolis Star*, May 30, 1925, p 1 & 12.

_____. "Hearne in Ballot Wins 15-Mile Race." *Indianapolis Star*, May 23, 1922, p 13.

_____. "List of Qualifiers Mounts to 24 As Five Speed Pilots Complete Four Fast Laps." *Indianapolis Star*, May 28, 1928, p 1.

_____. "Lockhart Wins Speedway Race." *Indianapolis Star*, June 1, 1926, p 1.

_____. "Meyer Wins 500-Mile Speedway Classic." *Indianapolis Star*, May 31, 1928, p 1.

_____. "Murphy Drives Record Race." *Indianapolis Star*, May 31, 1922, p 1.

_____. "Nineteen Cars Qualify for Speedway Marathon." *Indianapolis Star*, May 26, 1922, p 14.

_____. "Nineteen Pilots Qualify Cars for Long Grind." *Indianapolis Star*. May 27, 1928, p 33.

_____. "Observed from the Speedway Pits." *Indianapolis Star*, May 26, 1923, p 12 & 15.

_____. "Observed from the Speedway Pits." *Indianapolis Star*, May 25, 1924, p 23.

_____. "Observed from the Speedway Pits." *Indianapolis Star*, May 27, 1924, p 14.

_____. "Observed from the Speedway Pits." *Indianapolis Star*, May 25, 1925, p 12.

_____. "170,000 Will See Speedway Derby Today." *Indianapolis Star*, May 30, 1930, p 1.

_____. "160,000 Cheer As Ray Keech Wins Race." *Indianapolis Star*, May 31, 1929, p 1.
_____. "Schneider Wins Race; Rain Cuts Speed." *Indianapolis Star*, May 31, 1931, p 1.
_____. "Souders, in Duesenberg, Is Race Victor." *Indianapolis Star*, May 31, 1927, p 1 & 9.
_____. "Speedway Action Picks Up with Many Pilots on Track." *Indianapolis Star*, May 15, 1931, p 16.
_____. "Speedway Gossip." *Indianapolis Star*, May 14, 1930, p 13.
_____. "Speedway Race Occupies Spotlight of Sportdom with 26 Cars Ready." *Indianapolis Star*, May 30, 1922, p 1 & 3.
_____. "Speedway Victor Smashes Record." *Indianapolis Star*, May 31, 1924, p 1.
_____. "31 Cars Await Start of 500 Mile Race." *Indianapolis Star*, May 30, 1928, p 1.
_____. "33 Cars Are Ready for 500-Mile Whirl at Speedway Today." *Indianapolis Star*, May 30, 1927, p 1.
_____, "33 Cars Await $100,000 Speedway Race," *Indianapolis Star*, May 30, 1934, p 1.
_____. "33 Cars Await Start of Speed Classic." *Indianapolis Star*, May 30, 1929, p 1.
_____, "33 Cars Qualified for Speedway Grind." *Indianapolis Star*, May 29, 1934, p 1.
_____. "3 Duesenbergs Get Chance to Meet Test This Morning," *Indianapolis Star*, May 30, 1923, p 1.
_____. "28 Qualified for Race; 5 to Try Today." *Indianapolis Star*, May 29, 1928, p 1.
_____. "22 Street Chariots to Start in Speed Classic." *Indianapolis Star*, May 30, 1924, p 1 & 29.
"Pay Race Pilots Well." *Indianapolis Star*, June 19, 1910, p 32.
"Perfect Score by the Marmon in New England." *Indianapolis Star*, February 24, 1908, p 8.
"Pete Going Home to Make Try for Grand Prix Prize." *Indianapolis Star*, July 26, 1925, p 26.
"Peter DePaolo, Gulotta Qualify for Speed Grind." *Indianapolis Star*, May 26, 1930, p 1.
"Petition Asks Receiver for Premier Motor Firm." *Indianapolis Star*, December 11, 1921, p 8.
"Picks Balloon Officers." *Indianapolis Star*, May 20, 1909. p 9.
"Picture Shows Seek Winner." *Indianapolis Star*, August 4, 1912, p 29.
"Pilot Killed on Savannah Track." *Indianapolis Star*, November 21, 1911, p 9.
"Plan Big Contest." *Indianapolis Star*, August 12, 1908, p 4.
"Plans Being Made for Big Auto Race." *Indianapolis Star*, October 1, 1905, p 11.
"Plans Complete for Frisco Race." *Indianapolis Star*, February 21, 1915, p 17.
"Plans Factory Addition." *Indianapolis Star*, December 28, 1919, p 10.
"Plans New Surprise at Automobile Show." *Indianapolis Star*, September 6, 1914, p 13 & 23.
"Plans to Bring Plant Unit Here." *Indianapolis Star*, March 1, 1925, p 17.
"Plans to Start on Pak-Age-Car." *Indianapolis Star*, August 25, 1939, p 24.
"Plants Calling Workers Back." *Indianapolis Star*, January 20, 1918, p 12.
"Plant Enlarges Working Force 100 Men Daily." *Indianapolis Star*, August 22, 1924, p 18.
"Pope Automobiles." *Indianapolis Star*, February 3, 1907, p 30.
"Pope-Toledo Car First Across Line." *Indianapolis Star*, September 24, 1905, p 21.
"Pope-Waverley Electric." *Indianapolis Star*, September 28, 1904, p 7.
"Pope-Waverley Electrics." *Indianapolis Star*, January 27, 1907, p 10.
"The Pope Waverley Surrey." *Indianapolis Star*, September 19, 1904, p 7.
"Post War Car to Be Lighter." *Indianapolis Star*, March 9, 1919, p 64.
"Predict Great New York Show." *Indianapolis Star*, December 19, 1915, p 23.
"Premier Adopts New Gear Shift." *Indianapolis Star*, August 20, 1916, p 17.
"Premier Auto Company Makes Few Changes." *Indianapolis Star*, November 13, 1910, p 32.
"Premier Branches Out." *Indianapolis Star*, March 14, 1908, p 18.
"Premier Car First." *Indianapolis Star*, November 18, 1906, p 34.
"Premier Car Is in the Lead." *Indianapolis Star*, July 21, 1906, p 7.
"Premier Car Stands Test." *Indianapolis Star*, May 8, 1908, p 9.
"Premier Cars Perform Consistently." *Indianapolis Star*, July 28, 1907, p 29.
"Premier Directors Plan to Reorganize Company." *Indianapolis Star*, February 10, 1921, p 8.
"Premier Endures Trials at Pittsburg Auto Run." *Indianapolis Star*, May 4, 1909, p 9.
"Premier Gets Law's Aid." *Indianapolis Star*, July 26, 1910, p 9.
"Premier in New Test." *Indianapolis Star*, May 26, 1908, p 9.
"Premier Is Reinstated." *Indianapolis Star*, January 16, 1912, p 9.
"Premier Lays Case Before the A.A.A." *Indianapolis Star*, January 11, 1909, p 9.
"Premier Machine Is Entered in Big Run." *Indianapolis Star*, January 1, 1909, p 10
"Premier Motor Company Cuts Prices $710 to $910." *Indianapolis Star*, July 1, 1921, p 18.
"Premier Motor Company Formed." *Indianapolis Star*, December 8, 1915, p 2.
"Premier Named Victor." *Indianapolis Star*, July 3, 1910, p 31.
"Premier Plant Is Setting Fast Pace." *Indianapolis Star*, April 3, 1910, p 28.
"Premier Plant to Be Sold." *Indianapolis Star*, November 28, 1915, p 10.
"Premier Roadster or Touring Car $2,250." *Indianapolis Star*, June 23, 1907, p 34.
"Premier Sets Another Remarkable Record." *Indianapolis Star*, June 17, 1923, p 72.
"Premier Suit Settled." *Indianapolis Star*, November 3, 1923, p 13.
"Premier Takes Steps Toward Refinancing." *Indianapolis Star*, January 21, 1922, p 16.
"Premier Taxicabs Driven in Parade." *Indianapolis Star*, August 12, 1923, p 8.
"Premier Taxicabs Gain in Popularity." *Indianapolis Star*, December 31, 1924, p 10.
"Premiers Depart Today for Detroit." *Indianapolis Star*, July 6, 1909, p 11.
"Premiers Head Glidden." *Indianapolis Star*, June 19, 1910, p 35.
"Prepares for Big Speedway Contest." *Indianapolis Star*, March 26, 1911, p 36.
"Prepares for Season." *Indianapolis Star*, January 25, 1910, p 8.
"Presents New Duesenberg." *Indianapolis Star*, Mar 20, 1927, p 57 & 59.
"Price of Cole to Be Reduced Soon; Capital Doubled." *Indianapolis Star*, December 30, 1922, p 5.

"Price Rise Necessary for Pathfinder Twin Six Cars." *Indianapolis Star*, April 2, 1916, p 25.

Priest, Ray. "Auto Industry Reaching Radio and Air Fields." *Indianapolis Star*, December 9, 1928, p 65.

"Private Owners Enter Big Race." *Indianapolis Star*, April 8, 1914, p 8.

"Propose Parade of 2,000 Autos." *Indianapolis Star*, September 16, 1912, p 9.

"Propose Three Day Race of Stock Cars." *Indianapolis Star*, June 16, 1907, p 34.

"Proposes National Tour in Big Tent of Auto Show." *Indianapolis Star*, March 28, 1912, p 10.

"Public Auction Sale." *Indianapolis Star*, March 10, 1915, p 13.

"Pullen Wins Grand Prix; Ball Second." *Indianapolis Star*, March 1, 1914, p 45.

"Purdy Declares Payment Plan Reduces Automobile Costs." *Indianapolis Star*, July 25, 1926, p 57.

"Quantity Price Pathfinder Policy." *Indianapolis Star*, June 6, 1915, p 18.

"Quiet Prevails in Local Labor World." *Indianapolis Star*, June 13, 1904, p 5.

"Quits Racing Game." *Indianapolis Star*, February 17, 1910, p 9.

"Race Driver Home from Foreign Trip." *Indianapolis Star*, September 28, 1927, p 20.

"Race Germ Hits Restaurant Man." *Indianapolis Star*, May 1, 1913, p 13.

"Race Signals Are Vital." *Indianapolis Star*, October 16, 1910, p 41.

"Race Winners Given Prizes." *Indianapolis Star*, June 2, 1920, p 1.

"Racers Start Tuning Up for Big Race." *Indianapolis Star*, April 8, 1911, p 11.

"Races Place Cars Before Public Eye." *Indianapolis Star*, May 8, 1910, p 34.

"Racing Auto Runs over Mechanician." *Indianapolis Star*, August 18, 1909, p 1.

"Racing Autoists to Be Directed by Radio 'Phone.'" *Indianapolis Star*, April 8, 1922, p 1.

"Racing Campaign Aid to Customer." *Indianapolis Star*, March 12, 1911, p 22.

"Racing Engineers Select Marmons for Private Use." *Indianapolis Star*, March 6, 1924, p 12.

"Radio Is Available for Marmon Cars." *Indianapolis Star*, June 15, 1930, p 29.

"Railroad Earnings Make Unfair Comparison." *Indianapolis Star*, June 25, 1930, p 19.

Rankin, Allen C. "Cooper Is First at Road Race in Elgin." *Indianapolis Star*, August 21, 1915, p 8.

_____. "Resta Favorite in Speed Battle." *Indianapolis Star*, August 7, 1915, p 11.

Rankin, William H. "Lauds Decision Postponing Race." *Indianapolis Star*, May 30, 1915, p 1.

"Ray Harroun Cars Entered at Speedway." *Indianapolis Star*, April 21, 1914, p 7.

"Ray Harroun Wins Twice; Oldfield Lowers Record." *Indianapolis Star*, June 24, 1910, p 8.

"Ray McNamara Driving Premier in Hard Run." *Indianapolis Star*, September 27, 1908, p 14.

"Rays of Auto Light from Show Machines." *Indianapolis Star*, February 26, 1909, p 17.

"Ready for Auto Tour." *Indianapolis Star*, July 10, 1907, p 7.

"Ready for Hill Climb." *Indianapolis Star*, June 10, 1910, p 23.

"Real Estate News." *Indianapolis Star*, September 1, 1916, p 16.

"Real Estate Transfer Record." *Indianapolis Star*, July 19, 1911, p 11.

"Real Estate Transfer Record." *Indianapolis Star*, July 20, 1911, p 11.

"Real Estate Transfers." *Indianapolis Star*, April 6, 1911, p 14.

"Realty Board Wants Farm Loan Bank Here." *Indianapolis Star*, August 10, 1916, p 12.

"Realty Transfers in Marion County." *Indianapolis Star*, April 12, 1912, p 13.

"Recheck Shows DePaolo Wins First Laurel Race." *Indianapolis Star*, July 12, 1925, p 23.

"Receiver for Auto Firm." *Indianapolis Star*, December 4, 1910, p 64.

"Receivership Hearing of Motor Firm Continued." *Indianapolis Star*, July 19, 1923, p 18.

"Record Breaking Indianapolis Car." *Indianapolis Star*, May 24, 1916, p 12.

"Record Set by Cole Cars." *Indianapolis Star*, August 1, 1920, p 8.

"Record Trials to Be Next Feature." *Indianapolis Star*, October 24, 1909, p 36.

"Remy Will Pay Both." *Indianapolis Star*, July 29, 1910, p 9.

"Reorganization of Premier Motors Is Accepted by Court." *Indianapolis Star*, May 22, 1923, p 1 & 3.

"Reorganized Premier Motor Corporation Ready to Set New Mark in Industry." *Indianapolis Star*, April 2, 1916, p 22.

"Reports Stutz Car Production." *Indianapolis Star*, March 18 1932, p 20.

"Resta Captures Grand Prix in Peugeot." *Indianapolis Star*, February 28, 1915, p 45.

"Resta Wins with Cooper Next at Santa Monica." *Indianapolis Star*, November 17, 1916, p 10.

"Return with Trophies." *Indianapolis Star*, November 17, 1909, p 8.

"Rickenbacker to Drive Duesenberg in Vanderbilt." *Indianapolis Star*, November 1, 1916, p 11.

"Rickenbacker Wins Thrilling Race of 300 Miles." *Indianapolis Star*, July 5, 1914, p 23.

Ricker, Chester S. "Three Starter Types Defined." *Indianapolis Star*, December 3, 1911, p 36.

"Roosevelt Auto Put on Display." *Indianapolis Star*, March 29, 1929, p 12.

"Roosevelt Earns Public Approval." *Indianapolis Star*, June 16, 1929, p 58.

"Roosevelt Gets Great Reception." *Indianapolis Star*, April 7, 1929, p 62.

"Roosevelt No. 2 Nears 3rd Week." *Indianapolis Star*, June 26, 1929, p 24.

"Roosevelts Are Made Possible by Concentrating on Eights." *Indianapolis Star*, April 28, 1929, p 59.

"Roosevelts Smash All Marks; Continue Toward 250 Hour." *Indianapolis Star*, June 21, 1929, p 12.

"Route for Big Auto Contest Given Out." *Indianapolis Star*, May 17, 1908, p 10.

"Rules Committee Meets in Chicago." *Indianapolis Star*, January 29, 1911, p 28.

"Ryan-Lites." *Montreal Gazette*. March 9, 1929.

"Ryan to Start War on Banks." *Indianapolis Star*, November 28, 1920, p 2.

"Sarles Winner at Uniontown." *Indianapolis Star*, June 19, 1921, p 25.

"Savannah Is Ready for Big Auto Race." *Indianapolis Star*, November 7, 1910, p 10.

"Saves from 15% to 30% of Your Gasoline Bills." *Indianapolis Star*, November 29, 1914, p 22.

"Say Record Will Fall on New Track." *Indianapolis Star*, December 12, 1909, p 1.

Schleppey, Bloor. "Thirteen Drivers Will Make Elimination Trial Today." *Indianapolis Star*, May 27, 1921, p 1.

"Schwab Again Buys Stutz Motor Control." *Indianapolis Star*, July 8, 1931, p 18.

"Schwab Plans to Put More Money in Stutz Plant and Enlarge Operations." *Indianapolis Star*, August 12, 1922, p 12.

"Scoring System Devised for the Speedway Race." *Indianapolis Star*, May 29, 1914, p 6.

"Second Day Crowd Pleases Show Men." *Indianapolis Star*, March 30, 1910, p 9.

"See It at Our Salesroom." *Indianapolis Star*, July 3, 1929, p 12.

"See Waverley Boom." *Indianapolis Star*, September 27, 1908, p 15.

Seeds, Russel M. "Fisher's Vision and Allison's Brass Tacks Gave Premier Speedway of World to City." *Indianapolis Star*, May 30, 1924, p 1.

"Seeks Sanctions for Motor Races." *Indianapolis Star*, January 4, 1910, p 8.

"Seeks Unity in Advertising." *Indianapolis Star*, May 29, 1912, p 7.

"Sees Auto Boom in Spite of War." *Indianapolis Star*, September 4, 1914, p 6.

"Sees Great Benefit to City in Big Race." *Indianapolis Star*, April 27, 1913, p 36.

"Sees No Reason to Quit Racing." *Indianapolis Star*. September 11, 1903, p 1.

"Selden Patent Men Open Legal Fight." *Indianapolis Star*, April 16, 1910, p 9.

"Self-Starter Added to Cole Equipment." *Indianapolis Star*, November 12, 1911, p 30.

"Sets New World Record Mark for 24-Hours." *Indianapolis Star*, April 10, 1911, p 9.

"Seven Indianapolis Machines Capture Most of Prize Money." *Indianapolis Star*, May 31, 1921, p 1.

"17 Race Autos Forced to Quit." *Indianapolis Star*, May 31, 1935, p 11.

"71 Cars Entered in 500-Mile Race at Local Course." *Indianapolis Star*, May 3, 1931, p 1.

"Shows Vantage of 'Twin Six.'" *Indianapolis Star*, August 15, 1915, p 18.

Shuart, C. E. "Auto Pilots Set Marks in Safety." *Indianapolis Star*, May 28, 1910, p 1.

_____. "Crowds and Autos Set New Records." *Indianapolis Star*, May 31, 1910, p 1.

_____. "Victor Shatters Records in Race." *Indianapolis Star*, May 29, 1910, p 16.

"Shy at Entry in Final Race." *Indianapolis Star*, October 29, 1911, p 36.

"Simplex Car Wins in Eastern Grind." *Indianapolis Star*, May 15, 1910, p 32.

"Simplicity in New National." *Indianapolis Star*, March 21, 1915, p 16.

"Six Frontenacs Enter Big Race." *Indianapolis Star*, February 12, 1922, p 23.

"68 and 78 Series of Straight 8's Much Improved." *Indianapolis Star*, July 29, 1928, p 59 & 61.

"Skelton Takes Premier Helm." *Indianapolis Star*, October 15, 1919, p 13.

"Skinner Tells of Increase in 1922." *Indianapolis Star*, January 8, 1923, p 10.

"Smaller, Speedier Autos Predicted." *Indianapolis Star*, June 4, 1926, p 1.

"Smart Set Demands Tailor-Made Bodies." *Indianapolis Star*, May 10, 1914, p 46.

Smith, H.O. "Asks Better Route for Next Glidden." *Indianapolis Star*, July 10, 1910, p 22.

"Sparkling Array of New Motor Cars Bids for Acceptance As 1933 Show Season Is Opened at New York." *Indianapolis Star*, January 8, 1933, p 17.

"Speed Car Crash Kills Ansterberg." *Indianapolis Star*, October 17, 1924, p 1.

"Speed Defies Cold in Race for Marks." *Indianapolis Star*, December 18, 1909, p 1.

"Speed Demons in Oklahoma Race." *Indianapolis Star*, April 4, 1915, p 26.

"Speed Is Mania in America, Says a Well-Known Auto Man." *Indianapolis Star*, May 30, 1915, p 36.

"Speed King Harroun Quits Motor Strife." *Indianapolis Star*, November 20, 1910, p 44.

"Speed Kings in Big Race Here." *Indianapolis Star*, September 12, 1921, p 14.

"Speedway Almost Ready for Races." *Indianapolis Star*, November 28, 1909, p 22.

"Speedway Founders Honored at Smoker." *Indianapolis Star*, May 30, 1924, p 13 & 15.

"Speedway Pilots to Strive for Prizes Totaling $30,000." *Indianapolis Star*, May 8, 1916, p 10.

"Speedway Prize Melon Split at Driver's Dinner." *Indianapolis Star*, June 1, 1929, p 1.

"Speedway Race Can't Be 'Doped Out' Now." *Indianapolis Star*, March 22 1914, p 9.

"Speedway to Hold Six Meets in 1910." *Indianapolis Star*, November 21, 1909, p 23.

"Speedway Trials Will Start Today." *Indianapolis Star*, December 17, 1909, p 8.

"Sport Kaleidoscope." *Indianapolis Star*, May 12, 1929, p 37.

"Spring Automobile Industry in Prosperous Condition." *Indianapolis Star*, March 18, 1923, p 60.

"Stage All Set for N. Y. Auto Race Today." *Indianapolis Star*, October 9, 1915, p 10.

"Stamp Pledge Given As War Work Buzzes." *Indianapolis Star*, June 26, 1918, p 1.

"State Inventors Get 38 Patents." *Indianapolis Star*, April 10, 1932, p 3.

"State Pours Out $2,000,000 More." *Indianapolis Star*, June 1, 1917, p 1.

"Stearns Cuts Record in 24-Hour Race; Cole Star." *Indianapolis Star*, August 21, 1910, p 42.

"Steel Scarcity Threatens Auto." *Indianapolis Star*, May 12, 1917, p 8.

"Stock Duesenberg Makes Record Run." *Indianapolis Star*, April 30, 1923, p 3.

"Stock Is Oversubscribed." *Indianapolis Star*, October 26, 1919, p 67.

"Stock Motors Behind Speedway Specials." *Indianapolis Star*, May 17, 1931, p 25.

"Stock Trophy Event Won by Marmon 16." *Indianapolis Star*, October 16, 1931, p 1 & 5.

"Stop Put to Stutz Trading." *Indianapolis Star*, April 1, 1920, p 4.

"Stops Glidden Litigation." *Indianapolis Star*, June 28, 1911, p 9.

"Story Added from Bottom." *Indianapolis Star*, July 24, 1919, p 19.

"Strang Brings Case Team to Tune Motors for Big Race." *Indianapolis Star*, May 10, 1911, p 9.

"Strang to Pilot Marion." *Indianapolis Star*, May 5, 1910, p 9.

"Stratton Company Seeks Third Plant to Make New Car." *Indianapolis Star*, March 25, 1923, p 19.

"Strike of Machinists Will Affect Few Men." *Indianapolis Star*, June 6, 1904, p 8.

"Study Local Effect." *Indianapolis Star*, August 6, 1937, p 4.

"The Sturdy Stutz Wins Again." *Indianapolis Star*, February 28, 1915, p 22.

"Stutz Announces New Stock Plan." *Indianapolis Star*, October 20, 1930, p 1.

"Stutz Announces Production Boost," *Indianapolis Star*, November 6, 1935, p 22.

"Stutz Car, Wilcox Up, Sets Mark." *Indianapolis Star*, May 24, 1915, p 10.

"Stutz, Celebrating 20th Anniversary, Announces '31 Models in Three Lines." *Indianapolis Star*, October 26, 1930, p 29.

"Stutz Company Issues 50,223 Shares of Stock." *Indianapolis Star*, July 19, 1933, p 16.

"Stutz Company Will Double Local Plant." *Indianapolis Star*, August 8, 1919, p 1.

"Stutz 'Corners' Stirs Interest." *Indianapolis Star*, April 12, 1920, p 5.

"Stutz Declares Dividend." *Indianapolis Star*, July 11, 1916, p 21.

"Stutz Driven to Another Victory." *Indianapolis Star*, August 22, 1915, p 41 & 42.

"Stutz Enters Marions." *Indianapolis Star*, May 15, 1909, p 8.

"Stutz Factory Is Planned." *Indianapolis Star*, March 1, 1914, p 3.

"Stutz Factory Well Equipped." *Indianapolis Star*, April 9, 1922, p 54.

"Stutz Files Suit to Recover $30,000." *Indianapolis Star*, January 27, 1930, p 14.

"Stutz Firm Asks Bankruptcy Act," *Indianapolis Star*, April 3, 1937, p 3.

"Stutz Goes to Mill City." *Indianapolis Star*, August 29, 1915, p 43.

"Stutz in 3-Way Merger, Is Report." *Indianapolis Star*, March 20, 1930, p 3.

"'Stutz of Old' Comes Back in Spectacular H.C.S. Victory." *Indianapolis Star*, May 31, 1923, p 10.

"Stutz Orders Gain." *Indianapolis Star*, March 6, 1932, p 27.

"Stutz Outgrows Quarters; Leases Old 'Birthplace.'" *Indianapolis Star*, May 22, 1923, p 9.

"Stutz Production Increased to Meet Demand." *Indianapolis Star*, January 27, 1924, p 55.

"Stutz Racer Sets Wonderful Record." *Indianapolis Star*, September 12, 1915, p 22.

"Stutz Racers May Not Be in the 500-Mile Speedway Race." *Indianapolis Star*, March 30, 1915, p 10.

"Stutz Racers to Be Called in After Sheepshead Event." *Indianapolis Star*, September 21, 1915, p 11.

"Stutz Racing Team Makes High Speed in Time Trial." *Indianapolis Star*, April 22, 1915, p 3.

"Stutz Scores Again." *Indianapolis Star*, April 30, 1915, p 12.

"Stutz Shows Pak-Age-Car." *Indianapolis Star*, November 10, 1935, p 57.

"Stutz Stock Listed." *Indianapolis Star*, November 19, 1930, p 17.

"Stutz Stockholders Asked to Approve Loan." *Indianapolis Star*, January 17, 1935, p 15.

"Stutz to Start on Pak-Age-Car." *Indianapolis Star*, November 29, 1932, p 9.

"Stutz Victory Is Celebrated." *Indianapolis Star*, October 17, 1915, p 12.

"Stutz Will Build Racer Duplicates." *Indianapolis Star*, June 11, 1911, p 31.

"Stutz Will Exhibit Larger Pak-Age-Car to U.S. Bakers." *Indianapolis Star*, September 27, 1936, p 23.

"Stutz Wins Races." *Indianapolis Star*, April 9, 1910, p 8.

"Stutz Writes About Trip Abroad." *Indianapolis Star*, December 3, 1911, p 36.

"Substitute Glass Hood." *Indianapolis Star*, February 7, 1909, p 22.

"Substitute Plan Filed for Stutz." *Indianapolis Star*, November 14, 1937, p 3.

"Sues to Annul Skelton Policy." *Indianapolis Star*, May 18, 1921, p 18.

"Summary of Indiana Cup Race Shows No Auto Headed Monson in Marion Car." *Indianapolis Star*, June 19, 1909, p 9.

"Survey Shows Gain." *Indianapolis Star*, January 24, 1921, p 5.

"Syndicate Gets Parry Plant on $150,000 Bid." *Indianapolis Star*, January 11, 1911, p 16.

"Tablet Presented to Harry C. Stutz As Token of Esteem of Local Citizens." *Indianapolis Star*, May 24, 1916, p 3.

"Tardy Cars of Racing Game Will Be on Time This Year." *Indianapolis Star*, April 7, 1929, p 33.

"Tells Why Cars Are Not in Race." *Indianapolis Star*, May 25, 1913, p 70.

"Ten Motors Per Day for Cole Motor Car Company." *Indianapolis Star*, March 7, 1915, p 58.

"These Interesting Roosevelt Features." *Indianapolis Star*, March 31, 1929, p 70.

"Thinks Question Fully Answered." *Indianapolis Star*, November 15, 1914, p 25.

"Thirteen Drivers Will Make Elimination Trial Today." *Indianapolis Star*, May 27, 1921, p 1.

"'13' Figures Big in Race Lozier Wins." *Indianapolis Star*, November 8, 1910, p 10.

"Thirteen Pilots on Edge for Frays." *Indianapolis Star*, October 1, 1911, p 20.

"Thirty-Four Cars Entered in International Race at Speedway." *Indianapolis Star*, May 3, 1925, p 25.

"Thirty-Seven Cars to Go in Contest." *Indianapolis Star*, May 20, 1908, p 8.

"Thirty-Six Speed Creations Entered in 16th Annual 500-Mile Race." *Indianapolis Star*, May 2, 1928, p 13.

"33 of Fastest Cars in History Ready for Dash." *Indianapolis Star*, May 31, 1919, p 1.

"This Car Is Expected to Be a Winner." *Indianapolis Star*, May 17, 1915, p 54.

"Thomas Hurled from Auto." *Indianapolis Star*, September 4, 1906, p 11.

"Three Factories Increase Prices." *Indianapolis Star*, April 13, 1924, p 75.

"Three Factories May Go." *Indianapolis Star*, April 7, 1909, p 9.

"Three Indianapolis Firms Have Models in Gotham Show of Quality Models." *Indianapolis Star*, November 30, 1931, p 8.

"Three Monroes to Be in Race." *Indianapolis Star*, April 30, 1922, p 22.

"Three New Pilots to Drive Marmons." *Indianapolis Star*, September 23, 1911, p 9.

"Throng Attends Great Auto Show." *Indianapolis Star*, January 6, 1915, p 5.

Tibbetts, E. C. "Howdy Wilcox Record for Lap Would Mean 500 Miles in 5:03:20 Should This Speed Be Possible in Race." *Indianapolis Star*, May 31, 1915, p 11.

"Tire Effect Is Proof of Perfect Balance." *Indianapolis Star*, August 25, 1912, p 18.

"Tire Loss Halts Marmon Car." *Indianapolis Star*, April 12, 1910, p 35.

"To Attend Southern Races." *Indianapolis Star*, January 6, 1905, p 8.

"To Increase Overland Plant." *Indianapolis Star*, May 31, 1908, p 20.

"To Meet A.A. Board." *Indianapolis Morning Star*, May 17, 1907, p 7.

"Tommy Milton to Pilot Monroe in Auto Classic." *Indianapolis Star*, May 19, 1920, p 11.

"Tommy Milton Victor in 250-Mile Altoona Race." *Indianapolis Star*, June 14, 1925, p 25.

Trask, George K. "On Railroad Row." *Indianapolis Star*, March 20, 1909, p 10.

"Traveling Auto Show Is Boomed." *Indianapolis Star,* April 2, 1912, p 11.
"Tries New Auto Racer." *Indianapolis Star,* March 17, 1910, p 9.
"Trophy Question Rises." *Indianapolis Star,* February 20, 1910, p 48.
"Truck Test Run to Begin Today." *Indianapolis Star,* August 18, 1932, p 13.
"Twelve Lots Purchased." *Indianapolis Star,* September 30, 1911, p 7.
"Twenty Five Are Eligible for Classic." *Indianapolis Star,* May 25, 1915, p 11.
"$28,906 Tax Sum Returned to Stutz." *Indianapolis Star,* January 16, 1930, p 18.
"27 Cars Race Await Battle on Brick Oval." *Indianapolis Star,* May 30, 1913, p 14.
"Two Bridges Wrecked, Boulevard Is Broken." *Indianapolis Star,* March 26, 1913, p 5.
"2-Car-a-Family Trend of Today." *Indianapolis Star,* March 13, 1927, p 55.
"Two Closed Types Marions Announced." *Indianapolis Star,* September 28, 1913, p 33.
"Two Die in New York Feature Race Won by Eddie Rickenbacker." *Indianapolis Star,* May 14, 1916, p 62 & 63.
"Two Entries for Speedway Trials." *Indianapolis Star,* December 5, 1909, p 31.
"2 Firemen Hurt in $8,000 Blaze at Motor Plant." *Indianapolis Star,* April 10, 1915, p 1 & 14.
"Two Local Men Honored by American Auto Assn." *Indianapolis Star,* December 8, 1907, p 29.
"Two More Racing Cars Add Entries." *Indianapolis Star,* September 24, 1911, p 35.
"Two Past Presidents of S.A.E. on Engineering Staff at Marmon." *Indianapolis Star,* April 1, 1928, p 62.
"Two Scores Perfect." *Indianapolis Star,* November 27, 1907, p 5.
"Two Speedway Race Dates Set." *Indianapolis Star,* November 1, 1911, p 8.
"$2,500,000 Nordyke & Marmon 6% Serial Gold Notes." *Indianapolis Star,* July 2, 1919, p 15.
"$2,700,000 Airplane Contract Awarded Here." *Indianapolis Star,* June 9, 1917, p 23.
"Two Winners in Already Great Auto History of Indianapolis." *Indianapolis Star,* June 22, 1919, p 52.
"Two-Year Test Ushers in Car." *Indianapolis Star,* June 16, 1912, p 35.
"Ty Cobb Reels off Fast Mile in Auto." *Indianapolis Star,* April 5, 1911, p 10.
"'Type 646' Is Latest Car Announced by American Co." *Indianapolis Star,* September 7, 1913, p 18.
"Up-to-Date Vehicle Made by Local Firm." *Indianapolis Star,* March 29, 1905, p 2.
"U.S. at Brink of War with Germany Is Belief of Officials at Washington." *Indianapolis Star,* May 5, 1916, p 14.
"U.S. Government Loses on Appeal." *Indianapolis Star,* April 22, 1926, p 13.
"U.S. Stops Sale of Premier Assets." *Indianapolis Star,* June 22, 1923, p 24.
"Vacuum System Proves Popular." *Indianapolis Star,* December 6, 1914, p 23.
"Vanderbilt Sees Fastest Cup Race." *Indianapolis Star,* October 28, 1909, p 8.
"Veteran of Race Track on Marmon Technical Staff." *Indianapolis Star,* March 4, 1928, p 55 & 61.
"Wacker Completes New Power Complex." *Indianapolis Star,* July 29, 1918, p 5.
"Wagner's Visit Here Fruitless." *Indianapolis Star,* November 7, 1911, p 11.
"Wall Street Gossip." *Indianapolis Star,* May 11, 1921, p 16.
"Wake Up, Indianapolis." *Indianapolis Star,* December 19, 1916, p 10.
Watkins, E. C. "Dawson, Injured, Fights for Life." *Indianapolis Star,* May 31, 1914, p 1 & 7.
"Waverley Co. Ready with a New Electric." *Indianapolis Star,* December 31, 1915, p 23.
"Waverley Completes Four-States Run." *Indianapolis Star,* July 28, 1911, p 9.
"Waverly Electric Looks Like Gasoline Roadster." *Indianapolis Star,* March 10, 1912, p 39.
"Waverley Exhibits Its New Driving System." *Indianapolis Star,* June 2, 1909, p 8.
"Waverley Models Changed." *Indianapolis Star,* October 24, 1909, p 36.
"Waverley Will Build Bigger 1912 Electric." *Indianapolis Star,* August 20, 1911, p 30.
"Weidley Motor Now Used Here." *Indianapolis Star,* September 5, 1915, p 47.
"Weidley Motor on Display." *Indianapolis Star,* February 25, 1914, p 11.
"Well Known Tourist to Arrive Today." *Indianapolis Star,* December 14, 1912, p 10.
"Westgard to Make Three Other Tours." *Indianapolis Star,* April 27, 1913, p 34.
"What Motor Folk Are Doing." *Indianapolis Star,* May 15, 1910, p 48.
"What's The Answer?" *Indianapolis Star,* April 22, 1917, p 18.
"When a Duesenberg Stops—A Person of Note Steps Out." *Indianapolis Star,* April 19, 1926, p 9.
Whitney, B. M. "Aitken Confident Being There at Finish." *Indianapolis Star,* November 16, 1910, p 16.
_____. "Speed Kings Set for the Grand Prize Event." *Indianapolis Star,* November 18, 1916, p 4.
"Wide Range of Prices Offered at Motor Show." *Indianapolis Star,* February 16, 1927, p 1 & 9.
"Wilcox and Merz to Drive on Coast." *Indianapolis Star,* September 22, 1911, p 9.
"Wilcox Takes Two Sioux City Events." *Indianapolis Star,* July 9, 1916, p 57.
"Wilcox to Drive Third Premier." *Indianapolis Star,* May 28, 1916, p 68.
"Wilcox's Peugeot Wins Invitational Speed Race." *Indianapolis Star,* September 22, 1921, p 13.
"Will Build Cole Racer for the Trade." *Indianapolis Star,* January 15, 1911, p 17.
"Will Close Pope Option." *Indianapolis Star,* April 25, 1909, p 29.
"Will Contest Decision." *Indianapolis Star,* July 26, 1910, p 9.
"Will Hold Big Auto Races at Fair Grounds." *Indianapolis Star,* September 15, 1908, p 5.
"Will Market New Autos." *Indianapolis Star,* September 3, 1911, p 33.
"Will Produce LaFayette Cars." *Indianapolis Star,* October 7, 1919, p 1.
Willis, Paul P. "Motor Races Test Cars and Drivers." *Indianapolis Star,* July 2, 1910, p 5.
_____. "New York Auto Show Is Opened." *Indianapolis Star,* January 3, 1915, p 19.
_____. "Queen of Tragedy Hovers over Race." *Indianapolis Star,* May 31, 1911, p 1.
_____. "Resta Sets New Record at Chicago." *Indianapolis Star,* June 27, 1915, p 1 & 11.
_____. "Stars of Racing May Shatter Records." *Indianapolis Star,* May 23, 1915, p 49.
_____. "Thousands Wonder As Men Defy Time." *Indianapolis Star,* May 29, 1910, p 24.

"Winner Tells Reasons." *Indianapolis Star*, June 5, 1910, p 24.
"Winners of Speed Classic Rewarded." *Indianapolis Star*, June 1, 1924, p 1.
"Wins Motor Car Plant." *Indianapolis Star*, February 28, 1910, p 4.
"Wishes to Operate Factory." *Indianapolis Star*, December 20, 1910, p 3.
"Women Add Spice to Gala Auto Day." *Indianapolis Star*, March 24, 1909, p 11.
"Woolling Plans Big Apartment." *Indianapolis Star*, June 6, 1919, p 9.
"Work in New York Scarce, Is Report." *Indianapolis Star*, May 8, 1924, p 21.
"Work on New National Buildings Is Being Rushed to the Limit." *Indianapolis Star*, November 28, 1915, p 22.
"World Marks Twice Go on Coast Course." *Indianapolis Star*, October 15, p 41.
"World's Best Ready." *Indianapolis Star*, May 30, 1921, 13.
"Writes City's Name in Motor Archives." *Indianapolis Star*, February 26, 1911, p 17.
"Yes, Indeed, It's Nice to 'Enjoy' Funeral in Comfortable Autos." *Indianapolis Star*, March 7, 1915, p 69.
"Ziengal Makes a Record Trial Spin." *Indianapolis Star*, August 16, 1909, p 9.

Internet

Browne, Tiffany Benedict. "Industrial Building—Home of T. B. Laycock Manufacturing." HistoricIndianapolis.com, http://historicindianapolis.com/industrial-building-former-home-of-tb-laycock-manufacturing/. Accessed April 24, 2016.
"Hassler." *History of the American Automobile Industry.* http://www.earlyamericanautomobiles.com/american automobiles20.htm. Accessed February 24, 2016.
"The History of the French Grand Prix." http://unique-carsandparts.com/formula_one.htm. Accessed September 12, 2016.
Horvath, Dennis. "The American Underslung—'The Safest Car on Earth.'" HistoricIndianapolis.com, http://historicindianapolis.com/the-american-underslung-the-safest-car-on-earth/. Accessed March 12, 2016.
———, "Disappearing Indy Auto Landmarks," September 24, 2012, http://historicindianapolis.com/disappearing-indy-auto-landmarks/. Accessed December 11, 2015.
———, "Recycling the National Motor Vehicle Company Site," http://historicindianapolis.com/recycling-the-national-motor-vehicle-company-site/. Accessed October 31, 2016.
"Hume Body Corp." Coachbuiltwww. http://www.coach built.com/bui/h/hume/hume.htm. Accessed arch 5, 2016.
"Murray Body Corp./Murray Corp. of America." Coach builtwww. http://www.coachbuilt.com/bui/m/murray/murray.htm. Accessed March 7, 2016.
"The Original Savannah Races." *North American Motorsports Journal.* http://www.na-motorsports.com/Journal/1997/3/RussellJ.html. Accessed February 6, 2016.
"Overland." *History of the American Automobile Industry.* http://www.earlyamericanautomobiles.com/american automobiles12.htm. Accessed December 17, 2015.
"Parry Manufacturing." Coachbuiltwww. http://www.coach built.com/bui/p/parry/parry.htm. Accessed March 4, 2016.
"The Prest-O-Lite Vacuum Brake." *Automobile Trade Journal.* Sept 1916, Vol. 21, p 271. https://books.google.com/books?id=PnBIAQAAMAAJ&pg=RA3-PA271&lpg=RA3-PA271&dq=prest-o-lite+vacuum+brake&source=bl&ots=lJVXe21K7A&sig=zM-EPVsSayPAKllUj70T_BnY6nM&hl=en&sa=X&ved=0ahUKEwjG-t6H1JDLAhXKOz4KHeSbDH4Q6AEIHzAB#v=onepage&q=prest-o-lite%20vacuum%20brake&f=false. Accessed February 24, 2016.
RacingReference.info. http://racing-reference.info/race/1922–01/X. Accessed January 18, 2016.
"Reconstruction Finance Corporation." Wikipedia article. https://en.wikipedia.org/wiki/Reconstruction_Finance_Corporation. Accessed October 22, 2016.
Rothermel, Bill. "The Stutz Motor Car Company—The Car That Made Good in a Day." http://www.classiccarclub.org/info_garage/car_profiles/stutz.html. Accessed March 12, 2016.
"Sioux City's Mini Indy." http://www.siouxcityhistory.org/art-a-leisure/123-sioux-citys-mini-indy-sports-and-competition-have-been-an-important-part-of-sioux-citys-history-si. Accessed February 20, 2016.
"Stewart Vacuum Tank." *Motor Age*, Vol. 31, p 92. https://books.google.com/books?id=xFYfAQAAMAAJ&pg=RA1-PA92&dq=stewart+vacuum+gasoline+system&hl=en&sa=X&ved=0ahUKEwiQ2pOSl4TLAhXFNT4KHb4LDc0Q6AEIQjAD#v=onepage&q=stewart%20vacuum%20gasoline%20system&f=false. Accessed February 19, 2016.
"Weidley Motors Capitalized at $350,000." *Horseless Age*, Vol. 37, p 95. https://books.google.com/books?id=EVTmAAAAMAAJ&pg=PA95&lpg=PA95&dq=weidley+motor+company&source=bl&ots=KSLU5WJB1H&sig=s505tx11XXqiHNyFQTee_NJiv60&hl=en&sa=X&ved=0ahUKEwiK1tGD3JDLAhWMPT4KHQDKAYUQ6AEINTAE#v=onepage&q=weidley%20motor%20company&f=false. Accessed 2/24/2016.

Miscellaneous

Delancy, Howard R. *The History of the Cole Motor Car Company.* Indiana University Thesis.
Flanaghan, Philip. Untitled manuscript, April 15, 1937. (manuscript is at the Indiana State Library).

Index

Numbers in ***bold italics*** indicate pages with illustrations

Acme Works, Inc. 218
Agan, Frank 89
Aitken, Johnny 30–31, 34, 41, 43, 45–48, 51–53, 61–62, 64–69, 72–74, 79–82, 89, 94, 97, 113, 135, 140–141, 144, 152–154, 157–160
Alberti, Bill 250
Alco automobile 47
Alexander, H.A. 201
Alley, Tom 202
Allis-Chalmers 229
Allison, James 3–5, 16, 19, 23–24, ***40***–41, 49, 85, 95, 103, 141–142, 144, 153, 160, 166, 173, 175, 220
Allison Engineering Company 166, 168
Almy, Walter 125
American Automobile Association (AAA) 27–28, 30, 78, 91, 100, 126, 129–130, 156, 159, 166, 171, 188, 246, 251, 253; Contest Board 37, 45–46, 49, 54, 56–57, 60, 70–71, 78, 80–81, 97, 125, 173, 185, 195, 208, 226, 236
American Bicycle Company 8
American Foundry Company 201
American Motor Car Company 5, ***21***, ***26***, 30, ***35***, 37, 45, 49, 52, 56, 61, 67, 70, 72, 78–79, 97; racing 31, 34, 46, 53, 61–62, 64–65, 70, 73–74; American Motors Company 79, 86, 90–94, 96–97, 100, 102, 105, 109, 111–112, 114–116, 119, 123
American Motor Car Manufacturers' Association (AMCMA) 16, 46
American Motor Car Sales Company 30–31, 67
Andersen, Gilbert (Gil) 44, 63, 80, 83, 85, 89, 91, ***118***, ***120***, 123–124, 128–130, 135, 137–138, 140–145, 153–154, 157

Ansterberg, Eddie 220, 223
Anthony, Walter M. 215, 218
Apperson, Edgar 22, 27–28, 30, 33, 39
Apperson, Elmer 28, 86, 231
Apperson Brothers Automobile Company 19, 27, 31, 186
A.R. Sheffer & Company 163
Arnold, Billy 250
Ascari, Antoine 228
Associated Motor Industries 205, 207; *see also* National Automobile & Electric Company
Association of Licensed Automobile Manufacturers (ALAM) 16, 46, 53, 78, 81, 110
Atlanta Motor Speedway 47–49, 61–62, 74, 124
Atlas Engine Works 53; *see also* Lyons-Atlas
Automobile Board of Trade/Automobile Chamber of Commerce 81, 11, 110
Automobile Club of America 54, 140–141
Automobile Club of France 75, 125

Baker, Edwin G. ("Cannonball") 138–***139***, 140, 202–203, 214, 251
Balger, William 59
Ball, Guy 124
Ballinger, Charles 59
Barrows, Frederick 208–209, 224
Baruch, Bernard 165
Bash, Judge Mahlon E. 218, 224–225
Basle, Charles 63
Basle, Marcel 73
Basle, Maurice 86
Bass, Herbert L. 110
Batten, Norman 226
Bauman, Dutch 239
Baxter, Arthur R. 119
Beiling, Walter M. 131

Bennett, W.S. 125
Bentrup, William P. 246
Bergdall, Erwin 89
Besler, I.G. 11
Black, Charles 2–***3***, 7
Black, Merton S. 222
Boillot, George 124, 140
Bookwalter, Walter 10, 16, 28, 115
Bourque, Wilfred 45
Boyer, Joe 192–193, 195, 217, 219–221, 223
Bradley, Leon M. 32
Bradley, William F. 63
Brilli-Peri, Gaston 228
Brockway, Carl 31–32
Bromley, Wayne K. 77, 106
Brooklands speedway 54
Brown, A.C. 167
Brown, Ezra 215
Brown, Will H. 31, 42, 54, 86
Brown, W.M. 130
Bruce-Brown, David 80, 82, 85, 86, 97
Buck, Dave 72
Buick 92–93, 121, 126; Marquette-Buick 69, 71, 73; racing 3, 22, 24, 47, 67–68, 70–71, 82, 84, 89, 113
Burke, John J. 254
Burman, Bob 3, 68–69, 71, 74, 80–81, 85, 92, 118, 137, 143–144
Burt, Andy 144
Butler, Sam 91

Caccia, Joe 250
Caldwell, A.A. 135
Campbell, E.B. 31
Campbell, Henry F. 49, 67, 103, 125, 179, 222
Candler, Asa 62
Carlson, Billy 137
Carpenter, Captain 142
Carson, Oliver H. 31
Carter, L. 99
Carter, Judge Vinson 76

307

Index

Chalmers Motor Company 60, 81; Chalmers-Detroit 44, 48
Chamberlin, Judge Harry L. 219
Champion, Albert 195
Chase, Herbert 140
Chevrolet, Arthur 69, 74
Chevrolet, Gaston 185, 187, 198, 219
Chevrolet, Louis 47, 73–74, 175–176, 185, 187, 193, 197–198, 202, 208, 213, 220, 222, 246
Chevrolet automobile 175, 192
Christiaens, Josef 154
Christie, John Walter 33, 50, 52
Clarke, J.T. 28
Clemens, Jap 3, 19–20, 22–24
Clements, Frank 31
Clifford, A.V. 222
Cobb, Ty 81
Cobe, Ira A. 69
Cobe Trophy 44, 54, 66, 69, 71, 73, 129
Coey, C.A. 22
Cole, Joseph J. 38–**39**, 63, **83**, 86, 94–95, 103–104, 108, 110, **114**, 116, 123, 126, 133, 147, 155, 168, 195, 205, 210, 216, 228
Cole, Nellie 38–**39**
Cole Carriage Company 38
Cole Motor Car Company 4–5, **38–39**, 51–52, **55**, 63, 75, 78–79, 82, 86, 88, 90, 92, 94, **96**, 99–100, 102, 106–108, **107**, 110, 112–116, **115–116**, 123, **126**–127, 129, 132–**134**, 143, 145–147, 152–155, **153**, 159–160, 162, 164–170, 172, 174, 176–177, 182, 188–189, 194–196, **203**, 205, 207, 210, **212**, 214, 216, 220; racing 46, **50**–51, 53, 56–**59**, 61–63, 66–67, 69–71, 73–74, 81–84, **83**, 87, 89, 91, 130
Collins, E.J. 13
Columbia Axle Company 198
Commercial Club 31, 42
Cooley, William B. 35
Cooper, Earl 118, 123–124, 128–129, 135, 137–138, 140–145, 159–160, 168, 175, 217, 226, 236, 238
Cord, E.L. 231, 233, 237, 255
Corum, L.L. 202–203, 220–**221**, 235–236, 239, 250, 252
Cox, Allen 135
Cox, Clyde E. 10, 25, 31
Craig, B.L. 201
Crawford, Charles S. 38, 174
Cronk, Arnet B. 255
Cummings, Bill 250
Cummins Corporation 254
Cunard, C.H. 245

D'Alene, Wilbur 123, 135, 156, 202–203

Davidson, Homer 254
Dawson, Joe 44, 47, 62, 64–65, 67–69, 72–74, 80, 82–83, 85–86, 89–90, 92, 97–98, 112, 124, 127–128, 182, 239
DeFreet, Peter M. 2
DePalma, Ralph 79, 85, 124, 129, 140–144, 187, 192, 202–203, 208
DePaolo, Pete 187, 202, 220, 223–**224**, 226, 228–230, 250
Dermond, Mack 84
Devine, Thomas 85
Devore, Earl 236
Dick, J.P. 67
Dickson, George M. 30, 86, 103, 106, 112–113, 124, 128, 132, 140–141, 151, 156, 161, 165, 172, 195, 214–215
Dingley, Bert 23
Disbrow, Louis 70, 73, 79–80, 89, 137
Dixon, Arthur 209
Dolnar, Hugh 14
Dorn, Fred C. 167
Dougherty, Hugh 35
Dow, L.S. 8
Dubonnet, Andre 195
Duesenberg, August 4, 185–**186**, 211, 245, 250
Duesenberg, Denny 252
Duesenberg, Frederic 4, 185–**186**, 190, 192, 195, 211, 213, 221–223, 225–226, 229–232, 244, 252–253
Duesenberg Automobile & Motors Company 4–5, 185, 187, **189**–191, **194**, 201, 203, 206, 208, 210–211, 213–214, 216, 218, 223–224; Duesenberg, Inc. 231–**234**, 237–**239**, 240, **243**, 252, 253–255; Duesenberg Motors Company 225–226, 230
Duesenberg racing 156–157, 159, 175, 185–187, 192–193, 195–196, 201–203, 208, 211, 213, 216–217, 200, 220–221, 223–**224**, 226, 228–230, 235–239, 245, 250, 252–254
Dunn, James H. 225
Duray, Leon 128, 202–203, 226, 252

Earl, Clarence A. 215, 218
Edie, Lionel 234
Edmunds, Louis 67, 71, 81
Edward Jordan Company 192
E.J. Thompson Company 155
E.L. Cord Corporation 253
Elgin Motors, Inc. 210, 222
Elgin National Trophy 71–72, 118, 129, 142, 145
Ellingboe, Jules 193, 202–203

Elliott, Frank 226
Elliott, Frederick H. 27
Elstum, M.E. 215
Empire Automobile Company 95–96, 101, 110, 114, 121, 125, 129, 136–**137**, 142–143, 147, 150–152, 160–161, 166–167, 169–170, 174; Empire Motor Car Company 5, 41, 50, 52–53, 61, 65, 67–**68**, 78, 80, 84, 86, 94–95
Employers' Association of Indianapolis 13
Endicott, Bill 56, 58–**59**, 62–63, 67, 70–71, 73–74, 82, 84, 89, 91
Endicott, Harry 74
Erbstine, C.E. 124, 128
Evans, Dave 235–236

Fairbanks, Crawford 167
Federal Fuel Administration 169
Federated Motors Company 162–163
Federation of American Motorcyclists 45
Felicke, Karl 91
Fesler, J.W. 188
Fetterman, Isaac 187, 202–203
Firestone, Harvey S. 38, 219
Firestone Rubber & Tire Company/Firestone tires 216
Fisher, Carl Graham 1–5, **14**, 16–24, 28, 30, 33, 39–41, 45, 49, 52, 54, 80–81, 85–86, 88, 93, 95, 103, 114–115, 124, 138, 141–142, 144, 153–154, 173, 220, 229
Fitzgerald, F.N. 25
Flashaire, Georges 171
Fletcher, Stoughton 19, 159
Fletcher American National Bank 175, 191–192, 196, 198, 208
Fletcher Savings & Trust 201, 209, 225
flood of 1913 111–112
Flowers, J.C. 146, 174, 178
Flynn, John J. 254
Follansbee, S. 191
Forbes, Eben 67
Forbes, Thomas P.C., Jr. 67
Ford, Edsel 150
Ford, Henry 5, 30, 127, 150, 188
Ford, Percy 193
Ford Motor Company 16, 46, 124, 162, 203
Frame, Fred 239, 252–253
Franklin automobile 27, 33, 35
French, Charlie 92
French, L.S. 99
Frontenac Motor Company 5, 197–198; Frontenac Motors Corporation 222; Frontenac Motor Corporation of America, Inc. 198, 200, 207, 211; racing 175, 193, 195–196, 203

Fulton, H.F. 84

G & J Trophy 68, 128
Gardner Motor Car Company 195, 249
Garfield, Harry 169
Gates, Edward 208
Gates-Osborne Carriage Company 38
Gavin, James L. 109
Gelnaw, Frank 73
George W. Goethal & Company 191
Gibson, Cecil 29, 95, 125
Gibson Automobile Company 28–29, 39–40
Gilhooley, Ray 128
Gleason, Jimmy 238–239, 245, 252
Glidden Tour 28, 30, 32–34, 44, 58–60, 78, 81, 89
Gloetzner, Alwin A. 208, 215
Goetz, Phillip 8
Gorrell, E.S. 241, 248–250, 253–254
Goux, Jules 113, 125, 127–128
Grand Prize Race 30, 34, 73–75, 91–92, 123–125, 135, 144, 159–160
Grant, Harry 47, 73, 80
Greater Indianapolis Industrial Association 178
Green, E.A. 114
Greiner, Arthur 64–65, 69, 72–73, 85
Grubb, H.K. 222
Guaranty Trust Company 206–207
Gullotta, Tony 238–239
Gunn, Earl G. 166
Guyot, Albert 128, 192–193, 195

Habblett, Edward 67
Haibe, Ora 202–203
Hall, Ira 239, 253
Hall & Scott engines 166, 171
Hamilton, Marvin E. 255
Hammond, Bobby 252
Hammond, Harry 18, 28, 44
Hanch, Charles C. 81–82, 110
Handley, J.I. 79, 91, 96–97, 103, 115, 130, 134–135
Hardegen, E.C. 31
Harding, B.K. 223
Harlan, Austin 86
Harroun, Ray 46–48, 53, 55–58, 61–62, 64–69, 71–75, 80–85, **84,** **89**–90, 106, 109–110, 112, 115, 124–125, 127–129, 140
Hartz, Harry 201–202, 220–221, 226
Hassler, Robert H. 2, 10–11, 19, 23, 30, 41, 162
Haupt, Willie 46

Hay, Judge Linn 225
Hay, Tom 16
Hayes Body Corporation 239–240
Haynes, Elwood 86, 106
Haynes auto 30, 33–35
H.C.S. Cab Manufacturing Company 222
H.C.S. Motor Corporation 179, 181, **184**–185, 189, 192–194, **193,** 203, 207, 213–214, 216–217, 222, 226
Hearne, Eddie 68–69, 73, 87, 137, 185, 187, 192, 195–196, 202, 217, 219
Heinemann, Fred 73
Heinemann, Louis 72, 92
Henderson, Charles P. 39, 99–100, 127, 129, 165
Henderson, Pete 157
Henderson, Ransom P. 99, 103, 127
Henderson Motor Car Company 5, 38–39, 94, 99–100, **103**–104, 112, 114–115, 119, 127
Hepburn, Ralph 226
Herdman, C.P. 85
Herr, Don 65, 87, 89, 94, 97, **118**
Herreshoff Manufacturing Company 36
Herrick, Harvey 90, 94
Herrington, Col. Arthur W. 251
H.H. Franklin Manufacturing Company 225
H.H. Woodsmall & Company 216
Hill, Benny 192–193, 195–196, 208, 216, 219, 221, 230
Hilliard, Zeke 84
Hittle, J. Arthur 10–11
Hoblitt, F.W. 19
Hodson, Harry 31
Holbrook, H.L. 207
Holbrook & Company 155
Holcomb, Harry 45
Horan, Joe 74
Hottel, H.M. 201
Hough, Judge Charles M. 46
Howard, C. Glenn 202
Howard, Earle C. 179, 189
Hower Trophy 28, 33
Hughes, Hughie 70, 92
Hume Body Corporation 224
Hume Manufacturing Company 161
Humphrey, W.A. 219
Hunter, Melvin 2
Hutchinson, Newton P. 191, 201
Hydraulic Pressed Steel Company 127

Ideal Motor Car Company 4, 88, 90–92, 101, 111; *see also* Stutz Auto Parts Company
Imperial Automobile Company 134

Indiana Automobile Manufacturers Association 114, 130
Indiana Bicycle Company 2, 7
Indiana Brewing Company 17
Indiana State Fair 17, 98, 102, 129, 156; fairgrounds 14, 19–20, 22–23, 33, 129, 216
Indiana Trophy Race 44
Indianapolis Automobile Racing Association (IARA) 19, 22–23
Indianapolis Automobile Trade Association (IATA) 32–33, 82, 95, 112, 130, 188, 233
Indianapolis Board of Trade 31
Indianapolis Chain & Stamping 2, 8, 41
Indianapolis Motor Speedway 4, 40–41, 45–47, 49, 51–57, 61–64, 66–74, 79, 81, 104, 107, 117, 126, 129–130, 132, 137–138, 142, 144, 148, 157, 164, 166, 181–182, 188, 195–196, 198, 211, 220–221, 223, 228, 232, 235–237, 245, 253; Harvest Auto Racing Classic 157–158; Indianapolis 500 67, 76, 80–85, 91, 93–94, 97, 99, 106, 112–113, 118, 124, 127–128, 135, 138, 140–141, 144, 153–154, 173–174, 185–187, 192–193, 198, 202, 208, 220, 223, 226, 229–230, 235–236, 238–239, 240, 244–245, 250, 252–254
Inghibert, Louis 195

Jackson Automobile Company 46, 56–57, 78, 195
Jacoby, E.L. 222
Jagersberger, Joe 86
James Gordon Bennett Cup 13–14, 17
Jay, Webb 35, 44, 126
Jeffers, C.E. 182
Jeffries, James 49
Jenkins, Ab 254
Jenkins, Johnny 87, 92
J.I. Handley Company 115–116
J.J. Burke & Company 254
Johnson, Frank 136
Johnson, Harry **87**
Johnson, Herman 99
Johnson, Jack 80
Johnson, Wilbur C. 34–35
Jones, Ben 230
Joss, Fred A. 10

Kaiser, Paul 22
Kaminsky, Leo 140
Kateley, Frank A. 208
Keech, Ray 245
Keene, Bruce 46, 117, 128
Kelley, Judge William P. 60
Kellum, Claude 46
Kepperly, James E. 79

Kettering, Charles 5
Kimball & Company 155
Kincaid, Tom 23–24, 31, 47–48, 53, 61–62, 64, 66–70
King, F.A. 201
King Brothers 41
Kirkely, A.S. 238
Kiser, Earl 3, 18
Klaussman, Henry W. 135
Klein, Art 202–203
Knight, Harry 74
Knipper, Billy 112
Knobloch, A.F. 152, 155
Kothe, William Jr. 35
Kreis, Peter 226, 228, 236, 238
Krueger, Chief 17
Kuhn, William F. 35

LaFayette Building Company 182–183, 185
LaFayette Motors Company 5, **178**–179, 181–182, 188–189, 194, 196–197, 200
Lanarnick, N. 32
Landon, Archer A. 171
Landon, Hugh 16
League of American Wheelman 4
Leathers, Judge James M. 211
Leeds, Fred 215
Levey, Louis 28
Lewis, Dal H. 32
Lewis, Dave 118, 137, 157, 226
Liberty Bonds 165, 167, 174
Liberty engines 166, 168, 171–172, 174–175, 179
Lincoln Highway Association 103; highway 154, 156
Litz, Deacon 250
Livingston, Al 72–74
L.L. Harr & Company 250, 254
Lockhart, Frank 229, 235; estate 238
Longaker, V.A. 21, 31, 33, 56, 79, 86, 91, 105
Lorimer, Lee 48
Love, Hugh M. 35
Love, John R. 35
Lufkin, George I. 140
Lynch, Leigh 46, 56
Lyons-Atlas/Lyons-Knight automobile 5, 126, 132, 161–162
Lytle, Herbert 34, 45, 62, 64–65, 70

Mahan, Harry B. 225
Mais Motor Trucks 94, 146, 150
Maley, Henry 237, 250
Marean, Judge Josiah T. 81
Marion Motor Car Company 5, 10, 14, 16–17, 20, 23, 28, 30, 36–37, 44–46, 49, 52–53, 56, 60–61, 63, 67, 78–80, 94, 96, 100–102, 104–105, 111, 114–**117**, 121, 130, 133–135

Marmon, Daniel 11, 44
Marmon, Howard 4, 11, 19, 22, 28, 32–33, 44, 54, 57, 61, 65, 72, 75, 78, 80, 82–83, 92, 103, 110, 130, 132, 153, 165–166, 219–220, 238, 251
Marmon, Walter 4, 11, 13, 19, 33, 86, 97, 100, 123, 151, 165–166, 171, 174–175, 197, 220, 251
Marmon-Herrington 251–253, 255
Marmon Motor Car Company 229–234, 236–**244**, 245–253; Marmon Motor Company 1, 4–5, **12**, 14, 16, 20–22, 25–26, 29–30, 32–35, 37, 39, 43–45, 52–53, 62–63, 70, 75, 78, **84**, 94, 97–98, 100, 102, 106, 110–114, **111**–112, 117, 119, 121–123, **122**–**123**, 126–128, 130, 132–**133**, 141, **143**, 147–151, **149**–**150**, 154–157, 160–161, 167, 169–172, 174, 177, 180–182, 185–186, 192, 195, 197, 203, 206, 211, 216–217, 219, 223–225, 228–229; see also Roosevelt automobile
Marmon racing 4, 46–48, 50–51, 53, 55–58, 61–62, 64–69, 71–75, 80, 82–86, **84**, 89–92, 97, 123–124, 127–130, 238
Marshall, Cy 250
Marshall, Gov. Thomas R. 51
Martin, J.C.F. 201
Martin-Parry Corporation 205
Matson, F.E. 222
Maxwell, John M. 100
Maxwell, W.E. 25
Maxwell Motor 46, 59; racing 124–125, 127, 140, 144, 153
May, David 95
May, Rex 254
Maypole, Bob 125
McAdoo, William G. 161
McCutcheon, Charles 167
McDermid, H.M. 125
McDonough, Bob 226
McFarland, J.S. 165, 169
McGuire, Newton J. 91
McIntyre, William H. 86
McKee, Homer 102, 220
McLane, J.M. 67
McNamara, John J. 206
McNamara, Ray 19, 30, 32, 34–35, 40, 44, 59
Meddock, Emmett 84
Meeker, Ezra **163**
Menasco, D.S. 21
Mendelson, Joseph 254
Mercer Automobile Company 124–125, 129
Mery, Walter J. 218
Merz, Charlie 3, 19, 33–34, 43, 45–46, 53, 64–65, 79, 81–82, 85, 89, 94, **118**, 156, 157, 162, 246
Meyer, Louis 239
Miller, Blaine H. 209, 221
Miller, Charles 73
Miller, Eddie 187, 193
Miller, Harry 185, 221, 229–230; engine 202; Miller Specials 226, 239
Miller, S.J. 107–108
Milton, Tommy 185, 187, 193, 195, 198, 213, 217, 219–220, 226, 228–229, 245
Minshall, Charles 10
Mitchell, Robert K. 222
Mitchell Motor Car Company 46, 195;
Monckmeier, Gus 86
Monihan, J. Guy 133–135
Monroe Motor Company 5, 172–173, 176, 185, 187, 201–202, 204, 208–209, 215
Monsen, Adolph 53, 72
Moon Motor Car Company 249
Moore, Frank L. 16, 32–33, 54
Moore, Joe 24, 28, 36
Moore, Maurice J. 183
Morgan, M.B. 166
Morgan, W.J. 82
Moross, Ernest (Ernie) 33, 47–50, 54, 57, 62–64, 70–71, 80–81, 124
Morrison, John F. 38
Morton, Wade 226, 235
Moscovics, Frederick E. 121, 127, 143, 148–149, 174, 192, 211, 225, 241, 251
Mosher, George 167
Motor Car Manufacturing Company 77, 91, 100–101, 104, 106, 109, 119, 140; see also Pathfinder
Motsinger, Newell 50, 52–53, 65
Mourre, Antoine 226
Mulford, Ralph 72, 74, 85, 144, 168, 185, 187, 193, 202–203, 229
Murdock, A. Gordon 179, 222
Murdock, Samuel T. 179
Murphy, Jimmy 185, 187, 192–193, 195–196, 202–203, 208, 219–220, 221, 223
Murray Body Corporation 230, 237, 239
Mutual Motors Company 134
Myers, Theodore ("Pop") 142

Nash, Charles W. 179, 200
National Association of Automobile Manufacturers 110
National Automobile & Electric Company **8**; National Motor Car & Vehicle Company 158–159, 160–161, **164**, 166, 168–

170, 172, 174, 177, 179, 182, 185, 190, 192, 194–195, 198, 203, 205; National Motor Vehicle Company 3–5, *9*, 11–14, *13*, 16, 20–21, *25*–26, 28–30, 37, 39, 41, 43, 45–*47*, 52–53, 60–61, 64, 78–79, 86–87, 93–*95*, 97, 102, 104, 106, 111–113, 117, 120, 124, 128, 137–*138*, 140–141, 145–147, 151, 156–157; National Motors Corporation 207–208, 214–215, 218; racing 3–4, 12, 19–20, 22, 24, 30–31, 34, 41, 44–46, 48, 50–53, 56, 61–62, 64–66, 68–75, 79–80-82, 85–86, 89–90, 93–94, 97, 112–113, 124, 132, 135
National Automobile Dealers Association 210
Neely, H.A. 70
Nehrbas, F.P. 174, 188
New Haven Carriage Company 155
New Parry 77, 91
Newby, Arthur 3–5, 8–9, 11, 16, 19, 28, 30, 33, 40–41, 43, 46, 50, 52–53, 64, 74, 79, 81–82, 86 89, 91, 95, 141, 157, 173, 220
Newby, Charles 31
Newby Oval 4
Nikrent, Joe 89, 92
Nikrent, Louis 130
Nordyke & Marmon 4–5, 11–12, 16, 81–82, 97–98, *112*, 117, 121, 165–166, 168–169, 171, 174–175, 179, 182, 195, 219–220, 222, 225, 228, 229; *see also* Marmon Motor Car Company
Nutt, Frank 30, 35

Oakes Corporation 205
Oakes, W.E. 25
Oakes, W.D. 54
O'Brien, J.H. 201, 208
O'Donnell, Eddie 145, 185, 187
Ogborn, A.D. 79
Ohmer, Will I. 205
Oldfield, Barney 3, 22, 33, 45, 47–48, 50, 52, 64–66, 68, 70, 80–81, 118, 124–125, 128–130, 137, 143–144, 154, 186, *193*, 219
Olson, Ernie 187
Orr, Tom 144
Overland Automobile Company 5, 10, 25, 31–33, 35–37, 39, 42, 44, 52–53, 67, 71, 78–79, 93, 121
Owen, R.M. 40

Packard Motor Car 61, 140, 175
Pak-Age-Car 253, 255
Pardee, Phil 252
Parker Tire and Rubber Company 205

Parrott, Burton E. 35
Parry, David 13, 25, 31, *51*, 53, 77
Parry, Max *51*
Parry, St. Clair 10
Parry, Thomas 10
Parry Automobile Company 5, *51*–53, 66, 69–70, 76, *76*, 77
Parry Manufacturing Company 2–3, 10, 168
Patschke, Cyrus 71, 89–90, 92, 128–129
Pathfinder automobile 5, *90*–91, 94, 100–101, *104*, 106, *108*–109, *119*–121, 129, 132, 140–141, 145, *150*–*152*, 154, 162–164, *162*–*163*; Pathfinder Motor Company of America 167, 169; *see also* Motor Car Manufacturing Company
Patterson, E.C. 142
Pershing, Gen. John J. 168
Pfisterer, Peter A. 210–211
Pickens, William 80
Pierce, W.E. 224
Pierce-Arrow Motor Company 33, 35, 44, 109, 200
Pierson, Charles 2, 7
Polson Manufacturing Company 214
Poole, Al 71
Pope, Colonel Albert 42
Pope Manufacturing Company 7; Pope-Toledo Automobile Company 14, 17–18, 23; Pope-Waverley Electric Motor Company 7, 12–13, 16–17, 20, 22, 25, 31, 34; *see also* Waverley Electric Company
Premier Motor Car Company 146, 157, 160–161, 164, 166, 168–169, 174, 177–178, 186, 188, 191–192, 194, 196; Premier Motor Corporation 201, 207–209; Premier Motor Manufacturing Company 3–5, 9–10, 13–16, *15*, 20–21, *23*–*24*, 26, 29–30, 32–37, 39–41, 43–44, 46, 52–53, 58–61, 75, 78, 94, 100–102, 106, 114, 120–121, 125, 129–131, 133–*136*, 146; Premier Motors, Inc. 209–210, 214–218, 220, 223–225; racing 14, 18–19, 22–24, 27, 31, 81, 144, 150, 154, 156–157, 175
Prest-O-Lite Company 4, 16, 19, 93, 97, 105, 114, 161, 205; Prest-O-Lite Team Company 144, 153–154, 157, 159; Prest-O-Lite Trophy 41, 45, 61, 64, 70, 128, 153–154
Price, James A. 201
Pullen, Edward 125, 192–193
Pumpelly, James K. 9
Putman, Judge 60

Raiss, George 46
Ralston, Gov. Samuel 109
Rankin, L.M. 185
Rasmussen, William T. 218, 224–225
Raub, E.R., Jr. 222
Reconstruction Finance Corporation 254
Reep, Jack 61
Regal Motor Car Company 46, 127
Remy Electric Company 71, 121, 129; Remy Grand Brassard 62, 66, 68, 71–72, 128, 153–154
Reo Motor Car Company 33, 46
Resta, Dario 135, 140–144, 154, 159
Rice, Herbert 19, 34–35, 86, 112, 119, 123, 167
Richards, Charles W. 140
Rickenbacker, Eddie 144, 153, 157–160
Ricker, Chester 99, 182, 188, 211, 216, 218
Riley, F.A. 185
Robbins Body Corporation 205
Robert H. Hassler, Inc. 5, 162, 205
Roberts, J.E. 189
Roberts, Mort 196
Robertson, George 48, 50, 52–53, 66–67, 70
Rogers, E.E. 99
Rooney, Tom 144, 154, 185, 235, 237
Roosevelt automobile 241–243, *242*, 245–250; *see also* Marmon Motor Car Company
Root, C.J. 167
Rowe, S.E. 246
Russell, Charles J. 23
Russo, Joe 254
Rutherford, John A. 62
Ryan, Allan A. 155, 176, 183–184, 190, 197–198, 206–207

Samuel B. Stephens Trophy 234, 251
Samuel L. Wilternitz & Company 123
Sanders and Barth 205
Sarles, Roscoe 185, 192–193, 195, 202–203, 220
Savannah Challenge Cup 74, 91–92
Saylor, George H. 151
Schaefer, Ivan F. 191, 208–209
Schaeffer, E.F. 174
Schaf, Joseph C. 35
Schebler, George 54
Scheel-Frontenac 208, 213
Schnipper, Jay Edward 182
Scholler, Henie 154
Schroeder, Rockefeller & Company 255

Index

Schwab, Charles 190, 206–207, 214, 218, 252–253
Schweitzer, Louis 142
Sedwick, Charles 113, 141–142
Seifert, Frank 58
Selden Patent 16, 46, 53, 81
Seymour, Johnny 238
Shaefer, Jacob 186
Shafer, Phil 217, 223, 226
Shank, Mayor Samuel 99
Shaw, Wilbur 252
Sherer, Carl J. 236
Sherman, Joseph 254
Shideler, John E. 36
Shields, Bert 157
Shoaf, Ben 236, 239
Showers, W. Edward 134, 219
Simmeron, Dr. H. 74
Simon, G.O. 77
Skelton, Dr. Leslie S. 177–178, 191–192
Skinner, J.R. 206
Small, William 172, 188, 201
Smith, A.R. 119
Smith, Frank E. 130–131, 136, 146
Smith, Howard O. 4, 9, 19, 23, 27–28, 30, 33, 43–44, 54, 59–60, 81, 86, 103, 107, 134
Smith, Paul 33
Snare, C.K. 99
Snowberger, Russell 238
Sommers, Charles B. 19, 95, 142
Sommers, D.M. 103
Sourbier, Ed G. 63
Souders, George **235**–236, 239
Soules, Charles 33
Speedway Team Company 144, 150, 153–154, 157, 159–160
Spence, Bill 245
Staley, Frank 32
Stalnaker, W.E. 141, 151, 154
Standard Wheel Company 10, 25
Stapp, Babe 235–236, 250
Steinhart, E.W. 146, 178
Steinle, George A. 182
Stevens, Samuel B. 156, 234
Stewart-Warner Speedometer Corporation/Stewart Vacuum Gasoline System 126, 133, 146
Stillman, Harry 44, 46–48, 51, 53, 55, 57, 61, 154
Stoddard, W.J. 62
Stoddard-Dayton 22, 24, 31, 33, 56, 49, 93
Strang, Lewis 50–52, 63, 80
Stratton, Frank S. 208
Stratton Motors Corporation 208–209
Stubbs, Judge G.W. **23**
Stubbs, P.D. 30–31, 33, 37
Studebaker 33, 102, 120
Stutz, Charles 44–45, 49, 53, 56, 63
Stutz, Harry C. 4, 18–19, 21–22, 24, 28, 31, 44–45, 49, 56, 67, 80, 83, 87, 89, 92, 111, 118, 123–125, 129, 140, 144–145, 150, 153–155, 165, 176, 179, 184–185, 192–194, **193**, 213, 222
Stutz Auto Parts Company 49, 56, 80, 83, 85, **87**, 89–90, 92, 94, 101; Stutz Motor Car Company 4–5, **89**, 111, 114, 125–126, 130, 138–140, **139**, 145, 154–155; Stutz Motor Car Company of America 155, **157**–**158**, 161, 168–170, 173–174, 176–177, 179–180, 183–184, 190, 192, 196–**199**, 200, 203–207, **204**–205, 212, 217, 219, 225, **227**–229, 233–235, 237, 239–242, 247–255; see also Ideal Motor Car Company
Stutz Fire Engine Company 184–185
Stutz racing 112, **118**, 123–125, 128–130, 135, 137–138, 140–145, 150, 153–154, 157, 159–160, 168, 175, 235, 238–239, 250, 252
Sutherland, J.D. 191, 209
Sutterman, Leon 254
Sweet, Frank 40

Taggart, Mayor Tom 21
Teasdale, W.C. Jr. 77, 119
Test, Charles E. 9, 41
Tetzlaff, Teddy 90, 98, 127
Thayer, Eugene V.R. 206
Thomas, Charles 255
Thomas, H.H. 109
Thomas, Joe 185, 202–203
Thomas, Rene 137, 140–141, 175, 187
Thompson, William N. 184, 192, 196, 198, 225
Tone, Fred I. 54, 91
Tousey, William 65, 69
Triplett, Ernie 245, 252
Troescher, William F. 214
Tulasne, Major Joseph 171
Twyman, B.W. 95

Umphrey, William 134, 167
Updyke, Ed 223

Vail, Ira 202–203
Vanderbilt Cup 18–20, 22, 27, 46–47, 72–74, 91, 93, 123–124, 135, 144, 159–160
Van Nuys, Frederick 208
Van Ranst, Cornelius W. 196
VanZandt, Newton 185
Vaughn, Guy 19
Victory bonds 174
Vinton, A.E. 32
Von Hake, Carl 35
Vonnegut, Franklin 119

Wagner, A.B. 154
Wagner, Fred 87, 91
Wagner, Loring 34
Waldheim, A. 95
Walker, Madame C.J. **34**
Wall, W. Guy 18, 25, 32–33, 54, 79, 89, 92, 110, 166, 218
Wallace, William 73–74
Waltman, Cliff 22
Watson, Lee 38
Waverley Electric Company 9, 11, 14, **20**, 34–35, 45, 47, 52, 61, 75, 86–**87**, 94, 96, 107–**108**, 147
Weaver, C.V. 85
Webb, A.C. 18, 22–24
Weidley, George 4, 9, 14, 27, 29–30, 32–33, 54, 78, 120–121, 125, 134
Weidley, Walter 154
Weidley Motors Company 134, 145–146, 166, 185, 205, 215, 219, 225
Weightman, William 159
Western Storage Battery Company 9
Westgard, A.C. 101
Weymann bodies 235, 237, 247–248
W.H. Duval & Son 214
Wheatley Trophy Race 46–48, 73
Wheeler, Frank 4, 30, 40, 57, 142, 153
Wheeler-Schebler Carburetor Company 4, 51, 78, 182, 205; Wheeler-Schebler Trophy 41, 45–46, 53, 56, 61, 65–66, 70, 72, 78, 83, 124, 128, 153–154
Whipple, Merritt A. 196
White, D. McCall 179, 181, 196
White, Everett G. 166
White, Paul N. 167
Whiting, A.H. 59
Whitman, Hiram A. 196
Wilcox, Howdy 47, 64–65, 69, 72, 74, 79, 81–82, 89–90, 94, 97, 135, 137–138, 140–141, 144, 154, 156–157, 160, 175–176, 195–196, 213
Wildman, Edward 225
William Small Company 172, 176–177, 182, 187–188, 191, 198, 201; see also Monroe Motor Company
Williams, George M. 219–220, 222, 228, 232, 237, 240–241, 246, 248–249, 251–252
Willis, Frank B. 19
Willis, Fred I. 54
Willys, John N. 30–32, 36, 42, 67, 79, 96, 185
Willys-Overland Company 67
Wilson, Pres. Woodrow 151, 161, 168–169
Wing, Frank E. 30, 44, 224

Winn, Billy 253
Winnai, Freddy 245, 254
Winton Motor Company 18, 46
Wishart, Spencer 69
Wonderlich, Jerry 202–203

Wood, Johnny 92
Woodruff, F.W. 146
Woodruff, George 146
Worthington, B.A. 197
Wylie, Bruce M. 98, 172

Yarian, John L. 150, 154

Zengel, Len 45, 89
Zenite Metal Company 205
Zig Zag Cycle Club 3–4

www.ingramcontent.com/pod-product-compliance
Lightning Source LLC
Chambersburg PA
CBHW081539300426
44116CB00015B/2692